**Praise for *Introducing Quantitative Methods: A Pra***

'A much-needed text to help those new to quantita
writing is clear, examples easy-to-follow, and the inclu
stroke. Most importantly, Aidley puts the research ques
heart of the book and guides her readers through the apj ........us to gain meaningful
insight.'
— **Jackie Carter, Professor in Statistical Literacy, Cathie Marsh Institute for Social Research, University of Manchester, UK**

'A valuable resource for students and those of us who teach research methods at both undergraduate and postgraduate levels. Daniela Aidley guides students through the whole research process from identifying research questions suitable for quantitative inquiry through rigorous statistical analysis to writing up the project. It is this holistic approach that differentiates Daniela Aidley's book from other books on quantitative methods.'
— **Mikko Arevuo, Head of Postgraduate Management programmes, Regent's University London, UK**

'*Introducing Quantitative Methods* covers its subject very well: concepts are introduced and discussed without being belaboured; examples are numerous and diverse; and the writing style is clear and concise. Dr Aidley's knowledge and enthusiasm are evident on every page, and encourage the student to explore rather than fear the intimidating topic of conducting quantitative research. By including helpful reviews of various mathematical concepts as well, Dr. Aidley has created an ideal text for student and instructor alike. This is the text I wish I'd had as an undergraduate psychology major. It's the text I wish I'd have written as an instructor.'
— **Jacqueline Ralston, Adjunct Instructor, Psychology, Central New Mexico Community College, USA**

'A very comprehensive yet incredibly accessible introduction to quantitative methods. Students of all levels who need to embark on quantitative research projects will find this book user-friendly, easy to read, and anticipatory of most questions they'd be asking. I will be adding this to my reading list.'
— **Pamela Yeow, MBA Director, Central Saint Martins, University of the Arts London and Birkbeck, University of London, UK**

'*Introducing Quantitative Methods* has the potential to be a 'go to' resource at every stage of quantitative research, from pre-design right through to sharing research findings. It is particularly useful in providing choice between using Excel and SPSS for a wide range of statistical analyses, making the doing of quantitative research more achievable.'
— **Kate Mukungu, Lecturer in Social Sciences, University of Cumbria, UK**

'This textbook will make an excellent contribution to introducing research methods to undergraduates, postgraduates, and academics wanting to brush up on their statistical analysis. The text is logically ordered and accompanying online support provides further training to meet the needs of the user and help get their heads around the hard stuff! I found the clarification on associations and effects, particularly on casual language, an excellent and necessary section of the text. It is an important reminder for all readers both new to quantitative research and those refreshing their minds, that both their statistical models and writing up of findings must be aligned and well thought through before and after conducting advanced inferential statistical analysis.'
— **Ruth McKie, Lecturer in Criminology, De Montfort University, UK**

# INTRODUCING QUANTITATIVE METHODS

## A Practical Guide

Daniela Aidley

© Daniela Aidley, under exclusive licence to Springer Nature Limited 2019

All rights reserved. No reproduction, copy or transmission of this publication may be made without written permission.

No portion of this publication may be reproduced, copied or transmitted save with written permission or in accordance with the provisions of the Copyright, Designs and Patents Act 1988, or under the terms of any licence permitting limited copying issued by the Copyright Licensing Agency, Saffron House, 6–10 Kirby Street, London EC1N 8TS.

Any person who does any unauthorized act in relation to this publication may be liable to criminal prosecution and civil claims for damages.

The author has asserted her right to be identified as the author of this work in accordance with the Copyright, Designs and Patents Act 1988.

First published 2019 by
RED GLOBE PRESS

Red Globe Press in the UK is an imprint of Springer Nature Limited, registered in England, company number 785998, of 4 Crinan Street, London, N1 9XW.

Red Globe Press® is a registered trademarks in the United States, the United Kingdom, Europe and other countries.

ISBN 978–1–137–48721–6 paperback

This book is printed on paper suitable for recycling and made from fully managed and sustained forest sources. Logging, pulping and manufacturing processes are expected to conform to the environmental regulations of the country of origin.

A catalogue record for this book is available from the British Library.

A catalog record for this book is available from the Library of Congress.

*To Jack. My love, my rock; mein Fels in der Brandung.*

# Short Contents

| | |
|---|---|
| *Contents* | viii |
| *List of Figures* | xv |
| *List of Tables* | xviii |
| *About the Author* | xx |
| *Author's Acknowledgements* | xxi |
| *Publisher's Acknowledgements* | xxii |
| *Introduction* | xxiii |
| 1 The Research Question | 1 |
| 2 Basic Concepts of Empirical Research | 14 |
| 3 Data Collection | 55 |
| 4 Basic Mathematics | 95 |
| 5 Data Entry and Data Handling | 117 |
| 6 Basic Concepts of Data Description and Analysis | 155 |
| 7 Presentation and Illustration of Data | 191 |
| 8 Choosing your Statistical Analyses | 211 |
| 9 Statistical Analyses: Looking at Differences | 230 |
| 10 Statistical Analyses: Looking at Effects | 249 |
| 11 Statistical Analyses: Looking at Associations and Relationships | 275 |
| 12 Writing up Research | 289 |
| *Appendix 1 – Standard Error of Skewness for Small Sample Sizes* | 302 |
| *Appendix 2 – Critical Values for Wilcoxon Signed Rank Test* | 303 |
| *Exercise Solutions* | 304 |
| *General Glossary* | 329 |
| *Excel Functions Glossary* | 339 |
| *References* | 350 |
| *Index* | 357 |

# Contents

| | |
|---|---|
| *Contents* | viii |
| *List of Figures* | xv |
| *List of Tables* | xviii |
| *About the Author* | xx |
| *Author's Acknowledgements* | xxi |
| *Publisher's Acknowledgements* | xxii |
| *Introduction* | xxiii |

## 1 The Research Question — 1

    1.1  WHY IS A GOOD RESEARCH QUESTION IMPORTANT? — 2
    1.2  WHAT MAKES A GOOD RESEARCH QUESTION? — 2
    1.3  WHICH RESEARCH QUESTIONS ARE PARTICULARLY SUITABLE FOR QUANTITATIVE RESEARCH? — 5
    1.4  GOING FURTHER: EPISTEMOLOGY — 6
    1.5  HOW TO FIND A RESEARCH QUESTION — 6
        1.5.1  Replicating findings — 7
        1.5.2  Developing new questions — 8
    1.6  DEVELOPING YOUR OWN QUESTION — 9
    1.7  PLANNING YOUR RESEARCH PROJECT — 11
    A SHORT SUMMARY — 12
    RESEARCH METHODS AT WORK — 12
    CHECK YOUR UNDERSTANDING — 13

## 2 Basic Concepts of Empirical Research — 14

    2.1  WHAT IS A VARIABLE? — 15
    2.2  IN WHAT WAY CAN VARIABLES BE MEASURED? — 17
        2.2.1  Nominal scale data — 17
        2.2.2  Ordinal scale data — 18
        2.2.3  Interval scale data — 19
        2.2.4  Ratio scale data — 20
    2.3  MEASURE OR INDICATOR? — 21
    2.4  WHAT IS MEASURED: ASSOCIATIONS AND EFFECTS — 22
        2.4.1  Causal associations — 22
        2.4.2  Non-causal associations — 23
    2.5  WHAT IS MEASURED: DIFFERENCES BETWEEN GROUPS — 23
    2.6  WHAT KIND OF VARIABLES CAN BE MEASURED? — 24
        2.6.1  Control — 25
        2.6.2  Going further: Placebo effects and double-blind studies — 28
        2.6.3  Random allocation — 29
    2.7  EXPERIMENTS AND QUASI-EXPERIMENTS — 29

|  |  |  |  |
|---|---|---|---|
| 2.8 | TYPES OF RESULTS | | 32 |
| 2.9 | ETHICAL RESEARCH | | 35 |
| | 2.9.1 | Ethics guidelines | 36 |
| | 2.9.2 | Ethical research practice | 39 |
| 2.10 | HYPOTHESES | | 40 |
| | 2.10.1 | Hypotheses and effects | 40 |
| | 2.10.2 | Hypotheses and differences | 41 |
| | 2.10.3 | Hypotheses and associations | 42 |
| | 2.10.4 | Null hypothesis | 42 |
| 2.11 | IMPROVING RESEARCH QUALITY: RELIABILITY | | 43 |
| 2.12 | IMPROVING RESEARCH QUALITY: VALIDITY | | 46 |
| | 2.12.1 | Going further: Construct underrepresentation and construct-irrelevant variance | 48 |
| 2.13 | FROM THEORY TO PRACTICE: OPERATIONALISATION | | 49 |
| A SHORT SUMMARY | | | 51 |
| RESEARCH METHODS AT WORK | | | 52 |
| CHECK YOUR UNDERSTANDING | | | 52 |

## 3 Data Collection — 55

|  |  |  |  |
|---|---|---|---|
| 3.1 | PRIMARY AND SECONDARY DATA | | 56 |
| | 3.1.1 | Secondary data | 56 |
| | 3.1.2 | Primary data | 58 |
| 3.2 | DECIDING ON VARIABLES AND CONDITIONS | | 59 |
| 3.3 | DEVELOPING MATERIAL | | 60 |
| | 3.3.1 | Making your material accessible | 63 |
| | 3.3.2 | How to elicit responses | 64 |
| | 3.3.3 | Rating scales | 68 |
| | 3.3.4 | Semantic differential | 71 |
| 3.4 | DEMOGRAPHIC QUESTIONS | | 72 |
| 3.5 | PROCEDURAL QUESTIONS | | 74 |
| 3.6 | MUTUALLY EXCLUSIVE, COMPREHENSIVELY EXHAUSTIVE | | 75 |
| | 3.6.1 | Mutually exclusive | 75 |
| | 3.6.2 | Comprehensively exhaustive | 77 |
| 3.7 | AVOIDING BIAS | | 77 |
| 3.8 | RECRUITING PARTICIPANTS: SAMPLING | | 79 |
| | 3.8.1 | Sample size | 80 |
| | 3.8.2 | Sample composition | 81 |
| 3.9 | RECRUITING PARTICIPANTS: MAKING RESEARCH ACCESSIBLE | | 85 |
| 3.10 | ALLOCATING PARTICIPANTS TO CONDITIONS | | 85 |
| | 3.10.1 | Randomisation | 85 |
| | 3.10.2 | Order and sequence effects | 88 |
| 3.11 | PILOT STUDIES | | 88 |
| 3.12 | RELIABILITY TESTING | | 89 |
| RESEARCH METHODS AT WORK | | | 91 |
| A SHORT SUMMARY | | | 92 |
| CHECK YOUR UNDERSTANDING | | | 93 |

## 4 Basic Mathematics — 95

| | | |
|---|---|---|
| 4.1 | LARGER THAN, LESS THAN OR EQUAL TO SIGNS | 96 |
| 4.2 | PERCENTAGES AND PERCENT POINTS | 97 |
| 4.3 | DECIMAL POINTS | 100 |
| 4.4 | ROUNDING | 101 |
| | 4.4.1 Rounding in Excel | 102 |
| | 4.4.2 Rounding in SPSS | 102 |
| 4.5 | FRACTIONS AND RATIOS | 103 |
| 4.6 | SIGMA | 103 |
| 4.7 | RANGE | 104 |
| 4.8 | POSITIVE, NEGATIVE AND ABSOLUTE NUMBERS | 105 |
| 4.9 | READING EXPONENTIAL NOTATIONS | 107 |
| 4.10 | SCIENTIFIC NOTATION | 108 |
| 4.11 | SQUARES AND SQUARE ROOTS | 110 |
| 4.12 | CHANCE AND PROBABILITIES | 111 |
| | RESEARCH METHODS AT WORK | 112 |
| | A SHORT SUMMARY | 113 |
| | CHECK YOUR UNDERSTANDING | 114 |

## 5 Data Entry and Data Handling — 117

| | | |
|---|---|---|
| 5.1 | SAFE, CONFIDENTIAL AND ETHICAL DATA MANAGEMENT | 118 |
| | 5.1.1 Confidential handling of participant data | 118 |
| | 5.1.2 Reasonable precautions to save and back up your data | 119 |
| 5.2 | CHOOSING SUITABLE SOFTWARE: EXCEL | 120 |
| | 5.2.1 The basic setup | 121 |
| | 5.2.2 Entering data | 121 |
| | 5.2.3 Sorting data | 122 |
| | 5.2.4 Entering a function | 123 |
| | 5.2.5 Copying a function to other cells | 125 |
| | 5.2.6 Applying a filter | 126 |
| 5.3 | CHOOSING SUITABLE SOFTWARE: SPSS | 127 |
| | 5.3.1 The data file | 128 |
| | 5.3.2 The syntax file | 130 |
| | 5.3.3 The output file | 130 |
| | 5.3.4 Naming and labelling a variable | 131 |
| | 5.3.5 Naming and labelling variable values | 132 |
| | 5.3.6 Applying a filter | 133 |
| 5.4 | PREPARING A FILE FOR DATA ENTRY | 134 |
| 5.5 | ENTERING DATA | 135 |
| | 5.5.1 Data from open questions/sentence completion | 135 |
| | 5.5.2 Data from single choice questions | 136 |
| | 5.5.3 Data from multiple choice questions | 139 |
| | 5.5.4 Data from ordering/ranking tasks | 140 |
| | 5.5.5 Data from rating scales and semantic differentials | 141 |
| 5.6 | CHECK FOR DATA ENTRY ERRORS AND OUTLIERS | 142 |
| 5.7 | CODE AND RECODE YOUR DATA | 146 |
| | 5.7.1 Recoding data | 146 |
| | 5.7.2 Calculating new variables | 149 |

|  |  |  |  |
|---|---|---|---|
|  | 5.7.3 | Dummy variable | 150 |
|  | 5.7.4 | Going further: Scale transformations | 151 |
|  | 5.7.5 | Taking notes, taking names | 151 |
|  | RESEARCH METHODS AT WORK | | 151 |
|  | A SHORT SUMMARY | | 152 |
|  | CHECK YOUR UNDERSTANDING | | 153 |

## 6 Basic Concepts of Data Description and Analysis — 155

|  |  |  |  |
|---|---|---|---|
| 6.1 | FREQUENCIES | | 156 |
| 6.2 | PERCENTAGES | | 159 |
| 6.3 | MEASURES OF CENTRAL TENDENCY | | 160 |
|  | 6.3.1 | Mean | 161 |
|  | 6.3.2 | Mode | 161 |
|  | 6.3.3 | Median | 163 |
|  | 6.3.4 | Going further: Median split | 163 |
| 6.4 | COMPARING MEASURES OF CENTRAL TENDENCY | | 165 |
| 6.5 | MEASURES OF DISPERSION: VARIANCE AND STANDARD DEVIATION | | 166 |
| 6.6 | PARAMETERS AND STATISTICS | | 169 |
|  | 6.6.1 | Going further: Variations | 174 |
| 6.7 | NORMAL DISTRIBUTION | | 175 |
| 6.8 | Z-SCORES | | 178 |
| 6.9 | SKEW AND KURTOSIS | | 178 |
| 6.10 | SIGNIFICANCE | | 180 |
| 6.11 | POWER | | 182 |
| 6.12 | EFFECT SIZE | | 183 |
| 6.13 | DEGREES OF FREEDOM | | 184 |
|  | 6.13.1 | Going further: Yours or mine? Calculating effect sizes with pooled standard deviations | 185 |
|  | RESEARCH METHODS AT WORK | | 186 |
|  | A SHORT SUMMARY | | 186 |
|  | CHECK YOUR UNDERSTANDING | | 187 |

## 7 Presentation and Illustration of Data — 191

|  |  |  |  |
|---|---|---|---|
| 7.1 | BASIC DESCRIPTIVES | | 192 |
| 7.2 | USING TABLES EFFECTIVELY | | 193 |
| 7.3 | VISUALISING DATA | | 194 |
| 7.4 | CREATING A CHART | | 196 |
| 7.5 | CHART TYPES | | 197 |
|  | 7.5.1 | Column chart | 197 |
|  | 7.5.2 | Bar chart | 198 |
|  | 7.5.3 | Histogram | 198 |
|  | 7.5.4 | Pie chart | 199 |
|  | 7.5.5 | Scatter plot | 201 |
|  | 7.5.6 | Line chart | 201 |
| 7.6 | ACCESSIBILITY OF GRAPHS | | 202 |
| 7.7 | GOING FURTHER: SIGNIFICANCE IN TABLES | | 204 |
|  | RESEARCH METHODS AT WORK | | 207 |
|  | A SHORT SUMMARY | | 209 |
|  | CHECK YOUR UNDERSTANDING | | 209 |

## 8 Choosing Your Statistical Analysis — 211

- 8.1 PARAMETRIC OR NON-PARAMETRIC? — 212
- 8.2 DESCRIPTIVES IN EXCEL — 213
  - 8.2.1 Mean, median, skewness and kurtosis — 213
  - 8.2.2 Q-Q plot — 214
- 8.3 DESCRIPTIVES IN SPSS — 216
  - 8.3.1 Mean and median — 216
  - 8.3.2 Skewness and kurtosis — 216
  - 8.3.3 Q-Q plot — 216
- 8.4 INTERPRETING DESCRIPTIVES — 216
  - 8.4.1 Mean and median — 216
  - 8.4.2 Skewness — 216
  - 8.4.3 Kurtosis — 217
  - 8.4.4 Q-Q plot — 217
- 8.5 OVERVIEW OF ANALYSES — 219
- 8.6 LOOKING AT COMPARISONS OR DIFFERENCES — 220
  - 8.6.1 One-sample t-test — 220
  - 8.6.2 Paired-samples t-test — 220
  - 8.6.3 Wilcoxon signed rank — 221
  - 8.6.4 Independent-samples t-test — 221
  - 8.6.5 Mann-Whitney U-test — 222
- 8.7 LOOKING AT EFFECTS — 222
  - 8.7.1 Analysis of variance (ANOVA) — 222
  - 8.7.2 Analysis of covariance (ANCOVA) — 224
  - 8.7.3 Kruskal-Wallis — 224
- 8.8 LOOKING AT RELATIONSHIPS — 225
  - 8.8.1 Chi-square test — 225
  - 8.8.2 Chi-square test of independence — 225
  - 8.8.3 Chi-square test of goodness of fit — 226
  - 8.8.4 Pearson's correlation — 226
  - 8.8.5 Spearman's correlation — 226
- 8.9 HOW TO READ CHAPTERS 9, 10 AND 11 — 227
  - 8.9.1 Data set — 227
  - 8.9.2 How to read instructions in the following chapters — 228
- A SHORT SUMMARY — 228
- CHECK YOUR UNDERSTANDING — 228

## 9 Statistical Analyses: Looking at Differences — 230

- 9.1 ONE-SAMPLE T-TEST — 231
  - 9.1.1 One-sample t-test in Excel — 231
  - 9.1.2 One-sample t-test in SPSS — 232
  - 9.1.3 Reporting the results of a one-sample t-test — 233
- 9.2 WILCOXON SIGNED RANK — 233
  - 9.2.1 Wilcoxon signed rank in SPSS — 234
  - 9.2.2 Reporting the results of a Wilcoxon signed rank test — 235
- 9.3 PAIRED-SAMPLES T-TEST — 235
  - 9.3.1 Paired-samples t-test in Excel — 235
  - 9.3.2 Paired-samples t-test in SPSS — 237
  - 9.3.3 Reporting the results of a paired-samples t-test — 238

|       |          |                                                              |     |
|-------|----------|--------------------------------------------------------------|-----|
| 9.4   |          | INDEPENDENT-SAMPLES T-TEST                                   | 238 |
|       | 9.4.1    | Independent-samples t-test in Excel                          | 239 |
|       | 9.4.2    | Independent-samples t-test in SPSS                           | 240 |
|       | 9.4.3    | Reporting the results of an independent-samples t-test       | 241 |
| 9.5   |          | MANN-WHITNEY U-TEST                                          | 241 |
|       | 9.5.1    | Mann-Whitney U-test in Excel                                 | 242 |
|       | 9.5.2    | Mann-Whitney U-test in SPSS                                  | 245 |
|       | 9.5.3    | Reporting the results of a Mann-Whitney U-test               | 245 |
|       | A SHORT SUMMARY                                                         | 246 |
|       | RESEARCH METHODS AT WORK                                                | 246 |
|       | CHECK YOUR UNDERSTANDING                                                | 247 |

## 10 Statistical Analyses: Looking at Effects — 249

|       |          |                                                              |     |
|-------|----------|--------------------------------------------------------------|-----|
| 10.1  |          | ONE-WAY BETWEEN-PARTICIPANTS ANOVA                           | 250 |
|       | 10.1.1   | One-way between-participants ANOVA in Excel                  | 250 |
|       | 10.1.2   | One-way between-participants ANOVA in SPSS                   | 251 |
|       | 10.1.3   | Reporting results                                            | 255 |
| 10.2  |          | ONE-WAY WITHIN-PARTICIPANTS ANOVA/REPEATED MEASURES ANOVA    | 256 |
|       | 10.2.1   | SPSS guidance                                                | 256 |
|       | 10.2.2   | Reporting results                                            | 260 |
| 10.3  |          | TWO- OR THREE-WAY BETWEEN-PARTICIPANTS ANOVA                 | 260 |
|       | 10.3.1   | SPSS guidance                                                | 261 |
|       | 10.3.2   | Reporting results                                            | 263 |
| 10.4  |          | TWO- OR THREE-WAY WITHIN-PARTICIPANTS ANOVA                  | 263 |
|       | 10.4.1   | SPSS guidance                                                | 264 |
|       | 10.4.2   | Reporting results                                            | 268 |
| 10.5  |          | ANCOVA                                                       | 269 |
|       | 10.5.1   | SPSS guidance                                                | 270 |
|       | 10.5.2   | Reporting results                                            | 271 |
| 10.6  |          | KRUSKAL-WALLIS                                               | 271 |
|       | 10.6.1   | SPSS guidance                                                | 271 |
|       | 10.6.2   | Reporting results                                            | 271 |
|       | RESEARCH METHODS AT WORK                                                | 272 |
|       | A SHORT SUMMARY                                                         | 273 |
|       | CHECK YOUR UNDERSTANDING                                                | 273 |

## 11 Statistical Analyses: Looking at Associations and Relationships — 275

|       |          |                                                              |     |
|-------|----------|--------------------------------------------------------------|-----|
| 11.1  |          | PARAMETRIC DATA CORRELATION (PEARSON'S)                      | 276 |
|       | 11.1.1   | Pearson's in Excel                                           | 276 |
|       | 11.1.2   | Pearson's in SPSS                                            | 277 |
|       | 11.1.3   | Reporting Pearson's correlations                             | 278 |
| 11.2  |          | SPEARMAN'S CORRELATION                                       | 278 |
|       | 11.2.1   | Spearman's in Excel                                          | 279 |
|       | 11.2.2   | Spearman's in SPSS                                           | 280 |
|       | 11.2.3   | Reporting Spearman's correlations                            | 280 |
| 11.3  |          | COMPARING EXPECTED VERSUS OBSERVED FREQUENCIES: CHI-SQUARE GOODNESS-OF-FIT | 280 |
|       | 11.3.1   | Goodness-of-fit chi-square in Excel                          | 280 |

xiv  Contents

|  | | 11.3.2 | Goodness-of-fit chi-square in SPSS | 281 |
|  | | 11.3.3 | Reporting the outcome of a goodness-of-fit chi-square test | 282 |
|  | 11.4 | COMPARING EXPECTED VERSUS OBSERVED FREQUENCIES: TEST OF INDEPENDENCE CHI-SQUARE | | 282 |
|  | | 11.4.1 | Test of independence chi-square in Excel | 283 |
|  | | 11.4.2 | Test of independence chi-square in SPSS | 285 |
|  | | 11.4.3 | Reporting a chi-square test of independence | 286 |
|  | RESEARCH METHODS AT WORK | | | 287 |
|  | A SHORT SUMMARY | | | 287 |
|  | CHECK YOUR UNDERSTANDING | | | 288 |

## 12 Writing Up Research — 289

|  | 12.1 | LITERATURE REVIEW | | 292 |
|  | 12.2 | RATIONALE | | 293 |
|  | 12.3 | HYPOTHESES | | 293 |
|  | 12.4 | METHODS | | 294 |
|  | | 12.4.1 | Participants | 294 |
|  | | 12.4.2 | Design | 294 |
|  | | 12.4.3 | Procedures | 295 |
|  | | 12.4.4 | Data analysis | 295 |
|  | 12.5 | RESULTS | | 295 |
|  | 12.6 | DISCUSSION | | 296 |
|  | | 12.6.1 | Limitations | 296 |
|  | 12.7 | REFERENCES | | 297 |
|  | 12.8 | APPENDIX | | 298 |
|  | 12.9 | INTRODUCTION | | 298 |
|  | 12.10 | TITLE | | 299 |
|  | 12.11 | ABSTRACT | | 299 |
|  | RESEARCH METHODS AT WORK | | | 300 |
|  | A SHORT SUMMARY | | | 300 |
|  | CHECK YOUR UNDERSTANDING | | | 301 |

*Appendix 1 – Standard Error of Skewness for Small Sample Sizes* — 302
*Appendix 2 – Critical Values for Wilcoxon Signed Rank Test* — 303
*Exercise Solutions* — 304
*General Glossary* — 329
*Excel Functions Glossary* — 339
*References* — 350
*Index* — 357

# List of Figures

| | | |
|---|---|---|
| 1.1 | Requirements of a good research question | 3 |
| 1.2 | Requirements for a good research question for you | 9 |
| 1.3 | Relevance of the research question in each stage of the project | 11 |
| 2.1 | Scale types | 17 |
| 2.2 | Line chart showing main effect (data from Chu and Kamal, 2008) | 34 |
| 2.3 | Interaction of variables illustrated with a line graph (data from Chu and Kamal, 2008) | 35 |
| 2.4 | Plausible scenarios explaining a single outcome | 44 |
| 3.1 | Semantic differential with criteria from Kressmann et al. (2006) © Elsevier | 72 |
| 3.2 | Stonewall (2016) recommendations to collect data on gender and gender identity | 73 |
| 3.3 | Block randomisation | 86 |
| 3.4 | Order and sequence effects | 88 |
| 4.1 | 'Less than' sign | 96 |
| 4.2 | Moving decimal points | 100 |
| 4.3 | Rounding to the third decimal place | 101 |
| 5.1 | Linking files through participant IDs | 119 |
| 5.2 | Excel worksheet | 121 |
| 5.3 | Naming variables in Excel: by column | 122 |
| 5.4 | Naming variables in Excel: by row | 122 |
| 5.5 | Sorting in Excel | 123 |
| 5.6 | Entering a function manually | 123 |
| 5.7 | Formula Builder window in Excel | 124 |
| 5.8 | Sum formula in the Formula Builder window | 125 |
| 5.9 | Data menu in Excel | 126 |
| 5.10 | Filter window in Excel | 126 |
| 5.11 | Filter pick list | 127 |
| 5.12 | SPSS Data view | 128 |
| 5.13 | SPSS Variable view | 129 |
| 5.14 | Importing data into SPSS | 129 |
| 5.15 | SPSS syntax file | 130 |
| 5.16 | SPSS output file | 131 |
| 5.17 | Variable name mouse over information | 131 |
| 5.18 | Variable label in output file | 132 |
| 5.19 | SPSS Value Labels window | 132 |
| 5.20 | SPSS Select Cases window | 133 |
| 5.21 | SPSS 'Select Cases: if' window | 133 |
| 5.22 | Using questionnaire IDs | 134 |
| 5.23 | Excel insert menu | 147 |
| 5.24 | IF function | 148 |
| 5.25 | Recoding in Excel | 148 |
| 5.26 | Recoding in SPSS | 149 |
| 5.27 | SPSS Compute Variable window | 150 |
| 6.1 | Excel PivotTable menu | 157 |
| 6.2 | Excel PivotTable window | 157 |
| 6.3 | Excel PivotTable Builder | 158 |

## List of Figures

| | | |
|---|---|---|
| 6.4 | Excel pivot table | 158 |
| 6.5 | Dispersal of data points around a central measure | 160 |
| 6.6 | Example median split | 164 |
| 6.7 | Four samples from the same population | 170 |
| 6.8 | Descriptives for Sample 1 | 171 |
| 6.9 | Descriptives for all samples | 172 |
| 6.10 | Example of sources of variance in perceived stress | 174 |
| 6.11 | A prototypical normal distribution | 175 |
| 6.12 | Values one, two, three or more standard deviations from the mean | 176 |
| 6.13 | The shape of a normal distribution becoming more visible with growing sample size | 177 |
| 6.14 | Left- and right-skewed distributions | 179 |
| 6.15 | Types of kurtosis | 179 |
| 6.16 | Formula for pooled variance | 185 |
| 6.17 | Two groups in the pooled variance | 185 |
| 7.1 | Sample bars chart showing customer satisfaction scores before and after staff training | 197 |
| 7.2 | Sample stacked bar chart showing comparison of smoking habits by age bracket | 198 |
| 7.3 | Sample histogram showing frequencies of answers | 199 |
| 7.4 | Sample pie chart with fairly obvious distribution | 199 |
| 7.5 | Sample pie chart with small number of values | 200 |
| 7.6 | Sample pie chart with too many groups | 200 |
| 7.7 | Sample scatter plot | 201 |
| 7.8 | Sample line chart illustrating an interaction of Cognitive Behavioural Therapy (CBT) and exercise | 201 |
| 7.9 | Comparison of quality control measures over time | 202 |
| 7.10 | Using textures in a stacked chart | 203 |
| 7.11 | Using textures in a line chart | 204 |
| 7.12 | 100% stacked bar chart illustrating complaint types in Q1 and Q2 | 207 |
| 7.13 | Stacked bar chart illustrating complaint types in Q1 and Q2 | 208 |
| 7.14 | Relative number of complaints | 208 |
| 7.15 | Agreement data | 210 |
| 8.1 | Excel Q-Q plot for 'VerbalScore' | 215 |
| 8.2 | Excel Q-Q plot for 'NumericalScore' | 218 |
| 8.3 | Experimental design for sample data | 227 |
| 9.1 | How the t-test statistic is calculated | 232 |
| 9.2 | SPSS window one-sample t-test | 233 |
| 9.3 | SPSS output Wilcoxon signed rank | 234 |
| 9.4 | SPSS output paired-samples t-test, group 1 | 237 |
| 9.5 | SPSS output paired-samples t-test, group 2 | 238 |
| 9.6 | SPSS output for independent-samples t-test | 241 |
| 9.7 | Excel sheet to calculate Wilcoxon signed rank | 242 |
| 9.8 | Data for samples 1 and 2 | 243 |
| 9.9 | Completing calculations for Mann-Whitney U-test in Excel | 244 |
| 9.10 | A paired-samples t-test examining whether two variables are similar or different | 247 |
| 9.11 | Independent-samples t-test examining recall data of 2 and 12 days | 247 |
| 9.12 | Independent-samples t-test examining recall data of 2 and 20 days | 248 |
| 9.13 | Independent-samples t-test examining recall data of 12 and 20 days | 248 |
| 10.1 | Conducting a single factor ANOVA in Excel | 251 |
| 10.2 | Output for a one-way ANOVA with the independent variable 'CourseType' and the dependent variable 'VerbalScore' | 251 |
| 10.3 | Setting up a one-way ANOVA in SPSS | 252 |
| 10.4 | Setting options for a one-way ANOVA in SPSS | 252 |

| | | |
|---|---|---|
| 10.5 | Setting post-hoc multiple comparisons for a one-way ANOVA in SPSS | 253 |
| 10.6 | Descriptives for variable 'VerbalScore' across three conditions of 'CourseType' and overall | 253 |
| 10.7 | Test of homogeneity of variances for variable 'VerbalScore' | 254 |
| 10.8 | Result of ANOVA testing for effect of 'CourseType' on 'VerbalScore' | 254 |
| 10.9 | Test for equality of means for variable 'VerbalScore' | 254 |
| 10.10 | Multiple comparisons table listing post-hoc tests comparing all three groups | 255 |
| 10.11 | Repeated measures: defining factors | 256 |
| 10.12 | Repeated measures: defining measures | 257 |
| 10.13 | Repeated measures: defining within-subjects variables | 257 |
| 10.14 | Repeated measures: completed within-subjects variables field | 258 |
| 10.15 | Within-subjects factors | 258 |
| 10.16 | Descriptive statistics | 259 |
| 10.17 | Repeated measures: multivariate tests for variable 'Presentationformat' | 259 |
| 10.18 | Repeated measures: Mauchly's test of sphericity for variable 'Presentationformat' | 259 |
| 10.19 | Repeated measures: test of within-subjects effects for variable 'Presentationformat' | 259 |
| 10.20 | Setting up two-way univariate analysis in SPSS | 261 |
| 10.21 | Descriptive statistics for test scores across gender and education type | 262 |
| 10.22 | Levene's test of equality of error variances for variable 'C_Testscore' | 262 |
| 10.23 | Tests of between-subjects effects for dependent variable 'C_Testscore' | 262 |
| 10.24 | Repeated measures: defining two factors in SPSS | 264 |
| 10.25 | Repeated measures: defining individual within-subjects variables in SPSS | 265 |
| 10.26 | Repeated measures: completed definitions of within-subjects variables | 266 |
| 10.27 | Repeated measures: list of within-subjects factors 'Difficulty' and 'Length' | 266 |
| 10.28 | Repeated measures: descriptive statistics for six conditions | 267 |
| 10.29 | Repeated measures: Mauchly's test of sphericity for variables 'Difficulty' and 'Length' | 267 |
| 10.30 | Repeated measures: multivariate tests for variables 'Difficulty' and 'Length' | 267 |
| 10.31 | Repeated measures: tests of within-subjects effects for variables 'Difficulty' and 'Length' | 268 |
| 10.32 | Results of an independent-samples Kruskal-Wallis test in SPSS | 272 |
| 11.1 | Data analysis: Correlation window | 277 |
| 11.2 | Observed frequencies | 281 |
| 11.3 | Actual frequencies | 283 |
| 11.4 | Actual frequencies with row totals | 283 |
| 11.5 | Formulas to calculate expected frequencies | 284 |
| 11.6 | Calculated expected frequencies | 284 |
| 11.7 | Sample Excel formulas to calculate expected frequencies | 284 |
| 11.8 | Sample Excel formulas to calculate expected frequencies | 285 |
| 11.9 | SPSS data for chi-square test | 286 |
| 12.1 | A sample outline | 290 |
| 12.2 | Continuity in writing up | 291 |

# List of Tables

| | | |
|---|---|---|
| 2.1 | Sample age data | 16 |
| 2.2 | Sample nominal data | 18 |
| 2.3 | Sample ordinal data | 19 |
| 2.4 | Sample interval data | 19 |
| 2.5 | Sample description of interval data | 20 |
| 2.6 | Sample ratio data | 20 |
| 2.7 | Scale type properties | 21 |
| 2.8 | 2 × 2 × 2 × 2 × 2 study design in Velasco, Salgado-Montejo, Marmolejo-Ramos and Spence (2014). | 33 |
| 2.9 | 2 × 2 between-participants study with the independent variables 'blogger trustworthiness' and 'argument quality' (data from Chu and Kamal, 2008) | 34 |
| 2.10 | Average attitude scores per condition (data from Chu and Kamal, 2008) | 35 |
| 3.1 | Confidence level and z-score | 81 |
| 3.2 | Optimism pilot data | 90 |
| 3.3 | Item-total statistics from SPSS | 91 |
| 4.1 | Sample absolute responses | 98 |
| 4.2 | Responses in percentages | 98 |
| 5.1 | Recording selection for each response | 137 |
| 5.2 | Recording only selected response | 138 |
| 5.3 | Recording data from multiple choice questions | 139 |
| 5.4 | Recording data from ordering/ranking tasks | 140 |
| 5.5 | Data file excerpt | 144 |
| 5.6 | Data file showing data entry error | 145 |
| 6.1 | Frequencies of main reasons not to vote | 156 |
| 6.2 | Percentages of main reasons given | 159 |
| 6.3 | Complex table of percentages showing responses split by age and political affiliation | 159 |
| 6.4 | Frequencies of individual values | 162 |
| 6.5 | Mean and deviation from mean | 167 |
| 6.6 | Calculating the sum of squares | 167 |
| 6.7 | Comparison of symbols for population parameters and sample statistics | 170 |
| 6.8 | Mean and standard deviation for four samples from the same population, and for the overall population | 173 |
| 6.9 | Type 1 and 2 errors | 180 |
| 7.1 | Frequencies of main reasons not to vote | 193 |
| 7.2 | Reasons for non-voting by voting eligibility | 193 |
| 7.3 | Mean (SD) of average donation (in £) per condition | 194 |
| 7.4 | Mean (SD) of average suggested donations in £ | 195 |
| 7.5 | Average reaction time in ms, depending on priming and task difficulty | 205 |
| 7.6 | Correlation output in Excel | 205 |
| 7.7 | Correlation output in SPSS | 205 |
| 7.8 | Prototypical correlation table | 206 |
| 7.9 | Prototypical correlation table, with redundant cells shaded | 206 |
| 7.10 | Indicating significance in tables | 206 |
| 7.11 | Average arguments correctly and incorrectly recalled by time and type of recall | 207 |

| | | |
|---|---|---|
| 7.12 | Intent to purchase | 209 |
| 8.1 | Descriptives of 'VerbalScore' | 213 |
| 8.2 | Descriptives of 'NumericalScore' | 218 |
| 8.3 | Overview of statistical tests covered in Chapters 9, 10 and 11 | 219 |
| 9.1 | Results of a paired-samples t-test for Material 1 | 236 |
| 9.2 | Results of a paired-samples t-test for Material 2 | 236 |
| 9.3 | Excel result for f-test two-sample for variances | 239 |
| 9.4 | Excel result for t-test: Two-sample assuming equal variances | 240 |
| 11.1 | Correlation scores | 277 |
| 11.2 | Observed frequencies | 282 |

# About the Author

Daniela Aidley is a Professor of Business Psychology at the Applied University Westküste, Heide, Germany. Having first completed a Master's in Linguistics, Psychology and English, she worked at Harvey Nash HR Consulting and McKinsey, Inc. for five years before moving to the UK where she completed a PhD in Cognitive Psychology in 2012 at the University of Leicester. She then worked at the university until 2017 when she moved back to Germany. Daniela has supervised numerous dissertations at Bachelor, Master, PhD and Doctorate level and is a member of the Editorial Board at Sociological Research Online.

# Author's Acknowledgements

I thank Dr Richard Courtney for planting the seed of writing 'a quants book' a few years ago. First, I laughed. Then, I pondered ... and then I started writing. This is all your fault, Richard. My sincere thanks go to the staff at Red Globe Press: Peter Atkinson, Isabelle Cheng, Cathy Scott, Isabel Berwick, and previously Paul Stevens, for holding my hand throughout the process of publishing my first book. I regret nothing and I'd happily do it again. (I need a break though. I haven't had a guilt-free weekend for a few years now.) I gratefully acknowledge that parts of this book are based on modules I developed at the University of Leicester. Furthermore, I am genuinely grateful for the anonymous (to me) reviewers who read the proposal and the first full draft of the manuscript. Your feedback and your insight was invaluable and helped to make the book more rounded and, I hope, more useful to students and teachers. I thank Tikvah Rutz who read chapters of the book and gave helpful feedback, and my colleagues and friends for their support and their patience whenever I worried about deadlines and word counts and writing and did I mention deadlines? Last, but most definitely not least, my sincere gratitude and thanks go to my husband and best friend Dr Jack Aidley, my highly significant other ($p < .001$) who supported me throughout, providing encouragement, motivation, advice and understanding.

# Publisher's Acknowledgements

The figures taken from IBM SPSS Statistics software ("SPSS®") are reprinted courtesy of International Business Machines Corporation, © International Business Machines Corporation, © SPSS. SPSS Inc. was acquired by IBM in October 2009. IBM, the IBM logo, ibm.com, and SPSS are trademarks or registered trademarks of International Business Machines Corporation, registered in many jurisdictions worldwide. Other product and service names might be trademarks of IBM or other companies. A current list of IBM trademarks is available on the Web at "IBM Copyright and trademark information" at www.ibm.com/legal/copytrade.shtml.

The figures taken from Microsoft Excel © software are used with permission from Microsoft.

Figure 3.1. © Elsevier. Kressmann, F., Sirgy, M. J., Herrmann, A., Huber, F., Huber, S., & Lee, D. J. (2006). Direct and indirect effects of self-image congruence on brand loyalty. *Journal of Business Research*, 59(9), 955–964, https://doi.org/10.1016/j.jbusres.2006.06.001

Figure 6.13: The shape of a normal distribution becoming more visible with growing sample size. Reproduced with permission from BMJ Publishing Group Ltd. Alatman, D. G. and Gland, M. (1995). Statistics notes: The normal distribution. *British Medical Journal, 310,* p. 298.

# Introduction

If you're holding this book, chances are you are interested in how to conduct quantitative research; or you are undecided whether to conduct quantitative or qualitative research; or you have already started and found yourself stuck.

Whatever the case, I hope this book will be useful to you.

I have taught quantitative research methods for several years, and I have done so on programmes ranging from Bachelor's to Master's, PhD and Doctorate. The same issues have come up across all those different programmes, and seeing this made me wish textbooks would cover the basic concepts more thoroughly and in a more accessible way. Eventually I decided to write such a textbook myself. This book is partly based on module material previously developed for the School of Business at the University of Leicester, but most of it has been written afresh whilst drawing from my years of teaching experience. I wanted to achieve (at least) two things:

1. Provide a comprehensive guide for conducting a quantitative research study, from the conception of the research question to collecting data, analysing data and writing up.
2. Show that Excel can be used as an alternative to SPSS for a number of statistical analyses. Although Excel is a spreadsheet tool, it can be used for most descriptive statistics as well as for a range of inferential statistics.

This book is for you if:

- You are conducting a quantitative research project, be it as an undergraduate student or a postgraduate researcher who is suddenly faced with a quantitative research project.
- You need a complete overview of a quantitative research project from beginning to end.
- You seek guidance for some basic statistical analyses.
- You want to refresh your memory on some aspects of quantitative research.
- You want to conduct quantitative research in your workplace. Although the focus of this book is on quantitative research methods in an academic context, this book is also suitable for the interested practitioner.

The book takes a chronological approach. You can read it from start to finish if you would like to get an overview on how to conduct quantitative research, but you can also skip individual chapters if you already know what you are doing and are looking for guidance on specific topics.

**Chapter 1** helps you develop ideas for potential research questions, whether these questions are new or partly or fully based on existing research. At the end of this chapter you should be able to develop new research questions, examine whether they are suitable and feasible, and know what to look out for when planning your research project.

**Chapter 2** introduces and defines the basic concepts of quantitative empirical research, such as what constitutes a variable and what distinguishes a true experiment from a quasi-experiment or correlational study. Chapter 2 also introduces the requirements for conducting ethical research. At the end of Chapter 2 you should have a good overview on the type of research questions that can be answered in ethical quantitative studies and how the concepts of reliability and validity relate to your research methodology.

**Chapter 3** talks about the advantages and disadvantages of primary versus secondary data collection and what type of research question you might be able to answer with each type of collection. Chapter 3 guides you through means of data collection, sampling procedures and ways of avoiding or reducing bias. At the end of Chapter 3 you should be able to design material for data collection, decide on the type of sampling procedure you need, and appreciate that data collection has implication for data analysis.

**Chapter 4** reviews a range of basic mathematics concepts which will enable you to follow the discussion of statistical analyses later on. This ranges from being able to interpret signs such as <, > and $\Sigma$ to being able to understand and interpret fractions, exponents, scientific notation and absolute values. At the end of this chapter you should be able to follow the formulas and calculations in the chapters following Chapter 4.

**Chapter 5** covers the process of data entry and handling and bridges the gap between data collection and data analysis. This chapter describes how to eyeball your data for errors and how to search for and identify outliers. It provides guidance for entering different types of data into Excel and SPSS. At the end of the chapter you should be able to enter your data into the software you have chosen to work with, check your data for errors, and do some basic coding and recoding of variables. This chapter will also prepare you for the use of Excel and SPSS in Chapters 8, 9, 10 and 11.

**Chapter 6** looks more closely at data description and basic data analysis. This means introducing key concepts such as standard deviation and variance, outlining different ways of describing distributions of data and discussing the difference between a sample and a population. At the end of this chapter you should be able to provide basic descriptives of your data and have the knowledge to more fully understand the range of analyses described in Chapters 8, 9, 10 and 11.

**Chapter 7** discusses how to present your data to the reader by looking at different types of data presentation – tables and graphs – and when it might be appropriate to use either. This chapter also outlines how to present data in such a way that as many people as possible can access your findings. At the end of this chapter you should have a better understanding of the ways in which visualisation can – and cannot – complement your writing.

**Chapter 8** provides an overview of the analyses covered in this book. The chapter begins by discussing the concept of parametric and non-parametric tests and provides guidance on how to test data in both SPSS and Excel. It then describes the use and basic principles of every test described in more detail in Chapters 9, 10 and 11. At the end of this chapter you should understand how you can establish whether data is normally distributed and which test may be appropriate for which type of question, broadly categorised as looking either at effects, differences or associations.

**Chapter 9** describes how to conduct parametric and non-parametric tests which test for differences and comparisons: One-sample t-test, independent-samples t-test, paired-samples t-test, Mann-Whitney U-test and Wilcoxon signed rank. At the end of this chapter you should be able to conduct these tests and report the results.

**Chapter 10** describes how to conduct parametric and non-parametric tests which test for effects: (one-/two-/three-way) ANOVAs, ANCOVAs and Kruskal-Wallis. At the end of this chapter you should be able to conduct these tests and report the results.

**Chapter 11** describes how to conduct parametric and non-parametric tests which test for relationships and associations: Pearson's correlation, Spearman's correlation and chi square (goodness-of-fit and test of independence). At the end of this chapter you should be able to conduct these tests and report the results.

**Chapter 12** reviews how to document and write up your research process. It outlines the purpose of writing up and disseminating your research findings, while acknowledging the variations in requirements, depending on where and why you write. The chapter then discusses each element that may be needed in a write-up in more detail. At the end of this chapter you should know the rationale for including the individual elements of a write-up and know which information you need to report.

The aim of this book is to present accessible guides for the most frequently used statistical analyses. Each chapter starts with a brief overview of the topics that will be covered, a note on why this is relevant and a list of the learning outcomes that will be achieved. All chapters (except Chapters 9, 10 and 11 which contain guidance to conduct statistical tests) feature 'Review & Reflect' questions throughout, and each chapter ends with:

- *A short summary*: This section summarises the main points of the chapter.
- *Research methods at work*: This section takes the contents of the chapters and applies it in a setting outside the academic context to illustrate how the concepts discussed in the chapter are relevant and useful in the workplace.
- *Check your understanding*: This section provides a range of exercises to give you the opportunity to test your understanding before you move on to the next chapter. Where applicable, sample solutions are provided in the appendix.

*Going Further* sections contain optional content which allows you to examine some aspects in more detail, but you will not miss out on the overall understanding if you skip those sections.

❗ These sections highlight aspects you may find particularly tricky or troubling.

🌐 Additional content is available on the companion website: www.macmillanihe.com/companion/Aidley-Introducing-Quantitative-Methods.

Overall, I have tried to emphasise clarity, accessibility and inclusion. But as a social science researcher and psychologist I am painfully aware that I have blind spots. It is likely I got things wrong; in fact, I almost certainly did. Please do let me know what else I can do to make this book more accessible, more inclusive and more useful for you. You can get in touch with me at researchmethods@daniela.org.uk.

Content note: This book makes infrequent references to topics such as gender, depression, weight loss and self-esteem.

# 1 The Research Question

### WHAT IS THIS CHAPTER ABOUT?

This chapter starts by explaining why a clear research question is important for a successful research project before defining the qualities of a good research question in general, and of good *quantitative* questions in particular. Chapter 1 discusses several approaches to identifying and refining possible research questions, both through developing your own question and building upon existing ones. It then looks at determining whether a particular research question is appropriate and feasible for the individual researcher. The chapter ends by providing a brief overview on planning and scheduling your research project.

### WHY IS THIS IMPORTANT?

A clear research question informs and improves the relevance of the literature review, hypotheses, methodology, data analysis and conclusions. It serves as an objective that helps evaluate the success and outcome of your research. A well-thought-out research question provides more clarity, structure and guidance, which means fewer surprises and less stress.

### WHAT ARE THE LEARNING OUTCOMES FOR THIS CHAPTER?

When you have read this chapter and worked through the related exercises, you should be able to:

- Understand the ways in which a clear research question improves on different aspects of your research project
- Identify different sources and types of potential research questions
- Identify research questions appropriate for quantitative research
- Develop and refine your own research question while making sure that it is feasible and appropriate
- Develop a broad plan for your research project

## 1.1 WHY IS A GOOD RESEARCH QUESTION IMPORTANT?

A good question allows you to narrow down your literature research and save yourself considerable time. The clearer you are about what you are interested in, the easier it will be for you to distinguish between 'interesting' and 'interesting *and* relevant' information. A good question also determines the overall approach to the methodology and restricts the type of instruments that can be used and the analyses that can be performed on your data.

For an illustration of this we will look at an example question on the effect of ambient noise on concentration. Some people seem to like listening to music while working, while others are distracted by noise and prefer a silent work environment. This makes it an interesting topic for researchers to study in more detail. From this one general idea, a range of different research questions can be developed:

- Banbury and Berry (2005) examined whether background noise affected employees' job concentration, and subsequently motivation and job satisfaction. Their literature review focussed on the effects of background speech and non-speech noise, and their methodology combined taking sound measurements in an office and having the employees who worked there complete a survey (see Section 3.3 on surveys).
- Evans and Johnson (2000) were specifically interested in whether exposure to noise raised employees' stress levels. Their literature review focussed on the effects of noise on several indicators of health, and their choice of method was an experiment (see Section 2.7) where one group was exposed to noise whereas another group was not. In turn, Evans and Johnson measured the levels of stress hormones, examined whether participants would correct their posture, and observed employee performance in a variety of problem-solving tasks.
- Lercher et al. (2003) looked at the long-term effects of ambient noise on reading acquisition in children. Their literature review focussed on attention processes for visual tasks and outlined how children of different ages responded to noise. The children were recruited based on the noise level of their home environment, and the study (a quasi-experiment, see Section 2.7) consisted of them performing a variety of tasks in a carefully sound-controlled lab environment.

Although all three studies relate to broadly the same question, the different foci of these projects all require different perspectives on existing literature, and they lead to recruiting different groups of people (employees, participants recruited through ads, children selected from particular residential areas); different approaches (surveys, experiments, quasi-experiments); and different settings (in an office, in a lab). A clear research question is therefore necessary to filter and funnel your efforts early on.

### REVIEW & REFLECT

- How does defining the research question relate to the literature search?
- What are the consequences of a poorly defined research question?

## 1.2 WHAT MAKES A GOOD RESEARCH QUESTION?

The requirements for a good research question are deceptively simple. A good research question (Figure 1.1):

1. Is phrased as a question.
2. Tells you what you need to find out in order to answer the question.
3. Contributes usefully to the academic discussion.

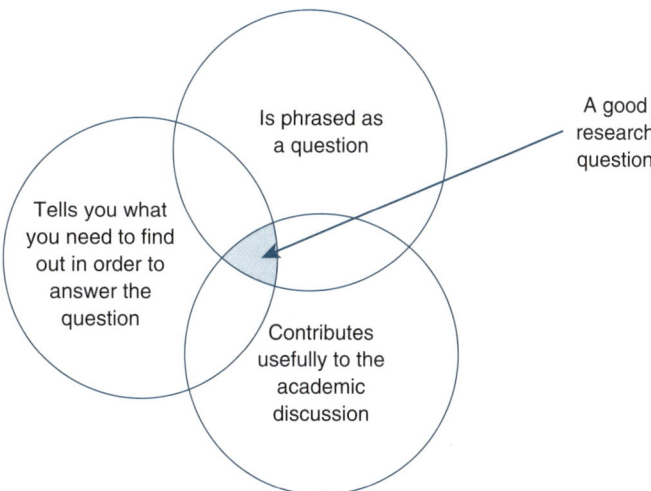

*Figure 1.1* Requirements of a good research question

We will now look at these requirements in more detail.

**Is phrased as a question:** A good research question can be summarised in a couple of sentences posing a clear question which can be addressed by your research. Although it is tempting to phrase your question in a general form describing an area of interest rather than a question, this will make it difficult for you to conduct an effective literature review or decide on a suitable methodology. Rephrasing your area of interest as a question helps you gain a clearer picture of what you need to do.

> **! LOOK OUT!**
>
> Try to avoid phrasing your research question in the form of 'The goal of this research is …' statements. Your research design and analysis should be guided by what you want to find out, not by what you want to do with the findings afterwards. Conducting research with a specific application in mind may bias your methods towards pursuing the more tangible, more 'useful' or 'beneficial', and therefore potentially bias your analysis, interpretation and further research.

That said, you can and should discuss the purpose of your research when writing the introduction to your dissertation or report, and you can certainly use the discussion section to examine to what extent the findings might contribute to your initial aim (see Chapter 12 for guidance on how to write up research findings). In business and management studies, it is also not unusual to talk about stakeholders (i.e., the people and groups for which the research would be interesting and relevant). A research question is a 'working title' for your research project. It determines your focus of interest and your methodology, and it helps you assess later whether you met the goal of your research project. To that extent, your research question is inward-facing: it is aimed at yourself and looks at the future because it tells you what you want to find out and what you need to do in order to achieve it. Your report or dissertation or paper, however, is outward-facing and looks at the past. It tells other researchers what you did and what your results were.

**Tells you what you need to find out in order to answer the question:** Let us assume that we have rephrased the previous example topic as a question: 'Are there individual differences in the effects of ambient noise?' This fulfils the requirement of having the form of a question but is still quite vague – which individual differences, what kind of effects, and what type of ambient noise? The research question needs to be precise enough to suggest or possibly name the variables (see Section 2.1) that need to be examined. A study could focus, for example, on the effects of ambient noise in the form of either music or noise on extraverts'[1] and introverts' task performance in a number of cognitive tasks (immediate recall, free recall, numerical and delayed recall, Stroop task) – as was done in a study by Cassidy and MacDonald (2007); alternatively it could examine the different effects of vocal and instrumental music on introvert and extravert performance in reading comprehension, a logic problem and a coding task (Furnham et al., 1999).

**Contributes usefully to the academic discussion:** If you are conducting research in an academic context, whether as a stand-alone study or for the purpose of an assignment or a final year dissertation, you will be expected to demonstrate your analytical skills and your ability to conduct meaningful research which contributes to the existing body of academic research. You will have to demonstrate that you can engage in a critical literature review and a critical analysis of your data and conclusion. For you, the third criterion becomes more relevant than for others (such as researchers outside an academic context), since it reflects on your ability to function as a critical and independent researcher. In practice, it means that you have to think ahead and subject your research question to a further test. For example, at a first glance studies aiming to quantify instances of behaviours, traits or individuals are suitable for a quantitative approach:

- 'What is the proportion of left- to right-handed individuals in a first-year student cohort at a large East Midlands university?'
- 'Who buys what kind of car?'
- 'To what extent does average monetary donation to animal shelters differ by political affiliation?'

However, simple 'counting questions' like the above are ill suited to demonstrate your skills and academic abilities, because what is missing for these answers to be useful is context. You can provide this context by linking questions to ongoing academic debates. For example, the number of left-handed vs. right-handed students in itself is not very informative, but might be crucial information in the context of discussing handedness and maths achievement (e.g., Casey et al., 1992) or when examining geographical variations in handedness (e.g., Raymond and Pontier, 2004).

Similarly, in the context of discussing individual differences and traits such as compassion and helpfulness, examining average monetary donation to animal shelters by political affiliation can provide useful information linking political affiliation to personal traits – something Bennett (2003) examined in a study on '[f]actors underlying the inclination to donate to particular types of charity'. A question like 'who buys what kind of car?' can be successfully transformed into a good research question, for example, by relating it to consumer willingness to pay for cleaner energy and lower consumption (Achtnicht, 2012) or underlying demographic factors affecting car purchase decisions (Prieto and Caemmerer, 2013).

But even if you are conducting research outside academia, simple counting questions are rarely useful. Instead they can be employed to gain a useful first impression and framework from which to develop more specific research questions:

- 'What are the user demographics of the new online car configurator tool?'

---

[1] We have here chosen to spell this term as extraversion but you will also see extroversion. For a discussion of the difference see https://blogs.scientificamerican.com/beautiful-minds/the-difference-between-extraversion-and-extroversion/

Here, too, the key is linking the question and the data to relevant concepts or frameworks. What do user demographics tell the provider about the appeal of online tools? Are they able to approach all users of the target audience, or does it give the provider new information on how to access notoriously inaccessible groups? The question could therefore be rephrased as:

- 'What are the demographics and personality traits influencing the use of the configurator tool?'
- 'Is there a gender difference in the use of the new configurator tool, and if so, why?'

## 1.3 WHICH RESEARCH QUESTIONS ARE PARTICULARLY SUITABLE FOR QUANTITATIVE RESEARCH?

For some questions, both quantitative and qualitative approaches can yield useful data and insight, but there are questions for which the quantitative approach is more appropriate. Here, you are most likely to find questions which aim at making definitive statements about the relationship between factors, in the form of making comparisons, examining associations or testing for a causal (cause-and-effect) relationship:

Comparisons: Two or more groups are examined at the same time to find out whether they are similar or different.

- Are women more risk-averse in their financial decision-making (e.g., Schubert et al., 1999)?
- Do monolingual and bilingual speakers react differently to affective priming (e.g., Altarriba and Canary, 2004)?
- Does citalopram work better than or equal to a placebo in treating major depression in children and adolescents (e.g., Wagner et al., 2004)?

Associations: Are two or more factors connected to each other?

- Is parental involvement linked with student performance (e.g., Desimone, 1999)?
- Is there a relationship between leadership style and employee satisfaction (e.g., Madlock, 2008)?
- Who listens to which style of music (e.g., North and Hargreaves, 2007)?

Causality: Are two or more factors causally connected such that a change in one factor brings about an effect in one or more other factors?

- Do children learn to imitate actions from watching TV (e.g., Barr et al., 2007)?
- Would a change in product packaging lead to higher appeal to customers (e.g., Underwood and Klein, 2002)?
- Will improved information lead to improved vaccination rates (e.g., Nyhan and Reifler, 2015)?

Of course the question 'Who listens to which style of music?' is not just about association but also differences. The same question can be asked in several different ways, each with its unique emphasis on particular aspects and each with implications for data analysis and interpretation. Knowing and understanding these types of relationships between variables is fundamental to quantitative research. We will look at each of these relationships and their implications for our methodology in the next chapter.

> **REVIEW & REFLECT**
> - What are the characteristics of a good research question?
> - Are there any characteristics that would immediately disqualify a research question, and if so, which and why?

## 1.4 GOING FURTHER: EPISTEMOLOGY

The terms **epistemology**, **positivist** and **interpretivist** refer to the broader philosophical framework within which researchers see their research. Epistemology means literally 'study of knowledge' and is a combination of 'episteme' = knowledge and 'logos' = study of (hence bio-logy, geo-logy, etc.). Different philosophical schools make different statements about the extent to which we can truly understand and know the real world, and the extent to which we can rely on empirical data to draw conclusions. On one end of the continuum, the 'positivist' approach assumes that objective truth exists and that we can examine data to formulate laws and models. On the other end of the continuum, we find the 'constructivist' approach, which assumes that reality and knowledge are socially constructed and hence inherently subjective.

Some of these approaches naturally ally with some research areas more than with others. Generally speaking, the positivist approach is more frequently associated with what we might consider the natural sciences. It is assumed that laws such as Avogadro's Law ('At the same temperature and pressure, any two given volumes of gas will have the same number of molecules') are objectively true and not socially constructed. Similarly, research examining samples to draw conclusions for populations (see Section 3.8 on the difference between sample and population) or aiming to make predictions about relationships between variables is more usually located in a positivist framework. On the other hand, a constructivist approach is more likely to ask questions relating to social issues: What is power? How are ideas developed and communicated? What shapes peoples' thinking and behaviour? This would typically align more with disciplines such as sociology. But the boundaries are debatable, and debated. Psychology, for example, as a discipline concerned with human behaviour and thought sits somewhat uneasily between the two approaches. One argument is that psychological research is more closely associated with the positivist approach, because it aims to make clear statements about objective truths and psychological research is as rigorous and empirical as any of the other natural sciences – possibly more so because psychologists know just how fallible human information processing is and therefore take extensive precautions against bias. A different argument, however, would be that precisely because psychology concerns human behaviour and thought, it is inherently subjective and research is necessarily of a constructivist nature. In the course of your studies you will likely frequently encounter these tensions and come to appreciate it as a source of debate inherent to the social sciences. Ultimately, however, it is your responsibility as a researcher to develop and define your position.

## 1.5 HOW TO FIND A RESEARCH QUESTION

As a researcher you are given a challenging and rewarding task: to independently plan and conduct your own piece of research. This means responsibility and independence in equal measures. Hopefully you have begun to see in the previous sections how a good research question will help you make the most of this, while an unsuitable research question can actively impede your progress. The following sections discuss possible sources of research questions.

## 1.5.1 Replicating findings

Research questions can range from exploring the new and unexamined, to refining or replicating previous research by conducting a study in a similar or identical way to an existing study. These **replication studies** are a vital element of research because flukes and statistical blips happen. We therefore rarely consider a single result conclusive and, in fact, the scientific process works through the continuous accumulation of evidence. Scientists collect data and over time this accumulated data will favour one explanation or one model over another. When you replicate studies you therefore contribute to the scientific process by expanding the amount of data and evidence available. There are many reasons why replicating a study might be appropriate. Sometimes a study yields surprising findings that do not align with related previous research. Other researchers might then try to replicate the study to see whether they get similar or different results. Of course no single study's results can be taken to prove or disprove a particular finding, but if subsequent studies fail to replicate the first study's findings this increases the probability that the earlier study's results were an anomaly. Likewise, if other studies do produce the same findings, it is more likely that initial findings constituted an accurate representation of matters. Much of research is based on people challenging or improving on existing research because they believe the original study to be flawed in design, analysis or conclusion. For example, several years ago, a technique called 'facilitated communication' raised the hopes of countless family members and carers of people hitherto seemingly unable to communicate with other people. Facilitated communication meant that a person who was unable to communicate with others (whether because of severe autism or a range of cognitive disabilities) was helped by another person to use a keyboard or a letter board. The assistant, also called 'facilitator', would hold the person's hand and interpret movement and touch as guidance to spell out individual letters, thus forming words and sentences. Some studies (e.g., Biklen and Schubert, 1991; Crossley, 1992) seemed to suggest that this was an effective technique of giving a voice to people who until then had not been able to speak. Others were more sceptical. Perhaps facilitators introduced their own bias and interpretation into the process? Eberlin et al. (1993) used a setup similar to the standard facilitation process but with some significant changes: screens blocked facilitators from seeing what their communication partner saw; headphones blocked them from hearing the questions their communication partner heard. It turned out that when facilitators did not hear or see what was asked, those extraordinary communication abilities disappeared completely. Fittingly, the title of Eberlin et al.'s paper is a poignant reflection on both their intention and the outcome of their study: 'Facilitated communication: A failure to replicate the phenomenon'.

Other times it is useful to replicate studies to examine how the findings hold up under different circumstances where social, political, economical, technological or cultural factors have changed to such a degree that it is a reasonable assumption original findings may no longer apply in the current context. For example, the increase of tuition fees may have led to a change in attitudes towards studying; consumption patterns may have shifted in the face of changing economies.

The constant need for (re-)evaluation does not only apply to the overarching research question that you start out to answer with your research – it will continue to apply throughout your research project and potentially through your life and work as a researcher. Was the result of your study unexpected but very interesting? Perhaps you want to try and replicate the finding in a second study. Or is the result implausible given what you know so far? You might critically assess the methodology and the data to find that you overlooked an important factor, and after slightly adapting the methodology you expect to find a different result when repeating the study.

> **REVIEW & REFLECT**
> - What are possible reasons to replicate studies?
> - Can you think of any studies you think should (not) be replicated?

### 1.5.2 Developing new questions

More obviously, new research is often prompted by new developments, be they technological or sociological. For example, the advent of the Internet and the home computer meant that whole new fields of research opened up, be they psychological such as exploring computer-user interaction, hypertext navigation or the use of online learning materials; business-related, such as online marketplaces or the birth of online-only retailers; technological, such as encryption, web design or the use of mobile data; or political, such as cyber warfare, the problem of fake news or web access and censorship. The impulse for new research can also come from new means to gather data – MRI scans, evermore capable microscopes, or even the scan of tweets for mention of flu symptoms to map the outbreak of a flu epidemic (e.g., Lee et al., 2013)!

Sometimes, researchers struggle not with the lack of questions but their abundance. Although it can feel overwhelming, having too many questions is a good place to start. It can be helpful to write all questions down, no matter how disconnected and random they seem, and then for each question to think about what type of data or information you would need to answer it. Another approach is to think about what you would like the outcome of your research to be, or who would likely read your research and be able to apply its findings or conclusions:

- Who is potentially interested in the research? For example, funding agencies, organisations, other researchers, etc.
- For whom would the results be relevant? For example, marketing agencies, consumers, Small and Medium Enterprises (SMEs), Non-Government Organisations (NGOs), patients, patient advocates, etc.

If you find it particularly difficult to choose just one question, it might be helpful to think of it as prioritising rather than choosing one and rejecting all other questions. If you are contemplating a question for your Bachelor's degree now, perhaps you could look into another question if and when you are pursuing your Master's degree. Framing it like this can help reduce the magnitude of the decision to more manageable levels because it will feel less like abandoning potentially interesting research – you merely postpone it.

It is perfectly normal to go through several stages of finding a topic, narrowing it down, revising it, then giving up on it in frustration and starting on a new topic. Research questions often are developed in loops of testing, refining and testing, using both quantitative and qualitative methods. This reflects the general iterative nature of research: you form hypotheses based on previous observations, test these hypotheses, and based on the results potentially revise your expectations and hypotheses for subsequent research. For example, you might be interested in learning more about people's motivation to volunteer for charities, so you start interviewing a small number of people. From what you have gleaned from the interviews you form an impression that people seem to either volunteer because doing so is consistent with their self-image as a compassionate person or because they think that their volunteer experience will be useful when applying for new jobs. This first impression leads you to devise two potential strands of enquiry: (a) Are there distinctive types of volunteers and how could they be identified? (b) How do employers look upon volunteering, does the absence or presence of volunteering in a CV make a difference? In the end you might decide to start with surveying past and future volunteers to see whether you can reliably identify different types of volunteers. This iterative nature also shows the importance of qualitative research and the importance of combining different methods that help you explore new areas, gain fresh perspectives and develop new hypotheses. In the same vein, this shows the importance of pilot studies (see Section 3.11) as they can help refine the research question, adjust the methodology or point out additional relevant variables or factors.

### ? REVIEW & REFLECT

- What are possible sources for new research questions?
- Which questions or topics can you think of that should have been addressed through research but (to your knowledge) have not been yet?

### www ONLINE CONTENT

On the companion website you can find a worksheet which helps you identify interesting topics you can then narrow down for a potential research question.

## 1.6 DEVELOPING YOUR OWN QUESTION

Earlier on we asked 'what makes a good research question?' The answer was that it:

1. Is phrased as a question.
2. Tells you what you need to find out in order to answer the question.
3. Contributes usefully to the academic discussion.

We are now going to rephrase the question as 'What makes a research question a good question *for you*?' and, in answer to this, we are adding two more requirements to the list (Figure 1.2):

1. You are genuinely interested in this question, and
2. You have the resources to conduct the research required to answer the question.

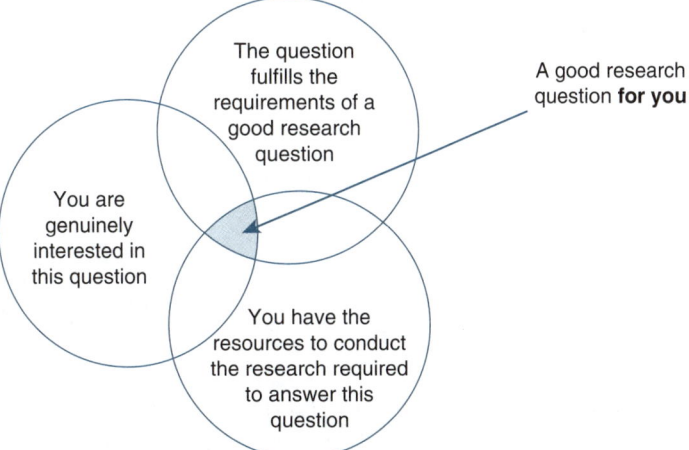

*Figure 1.2* *Requirements for a good research question for you*

**You are genuinely interested in this question**: This does not mean that your methodology should be determined by your preferences; instead, your methodology should follow logically from your research question. But if you have a degree of freedom in choosing your research question, being aware of your own strengths and interests can be very helpful. Doing any research project is challenging, time consuming and often frustrating. You will cope with setbacks and frustrations much better if you work on a project you like and are personally interested in. It is certainly useful to keep your future career prospects in mind. However, if you have a choice between a project that would look good on your CV and a project that excites you, makes you want to read all related papers, and you cannot resist telling other people about, consider picking the latter. Career prospects are abstract and will not keep you awake when you are working on your project late at night for the 15th day in a row – excitement and personal interest will.

 **ONLINE CONTENT**

On the companion website you can find a worksheet which helps you identify your research preferences.

That all said, this may not always be possible. Perhaps you have been assigned a particular question by a teacher, manager or supervisor; perhaps you had a limited list of options and you chose the least off-putting option. In that case, take this requirement as encouragement to try and link whichever topic you end up with to something you *are* genuinely interested in. Talk to people in the field or to people teaching the subject you are researching to catch some of their enthusiasm. Find out how the research can help you progress in your studies or in your later career. Above all: Avoid apathy. (Also, avoid alliteration. Always.)

**You have the resources to conduct the research required to answer the question**: Whatever research question you choose, you need to be able to conduct the required research in good time and to a satisfactory standard. Think about the amount of work you can *realistically* do in the time available. Plan with setbacks and failures and allow for buffer in your planning. Keep the methodology simple – a simple study well conducted and documented is preferable to a complex study only half executed and poorly written up. However, feasibility does not only concern timing; it also means being realistic about skills, access to participants, and so on.

 **ONLINE CONTENT**

On the companion website you can find a worksheet which helps you decide whether your project is feasible.

**REVIEW & REFLECT**

- What are your requirements for a good research question?
- Which are more difficult than others? Why?

## 1.7 PLANNING YOUR RESEARCH PROJECT

Earlier on we mentioned time and resource constraints as important factors influencing the final shape of the research question. Those same time and resource constraints then need to be taken into account when planning your research project. Although every project is unique and requirements for individual steps differ, there is a very basic common structure to all of them. You can see in Figure 1.3 how the research question affects and guides individual stages, and is in turn influenced by some of them.

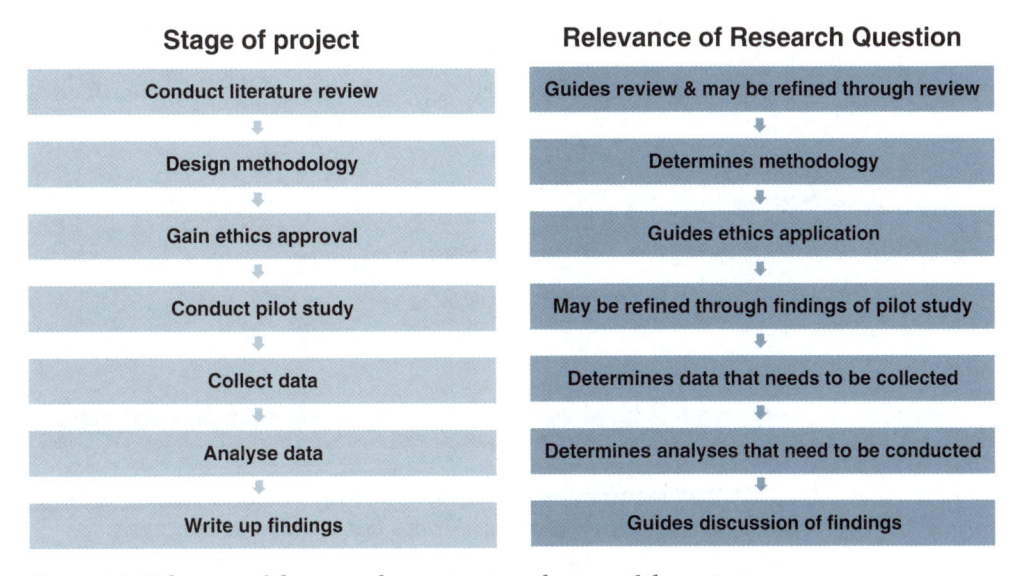

| Stage of project | Relevance of Research Question |
|---|---|
| Conduct literature review | Guides review & may be refined through review |
| Design methodology | Determines methodology |
| Gain ethics approval | Guides ethics application |
| Conduct pilot study | May be refined through findings of pilot study |
| Collect data | Determines data that needs to be collected |
| Analyse data | Determines analyses that need to be conducted |
| Write up findings | Guides discussion of findings |

*Figure 1.3* *Relevance of the research question in each stage of the project*

The literature review needs to come first, because it helps refine the research question and develop the methodology. If you need ethics approval (see Section 2.9), you cannot start data collection until you have received approval. Similarly, if you conduct a pilot study (see Section 3.11), this can only be done after ethics approval, but needs to be completed before the actual data collection. You can only start your analysis once you have collected most of your data, but you can start writing up your methods section even when you are still in the planning stages. Of course the figure above is a simplified illustration of the process. In practice, for example, the literature review not only informs your research question and your methodology, it also feeds into the discussion part of your research. The review is therefore a continuous process rather than a one-off task at the start of your research project. But even in this simplified illustration, you can get a broad sense of the required milestones and stages of your project. You can also use mind maps or decision trees to work out further required milestones: For example, what are the consequence of only recruiting [this many] participants? What might you be able to do if you get access to a particular population? If you decide to use an online survey, what does this mean in terms of cost, time and potential size of sample as opposed to using a paper-based questionnaire?

Once you have defined your milestones, use them to work your way back from your intended deadline while a) allowing for enough buffer and b) including drafts in your planning.

- **Allowing for enough buffer:** Try to not plan to the very last day. If you need to be finished by day X, try to plan your work such that you would be finished by day X – 10.

- **Including drafts in your planning:** If you have the opportunity to have others read over all or parts of your work – whether colleagues, friends, peers, teachers, etc. – make use of that. Make sure that you schedule for enough time for others to read and for you to act on the feedback.

Keep in mind fixed dates and existing tasks and responsibilities. When are you unavailable or unable to work on your research because of a busy period at work or because of exams? If you rely on recruiting participants, watch out for periods of unavailability – many people will be on annual leave over the summer, and students often go home during the summer holidays. Lastly, it helps remembering that simpler is often better. A simple research question examined thoroughly can be more rewarding than a very complex question that requires extensive materials and procedures. Research thrives on simple, succinct and effective studies: Think of the Stroop effect study (Stroop, 1935) comparing times of reading colour words coloured either in congruent or incongruent colours.

## REVIEW & REFLECT

- Which parts of the research project are dependent on each other?
- Are there parts that are more critical than others?

## A SHORT SUMMARY

- Your research question guides the scope of your literature review and the choice of your methodology. A good question helps you make decisions faster and more effectively.
- A good research question is phrased as a question, hints at the variables or factors to be examined and contributes usefully to existing academic research.
- Some questions are more suitable for quantitative research than others. The most suitable types are a) comparisons, b) examinations of associations and correlations or c) examinations of possible causal relationships.
- Research questions can range from exploring new topics to expanding the coverage of previous findings or replicating existing research.
- Choose a research question that is both interesting for you and relevant for your future endeavours, whether you are planning to stay in academia or work in industry.
- When planning your research, define milestones, then start with your deadline and work your way backwards. Include drafts as your milestones and plan with a buffer.

## RESEARCH METHODS AT WORK

Jon works in the HR department and has been asked by his manager to think about ways of finding out how employee morale is overall. Jon already knows that simply asking 'How do you feel about the organisation?' is far too broad, and that asking about every single aspect of work is far too detailed. Thinking about why the organisation wants to know how happy their employees are, Jon realises that happiness is likely to impact on their motivation and therefore their performance; unhappy employees are also more likely to leave. This tells Jon that in addition to overall happiness, questions regarding wellbeing and intention to leave could be useful. Because Jon is planning to conduct this study within the organisation with no intent to publish the results in an academic context, he does not have to think about whether the findings would contribute to existing research – all that matters is that the findings are useful for the organisation.

The mental health charity Sansa is working for has been offering Wednesday afternoon drop-in sessions in addition to their regular home visits. While the charity is happy with the number of people using the service, there is some concern whether the offer reaches enough people; volunteers report that they seem to see primarily male and elderly clients, but fewer of their female or younger clients. Sansa wants to find out whether the volunteers' impression is accurate, but she knows that just counting who turns up will not give the charity useful information; what would be more useful is knowing who does not turn up and *why*. Sansa therefore pursues two lines of investigation: she conducts a literature review to find out what is already known about different groups' willingness to access services; and she also plans to survey all of their client base. That way she can establish how many of their clients know of their service, and what, if anything, keeps them from making use of it.

### CHECK YOUR UNDERSTANDING

1. When might it make sense to repeat a study that has already conducted?
2. Are some areas of research more likely to benefit from replicating studies than others? Why or why not?
3. Assume that you want to find out why people still use their mobile phones while driving and how their usage of phones might affect their driving. List at least eight different research questions that could help shed light on this issue:
    a.
    b.
    c.
    d.
    e.
    f.
    g.
    h.
4. Now work through as many questions in Exercise 3 as you think are necessary:
    a. What would an answer to this question look like?
    b. Does it indicate which type of data analysis is likely needed?
    c. Does it indicate which variables need to be examined?
    d. Does it contribute usefully to existing research? For this exercise, the fourth criterion can be relaxed not to require extensive literature research. Which theoretical concepts can you usefully discuss in the context of your question(s)?
5. Of your eight questions in Exercise 3, which (if any) are suitable for quantitative research and why?

# 2 Basic Concepts of Empirical Research

## WHAT IS THIS CHAPTER ABOUT?

Chapter 2 introduces the basic concepts that are needed to begin planning and designing research methods. It starts by defining what a variable is and what forms it can take before looking at different types of questions that may be answered with quantitative research. It then explains how to design studies in an ethical way and how to minimise bias; to do so, the concepts of control and random allocation are introduced before discussing the criteria of reliability and validity in more detail. Chapter 2 ends by discussing operationalisation – the process of turning theory into practice.

## WHY IS THIS IMPORTANT?

The concepts explained in this chapter lay the foundations for the following chapters. Before we can embark on any kind of research, we need to know what can and cannot be measured and what the implications of different types of measurements are. Reliability and validity are two fundamental concepts which affect the decisions we make regarding our research design and the ways in which we can move from theoretical concepts to practical measurements. These concepts are all important to reduce bias in the way in which we collect and analyse data.

## WHAT ARE THE LEARNING OUTCOMES FOR THIS CHAPTER?

At the end of this chapter you should be able to:
- Explain what a variable is, distinguish between different types of variables, and understand how they can be described
- Explain why research needs control groups or control conditions
- Carefully consider the ethical implications of your methodology and ensure that your methods comply with relevant ethical standards
- Form and interpret one- and two-tailed hypotheses
- Understand what reliability and validity are and how they apply to your research method
- Translate your (theoretical) variables into practical measurements

## 2.1 WHAT IS A VARIABLE?

Broadly speaking, a **variable** is whatever quantifiable information we measure and record, from reaction time to IQ, salary, correct answers in a test, number and direction of eye movements, number of GP visits in the last year, average household spending, willingness to donate to a charity, etc.

But that is only part of the story. What makes data quantifiable is what we do with it. In fact, it is perfectly possible to conduct quantitative analyses on qualitative data. Consider, for example, a study conducted by Kolek and Saunders (2008) in which they analysed publicly available Facebook content from undergraduate students by searching for, and counting references to, learning or studying and partying in order to examine the degree to which students disclosed details of their private life to the public. Note, therefore, that the distinction between qualitative and quantitative is not as simple as 'words' or 'numbers'. You need to look carefully not only at what you are measuring but also how you analyse your data to determine whether you are conducting qualitative or quantitative research, or are using a **mixed-method approach**, which is an approach combining qualitative *and* quantitative elements.

Variables are a type of data that has been classified as having two or more distinct values. But it is not always clear how many values can or should be measured because information about the same individual, item or entity can be collected in many different forms. For example, you can measure participants' reaction time in milliseconds; this would mean that the variable is a **continuous variable** as (potentially) all values are possible – 251 ms, 373 ms, 252 ms, 401 ms, 402 ms, 403 ms and so on. However, you can also collect reaction time as a **discrete variable**, which means that the variable can only take on certain, defined values. For reaction time this could mean creating brackets of values, for example 'less than 200 ms', 'between 201 and 300 ms', 'between 301 and 400 ms' and 'more than 400 ms'. Similarly, you could measure work experience continuously in years and down to months or even weeks, or discretely (but not discreetly) by defining brackets of 'less than 2 years', 'between 2 and 5 years', etc. In practice, you often take shortcuts in your daily life by treating continuous data as discrete – for example, despite the incredible variety of body shapes and sizes (continuous data), clothing still comes only in few different sizes (discrete data).

Defining how a variable is measured can be challenging because it often reveals your own or societal expectations. How you choose to define variables can affect how those expectations are communicated and perpetuated. For example, you will be used to seeing gender represented as a binary variable (i.e., as either male or female). But there is a growing understanding that gender identity and gender expression are far from binary, but rather lie on a continuum; that someone's gender identity can differ from the identity they were assigned at birth; that there are many nuanced identities between the 'male' and 'female' end poles of the continuum; and that these identities can be fluid and non-fixed. Defining gender as a binary variable means participants with non-binary or gender non-conforming identities will not be able to adequately represent their own identity. Because this is such an important aspect, we will take a closer look at how to collect data on gender and sexual orientation in the section on demographic questions in Chapter 3; for now, we want to emphasise that with many variables there is a degree of choice involved in how you represent those variables, and with that choice often comes responsibility.

For many variables, it is up to you as the researcher to decide whether to treat a variable as discrete or continuous, but there are advantages to collecting data in its continuous form in the first instance because you can transform – that is, change – continuous data to discrete data but not the other way round (more on that in Section 5.7.4). Let us have a brief look at an example of why and how it makes a difference whether you collected data in discrete or continuous form; more precisely, we will discuss why it is usually a good idea to collect data in continuous form to start with. In this example we have decided to treat age as a discrete variable and have presented participants with age brackets such as *under 19, 20–29, 30–39, 40–49, 50–59, 60 and over* (you will see in a second why this is usually not a good idea). At the end our data looks like this (Table 2.1):

*Table 2.1* Sample age data

| Age bracket (in ascending order) | Number of participants (N = 25) |
|---|---|
| Under 19 | 4 |
| 20–29 | 5 |
| 30–39 | 3 |
| 40–49 | 5 |
| 50–59 | 6 |
| 60 and over | 2 |

Unfortunately, with this kind of data we are unable to answer simple questions such as:

1. What is the age range of our participants?
2. How old is our oldest participant?
3. What is our participants' average age?

For 1., our unsatisfactory answer is 'from under 19 to over 60'; for 2., 'over 60' – but we do not know whether they are aged 61 or 91. For 3., we simply have to shrug our shoulders and say 'Don't know'.

If, on the other hand, we had collected our data in continuous form by asking participants how old in years they are, our data from the same set of participants might look like this:

Age data (sorted in ascending order):

17, 18, 18, 18, 20, 20, 23, 24, 25, 37, 37, 39, 43, 44, 48, 48, 48, 50, 51, 51, 52, 54, 58, 62, 71

This set of data then would allow us to answer all of these questions, and if we wanted to we can *still* sort our data into brackets:

1. Their age ranges from 17 to 71.
2. Our oldest participant is 71.
3. The average age of our participants is 39.04 years (see Section 6.3 on a definition of the average and alternative ways to describe the same kind of data).

Of course, sometimes there might be other considerations for the format of your question. In some cultures, it is considered impolite to ask for a specific age so we might decide to forgo detailed age data in exchange for the goodwill and co-operation of our participants.

This is your decision to make and it may be a trade-off you are willing to make. Some variables, however, are less open to interpretation and lend themselves more naturally to either a discrete or continuous measurement. For example, *nationality* is more likely to be a discrete variable and would not generally be measured on a continuous scale between, for example, *Swedish(ness)* and *French(ness)*. On the other hand, properties such as length, distance, income or temperature which, theoretically, could be measured in ever-increasing detail depending on the measuring instrument, are more likely to be collected in continuous form – unless the research design requires categorisation such as 'tall/short', 'liberal/conservative', etc.

## 2.2 IN WHAT WAY CAN VARIABLES BE MEASURED?

A different way of looking at variables and the data they describe is classifying data as measured on *nominal*, *ordinal*, *interval* or *ratio* scales. (You might also have heard of the Likert scale, though this is a different type of scale and covered in more detail in Section 3.3.3.) There is a hierarchy to **scale types** such that ratio type data contains the most information, interval data contains less information than ratio but more than nominal and ordinal, and nominal contains the least amount of information. We will now have a closer look at the individual scale types (Figure 2.1).

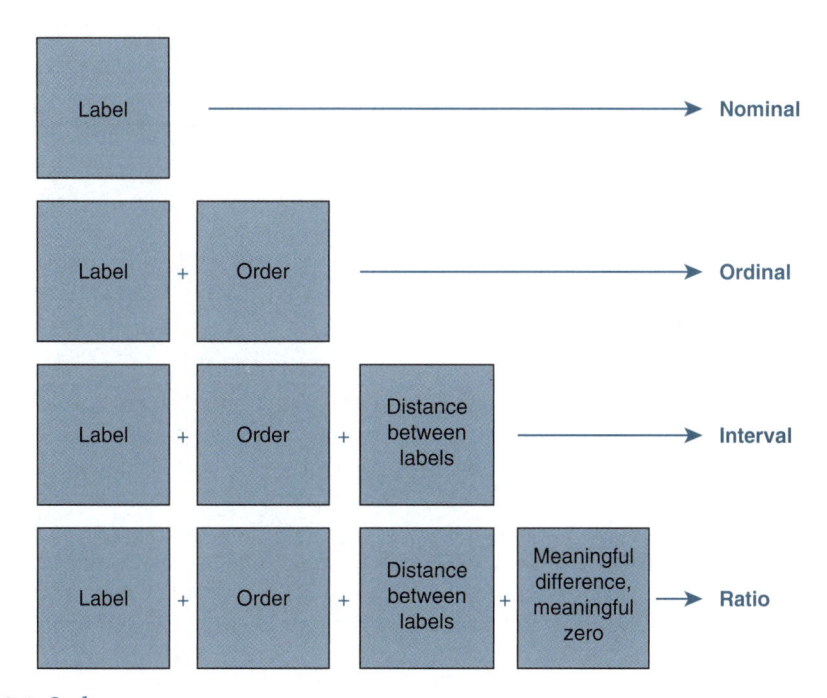

*Figure 2.1 Scale types*

### 2.2.1 Nominal scale data

**Nominal scale** data refers to data that can be named (from lat. *Nomen* = name) and categorised; because of this it is also referred to as **categorical data**. For example, music styles like Blues, Rock, or Punk are categorical data – because items are sorted into categories. Other examples of nominal data would be participants picking their preferred packaging design out of a range of options or indicating whether they would buy a certain product or not.

Sample prompts:

- *What is your favourite music style? ____.*
- *Of the music styles listed below, which is your favourite?*

The table below provides an example of the data you would collect (Table 2.2).

*Table 2.2 Sample nominal data*

| Participant | Response | Participant | Response |
|---|---|---|---|
| 1 | Rock | 6 | Punk |
| 2 | Jazz | 7 | Jazz |
| 3 | Rock | 8 | Pop |
| 4 | Classical | 9 | Pop |
| 5 | Punk | 10 | Rock |

This data can be counted and described by frequencies (see also Section 6.1). You can categorise and summarise data, but only as a tabulation of the frequency of individual categories (e.g., 'In total, 67 participants (45%) indicated that their favourite style of music was *Rock*)'; you cannot calculate average values. However, the use of dummy coding (more on that in Section 5.7.3) may allow conducting additional statistical analyses.

## 2.2.2 Ordinal scale data

Data that can be ordered or ranked is measured on an **ordinal scale**. For example, you might ask participants to sort a range of brands or styles of music by order of preference; sort a group of candidates from least to most qualified; or sort product qualities from most to least important. In doing so, each item is allocated a **rank** (i.e., a position in a sorted list). Although this is more than you can do with nominal data, ordinal data has in common with it that it does not allow calculation of an average, either. For example, although education data allows ordering by level of education (A-level, college, Bachelor's, Master's, PhD) you cannot calculate average education level: if ten participants have a Bachelor, and ten have a PhD, this does not mean that, on average, they have a Master's. Nominal and ordinal data can only be measured as discrete variables but not as continuous variables.

Sample prompts:

*Please list at least three different styles of music you regularly listen to, and rank them in order of preference, starting with the music you like most.*

*Please assign a rank from 1 (most preferred) to 5 (least preferred) to each of the music styles listed below. Please make sure you only use each rank once.*

This yields data as depicted in the sample table below (Table 2.3):

*Table 2.3* Sample ordinal data

| Participant | Rank of 'Jazz' | Rank of 'Classical' | Rank of 'Punk' | Rank of 'Rock' | Rank of 'Pop' |
|---|---|---|---|---|---|
| 1 | 4 | 5 | 2 | 1 | 3 |
| 2 | 1 | 2 | 3 | 4 | 5 |
| 3 | 5 | 3 | 2 | 1 | 4 |
| 4 | 2 | 1 | 3 | 4 | 5 |
| 5 | 5 | 2 | 1 | 3 | 4 |
| 6 | 2 | 3 | 1 | 5 | 4 |
| 7 | 1 | 4 | 5 | 3 | 2 |
| 8 | 3 | 4 | 2 | 5 | 1 |
| 9 | 5 | 4 | 3 | 2 | 1 |
| 10 | 2 | 3 | 4 | 1 | 5 |
| Total | 30 | 31 | 26 | 29 | 34 |

This type of data allows you to calculate the least and most preferred music style across all participants and for every individual participant: 'Overall, participants most preferred Punk, followed by Rock, then Jazz, Classical; the least preferred music style was Pop.'[1] We will show later which tests you can use to examine whether the difference in ranks is (statistically) meaningful.

### 2.2.3 Interval scale data

**Interval scale** data allows ranking and the calculation of an average. In addition, it is assumed that the intervals between individual values are of the same size (Table 2.4).

Sample prompts:

*On a scale from 1 to 7 (with 1 = not at all, and 7 = very much), how much do you like each of the following music styles?*

*Table 2.4* Sample interval data

| P | Jazz | Classical | Punk | Rock | Pop |
|---|---|---|---|---|---|
| 1 | 2 | 1 | 5 | 7 | 3 |
| 2 | 6 | 5 | 4 | 3 | 2 |
| 3 | 2 | 5 | 5 | 7 | 5 |
| 4 | 4 | 6 | 4 | 2 | 1 |
| 5 | 1 | 3 | 6 | 2 | 2 |
| 6 | 7 | 6 | 7 | 6 | 6 |
| 7 | 5 | 3 | 1 | 3 | 3 |
| 8 | 2 | 2 | 2 | 2 | 4 |
| 9 | 2 | 4 | 6 | 6 | 6 |
| 10 | 6 | 4 | 4 | 7 | 4 |
| Total | 37 | 39 | 44 | 45 | 36 |

---

[1] Remember that we have summed up ranks, and that the highest rank (in terms of preference) is 1, therefore lower sums mean higher preference.

When interpreting interval data, it is assumed that similar-sized differences in responses reflect similar-sized differences in properties measured: The difference between responses '3' and '5' (=2) is considered to be equivalent to the difference between responses '2' and '4' (=2). This is important because the same is not true for the items measured on an ordinal scale. For example, there is no meaningful way in which the difference between the second and fourth most liked music style is similar to the difference between the third and fifth most liked style; it is simply not the kind of data for which talking about differences makes any sense. In contrast, for statistical analyses of data on an interval scale it is assumed that the difference between a rating (e.g., of a musical style) of 2 and 4 is equal to a difference of ratings between 3 and 5. Interval data allows the calculation of measures of central tendency (see Section 6.3) and distribution (see Sections 6.5 and 6.7) as well as most statistical analyses such as t-tests (see Sections 9.1, 9.3, 9.4), correlations (see Sections 11.2 and 11.3) and analyses of variance (see Sections 10.1 to 10.5) (Table 2.5).

*Table 2.5* Sample description of interval data

| Style | Total | Mean | Standard Deviation |
| --- | --- | --- | --- |
| Jazz | 37 | 3.7 | 2.05 |
| Classical | 39 | 3.9 | 1.58 |
| Punk | 44 | 4.4 | 1.74 |
| Rock | 45 | 4.5 | 2.16 |
| Pop | 36 | 3.6 | 1.62 |

### 2.2.4 Ratio scale data

Lastly, the **ratio scale** combines the properties of all preceding scales and adds the requirement for an absolute, or natural, point of zero. Asking for amounts of time spent doing X, such as listening to a particular type of music, means there is an absolute point of zero: not listening to that music at all. Length, weight, or amount of money spent are measured on a ratio scale: an absolute (i.e., non-arbitrary) point of zero exists and the measurement intervals are meaningful and allow mathematical operations. Unlike nominal or ordinal data, interval and ratio data can also be elicited as continuous data. Although most data on attitudes, traits or preferences is measured as ordinal or interval data, there are ways of defining (also referred to as *operationalising*, more on this in Section 2.13) your variables in a way that allows you to measure data on a ratio scale. For example, you could take amount of time listened to each music style as ratio data:

*Table 2.6* Sample ratio data

| Participant | Music Style | Time listened to in last seven days (in minutes) |
| --- | --- | --- |
| 1 | 1 | 23 |
| 1 | 2 | 66 |
| 1 | 3 | 0 |
| 1 | 4 | 15 |
| 1 | 5 | 120 |
| 2 | 1 | 12 |
| 2 | 2 | 30 |
| 2 | 3 | 180 |
| 2 | 4 | 62 |
| 2 | 5 | 90 |

'Time listened to' has an absolute 0, and the difference between 30 and 90 minutes is equivalent to the difference between 120 and 180 minutes. All types of data analysis are available. You can report results in a similar way to Table 2.5 above.

The definition of the ratio scale belies its roots in the natural sciences where non-arbitrary points of zero are much more readily found. In some subject areas, they are easier to find than others: stock levels, price, income all have a point of zero. In other social sciences, such as psychology and related disciplines, true points of zero are difficult to find and define. Even the use of interval scales is somewhat fraught with problems: using an interval scale to assess motivation assumes, strictly speaking, that the difference in motivation between the scores 15 and 30 is equivalent to the difference between scores 60 and 75. This assumption is made on principle, and using the interval scale indicates that this type of data is considered to convey more information than data on an ordinal or nominal scale would. Table 2.7 gives you a quick overview of what you can and cannot do with different scale type data:

*Table 2.7* Scale type properties

|  | Nominal | Ordinal | Interval | Ratio |
| --- | --- | --- | --- | --- |
| Can be measured as discrete data | ✓ | ✓ | ✓ | ✓ |
| Values allow calculation of frequencies | ✓ | ✓ | ✓ | ✓ |
| Values allow calculation of means | ✗ | ✓ | ✓ | ✓ |
| Values allow calculation of and with intervals | ✗ | ✗ | ✓[2] | ✓ |
| Can be measured as continuous data | ✗ | ✗ | ✓ | ✓ |

> **REVIEW & REFLECT**
>
> - Are there variables which can only be measured on a nominal scale?
> - Assume you have collected data in nominal form. Could you change it to ordinal or ratio data? Why or why not?

## 2.3 MEASURE OR INDICATOR?

In the example above, we have taken the easy route of choosing properties where what you are interested in and what you measure is identical: *nationality* is described by nationality, *age* is described in years or months, *income* is described by a salary figure. In this way, years are a **measure** of age; salary is a measure of income. But we have already pointed out that it is not always this simple by looking at *gender*: What you want to measure by asking for a participant's gender can range from referring to the social construct of gender consisting of learned behaviour related to the gender role to assumptions on sex-specific traits based on a differential exposure to male and female hormones, which are therefore more likely to be a biological phenomenon. Instead of enquiring in detail after perception of social roles or exposure to hormones, gender is used as a proxy, as a shortcut for a *presumed* set of physiological and psychological traits and abilities. A similar approach is taken by using the result of an extraversion scale as a proxy, a so called **indicator**, for extraversion because you cannot measure extraversion or introversion in

---

[2] Yes, with some reservations. It is usually interpreted that way to make things easier and allow for more operations.

the same way you can measure length, weight, temperature or pressure. Whether a variable is a measure or an indicator depends entirely on the context of the research question. 'Money spent on a product' is a measure of consumption, but could also be an indicator of brand affinity or preference, perception of value, etc.; reaction time, on the other hand, is a *measure* of reaction speed, but may also be used as an *indicator* of attention, motivation to attend to a stimuli, perception of a priming stimuli, etc. The difference between measure and indicator becomes particularly relevant when deciding how to transform abstract concepts into concrete, measurable variables, a process also referred to as operationalisation; this will be discussed in more detail in Section 2.13.

> **REVIEW & REFLECT**
>
> - What are the implications of using measures or indicators?
> - Are there situations where it might be preferable to use indicators rather than (direct) measures?

## 2.4 WHAT IS MEASURED: ASSOCIATIONS AND EFFECTS

In Chapter 1 we briefly introduced three main types of research questions that are particularly suitable for quantitative research. Having now had a closer look at how to measure and categorise variables, we are going to look at these question types again in more detail.

Generally, a variable can have an *effect* on another variable; variables can be *associated* with each other; or there can be a *difference* (in a variable) between groups. In the context of quantitative research methods, these three terms are clearly defined and distinct; this is especially important for the difference between effect and association.

*Relationships* or *associations* between variables mean the variables are not independent of each other, but are linked to some extent. Some associations may be causal, that is, one variable directly affecting another variable in a cause-and-effect relationship. Other variables may be linked in a non-causal way. For example, age and musical preference are broadly related, but no one would suggest that a certain age 'causes' someone to have a particular musical preference, or that a musical preference causes a certain age.

### 2.4.1 Causal associations

Talking about **effects** implies a causal (cause-and-effect) relationship of at least two variables, at least one of which directly influences the other variable(s). For example, Dixon et al. (2011) showed that parents were more likely to choose a certain type of food if it had been endorsed by a celebrity. There was an *effect* of celebrity endorsement on purchasing decision – those decisions were *affected* by the endorsement.

> **LOOK OUT!**
>
> Make sure you know the difference between **effect** and **affect**. **Effect** is a **noun**: 'There is an **effect** of celebrity endorsement on purchasing decision.' Similarly, in this context, **affect** is a **verb**: 'Celebrity endorsement **affects** purchasing decision.' Remember **E** for **E**vent and **E**ffect; **A** for **A**ction and **A**ffect.

## 2.4.2 Non-causal associations

If two variables are systematically related to each other but not in a causal manner this can be referred to as **association**, which means that the variables are not independent of each other. For example, you might have consumers choose one of four products which are identical in functionality, but each product is in a different design. If the four products are equally appealing, and therefore design does not play a role, then you would expect consumers picking a product more or less randomly, and roughly equal numbers of participants picking each product. If that is not the case (i.e., participants are using one product more than you would expect by chance), then the variables 'design of product' and 'customer choice' are not independent – they are associated with each other.

**Correlations** are a special type of association where variables vary systematically with each other. For example, students who are more stressed achieve lower grades (Struthers et al., 2000); people who have more positive pro-environmental attitudes are more likely to exhibit pro-environmental behaviour (Bamberg and Möser, 2007). Although causal relationships are usually accompanied by correlations, not all correlations reflect causality. It has been observed, for example, that 'as air temperature falls from 15°C to 10°C, sales of fresh fruit would increase by 12% whereas the sales of cooked chicken would fall by 12%.' (Agnew and Thornes, 1995, referring to data by Harrison, 1992). This is not a direct causal relationship – the drop in temperature does not *cause* more sales of fresh fruit. Rather, cooler weather means more people are staying inside and overall they are in more of a mood for fruit. Correlations are either **negative** (as one variable's values increase, the other variable's values decrease) or **positive** (as one variable's values increase, the other variable's values increase too). Note that we are only talking about *directions* here; a correlation does not automatically mean that both variables' values change at the same *rate*. The rate of change is described by the correlation size, which Section 11.1.3.3 discusses in more detail.

Examples of positive correlation:

- Demand/Price: As demand for a product increases, so does the price.
- Stock Price/Organisational Performance: Stock price increases with organisational performance.
- Education/Income: People with a higher level of education tend to have a higher level of income.

Examples of negative correlations:

- Vaccinations/Flu cases: As more people get vaccinated, fewer people contract the flu.
- Spending/Savings: The less money you spend, the more money you have available for savings.
- Practice/Mistakes: The more you practice a task, the fewer mistakes you will make.

Correlations and associations are frequently but not exclusively used in business and economics research where existing population-scale data is examined to find patterns and trends, such as Tang's (2009) examination of Malaysian energy consumption between 1970 and 2005, or the relationship between international trade and national rise of inequality in the UK (Haskel and Slaughter, 2001).

## 2.5 WHAT IS MEASURED: DIFFERENCES BETWEEN GROUPS

A different approach to describe data is to talk about differences between groups:

- Do pupils from private schools have better employment chances than pupils from public schools?

- Were people who received the leaflet on solar energy subsidies more likely to install solar panels on the roof than those who did not receive the leaflet?
- Do investors with a low-risk strategy fare better or worse than investors with a high-risk strategy?

We will often find that the same question can easily be asked as a question about differences, associations or effects. Looking at investment strategy and success we can phrase the question in terms of differences:

- Is a low-risk investment strategy more or less successful than a high-risk strategy?

or in terms of associations:

- Is a riskier strategy associated with more success?

Each of these questions has a slightly different focus, and requires different statistical analyses to answer.

You might have noticed that some of those definitions overlap, and this is an important observation. There is a hierarchy to relationships from the least stringent and demanding to the most direct and exhaustive. The most stringent and demanding is the effect. This requires a direct, causal relationship (e.g., celebrity endorsement affects purchases). Variables which exhibit a cause-and-effect relationship also demonstrate a correlation. The strength of purchase intentions will correlate with the extent of celebrity endorsements. But the reverse is not true. Variables can correlate with each other without being linked through cause and effect, for example ice cream sales and weather.

The language of effects, differences and associations often projects a clarity and precision that can easily be misinterpreted as certainty. In reality, all of these statements talk about tendencies and probabilities (more on that in Section 4.12). Not everyone who practices will make fewer mistakes, but over a period of time and looking across a group of people, those who practice are less likely to make mistakes. Not everyone who received a leaflet promoting solar energy will be willing to install a solar panel on their roof, but we would expect more people of the group who did receive the leaflet to change their behaviour than those who did not receive the leaflet. All of these statements also talk about tendencies and probabilities across *groups*, not individuals. Knowing that there is an effect, or a difference, does not allow us to predict which individual might make fewer mistakes or who might install a solar panel on their roof.

## REVIEW & REFLECT

- What is the use of psychological research if we cannot predict individual behaviour?
- Which research questions might only be examined in terms of associations but never effects?

## 2.6 WHAT KIND OF VARIABLES CAN BE MEASURED?

In the context of any study, variables are mainly referred to as either independent or dependent variables. One or more **independent variables** (IV) are usually manipulated to observe whether they affect the **dependent variable** (DV) (i.e., the variable that is presumed to depend on the independent variable). Dependent and independent variables are named in a counterintuitive fashion because the independent variable is the one that is controlled (also referred to as 'manipulated') by the researcher. Perhaps the easiest way to remember is that the dependent variable is called that way because you, the researcher, hope that it depends on the independent variable – in other words, the dependent variable changes in response to changes in the independent variable. For this reason, the dependent variable is also sometimes referred to as the **response variable** whereas the independent variable is referred to as the **explanatory variable**.

Example questions referring to independent and dependent variables are:

- Does 'package design' (IV) affect 'consumer choice' (DV)?
- Can a 'training intervention' (IV) increase 'treatment compliance' (DV)?
- Does increasing the 'marketing spend' (IV) improve 'overall firm value' (DV)?
- Does 'practice' (IV) improve 'performance' (DV)?
- Does 'employee training' (IV) increase 'employee satisfaction' (DV)?

If we look at the impact of practice on task performance, 'practice' is considered the independent or explanatory variable, and 'task performance' the dependent or response variable – but crucially only if we as the researcher actively control how long each participant can practice. Consider the difference between *measuring* amount of practice and *manipulating* amount of practice: If we simply measure amount of practice and relate it to task performance, we might find that people who practice more perform better in the task. But people who are motivated tend to practice longer. Participants' individual motivation therefore interferes with our examination of the relationship between practice and performance since the variation in performance might be partially or wholly due to the variation in motivation and not *only* due to the difference in practice. In this case motivation would be considered a **confounding** or **intervening variable**, or a **confound**. Variables influencing or intervening on the effect of the independent variable on the dependent variable(s) are also referred to as **covariates**. In a different scenario we might find that after a department started sending its employees to more training than in previous years, overall employee performance and employee satisfaction pick up. Is that a consequence of sending employees to training? Does it mean that training increases employee satisfaction? Perhaps, but we cannot say for sure. Perhaps it was because the department has been allocated a bigger budget (so it can finally send more employees to training in the first place) and the bigger budget means it also has been able to hire more staff, thus reducing overall individual workload, in turn reducing stress and increasing employee satisfaction. Or perhaps the department has been assigned a new manager, who turned out to be more responsive to the employees and understood that training was sorely needed. If we just observed the variables 'amount of training' and 'employee satisfaction', we might assume that one directly affects the other, but we would have overlooked possible confounds such as economic factors, manager leadership style, etc. Confounds can come from the participants (personality traits, demographics, abilities and skills) or the setup itself, for example if one task always comes first and allows participants to practice for a subsequent task (see Section 3.10.2 on order and sequence effects), thus making the second task easier; or if one argument is presented in plain text and the other argument supported by graphics and statistics, and so on.

### 2.6.1 Control

To deal with potential confounding variables, we need control; to be more precise, we need **control conditions** or **control groups**. Consider a scenario where participants are allocated to one of two groups. In the first group, participants are asked to rate a CV of a candidate called Laura Smith, in the second group, participants are given an identical CV but are told the candidate's name is Latisha Ayoade. If participants judge candidates purely on their qualifications, both should receive similar ratings. In practice, studies of this kind (e.g., Booth et al., 2012, or Carlsson and Rooth, 2008) usually find that applicants with what participants or raters perceive to be 'ethnic' names fare worse than those with non-ethnic names.[3] Keeping the CV identical but only varying the name given to the applicant is a simple but elegant example of a control condition. Because all but one variable (the name) are kept constant, any difference in evaluation is likely to be due to the only difference in conditions – and that is the name.

Have a look at another example. Assume that we want to find out whether providing meditation training in the workplace is effective at reducing stress levels.

**Step 1:** Participants complete Cohen et al.'s (1983) *Perceived Stress Scale (PSS)*, ranging from 0 to 40, with higher numbers indicating more perceived stress. The average score for participants is 21, indicating moderate levels of perceived stress.

**Step 2:** Over the course of four weeks, participants attend weekly meditation sessions. This is the *intervention*.

**Step 3:** After four weeks, participants complete the PSS again. The average score across participants is now 17.

Looking at the perceived levels of stress before and after participants attended the meditation settings, can we reasonably conclude that the meditation sessions were successful in improving participants' stress levels? (Note: Assume for the moment that the decrease in perceived stress as indicated by the difference between 21 and 17 is substantial and meaningful. We will see in later chapters that not all differences are created equal and that some are more important than others.) The simple answer is no. For example, participants' stress levels may have improved (i.e., decreased) naturally over time. To find out whether this improvement was due to the mere passage of time and not the specific intervention, we need to add a control group: a group of participants who serves as a comparison to the group we are interested in. (For the purpose of this example, we will assume that the groups are identical in any possible aspect but for the fact that participants in group A attend the sessions and participants in group B do not.)

| Group A | Group B |
| --- | --- |
| **Step 1:** Participants complete Cohen et al.'s (1983) *Perceived Stress Scale (PSS)*, ranging from 0 to 40, with higher numbers indicating more perceived stress. The average score for participants is 21, indicating moderate stress. ||
| **Step 2:** Over the course of four weeks, participants attend weekly meditation sessions. This is the *intervention*. | **Step 2:** Participants do not attend any meditation sessions. These participants constitute the control group. |
| **Step 3:** After four weeks, participants complete the PSS again. ||
| The average score across participants in group A is 17. | The average score across participants in group B is 21. |

---

[3] What is considered 'ethnic' depends on the region and culture in which a study is conducted; while the *patterns* of discrimination can be found in different countries, the precise *names* subject to discrimination will differ from country to country.

While this is not conclusive proof, this design allows us to discount the mere passing of time as the source for the improvement in perceived stress levels. Participants in group B had a similar waiting period between the first and second completion of the PSS and their scores did not improve.

In this example we have introduced one of the most important principles in research design: **control**. By keeping group size, group composition and timing of measurements similar between groups we can be reasonably confident that any differences we do find are due to the only difference we introduced, in this case, the meditation sessions. When participants are allocated to different groups in a study, such as 'group which attends sessions' and 'group which does not attend sessions', these groups are referred to as **levels**, **conditions**, **treatments**, or as **factors** (though see Section 2.7 on a specific meaning of factor). In the example just described, the variable 'intervention' had two levels: 'meditation session' and 'no session'. Varying the values of an independent variable (or factor) is called **manipulation** – it means that the researchers exert control over the variable rather than just observing matters. Likewise, a condition or level of a variable where no manipulation is applied to the independent variable is called a control condition because it constitutes a measure of control over the experimental setup by allowing a comparison, in this case, between attending meditation sessions and not attending. A **manipulation check**, in turn, is any kind of measurement by the researcher to check whether the conditions really were different – different enough, that is, to collect the data for the study. For example, if you wanted to manipulate difficulty of tasks to create easy/medium/difficult conditions, you will want to check later on that the tasks actually were different in difficulty.

Using a control group allows us to eliminate one possible reason for any difference between groups, but not all. Another possible reason might be the mere fact of receiving an intervention at all, as opposed to no intervention. In this example, participants in group A had the opportunity to take time out of work each week and relax under the guidance of a professional. This alone may have had a positive impact on their stress level. In contrast, participants in group B did not receive an intervention at all. How do we know whether it was the meditation sessions specifically and not just the break in routine every week?

This tells us that the nature of the comparison matters. It is not enough to compare 'doing something' with 'doing nothing', we also need to compare 'doing something' with 'doing something else'. For example, we could have compared group A attending meditation sessions with group B attending simple relaxation sessions, or just taking an extra hour of break at the same time the other group does. This then would be more useful in telling us whether it is meditation or the extra hour of break time once a week:

| Group A | Group B |
| --- | --- |
| **Step 1:** Participants complete Cohen et al.'s (1983) *Perceived Stress Scale (PSS)*, ranging from 0 to 40, with higher numbers indicating more perceived stress. The average score for participants is 21, indicating moderate stress. ||
| **Step 2:** Over the course of four weeks, participants attend weekly meditation sessions. This is the *intervention*. | **Step 2:** Over the course of four weeks, participants meet for coffee and a chat once a week during an extra hour of break. This is the control condition. |
| **Step 3:** After four weeks, participants complete the PSS again. ||
| The average score across participants in group A is 17. | The average score across participants in group B is 21. |

The difference between scores at the end of the four weeks means that it is likely not the regular time out from work that affected group A's stress levels, but that it was indeed the meditation session itself.

Wherever research is concerned with human thought and behaviour, designing studies becomes particularly challenging. Participants have their own individual reasoning and motivation and may try to guess the study's aim or to help the researcher. In this example, it would have been easily possible that participants did not experience a decrease in stress levels but guessed at the purpose of the study and did not want to disappoint the researcher (see, e.g., Nichols and Maner, 2008). Or perhaps they grew to like the meditation trainer they had been seeing regularly and did not want to give 'bad' feedback by saying their stress levels did not decrease. Including a control condition with a different intervention allows the true effect to stand out more because if there is a genuine beneficial effect of the true intervention, it will be more likely to be visible over and above the effects of participants trying to be 'helpful'. Coincidentally, this is the reason medical research in particular is making use of the **placebo** (from the Latin *placebo*, 'I shall please'). Rather than comparing participants who receive a treatment token (a new medication, physiotherapy, a diet regimen) with participants who do not, researchers use a 'decoy' intervention so that all participants receive treatment and cannot guess from (not) receiving a treatment whether they experience what they perceive as the more helpful or beneficial option. When participants do not know which condition they have been allocated to, they are **blind** to the condition. Studies making use of blinded (not blind!) participants are called **blind studies** or **blind trials**. Compare this with participants who might participate in a study on meditation and stress levels: each participant will know whether they have attended meditation sessions although, depending on the briefing they receive at the beginning of the study, they may not necessarily know whether and how many other conditions exist.

### 2.6.2 Going further: Placebo effects and double-blind studies

The **placebo effect** is one of the reasons we have stressed that we cannot simply compare 'intervention' with 'no intervention'. Particularly in a context of treatment and recovery, receiving attention and care of any type can provide an uplifting and beneficial effect on its own, and we need to make sure that we do not mistake this effect for a consequence of the actual intervention. It is one of the possible explanations for seeing positive effects of homeopathic treatments of young children (e.g., Frei and Thurneysen, 2001) or even animals (Løken, 2002). Even though the treatment itself has no scientifically plausible mechanism of effect (see, e.g., Grimes, 2012), the very act of administering treatment and spending extra care and attention may be beneficial (Shang et al., 2005). To really find out whether these treatments are effective we need to provide a treatment established to be neutral or inert (e.g., a placebo) and apply it in the exact same caring and attentive manner. But researchers are humans and their expectations, too, can potentially bias research results. For example, a study might rely on a researcher assessing their participants' mood and alertness. But their own perception and attention is more often than not coloured by what they expect to find; if the researcher knows who has received the treatment and who has not, they might therefore tend to see improvements in participants they know received the treatment, or fail to notice improvements in participants who they know to be a member of the control group (see, e.g., Rosenthal, 1963). Similarly, researchers might prefer one statistical analysis over another because they expect it to yield 'better', more suitable results. For these and other biases to influence our work, our data and our conclusion we do not even have to be aware of them; in fact, most of the time there is no malice or deception at work, just the vulnerability of human thought and processing. Therefore, where there is a risk that the researcher's expectations potentially influence the result, a **double-blind study** is often the solution: a study where neither the researcher nor the participants know which condition they are allocated to. Sometimes this means having different tasks in the study performed by different people, for example, an outside party who allocates participants to conditions, and a researcher who assesses data regarding the effectiveness of a treatment. Any such setup reduces the possibility that the researcher's expectations impact on the data collection or analysis.

### 2.6.3 Random allocation

In our description of the meditation intervention study above we said that for the purpose of the example we assume that the two groups which are being compared are identical. We have made this assumption for the sake of simplicity, but in reality humans are of course unique. It is simply impossible to find participants identical in physical and psychological makeup, with the same upbringing, experience, economic circumstances and personality traits. Fortunately, this is not necessary: rather than aiming for perfect similarity, the solution is **randomisation** in the form of **random allocation** to groups. To demonstrate the usefulness of random allocation, consider a variation of the study described above but instead we forego random allocation and let participants sign up to the experimental condition of their choosing. It would then be plausible – and quite likely – that participants' choice of condition reflects on their approach to meditation and on the nature of their stress issues. For example, participants who are more aware of their stress levels might choose the condition to attend the meditation sessions because they are more willing to work on reducing their stress levels. Likewise, participants who are either not aware of their stress levels or dislike being alone with their thoughts might prefer to sign up to the coffee-break-with-no-meditation sessions. This is also referred to as **self-selection**, and the corresponding bias **self-selection bias**. Wherever research relies on voluntary participation – and we will see later in Section 2.9 that the ability to voluntarily participate or cease participation is essential to good research ethics – self-selection bias is a potential issue and needs to be considered when interpreting the findings. As a result, if we allow participants to self-select, we can then no longer be sure that any difference in the resulting stress levels are due to the type of intervention (meditation/no meditation): the differences could also be due to different levels of awareness, different levels of interest in meditation, or any number of reasons that might influence participants' choices. Random allocation of participants to groups therefore is crucial. It ensures that whatever else may be relevant to participant-related outcomes (e.g., skill, experience, motivation) is randomly allocated to the two or more groups and any effects of potential confounding variables is minimised.

Section 3.10.1 discusses randomisation methods for testing items, but many of the methods described therein can be adapted to ensure random participant allocation to groups. An alternative to random allocation of participants is **matching**, which means ensuring that two or more groups are as similar as possible in all the relevant variables, for example age, gender, experience, etc. However, this approach is most likely to be important in clinical and pharmacological trials where matching is largely based on physiological factors such as age, weight, illness progression, prognosis, etc.

## 2.7 EXPERIMENTS AND QUASI-EXPERIMENTS

Random allocation and control are the two key requirements for a study to be considered a true **experiment**. Only if *both* conditions are met can the empirical study be called an experiment. This makes experiments the most stringently defined type of research. In turn, they can yield valuable information on causal relationships.

To demonstrate why this is the case, consider briefly what would happen if you relaxed either of the two requirements:

1. **Relaxing the 'control' requirement:** The key for control is to vary only the variable(s) we have defined as independent variable(s) and hold all other variables constant. Lack of control means we have not excluded other potential reasons for changes in the dependent variable. The changes *could* be due to the changes in the independent variable … or not. If we do not exercise sufficient control, we cannot reliably tell which is which and this affects the *validity* of our conclusions (see Section 2.12). For example, if the participants in the experimental group received not only a weekly meditation session but also received guidance on healthy nutrition whereas the control group did not, we would not be able to tell whether any changes in reduced levels of stress are due to meditation, better nutrition or a combination thereof.
2. **Relaxing the 'random allocation' requirement:** If we let participants self-select which intervention to receive, participants with similar personality traits and perceived stress levels may choose similar conditions such that specific personality traits are more prevalent (i.e., widespread) in one group than in the other. Ultimately this might mean that the two groups, A and B, do not differ only in the type of intervention they receive, but also in their participants' personality traits and preferences. We then cannot be sure whether any differences in outcome are due to the different interventions or due to differences in group composition.

In this manner, the requirement for random allocation is a logical extension of the requirement for control. Random allocation allows for better control.

It is important to note that most variables are not inherently independent or dependent variables; or explanatory and response variables, respectively. A variable can be a dependent variable in one study and an independent in another setup. In the previous example, (not) attending a meditation session was the independent variable whose effect on stress levels we wanted to examine. In a different setup, researchers may offer participants a range of coping strategies to find out whether individual traits are associated with preferences for particular strategies; in this context, (non)attendance would be a dependent variable. That said, there are some variables that by their inherent quality can never be genuine independent *or* dependent variables. Neither nationality, gender nor age, for example, can ever be independent variables as we cannot assign participants to a nationality, gender or age of our choosing. At the same time, neither can ever be a truly dependent variable as they are unlikely to be affected by any variables we are able to manipulate. Yet these variables such as age are of interest for a wide range of research questions, from the relationship between age and seafood consumption (e.g., Olsen, 2003) to the effect of age, gender and experience on attitude towards computers (e.g., Pope-Davis and Twing, 1991).

Nationality and age are two very obvious examples, but there are numerous not-so-obvious examples such as level of education, extraversion, socioeconomic status, IQ, employment, etc. Variables of this kind are referred to as **factors**; if a study uses this type of variable to allocate participants to different groups and adheres to all other requirements of an experimental setup, such as experimenter control and measurement of dependent variables, etc., it is referred to as a **quasi-experiment** – almost, but not quite, an experiment since participants cannot ever truly be randomly allocated to groups but are already inherently members of one group over another. A study looking at the effects of background music for people high or low on extraversion (such as the one by Cassidy and MacDonald, 2007, mentioned in Section 1.2) therefore can not be conducted as an experiment, but at the most as a quasi-experiment. The existence of quasi-experiments shows that although the requirements for control and random allocation are linked, they are distinct: it is possible to have studies that fulfil one requirement (control) but not the other (random allocation).

> **! LOOK OUT!**
>
> The term 'experiment' is frequently used as a generic term to refer to empirical research, particularly in layman's speech and writing. However, in the context of academic research, the term is very narrowly defined. When you write papers, reports or dissertations make sure that you only refer to a study as 'experiment' if the conditions of both random allocation and experimenter control are met. Informed readers will assume that when you write 'experiment' you are referring to this very specific subset of empirical research.

So far we have mainly discussed **univariate** research designs consisting of only one independent variable and an unspecified number of dependent variables; a study employing only one factor is also called a **unifactorial** study. Consequently, **multivariate** studies employ more than one independent variable, whereas **multifactorial** studies employ more than one factor. A study employing multiple independent variables and factors is referred to as a **mixed factorial** study.

Regardless of any study's exact design, there will always be at the very least two conditions – if a variable had fewer than two values, it would be a constant! This then means that for every variable we need to determine who experiences which value, or level, of the variable, that is, which participant is allocated to which condition.

There are two ways of allocating participants to conditions, and these are referred to as either **within-participants** or **between-participants** design. Occasionally this is still referred to as **within-subjects** or **between-subjects** designs, respectively. They are so named because research used to refer to participants as 'subjects'. Nowadays it is generally frowned upon to refer to human participants as 'subjects' since this implies lack of agency and lack of respect, but the history lives in the terms still employed. Within-participants design means that the individual participant experiences all conditions of the independent variable, including any control conditions, whereas between-participants design describes a method where participants are divided into groups and every group experiences a different condition. In the meditation session example described above, participants experience *either* the meditation sessions *or* the extra coffee break; this would be described as a between-participants design. A mixed between/within design is, coincidentally, described as **mixed** or **mixed between-within**.

Both methods have their advantages and disadvantages. We will see later that with a growing number of variables, the number of possible conditions can easily grow quite large so that it can be impractical or impossible to recruit sufficient participant numbers to allocate unique participants to each condition. For these cases, a within-participants design can be a good compromise. That said, within-participants designs are more prone to certain biases, such as testing fatigue from experiencing several conditions or very long tasks, practice effects or order effects; we will have a closer look at this in Section 3.10.2.

Often a shorthand notation is used to indicate for any study how many variables with how many conditions are used. This shorthand focusses on factors and independent variables and does not include information on the number of dependent variables. In its simplest form the shorthand consists of two elements 'A × B' (read as 'A by B') showing that there are two variables which could be factors or independent variables. 'A' and 'B' are expressed as numbers (i.e., '2 × 2' or '4 × 3') expressing the number of conditions for each variable. A 2 × 3 design therefore consists of two variables, one with two and one with three levels. Conveniently, this provides an easy way to work out the number of conditions by multiplying the individual numbers. A 'two by two' design has four (two times two) conditions; a '4 × 3 × 2' design 24 conditions (four times three times two):

| 4 | × | 3 | × | 2 |
|---|---|---|---|---|
| Variable A, with four levels | | Variable B, with 3 levels | | Variable C, with 2 levels |

This shorthand notation only includes independent variables and factors and ignores the number of dependent variables. Neither does the order of A, B, C etc. have any meaning; the study described above as '4 × 3 × 2' can be described as '4 × 2 × 3' or '2 × 3 × 4' or any possible order of the three elements, and all descriptions are equivalent.

Sometimes variables and conditions can add up fast. Velasco et al. (2014) wanted to find out to what extent packaging design evoked sensor impressions of sweet- or sourness and used a 2 × 2 × 2 × 2 × 2 design for this. Participants were presented with packaging designs varying in container shape (angular or rounded), typeface (angular or rounded), letter shape (angular or rounded) and accompanying sound (high or low pitch); half of the time participants had to decide whether the packaging evoked a sweet sensory impression or a sour sensory impression. The dependent variable was participant reaction time. To derive the number of different conditions overall, the individual levels are multiplied with each other. Five independent variables with two values each means 32 individual conditions: 2 × 2 × 2 × 2 × 2 = 32 (two times two times two times two times two) different conditions in the entire study. The table below spells out all combinations. Each cell represents one specific condition. Participants allocated to condition 17, for example, would be presented with a round-shaped container, with a label with angular typeface and angular letter shapes, accompanied by a high-pitched sound and asked to indicate whether this evoked a sweet taste sensation (Table 2.8).

## 2.8 TYPES OF RESULTS

In a previous example we discussed how changing a candidate's name while keeping their CV otherwise identical (see, e.g., Booth et al., 2012, or Carlsson and Rooth, 2008) affected how participants evaluated their qualifications. In doing so, we looked at the effect of a single variable. We refer to such an effect as a **main effect**. When we look at multivariate or multifactorial studies, however, that is, studies varying more than one variable, we now need to distinguish between main effect and **interaction**.

Chu and Kamal (2008) looked at the perception of brand-related messages in blogging; more specifically, they examined how perceived trustworthiness and perceived argument quality impacted on attitudes towards the brand and the extent to which the information was processed by the reader. They tested this with a 2 × 2 between-participants design with the two independent variables 'perceived blogger trustworthiness' and 'argument quality'. Both had two levels. One group of participants read blog posts on a fictitious product by a blogger they were told is honest and can be trusted, the other group was told the blogger is dishonest and cannot always be trusted. Each group was further split into two halves, one of which was presented

**Table 2.8** 2 × 2 × 2 × 2 × 2 study design in Velasco, Salgado-Montejo, Marmolejo-Ramos and Spence (2014).

|  |  |  |  |  | Taste (T) ||||
|---|---|---|---|---|---|---|---|---|
|  |  |  |  |  | Sweet || Sour ||
|  |  |  |  |  | Sound (S) || Sound (S) ||
|  |  |  |  |  | High Pitch | Low Pitch | High Pitch | Low Pitch |
| Container Shape (CS) — Angular | Typeface (TF) — Angular | Letter Shape (LS) — Angular | | | **Condition 1**<br>CS: Angular<br>TF: Angular<br>LS: Angular<br>T: Sweet<br>S: High Pitch | **Condition 2**<br>CS: Angular<br>TF: Angular<br>LS: Angular<br>T: Sweet<br>S: Low Pitch | **Condition 3**<br>CS: Angular<br>TF: Angular<br>LS: Angular<br>T: Sour<br>S: High Pitch | **Condition 4**<br>CS: Angular<br>TF: Angular<br>LS: Angular<br>T: Sour<br>S: Low Pitch |
| | | Letter Shape (LS) — Rounded | | | **Condition 5**<br>CS: Angular<br>TF: Angular<br>LS: Rounded<br>T: Sweet<br>S: High Pitch | **Condition 6**<br>CS: Angular<br>TF: Angular<br>LS: Rounded<br>T: Sweet<br>S: Low Pitch | **Condition 7**<br>CS: Angular<br>TF: Angular<br>LS: Rounded<br>T: Sour<br>S: High Pitch | **Condition 8**<br>CS: Angular<br>TF: Angular<br>LS: Rounded<br>T: Sour<br>S: Low Pitch |
| | Typeface (TF) — Rounded | Letter Shape (LS) — Angular | | | **Condition 9**<br>CS: Angular<br>TF: Rounded<br>LS: Angular<br>T: Sweet<br>S: High Pitch | **Condition 10**<br>CS: Angular<br>TF: Rounded<br>LS: Angular<br>T: Sweet<br>S: Low Pitch | **Condition 11**<br>CS: Angular<br>TF: Rounded<br>LS: Angular<br>T: Sour<br>S: High Pitch | **Condition 12**<br>CS: Angular<br>TF: Rounded<br>LS: Angular<br>T: Sour<br>S: Low Pitch |
| | | Letter Shape (LS) — Rounded | | | **Condition 13**<br>CS: Angular<br>TF: Rounded<br>LS: Rounded<br>T: Sweet<br>S: High Pitch | **Condition 14**<br>CS: Angular<br>TF: Rounded<br>LS: Rounded<br>T: Sweet<br>S: Low Pitch | **Condition 15**<br>CS: Angular<br>TF: Rounded<br>LS: Rounded<br>T: Sour<br>S: High Pitch | **Condition 16**<br>CS: Angular<br>TF: Rounded<br>LS: Rounded<br>T: Sour<br>S: Low Pitch |
| Container Shape (CS) — Rounded | Typeface (TF) — Angular | Letter Shape (LS) — Angular | | | **Condition 17**<br>CS: Rounded<br>TF: Angular<br>LS: Angular<br>T: Sweet<br>S: High Pitch | **Condition 18**<br>CS: Rounded<br>TF: Angular<br>LS: Angular<br>T: Sweet<br>S: Low Pitch | **Condition 19**<br>CS: Rounded<br>TF: Angular<br>LS: Angular<br>T: Sour<br>S: High Pitch | **Condition 20**<br>CS: Rounded<br>TF: Angular<br>LS: Angular<br>T: Sour<br>S: Low Pitch |
| | | Letter Shape (LS) — Rounded | | | **Condition 21**<br>CS: Rounded<br>TF: Angular<br>LS: Rounded<br>T: Sweet<br>S: High Pitch | **Condition 22**<br>CS: Rounded<br>TF: Angular<br>LS: Rounded<br>T: Sweet<br>S: Low Pitch | **Condition 23**<br>CS: Rounded<br>TF: Angular<br>LS: Rounded<br>T: Sour<br>S: High Pitch | **Condition 24**<br>CS: Rounded<br>TF: Angular<br>LS: Rounded<br>T: Sour<br>S: Low Pitch |
| | Typeface (TF) — Rounded | Letter Shape (LS) — Angular | | | **Condition 25**<br>CS: Rounded<br>TF: Rounded<br>LS: Angular<br>T: Sweet<br>S: High Pitch | **Condition 26**<br>CS: Rounded<br>TF: Rounded<br>LS: Angular<br>T: Sweet<br>S: Low Pitch | **Condition 27**<br>CS: Rounded<br>TF: Rounded<br>LS: Angular<br>T: Sour<br>S: High Pitch | **Condition 28**<br>CS: Rounded<br>TF: Rounded<br>LS: Angular<br>T: Sour<br>S: Low Pitch |
| | | Letter Shape (LS) — Rounded | | | **Condition 29**<br>CS: Rounded<br>TF: Rounded<br>LS: Rounded<br>T: Sweet<br>S: High Pitch | **Condition 30**<br>CS: Rounded<br>TF: Rounded<br>LS: Rounded<br>T: Sweet<br>S: Low Pitch | **Condition 31**<br>CS: Rounded<br>TF: Rounded<br>LS: Rounded<br>T: Sour<br>S: High Pitch | **Condition 32**<br>CS: Rounded<br>TF: Rounded<br>LS: Rounded<br>T: Sour<br>S: Low Pitch |

34  *Introducing Quantitative Methods*

with arguments previously designed to be strong arguments; the other group was presented with weak arguments (Table 2.9):

***Table 2.9*** *2 × 2 between-participants study with the independent variables 'blogger trustworthiness' and 'argument quality' (data from Chu and Kamal, 2008)*

|  |  | IV: Perceived blogger trustworthiness |  |
|---|---|---|---|
|  |  | High | Low |
| IV: Argument quality | Strong | Condition 1 (N = 32) Participants are presented with strong arguments they are told are written by an honest blogger. | Condition 2 (N = 30) Participants are presented with strong arguments they are told are written by a dishonest blogger. |
|  | Weak | Condition 3 (N = 50) Participants are presented with weak arguments they are told are written by an honest blogger. | Condition 4 (N = 33) Participants are presented with weak arguments they are told are written by a dishonest blogger. |

Each group was asked to rate the product along five traits which were consolidated into a single index expressing participants' attitude towards the product (the higher the score, the more positive the attitude towards the product). To measure the extent to which participants thought about the information presented, they were asked to list as many thoughts regarding the product as they could; based on this Chu and Kamal calculated the measure *elaboration index*. This index averaged 1.2 in the conditions with high perceived blogger trustworthiness and 1.8 for conditions for low trustworthiness, meaning that participants thought more about the blogger's arguments when they were told that they were dishonest (all effects and interactions mentioned here are significant – a concept which is explained in more detail in Section 6.10). Figure 2.2 illustrates this main effect:

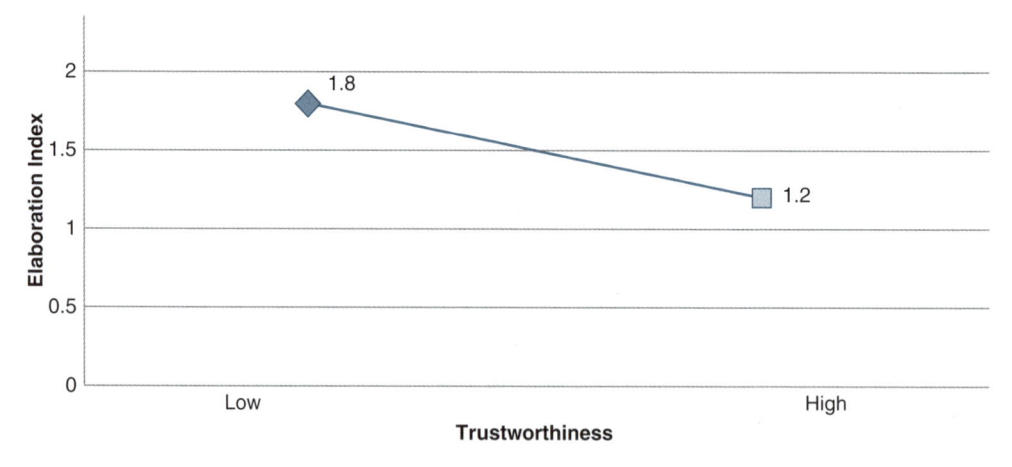

***Figure 2.2*** *Line chart showing main effect (data from Chu and Kamal, 2008)*

Looking at the data in the table below we can similarly see a main effect of 'argument quality' on attitude towards the product: participants in the two conditions with strong arguments had higher attitude scores towards the product than participants in the two weak argument conditions. But Chu and Kamal also observe an interaction: the impact of strong arguments is higher when the blogger is perceived to be honest than when they are perceived to be dishonest (Table 2.10).

*Table 2.10 Average attitude scores per condition (data from Chu and Kamal, 2008)*

|  |  | Perceived blogger trustworthiness | |
|---|---|---|---|
|  |  | High | Low |
| Argument quality | Strong | 23.1 | 19.7 |
|  | Weak | 12 | 13.8 |

When illustrated with a line graph, an interaction will show typically as a diagonal line because the values of one variable change as the other variable changes (Figure 2.3):

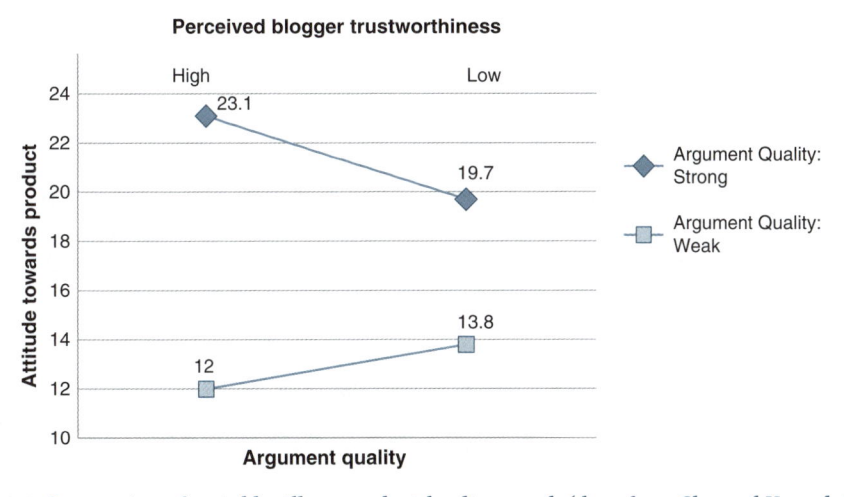

*Figure 2.3 Interaction of variables illustrated with a line graph (data from Chu and Kamal, 2008)*

In the same graph, the main effect is still visible in the way the 'Strong' line stays above the 'Weak' line. Note that although the Weak line also appears diagonal, we know from the statistical analyses and the non-significant (see Section 6.10 on significance) result that this does not reflect an interaction – an important reminder that graphs can be misleading and should always be presented in a context and with supporting information.

## ? REVIEW & REFLECT

- What is the difference between an effect and an interaction?
- What are advantages and disadvantages of using line charts to illustrate results?

## 2.9 ETHICAL RESEARCH

Issues such as experimenter control and blind studies raise another important question. If we are testing the effect of a new treatment (or therapy or intervention) which, presumably, we think might be more effective than the old treatment, would that not mean that the participants in the control group receive a treatment that is potentially less effective? And in blind studies, are we not cheating participants by potentially administering a placebo rather than a real drug? Thinking through these questions is part of the planning and designing process and forms part of the ethics considerations.

## 2.9.1 Ethics guidelines

Some of the more famous psychological studies have caused severe and, in some cases, long-term harm to their participants. In Zimbardo's prison study (Haney et al., 1972, 1973a, 1973b), for example, participants were reported to be deeply traumatised from the experience, with some having to leave the study prematurely and under great distress:

> The most dramatic evidence of the impact of this situation upon the participants was seen in the gross reactions of five prisoners who had to be released because of extreme emotional depression, crying, rage and acute anxiety. (Haney et al., 1973b, p. 81)

In another example, Stanley Milgram reported on the results of his 1963 obedience experiment (Milgram, 1963) with observations of the participants' distress:

> Many subjects showed signs of nervousness in the experimental situation, and especially upon administering the more powerful shocks. In a large number of cases the degree of tension reached extremes that are rarely seen in sociopsychological laboratory studies. Subjects were observed to sweat, tremble, stutter, bite their lips, groan, and dig their fingernails into their flesh. These were characteristic rather than exceptional responses to the experiment. (p. 375)

Researchers would not be able to conduct these experiments today, as most if not all disciplines have now formulated stringent guidelines on the treatment for the safeguarding and protection of (potential) research participants. While individual guidelines may differ to some extent, they usually agree on a core set of expectations and assumptions that should apply to how research is conducted:

- Avoiding or minimising harm to participants
- Treating participants respectfully
- Avoiding deception
- Avoiding coercion
- Maintaining anonymity and confidentiality of participants and their data.

We will now have a closer look at each of these expectations.

**Avoiding or minimising harm to participants:** In many ways, this is the overarching guideline from which the others are derived. Akin to the medical doctors' credo 'First, do no harm', researchers working with human participants are required to minimise both physical harm, such as pain, hunger or fatigue; and psychological harm, like causing participants to be distressed or upset. At the same time, this puts enormous restrictions on the kind of research that is possible. For example, how do we conduct research on the ways in which participants experience pain or hunger? How do we find out more about what makes people upset or anxious, and in turn work on alleviating their upset or anxiety?

[Content note: Mention of domestic violence in the next paragraph.]

In practice, then, it is often about weighing up the extent of potential harm or upset caused against the potential benefit. Institutional review boards and ethic committees exist so that researchers do not have to grapple with these questions on their own and, more importantly, do not have their judgement clouded by their own assumptions and expectations. For example, research (in the form of surveys or interviews) on the prevalence of domestic violence and on the experiences of domestic violence survivors is extremely important if we want to find out how to help those experiencing abuse. But interviews on the experience of domestic violence can be traumatic and upsetting for participants recounting their experiences. In these cases, ethical research design would include, among other precautions, having appropriately trained interviewers and providing extra sources of support for the interviewees (see, e.g., the WHO, 2001, guidelines on research on domestic violence against women).

**Treating participants respectfully:** Participants should be treated in a courteous and professional manner, regardless of their faith, gender, sexual orientation, transgender status, disability, race/ethnicity or age. This also means avoiding any insensitive or offensive jokes and any and all racist or sexist language, such as addressing female participants with 'girl' or 'sweetheart', etc.

[Content note: Mention of sexual harassment in the next paragraph.]

Of course, the same caveats apply as the ones mentioned two paragraphs earlier. Where we want to examine how people respond to offensive or insensitive language, researchers (and, more importantly, associated ethics review boards) may determine that a minimal, short-term exposure to discourteous/offensive material can be acceptable. For example, Woodzicka and LaFrance (2005) examined the effect of sexual harassment on women's performance in a job interview: Female participants were invited to what they believed was a genuine job interview, and the harassment consisted of up to three inappropriate questions during the interview, such as asking the women whether it was important to wear a bra at work.[4] The fact that participants believed to be invited to a genuine job interview also touches on another ethical issue, namely that of deception.

**Avoiding deception:** While the idea of avoiding deception seems very simple in theory, in practice it is much more difficult to fully avoid deception in research with human participants. Because human participants are likely to try and gauge a study's purpose and the experimenter's expectations towards them as well as then try to react towards these expectations, it is often necessary to obscure a study's true nature for the duration. For example, Keating et al. (2016) asked their student participants to argue the merits of the US presidents Barack Obama and George W. Bush. Their primary interest, however, was to find out whether and how group discussions polarise existing attitudes. In this context, any knowledge of the research question would have affected and thus biased the participants' behaviour and attitudes. Arguably, this is a relatively minor deception, whereas the deception described in the previous paragraph was of a much greater nature since participants were under the impression that they were coming in for a job interview. In fact, the Woodzicka and LaFrance state explicitly that '[d]espite its covert nature, the current study received approval from the Institutional Review Board at Boston College, where the study was conducted' (p. 69), thus acknowledging that the covert nature was a potentially critical issue.

**Avoiding coercion:** This means that participants should not be coerced to participate in a study and should be free to withdraw their participation at any time, without having to give any reason. Although some institutions require students to participate in research as part of their course requirements, those institutions normally also offer alternatives to fulfil these requirements, for example, in the form of short essays, etc. The requirement to avoid coercion derives from the expectation to avoid or minimise harm: Because everyone's lived experience is unique, we cannot always know whether a particular setup or topic may be distressing or upsetting to a participant, and we therefore have to give our participants the option to leave at any time, without having to explain themselves. Similar to what was discussed in the previous paragraphs, though, this does not mean that coercion cannot be part of a research method, particularly where research is interested in how coercion works and how people respond. In contrast to some of the more (in)famous classical psychology experiments of Milgram and Zimbardo, however, coercion in more recent studies usually consists of the experimenter repeating a request once and upon

---

[4] In this study, sexual harassment had an immediate negative effect on the women's performance in the job interview in comparison to women who completed an otherwise identical interview without sexually harassing questions.

another refusal, terminating the study and debriefing (more on that on p. 39 the participant – a strategy employed, for example, by Saulnier and Sivasubramaniam (2015) in their study of the effects of coercion on offering apologies for misconduct.

**Maintaining anonymity and confidentiality of participants and their data:** This expectation, too, derives from the overarching principle of avoiding or minimising harm to participants. Maintaining anonymity and confidentiality helps avoid the harm that participants might suffer if their personal data was made public or fell into the wrong hands, from personal contact details (name, email address, phone number), to sensitive demographic information (income, marital status, number/age of children), to sensitive personal information (attitudes on specific topics, IQ test results, data on shopping preferences, anxiety issues and so on). Equally, if you conduct research in an organisation, employees' livelihoods might be at stake if carelessly handled data of their satisfaction with their employer, their superior or colleagues was to become known within the organisation. Lastly, if you collect data on aspects like people's sexual orientation, gender, faith or disability, you need to be aware that in some cases a breach of anonymity or confidentiality can put those participants at risk of violence or persecution. Section 5.1 gives some practical advice on how to safely store participant data.

You will see the guidelines listed above reflected in codes and guidelines issued by a range of different organisations, complemented by a number of additional recommendations. The British Psychological Society, for example, has issued extensive guidelines to its members, detailing the high levels of professional standards expected (BPS, 2014). The code describes a range of standards such as 'general respect', 'privacy and confidentiality', 'informed consent', etc. (p. 10) which should inform members' behaviours, decisions and research methodologies – and which reflect the expectations we have described earlier. The British Academy of Management expects its members to comply with the guidelines laid out in their 'Code of Ethics and Best Practice for Members' (British Academy of Management, 2013), advising to behave with 'integrity and honesty' and 'respect and fairness'; to maintain 'privacy and confidentiality'; and to avoid 'personal gain' and 'conflicts of interest' (p. 6). Similar guidelines are issued by major funding bodies such as the Economic and Social Research Council (ESRC, 2015), Research Council UK (RCUK, 2013) or the Wellcome Trust (Wellcome Trust, 2005). In addition, almost all research-active institutions have codified (that is, put rules into writing) their expectations towards ethical behaviour of their members, staff and students alike. To make matters slightly more complicated, institutions such as universities may further have department- or degree programme–specific guidelines complementing overall, institution-wide policy. Most institutions will require researchers to have their research methods approved by an ethics committee or institutional review board before embarking on the actual research. This is to ensure that all research meets the standard required through the regulations, codes and guidelines, not the least because we as researchers are representatives of our organisation and our discipline and how we conduct ourselves may affect the reputation of both in the eyes of our current and future participants.

### REVIEW & REFLECT

- Do you think the harm caused to participants in the experiments by Haney et al. (1972, 1973a, 1973b) or Milgram (1963) was justifiable given the importance of their findings? Why or why not?
- Can you think of research methods which might give similar insight into human behaviour but which are less harmful to the participants?

## 2.9.2  Ethical research practice

What does this all mean for you and your research project? It means that you need to consider the ethical implications of your research question and your research methodology well in advance of ever contacting the first (potential) participant. Plan your research methods in a way that avoids or minimises harm to participants:

- Make sure that your participants are well aware of their rights as participants, such as their data being handled in confidentiality, their right to withdraw at any time without having to give any reason, etc. This usually means having to provide a **participant information sheet** and a **consent form** to participants in advance of their participation. The participant information sheet gives them as much information on your study and its purpose as you can provide without compromising your method: the consent form details the participants' rights. This form should be signed by the participant to acknowledge that they have been informed, and the form then retained by you.

> **ONLINE CONTENT**
>
> On the companion website, you can find a sample Participant Information Sheet as well as a sample Consent Form.

- If you think deception or temporary harm is necessary, you will have to carefully think about how you can mitigate that harm: Can you offer support, either straight away or by referring them to other sources of support?
- Are you confident that you are able to spot when a participant is in distress? Can you get interviewer or researcher training to improve your ability to do so?
- Make sure that participants are informed as much as possible about the research and what it entails.
- Where the setup of the study does not allow you to tell the participants the actual research question, make sure to do so during the debriefing (see below).
- Where possible, have a **debriefing** take place after a participant has completed a study. This usually entails several parts:
  - If you used any deception, ask participants what they thought the research question was. If their guess is correct or close to correct, you will have to exclude their data because it is likely that their responses are biased.
  - Inform them of the true research question.
  - Ask whether they are okay or would like any support or help, such as counselling services.
  - Let them know where to contact you with questions or concerns that may arise later on.
  - If data is collected in a non-anonymous way, it is customary to give participants a period of time during which they can ask you to remove or delete their data. It is vital that these requests for deletion and removal are honoured.

Lastly, make sure to think about ethical issues and how to avoid or mitigate them well in advance. Most research-active institutions will require you to gain ethics approval before starting your data collection, and this approval will depend on you being able to show that your research has minimal negative impact on your participants. This approval also often takes time, particularly if the review board is asking you to explain things further or amend your methods.

## 2.10 HYPOTHESES

Unless our research is purely exploratory we usually approach our research question with a certain expectation towards the result. We consider one type of outcome somewhat more likely than another based on what we know from the literature and previous research. In fact, part of being a good researcher is learning to resist using our gut instinct and our own experiences, or what is considered 'common sense', as our guide in formulating our expectations towards the outcome in the form of **hypotheses** – they need to be based on existing research, be it our own or that of others. It may seem paradoxical that we rely on existing research in order to predict the outcome for our research. But as we have mentioned previously, research is fundamentally about probabilities and tendencies. Hypotheses are expressions of such predictions or reasonable estimates towards similar or related variables rather than of absolute expectations. For example, we know that information from sources perceived to be high in trustworthiness will be scrutinised less (e.g., Chu and Kamal, 2008). Knowing that previous research has established that people with higher social status are perceived to be more trustworthy, (e.g., Linke et al., 2016), it is therefore a plausible expectation, or hypothesis, that persuasive information from high-status sources will be scrutinised less.

Testable hypotheses are considered a hallmark of good science, and the predictive power of a theory is one of its quality criteria. A good theory allows making predictions regarding the association(s) of at least two variables, and it makes those predictions in a form that allows them to be proven wrong: It makes **falsifiable** hypotheses, that is, hypotheses that can be disproven. Conversely, a theoretical framework that merely describes the state of things is of limited use for you as a researcher. Rather, we want to be able to explain and, eventually, predict. Given what we know, and assuming an individual or group encounters a particular context, what are the chances they will act in a specific way?

Hypotheses spell out expectations towards the result. While this may seem initially restricting, it is a prerequisite to a large number of statistical analyses and is needed in order to declare the result meaningful and valid, because the type of hypothesis determines the type of data needed, and the type of analysis available. Testing whether variables correlate with each other requires a different test than examining whether there is an effect of one variable on another. Hypotheses are classed as either **directional hypotheses** [or **one-tailed**; the 'tail' refers to the shape of a normal distribution (more on this in Section 6.7)] or **non-directional hypotheses** (or **two-tailed**). Non-directional hypotheses are less restrictive as they only predict the *existence* of a difference, effect or relationship but make no statement about its *direction*. When testing hypotheses, one- and two-tailed hypotheses have different requirements and success criteria; what constitutes a good finding for a one-tailed hypothesis is not necessarily a positive finding for a two-tailed hypothesis. One-tailed hypotheses are, in a manner of speaking, bolder. They make more specific predictions and narrow the field of results that would be considered successful in testing the hypothesis. We will see later on that in return we are given more leeway in establishing statistical significance.

### 2.10.1 Hypotheses and effects

Two-tailed hypotheses state the *existence* of an effect but make no predictions on its direction. For example, in their 2008 study on the effect of newscasters' gender and age on their perceived credibility, Weibel et al. (2008) noted conflicting existing research regarding the effect of gender and concluded that 'there is no consensus about the direction of the effect' (p. 473). Their two-tailed hypothesis was as follows:

> $H_1$: The gender of the newscaster has an influence on the perceived credibility of the message. (Weibel et al., 2008, p. 473)

Note that this only predicts the existence of an influence but not the direction; Weibel et al. did not specify which gender influences credibility in which way. When examining participants' evaluation of the newscasters presented to them, Weibel et al.'s findings could have fallen into one of three categories:

1. An effect of gender such that participants perceive the female newscasters' message to be *more* credible than the male newscasters'.
2. An effect of gender such that participants perceive the female newscasters' message to be *less* credible than the male newscasters'.
3. No effect; participants find messages from male and female newscasters equally credible.

Because $H_1$ was phrased as a two-tailed hypothesis, either of the first two outcomes would have supported $H_1$ and only the third – no significant difference – would have contradicted it. In contrast, a one-tailed hypothesis predicts the existence of an effect *and* its direction. For example, if Weibel et al. had looked at age of a newscaster and predicted that higher age would lend more credibility, this would have been a one-tailed hypothesis (though we will see below that Weibel et al. looked at age from the perspective of differences rather than effects):

> $H_1$: Age has a positive effect on perceived credibility.

## ! LOOK OUT!

Note the phrasing of 'would have supported $H_1$' in the preceding paragraph. A recurring theme in this chapter has been the observation that research in general, and statistics in particular, is fundamentally about probabilities and tendencies rather than about absolutes and certainty. At the same time, empirical studies almost always open only small windows into reality. Weibel et al.'s study examines the effects of a small range of age for a small selection of newscasters on a small sample of participants, but of course their research fundamentally aims at drawing conclusions for a wider range of newscasters and how they are perceived by a larger part of the population (see also Section 2.12, in particular the passage on ecological validity, and Section 3.8 on sampling). Even the strongest correlation, effect or difference can only provide further support in the underlying assumptions and models, but not prove them conclusively.

### 2.10.2 Hypotheses and differences

When looking at differences, a one-tailed hypothesis predicts the existence of a difference but does not specify the way in which groups or conditions will differ. For example, Weibel et al. (2008) expected a newscaster's age to play a role in how credible they would be perceived to be by their audience:

> $H_4$: Older newscasters are perceived as being more credible than younger newscasters. (p. 473)

In contrast, a two-tailed hypothesis only states the existence of a difference without specifying the manner or direction of the difference. In Chapter 1 we described Cassidy and Macdonald's (2007) study on the effect of background noise on task performance of introverts and extraverts. In their study, they posited a difference between introverts' and extraverts' preferences, without specifying the manner or direction of the difference. For this, they employed a two-tailed hypothesis:

> Thirdly, it was hypothesized that introverts and extraverts would report differential preferences for music listening and studying in the presence of music and noise. (p. 521)

### 2.10.3 Hypotheses and associations

For associations and correlations, a two-tailed hypothesis specifies the existence of a correlation. For example, Wahab and Rahman (2009) examined the relationship between institutional ownership and director remuneration. Existing research suggested that an argument could be made for both a negative and a positive relationship, which led Wahab and Rahman to formulate a non-directional hypothesis:

> Therefore, based on the arguments presented above, we predict a non-directional relationship between institutional participation in politically connected firms and director remuneration. (p. 148)

A one-tailed hypothesis, on the other hand, specifies the direction of the association. Flanagin and Metzger (2000), for example, examined to what extent the use of a medium, such as the Internet, was associated with the perception of the medium's credibility. Their expectation was that greater use was associated with higher perceived credibility:

> $H_2$: Internet users with greater experience will perceive it to be a more credible source of information, in relation to conventional media such as the television, newspapers, radio and magazines, than will less experienced users. (p. 520)

### 2.10.4 Null hypothesis

Hypotheses are another reason why the exact phrasing of our research question and the definition of our variables matters so much. By stating our hypothesis at the very beginning we avoid rephrasing our research question so as to fit the findings – the equivalent of firing our arrow first and then drawing a bullseye around the point of impact. Researchers often use the concept of the **null hypothesis** to clarify their predictions. Simply put, the null hypothesis $H_0$ – as opposed to the **alternative hypotheses** $H_1$, $H_2$, $H_3$, etc. – explicitly states the opposite of what we are expecting to find. If our hypothesis predicts that variables A and B correlate, our null hypothesis states they are not associated; our research effectively tries to disprove the null hypothesis. Note that null hypothesis does not necessarily mean 'no association' or 'no effect'! If our hypothesis is that variables C and D are unrelated, our null hypothesis states that C and D are, in fact, associated. Since our goal is to disprove the null hypothesis, however, we would be ill advised to choose a null hypothesis that claims an existence of association, effect, or difference because prediction of non-existence is easier to disprove than prediction of existence. A null hypothesis claiming an absence of an effect is conclusively and decisively disproven by finding an effect. If our claim is that there are no purple unicorns, a single purple unicorn disproves our claim. On the other hand, a null hypothesis claiming the existence of an effect is not easily disproven by the absence of an effect. If we claim that there is at least one purple unicorn, the failure to sight one such thing is not proof that no purple unicorns exist; we might simply have looked in the wrong place. Or, shorter: absence of evidence is not evidence of absence!

> **! LOOK OUT!**
>
> The null hypothesis is usually used as a theoretical construct to help you develop your actual hypotheses. When you write up your research, state your hypotheses and do not include the null hypothesis in your paper, unless explicitly instructed to do so.

Designing a new study is guided by two main principles: to ensure reliability and to increase validity. Both concepts apply to a study as a whole as well as to individual instruments used within the study. We now turn to discussing these two key principles in research design, starting with reliability.

## 2.11 IMPROVING RESEARCH QUALITY: RELIABILITY

**Reliability** refers to the extent to which an experiment or an instrument's measurements are *consistent*. We have stressed in Section 2.7 that the experimental method relies on keeping all other factors constant, manipulating only the independent variable(s) and then examining whether the dependent variable(s) have changed. It follows that when we are using any instrument for measurements we need to be as certain as possible that any changes we observe are due to the manipulation of the independent variable and not due to variations in the instrument we used. For example, a tape measure is a reliable instrument because if we apply the same tape measure to the same item, we have a very high chance of getting the same result – in fact, one would hope that there is a 100% chance to arrive at the same measurement, assuming that the object we are measuring has not changed shape in the meantime. Unfortunately, where human thought is concerned, reliability becomes a much more difficult issue. After all, attitudes and behaviour can and do change over time. People make new experiences and acquire new skills; cultural or political environments change; attitudes may become more negative or positive simply by virtue of repeated exposure to the attitude object, and so on. Any athlete or musician knows that they have good days and bad days: a piece or exercise that went very well just yesterday suddenly falls apart today – but the next day everything is back to normal, perhaps even better. But at the same time, musicians and athletes can also tell that there is a difference between the individual day-to-day fluctuations and genuine progress. Therefore, wherever we measure traits, skills or attitudes we want to be able to distinguish between normal variation and fluctuation and meaningful, effective change.

In Section 2.6.1 we mentioned using the Perceived Stress Scale to measure perceived stress levels. Consider a participant who scored a 16 on the scale before the intervention, then attended all four sessions and now scores 13 on the same scale. This *may* indicate that their stress levels have been lowered, but of course it assumes that the scale is reliable and has accurately measured the improvement (i.e., reduction in stress). Unfortunately, there are several plausible scenarios that may all lead to the same outcome but individually lead us to completely different conclusions. These scenarios are illustrated in the graphic below:

44  Introducing Quantitative Methods

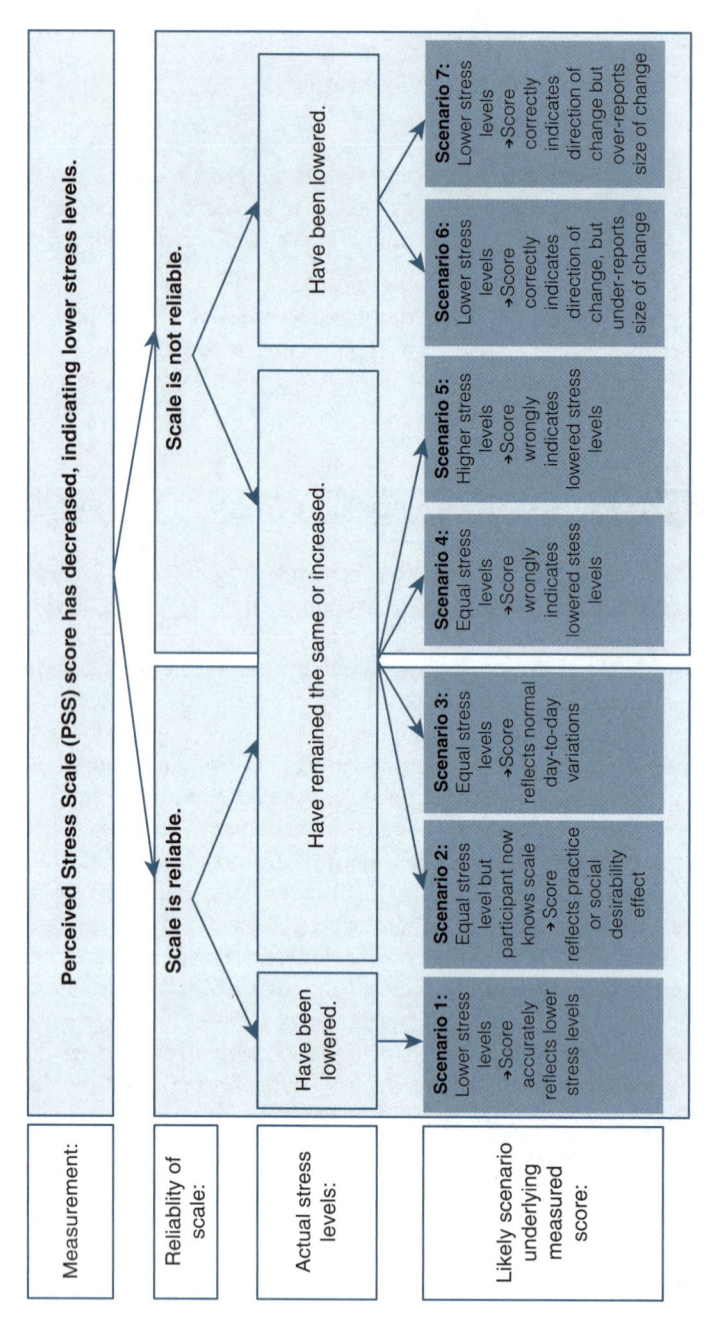

*Figure 2.4* Plausible scenarios explaining a single outcome

This example starts with the observation that the PSS score has decreased. This may indicate that stress levels have been lowered and that the scale has adequately measured direction and extent of change in stress levels (scenario 1). However, a lowered score alone is not sufficient evidence to demonstrate that stress levels are actually lower. For example, the participant may remember some of the questions from the first time of completing the scale and is now trying to achieve a lower total score (scenario 2), or their stress level usually fluctuates between 12 and 17 and the intervention has not made any lasting impact on overall stress levels (scenario 3). Those are plausible scenarios assuming the scale may be a reliable instrument. Of course, the scale may well not be reliable. The score may inaccurately indicate a decrease in stress levels despite actual stress levels remaining the same (scenario 4) or increasing (scenario 5). It may be accurately reporting the direction of the change but not the size of the change by either under-reporting a change from 16 to 10 as 16 to 13 (scenario 6) or over-reporting change of stress levels of 16 to 15 as 16 to 13 (scenario 7). For the purpose of our study we want to be sure that what we are observing is scenario 1 – stress levels have been lowered, and the scale is accurately reporting both direction and size of change – rather than any of the other scenarios. Much of what we talk about regarding research methodology and what will be discussed in this and the following chapters aims to help show that we are observing scenario 1 by establishing to a reasonable degree of certainty that we are *not* observing scenarios 2 to 7. For example, Section 3.12 describes how to measure, describe and improve instrument reliability. As we increase our confidence that the instrument is reliable, we decrease the likelihood that we are observing scenarios 4 to 7. Equally, a large part of research methodology is to reduce the likelihood of introducing sources of bias such as practice effects, etc. so as to reduce the likelihood of scenarios similar to scenario 2. Scenario 3 emphasises the need to compare and examine groups rather than individuals to allow us to distinguish variations based on individuals from variations based on groups (Section 6.5 on the different sources of variance explains this difference in more detail).

It is difficult to overstate the importance of reliability. The very essence of quantitative research is to examine fluctuations and changes in one or more variables in relation to one or more additional variables. Knowing which of these changes in variables reflect actual change in the entities and properties they represent, and which changes are superficial, temporary or simply a consequence of inaccurate measurements is a fundamental requirement for drawing accurate conclusions from our data. That said, reliability is only part of the equation. Reliable instruments and reliable data are ineffective if interpreted wrongly or if the method itself is flawed. A tape measure is a reliable instrument to measure length, height, width or depth. But it is not an adequate measure of intelligence or self-esteem: it would yield reliable but useless data because height is not an appropriate measure of intelligence. To express whether we are measuring the right thing and drawing the right conclusions, we look at validity rather than reliability. The following section discusses the concept of validity in more detail.

### ❓ REVIEW & REFLECT

- Why is it difficult to establish reliability of measurements where human skills and traits are concerned?

## 2.12 IMPROVING RESEARCH QUALITY: VALIDITY

Whereas reliability focusses on the accuracy of measurement, **validity** refers to the extent to which our conclusions are a sound and true reflection of the real relationships between the variables and of the conclusions we draw from the data. In other words, is the change in measurements due to the factors we manipulated and examined? How well have measurements captured the essence of the 'real world' outside the lab? Are there alternative explanations that could equally well or better account for the change in measurements? A different way of putting this would be to state that our task is not only to show 'X does Y', but to show that 'A does not do Y, B does not do Y, C does not do Y, ...'. Looking back to Figure 2.4, establishing validity means showing that scenario 1 is most likely true but scenarios 2 and beyond are not.

This process of excluding other explanations was modelled in our approach to the study establishing whether meditation sessions had a beneficial effect on stress levels in the workplace. The control group was added to reduce the likelihood that it was mere passage of time that explained the lowered stress levels; a control condition was added to reduce the likelihood that it was simply the extra hour of break which explained lower stress levels; we introduced random allocation to avoid introducing bias through self-selection, and so on.

Among threats to validity, **practice effects** are quite common. Practice effects can occur when participants complete the same task or the same test more than once. There is then a chance that all but the initial completion are affected by the experience and practice gained from previous completions. Practice effects are most likely:

- If the exact same version of a testing instrument is used: because participants may be less nervous at the second time of exposure.
- If the tasks require adopting a particular type of strategy: because participants may avoid previously unsuccessful strategies.
- Or if the tasks are very unusual and require training: because participants may have practiced the relevant skills in the meantime.

Note, however, that practice effects do not affect the *reliability* of the instrument as such: all things being equal, any increases due to practice effects would accurately reflect improved performance, though of course those effects may still be over- or under-reported. A possible strategy to minimise practice effects is to have participants work on a few practice tasks before the actual testing so nervousness or unfamiliarity do not affect their performance too much once you start taking records of their performance (Collie et al., 2003). Alternatively, different variants of a test can be used to reduce the likelihood and magnitude of practice effects (Benedict and Zgaljardic, 1998) – one of the reasons intelligence tests often come in more than one version or variant. In contrast to practice effects, **testing fatigue** can have the opposite result: very long or challenging tasks are likely to demotivate the participant and test results may reflect ensuing lack of attention rather than genuine low performance or ability.

Of the numerous types of validity, there are five particular types that are most frequently referenced and which will therefore be discussed in more detail:

- Construct validity
- Conclusion validity
- Internal validity
- External validity
- Ecological validity.

**Construct validity** refers to the extent to which our instruments measure what we intend to measure. It is particularly important whenever we are trying to measure abstract and theoretically defined concepts such as risk affinity, motivation, aptitude, resilience, attitude, etc., where no obvious direct measurement exists – as opposed to, for example, reaction time, money spent, age or weight. You can see this in the history of how intelligence tests were developed and refined (for a more comprehensive overview of this development see Boake, 2002). Conceptualisations of intelligence ranged from Binet-Simon's test focussing on verbal intelligence and establishing mental age (Binet and Simon, 1916) to Thurstone's seven factors of verbal comprehension, word fluency, number facility, spatial visualization, associative memory, perceptual speed, reasoning and induction (Thurstone, 1934). Intelligence was differently conceptualised by Spearman's general factor $g$ (1946) and Cattell's two-factor approach of fluid and crystallised intelligence (1963) … and still the concept of intelligence and its measurement is being refined, revised and re-examined. Each conceptualisation has its advantages and disadvantages. The extent to which these advantages and disadvantages are balanced out to provide a good approximation of the underlying construct is what is described by construct validity. Additionally, intelligence tests with their different tests measuring different aspects of intelligence are a good example of how we can increase **convergent validity**, the degree to which multiple measures of the same construct arrive at the same or similar result.

**Conclusion validity** describes the extent to which the conclusions we draw from our study in terms of support or rejection of hypotheses are valid. If in the study examining the effect of meditation on workplace stress we had left it at pre- and post-measurement of stress levels but not included a control group, the conclusion validity would have been low because we did not account for the possibility that mere passage of time may have lowered stress levels.

**Internal validity** specifically refers to the extent to which we can appropriately infer a causal relationship between independent and dependent variables. Internal validity is threatened if we fail to ensure random allocation of participants to conditions or control confounding variables. If in the study above we had allowed self-selection of participants to the different conditions, this would have introduced a source of bias into the study, because changes in stress levels could have been caused by the personality traits on the basis of which participants self-selected their condition rather than the treatment they received in either condition. In this instance, we could not readily have inferred a causal relationship between intervention and lowered stress levels because we did not control for confounding variables. Randomly allocating participants to conditions therefore helps improve internal validity.

**External validity** refers to the extent to which findings can be generalised to other participants, at other times, in other places. External validity can be compromised if our sample is not representative of the overall population (more on sampling in Section 3.8) or if research is very specific to a particular place, time or era. Other threats to external validity are far more subtle: For example, online questionnaires only reach potential participants who have Internet access and sufficient computer skills. Any study for which participants are primarily recruited online or where the study itself is conducted online may therefore be skewed towards a younger and potentially more affluent demographic (i.e., people who are more likely to be comfortable online and have reliable access to the technology). This is a problem if any of the variables examined in the study are likely to be related to age, status, affluence and in turn related to levels of education, etc. Similarly, eliciting student attitudes on tuition fees is unlikely to represent the general population's attitude towards the same topic. In fact, students are a weird demographic in many ways because they tend to form a fairly narrow subset of the overall population in terms of background and ability, and yet a fair share of research relies almost exclusively on more or less willing student participants. Using the term 'weird' is no coincidence: the acronym WEIRD is sometimes used to refer to the observation that students appearing as participants in research tend to come from a predominantly *Western* background, are fairly well *Educated*, come from *Industrialised* nations, are comparatively *Rich* (as they can afford to attend university) and come predominantly from *Democratic* societies. The differences between students and non-students may even be further-reaching: Scholars such as Henrich et al. (2010) argue that students are not representative of the general population in terms of abilities such as visual perception and spatial reasoning, for example. This means that conclusions based on research with student samples may not always hold true for the general population, and hence potentially have low external validity. On a related note, in Chapter 1, we have argued that it can be useful and illuminating to repeat previous studies. Hopefully it now becomes clearer that it is not only useful but often necessary to re-examine observations and conclusions formed on the basis of very narrow participant groups.

**Ecological validity** is a subtype of external validity that refers to the extent to which our findings and inferences can be generalised, or extrapolated, from the testing environment to the 'real world'. Most research situations are inherently artificial because the very virtue of sound research methodology is to isolate the specific variables and factors we are interested in, and to control those we are not. But this means that the tasks participants have to perform are often abstract, removed from their day-to-day life and presented with little context. For example, although Mir et al. (2011) could show that the offer of monetary rewards can speed up reaction time in a carefully controlled experiment, this is only a theoretical ideal of the situation we really want to explore. It is only a pale approximation of an employee working on tasks of varying complexity and interest, whilst being instructed and managed by managers with different types and skills of leadership, with deadlines breathing down their neck, and assorted financial pressures in their private life. In addition, nearly all research takes place in a context where participants are fully aware of the fact that they are taking part in research. Of course, there are exceptions to this: children up to a certain age may not be aware of participating and in rare cases the research question may require the use of deception (see Section 2.9). But for the most part we can assume that participants know that they are participating in a study of some sort, regardless of whether it takes place in a lab, through an online questionnaire or by an interviewer with a clipboard in their hands. All these factors contribute to the artificial context of the research situation and are likely to influence respondent behaviour. The actual influence may be marginal, but a good many results live in the margins.

### 2.12.1 Going further: Construct underrepresentation and construct-irrelevant variance

Messick (1989, as cited in Messick, 1995) defines validity as 'an overall evaluative judgement of the degree to which empirical evidence and theoretical rationales support the adequacy and appropriateness of interpretations and actions on the basis of test scores or other modes of assessment' (p. 741). The two key parts in this definition are 'theoretical rationales' and 'test scores or other modes of assessment' as this is a reminder that in many cases we are not measuring an ability or trait directly, but rather through indicators (see Section 2.3). Messick (1995) describes two construct-related threats to validity; **construct underrepresentation**, and **construct-irrelevant variance**. A construct is underrepresented in a methodology when 'assessment is too narrow and fails to include important dimensions or facets' (p. 742). For example, Hinkin and Schriesheim (2008) conclude that leadership encompasses several distinct dimensions, such as communication, procedural justice, organisational influence, goal clarification and technical competence. If a study which uses leadership as a variable only examined the leader's communication skill, Hinkin and Schriesheim (and others) could then argue that the construct 'leadership' has not been adequately represented; it has been underrepresented.

Construct-irrelevant variance, on the other hand, is introduced when unrelated facets of a task or experimental treatment cause changes to the measurements. For example, we might employ an idea-generating task to test participants' creativity and as part of that assessment include a timed writing task that requires participants to type a list of associations to a given term. Chances are that such a task would not (primarily) examine creativity but familiarity with computers and typing skills. This is a skill likely to be varying widely from participant to participant and, as such, performance in this task will be heavily influenced (or confounded) by the participants' ability to handle computer-based tasks rather than creativity alone.

## 2.13  FROM THEORY TO PRACTICE: OPERATIONALISATION

Having now introduced the concepts of validity, and in particular construct validity and ecological validity, we return to **operationalisation**, the process of translating the variable we are interested in into something measurable and quantifiable. This is more difficult the more abstract the concept is. Measuring age is easy: we usually measure it in years, months, or perhaps down to weeks and days. But how do we measure concepts such as 'self-esteem' or 'motivation'? Is this a subjective perception of self ('I don't feel very motivated') or others ('This person acts in a very motivated way') or is it something that can be objectively measured, perhaps through quality of work, time needed to finish a task, or by how little extra payment is needed to persuade an individual to perform a specific task? For most research concerned with human thought and behaviour, operationalisation comes with the added difficulty that most of what researchers are interested in is only indirectly observable and, therefore, reliant on either self-reports or the observation of behaviour thought to be indicative of underlying traits, opinions or abilities. The centuries-long discussion on the definition and measurement of intelligence is just one such example; similar effort has gone into defining and measuring motivation, extraversion, confidence, etc. In fact, in some cases there is still disagreement on whether personality traits are distinct or different manifestations of the same; see, for example, Bates (2015) on whether optimism and pessimism are one or two distinct traits.

Not all variables are difficult to operationalise, but the more abstract our variable(s), the more challenging the process of operationalisation. Attention or interest elicited by a banner or link may be measured through click-through rates; risk-affinity or risk-aversion may be operationalised by the amount of money a participant is willing to risk on a given bet; reading speed can be operationalised by the number of words read per minute. On the other end of the spectrum, abstract concepts such as motivation, introversion, self-esteem, depression, etc. are often measured by eliciting (dis)agreement to a range of statements which approach the same concept from different angles. For example, the **Beck's Depression Inventory** (Beck et al., 1996) consists of 21 questions, ranging from asking about changing sleep patterns or feelings of sadness and guilt to whether the patient (or participant) has lost interest in other people and how they feel about their appearance. The level of depression can then be expressed by a score out of 21 (such a score would also be referred to as a **composite measure** since it summarises several responses into one); the elaboration index used by Chu and Kamal (2008) mentioned on p. 34 is another example.

To show the range of options to operationalise variables, consider prejudice. We could operationalise prejudice by asking participants to what extent they considered themselves prejudiced towards, for example, women or people with a minority ethnic background. This could easily be done by just one or two questions. It could also easily generate useless data – because the social desirability bias to not appear prejudiced can be very strong. Alternatively, we could measure prejudice (to some extent) through reaction time, for example, by using the Implicit Association Test (IAT).[5] At its core, the IAT is a simple category recognition test which relies on the assumption that reaction time will be slower if elements of a category we are prejudiced towards are paired with positive terms, but faster if they are paired with negative terms (though for a critique of the IAT and its construction and interpretation see Fiedler et al., 2006). Yet another approach would be to examine how people actually behave towards members of a prejudiced group. Consider LaPiere's (1934)[6] seminal study on the difference between racism in attitude and action in the United States. He accompanied a Chinese couple during their travels in the United States, during which they stayed at 66 hotels and B&Bs and were only refused accommodation once; in the course of their travels they ate at more than 180 restaurants. Six months later LaPiere phoned the very same establishments to ask whether they would consider accepting Chinese visitors at their establishments. Over 90% of the respondents said they would not, thus demonstrating a striking difference between their attitude towards an abstract concept and their actual behaviour towards real people. This illustrates how there are different approaches to the same underlying construct, each with their own advantages and disadvantages as they differ in the ease with which they could be implemented in a laboratory setting, vary in their degree of ecological validity and are more or less removed from the underlying construct.

When deciding on how to operationalise variables in our study, keep the following recommendations in mind

- Do not re-invent the wheel.
- Triangulate and confirm.
- Do not mistake reliability for validity.

**Do not re-invent the wheel:** Unless your research is mostly exploratory, or you are explicitly looking to examine whether a particular concept exists or can be measured in a particular way, you may be able to find examples of how your variable of interest has been successfully operationalised before.

**Triangulate and confirm:** Most of the time it makes sense to try and use additional variables already confirmed as predictors or indicators for your variable of interest, a process called **triangulation** because it essentially consists of using two points of reference to identify a third point. If existing research gives you reason to believe that variables B and C correlate highly, and you believe that variables A and B correlate, then A and C should also show some association. You would, of course, not expect perfect correlation, but if those two variables do not correlate at all it should give you pause for thought.

For example, we might be interested in examining leadership success (variable A) and self-esteem (variable B), and we know that the literature research suggests that self-esteem correlates with internal locus of control (variable C) i.e., the idea that most of what happens to you is under your control as opposed to outside influences. You could then use an established instrument such as Rotter's (1990) locus of control scale to measure locus of control and use the data to further confirm whatever variable(s) you use to measure self-esteem.

**Do not mistake reliability for validity:** Remember that an instrument can be absolutely reliable (e.g., a tape measure or a ruler) but be absolutely useless for your variable of interest (e.g., intelligence or motivation).

---

[5] You can try it out yourself here: https://implicit.harvard.edu/implicit/takeatest.html.
[6] Content note: This is a paper written in 1934 and contains language which by today's standard would be considered racist and to an extent sexist, but was considered appropriate at the time.

## REVIEW & REFLECT

- Are there any stages in your research process where you might not need to consider validity? Why or why not?
- Conversely, are there any types of validity that are particularly critical to your research project?

## A SHORT SUMMARY

- Variables can be *continuous* (all values available) or *discrete* (defined brackets of values).
- Quantitative research is likely to either look at comparisons, associations or causal relationships between variables.
- Correlations can be negative (values move in opposite directions) or positive (values move in same direction).
- In a study, you manipulate the independent variable (IV) and observe whether the dependent variable (DV) changes in response. Variables which may affect the relationship between IV and DV and which are not controlled for are considered confounding variables. A variable can affect another variable directly (main effect) or contingent on another variable's value (interaction).
- Control groups provide a comparison to the groups allocated to the main conditions.
- Random allocation of participants ensures that any potential confounding variables (traits, abilities) inherent to the participants are mitigated by being roughly equally distributed across conditions. A true experiment requires full control and random allocation of participants to conditions.
- Nominal data can be counted; ordinal data can be ranked. Interval and ratio data have meaningful intervals, but ratio data also has a natural point of zero.
- An important part of research design is operationalising your variable, that is, turning it from an abstract concept into something measurable.
- 'X by Y' describes the setup of independent variables or factors for a given study where each X, Y, etc. designates one variable and the value of X, Y, etc. indicates number of variable levels.
- Ethical research is based on the overarching principle of avoiding or minimising harm to participants. This includes respectful interaction, maintaining confidentiality and anonymity, and the avoidance of deception and coercion.
- To make sure participants' rights are protected, it is best practice to hand out a participant information sheet, to inform participants about the study, and a consent form to demonstrate participants have been informed. Where possible, participation should be followed by debriefing.
- Stating hypotheses in advance helps reduce researcher bias by defining a study's success criteria in advance. Hypotheses ($H_1$, $H_2$, etc.) which state the existence of an effect/difference/association are called non-directional or two-tailed; hypotheses which additionally state a direction are referred to as directional or one-tailed.
- Reliability describes the extent to which an instrument truthfully measures what it purports to measure, whereas validity describes the extent to which findings truthfully reflect the real state of affairs, and to what extent design and conclusions are sound and justified.

## RESEARCH METHODS AT WORK

Evelyn works for a small construction company producing timber frames. Her manager has asked her to think about how they could establish a system of structured quality control so that the company can track the quality of their work output over time. Evelyn's first task is to operationalise the concept of quality. What characterises good or poor quality of a timber frame? After some consideration, Evelyn defines several quality criteria, some relating to dimensions of the finished product being within defined tolerances from the dimensions specified in the order and some relating to the aesthetic appearance of the finished product.

Rick works for a supermarket chain which wants to trial a new store layout. His manager initially suggests to try the new layout at the same time they introduce the new cash register, because she wants to minimise disruption. However, Rick argues that changing two things at the same time means they will not be able to tell which effects are due to which change, the layout or the register, or a combination of the two. Instead, he suggests to start by selecting a number of stores in which to trial the changed store layout first. This will allow them to study the effects of the store layout change in isolation, and by doing it in several branches they will also be able to look for a general trend rather than relying on the observations in one particular branch.

## CHECK YOUR UNDERSTANDING

1. For the following information, list an option to perform measurements in continuous or discrete form (one example is given):

   |  | Discrete | Continuous |
   | --- | --- | --- |
   | Reaction time | <200<br>201 – 300<br>301 – 400<br>>400 ms | In ms as measured |
   | Temperature |  |  |
   | Literacy |  |  |
   | Socioeconomic status |  |  |
   | Risk aversion |  |  |
   | Willingness to donate |  |  |

2. Looking at the following topics, describe how you might phrase and examine research questions in terms of associations, differences or effects:
   a. Type of information provided and compliance with medication regimen
   b. Educational background and reading skill
   c. Product scarcity and perceived product value
   d. Socioeconomic status and political affiliation

3. How would you describe the following study in the shorthand of the 'A by B' type: an examination of the relationship between 'product price', 'product scarcity' and 'intent to

purchase', with the independent variables 'product price' (high/medium/low), 'product scarcity' (rare/common) and the dependent variable 'intent to purchase'? How many unique conditions does this study have?

4. If you want to compare willingness to donate between participants identifying as either liberal or conservative, would this be within-participants or between-participants? Would you refer to this as an experiment? Why or why not?

5. For each of the following variables, determine whether this can be used as an independent variable:
   a. Age
   b. Time allowed to complete a task
   c. Importance of individual answer
   d. Time pressure to complete a task
   e. Life satisfaction
   f. Familiarity with a task
   g. Numeracy

6. Note for each statement whether it is true or false, and why.
   a. Participants do not have to be told the purpose of a study before they participate.
   b. Once participants have completed a questionnaire, they cannot withdraw from the study anymore.
   c. Participants have to sign a consent form before you can collect data.
   d. Participants have to explain their reasons if they want to withdraw participation in the middle of the study.
   e. It is always okay to coerce participants to do things as long as that is part of the research question.
   f. Debriefing is also a way of checking whether participants feel okay after participation and offering potential further sources of support.

7. Are the following hypotheses directional or non-directional?
   a. Depressed participants will report less exercise per week than non-depressed participants.
   b. Contacting customers by email and text leads to different retention rates than contacting customers by email alone.
   c. There will be no significant difference in self-esteem between participants high or low in extraversion.
   d. There will be an association between age and musical preference.
   e. Participants who kept a diary are more likely to report a change in exercise habits than participants who did not.

8. For each of the hypotheses listed in Exercise 7, state the null hypothesis.

9. The following are all potential operationalisations of the abstract concept of hunger. To what extent do you think they adequately reflect the underlying concept, and why?
   a. Volume of rumbling stomach noise
   b. Answer to the question 'On a scale from 1 to 10, how hungry are you right now?'
   c. Speed with which participant reaches for food offered
   d. Amount of money participant is willing to pay for food
   e. Combination of skin conductivity and heart rate measurements

10. Assume that you want to examine whether there is an association between numeracy and risk-taking in financial decisions. How could you operationalise numeracy?
    a. In a questionnaire setting
    b. In a lab-based study
    c. Relying only on secondary data

    Can you think of other possible operationalisations? What are their advantages and disadvantages?

# 3 Data Collection

## WHAT IS THIS CHAPTER ABOUT?

Chapter 1 discussed how to find your research question; Chapter 2 outlined the key concepts of research design. Chapter 3 now looks at how to turn your research into practice and collect the data you need to answer your research question. The chapter discusses a range of testing instruments as well as a range of response designs and their implications for data analysis. A large focus of this chapter is avoiding bias, both in the design of the testing material and in terms of overall methodology; therefore, concepts such as sequence effects, randomisation and reliability testing are examined. Lastly, pilot studies are introduced as an essential research tool and part of good practice.

## WHY IS THIS IMPORTANT?

The data you analyse can only be as good as the data you collect. You will see in this chapter that different data types allow different types of statistical analyses; it is important you know these restrictions before you start your data collection. Planning a study's methodology often involves a trade-off between things you would like to do and things you can reasonably and feasibly achieve, and this chapter will give you some guidance on how to make the best decision for your study. Another focus of this chapter is the avoidance of bias: this is important so that the data you collect helps you answer your question in the best way possible and is unaffected by your own bias and that of your participants.

## WHAT ARE THE LEARNING OUTCOMES FOR THIS CHAPTER?

At the end of this chapter you will be able to:

- Come to an informed decision whether to use secondary data and/or collect your own (primary) data
- Select a method of data collection that is appropriate to your research question
- Design questions for questionnaires and tests, and select appropriate response options
- Avoid bias in constructing your testing instruments
- Appreciate the purpose of a pilot study and what you might examine with it

## 3.1 PRIMARY AND SECONDARY DATA

One of the first choices you face when designing your research is whether to use existing data or create and collect your own. Data you collect yourself is called **primary data**; data you use for your research but have not collected yourself is called **secondary data**.

Regardless of whether you plan on using primary or secondary data, we advise you to read the sections for both. No matter which type of data you are planning to use yourself, it is likely that the papers you read will make reference to either type and you need a keen understanding of the challenges of data collection.

### 3.1.1 Secondary data

Using secondary data means you are using existing data you have not collected yourself. These sources can be classified as follows:

- Data collected through previous research
- Data collected by official sources
- Other secondary data

**Data collected through previous research:** This is data researchers have collected in the course of their own studies – often with much more extensive means and resources than are available to you. For example, Coyle-Shapiro and Kessler (2000) conducted a large-scale **survey**, that is they sent out questionnaires to 1130 potential participants in the first part and 23,000 in the second; such participant numbers are very difficult to achieve for any one student researcher. Similarly, student projects are by their very nature and their limit on time and effort mostly unsuitable for **longitudinal** studies, that is, studies which collect measurements from a group or cohort of participants over a long period of time to examine trends, fluctuations and developments. The famous 'marshmallow study' is such a longitudinal study. In the 1960s, researchers looked into the concept of delayed gratification by observing whether children were able to refrain from eating a marshmallow immediately to obtain a second marshmallow as a reward shortly thereafter (Mischel et al., 1972). Researchers then tracked the children's progress over the years to see how their (in)ability to delay gratification related to other aspects of their personality and development. One such follow-up study found that the extent to which children were able to delay gratification was significantly associated with their Body Mass Index (BMI) almost 30 years later (Schlam et al., 2013). While it would be impossible for you to conduct such a longitudinal study as part of your research project, you could in turn use Schlam et al.'s data as a basis for a project of your own. Some studies require co-operation of a number of researchers across several countries. For example, Campbell and colleagues (1988) examined the difference in marketing negotiations in the United Kingdom, the United States, France and Germany, respectively, each conducting part of the research in the country of their residence. Again, you would likely not be in a position to conduct such international research on your own, but could potentially use the data thus collected as secondary data for further analysis. Some journals require their authors to submit the data set with their paper, so if you would like to use other researchers' data, it is worth checking whether the paper contains any link or references to the existing data set. Alternatively, check whether the report (in a paper or chapter) gives any contact details for the author or part of the team; often you will find a designated author to contact for enquiries ('Please address your correspondence to …').

**Data collected by official sources:** This is data collected by institutions such as ministries, government departments, registries, etc. Secondary data is also sometimes referred to as **archival data**, although some make a distinction between secondary data, which has previously been analysed, and archival data, which has not. Data provided by official institutions is often collected without specific research purposes in mind other than to forecast developments and plan provisions of services. Like the studies described in the previous section, the data collected sets are often very large in sample size and can cover entire regions or even countries and span years or decades; on the OECD's website (http://stats.oecd.org/), for example, you can find data on graduation rates for 30 countries, covering years from 1998 to 2012 (results of the query can be found at http://stats.oecd.org/Index.aspx?DatasetCode=RGRADSTY). The fact that the data already exists saves you a lot of time and effort, but it means that you have to accept the data as given. You can only *reduce* the data set but never *expand* it, though you can combine it with other new or existing data sets, like Schlam et al. did by combining recent BMI data with decade-old data on delay of gratification. Depending on the data set, you might not be able to change which values or records are excluded as **outliers** – values so distinctly different from the rest of the data set that including them would substantially skew the results and interpretation – or how individual values have been coded or labelled (more on this in Sections 5.5 on data entry and 5.7 on coding and recoding your data). This is problematic because the definition and identification of what is a genuine data entry mistake or what is an outlier will have been guided by the original researcher's own assumptions and interpretations, with which you may or may not agree, or which may not even be known.

The sampling procedure (see Section 3.8) is similarly out of your control. For example, you might find that a 20-year-old data set from a survey on attitudes towards renewable energy sources only included respondents who (were) identified as male. You cannot simply repeat the survey with additional participants, because you cannot combine data collected 20 years apart in a single sample – unless, of course, you are conducting longitudinal research and this is part of the design. Instead you could repeat the survey with male-identifying participants to compare attitudes now and 20 years ago, or repeat the entire survey without any restrictions on the gender of participants. Secondary data comes with a further limitation that your research question cannot involve cause and effect because you are not actively manipulating any factors and, therefore, do not have full control (see Section 2.6.1). Possible analyses do include examinations for associations (see Section 2.4) and differences (see Section 2.5). In fact, register data or data from large-scale surveys is particularly suitable for examining how a range of variables may predict the outcome of others. For example, Hentschel et al. (2000) combined data from a large-scale household survey (approximately 3400 households) and census data from approximately two million households to develop a statistical model that could predict the geographical distribution of poverty across Ecuador.[1]

Although secondary data of any type comes with some restrictions, the advantages can often outweigh the disadvantages. If you do decide to use secondary data, the following websites offer a good starting point. You can find data such as census data, employment rates, key indicators on national and regional levels, but also data on cultural activities, crime rates, housing statistics and so on.

- Australia: http://www.abs.gov.au/
- Canada: http://www.statcan.gc.ca/ (also available in French)
- India: https://www.indiastat.com/default.aspx
- Ireland: http://www.cso.ie/
- New Zealand: http://www.stats.govt.nz/
- South Africa: http://www.nrf.ac.za/information-resources/databases
- UK: http://www.data-archive.ac.uk/, http://www.statistics.gov.uk/
- USA: https://www.data.gov

---

[1] A prediction is the result of a mathematical formula, also called a model. Normally, such a model and its prediction are compared against existing data for the variable of interest to see how well the output of the model matches reality. In the study above, this means that researchers compared how well their mathematical model of what influences the distribution of poverty matched actual distributions of poverty across Ecuador.

- Data from the OECD countries: https://www.oecd.org/std/business-stats/structuraland demographicbusinessstatisticssdbsoecd.htm
- Data for the EU nations: https://ec.europa.eu/eurostat/home

A more comprehensive list of resources of social science data is available on this website which collates international databases and archives:

http://www.sociosite.net/databases.php

Last but not least, you can also find data from existing large-scale surveys online, such as the European Social Survey, the British Election Study or the British Social Attitudes Survey, to name just a few. Data available through these sources can be a good starting point for a student thesis, because a substantial part of research is based on analysing existing data through new lenses and perspectives. In fact, the author of this book was part of such a research team (Wood et al., 2015) analysing existing data from the UK Commission's 2011 Employer Skills from a fresh theoretical perspective – in this case, aspects of high-involvement management.

### ONLINE CONTENT

You can find the URLs to all the websites mentioned in this chapter on the companion website.

**Other secondary data:** Lastly, you may want to use existing data which has been collected for very practical purposes but which may be interesting to analyse in a more systematic and theory-based approach: online application data, hospital records, police reports, insurance claim forms, sales receipts, activity logs, diaries, exam papers, interview recordings, household bills, bank account statements, page impressions, library borrowing records, text messages, visitor statistics ... wherever data can be usefully extracted to draw conclusions on people's behaviour, motives or attitudes. In the list above, text messages may for example be used to look at patterns of sending and receiving texts to establish how well connected individuals are, or for the analysis of text contents themselves.

### 3.1.2 Primary data

Collecting your own data means that you are in control of selecting or designing data collection tools and selecting individual testing items, variable measurements and samples. Conducting your own research and gathering primary data also gives you the opportunity to conduct pilot studies, which in turn allows you to identify potential problems and adapt your procedures and instruments accordingly. This puts you in a better position to interpret data because you are aware of its origin and limitations: you know that participants filled out the survey while sitting in a noisy university cafeteria or while waiting at a bus stop out in the cold; you know this may have affected how well they concentrated on the questions and how much time they took to think about the questions.

Regardless of the exact nature of your research, if you use primary data there are usually a few key elements of your methodology:

1. Deciding on variables and conditions.
2. Developing material to use in your study to elicit and record data from conditions.
3. Recruiting (human) participants.

The rest of this chapter will discuss all of these steps in turn.

## 3.2 DECIDING ON VARIABLES AND CONDITIONS

If you have followed the steps outlined in Chapter 1, your research question will likely already be phrased in terms of variables or hint at the variables you are interested in. If that is not the case, now is the time you need to decide what you will be measuring. How directly your measurements relate to what you are interested in depends on the operationalisation of your research (see Section 2.13) while at the same time aiming for high reliability and validity (see Sections 2.11 and 2.12, respectively). There are a few things you should keep in mind when deciding *what* to measure:

- Consult the literature.
- Use more than one measurement tool.
- Use more than one measurement for constructs.
- Remember Garbage In, Garbage Out (GIGO).

**Consult the literature:** Make sure to determine whether adequate testing instruments for the type of data you are looking for already exist. For example, if you want to know whether stress-coping strategies differ between introverted and extraverted people, look for existing instruments that measure introversion and extraversion; if you are interested in examining leadership styles across different organisations, consider using instruments developed within frameworks of existing leadership models. If papers using these studies have been published in academic journals, they have already undergone rigorous peer review and you will, in most cases, be able to find statistics indicating how well the tests measure what they purport to measure (see Cronbach's alpha later in Section 3.12). If you find that the tests do not measure exactly what you are looking for, you can still try and adapt the existing instrument for your needs.

**Use more than one measurement tool:** If you decide to develop your own measurement tool, try and provide some validation through using a second, more established tool at its side. If you are measuring the same construct, the two sets of results should be roughly similar – a property referred to as *convergent validity* in the previous chapter.

**Use more than one measurement for constructs:** Try to take multiple measures to capture different facets or dimensions of the same variable. Where we refer to an instrument as a **scale** – in other words, a tool consisting of multiple items – this usually indicates that the set of items is testing different facets of the same construct. Here, a **construct** is defined as an abstract concept which is intangible – for example, socioeconomic status, risk aversion, curiosity or intelligence. Concepts like these cannot be measured directly but can be inferred from traits or behaviours related to the one you are interested in. For example, you might try to elicit information about a participant's self-esteem by asking 'On a scale from 1 to 5, with 1 = Very High and 5 = Very Low, how high would you rate your self-esteem?' Although this gives you a neat single value to describe self-esteem, you would be better advised to develop multiple items to test the relevant construct, for example by asking about feelings of self-worth, confidence to meet new people, happiness with own body, etc. These items should be based on a thorough appraisal of the relevant literature. In a second step, responses to the items can then be consolidated into a single value. Because you have considered multiple facets of the self-esteem construct, this value is more likely to give you a true assessment of the participant's self-esteem than their answer to a single question would.

**Remember Garbage In, Garbage Out (GIGO):** We use it here as a reminder that your data collection affects the kind of data analysis you can do later on. Only high-quality data allows you to conduct high-quality analyses. Section 2.2 introduced a way of describing data by referring to nominal, ordinal, interval or ratio scale data. Different scale types allow different statistical analyses, and you can influence the scale type by the way in which you measure and record your data. For example, even though level of education lends itself to an ordinal scale, it could also be measured by years spent in secondary and higher education; a company's financial success can be expressed by annual income or turnover (ratio data), or position on a ranking such as the Forbes 500 or its rank in a given sector/region/industry (ordinal data). Conversely, while time usually is considered to be data of the ratio scale type, recording the order in which participants in a group finish a task (first, second, fifth, etc.) measures data into an ordinal scale but would result in a loss of detail. In fact, **data transformation** or **scale transformation** (i.e., changing data from one scale type to the other) always results in a loss of detail because you can only transform downwards (ratio to interval, ordinal or nominal; interval to ordinal or nominal; ordinal to nominal) but never upwards. The only way to add detail is to collect additional data.

## LOOK OUT!

A similar loss of detail takes place whenever test results are used to group participants into subgroups, for example using extraversion scores to classify participants as either high or low in extraversion. There may be valid reasons for doing so, but it is important to be aware of the resulting change in data type. When you transform data, you lose the detail such as the exact test score. To mitigate against mistakes and change of mind, make sure that you create a new variable (see Section 5.7.1 on how to do that) and retain the old one with the original value.

## REVIEW & REFLECT

- When might it be more suitable to use secondary data?
- Can you conduct an experiment with secondary data? Why or why not?

## 3.3  DEVELOPING MATERIAL

Quantitative studies can take a variety of forms, both in terms of settings (laboratory, online, collecting data from pedestrians on a busy street, etc.) and material (online tests, online surveys, videos, lost letters, staged scenarios in a public place, etc.), so this section will not be able to give a comprehensive overview. The list below demonstrates a range of possible approaches but it is by no means exhaustive:

- Providing auditory, visual, tactile or olfactory stimuli and asking participants to identify, categorise or evaluate them to specific criteria, for example, 'How pleasant is this sound?' 'Which word was shown on the screen?' 'Is this an acceptable word in English?' 'Was this an image of a man or a woman?' 'Which of the two pictures did you like better?'
- Observing or measuring spontaneous responses to stimuli, for example, measuring eye movements when participants are presented with a particular picture or text; recording heart rate or skin conductivity while being shown a video or audio clip; recording facial movements and identifying them as disgust, surprise or joy

- Observing group behaviour, for example when having to come to a unanimous decision; response to peer pressure with or without an ally present; recording dyads (two people) or triads (three people); group responses to given stimuli or environments, such as different leadership styles; watching toddlers interact with each other in a playgroup
- Observing individual behaviour, such as being asked to think aloud when solving a problem; observing a musician improvise; observing a participant work through an in-tray exercise; asking participants to interact with technology such as virtual reality glasses or a new software
- Observing responses to group or individual behaviour, such as helping behaviour in situations where other people are perceived to be in need of assistance; response rates to advertisements; response rates in a **lost-letter setup** (for a brief explanation see Glossary)
- Eliciting attitudinal data by asking participants to complete questionnaires
- (Cor)relating different personality traits and characteristics by having participants complete several personality tests.

The list could go on and on. Hopefully it becomes clear that there is a huge range of options, and with it a huge range of possible material that may need to be developed. This variety also extends to the environment: research may be conducted through online tests which participants can complete in the privacy of their own home; it may require a complex technical setup and can only be conducted in a university laboratory; it may be paper-based and has to be filled out during a strictly time-limited session or can be mailed and returned through the post, etc. Some of the most frequently used methods are:

- Observations,
- Questionnaires/Surveys, and
- Tests.

**Observations**, that is, the monitoring and possible recording of behaviour of one individual or interactions between two more individuals, are more commonly associated with qualitative research but can, with the right adaptations, be used for quantitative research. The key here is to define countable categories of observable behaviour, for example counting the number of times participants who are speaking are interrupted by others; recording how often participants preferred one product over the other; or noting the sequence of problem-solving steps in a task requiring manipulation of physical objects. In another example, you might be interested in examining turn-taking in group discussions and therefore observe a group of participants trying to reach an agreement. You make a note whenever a participant speaks and jot down whether they (1) started talking during a gap in conversation; (2) talked over another participant but relented and let the other participant finish their part; or (3) continued to talk over the other participant until the other participant stopped talking. This then gives you a list of countable instances of a specific behaviour. The key requirements to successfully generating data from observations are:

- An unambiguous definition of what the specific behaviour looks like;
- An examination of observer reliability, for example by correlating two or more observers' data; and
- Comparable situations for participants to be observed in so that observations can also be compared.

For an example of an observational study, consider work by Aitken and Jahoda (1983) on the demographics of young adult alcohol consumption. Aitken and Jahoda and a couple of colleagues spent quite a lot of time in bars (for science, obviously) and observed a total of 200 groups of young adults in an attempt to identify demographic information (such as age and gender) and consumption patterns (such as who bought what drink, who pressured whom into buying/consuming alcohol):

> throughout the study the observers were instructed to record the following information with respect to each group member: time of arrival; sex; age (under 18, 18–21, 22–25, over 25); identity of purchaser and method of purchase for each round (round-buying by one person, shared round-buying, 'kitty', individual purchase); type of drink consumed for each round (nothing, non-alcoholic drink, beer/lager, spirits, wine/cocktail); amount consumed at each round (pint or half-pint for beer/lager, single or double measure for spirits, glass for wine/cocktail); time received each drink, time started each drink, and time finished each drink. The information was recorded ... on prepared record forms concealed in newspapers or magazines. (p. 136)

Some of this information was easier to observe than others. For example, the type of drink consumed by round or the time received for each drink was relatively easy to observe and record; other information, such as the age, was much more difficult to establish and Aitken and Jahoda subsequently described the measures they took to establish reliability:

> In the present study each observer recorded information with respect to all members of the group. For this reason, each observer received several training sessions under the guidance of an experienced observer. Subsequent reliability tests showed that all but one of the factors or variables listed above achieved levels of agreement of over 90% between pairs of observers. The age rating achieved a much lower level of agreement, ranging from 63 to 73%. This is not surprising given the difficulties involved in making relatively fine judgements of the ages of young adults. (p. 136)

**Questionnaires/Surveys** are particularly well suited for eliciting responses from a large number of people in a relatively short period of time, provided the questions are unambiguous and not too complex. They can also be posted, emailed, linked online or shared via social networks, etc.; the survey on the website http://futureconservation.org/ is such an example (though note that the questions on the survey are not all as unbiased as would be ideal). This makes them relatively cost-efficient and easy to administer, and recipients can complete them at their own time in their own space. On the downside, if you are not present when your participant attempts to complete the questionnaire you cannot respond to any of their questions for clarification or address any ambiguities in the material. Questionnaires can be distributed in paper form or electronically, which can (but does not have to) mean online; for example, you could set up a computer on which your participants complete the questionnaire in a quiet environment. Electronic and online questionnaires can easily be changed and allow fast responses to pilot study results or participant feedback. Because you only have to make changes once in the programming of the questionnaire (rather than printing new questionnaires and posting them out to participants), online questionnaires are particularly suitable for administering to a large number of people at the same time, which is advantageous if you are conducting international research or need a very large sample. However, changing the content of an active questionnaire may invalidate part or all of your data because you cannot easily compare data sets where questions or response options differ. Online tools are easy to promote and distribute via links to online tools in emails, tweets or Facebook posts, but the easy online contact often translates into only superficial interest for your questionnaire and, subsequently, into low completion rates.

Advanced online tools sometimes offer *conditional logic*, a system where different sections or questions are presented to a participant depending on their answer to earlier questions (e.g., if a participant responds that they do not own a car, the set of questions relating to car ownership will be skipped); *branching*, a system where X% of respondents will be allocated to version A, Y% to version B and so on; and *logs*, records which can tell you how many people started the questionnaire, how many completed it and how long it took. The list below gives just a few examples of popular online survey tools (all links also available on the companion website):

- http://www.surveymonkey.com
- http://www.surveygizmo.com
- http://www.google.com/google-d-s/forms/
- https://www.qualtrics.com

However, before you use a tool from an external provider, check with your university's or employer's IT department. Many organisations have very strict requirements about how and where data can be stored (i.e., not in the Cloud) and may not allow you to use a tool that does not fit those requirements and/or require that you use an in-house tool.

**Tests** can be conducted in paper form or electronically, both online and offline: a test measuring reaction time or pattern recognition may well be presented on a computer (or tablet, etc.) without necessarily containing an online component. For example, in the UK, learner drivers have to successfully complete the Hazard Perception Test (HPT), a computer-based task which consists of a video being shown from the perspective of a driver. You can try the HPT here:

https://www.safedrivingforlife.info/practice-hazard-perception-test

The learner has to carefully monitor the traffic situation presented on the screen and click whenever a potentially dangerous situation is developing. With this setup, the HPT is an example of an offline electronic test.

If you are associated with a university or school, you may have access to special in-house software which can be programmed to run a number of tests. For example, many departments offer training in and use of e-Prime, a well-known testing software package.

### 3.3.1 Making your material accessible

Whatever means of data collection you use, try and make sure that it is accessible to as many participants as possible:

- Offer large-print versions of your printed materials.
- If your material contains potentially disturbing content, for example by referring to illness, bereavement, abuse or self-harm, or by containing pictures of objects participants might be phobic of, such as spiders, snakes, weapons, etc., consider the use of **content notes** or **trigger warnings** (see Glossary).
- Be careful with using humour or metaphors unless you are explicitly researching any of these topics; humour or non-verbal cues may be difficult to pick up by non-neurotypical (see Glossary for a definition of **neurotypical**) participants.
- If you use graphics, either on screen or on paper, make sure that no vital information depends on colours or colour contrasts, such as red-green, which would not be visible to any colour-blind participants. Websites such as http://colorbrewer2.org/ can suggest colour-blind safe colour schemes to use.

- Similarly, avoid relying on different colours to indicate differences. If possible, use different shadings or differences in intensity/saturation (see also Section 7.6 on designing accessible graphs).
- If you use online content, make sure that it can be easily navigated with screen readers. Screen readers are software tools which read out loud the text from a computer screen so that visually impaired people can access digital content. You can find free tools to check accessibility for screen readers at http://www.nvaccess.org/ and you can submit your website for testing with http://wave.webaim.org/.
- Audio material or video material: If you use video clips or movies, check whether you can present them with captions or transcripts for auditory impaired participants and voice-over for visually impaired participants.

When deciding which items to include in your instrument, you always need to keep in mind how you will be able to analyse the data later on. Taking more time to carefully design an instrument will pay off in less effort to code, enter and analyse the data, whereas a poorly defined or phrased question can render your data unsuitable for more sophisticated analyses or, at the worst case, unusable for any analysis at all.

The following section will describe a variety of different options to elicit data. It draws from a broad range of examples to show how many of these options can be used in a wide variety of contexts.

### LOOK OUT!

There is often some confusion about the use of the term 'scale' as this can refer to a complete testing instrument, for example the 'Wechsler Adult Intelligence Scale' (an IQ test); a means of measuring an item (e.g., 'answers to a question can be given on a scale from 1 to 10'); or a type of data that has implications for the statistical tests that can be used. From here on, the term scale itself will be reserved for scales measuring responses. If you encounter this term in your reading, make sure to check in which context and meaning it is used.

### REVIEW & REFLECT

- How can making your research more accessible improve your data quality?
- What are the advantages and disadvantages of tests, observations and surveys?

### 3.3.2  How to elicit responses

**Open question:** A question allowing a free response, ranging from a single word to paragraphs or short essays.

Examples:

- How do you deal with stress?
- How satisfied are you with your current role?
- If there was a general election next week, which party would you vote for and why?
- What does your ideal relationship look like?
- Can you please describe how you solved this problem?

At a glance, this seems like the most direct and easiest way to elicit answers to a question. However, the responses to open answers may require the use of specialist software such as NVivo, SPSS Modeler or SAS Enterprise Minder for quantitative analysis, as free-text answers pose a number of challenges:

- Participants' answers can range from single-word answers to answers several paragraphs long. This means data cannot simply be sorted and counted but needs to be looked at individually.
- The same answer can be given in different forms. For example, people might respond to the question 'How do you deal with stress?' with answers such as 'exercise' or 'sport' and for the purpose of your analysis, you would want to combine those two answers in one category. But to identify both responses as referring to the same concept you need to manually examine the data. You can of course search for key words to identify multiple answers relating to the same concept but that, too, means you introduce your assumptions and expectations of what you might find and you risk *not* finding answers you do not *expect* to find. You can only identify these almost-but-not-quite-the-same answers by reading every single answer yourself. This may be feasible for small data sets, but with large-scale studies reading every individual answer will not be an option.

**Asking to complete sentences:** When using the method of **sentence completion**, participants are asked to complete a given sentence.
Examples:

- What I'm most looking for in a new car is ____.
- When I go shopping, I am primarily looking for ____.
- My friends would describe me as ____.
- ____ is the most important thing in a relationship.
- The thing I'm most looking for in a new job is ____.

This likely will generate shorter answers, but you still need to examine every answer individually to be able to group answers under certain categories or recognise them as different variants of the same answer.

> **! LOOK OUT!**
>
> If you do decide to use free-text responses for some of your questions – perhaps for comments, feedback and enquiries – keep in mind that some database software puts size limits on text fields. Entering free-text data in a Word or Excel table will pose no problem, but for other software you might want to check in advance. You do not want to find yourself in a position where a participant's thoughtful 560-character response does not fit into a 256-character database field, so that you have to truncate or summarise the response and thus lose data and detail.

**Choice question:** The question lists several possible responses and indicates how many responses are allowed. This can range from one (e.g., 'pick the option that most applies to you/is most typical for you/you agree with most') to multiple or all responses (e.g., 'tick all that apply'). It is usually advisable to add a further option 'Not applicable (n/a)'/ 'Does not apply' so that the participant can indicate that none of the options are suitable for them.

Examples:

Single choice question: 'If you didn't vote in the last election, please indicate below why (please select your main reason)'

|  |  |
|---|---|
| ☐ | I didn't think my vote would count |
| ☐ | None of the parties reflected my own values |
| ☐ | I didn't have time to vote |
| ☐ | I couldn't make up my mind |
| ☐ | I'm not interested in politics |
| ☐ | I didn't know there was an election |
| ☐ | Don't know |
| ☐ | Not applicable |

Multiple choice question (MCQ): 'If you applied for a job in the last six months, please indicate which criteria you used to select the positions you applied for (tick all that apply):'

|  |  |
|---|---|
| ☐ | Geographical location |
| ☐ | Salary |
| ☐ | Job description |
| ☐ | Employer reputation |
| ☐ | Investor in People accreditation |

'Please indicate for each item whether it is an acceptable English word:'

- ∘ 'kwimble'   [ ] Yes   [ ] No   [ ] Can't decide
- ∘ 'fthagn'    [ ] Yes   [ ] No   [ ] Can't decide
- ∘ 'tippy'     [ ] Yes   [ ] No   [ ] Can't decide
- ∘ 'rpawn'     [ ] Yes   [ ] No   [ ] Can't decide

Questions with fixed choices have a distinct advantage over the two methods previously described: all possible answers are already defined and can be counted more easily. This makes entering and coding data much easier since you no longer have to examine every response individually. You can include a 'Don't know' option, which will reduce the likelihood of missing data, or 'Don't wish to say' which allows participants to indicate that they have read and understood the question and have actively chosen not to disclose the information. The fixed selection of possible responses is both an advantage and a disadvantage, as in its restricted form the instrument only allows eliciting responses you were aware of and expected to receive. This can lead to very misleading results and can be remedied by including an additional option:

|  |  |
|---|---|
| ☐ | Other, please specify: |

While not perfect, this allows you to gather responses that you had not considered initially. Particularly when used in a pilot study, 'Other, please specify' is often helpful in identifying additional required answer options.

**Ranking questions:** These questions ask respondents to rank a number of options according to a criterion defined by you; this procedure is also known as **rank ordering**.

Examples:

'Thinking about the five candidates whose CVs you have just read, please rank them from least qualified to most qualified for the job role:'

Rank (1 = Most qualified, 5 = Least qualified)

| 1 | Candidate _____ |
| 2 | Candidate _____ |
| 3 | Candidate _____ |
| 4 | Candidate _____ |
| 5 | Candidate _____ |

'How important are these characteristics in a romantic partner? Please rank the following factors in order of importance, ranging from 1 = Least important to 10 = Most important.'

| Rank | |
|---|---|
| [ ] | Physically attractive |
| [ ] | Well educated |
| [ ] | Has great sense of humour |
| [ ] | Intelligent |
| [ ] | Gets along well with my friends |
| [ ] | Shares my hobbies and passions |
| [ ] | Finds me attractive |
| [ ] | Shares my political views |
| [ ] | Is supportive of my dreams and ambitions |
| [ ] | Communicates openly and honestly |

Gathering data on the explicit preferences of participants can be extremely valuable; however, data issues can arise if participants do not assign all possible values or assign the same value twice by mistake, which may render the entire set of data for that participant unusable. Some online surveys or computer testing software allow the definition of validation rules such as 'all values have to be used', 'no value can be assigned twice', 'value must be between 1 and 5', etc.

**Pairwise comparison:** A **pairwise comparison** presents two options and asks respondents to choose one of the two.

Example:

'Consider the presenters you just saw on video. For each of the comparisons, pick the presenter you think was more trustworthy.'

| Maggie | Or | Charlie |
|---|---|---|
| [ ] | | [ ] |
| Charlie | Or | Bruce |
| [ ] | | [ ] |
| Kira | Or | Maggie |
| [ ] | | [ ] |
| Quincy | Or | Tipsy |
| [ ] | | [ ] |
| Quincy | Or | Kira |
| [ ] | | [ ] |

Participants may find it difficult to assign an order to a list of options, but less difficult to indicate a preference between two items. Pairwise comparisons are not always practical, however, as the number of pairs very quickly becomes too large to manage as items are added. You can calculate the number of required pairwise comparisons with the following formula, where n is the number of items you want to compare:

$$\frac{n \times (n-1)}{2}$$

Therefore, to find out the number of pairwise comparisons you need for comparing five items, replace n with 5:

$$\frac{5 \times (5-1)}{2} = \frac{5 \times 4}{2} = \frac{20}{2} = 10$$

Each participant in the above example has to assess ten pairs. However, if you were to increase the number of items somewhat, say to ten (only five items more), you need a much larger number of comparisons:

$$\frac{10 \times (10-1)}{2} = \frac{10 \times 9}{2} = \frac{90}{2} = 45$$

By adding five more items to the list, you have already increased the number of required comparisons from 10 to 45. And just to drive home the point, have a look at an example with 20 items – only 10 more items than in the last example:

$$\frac{20 \times (20-1)}{2} = \frac{20 \times 19}{2} = \frac{380}{2} = 190$$

One-hundred ninety pairwise comparisons will sorely test the patience and stamina of any participant, and it would only be fair and kind to develop a different questionnaire design that does not threaten your participants' sanity. Because pairwise comparisons are challenging to record and analyse, we show them here for completeness' sake but will not cover them in the remainder of this book in terms of data entry and analysis.

### 3.3.3 Rating scales

A different approach of eliciting data is using rating scales which allow participants to evaluate items individually along a number of criteria. **Rating scales** can be used to assess attitude, (dis)agreement with statements, preference, (dis)approval, (un)certainty and many other purposes. As mentioned before, there is some ambiguity in the use of the term scale as it can take on a number of meanings, ranging from collecting a response to a single item to forming a complete test instrument. When the term is used to refer to an entire test instrument, that instrument often in itself contains a number of individual rating scales. Last but not least, the term scale is also used to refer to the type of data and the properties associated with the type; this is discussed in more detail in Section 2.2. Where this and the following sections refer to scales, unless mentioned otherwise, it is meant to refer to single-item rating scales along the lines of 'On a scale from 1 to 5, with 1 = Not at all and 5 = Very much, how much would you like to stop reading about scales right now?'

When you think of using rating scales, you have a number of decisions to make:

- Unipolar or bipolar?
- Neutral option: Yes or no?
- Symmetric or asymmetric?
- How detailed?

**Unipolar or bipolar? Unipolar rating scales** mean collecting data on one specific trait or property, starting from a point of zero and pointing towards an end point (or end pole) you have defined; bipolar rating scales means collecting data which spans a continuum between two end points, for example like/dislike or agree/disagree. Whether something should be measured on a unipolar or bipolar scale is not always inherent to the variable; in some cases, it can depend on theoretical considerations. For example, different strands in the literature view optimism and pessimism as (a) two opposite poles of one scale (You are either a pessimist or an optimist) or (b) as traits which are distinct (You can be a pessimist in some regards and an optimist in others). Similarly, agreement with a statement could be either examined by defining it as something that could be absent or present to varying degrees, for example:

To what extent do you agree with the statement: 'I am usually a confident person'?

| ☐ | ☐ | ☐ | ☐ |
|---|---|---|---|
| Not at all | Agree somewhat | Agree | Agree very strongly |

Here, you use a unipolar scale as the answers range from a point of zero to whatever end point you define. But the same question could be asked and analysed in a slightly different way, such that agreement and disagreement are seen as two end points of a continuum, expressed through a bipolar scale:

To what extent do you agree or disagree with the statement: 'I am usually a confident person'?

| ☐ | ☐ | ☐ | ☐ |
|---|---|---|---|
| Disagree strongly | Disagree somewhat | Agree somewhat | Agree strongly |

Questions about frequencies can suggest using a unipolar scale:

On average, how many hours a day have you spent surfing the Internet in the last two weeks?

| ☐ | ☐ | ☐ | ☐ | ☐ |
|---|---|---|---|---|
| None | Less than 2 hours | Between 2 and 4 hours | Between 4 and 6 hours | More than 6 hours |

However, depending on the type of frequency, a bipolar scale is possible if the subject allows the two end points of 'Always' or 'Never', for example:

For the last month, how often have you felt feelings of despair?

| ☐ | ☐ | ☐ | ☐ | ☐ |
|---|---|---|---|---|
| Never | Rarely | Sometimes | Very often | All the time |

**Neutral option: Yes or No?** This design decision relates to whether you allow your respondents to be indecisive or give a neutral answer, or whether you would like to gently coerce them to express a preference, one way or the other. Note the difference between the two following options:

To what extent do you agree or disagree with the statement: 'I'm willing to take risks and try new things'?

| ☐ | ☐ | ☐ | ☐ | ☐ |
|---|---|---|---|---|
| Strongly disagree | Disagree | Neither agree nor disagree | Agree | Strongly agree |
| Disagreement || Neutral | Agreement ||

To what extent do you agree or disagree with the statement: 'I'm willing to take risks and try new things'?

| ☐ | ☐ | ☐ | ☐ |
|---|---|---|---|
| Disagree strongly | Disagree somewhat | Agree somewhat | Agree strongly |
| Disagreement || Agreement ||

The first option allows participants to be indecisive, the second option does not. Including a central option will increase the chances of participants 'going for the middle'. This is known as the **central-tendency bias** (i.e., avoiding extreme values in responses); scales without a neutral central option employ what is called a **forced-choice method**.

**Symmetric or asymmetric?** Coincidentally, the first of the two scales above is also an example of a five-point **Likert scale**, which refers to a type of bipolar rating scale expressing a degree of disagreement and agreement (with or without a central option), and ranging from four-point scales to any reasonable number of response options beyond that. Likert scales are considered to be **symmetric rating scales**. In fact, both scales above are symmetric as you can see from the distribution of agreement and disagreement responses. This is a special type of bipolar scale and means that response options are balanced with an equal number of response options (with or without a neutral central option) for both poles of the scale. In contrast, below is an example of an **asymmetric rating scale**:

To what extent do you agree with the statement, 'I usually try to play it safe'?

| ☐ | ☐ | ☐ | ☐ | ☐ |
|---|---|---|---|---|
| Disagree | Agree slightly | Agree somewhat | Agree strongly | Agree very strongly |
| Disagreement | Agreement ||||

Respondents have four options to express a degree of agreement and only one option of disagreement. You have to be careful when you design your rating scale so that it can still capture the full range of participants' responses. Alternatively, you can use numbers rather than labels such as 'agree' or 'disagree', or you can use them in combination – but this then leads to the question how to label your response options. Do you start at 0 and increase by 1, do you start with a negative number and use 0 as the central point, or do you not provide any numerical value labels at all? All of the following versions are acceptable, but all can carry slightly different connotations for the participant.

| ☐ | ☐ | ☐ | ☐ | ☐ |
|---|---|---|---|---|
| (1) Strongly disagree | (2) Disagree | (3) Neither agree nor disagree | (4) Agree | (5) Strongly agree |

| ☐ | ☐ | ☐ | ☐ | ☐ |
|---|---|---|---|---|
| (−2) Strongly disagree | (−1) Disagree | (0) Neither agree nor disagree | (1) Agree | (2) Strongly agree |

| ☐ | ☐ | ☐ | ☐ | ☐ |
|---|---|---|---|---|
| Strongly disagree | Disagree | Neither agree nor disagree | Agree | Strongly agree |

The first version may suggest that agreement is unipolar, ranging from no agreement to strong agreement; the second and third versions are more likely to suggest that disagreement and agreement are opposites. Ultimately the choice is yours. You can also decide to not show your participants any numerical labels and only use the numerical values when you need them for your statistical analyses.

**How detailed?** In theory, your scale can be as fine-grained as you like. Everything from scales with 3 responses to up to 100 and more is possible. You need to decide how many different levels of response are practical and useful. If you measure motivation, will allowing participants to answer from 1 to 20 really give you better data than just allowing responses between 1 and 10 or even between 1 and 5? It is unlikely that your participants can accurately distinguish whether their motivation is more a 16 or a 17 (of 20); instead, it is more likely that they will be able to perceive a difference between 4 and 5 (of 5).

> **! LOOK OUT!**
>
> It is easy to rely on rating scales measuring agreement. You develop a list of statements and have your participants rate to what extent they agree – quickly done, quickly analysed! But depending on the question, you might short change yourself of information that could be quite useful. Consider the following question. To what extent do you agree with the statement 'I am happy with the amount of attention I am getting from my line manager'? Here, agreement is easily understood, but disagreement is more difficult to interpret. Does a disagreeing participant think they are getting too much or too little attention? A better way to phrase the question would be: 'How much attention are you getting from your line manager?' combined with perhaps a five-options answer of 'Far too little/Too little/Just right/Too much/Far too much'.

### 3.3.4 Semantic differential

If you are interested in respondents' perception or feelings regarding a certain issue or concept, you can use a **semantic differential**. This lists a number of contrasting terms such as 'good'/'bad' as two end poles and the respondent has to indicate where they perceive the item concerned fits between the two extremes. Kressmann et al. (2006), for example, used a semantic differential when asking their participants to assess both their own car as well as that 'of the ideal car of that class' along a range of criteria such as engine power, appearance, etc. Each semantic differential then illustrated a personality 'profile' of the owned and the ideal car (Figure 3.1).

| Engine Power: | Very poor | ○ ○ ● ○ ○ ○ ○ | Very strong |
| Appearance: | Very plain-looking | ○ ○ ○ ● ○ ○ ○ | Very good-looking |
| Safety: | Very unsafe | ○ ● ○ ○ ○ ○ ○ | Very safe |
| Quality: | Very low-grade | ○ ○ ○ ○ ● ○ ○ | Very high-grade |
| Gas Consumption: | Very low | ○ ● ○ ○ ○ ○ ○ | Very high |
| Cost: | Very expensive | ○ ○ ○ ● ○ ○ ○ | Very reasonable |

**Figure 3.1** *Semantic differential with criteria from Kressmann et al. (2006) © Elsevier*

If participants have to answer long lists of questions, consider reversing the order of positive and negative terms every now and then so that participants do not fall into a routine of selecting only the leftmost or rightmost option; although opinion is divided whether this really is a good strategy. This process is referred to as **reverse coding** and will subsequently require more vigilance on your side when you collect, analyse and present your data.

## ? REVIEW & REFLECT

- How might the researcher's assumptions affect the design of rating scales?
- How does response design affect data analysis?

## 3.4 DEMOGRAPHIC QUESTIONS

Demographic data such as age, gender, level of education, etc. is important because it allows you to examine the composition of your sample and estimate how similar your sample is to the overall population. This in turn tells you to what extent your study's findings can be generalised. If participants in your study are overwhelmingly students, but the population you are interested in is a mixture of school pupils, students, employees and retirees, then the sample will not reflect on the population as a whole. The collection of additional demographic information through **demographic questions** (i.e., questions establishing key demographic information on your sample) depends upon the specific research question and the factors you consider to be relevant. Of interest to you is data which is intrinsically related to the topic and which can be elicited unobtrusively, that is, without detracting from the main topic and main data of interest. For example, when conducting research on nutrition and exercise you might want to know levels of income or amount of available spending income, as this affects the choices that are available to your participants in terms of quality of food, frequencies of eating out, affordability of gym membership and private trainers, etc. Other demographic variables that are potentially of interest in this or other contexts are relationship status, number of children, type of employment, nationality, first language, ethnicity, etc. However, only collect data if you have sufficient reason to believe it may be relevant to your research question. Not every research question will be compromised by a sample with a limited age; cohabitation (who lives with whom) can be a relevant demographic variable where research concerns household spending patterns, but not for research on learning preferences.

In this context we want to urge you as a researcher to acknowledge the lived experience of many individuals. Always think carefully about what information you are asking for, and why and how. In the case of gender, be mindful of the distinction between sex (considered to be based on biological and physiological differences) and gender or gender identity (considered to be culturally and socially constructed). Make sure that you know which of the two, if either, is relevant for your research, and consider including options in addition to male and female, such as intersex (e.g., exhibiting physiological characteristics of both sexes); gender-fluid (i.e., with changing and fluctuating gender identity); or non-binary or gender-queer, an identity that does not match either of the binary definitions. Allow participants to not disclose their gender by including an option 'do not wish to disclose', but do make sure you only use the option 'Prefer to not say'/'Do not wish to disclose' in conjunction with a comprehensive set of response options. The use of this response option on its own is quite contentious, because it implies that participants chose not to disclose their gender, when more often the choice was taken away from them because no response option adequately described their gender identity.[2]

You can tackle this question in varying degrees of complexity. For example, in their guidelines on collecting data in the workplace, the UK LGBT charity Stonewall recommends to split the question in three parts (Figure 3.2):

What best describes your gender?

| [ ] | Male |
| [ ] | Female |
| [ ] | Prefer to self-describe:_____ |
| [ ] | Prefer not to say |

Do you identify as trans?

| [ ] | No |
| [ ] | Yes |
| [ ] | Prefer not to say |

Is your gender identity the same sex as you were assigned at birth?

| [ ] | No |
| [ ] | Yes |
| [ ] | Prefer not to say |

**Figure 3.2** *Stonewall (2016) recommendations[3] to collect data on gender and gender identity*

In contrast, these are the options researchers used when looking explicitly at gender and sexual orientation (Boncori, 2017):

---

[2] Thanks go to Dr Ilaria Boncori for first making the author of this book aware of this.
[3] Stonewall (2016), Do Ask, Do Tell. Available at https://www.stonewall.org.uk/sites/default/files/do_ask_do_tell_guide_2016.pdf. (Last accessed 22 June 2018).

Gender:

| [ ] | Cisgender Male (Male and was assigned Male at birth) |
|---|---|
| [ ] | Cisgender Female (Female and was assigned Female at birth) |
| [ ] | Transgender Male |
| [ ] | Transgender Female |
| [ ] | Agender |
| [ ] | Bigender |
| [ ] | Demiboy |
| [ ] | Demigirl |
| [ ] | Gender Fluid |
| [ ] | Non-binary |
| [ ] | Trigender |
| [ ] | Two-spirited |
| [ ] | Other (explain) |

Sexual Orientation:

| [ ] | Heterosexual (Straight) |
|---|---|
| [ ] | Gay |
| [ ] | Lesbian |
| [ ] | Asexual |
| [ ] | Bisexual |
| [ ] | Pansexual |
| [ ] | Other |

Last but decidedly not least, if and when you do decide to collect data referring to individuals' sexuality or gender expression, please remember that many people still encounter violence prompted by homophobia or transphobia. You should always treat your data with utmost care and confidentiality, but even more so here where losing or publicly disclosing your data might put individuals at risk of severe harm, physically and psychologically.

## 3.5 PROCEDURAL QUESTIONS

**Procedural questions** do not refer to factors or variables related immediately to the research question but rather help improve overall conclusion validity (see Section 2.12). For example, you want to make sure that participants understand the instructions and the testing material in order to be able to draw any conclusions from the results. Hence it is good practice to include a question to check how and to what extent participants encountered any difficulties with the material: 'How difficult to read was the material? Were the questions easy/difficult/too difficult?' etc. This helps identify participants who may have struggled with the instructions and whose data may skew the results. Questions of this type can be an integral part of a pilot study and inform your decision as to whether further methodological refinement is needed or material and procedure are sufficiently developed.

If you conduct an experiment, by definition you aim to manipulate variables. To increase conclusion validity, you want to make sure that the manipulation was successful. For example, you might be interested in the interaction between *difficulty of task* and *background noise* on *accuracy* in a letter-search task – a 2×3 within-participants experiment with two levels of difficulty (easy, difficult) and three levels of background noise (none, low, high). To conclude whether difficulty has an effect on accuracy you need to make sure that the three different conditions of difficulty did indeed present different levels of difficulty to participants; you need to conduct a **manipulation check**. How do you find out whether there was a distinct difference in difficulty between each condition? You can either use an indicator for difficulty – for example, reaction speed – or you can ask every participant in each condition how difficult they found the tasks. You may also check their understanding of the instructions and their interpretation of the study during debriefing (see Section 2.9.2).

### ! LOOK OUT!

Whatever variable you use to conduct your manipulation check, it is important that you use a different indicator than the dependent variable. For example, if you use 'accuracy' as a dependent variable, it would not make sense to use 'accuracy' as a manipulation check for 'difficulty' because this would result in a circular argument: 'Accuracy decreases in this condition because the task is more difficult. How do I know that the task is more difficult? Because accuracy has decreased ...' If you find that levels of accuracy are not significantly different across all two conditions (and in the right direction, i.e., longer reaction time in the more difficult conditions, shorter reaction time in the less difficult conditions), your manipulation was not successful. At that point you can still draw conclusions about the effect of background noise on accuracy, but you cannot say anything about difficulty or the interaction between difficulty and background noise.

## 3.6 MUTUALLY EXCLUSIVE, COMPREHENSIVELY EXHAUSTIVE

When designing response options, it is good practice to make responses **MECE** (pronounced *'mI: sI:'*) – **Mutually Exclusive, Comprehensively Exhaustive**. Simply put, response options should be *complete* but not *overlap*; mathematicians call this a *non-overlapping cover*. Mutually exclusive means an answer has to be clearly either one response or another; comprehensively exhaustive means that the sum of all answering options should cover any possible participant responses. Of course these requirements do not apply if you are aiming for a 'Pick all that apply' type of question.

### 3.6.1 Mutually exclusive

Have a look at the following list of response options. What do you notice?

|   |   |
|---|---|
| ☐ | 19–30 years |
| ☐ | 30–39 years |
| ☐ | 40–49 years |
| ☐ | 50–59 years |
| ☐ | Over 60 |

The list of options is not mutually exclusive: Participants aged 30 years have two options they can pick, '19–30' and '30–39'. Neither is the list comprehensively exhaustive, as it does not cover all possible options: Participants aged 60 or participants younger than 19 have no option applicable to them. This is problematic because poorly defined answer options like this force your participants to guess or enter wrong data, and this impacts on your data quality. A couple of wrong entries on participant age data can become critical if age is an important variable in your research question.

With a few simple steps you can make this list MECE: In the revised list below we have made sure that options do not overlap by changing '19–30' to '19–29'. We have added a category for participants under 19 years, and have renamed the last option to '60 years or over'. For every possible participant, whether they are two years old or 102 there is now one and only one option available to them:

| ☐ | under 19 years |
|---|---|
| ☐ | 19–29 years |
| ☐ | 30–39 years |
| ☐ | 40–49 years |
| ☐ | 50–59 years |
| ☐ | 60 years or over |

The following list of questions is another example of items not being mutually exclusive because it conflates two questions into one, namely housing accommodation and living arrangements.[4]

Please choose the option that describes your current housing situation:

| ☐ | Living in rented accommodation |
|---|---|
| ☐ | Living in own accommodation |
| ☐ | Living with a partner |
| ☐ | Living with parents |
| ☐ | Student accommodation |

Living with a partner could take place both in rented or own accommodation, and it is not uncommon to share a house with both partner and parents. At the same time, the list reflects assumptions on how accommodation arrangements progress over time. First living with your parents, then at student accommodation, then either with a partner or in rented accommodation and ultimately in own property. Real life tends to be more chaotic and non-linear. Someone may move back to living with their parents to find their feet after a breakup, while renting out their previous flat. In times of transition, people sometimes live at hotels or hostels; other people may not reside at a permanent address at all. A more precise answer thus requires the question to be split up, for example, by asking separately about housing arrangements (renting, living at own property, student accommodation, non-permanent, etc.); living arrangements (alone, with partner, with parents, with parents and partner, shared housing, etc.) and property ownership (yes/no). Sometimes options are not mutually exclusive because they are phrased ambiguously or because different circumstances applied to participants at different times in their life. It helps if you phrase your question in a way that allows participants to pick several answers if more than one option applies to them, for example, by asking for the response that applies to their most recent, most frequent or most representative experience.

---

[4] Thanks to Dr Kine Dørum who first made the author aware of this example.

### 3.6.2 Comprehensively exhaustive

In the previous housing example, the answers were not comprehensively exhaustive as there are circumstances a respondent could live in that did not appear among the options (i.e., living in assisted housing, living in a hostel, living in a trailer park). If you want to make sure that you do not miss any options you might not even be aware of, make careful use of answering options such as

| ☐ | Neither |
| --- | --- |
| ☐ | All of the above |
| ☐ | Other, please specify |

Ultimately, the appropriate choice of items will be based on the exact research question, and on the literature underpinning your research which carries assumptions on how concepts and choices are related. At the same time, it is crucial that you are aware of the assumptions you make and that you make your data collection as flexible as possible. You need to make sure that the absence of a particular answer is a consequence of that answer not reflecting any respondents' opinion rather than the absence of the respective response option. Or, shorter – it is easy to conclude 'Everyone loves coffee!' if you forgot to include 'I prefer tea' as an option.

## 3.7 AVOIDING BIAS

Hambleton and Rodgers (1995) define bias as 'the presence of some characteristic of an item that results in differential performance for individuals of the same ability but from different ethnic, sex, cultural, or religious groups' (p. 1). Questions of any type need to be phrased very carefully to avoid any bias. While your participant may not always consciously notice the bias (and perhaps neither did you) in the phrasing of open questions, he might react unconsciously to it – worse, he might notice and be influenced by his reaction to the bias. Coincidentally, gender bias is one such example:

> While your participant may not always consciously notice the bias (and perhaps neither did you) in the phrasing of open questions, **he** might react unconsciously to it – worse, **he** might notice and be influenced by **his** reaction to the bias.

Aim to avoid bias throughout your research, from phrasing your research question to designing your method to analysing and interpreting your data. Research has consistently shown that the mere activation of stereotypes does impact on participant performance. For example, children perform better when reminded of positive stereotypes and worse when reminded of negative stereotypes (Ambady et al., 2001); students of colour perform worse than white students when told that a test is diagnostic of their abilities, but similar to white students when told a test is non-diagnostic (Steele and Aronson, 1995). Avoiding bias is therefore the morally right thing to do, because it gives your participant the opportunity to perform to the best of their knowledge and ability. Avoiding bias requires not only excluding items that could upset or offend a group, but also avoiding items that would be particularly easy or difficult for any subgroup of participants. For example, a scholastic aptitude test which includes items requiring knowledge of national customs would disadvantage pupils with a different cultural background. To avoid bias, make sure that you screen out questions which may require specific subject knowledge which is dependent on upbringing, ethnicity, gender or religion. Examples for biased language include (this is by no means an exhaustive list!):

- Making an assumption about the respondent's opinion.
- Making an assumption about the respondent.

- Using loaded language.
- Asking questions where social norms would favour one answer over another.
- Asking more than one question in one item.

**Making an assumption about the respondent's opinion:** 'What are your objections to the hiring freeze?' This assumes the respondent opposes the hiring freeze, which may not be the case. A better way would be to split up the question into two parts: 'Are you for or against the hiring freeze? Why or why not?'

**Making an assumption about the respondent:** To avoid bias, aim to make your questions and their answers as inclusive as possible. Be careful to not let your own assumptions guide your choice of questions and answers. For example:

- The partner of a participant who identifies as male is not always female; neither is the partner of a participant who identifies as female always a male partner.
- Not all couples who have children are married; not all married couples plan to have children; not all childless couples are childfree by choice.
- Not all participants know their parents; not all participants have been raised by one father and one mother.
- Not all participants who are in a relationship are monogamous (here, we refer to the existence of consensual non-monogamy, not cheating); not all relationships consist of only two partners; not all single participants are looking for a partner.
- Not all participants celebrate anniversaries, or observe religious or public holidays.

**Using loaded language:** 'Do you agree that hunting is cruel and inhumane?' This question is not asked in a neutral manner and hints at the researcher's personal opinion. A question can be positively loaded:

> The city council is consulting on the closure of the central library. Should this essential facility which provided so much joy and knowledge to many generations be closed down?

Or negatively:

> Do you support the cruel and inhumane sport of hunting?

If you want to elicit participants' unbiased opinion, you could use an open question, 'What do you think about hunting?', or a list consisting of equal numbers of positive and negative descriptors. Lastly, if for whatever reason you want to know your participants' response to those two terms in particular, a better way to phrase the question would be to ask, 'To what extent do you agree or disagree with the statement: "Hunting is cruel and inhumane"?'

**Asking questions where social norms would favour one answer over another:** 'To what extent do you agree that it is important to treat others fairly?' It will be difficult to find participants who would disagree, even if they can answer the question with complete anonymity and confidentiality. This is termed **social desirability bias**. It is socially desirable to be seen as someone who treats others fairly, and respondents will be very reluctant to answer in the negative to this type of question.

**Asking more than one question in one item:** 'To what extent do you agree that treating others fairly is important because it will make them like you more?' This contains a question about the participant's perception of treating others fairly as being important, and it is combined with a potential reason for that perception, which may not be the only reason. For example, a participant may think treating others fairly is the morally right thing to do; or they have experienced unfairness and do not want to inflict this on others; or they have a strong belief in a just world and so on. Unless you are specifically concerned about participants' opinions about what makes others like them more, this question would better be split up into two or more: 'To what extent to you agree treating others fairly is important?' and 'Do you think treating others fairly will make them like you more?'

For a prime example of a poorly designed questionnaire with a multitude of loaded questions we refer you to the recent Mainstream Media Accountability Survey conducted by the US Republican government:[5]

- *'On which issues does the mainstream media do the worst job of representing Republicans? (Select as many that apply.)'* 'Worst' is a relative term. Relatively speaking, the winner of an Olympic bronze medal is the worst of the three athletes on the podium; absolutely speaking their performance is literally a world class performance.
- *'Do you believe that contrary to what the media says, raising taxes does not create jobs?'* Good luck figuring out what a 'yes' or 'no' answer to this question even means.

Please, *please*, do not design that kind of survey.

### REVIEW & REFLECT

- What is the harm of conducting biased research?
- How do the guidelines on ethical research relate to the issue of biased research?

## 3.8 RECRUITING PARTICIPANTS: SAMPLING

Working with human participants requires particular attention to the process of recruiting participants and making participation in research as accessible as possible. However, before you approach your first participant, let us have a look at the process of **sampling**, that is, the process of deciding who to approach, and how. Your study's external validity is determined by the extent to which your results apply to the general population, so you want to make sure that your participant selection – your sample – reflects the population you are interested in as closely as possible. First, let us clarify the terms. Broadly speaking, the **population** is everyone of interest for your research question, whereas the **sample** is the group of participants chosen for your research project. If you are interested in employee motivation, your population is the sum total of all employees; if you are interested in the effects of depression, your population is everyone currently suffering from depression. Of course, you will not be able to ask or survey every single employee in the world, and for many questions regional and cultural differences will preclude a global population. This is where a narrowly defined research question is important because it helps you narrow down the population and in turn reduces the size of the required sample. For example, you could reduce the size of population relevant to you by revising your research question to the motivation of employees *in a particular organisation.* In doing so, your population now only comprises all employees in this organisation, potentially allowing you to

---

[5] Archived through the Internet Archive Wayback Machine here: https://web.archive.org/web/20170217023015/https://gop.com/mainstream-media-accountability-survey/.

80  *Introducing Quantitative Methods*

examine the entire population (depending, of course, on the size of the organisation), as well as allowing a smaller sample size. Sampling is so important because as a researcher you want the conclusions drawn from your studies to hold true and be applicable beyond the research lab; you want to be able to generalise your findings. But if you cannot look at the entire population relevant to your research question, you have to work with a sample (i.e., a fraction or a part of the population). In your research, this sample *represents* the population you are interested in. The more representative of, and similar to, the population, the higher the chance that any conclusions drawn from your research may to a greater extent also apply to the larger population.

### 3.8.1  Sample size

Apart from knowing which population to draw the sample from, you also need to know how large your sample should be. To calculate required sample size you need to know, broadly speaking, how precise you want your result to be and how certain you are of the result (this is a simplified explanation, but it will suffice for now). The precision of your result is expressed by what is called **margin of error** or **confidence interval**, and your certainty is expressed through the **confidence level**. Take the following statement:

> In a recent survey, mean satisfaction with the ordering process was 50.6 (margin of error 3%, confidence level 95%).

Here, the precision of the result is expressed by the margin of error, the confidence in the result itself by the confidence level. The margin of error is the degree to which the result may vary: here, plus/minus 3 percent points away from 50.6%. In turn, the confidence interval (not level!) spans from the lower margin to the higher margin: from (50.6 − 3) = 47.6 to (50.6 + 3) = 53.6. The confidence interval here ranges from 47.6 to 53.6. Together with the confidence level it means that if the survey was repeated, we would expect mean satisfaction to fall between 47.6 and 53.6 around 95% of the time. You can find a simple Excel tool on the companion website that allows you to calculate a rough guide for a required sample size as well as links to other sample size calculators available online.

> **ONLINE CONTENT**
>
> The sample size calculator as well as links to other online tools are available on the companion website.

All of these tools, however, still require you to input some data in order to calculate the required sample size. To explain those terms and the process, we will work through calculating the required sample size for an example study testing customer acceptance of a new online account tool. To follow the calculation, open the Excel tool provided on the companion website. This calculation will make reference to some terms that will later be introduced in more detail and we will point out where you can read up on those terms. For now just note that these are the pieces of information you need which will enable you to estimate needed scenario size.

- **Population size:** The population size is the number of people you could potentially draw from. In other words, if you are looking to recruit participants from an organisations' customer database, your population size is the total number of customers included in the database. In this example, we will assume that there are 23,000 customers using the current online account tool, and population size is therefore 23,000.
Enter this value under N.

- **Margin of error/confidence interval:** Here you need to decide how much precision you are aiming for, or rather, how much imprecision you are willing to tolerate. Higher precision requires smaller margin of errors. If you are at all unsure, try a standard margin of error of 5% first and see which sample size this would require. In this example we will similarly pick a margin of error of 5%. Enter this as a decimal figure, that is, '.05' under Margin of Error (see Section 4.4 on handling decimal places and Sections 4.2 and 4.3 on conversions between percentages and decimal figures).
- **Confidence level:** A simplified explanation of the confidence level is the degree of confidence in your results that you would get the same results if you repeated the same study; you will see later in Section 6.10 how the confidence level relates to the so-called alpha value, or $p$. For now, it is enough to know that the more confident you want to be in your results, the larger the required sample size. Having picked your confidence level, select the matching z-score (more on that in Section 6.8) from the table below (See Table 3.1). Since we picked a confidence level of 95%, we need to enter a value of 1.960 into the field in Excel.

*Table 3.1 Confidence level and z-score*

| Confidence Level in % | Z-score |
| --- | --- |
| 80 | 1.282 |
| 85 | 1.440 |
| 90 | 1.645 |
| 95 | 1.960 |
| 99 | 2.576 |
| 99.5 | 2.807 |
| 99.9 | 3.291 |

In this example, the sample size calculator tells us that we would need 378 participants in our sample. There are also more sophisticated tools available which calculate required sample size based on the size of the associations, differences or effects you expect to find, but discussing these would go beyond the scope of this chapter. That all said, while you should always aim for a fairly large sample size (and ideally one that allows you to express your results with both accuracy and confidence), it is understood that research projects conducted by students with limited time and resources cannot always reach required sample sizes. Nevertheless, knowing which sample size would be appropriate gives you more context on how to interpret and discuss your results, and possibly discuss sample size issues as part of the limitations of your research.

## REVIEW & REFLECT

- What happens if you were to conduct research with very small sample sizes?
- Are there any circumstances where precision might not be the focus of the study?

### 3.8.2 Sample composition

Having determined the size of the sample, the next step is to determine its composition. Please note that for ease of reference we will be talking about human participants in this and subsequent sections relating to sampling; however, the techniques can, with adjustments, also be applied to organisations, items, groups, etc.

### 3.8.2.1 Probability sampling
Sampling techniques are most commonly categorised as either probability or non-probability sampling techniques. **Probability sampling** means that every element of the target population has the same theoretical chance of being included in the sample, and the exact probability of being included can be specified. This does not mean that the probability has to be specified, just that it could potentially be calculated. Types of probability sampling include:

- Simple random sampling
- Systematic sampling
- Stratified sampling
- Cluster sampling

**Simple random sampling** refers to any technique where every individual in the population has an equal probability of being selected for the sample. If your population consists of all the employees of one organisation, simple random sampling requires every employee to have the same probability of being selected. This can be achieved by randomly drawing slips of paper with employee numbers, creating lists of employee names and using a random number generator to select names, or any other method of random selection as long as every member of the population is included and the means of selection ensure randomness.

For large populations and large samples, the outcome of such a process might be very time consuming to put into practice even though the process of determining the composition of the sample can be fast and simple. Consider the following scenario. You are conducting research for a large cancer research charity (>200 branches across the country) which has recently implemented a new training programme for their branch staff, including everyone from receptionist to case worker to fundraiser. You are tasked to find out how well the training objectives have been met by interviewing members of staff who have received the training. You plan to conduct brief face-to-face-interviews with members of staff and aim for a sample size of 150. If you are using a truly random sampling method to select 150 members of staff for your research, you might end up with staff from up to 150 different branches, requiring enormous time and effort to visit each and every one of them. With limited resources (time, money, sanity) visiting 150 different branches may simply be not feasible. In such a situation, **cluster sampling** allows you to define clusters within the population and then apply additional random sampling techniques within those clusters. For example, you randomly select 5 branches with any of the techniques described above, and you then randomly select 30 members of staff each in those 5 branches.

**Systematic sampling** retains the random element but provides more structure to the selection process. In the previous example, your population contains all members of staff of the cancer charity. For the sake of the example, assume that there are 1200 employees in total and that you have determined your sample needs to contain at least 150 participants. To select participants for your sample, you source a file with the names of all members of staff.
First determine the fraction that describes the relationship between the population and the sample by dividing population size (1200) by sample size (150):

$$1200 / 150 = 8.$$

As a next step, determine the starting point in the first set of eight participants by rolling a dice or using any other means of picking a random number between 1 and 8. In this case, you roll an eight-sided dice and generate 3 as your random starting number. Starting with item (i.e., participant name) number 3 in the list, you add 8 to 3, add the name at position 11 to your list of participants, add 8 again to arrive at and select 19, and so on until you have selected 150 participants. While relatively easy to use, there is some risk of introducing a bias depending on how the original list from which you select your participants is constructed. For example, consider applying the same technique to sampling households along a street by picking addresses (i.e., house numbers from a list). If you are using the same increment throughout, for example, every second house, the starting number will determine whether the house numbers are all odd or even. This could potentially introduce bias in cases where odd and even house numbers are separated on either side of the street and as such might be related to different types of neighbourhood (after an example of Harris and Jarvis, 2013, p. 101). However, if the lists are created without bias, every participant has the same chance of being included in the sample.

In organisations and groups where individuals have different roles and responsibilities (frontline staff vs. admin, doctors/nurses, or in organisations managers/salespeople/HR, etc.) you might find that some roles or some groups are over- or underrepresented. If you worry that with a random distribution your final sample may not represent all groups equally, **stratified sampling** would be more appropriate (*stratum* = level, layer; plural *strata*). To achieve this, you need to identify the relevant strata and then decide whether you want the strata to be (a) all be of equal size or (b) be proportionate to their size in the population.

Let us assume the cancer charity employs staff in five broad areas:

| Outreach | 240 |
| Fundraising | 360 |
| Administrative | 120 |
| Case workers | 180 |
| Clinical staff | 300 |

To accurately represent this stratification, you need to make sure that the resulting sample contains employees from the five areas of responsibility in the same distribution. First, you establish the relative strata sizes of the existing population. The shares have been calculated below (see Section 4.2 for calculation of percentages):

| Size | Department | Share |
|---|---|---|
| 240 | Outreach | 20% |
| 360 | Fundraising | 30% |
| 120 | Administrative | 10% |
| 180 | Case workers | 15% |
| 300 | Clinical staff | 25% |

The required absolute number of participants per strata has been calculated based on a sample size of 200. The next table shows the resulting strata sizes.

| Population Strata | Population Share = Sample Share | Sample Strata |
|---|---|---|
| 240 | 20% | 40 |
| 360 | 30% | 60 |
| 120 | 10% | 20 |
| 180 | 15% | 30 |
| 300 | 25% | 50 |
| 1200 employees | 100% | 200 participants |

Alternatively, all five areas could be represented by 20 participants each, to make all the strata of equal size.

### 3.8.2.2 *Non-probability sampling*

In contrast to the probability sampling techniques described above, **non-probability sampling** techniques usually require less effort and time, an advantage that is paid for by poorer quality and a more likely bias in the sample.

**Convenience sampling, opportunity sampling**, and **accidental sampling** all refer to the same technique of approaching members of the population in a manner that does not give everyone equal opportunity to be part of the sample. Distributing questionnaires while standing at a busy shopping street means that only the part of the population that goes shopping at that particular time in that particular location has a chance of being approached; members of the population who shop at different times are excluded from the sample. If there are systematic reasons for why some people shop at a particular time – for example, unemployed or self-employed people might be likely to shop during the day; employed people will be more likely to shop either before or after work – this will introduce a bias into your sample, just as selecting people who shop near a very expensive shopping quarter will lead to a more affluent sample than approaching people in front of a large discount store. This is further likely to be influenced by your tendency to approach people who look more amenable to being approached. You will be less likely to approach grumpy and sleepy shoppers than people who look friendly and approachable; you will be more likely to approach people similar to yourself in terms of age, class, gender or ethnicity. This bias is mostly problematic if the sample is biased in a way that is directly related to the research. For example, if you have reason to believe that employment or income or class have an impact on the answers you get when trying to elicit attitudes on income taxation, opportunity sampling in the manner described above would likely lead to a bias in your participants' responses. However, in a scenario where you are interested in peoples' attitudes on shopping and spending, the busy high street may be a good recruiting area and the shoppers part of your population. You could introduce a random element – such as approaching every tenth person walking past you – and thus further improve the quality of your sample.

If you are a student planning your research project, chances are high that you will have to resort to convenience or opportunity sampling simply because true probability sampling may not be possible in the time you have available. These restrictions will likely be understood by your instructors and your institution. Even so, it is worthwhile acknowledging the limits that come with this sampling technique in your write-up.

Very small or specific populations also often require special sampling techniques. Suppose you want to recruit experts in a very limited field for your research, or need participants with a very specific profile, but only know a handful and have few or no means of identifying further potential participants. One way of identifying more suitable participants is to ask every existing participant to help recruit other participants, either by approaching them or by providing contact details. This technique is referred to as **snowball sampling**, in reference to a snowball rolling downhill and growing larger very quickly on its way down. Particularly when participants are asked to generally promote the study rather than recruit another single participant, this can dramatically increase the number of potential participants. By participants recruiting participants, the sample is susceptible to bias, however, as people tend to know and approach people they like and who share similar interests. Again, depending on your population and research interest that may be problematic but not necessarily so – for a research question with a student population, snowball sampling might be quite effective as students are more likely to be successful in recruiting other students to the sample.

Quota sampling and panel sampling are two more common sampling techniques. **Quota sampling** is more often associated with market research when sample sizes of two or more very specific groups are required (full-time employed women under 30/under 40/under 50, etc.), and a non-random technique such as accidental sampling is used until the quota is fulfilled. Lastly, **panel sampling** refers to a panel of participants who are randomly selected but are asked the same set of questions several times; as such, this technique is more appropriate for longitudinal studies over a longer period of time.

## 3.9 RECRUITING PARTICIPANTS: MAKING RESEARCH ACCESSIBLE

The key point to keep in mind is that you are asking your potential participants to volunteer their time and effort for you. You are asking them a favour which they are under no obligation to provide, so it is your responsibility to be transparent about the process and to make participation accessible to as many as possible (this is also part of the research ethics, see Section 2.9). This starts with the way in which you contact participants. Are you reaching out to marginalised groups or are you relying on students/acquaintances/people who can afford to take time out to participate in your study/people who can afford the travel costs to wherever they need to be? Make sure to communicate accessibility or the lack thereof to your participants in advance. Having to ask whether accommodations can be made puts a burden on the potential participant and this burden can act as a barrier to participation. For example, if the premises have too narrow doorframes which do not allow wheelchair entry or the office is on the second floor with no lift access, let your participants know in advance to save them the trip and the potential disappointment.

Questions to consider:

- Are the premises well lit and with little or no background noise?
- If participants have to physically attend a testing session, check that the premises are accessible (e.g., Is there a lift available for a wheelchair user? Can the premises be reached without having to navigate stairs, high doorsteps or narrow doorframes?).
- Can the location be reached by public transport?
- Is parking reserved for disabled users? Are there accessible toilets nearby?
- Do not assume that a building is accessible just because it is a public building or it is new.

Sometimes the nature of your research question will require that participants fulfil certain criteria (e.g., they need to be of a certain age, need to have normal or corrected-to-normal vision, have a specific language as a first language, are not dyslexic, etc.). Make sure to communicate these criteria very clearly and transparently. Again, you do not want participants to go to the time and effort to turn up for your study only to be turned away because they do not meet the criteria.

## 3.10 ALLOCATING PARTICIPANTS TO CONDITIONS

This step takes place after you recruited your participants. Whether you do it in advance or on the day depends on the setup of your study. If you use an electronic test, participants may be randomly allocated the moment they start up the programme, but you can also perform the allocation days in advance once you know the exact size of your sample. Earlier on we mentioned the need to decide whether you are using a between-participants or within-participants design. Section 2.6.3 stressed that random allocation to condition is a key requirement to maintain and improve a study's validity. The methods described in the next sections can be used to allocate participants to condition or to randomise items across conditions.

### 3.10.1 Randomisation

A **randomised presentation** means the exact sequence of items is determined randomly for every individual participant and every item has an equal probability of preceding or following another item. Even though some participants will still be subjected to a sequence of items that may influence them towards a particular question, every other combination is just as probable and any potential effect is likely to be balanced out by the number of participants who were not subjected to that particular sequence.

86    *Introducing Quantitative Methods*

There are very useful, free random number generators available online, for example:

- https://www.randomizer.org/
- https://www.random.org/sequences/

### ONLINE CONTENT

You can find links to a range of random number generators on the companion website.

For example, randomising a list of ten items you might get the following sequence:

$$3, 8, 1, 4, 5, 10, 9, 7, 2, 6^6$$

Whatever tool you choose, if you are looking to determine sequences make sure that the list of numbers only includes *unique* numbers so that each number only appears once.

### LOOK OUT!

Do not attempt to randomise sequences manually. Humans are notoriously bad at understanding and processing genuine randomness. If you tried to manually randomise sequences, there would be a substantial risk of introducing bias into your data. Human randomisers are prone to trying to make sequences 'look random'. For example, in trying to create a sequence of 1 and 0, humans will be more likely to come up with sequences such as '01011001010101011010' whereas true random sequences might look like 111110110011111110 with much more clustering of values than you would expect.

If you have to deal with a large number of items, such as questions in a questionnaire, you can employ **block randomisation**. For example, one hundred items can be divided into 5 blocks of 20 questions each. You can then use one of the random number generators to generate a random sequence for five items and then sort your blocks into this sequence, as shown in Figure 3.3:

| Block 1 | Block 2 | Block 3 | Block 4 | Block 5 |   | Block 5 | Block 3 | Block 4 | Block 2 | Block 1 |
|---|---|---|---|---|---|---|---|---|---|---|
| 1 | 21 | 41 | 61 | 81 |   | 81 | 41 | 61 | 21 | 1 |
| 2 | 22 | 42 | 62 | 82 |   | 82 | 42 | 62 | 22 | 2 |
| 3 | 23 | 43 | 63 | 83 |   | 83 | 43 | 63 | 23 | 3 |
| 4 | 24 | 44 | 64 | 84 |   | 84 | 44 | 64 | 24 | 4 |
| 5 | 25 | 45 | 65 | 85 |   | 85 | 45 | 65 | 25 | 5 |
| 6 | 26 | 46 | 66 | 86 |   | 86 | 46 | 66 | 26 | 6 |
| 7 | 27 | 47 | 67 | 87 |   | 87 | 47 | 67 | 27 | 7 |
| 8 | 28 | 48 | 68 | 88 |   | 88 | 48 | 68 | 28 | 8 |
| 9 | 29 | 49 | 69 | 89 |   | 89 | 49 | 69 | 29 | 9 |
| 10 | 30 | 50 | 70 | 90 |   | 90 | 50 | 70 | 30 | 10 |
| 11 | 31 | 51 | 71 | 91 |   | 91 | 51 | 71 | 31 | 11 |
| 12 | 32 | 52 | 72 | 92 |   | 92 | 52 | 72 | 32 | 12 |
| 13 | 33 | 53 | 73 | 93 |   | 93 | 53 | 73 | 33 | 13 |
| 14 | 34 | 54 | 74 | 94 |   | 94 | 54 | 74 | 34 | 14 |
| 15 | 35 | 55 | 75 | 95 |   | 95 | 55 | 75 | 35 | 15 |
| 16 | 36 | 56 | 76 | 96 |   | 96 | 56 | 76 | 36 | 16 |
| 17 | 37 | 57 | 77 | 97 |   | 97 | 57 | 77 | 37 | 17 |
| 18 | 38 | 58 | 78 | 98 |   | 98 | 58 | 78 | 38 | 18 |
| 19 | 39 | 59 | 79 | 99 |   | 99 | 59 | 79 | 39 | 19 |
| 20 | 40 | 60 | 80 | 100 |   | 100 | 60 | 80 | 40 | 20 |

**Figure 3.3** *Block randomisation*

---

[6] Generated with https://www.randomizer.org/.

A different way to generate randomness, particularly for smaller numbers, is simply rolling a dice. If you have six different conditions for your between-participants study, you can role a dice for participants signing up to decide which condition they are allocated to. Do not worry if you need different numbers than six: dice exist in a number of different shapes and there are four-, six-, eight-, ten-, twelve- and even twenty-sided dice; there are also dice rolling apps for tablets and mobile phones. A method often used to prevent order or sequence effects of conditions or presentation of items is the **Latin Square**. In its simplest form a Latin Square consists of four cells, where the rows should be read as different groups of participants, with the individual cells denoting the type of experimental condition. The easiest way to think of the Latin Square method is to compare it to sudoku in that every item appears once only per row and column:

| A | B |
|---|---|
| B | A |

For two items or two conditions, this would be equivalent to a simple reversal of order where one group first encounters condition A, then condition B, and the second group first receives condition B, then condition A. A 3×3 Latin Square could look like this:

| C | A | B |
|---|---|---|
| A | B | C |
| B | C | A |

There is more than one possible solution. The examples below are different, equally valid versions of a 3 × 3 square:

| B | C | A |
|---|---|---|
| A | B | C |
| C | A | B |

| B | A | C |
|---|---|---|
| C | B | A |
| A | C | B |

Whereas a 4 × 4 Latin Square might look like this:

| A | B | C | D |
|---|---|---|---|
| B | C | D | A |
| C | D | A | B |
| D | A | B | C |

If you have a large number of conditions but not enough participants to allocate them to different conditions, you can use the **counterbalancing** method instead. In this case you present group 1 with the conditions A, B, C and D and group 2 with the same conditions but in reverse order (i.e., D, C, B and then A):

Group 1

| A | B | C | D |
|---|---|---|---|

Group 2

| D | C | B | A |
|---|---|---|---|

## 3.10.2 Order and sequence effects

Occasionally a task or question can be influenced by the nature of a task or question preceding. This refers both to the sequence of items in a test or questionnaire and the sequence of treatments and conditions in an experiment. If a participant's answer or performance in a task is affected by one item (A) preceding another item (B) at any point in the process, for example by providing a potential answer to a question or by directing the participant's thought into a particular direction, this is referred to as an **order effect**. A **sequence effect** refers to a specific type of order effect where the two interacting items follow each other immediately (Figure 3.4).

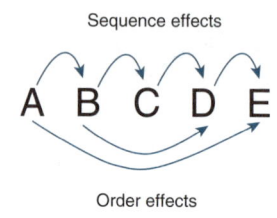

**Figure 3.4** *Order and sequence effects*

An example for an order effect would be an experimental setup where two tasks are inadvertently presented such that a question A asks participants about treating others fairly, thus activating their self-image as someone who treats others fairly, and a question D later on asks participants whether cheating is sometimes okay. In this scenario answers for question D will likely be different than if D had been presented before A because participants will want to maintain a consistent self-image. You can avoid order effects of any type by employing either a randomisation technique or a systematic variation of items or treatments, for example by using the Latin Square technique. Often the exact nature of the method you choose depends on how many participants you have and to what extent you can make use of a true randomisation procedure.

## 3.11 PILOT STUDIES

In the previous sections we have emphasised how carefully you need to choose and phrase the questions you include and how much care needs to go into designing the scales with which you measure your participants' answers. But we are blind to our own assumptions and biases, and relying on our own judgement and objectivity would be ill-advised. This is why **pilot studies** are useful. A pilot study is a small-scale version of parts or all of your main study. You usually conduct it to test the instrument(s) you plan to use. A pilot study can tell you whether participants understood the instructions. You will be able to tell from the range and scope of answers whether the questions are clear and whether you need to rephrase any or all of them. Receiving a number of questionnaires where participants only completed the first three pages tells you that the material is too long or participants were not sufficiently made aware of the length of the material. A pilot study might make you aware that a question could be interpreted in a manner different from the one you intended; a participant may point out to you that the phrasing is considered offensive to some people. All of this is information you want to know before you present your questions to a larger number of people. To identify potential problems and potential improvements, consult both data and participants. Often it is useful to ask participants what they thought the aim of the study was. This is important because it can help identify possible sources of desirability bias (see Section 3.7). If you conduct computer-based tests, make sure to stress-test the system before you let participants use it. What happens if you enter responses too soon or too late? What if you type in too much or not enough? If you have the same test run on several computers, can the network cope with several instances of the same test?

The following is a (by no means exhaustive) list of research elements you might want to examine more thoroughly in a pilot study:

- Clarity of instructions
- Participants' understanding of questions and material
- Distribution of answers
- Shape and type of data
- Validity and reliability of procedure
- Timing

### ONLINE CONTENT

A more detailed checklist is available on the companion website.

## 3.12 RELIABILITY TESTING

Whether you design your own instrument or use an existing one, you will want to make sure that it is internally consistent and, hence, reliable (see Section 2.11 for a more detailed discussion of reliability). All suitable testing methods are based on the assumption that while answers may vary from participant to participant, overall responses are required to display a certain consistency (i.e., be similar to an extent for any one dimension you measure). For example, you might conceptualise motivation as a construct with both internal and external motivation, and you then develop a test for both dimensions. Responses relating to external and internal motivation respectively should then show a basic level of consistency.

Eyeballing the data gives you a first indication of how consistently your items measure the same construct, but this is not very reliable, and it is only feasible for smaller data sets. For larger sets you need a more objective method of testing. Below we have listed a number of questions all purporting to measure optimism; all responses are given on a scale from 1 = Not at all to 5 = Very much:

To what extent do you agree with the following statements:

1. Generally, things tend to work out over time.
2. I believe that people tend to be good.
3. If I work hard enough, I can achieve my goals.
4. I believe that I alone am in control of my fate.
5. Most problems have a solution.
6. I am excited about the future.
7. I welcome challenges because they help me grow and learn.

Imagine you did a small pilot study with ten participants. The data you collected then might look like this (the headings refer to question 1 to question 7) (Table 3.2):

**Table 3.2** *Optimism pilot data*

| P | Q1 | Q2 | Q3 | Q4 | Q5 | Q6 | Q7 |
|---|----|----|----|----|----|----|----|
| 1 | 2 | 3 | 2 | 5 | 3 | 2 | 3 |
| 2 | 4 | 5 | 3 | 1 | 4 | 3 | 4 |
| 3 | 2 | 2 | 3 | 4 | 1 | 2 | 1 |
| 4 | 4 | 3 | 3 | 1 | 4 | 5 | 3 |
| 5 | 3 | 4 | 3 | 5 | 2 | 3 | 1 |
| 6 | 1 | 3 | 2 | 4 | 2 | 1 | 2 |
| 7 | 4 | 3 | 5 | 2 | 4 | 3 | 3 |
| 8 | 3 | 4 | 3 | 2 | 4 | 3 | 4 |
| 9 | 2 | 1 | 2 | 4 | 2 | 1 | 2 |
| 10 | 3 | 3 | 2 | 4 | 2 | 3 | 2 |

## ONLINE CONTENT

You can find the SPSS and Excel sample data files for this analysis on the companion website.

This is a very small sample and a very small set of testing items for the purpose of illustrating the underlying principle – in 'real life' research, the number of items would be considered too small to draw any meaningful conclusions, because small sets overemphasise differences. The degree to which different items measure the same thing can be expressed by **Cronbach's alpha**, which serves as a coefficient of consistency and therefore allows **scale reliability testing**. Cronbach's alpha is expressed as a value between .000 and 1.000 where higher is better and 1.000 means all items have identical values. The size of acceptable alpha values varies within disciplines – in psychology, a minimum value of .7 is required for a scale to be considered reliable, whereas in sociology and education studies frequently .8 or even .9 are required. Unfortunately, the only reasonably simple and accessible solution for conducting a Cronbach's alpha reliability analysis in Excel requires a software add-on for Excel, which as of now only works for Excel 2011. Since this book aims at providing guidance for software easily available in most institutions' infrastructure and IT setup, the process will be described only for SPSS. We are introducing this procedure here since it is closely related to the development and testing of materials. You will find guidance on how to use SPSS in Section 5.3 and information on how to interpret the outcome of correlational analyses in Sections 11.2 and 11.3.

- In SPSS, go to Analyze → Scale → Reliability Analysis. Move the variables you are interested in to the right column 'Items:'.
- Click on the Statistics ... button and find the left top corner labelled Descriptives for. Tick the boxes for Item, Scale and Scale if item deleted.
- For additional information, tick Correlations in the Inter-Item top right corner.
- Click Continue which brings you back to the Reliability Analysis window, and click OK.
- The output consists of several elements. The second element, headed Reliability Statistics, tells you the overall Cronbach's alpha for the set of seven questions; in this example, .769.
- If you look at the item headed Item-Total Statistics, however, you will find something much more interesting. Look at the rightmost column in Table 3.3:

*Table 3.3* Item-total statistics from SPSS

**Item-Total Statistics**

|  | Scale Mean if Item Deleted | Scale Variance if Item Deleted | Corrected Item-Total | Squared Multiple Correlation | Cronbach's Alpha if Item Deleted |
|---|---|---|---|---|---|
| Q1 | 18.40 | 22.933 | .962 | .980 | .623 |
| Q2 | 18.70 | 25.567 | .883 | .897 | .658 |
| Q3 | 18.50 | 27.389 | .878 | .976 | .675 |
| Q4 | 19.00 | 54.889 | −.753 | .751 | .976 |
| Q5 | 18.50 | 24.278 | .930 | .977 | .640 |
| Q6 | 18.40 | 27.600 | .823 | .884 | .682 |
| Q7 | 18.10 | 24.100 | .892 | .977 | .645 |

- This column tells you for each item how well it fits in with the other items by measuring what difference it would make to remove it from the scale. For all items *except* item 4, removing it would lower overall Cronbach's alpha from .769 to a value below .7. However, removing item 4 would dramatically improve Cronbach's alpha from .769 to .976. This tells you that question 4 appears to be measuring something different from the remaining questions and that it would increase the quality of your questionnaire to remove question 4 from the set.

## RESEARCH METHODS AT WORK

Jonathan is the marketing manager of a traditional highland whisky distillery whose sales have slumped recently after previously enjoying a long period of prosperity. Jonathan decides to establish a brand personality for the distillery's whisky which would help him determine who the product appeals to and why; he also wants to know how the distillery's own product compares against the competitors. He settles on using five factors – Sincerity, Excitement, Competence, Sophistication and Ruggedness[7] – to compare the brand against four competitors through a series of pairwise comparisons. However, he quickly realises that this will ask too much of potential participants: Although 5 products only require 10 comparisons[8] in total, it would mean 10 comparisons *per* personality trait (i.e., 10 × 5 = 50 comparisons in total). Jonathan does not want to reduce the brand personality traits, and he does not want to use a different method; therefore, he has to make do with comparing only three products, the own brand against two competitors. This means 3 comparisons[9] for each brand personality trait – with 5 brand personality traits, that still gives him 5 × 3 = 15 comparisons in total.

---

[7] These are actual brand personality traits as first developed through Aaker's (1997) work.
[8] Number of pairwise comparisons calculated through formula described on p. 68:
$$\frac{5 \times (5-1)}{2} = \frac{5 \times 4}{2} = \frac{20}{2} = 10$$
[9] Number of pairwise comparisons calculated through formula described on p. 68:
$$\frac{3 \times (3-1)}{2} = \frac{3 \times 2}{2} = \frac{6}{2} = 3$$

> In the previous chapter, you have already encountered Evelyn who is trying to develop a quality testing procedure for the small timber-frame construction company. In addition to the quality criteria, Evelyn also thinks about the frequency of sampling. Because measuring the dimensions of all individual elements for an entire frame would take up a lot of time, and because it takes several days to produce a single frame, Evelyn settles on sampling 5% of the overall production while defining individual elements as sampling items rather than complete frames. Lastly, Evelyn needs to decide on how the sample is selected. This is helped by all individual elements being consecutively numbered by a unique production ID. By using a random number generator to pick a random number from a given set, Evelyn makes sure that the selection process is random and cannot be biased by workers knowing which elements may be inspected and focussing on those to the detriment of others.

## A SHORT SUMMARY

- Before you start your data collection, make sure you consult the literature. Use more than one measurement tool, and use more than one measurement for each construct.
- Primary data is data you collected yourself; it takes more effort but gives you more control. To use secondary data (data which has been collected by someone else) takes less effort but gives you less control.
- The sum total of entities or people to which findings should apply is considered the population. Research is conducted with a subset of the population, the sample. Sampling procedures where every member of the population can potentially be selected are called probability sampling. Sampling procedures which do not potentially allow any member of the population to be selected are referred to as non-probability sampling.
- Quantitative data is best collected through tests or questionnaires, both online or offline. The type of question determines the shape of data you collect and what analyses you can conduct on it. Example question types are open questions, sentence completion questions, (multiple) choice questions, ranking questions, pairwise comparisons or semantic differentials.
- Answering scales can be described by their polarity (unipolar or bipolar); symmetry, absence or presence of a neutral response. and the number of options they offer.
- Response options should not overlap and should cover all scenarios.
- Data can be classified as nominal, ordinal, interval or ratio data – here listed in ascending order of information contained and data analysis available. The type of data collected can be influenced by the manner in which the data is elicited.
- Research methods and material need to avoid bias and be accessible to as large a part of the population as possible. One type of bias can be introduced by sequence effects or ordering effects. To minimise this source of bias, you can use randomisation techniques such as block randomisation, counterbalancing or Latin Squares.
- Demographic questions are useful to examine how closely your sample mirrors your target population.
- A pilot study helps you to identify possible sources of bias, misunderstanding of instructions and to check whether manipulation of independent variables was successful.
- Reliability testing allows you to examine to which extent individual items of a questionnaire measure the same construct.

## CHECK YOUR UNDERSTANDING

1. You want to know whether the depiction of violence on TV can raise aggression levels in the short term. You could design your own experiment, for example, presenting either violent or non-violent TV clips to participants and then measuring aggression by examining behaviour in a co-operation task or a negotiation exercise. Alternatively you could use data collected by Tel-Stats,[10] an organisation run and funded by ten major private broadcasters. Tel-Stats has recently published a report looking into the prevalence of crime on TV in relation to the crime rates developing over the past ten years, using data from over one million hours of television material. What are the advantages and disadvantages of using Tel-Stats data or developing your own study?

2. Using the Excel tool on the companion website, calculate the required sample size for a study with the following parameters:
    a. Population size 800, alpha level 5%, margin of error 5%
    b. Population size 430,000, alpha level 1%, margin of error 2%
    c. Population size 60,000, alpha level .5%, margin of error 5%

3. A local school has recently trialled a new anti-bullying scheme. This consisted of mandatory training sessions for all pupils across all years and classes. The school now wants to find out whether and to what extent pupils' attitudes towards bullying have changed. You want to survey a sample of 100 out of the 1500 pupils. Identify the sampling techniques listed below:
    a. You position yourself at the entrance of the cafeteria at 12:30 and approach every tenth pupil.
    b. You have a numbered list with the names of all 1500 pupils. You use a random number generator to generate random numbers between 1 and 1500 and pick the student listed at that position on the list.
    c. You have a numbered list with the names of all 1500 pupils. You generate a random number between 1 and 15. Starting with the pupil listed at that position on the list, you then pick every 15th pupil.
    d. You send around an email to all pupils asking them to fill out an online questionnaire at a link given in the email.
    e. You are given a list with class cohorts. From that list you establish that there are 30 class cohorts in the school. You randomly pick 20 classes from the list and subsequently randomly pick 5 students per class.
    f. You think that bullying might be perceived differently by pupils of different ages. You consider 'age' a relevant variable to the study and thus want to re-create the distribution of 'age' across the school in your sample. You establish that 40% of the pupils are aged 14 or under, 40% between 15 and 16, and 20% are aged 17 and above. When approaching pupils, you recruit as many pupils as you need until your sample consists of 40 pupils aged 14 or under, 40 pupils aged between 15 and 16, and 20 pupils aged 17 or older.
    g. You are particularly interested in comparing male versus female pupils' views on the anti-bullying campaign. You are approaching students identifying as one of either gender until your sample consists of exactly 50% male- and 50% female-identifying students.

4. (Content Note: Weight loss.) You are interested in people's weight loss successes and failures. You want to know which diets people may have attempted in the past and how

---

[10] An entirely fictitious organization.

effective they were. How could you phrase related questions in each of the formats listed below, and what would the data look like?
   a. Open-ended
   b. Multiple choice
   c. Rank order
   d. Semantic differential
   e. Sentence completion

5. How many pairwise comparisons would you need for seven items?

6. Design both a unipolar and a bipolar scale to ask participants how happy they are with their life at the moment.

7. Look at your scales from Exercise 6. Are they symmetric or asymmetric?

8. Consider the following set of response options to the question: 'What is your employment situation right now?' Unemployed/Employed (part-time)/Employed (full-time)/In full-time education.
   a. Why would this not be considered MECE?
   b. What could you do to make the set of options mutually exclusive and comprehensively exhaustive?

9. For each of the following variables, note whether it is data on a ratio, interval, ordinal or nominal scale:
   a. Level of education
   b. Products ranked by perceived quality
   c. Outside temperature
   d. Satisfaction with service
   e. Distance between home and workplace
   f. Agreement with a statement
   g. Time per day spent at the computer
   h. Traits to describe self, ranked from most applicable to least applicable

10. How are the following questions biased and how could you change them to reduce bias?
    a. 'Do you agree that it is important to give to charity?'
    b. 'Many people oppose the recent cuts in benefits, saying that they hit the poorest most. Are you for or against benefit cuts?'
    c. 'How often do you ask your boss for his opinion?'
    d. 'At what age did you start cheating in school exams?'
    e. To male participants, 'How would you describe your relationship with your partner? To what extent do you feel supported by her?'
    f. 'With which character from Hollyoaks do you identify most?'

11. You are conducting a 2 × 2 within-participants study. Your two independent variables are 'background noise' (absent/present) and 'task difficulty' (high/low). This gives you four different conditions:
    AH: Background noise **a**bsent, **h**igh difficulty
    AL: Background noise **a**bsent, **l**ow difficulty
    PH: Background noise **p**resent, **h**igh difficulty
    PL: Background noise **p**resent, **l**ow difficulty
Create a Latin Square which gives you four different sequences in which participants can experience all four conditions.

# 4 Basic Mathematics

## WHAT IS THIS CHAPTER ABOUT?

This chapter reviews a few basic mathematics concepts to give you a solid basis of understanding from which to tackle Chapters 6 to 11. If you feel confident in handling and calculating percentages; can tell whether .3 is greater or less than .05; can handle fractions, exponents and the sigma sign; and know your way around '<', '>' and '≤', then you can skip this chapter. But if you are at all unsure or your last brush with mathematics was a long time ago and left you traumatised and resentful, then this chapter gives you a brief and hopefully painless overview into what you need to know. The information in this chapter will also help you to understand and interpret test results.

## WHY IS THIS IMPORTANT?

The aim of this book is to give you a solid foundation from which to conduct a quantitative research project. To this end, we also want to give you the basic tools and skills to understand the mathematics contained in this book. We want to make sure that you can not only run the required statistical tests, but also that you are capable of correctly interpreting the results. You can either work through this chapter in a linear way, as the topics build on each other; pick and choose the topics where you feel you might benefit from a brief refresher; keep this chapter in mind as a resource as you work your way through the book; or, if you feel confident about your skills, ignore this chapter entirely. (And if you do decide to look up things every now and then, we will not tell anyone.)

## WHAT ARE THE LEARNING OUTCOMES OF THIS CHAPTER?

At the end of this chapter you will be able to:
- Correctly interpret 'greater than' and 'less than' signs
- Understand and calculate percentages
- Distinguish between percentages and percent points
- Manipulate decimal points
- Correctly round to a specific decimal place
- Read and understand fractions and ratios
- Interpret the sigma sign
- Identify the range of a distribution
- Understand and calculate with positive, negative and absolute numbers
- Read and calculate exponential expression
- Interpret numbers displayed in scientific notation
- Understand and calculate with squared numbers and square roots
- Have a basic understanding of chance and probability

## 4.1 LARGER THAN, LESS THAN OR EQUAL TO SIGNS

### THIS IS IMPORTANT FOR:

- Interpreting *p*-values to establish (non-)significance (see Section 6.10)

If you have read any published papers you will most likely have come across statements such as 'the difference was statistically significant at $p < .05$.' Later chapters will discuss in more detail what a statement like this means, but this chapter wants to make sure you can understand and correctly interpret expressions like this. We will start with the 'less than'/'greater than' signs. These signs make a statement about the relationship between two values. The way to read them is as follows:

| Number A | sign | Number B |
|---|---|---|
| [Item to the left ← ] | [specific relationship to] | [ → item to the right] |

The signs' shapes themselves give the clue for their interpretation: they indicate relative size, and the larger side of the sign points to the larger of the two values (Figure 4.1):

**Figure 4.1** *'Less than' sign*

When you see '$x < y$', you can tell that '$x$' is less than '$y$' because the smaller, pointier side of the sign is on the side of x, whereas the larger side of the sign is on y's side. The same relationship can be described the other way around: '$x < y$' (read as *x is less than y*) is equivalent to '$y > x$' (read as *y is greater than x*).

We will now look at the different versions of *greater than/less than* in detail.

$$X = Y$$

This is read as 'X equals Y' and means the following:

($A_1$) X and Y are equivalent. For example:

- $2 = 2$   2 is identical with itself; two equals two.
- $\frac{6}{3} = 2$   Six divided by three equals two.

$$X < Y$$

This is read as 'X is less than Y' and means the following two statements are true:

($B_1$) X is less than Y.
($B_2$) Y is greater than X.

For example:

- $3 < 5$          3 is less than 5; 5 is greater than 3.
- $3\% < 5\%$     3% is less than 5%; 5% is greater than 3%.
- $X < X + 1$    X is less than X + 1; and X + 1 is greater than X alone.

$$X \leq Y$$

This is read as 'X is less than or equal to Y' and means that *either* $A_1$ is true (see above), *or* $B_1$ and $B_2$ are both true. The only thing we know for sure is that X is *not* greater than Y. For example:

- $1 + 1 \leq 2$      1 plus 1 *either* equals *or* is less than 2. (1 + 1 equals 2.)
- $\frac{6}{3} \leq 2$        $\frac{6}{3}$ *either* equals *or* is less than 2. ($\frac{6}{3}$ equals 2.)
- $3\% \leq 5\%$    3% *either* equals *or* is less than 5%. (3% is less than 5%.)
- $X \leq X + 1$    X *either* equals to *or* is less than X + 1. (X is less than X + 1.)

$$X > Y$$

This is read as 'X is greater than Y' and means the following two statements are true:

($C_1$) X is greater than Y.
($C_2$) Y is less than X.

For example:

- $20 > 15$       20 is greater than 15.
- $X + 1 > X$    X plus 1 is greater than X alone.

$$X \geq Y$$

This reads as 'X is equal to or greater than Y' and means that *either* $A_1$ is true (see above), *or* $C_1$ and $C_2$ are both true. The only thing we know for sure is that X is *not* less than Y. For example:

- $6 \geq 6$         6 *either* equals *or* is greater than 6. (6 equals 6.)
- $X + 2 \geq X$    X + 2 *either* equals *or* is greater than X. (X + 2 is greater than X.)

Before you move on, test yourself with Exercises 1 and 2 on page 114.

## 4.2 PERCENTAGES AND PERCENT POINTS

### THIS IS IMPORTANT FOR:

- Alpha levels (see Section 6.10)
- Confidence levels (see Section 3.8.1)
- Using descriptive statistics (see Section 6.2)
- Performing sampling procedures (see, e.g., Section 3.8)

The following two statements appear contradictory but can both be true at the same time.

- Fantastic! Test scores have improved by 50%!
- Awful: Test scores only increased by 1 percent point!

No wonder that calculating and understanding percentages can be frustrating!

First things first. What does percent even mean? It literally means 'pro (one) hundred', in other words, 'a one-hundredth', from the Latin word *'centum'*, meaning hundred. This is the same *'centi'* in centimeter (i.e., a centimeter is one hundredth of a meter), centiliter (i.e., one hundredth of a liter), and even centipede (here referring to an animal with figuratively one hundred legs). It is also the reason a Euro is equivalent to 100 cents. Percentages describe a ratio of one group of items to another with a basis of 100 items for comparison. This means that you can easily compare ratios between groups of very different sizes. Consider the following scenario.

Your study looks at willingness to donate to charity across different age brackets. You surveyed 450 participants and have tabulated their responses to the question whether they would be willing to donate £5/month to a charity by age group. Using only **frequencies** (i.e., counting how often a particular value appears) your table will look like this:

*Table 4.1 Sample absolute responses*

| Age group | Total number of participants | Number of participants responding with 'yes' | Number of participants responding with 'no' |
|---|---|---|---|
| ≤19 years | 50 | 22 | 28 |
| 20–29 | 70 | 40 | 30 |
| 30–39 | 160 | 40 | 120 |
| 40–49 | 80 | 40 | 40 |
| 50–59 | 50 | 17 | 33 |
| ≥60 | 40 | 15 | 25 |

Using this format, you will find it difficult to compare individual groups. Three cells contain '40' as the number of responses, but in each instance '40' has a different connotation because the group sizes differ so much: for the 20–29 year olds, 40 represents a majority (40 out of 70); for the 30–39 year olds it is a minority (40 out of 160); for the 40–49 year olds it represents a half-half split (40 of 80). Knowing only that 40 people responded with 'yes' therefore does not tell you much. If you use one hundred as your base though, you can compare ratios of participants responding with 'yes' and 'no' directly (Table 4.2):

*Table 4.2 Responses in percentages*

| Age group | Total number of participants | Number of participants responding with 'yes' | Number of participants responding with 'no' |
|---|---|---|---|
| ≤19 years | 50 | 44% | 56% |
| 20–29 | 70 | 57% | 43% |
| 30–39 | 160 | 25% | 75% |
| 40–49 | 80 | 50% | 50% |
| 50–59 | 50 | 34% | 66% |
| ≥60 | 40 | 38% | 62% |

But how do you calculate percentages? You need to know two numbers: the total number of cases, and the number of cases you want to express as a percentage. Have a look at the first line in Table 4.1:

| ≤19 years | 50 | 22 | 28 |

You want to know how many percent 22 out of 50 are. To find out, divide 22 by 50. If you do so on a calculator you will get 0.44. To derive the percentage from this, multiply by 100 to get to 44, or interpret 1.0 as 100%, which helps you to read 0.44 as 44% straight away:

$$1.0 = 100\%$$
$$0.5 = 50\%$$
$$0.05 = 5\%$$
$$0.005 = 0.5\%$$
and so on

Note: For clarity's sake we are here displaying the 0 before the decimal point. In later chapters we will adopt the American Psychological Association's (APA) style guidelines which state to 'not use a zero before a decimal fraction when the statistic cannot be greater than 1 (e.g., correlations, proportions, and levels of statistical significance)' (2010, p. 113). In the example above, this would mean the numbers would be displayed as .5 and .05, respectively. Displaying percentages in this format has another benefit. It helps you work out how much X percent of Y is. For example, if you want to calculate 7% of 50, you now know that 7% can be expressed as 0.07, so you can compute 7% of 50 by multiplying 50 by 0.07:

$$50 \times 0.07 = 3.5 \rightarrow 7\% \text{ of } 50 \text{ equals } 3.5.$$

If you want to add 7% to the existing value, it means that you want to know what equals 107% of 50, thus you multiply 1.07 by 50:

$$50 \times 1.07 = 53.5 \rightarrow \text{Adding } 7\% \text{ to } 50 \text{ gives } 53.5.$$

But perhaps you want to subtract 7% off the existing value? Taking 7% off means you want to keep the remaining 93%, so to calculate this you multiply 50 by 0.93:

$$50 \times 0.93 = 46.5 \rightarrow \text{Decreasing } 50 \text{ by } 7\% \text{ gives } 46.5.$$

### ? REVIEW & REFLECT

- When might it be preferable to use percentages rather than frequencies?
- How does the calculation of percentages relate to the decimal system?

So far we have referred to *percentages*, which refer to fractions or ratios. A 50% reduction in reaction time from 600 ms to 300 ms means half the reaction time; if the average test score increases from 20 to 22, that is a 10% increase – because you take the score of 20 as your basis. But if test scores improve from 50% to 52% you would describe it in terms of **percent points** by saying 'there is an increase of 2 percent points'. The difference is that this talks about the *absolute* increase of percentages, not the increase *relative* to the base value of 20. And this explains the two seemingly contradictory statements at the start of this section:

*Fantastic! Test scores have improved by 50%!*
*Awful: Test scores only increased by 1 percent point!*

If the initial test scores were 2% (perhaps a very difficult test?), then a change to average test scores of 3% means both an absolute difference of 1 *percent point* and a relative difference of 50% (50% of 2 equals 1, thus 2 + 1 = 3).

Before you move on, test your understanding with Exercises 3 and 4 on page 114.

## 4.3 DECIMAL POINTS

### THIS IS IMPORTANT FOR:

- Pretty much everything, including but not limited to
- Understanding and interpreting output from Excel and SPSS (from Chapter 6 onwards)
- Performing simple calculations manually (e.g., Sections 6.5, 6.10, 6.13)

Some calculations above required you to multiply a value by 100, which you achieved by moving the decimal point by two places to the right. But why? The start of this chapter introduced '*centi*' as a word fragment meaning '100'. The word 'decimal' is based on '*decem*' (10) and *decimus* ('tenth'). A *decimeter* is a tenth of a meter (=10 cm), a *deciliter* a tenth of a liter (=100 ml). The numeral system you are most likely used to operating with is a *decimal system* – it works on the basis of multiples of tens.

Because this system operates with multiples of ten, moving the decimal point one place to the right means multiplying by ten; moving it one place to the left means dividing by ten. Each place further to the right or the left adds one order of magnitude: from 10 to 100 to 1000 to 10,000 and so on (Figure 4.2).

13,437.0

| Moving the decimal point one place to the left divides the original number by 10 | 1,343.70 ← | 134,370.0 → | Moving the decimal point one place to the right multiplies the original number by 10 |
| Moving the decimal point two places to the left divides the original number by 100 | 134.37 ← | 1,343,700.0 → | Moving the decimal point two places to the right multiplies the original number by 100 |

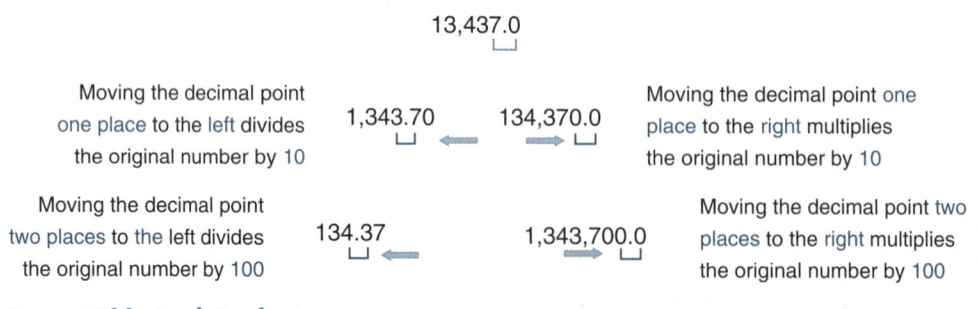

**Figure 4.2** *Moving decimal points*

### ❗ LOOK OUT!

The use of symbols for decimal points and decimal separators can differ between countries and regions. We have adopted the British and American notation of using a comma for decimal separators and a period for the decimal point; be aware that in some countries (e.g., Germany or Russia) the usage is reversed by using a comma for the decimal point and a period for decimal separators. To add to the confusion, not all systems use decimal separators. In some countries the use is different when writing by hand and when used anywhere else (e.g., Switzerland). Even the International System of Units (SI, from its French name Système International d'Unités) has two versions, a French and an English one, where the French version uses the comma for the decimal point and the English version the period.

Before you move on, test your understanding with Exercises 5 to 8 on page 114.

## 4.4 ROUNDING

### THIS IS IMPORTANT FOR:

- Reducing the number of decimal figures to a given number (e.g., reducing a t-value or F-value from its precise value to the more usual standard of three decimal places that you would use when writing up your results)

When you start calculating ratios and percentages you will often find that the result of your calculations is much more detailed than you really need. You might get a figure with many numbers after the decimal point, for example a number like 3.45825. Most statistical testing software will give you output data with up to four or five numbers after the decimal point, which is a degree of detail you do not always need. Or perhaps the assignment or formatting requirements ask you to 'round to the third decimal place'. How do you interpret these requests? Take a number with four places after the decimal point. For demonstration, we will present this number as A.BCDE such that BCDE are the numbers after the decimal point. To round A.BCDE to the third decimal place, proceed as follows (Figure 4.3):

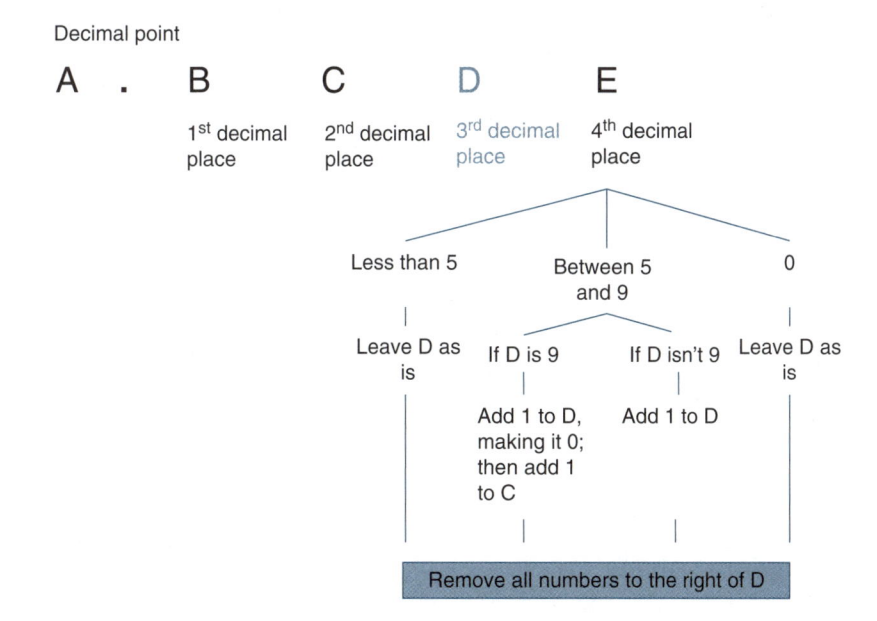

**Figure 4.3** *Rounding to the third decimal place*

1. Identify the number in the third decimal place – here, D.
2. Look at the number immediately to the right of D – here, E.
    a. If E is less than 5, keep D as is. Example: 1.2344 is rounded to 1.234.
    b. If E is between 5 and 9, add 1 to D. Example: 1.2348 is rounded to 1.235.
       If D is already 9:
       1. Add 1 to turn D into 0
       2. Add 1 to the number preceding D (i.e., C).
       Example: 1.2397 is rounded to 1.240.
    c. If E is 0, keep D as is. Example: 1.2340 is rounded to 1.234.
3. Remove all numbers to the right of the third decimal place.

For the example given above (3.45825), this would mean the following:

1. Identify the third decimal place: 8.
2. The number immediately right to 8 is 2. 2 is less than 5, therefore 8 remains unchanged: 3.45825
3. Remove all numbers to the right of the third decimal place: 3. 458.

How would this have looked if, instead of a 2, you had found a 9 (e.g., if the original number had been 3.45985)?

1. Identify the third decimal place: 9.
2. The number immediately to the right of 9 is now 8.

8 is greater than 5 therefore you add 1 to 9. Because this turns 9 into 0, you add 1 to the number immediately preceding it, thus turning 5 into 6: 3.46075.

3. Remove all numbers to the right of the third decimal place: 3.460.

> **REVIEW & REFLECT**
>
> - What does rounding to the third decimal place mean?
> - Why is it important to know how to round numbers to a specific decimal place?

### 4.4.1 Rounding in Excel

You can tell Excel to which decimal place you want numbers rounded. Go to Format → Cells, and click on the Numbers tab. Select the category Numbers in the left-hand list, then set the number of decimal places you want in the right-hand side of the window. Note that this will only change the number of displayed decimal places; if you reduce the number of decimal places displayed, Excel will retain the original information so that you could change back the display to more decimal places if you decided to later on.

### 4.4.2 Rounding in SPSS

In SPSS you can change the number of decimal places displayed in the Decimal setting in the Variable view (see also Section 5.3.1).

You can test your understanding of rounding with Exercises 9 and 10 on page 114–5.

## 4.5 FRACTIONS AND RATIOS

### THIS IS IMPORTANT FOR:

Understanding the instructions for the manual calculation of any of these values:
- Variance (see Section 6.5)
- Standard deviation (see Section 6.5)
- Mean (see Section 6.3.1)
- Median (see Section 6.3.3)
- Z-score (see Section 6.8)

In this context, 'fraction' usually refers to an arrangement of two parts of the form $^A/_B$ or $\frac{A}{B}$ or, for example, ¾ or $\frac{n \times (n-1)}{2}$, the formula used in Section 3.3.2 to calculate the number of pairwise comparisons.

In these examples, the part above the line or to the left of the dash is called the **numerator**, and the part below the line or to the right of the dash is called the **denominator**:

$$\frac{Numerator}{Denominator}, \text{ or } ^{Numerator}/_{Denominator}$$

Probabilities can be expressed as fractions, for example, a '1 in 5' chance is a chance of $\frac{1}{5}$, that is, one-fifth. But they can also be expressed as divisions, such as 3:4 (i.e., 'three divided by 4', equalling 0.75), which means they can sometimes be mistaken as **ratios**, such as 'the ratio of smokers to non-smokers was 3:4'. Although looking similar, the interpretation of a ratio is different from the interpretation of a fraction. As a ratio, 3:4 of A to B means that for every three As there are four Bs. Exact word choice as well as order of words is important:

- A success ratio of 1 *in* 10 tries means there is *one success* and *nine failures* (basis for the comparison is a group of 10).
- A ratio of *1 to 10* successes to failures means there is *one success* for every *ten failures* (basis for the comparison is a group of 11).
- A ratio of *10 to 1* successes to failures means there are *ten successes* for every *one failure* (basis for the comparison is a group of 11).

You can test your understanding with Exercises 11, 12 and 13 on page 115.

## 4.6 SIGMA

### THIS IS IMPORTANT FOR:

- Manually calculating variance (see Section 6.5)
- Manually calculating standard deviation (see Section 6.5)

This is the Sigma sign:

$$\Sigma$$

If you see this sign, it usually means to add up several elements repeatedly. For example, you might see this part of the formula to calculate the sum of squares (see Section 6.5):

$$\sum X$$

This tells you to add up all values of X, that is, all the values of the variable you want to calculate the sum of squares for. If you had collected the following values: 1, 2, 3, 4, 5, 6, 7, 8, this would mean adding them up as follows:

$$\sum X = 1 + 2 + 3 + 4 + 5 + 6 + 7 + 8 = 36$$

But you can also sum up more complex expressions. For example, if the formula looked like $\sum (X + 2)$, this would mean performing the operation for every given value of X:

$$\sum (X + 2)$$
$$= (1 + 2) + (2 + 2) + (3 + 2) + (4 + 2) + (5 + 2) + (6 + 2) + (7 + 2) + (8 + 2)$$
$$= 3 + 4 + 5 + 6 + 7 + 8 + 9 + 10$$
$$= 52$$

In the examples above, we have simplified matters a bit by leaving out some elements. Normally, a Sigma sign has three components: a formula or function that is being calculated and two components telling you where to start and stop your calculations, respectively. For example, if you wanted to add up all squares from 1 to 10, the formula would look like this:

$$\sum_{i=1}^{i=10} X_i^2$$

This formula tells you to square the variable X, and to do so for the first to tenth value of X. If you want to square all values of X, like you would want to do for calculations of variance and standard deviations, you can omit the upper and lower limit and just refer to the variable itself:

$$\sum X^2$$

This means to square every value of X and add them all up.

Before moving on, test your understanding with Exercise 14 on page 115.

## 4.7 RANGE

### THIS IS IMPORTANT FOR:

- Understanding and providing descriptive data (also see Section 6.5)
- Performing an initial data check after data entry (see Section 5.6)

The **range** is a concept describing the span or width of values present in a distribution (i.e., a set of values; see also measures of dispersion in Section 6.5). You calculate the range by subtracting the lowest value from the highest. For example, if you have a set of values, first sort them from lowest to highest:

$$1, 2, 4, 6, 8, 9, 12, 15, 17, 18, 20, 20,$$

The range is then calculated by subtracting the lowest value (1) from the highest (20):

$$20 - 1 = 19; \text{ in this example the range is 19.}$$

The range gives only limited information about a set of values, though, because it only considers the highest and lowest number without regard for how the values are distributed between those two numbers. In other words, all the following sets of values have the same range of 19:

- Set 1: 1, 2, 4, 6, 8, 9, 12, 15, 17, 18, 20, 20.
- Set 2: 1,1,1,1,1,1,1,1,1,1,1,1,1, 20.
- Set 3: 1, 20, 20, 20, 20, 20, 20, 20, 20.

Note that you can also describe a distribution in terms of 'ranging from [lowest value] to [highest value]'; this is different from referring to the range itself:

'Values range from 1 to 20'.
But: 'The range is 19'.

**EXCEL** To calculate the range for a set of values in Excel, you can use a combination of the MIN and MAX functions to identify the minimum and maximum value and then subtract the minimum from the maximum value. See Section 5.2 for a basic introduction to Excel, and see the Excel Functions Glossary for a detailed description of individual functions. In this example we are calculating the range of the values entered in cells A1 to A13; note how the first part of the formula calculates the maximum value, the second part the minimum value, and the overall formula calculates the difference between the two:

$$= MAX(A1:A13) - MIN(A1:A13)$$

**SPSS** Navigate to Analyse → Descriptive Statistics → Descriptives.... Click Options, and tick the option Range.

You can test your understanding with Exercise 15 on page 115.

## 4.8 POSITIVE, NEGATIVE AND ABSOLUTE NUMBERS

### THIS IS IMPORTANT FOR:

- Understanding why the formulas for variance and standard deviation use squared values rather than the unsquared values (see Section 6.5)

Negative numbers become relevant, for example, where we work with differences from averages. Take the following set of values, ranging from 1 to 30, with an average of 14:

$$1, 5, 10, 12, 12, 15, 15, 17, 18, 19, 30$$

Now suppose you want to find out for each individual value the difference to the average:

$$1 - 14 = (-13)$$
$$5 - 14 = (-9)$$
$$10 - 14 = (-4)$$
$$12 - 14 = (-2)$$
$$12 - 14 = (-2)$$
$$15 - 14 = 1$$
$$15 - 14 = 1$$
$$17 - 14 = 3$$
$$18 - 14 = 4$$
$$19 - 14 = 5$$
$$30 - 14 = 16$$

Suppose further that you want to know the sum of the individual differences to the mean. To do so, you would add up the individual results; note that we have put the negative numbers in brackets for clarity.

$$(-13) + (-9) + (-4) + (-2) + (-2) + 1 + 1 + 3 + 4 + 5 + 16 = 0.$$

This could also be expressed as:

$$-13 - 9 - 4 - 2 - 2 + 1 + 1 + 3 + 4 + 5 + 16 = 0.$$

Clearly, just adding up the individual results is not very helpful, because the positive and negative values cancel each other out. Instead, you can use the absolute values. In the next equation, the symbol shows that we are using the absolute value of whatever is contained between the two bars:

$$|-13| + |-9| + |-4| + |-2| + |-2| + |1| + |1| + |3| + |4| + |5| + |16| =$$
$$13 + 9 + 4 + 2 + 2 + 1 + 1 + 3 + 4 + 5 + 16 = 60$$

There are a few simple rules when calculating with negative numbers:

- Negative numbers are smaller than positive numbers, even if their absolute values are larger: $15 > 1$, but $(-15) < 1$.
- A negative number plus a negative number will equal a negative number, for example, $(-5) + (-7) = -5 - 7 = (-12)$.
- A negative number multiplied with a positive number will give a negative result: $(-3) \times 4 = (-12)$.
- A negative number multiplied with a negative number will give a positive result: $(-3) \times (-4) = 12$. This also means squaring negative numbers always gives a positive result.

> **EXCEL** To calculate the absolute value of a number in Excel, you can use the ABS function. See Section 5.2 for a basic introduction to Excel, and see the Excel Functions Glossary for a detailed description of individual functions.

> **SPSS** If you needed to calculate the absolute value, the ABS function is also available in SPSS for computing or recoding a variable (see Sections 5.5 and 5.7, respectively).

Before moving on, test your understanding with Exercises 16 and 17 on page 115.

## 4.9 READING EXPONENTIAL NOTATIONS

### THIS IS IMPORTANT FOR:

- Understanding the formula for variance (see Section 6.5)
- Understanding the formula for standard deviation (see Section 6.5)
- Understanding the formula for sample size calculation (see Section 3.8.1)

Occasionally you will come across numbers expressed in the following formats:

- $12^3$
- $7^{-2}$

The superscript (from Latin *super*, broadly meaning *above* or *over*) is called **exponent** and the numbers it is applied to is called **base**:

$$\text{Base}^{\text{Exponent}}$$

This expression is read as '[Base] to the power of [Exponent]'. You would therefore describe the expressions above as 'twelve to the power of three' or 'seven to the power of minus two'.

Exponents can be positive or negative. *Positive exponents* tell you how often to multiply the base with itself: $X^n$ equals 'X multiplied with itself n times'. For example, $12^3$ means multiplying 12 three times with itself; $2^5$ means multiplying 2 five times with itself:

$$12^3 = 12 \times 12 \times 12 = 1{,}728$$
$$2^5 = 2 \times 2 \times 2 \times 2 \times 2 = 32$$

*Negative exponents* express a fraction by telling you how often to divide 1 by the base: $X^{-n}$ equals '1 divided by X n times'. For example, $7^{-2}$ means dividing 1 two times by 7; $8^{-3}$ means dividing 1 by 8 three times.

$$7^{-2} = (1/7)/7 = 0.020$$
$$8^{-3} = ((1/8)/8)/8 = 0.002$$

## 108  Introducing Quantitative Methods

A better way to express this is as a fraction:

$$1/(X^n)$$

For example:

$$7^{-2} = \frac{1}{7^2} = \frac{1}{7 \times 7} = \frac{1}{49} = 0.020$$

$$8^{-3} = \frac{1}{8^3} = \frac{1}{8 \times 8 \times 8} = \frac{1}{512} = 0.002$$

The greater the negative exponent, the smaller the fraction:

$$4^{-7} = \frac{1}{4^7} = \frac{1}{4 \times 4 \times 4 \times 4 \times 4 \times 4 \times 4} = \frac{1}{16384} = 0.00006103515625$$

Before you move on, test your understanding with Exercise 18 on page 115.

## 4.10  SCIENTIFIC NOTATION

### THIS IS IMPORTANT FOR:

- Understanding the output of Excel

Looking back at the result of $4^{-7}$, the last result looks quite unwieldy. Fortunately, there is a different way of displaying the same number, and it will explain the type of Excel cell information you might have seen in the past:

$$\boxed{6.10352\text{E-}05}$$

The information displayed here consists of four parts: '6.10352', the letter 'E', the '–' sign, and the number '05'. Together, these parts form a construction kit, so to speak, to put together the actual number. The 'E' is the crucial part. It tells you that this way of displaying the data is the E-notation because you make use of **E**xponents; this is also referred to as scientific notation. In this notation, the base (see above for the definition of 'base') is always 10. In the example above, '–05' describes the exponent. The exponent is negative so you have to divide 1 five times by 10: ((((1:10):10):10):10):10 as described above. You can also express this as a fraction:

$$10^{-5} = \frac{1}{10^5} = \frac{1}{10 \times 10 \times 10 \times 10 \times 10} = \frac{1}{100,000} = 0.00001$$

Once you have applied the exponent to the base of 10, you multiply it with the part of the string that comes before 'E' – here, '6.10352':

$$6.10352 \times 0.00001 = 0.0000610352$$

Note that if you compare this number to the initial result of $\frac{1}{16384}$ (which was 0.00006103515625), you can see that Excel has rounded the number to the tenth decimal place.

> **? REVIEW & REFLECT**
>
> - What might be the advantages and disadvantages of using the scientific notation?

There is an easier alternative to calculate these numbers. Remember that the start of the chapter introduced the decimal system as a system based on sets of 10; and dividing or multiplying by 10 moves the decimal point to either side. This means that rather than doing the work of multiplying ten by ten by ten and so on, for numbers displayed in the E-notation you can simply move the decimal point in the appropriate direction and by the appropriate number of places. If the exponent is negative, you need to make the number smaller and therefore move the decimal point to the left; if the exponent is positive, you need to make the number bigger and therefore move the decimal point to the right. Have a look at '2.57873E05'. The exponent is positive, so you need to move the decimal point to the right, and '05' tells you that you need to move the decimal point *five* places to the right:

|   | 2.57873 |   |
|---|---|---|
| → | 25.7873 | Moved 1 decimal place to the right |
| → | 257.873 | Moved 2 decimal places to the right |
| → | 2,578.73 | Moved 3 decimal places to the right |
| → | 25,787.3 | Moved 4 decimal places to the right |
| → | 257,873.0 | Moved 5 decimal places to the right |

What if your number has fewer digits than you are asked to move decimal points? You just keep adding zeroes to it. Have a look at the example below, taking the same number but with one additional decimal place:

|   | 2.57873 |   |
|---|---|---|
| → | 25.7873 | Moved 1 decimal place to the right |
| → | 257.873 | Moved 2 decimal places to the right |
| → | 2,578.73 | Moved 3 decimal places to the right |
| → | 25,787.3 | Moved 4 decimal places to the right |
| → | 257,873.0 | Moved 5 decimal places to the right |
| → | 2,578,730.0 | Moved 6 decimal places to the right |

You can apply the same technique to expressions with a negative exponent. Take the earlier example, '6.10352E-05'. The exponent (05) is negative which means you have to make the number smaller and therefore move the decimal point to the left:

|   | 6.10352 |   |
|---|---|---|
| → | 0.610352 | Moved 1 decimal place to the left |
| → | 0.0610352 | Moved 2 decimal places to the left |
| → | 0.00610352 | Moved 3 decimal places to the left |
| → | 0.000610352 | Moved 4 decimal places to the left |
| → | 0.0000610352 | Moved 5 decimal places to the left |

Test your understanding of this section with Exercises 19 and 20 on page 116 before you move on.

## 4.11  SQUARES AND SQUARE ROOTS

### THIS IS IMPORTANT FOR:

- Understanding the formula for variance (see Section 6.5)
- Understanding the formula for standard deviation (see Section 6.5)
- Understanding the formula for sample size calculation (see Section 3.8.1)

The statistical analyses you are most likely to conduct will mostly require no more complex exponential expressions than squared numbers which are expressions where the exponent is 2. These expressions are therefore read as 'X to the power of two' or 'X squared'. A squared number is the product of multiplying the number with itself, and the result will always be positive (you will see in Section 6.5 that this is an important property to calculate the standard deviation):

$$12^2 = 144$$
$$7.5^2 = 56.25$$
$$(-1.2)^2 = 1.44$$
$$5^2 = 25$$
$$(-5)^2 = 25$$

Conversely, if you want to compute the square root of a number Y, you are trying to find the number X which, when multiplied with itself, yields Y. The square root of 25 is 5, the square root of 1.44 is 1.2 and so on:

$$\sqrt{25} = 5$$
$$\sqrt{1.44} = 1.2$$
$$\sqrt{56.25} = 7.5$$

The calculations to conduct statistical analyses will not involve square roots of negative numbers – this requires a special category of numbers called complex numbers. For the intents and purposes of this book, assume that you can square negative numbers but cannot calculate the square root of negative numbers (because normally we assume that −4 multiplied by −4 equals 16). Lastly, because squared numbers are the product of a number multiplied with itself, multiplying a square root of X with a square root of X equals X itself:

$$\sqrt{56.25} \times \sqrt{56.25} = 7.5 \times 7.5 = 7.5^2 = 56.25$$

**EXCEL**  To calculate the square root in Excel, you can use the SQRT function. See Section 5.2 for a basic introduction to Excel, and see the Excel Functions Glossary for a detailed description of individual functions.

Before moving on to the next chapter, test your understanding with Exercises 21 and 22 on page 116.

## 4.12 CHANCE AND PROBABILITIES

### THIS IS IMPORTANT FOR:

- Understanding the chi-square test (see Sections 8.8.1 to 8.8.3)
- Understanding concepts of *p*-value and normal distribution (see Sections 6.10 and 6.7, respectively)

This section briefly describes some of the main concepts you need to know in order to understand and apply the analyses described later in the book. Our focus is here on the basic understanding on how probabilities work rather than on being able to use specific formulas.

The most vexing aspect of chance and probability is that you can often describe and analyse overall patterns of behaviour without being able to describe an individual entity or object's behaviour. Take something as simple as rolling a dice. Overall, we know that the chance of all sides of the dice are exactly identical. For each side, it is exactly 1 out of 6, or $\frac{1}{6}$ (one sixth). Yet for each individual roll of the dice the behaviour of the dice is unpredictable. The same applies when we talk about behavioural tendencies or differences or effects. For example, although we know that on the whole children of academics will perform better in school, this does not help us predict the school performance of an individual child from an individual family. Another aspect that is often confusing is the difference between individual and combined probabilities. For example, imagine you have rolled a dice ten times and it has always come up with 1. When you roll it the 11$^{th}$ time, you might now expect it to come up with something other than 1, because it has already happened so often and surely another side of the dice should now come up. Alas, for the next roll of the dice the chances are exactly $\frac{1}{6}$ for any possible result – including yet another 1. What we intuitively consider improbable is based on the perception of the events (rolling the dice) as a series of events rather than an individual roll of the dice – and surely such a series should be less probable? Yes, and that is the (often confusing) difference. The probability of rolling twelve 1s in a row is calculated by multiplying each individual chance with each other, in this case:

$$\left(\frac{1}{6}\right)^{12} = \frac{1}{6} \times \frac{1}{6} \times \frac{1}{6} \times \frac{1}{6} \times \frac{1}{6} \times \frac{1}{6} \times \frac{1}{6} \times \frac{1}{6} \times \frac{1}{6} \times \frac{1}{6} \times \frac{1}{6} \times \frac{1}{6} = \frac{1}{2,176,782,336}$$

Again, this is the probability for rolling twelve 1s in a row (i.e., the probability for a sequence of events). However, *at the point of rolling the dice* the probability is the same each time: exactly $\frac{1}{6}$.

This misunderstanding of individual events and sequences of events is also at the root of the Monte Carlo Effect: the gambler's fallacy that, for example at the roulette table, black has come up so often that with every game it is much more likely that red will finally come up. For a sequence of events this is certainly correct:

A sequence of two blacks in a row has a chance of $\left(\frac{1}{2}\right)^2 = \frac{1}{2} \times \frac{1}{2} = \frac{1}{4}$

A sequence of three blacks in a row has a chance of $\left(\frac{1}{2}\right)^3 = \frac{1}{2} \times \frac{1}{2} \times \frac{1}{2} = \frac{1}{8}$

A sequence of four blacks in a row has a chance of $\left(\frac{1}{2}\right)^4 = \frac{1}{2} \times \frac{1}{2} \times \frac{1}{2} \times \frac{1}{2} = \frac{1}{16}$

But as you can see from the way it is calculated, each individual event still has the same ½ chance. For the gambler at the table, this means that although their overall string of bad luck is quite unlikely, their individual chance of seeing one or the other colour on the roulette wheel does not change for each new try.

> **REVIEW & REFLECT**
>
> - Why are probabilities so counterintuitive to human cognition?
> - How does this relate to the recommendation a human researcher never design a random sequence manually?

That said, there are instances when the probability of one event occurring depends on another event. For this consider playing cards rather than roulette: With every card drawn from a deck, the probability of drawing a card of the same colour is reduced slightly because there are now fewer cards of that colour in the deck. This is referred to as **conditional probabilities**, whereas so far we have talked about **unconditional probabilities**. If you draw a card from a fresh deck of 52 cards (no jokers), the chances of drawing a red card are 26 out of 52, which equals $\frac{26}{52} = \frac{1}{2} = 50\%$. Depending on which card you draw in the first attempt, the probabilities for the next card change as follows:

- If you draw a red card first, then there are 25 red cards and 26 black cards left, which makes 51 cards in total.
  - The probability for a black card next is now: $\frac{26}{51} = 50.98\%$
  - The probability for a red card next is now: $\frac{25}{51} = 49.02\%$
- If you draw a black card first, then there are 25 black cards and 26 red cards left, which makes 51 cards in total.
  - The probability for a black card next is now: $\frac{25}{51} = 49.02\%$
  - The probability for a red card next is now: $\frac{26}{51} = 50.98\%$

You can see how the probability for a black card in the second draw changes depending on whether a red or a black card was drawn in the first draw. Dealing with conditional probabilities changes the probabilities themselves but not the underlying calculation rules, and we will therefore not pursue this distinction further in this chapter.

Before you move on, you can test your understanding with Exercises 23 and 24 on page 116.

> **RESEARCH METHODS AT WORK**
>
> Taylor is designing an Excel sheet which helps them track payment transfers between different international branches of the multi-national company Taylor works for. Because of the international payments, the Excel form needs to be able to convert between currencies. This gets Taylor thinking about currency rates and decimal places: Currency conversion rates are often given with up to five decimal places, which initially seems like gratuitous accuracy: whether £1 converts to €1.11642 or €1.11643, does not make much of a difference to a tourist when exchanging £100 – it either converts to €111.642 or €111.643, which in practice means €111.64 in both cases. Even when exchanging £1000, a change

in the fifth decimal place still only makes a difference of one cent: €1116.42 vs. €1116.43. However, Taylor then realises that over time or with large enough expenses, these small differences start to matter: £1,000,000 convert to either €1,116,420 or €1,116,430 and suddenly the different fifth decimal place has translated into a €10 gap. They therefore decide to require currency rates to be entered to five decimal places.

Raj is a marketing manager for a small independent online bookstore. To get a sense of how satisfied their customers are with their service, he is using the Net Promoter Score (NPS, described for example in Reichheld, 2003): Customers are asked how likely they are to recommend the company to a friend or colleague, with answers on a scale from 1 to 10. Customers with an answer between 1 and 6 are classed as 'detractors', with 7 or 8 as 'passives', and 9 or 10 as 'promoters'. The NPS is then calculated by deducting the percentage of detractors from the percentage of promoters.

Last week, 554 customers responded to the survey questions, of which 83 gave an answer of 6 or below, 266 chose 7 or 8, and 205 answered 9 or 10. Raj first calculates the individual percentage values, rounding them up to the nearest full number:

- Detractors: $\frac{83}{554} = 0.1498 = 14.98$, rounded to 15%
- Passives: $\frac{266}{554} = 0.4801 = 48.01$, rounded to 48%
- Promoters: $\frac{205}{554} = 0.3700 = 37\%$

He then deducts the percentage of detractors from the percentage of promoters:

$$37\% - 15\% = 22\%,$$

giving him a Net Promoter Score of 22%. Raj is delighted. The previous week's NPS score was 18% and although the new score is only 4 percent points higher, it represents a 22% increase, which means the improved order handling process seems to have been received well.

## A SHORT SUMMARY

- To correctly interpret '<' and '>' signs, remember that the larger side of the sign points towards the larger of the two values. The signs '≤' and '≥' mean that *either* the 'is less than' or 'is greater than' relationship, respectively, is true, *or* the values are equal.
- Percentages indicate a ratio or fraction, standardised to a base of 100. Percentages talk about relative differences; percent points indicate absolute differences between percentages.
- The decimal system is based on multiples of ten. Moving a decimal point to the right means multiplying a value by 10, moving a decimal point to the left means dividing a value by 10.
- Rounding to the *nth* decimal place (here called X) requires looking at the number immediately to the right of the X. For numbers equal to or greater than 5, add 1 to X; for numbers less than 5, leave X as is. An extra step is added if X is already 9. Having done so, remove all numbers to the right of X.
- Exponential notation uses a base and an exponent which can be either positive or negative. Positive exponents express the number of times with which the base number has to be multiplied with itself; negative exponents express the number of times with which the number 1 should be divided by the base.

- To interpret figures presented in scientific notation of the form [number]E[exponent] (e.g., 1.54E04), first focus on the part starting with 'E'. For this kind of notation, the base is always 10. Work out the result as with regular exponential notation, then multiply it with the figure given before 'E'.
- To square a number, multiply it with itself. The square root of a given number X is the number Y which, when multiplied with itself, yields X.

### CHECK YOUR UNDERSTANDING

1. Decide for every statement whether it is true or false:
   a. $X < X + 1$
   b. $X > X + 1$
   c. $7 \leq 5$
   d. $.05 \leq .05$
   e. $.01 \leq .05$
   f. $.03 \geq .001$
   g. $.2 \leq .05$
   h. $5 \geq 4$
   i. $5 \leq 7$

2. Express the following statements using the correct greater than/less than sign:
   a. 3 is less than 5
   b. .001 is less than or equal to .01
   c. X is greater than X-1
   d. .04 is less than .4

3. Calculate the following percentages:
   a. 15 of 58 =
   b. 34 of 200 =
   c. 3000 of 23,481 =
   d. 17 of 100 =
   e. 5% of 17 =
   f. 50% of 170 =
   g. 150% of 20 =

4. Give the results for taking off ten percent points from the results of 3a–d:
   a. =
   b. =
   c. =
   d. =

5. Move the decimal point in 9.34281 four places to the right.

6. Move the decimal point in 0.0342 six places to the left.

7. Multiply .009 by 1000.

8. Divide 1202094 by 10,000.

9. Round the following numbers to the second decimal place:
   a. 2.874
   b. 35.988

c. 9.809348
   d. 234.54
   e. 98.870

10. Round the following numbers to the third decimal place:
    a. .0094
    b. .8721
    c. 1.8379
    d. .0121
    e. 1.2098

11. In the fraction $\frac{17}{18}$, which is the numerator and which is the denominator?

12. In a group of 20 consumers, there are 15 non-smokers and 5 smokers. Express this as a ratio of
    a. Smokers to non-smokers
    b. Non-smokers to smokers

13. Express the statements below in the form of 'Of _____ treatments, _____ succeed and _____ fail.'
    a. 'This treatment has a 1 **in** 5 success **rate**.'
    b. 'This treatment has a 1 **to** 5 success **ratio**.'

14. Perform the calculations expressed in the formulas below based on the following set of values: 10, 12, 20, 15, 22, 25
    a. $\sum x$
    b. $\sum (x-5)$
    c. $\sum x^2$
    d. $\left(\sum x\right)^2$

15. What is the range for the following sets of values (note that the sets are not ordered)?
    a. 5, 10, 12, 16, 20, 22, 20, 20
    b. 123, 155, 167, 188, 120, 125
    c. 4, 6, 2, 5, 8, 4, 12, 16
    d. 1.23, 1.45, 1.17, 1.18, 1.22, 2.01

16. For the following set of values, first calculate the average, then the total of the absolute differences to the average: 12, 16, 24, 26, 28, 30, 32, 35, 40.

17. Work out the results for the following equations:
    a. $-3 - 4 =$
    b. $(-3) \times (-4) =$
    c. $3 \times (-4) =$
    d. $|7| + |-5| + |-12| =$

18. Calculate the following exponential expressions. First express them as a fraction, then work out the result. The solution for the first item is provided:
    a. $3^{-7} = \frac{1}{3 \times 3 \times 3 \times 3 \times 3 \times 3 \times 3} = \frac{1}{2187} = 0.000457247$

b. $2^6 =$
c. $4^{-3} =$
d. $13^{-2} =$
e. $980^2 =$
f. $(1.5)^{-2} =$
g. $(0.6)^2 =$
h. $(0.06)^2 =$

19. Work out the results for the following exponential expressions:
    a. 1.2398E-04
    b. 9.82E07
    c. 1.09385E-08
    d. 5.342342E06

20. Express the following numbers in scientific notation:
    a. 2,983,000
    b. 4398
    c. .0000456
    d. .0000000384
    e. 983,349,923,982
    f. 1500
    g. .0034928736

21. Express the square of the following numbers as a product, then calculate the result. The first solution has been provided for you:
    a. $25^2 = 25 \times 25 = 625$
    b. $17^2 =$
    c. $(-45)^2 =$
    d. $9^3 =$
    e. $(0.5)^4 =$
    f. $(-14)^2 =$
    g. $(-2.3)^2 =$

22. Calculate the result of the following expression: $\sqrt{70} \times \sqrt{70} =$

23. Assume that you are taking a multiple choice test on a topic you do not know anything about. There are four questions, each with three answer options. What are your overall chances to get a perfect score if you guessed the answer for every single question?

24. You and your colleagues are drawing straws to determine who is to work on the boring task you all dislike. You are in a group of 7 people in total, and there are six long straws and one short one. What is your chance to draw a short straw if you are drawing your after two people already drew a long straw?

# 5 Data Entry and Data Handling

## WHAT IS THIS CHAPTER ABOUT?

Chapter 5 continues the quasi-chronological approach of following the research process by looking at the practicalities of data entry. This chapter is designed to help ensure the data you collected is processed and analysed in an objective and structured manner. We start by briefly introducing the two software packages this book covers so that you are able to use their main functions. We then explain how to validate data, identify data entry errors, and identify and treat outliers before moving on to how to prepare data for analysis by coding and recoding variables.

## WHY IS THIS IMPORTANT?

This chapter forms the link between data collection and data analysis. Decisions you make here can affect the type of analyses available to you, and with that, the type of conclusions you can draw from the data. Data handling, and particularly the identification and potential exclusion of outliers, is another aspect of avoiding bias in either direction, that is, excluding what should not be excluded or using what should not be used. This chapter also gives you the basic skills to use the two software packages we are covering (SPSS and Excel), which will help you conduct the analyses we introduce in more detail in later chapters.

## WHAT ARE THE LEARNING OUTCOMES FOR THIS CHAPTER?

At the end of this chapter you will be able to:
- Perform basic functions in Excel and SPSS
- Enter your data into the software you have chosen
- Eyeball your data to see whether data has been entered correctly
- Identify potential data entry errors and outliers
- Create new variables and recode existing ones

The process of data handling starts the moment your participant(s) complete their part, whether in the form of an online questionnaire, a paper test, a computer-based test or something else. To keep with the chronological structure of this book, this chapter follows the steps from just after data collection to just before data analysis.

1. Throughout the entire process you need to ensure safe, confidential and ethical data handling.

You then need to

2. choose suitable software for data analysis, and
3. prepare a file for data entry.

In doing so, you have to

4. check your data for data entry errors and outliers, before you can start to
5. code and/or recode your data.

The following sections will cover all of these steps in more detail.

## 5.1 SAFE, CONFIDENTIAL AND ETHICAL DATA MANAGEMENT

Data is a researcher's second most valuable asset, right after your most valuable asset which is your participant's trust and confidence in you. If your research involves human participants, these participants volunteer their time and effort in order to assist you with your research and, often, they are not adequately compensated for their participation; in some cases, you are asking participants to trust you with information that makes them potentially very vulnerable. If your data is compromised or lost, all sides lose. What does responsible data management look like? It means:

- Confidential handling of participant data
- Reasonable precautions to save and back up your data.

### 5.1.1 Confidential handling of participant data

Confidential handling of participant data does not start with data collection but begins when you communicate with participants. For example, if you use email to communicate with participants, make sure that your computer is protected by a virus scanner so as not to infect your participants' computers. If you send out emails to more than one participant, use the *Bcc* function so you do not accidentally disclose their email addresses to other parties; do not forward your participants' emails to other participants. When conducting your research offline or printing out questionnaire responses, make sure that you do not leave identifiable participant data lying around where other people might have access to it. During and after data collection, ensure confidential treatment of your participants' data by storing research data and identifying information separately.

Remember that you have to give participants the opportunity to remove their data even after participation. The best way to do that is to assign a unique ID to every participant and create a separate look-up document which matches participant ID and identifying information. Save this document in a different space and then continue working with the raw data *minus* the identifying information (see Figure 5.1).

## Excerpt of raw data, containing identifying information (name, age and gender, and the data relating to the study)

| First name | Last name | Gender Identity | Age | Answer _Q1 | Answer _Q2 |
|---|---|---|---|---|---|
| Theodore | Roosevelt | M | 61 | 5 | 3 |
| George | Washington | M | 67 | 7 | 4 |
| Barack | Obama | M | 56 | 5 | 6 |
| Hillary | Clinton | F | 70 | 6 | 6 |

This file contains identifying information, but no data relating to the study.

| Participant ID | First name | Last name | Gender Identity | Age |
|---|---|---|---|---|
| 1 | Theodore | Roosevelt | M | 61 |
| 2 | George | Washington | M | 67 |
| 3 | Barack | Obama | M | 56 |
| 4 | Hillary | Clinton | F | 70 |

This file contains only the information relating to the study, but no identifying information.

| Participant ID | Answer _Q1 | Answer _Q2 |
|---|---|---|
| 1 | 5 | 3 |
| 2 | 7 | 4 |
| 3 | 5 | 6 |
| 4 | 6 | 6 |

The two files are linked by the same unique participant ID.

*Figure 5.1* *Linking files through participant IDs*

In the example above the initial data set contained identifying information (names, age and gender) plus sensitive information such as responses to employee satisfaction or willingness to change jobs. This file was then split into two separate files. One with the information needed to select the individual data set should one of the participants ask to remove their data; and one which contains the actual data but no identifying information. You can now work with the data without knowing which individual participant each data set refers to; however, should Theodore Roosevelt approach you later to have his data deleted, you know that you have to remove the data record for participant ID 1.

### REVIEW & REFLECT

- Why is confidentiality so important?
- What would be the consequences if you could not identify (and delete) participant data if requested to do so by the participant?

### 5.1.2 Reasonable precautions to save and back up your data

We have previously mentioned that in research, data analysis can easily be biased by your assumptions and expectations. The very definition and identification of outlier data is potentially fraught with bias, and excluding data that does not conform to your expectations as to what should fall within the normal distribution from analysis can impact on the validity of your results. It is thus important to always retain a copy of the original full data set before making any changes. That way, if at some later point you consider your original assumptions to be incorrect, or decide that you needed that variable that you deleted after all, you can always go back to the original data set.

How can you save your data? Your data will come in either physical form (e.g., completed paper questionnaires, test forms) or digital form (e.g., data from online questionnaires, computer-based tests, eye-tracking data, videotapes, audio recordings, etc.). Where possible, try to transform physical data into digital data as soon as possible so you can create backup copies: If you used paper questionnaires, scan them in or take photographs with a digital camera or your mobile phone. Similarly, if you made notes on paper, scan them in or take a photo so that you still have your data even if you lose the piece of paper.[1] The best way to protect yourself from (data) loss is to:

- Make copies, for example on several different computers, a USB stick, or the Cloud. If you make several copies, do not keep the copies at the same place or in the same computer.
- Use data protection, such as virus scanners and encryption.

## 5.2  CHOOSING SUITABLE SOFTWARE: EXCEL

In this section we will give you a brief introduction to Excel. You can skip this section if you already know how to:

- Enter data
- Sort data
- Enter a function
- Copy a function to other cells
- Apply a filter

This book and the analyses described later *do not* assume or require knowledge of macros, and we generally aim to keep the Excel skills required as basic and simple as possible. The easier descriptive analyses can be conducted with the basic versions of Microsoft Excel for Mac or for Windows; to perform some of the more advanced analyses you will have to activate the *Data Analysis ToolPak* add-on. Where it is available (see below) it is included with the installation software but needs to be explicitly activated to be used from within Excel. Availability of the add-on depends on whether you work with a Mac or Windows operating system:

Mac OS

- Excel 2016: add-on is included
- Excel 2011: if you have Service Pack 1 installed, the Data Analysis ToolPak is not included. Microsoft suggests to install a third-party analysis tool such as StatPlus:mac:LE
- Excel 2008: does not include Data Analysis ToolPak. Microsoft suggests to install a third-party analysis tool such as StatPlus:mac:LE

Windows

- Data Analysis ToolPak is included in Excel, starting from version Excel 2007

---

[1] If you use your phone to take photos of confidential documents, make sure your phone is protected by a pass lock or a fingerprint scan.

The screenshots in this handbook are based on Microsoft Excel for Mac 2016. For analyses not requiring the Data Analysis ToolPak, the main functionalities described will also apply to Lotus 123, Open Office Calc or similar spreadsheet programmes, although some searching for the corresponding similar-but-not-identical-named menu items may be required.

Some of the analyses described later in the book can also be conducted with an Excel tool called Real Statistics, which is (at the point of writing) freely available. However, this tool is not officially associated with Microsoft. If you work on a computer issued by your organisation, you may not be able to install such a programme on your computer. We have therefore not included any guidance to Real Statistics in this book.

### 5.2.1 The basic setup

If we look at an open, empty Excel file, the file name is displayed at the top (1); here the name is still Workbook1 because this is a new file that has not been saved yet under a specific name. Every Excel file consists of at least one worksheet, which you can see named Sheet1 (2). You can add further data sheets by right-clicking on the name tab of any sheet and selecting Insert Sheet. Data is entered by typing directly into the cell (3) or the function bar above the spreadsheet (4). You find menu functions in the menu bar (5), and the buttons for saving the current file or opening or closing files just above that (6).

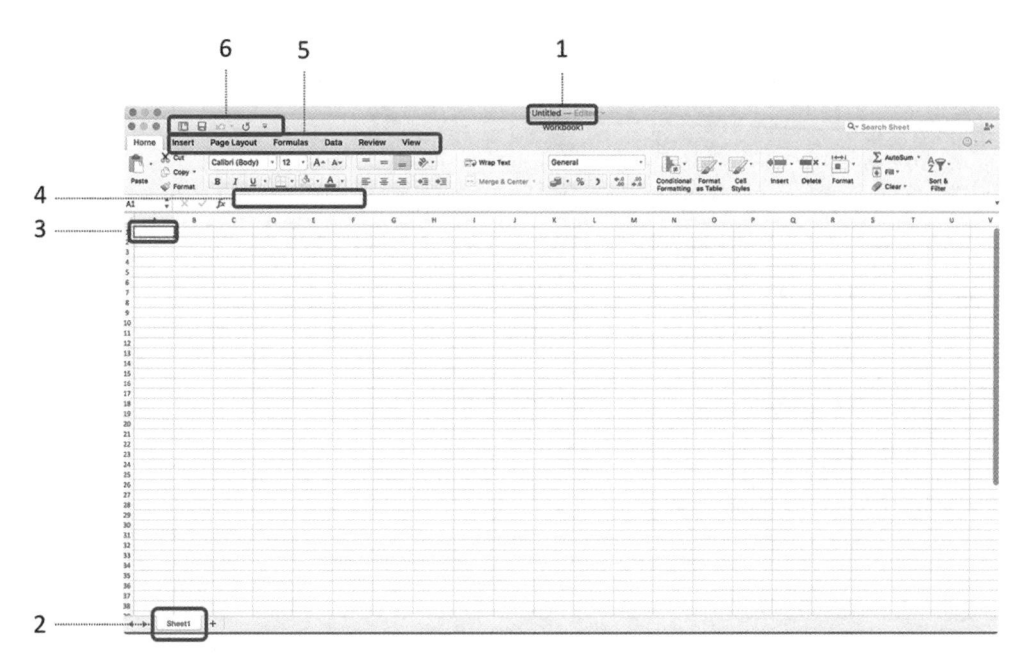

*Figure 5.2* Excel worksheet
Used with permission from Microsoft.

### 5.2.2 Entering data

Entering data into Excel can be done by typing straight into the cells or typing into the function bar (see (4) in Figure 5.2). Since Excel is a spreadsheet programme rather than a database or an analytics software, you cannot create variables as independent objects or items in Excel without using VBA (Visual Basic for Applications, a programming language). Instead you have to name the column or row that contains your data by entering the variable name into the first cell in the column or row. The combination of row and column ID is a unique ID for every individual cell. For example, cell A11 is the 11$^{th}$ cell in column A and contains participant ID '10'. You will see these references to cells when we use functions which take individual cells or cell ranges as input. To refer to a range of cells we use the colon; if we wanted to refer to the range of cells containing responses, it would look like this: B2:B11.

The picture below shows an example of the variables 'Participant ID' and 'Response' being identified as such. Note that the variable name does not change the column ID (which is still A and B, respectively) (Figures 5.3 and 5.4).

|    | A | B |
|----|---|---|
| 1  | Participant ID | Response |
| 2  | 1 | 2 |
| 3  | 2 | 3 |
| 4  | 3 | 2 |
| 5  | 4 | 3 |
| 6  | 5 | 1 |
| 7  | 6 | 2 |
| 8  | 7 | 4 |
| 9  | 8 | 3 |
| 10 | 9 | 1 |
| 11 | 10 | 2 |

*Figure 5.3* Naming variables in Excel: by column
Used with permission from Microsoft.

|   | A | B | C | D | E | F | G | H | I | J | K |
|---|---|---|---|---|---|---|---|---|---|---|---|
| 1 | Participant ID | 1 | 2 | 3 | 4 | 5 | 6 | 7 | 8 | 9 | 10 |
| 2 | Response | 2 | 3 | 2 | 3 | 1 | 2 | 4 | 3 | 1 | 2 |

*Figure 5.4* Naming variables in Excel: by row
Used with permission from Microsoft.

### 5.2.3 Sorting data

If you want to sort your data by a certain variable's values, make sure that you select the entire range of your data (you can do that by clicking on the rectangle at the top left of the worksheet, to the left of column heading 'A' and the top of cell heading '1'). Otherwise the sorting will only apply to that particular row or column, but leave the remaining data untouched, which will break up the data sets. Having selected the entire range, navigate to Data → Sort: which will open the Sort window (see Figure 5.5). In this example, we have ticked 'My list has headers' as the first cell of each column contains the variable names so Excel interprets the headings as variable names and then offers those in the Column field to pick. The Sort On field also offers options to sort by cell, font colour or cell icon; however, for the analyses and procedures described in this book, the 'values' option is the one you require. Lastly, the Order field asks you to pick the sorting order.

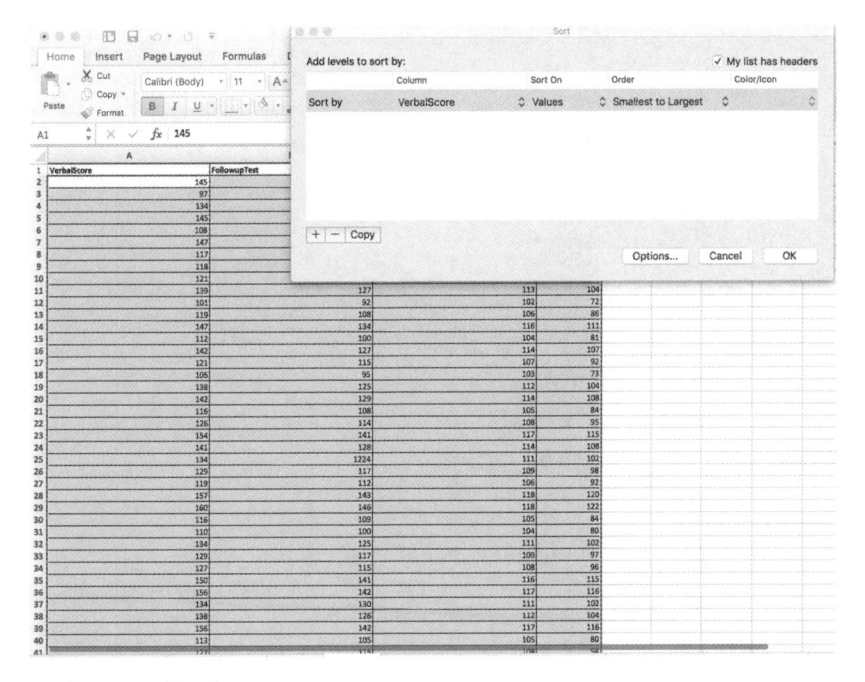

**Figure 5.5** Sorting in Excel
*Used with permission from Microsoft.*

### 5.2.4 Entering a function

There are three main ways to enter a function: entering it manually; through the function bar; or through the function window. To enter a function manually, first select the cell in which you would like the result of the function to appear. While typing in the formula, Excel will search for existing functions and offer to autocomplete your entry, but you do not have to select anything. In the image below you can also see that Excel highlights the cell you are referring to so you can visually confirm that you are referring to the right cells. Remember to hit 'Enter' once you completed typing in the formula (Figure 5.6).

**Figure 5.6** Entering a function manually
*Used with permission from Microsoft.*

Alternatively, you can use the formula builder, first selecting the cell you want the result to appear in and then navigating to Insert → Function .... This will open the Formula Builder window (Figure 5.7):

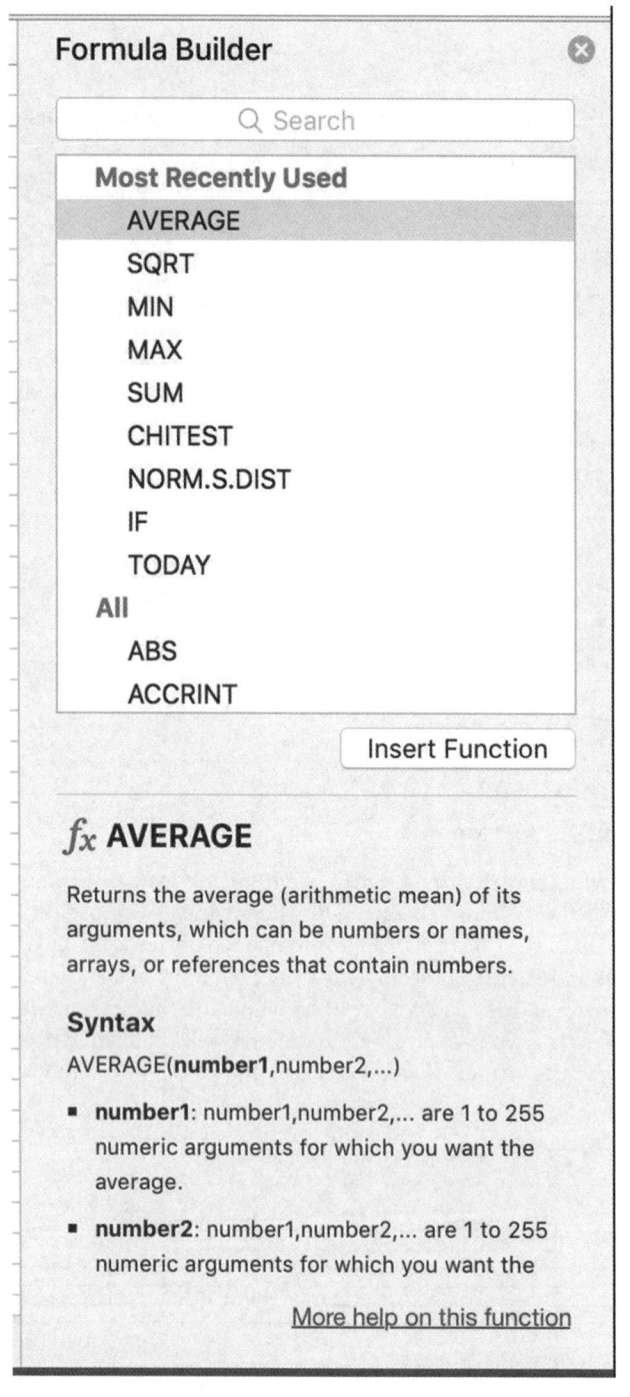

**Figure 5.7** *Formula Builder window in Excel*
Used with permission from Microsoft.

You can search for functions in the Search field. Double-click on the function you want to use and a window opens that lets you enter the required parameters for a function into separate fields (Figure 5.8):

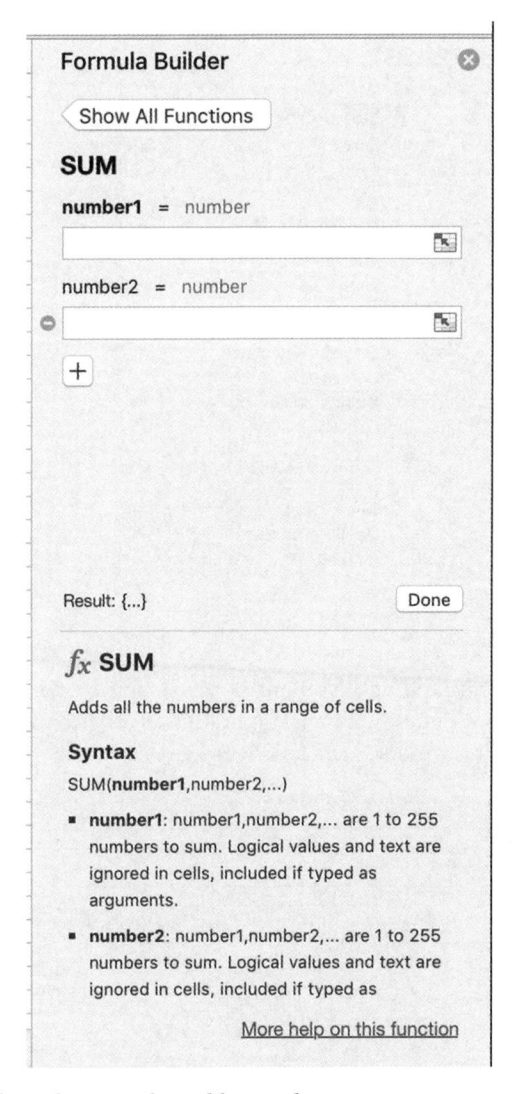

**Figure 5.8** *Sum formula in the Formula Builder window*
Used with permission from Microsoft.

You can then enter either numbers or cell ranges into the individual fields; you can add new fields by clicking on the plus sign. Click Done when the formula is completed.

### 5.2.5 Copying a function to other cells

If you want to copy the content of a cell to another cell, you can use the standard copy and paste function of the operating system you are using (ctrl or apple key + c or v, respectively). Alternatively, if the cell you are copying from is adjacent to the cell you are copying to, you can move the cursor near the bottom right of the cell until a plus sign appears; click on the plus sign and, keeping the mouse button pressed, expand the marked area to cover the cells you want to copy the content to.

126  *Introducing Quantitative Methods*

### 5.2.6   Applying a filter

To apply a filter, select the column which contains the data on the basis of which you want to filter and make sure the entire column is highlighted. Navigate to Data and click once on Filter so that it appears ticked (Figure 5.9):

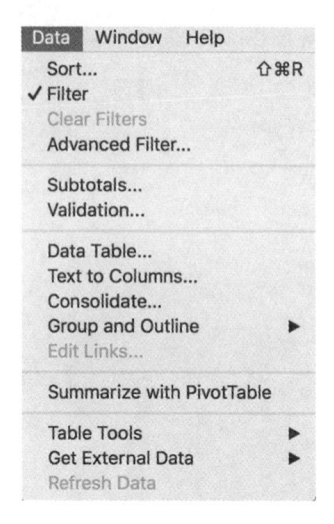

**Figure 5.9**  Data menu in Excel
*Used with permission from Microsoft.*

When you have done this and until you untick this line, the column you selected will now have a small triangle to the right of its name, indicating that its content can be filtered. If you click on that triangle, a filter window appears (Figure 5.10):

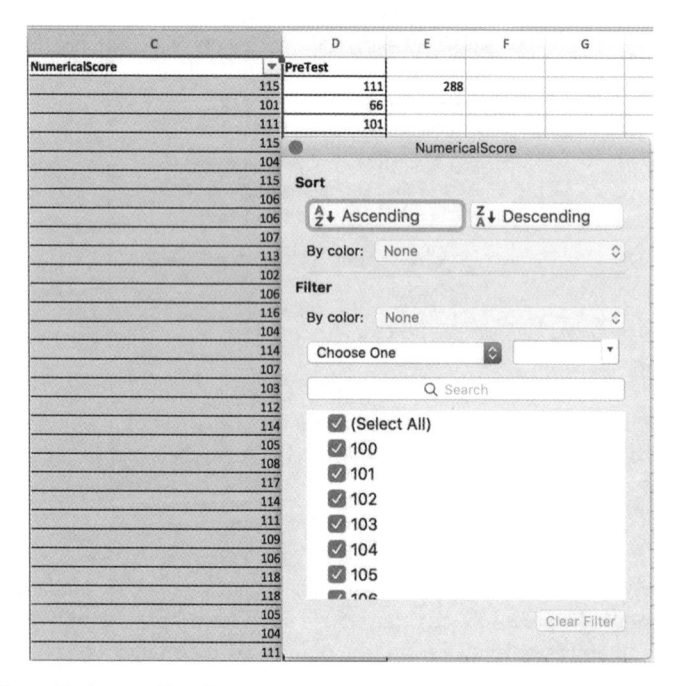

**Figure 5.10**  Filter window in Excel
*Used with permission from Microsoft.*

In this window you can sort by the variable you have selected. You can also filter data records by selecting and de-selecting values in the bottom field. Currently all values are displayed. If you unclick 100, for example, cells in the NumericalScore column which contain a value of 100 will not be displayed. Lastly, if you click on Choose One, you can specify your filter in much more precision by indicating that you only want cells displayed where the content equals a certain value or is greater than/less than a given value, etc. (Figure 5.11).

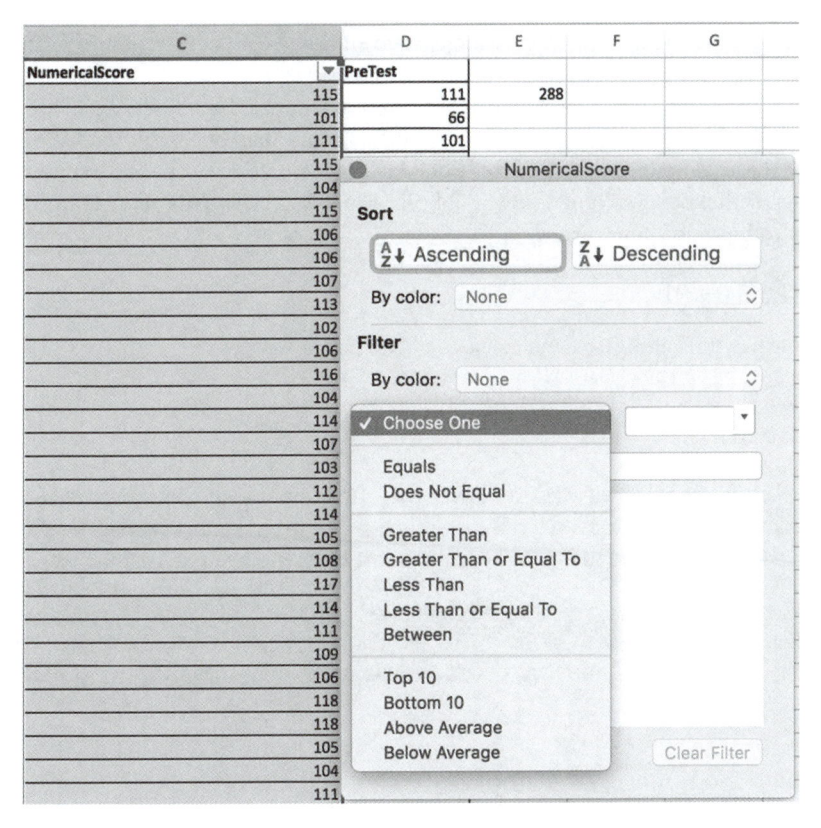

**Figure 5.11** *Filter pick list*
*Used with permission from Microsoft.*

## 5.3 CHOOSING SUITABLE SOFTWARE: SPSS

If you are a student at a university, chances are you will be able to acquire an SPSS license through your IT department. The software itself is available on the Internet with a 30-day free trial; after that a license key is required to keep the software operating.

The scope of this handbook does not allow a comprehensive introduction to SPSS (and the rapid life cycle of versions makes it difficult to recommend specific books rather than series or authors). Hence this section will give you a brief introduction to SPSS; you can find more detailed guidance available in, for example, *SPSS for Psychologists* by Brace et al. (2016). You can skip this section if you:

- Understand the basic structure of SPSS's data, output and syntax windows and know how to switch between them

128  *Introducing Quantitative Methods*

- Know how to:
  - Enter data in the Data view
  - Define variables in the Variable view
  - Name and label variables
  - Access functions from the menus
  - Access output in the output window.

SPSS guidance and screenshots in this book are from the latest (at the point of writing) SPSS version 25.

Since SPSS was created and developed for different purposes, the setup is distinctly different. In Excel, it is possible to enter data, analyse and display data all in one single worksheet whereas SPSS splits these components up into three files: a data file, an output file and a syntax file, with the data file further being split up into Variable view and Data view. **This also means that every file needs to be saved separately!**

### 5.3.1 The data file

The *data file* has the ending *.sav* and consists of two parts:

- Data view
- Variable view

Data is displayed in the Data view (1), see Figure 5.12. Column headers show the variable names (2) and the yellow shading indicates the cell currently selected (3). You can sort data by simply right-clicking on the variable name and then choosing to sort in ascending or descending order.

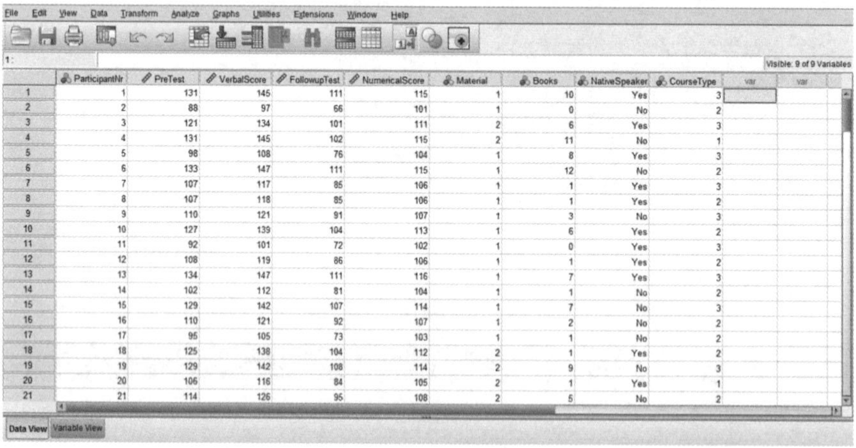

*Figure 5.12  SPSS Data view*
Reprint Courtesy of International Business Machines Corporation, © International Business Machines Corporation.

Variables are defined in the Variable view (4) (see Figure 5.13), including variable name (5) and type (6) and to how many decimal points they are measured (7). You can add additional explanation for the variable into the Label field (8). A separate field Measure (9) defines the type of measure limiting the analyses available for this variable as either scale, ordinal or nominal; here scale means either interval or ratio.

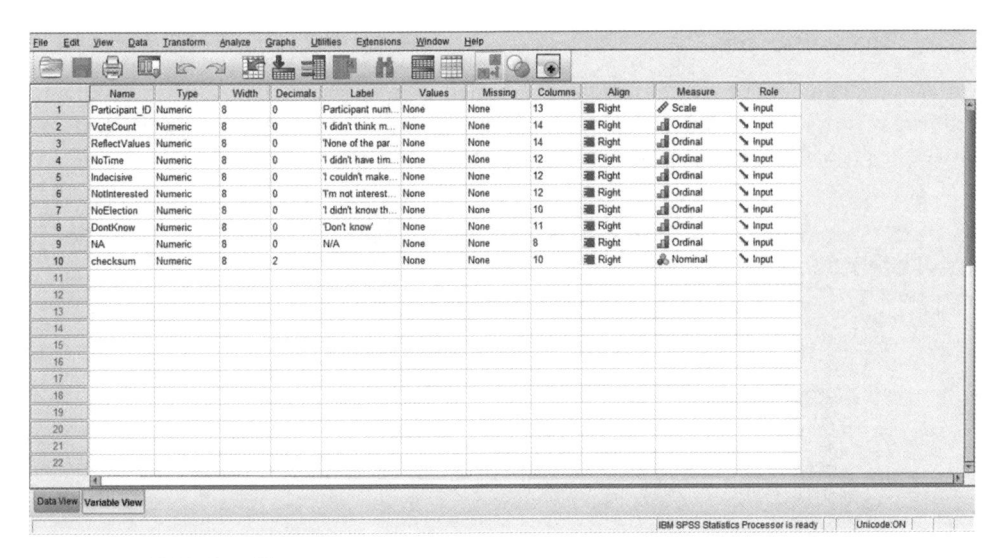

*Figure 5.13* SPSS Variable view

*Reprint Courtesy of International Business Machines Corporation, © International Business Machines Corporation.*

You can either enter your data directly into the data file or import your data from other sources. If you go to File → Import Data, you will see that SPSS offers a range of importing options. Click on the format for the file you want to import and SPSS will guide you through the remainder of the importing process (Figure 5.14).

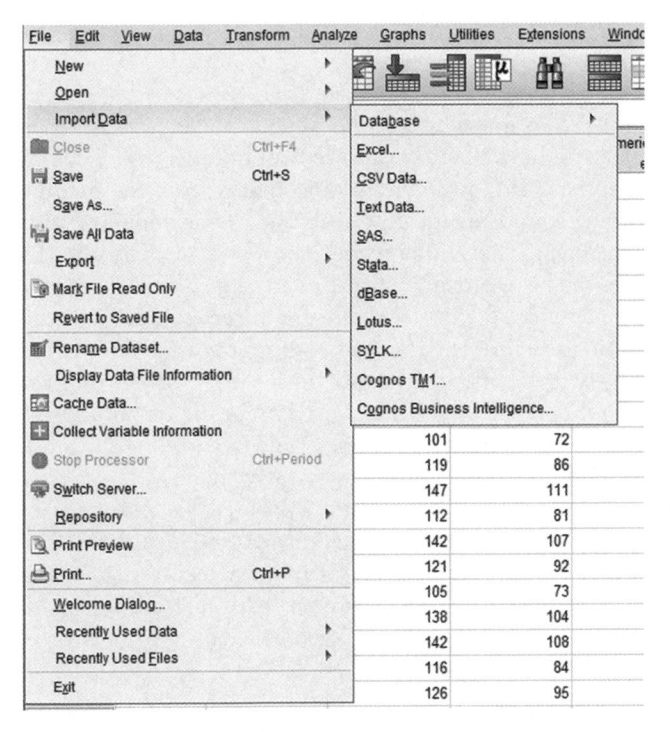

*Figure 5.14* Importing data into SPSS

*Reprint Courtesy of International Business Machines Corporation, © International Business Machines Corporation.*

## 5.3.2 The syntax file

Analyses are run either by navigating through menus or by giving SPSS explicit commands conforming to a set structure, the SPSS syntax. This syntax is saved in a different file, the *syntax file* (see Figure 5.15). Syntax files end with *.sps*.

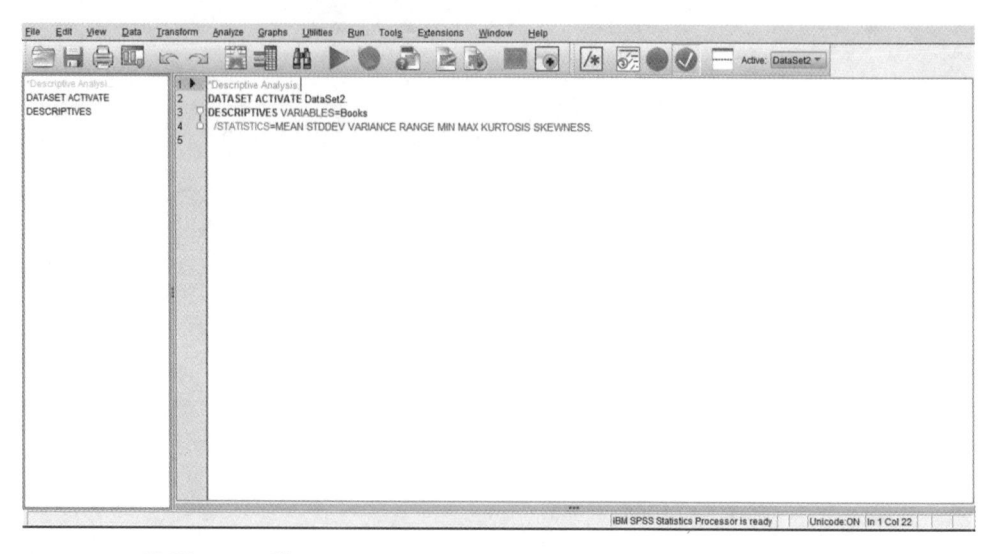

**Figure 5.15** SPSS syntax file
Reprint Courtesy of International Business Machines Corporation, © International Business Machines Corporation.

The results will be the same whether the same analysis is run through a menu or by using SPSS syntax; in addition, before running any analysis from a menu, there is always an option to 'paste' (i.e., saving the underlying syntax from the menu command to the syntax file). This may sound technical, but it has an enormous advantage that cannot be stressed enough. Saving the syntax from the conducted analyses (10) means that the exact same analyses can be run again on a different (e.g., larger or smaller) data set at any later point of time. Combined with the ability to insert comments into the syntax (11) file simply by starting the line with '\*' and ending it with a '.' – without the quotation marks – makes this extremely powerful. You can see in the screenshot that comments are displayed in a different colour to set them apart from the remaining syntax. Comments can range from 'Here I'm checking whether X and Y correlate' to longer text passages detailing possible data interpretations. Particularly when working on a longer piece of work where years can pass between the initial data analysis and the eventual writing up, comments on what you did to the data and why can be invaluable! Documenting your analyses this way and adding comments on why variables were calculated in a particular way, or analyses conducted in a specific manner helps developing an audit trail on your methodology.

## 5.3.3 The output file

Regardless of whether we use syntax or navigate through menus to tell SPSS what to do, the output is displayed in a different file, the *output file*. Output files end with *.spv*.

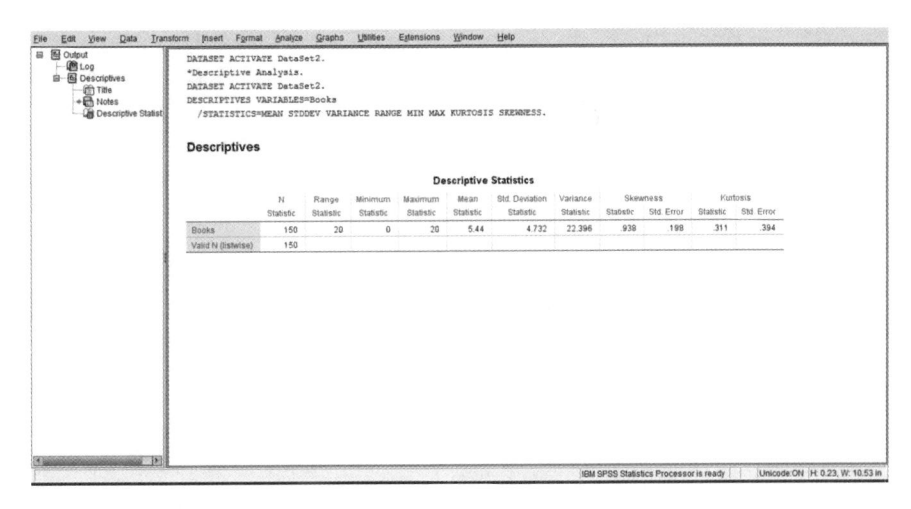

***Figure 5.16*** *SPSS output file*
Reprint Courtesy of International Business Machines Corporation, © International Business Machines Corporation.

The navigation pane on the left (12) helps navigating to individual entries. The output always is preceded by the syntax used to define the analyses (14) before the result is displayed (15). In this example, comments had been added to the syntax file (Figure 5.16) and these comments are displayed in the output file too, preceded by the asterisk to mark them as comments (13).

### 5.3.4 Naming and labelling a variable

Note that in SPSS you have the option to provide two names: a *variable name* and a *label*:

- The *variable name* can be up to 64 characters long, has to start with a letter, may not include any spaces and can contain only one of four special characters ($, #, _ or @).
- The *label* can be up to 256 characters long, may include spaces and can include a wider range of characters.

The label can be incredibly useful for documenting and commenting on your data because it allows you to explain what a variable describes.

In the following example our SPSS file contains a variable named 'CourseType'. You can enter the description of what the variable refers to in the Label field in the Variable view (item 8 in Figure 5.13). In this example, we have added the description 'Whether the old or new set of material was used'. If we now change back to the Data view and mouse over the variable name, a short description of the variable appears, which includes its name and its label but also type and measure (Figure 5.17):

***Figure 5.17*** *Variable name mouse over information*
Reprint Courtesy of International Business Machines Corporation, © International Business Machines Corporation.

132  *Introducing Quantitative Methods*

If you are setting up new analyses, the lists and output will now show the label rather than the name; you can change this by going to Edit → Options. In the General tab there is a section called Variable lists in the top left where you can select either 'Display labels' or 'Display names' (Figure 5.18).

**➔ Frequencies**

**Statistics**

Whether the old or new set of material was used

| N | Valid | 150 |
|---|---|---|
|  | Missing | 0 |

**Whether the old or new set of material was used**

|  |  | Frequency | Percent | Valid Percent | Cumulative Percent |
|---|---|---|---|---|---|
| Valid | 1 | 75 | 50.0 | 50.0 | 50.0 |
|  | 2 | 75 | 50.0 | 50.0 | 100.0 |
|  | Total | 150 | 100.0 | 100.0 |  |

***Figure 5.18*** *Variable label in output file*
*Reprint Courtesy of International Business Machines Corporation, © International Business Machines Corporation.*

### 5.3.5 Naming and labelling variable values

Just as you can enter labels for variables to make the data easier to read and understand in SPSS, you can enter labels for data values, too. Consider an example where participants are asked to indicate their agreement on a four-point scale from '1 = Disagree Strongly' to '4 = Agree Strongly'. You would then enter the values 1 to 4 in your data file but that means, of course, that when looking at your data all you see is 1s, 2s, and so on. SPSS allows you to add labels to these values so that instead of seeing values from 1 to 4 you can see what the actual responses were. To do so, go into the Variable view and click onto the Value field for the variable whose labels you want to change. In the window that opens, enter the value into the Value field, the associated label in the Label field below, then click Add. Repeat for all available values (Figure 5.19).

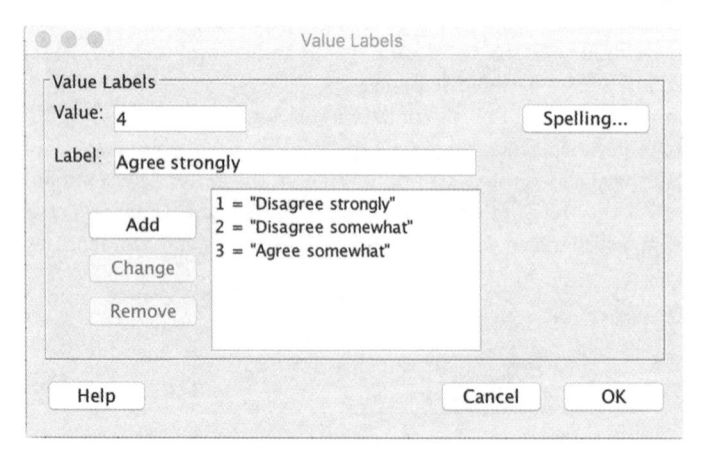

***Figure 5.19*** *SPSS Value Labels window*
*Reprint Courtesy of International Business Machines Corporation, © International Business Machines Corporation.*

Once you have done this, you can switch views by going to the menu View and ticking the option Value Labels. If Value Labels is ticked (✓), you will see the labels (e.g., 'disagree strongly'); if it is not ticked, you will see the values (e.g., '1').

### 5.3.6 Applying a filter

To apply a filter, go to Data → Select Cases (it is the second to last option in a very long list). This opens the Select Cases window (Figure 5.20):

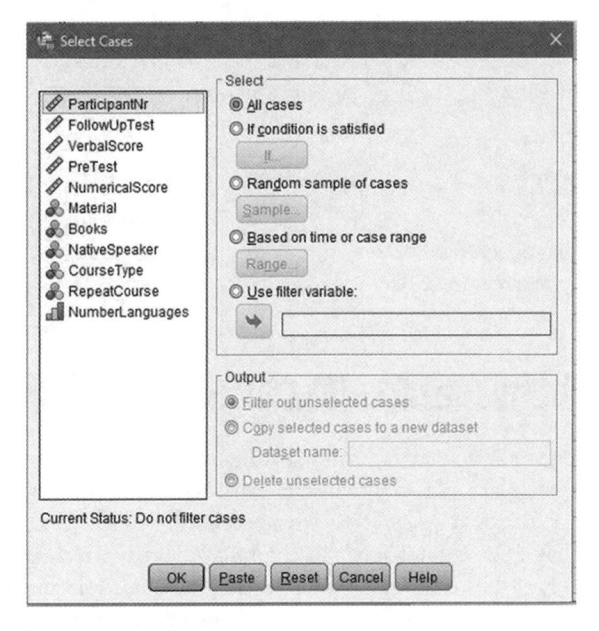

***Figure 5.20*** *SPSS Select Cases window*
Reprint Courtesy of International Business Machines Corporation, © International Business Machines Corporation.

You can see that SPSS offers a range of different filter options. The one you will be most likely using in the procedures described in this book is the first filter, 'If condition is satisfied'. If you select this option, you can then define the condition and the variable it should apply to. Click on If ... which opens a new window (Figure 5.21):

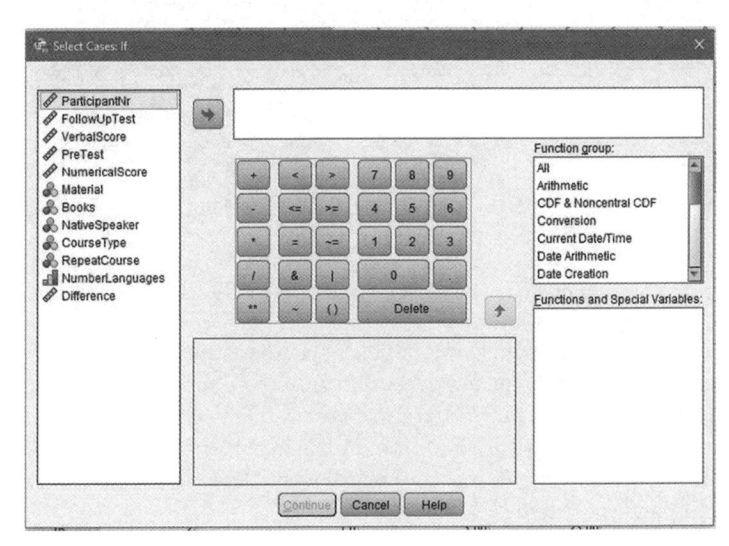

***Figure 5.21*** *SPSS 'Select Cases: if' window*
Reprint Courtesy of International Business Machines Corporation, © International Business Machines Corporation.

Here you can either move the selection variable (in this case, 'Material') to the right field via the arrow or type it in directly. 'Material = 1' means that only the cases where the value for 'Material' equals 1 are selected. After clicking Continue and then clicking OK, SPSS applies the filter to the data. If you look at the Data view again, a new column called *filter_$* has appeared, and the row number of data sets where 'Material' equals 2 is crossed out. This will remain in place for any further data display and analyses until the filter is removed by entering the Data → Select Cases menu and selecting the All Cases option again.

> **REVIEW & REFLECT**
>
> - What are the main differences between SPSS and Excel?
> - Is it fair to even compare the two?

## 5.4 PREPARING A FILE FOR DATA ENTRY

If you have to manually enter your data, whether from a sheet of paper or a questionnaire, it is important not to lose your place and know which data set belongs to which questionnaire because once you have identified a mistake you will have to go back and check what the original value was – but you can only do that if you can reliably and accurately identify which data set contained the mistake. The easiest way to do so is to number your data sets or questionnaires before you begin data entry and then keep track with a variable 'Questionnaire ID'. For example, while eyeballing the data below, you have noticed that the salary for participant 4 looks very different from the other salaries. You wonder whether perhaps you entered this with one zero less than it should have been so you want to go back and check the participant's answer on the original questionnaire. Because you numbered the questionnaires and kept track of which questionnaire belonged to which participant, you now know that you have to check questionnaire number 25 (Figure 5.22).

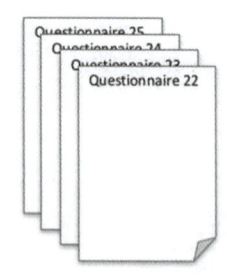

| Participant ID | Questionnaire ID | Annual Salary | Job Satisfaction |
|---|---|---|---|
| 1 | 22 | 45.000 | 8 |
| 2 | 23 | 65.000 | 5 |
| 3 | 24 | 80.000 | 7 |
| 4 | 25 | 5.500 | 6 |

*Figure 5.22* Using questionnaire IDs

Regardless of whether you import your data from a different source, such as from an online survey, or enter it straight from a (paper) questionnaire, before you can start analysing your data you need to bring it into a form in which it can be easily handled and examined. Keep in mind that you will often have to select variables from pick lists in menu tabs and that you might not see the full name in those fields. To make it easier for you, label your data clearly by keeping it informative, short and consistent.

**Informative:** Where you can, use the actual variable name. For example, when you look at the impact of introversion on self-esteem, use variable names such as 'motivation', 'attitude_total',

'Job-Satisfaction subtotal Section 1', etc. rather than 'Answer to Q1'. Informative also means sensibly recording conditions and levels of variables. For example, if you collect job satisfaction data three times (once at the start to establish a baseline, at the end of the intervention period, and half a year after the last intervention) make sure your variable names reflect the individual levels: You could name your job satisfaction variables 'js_before', 'js_after', 'js_after6mo'; alternatively, you can count in months since beginning the study so that your variables would be 'js_1', 'js_5', 'js_11', etc.

**Short:** Shorter names are better because they help you pick variables from lists faster and more accurately.

**Consistent:** For the same reason, make sure that you apply labels in consistent style. If three variables are named 'Something1', 'Something 2' and 'Something3', the second variable will appear first in the list because of the space between 'Something' and '2'.

## 5.5 ENTERING DATA

In Chapter 3 we looked at the following ways of asking questions and eliciting data:

- Open questions/sentence completion
- Single choice questions
- Multiple choice questions
- Ordering/ranking questions
- Pairwise comparison
- Rating scales and semantic differentials

The following sections will be looking at how to enter data elicited through these methods.

### 5.5.1 Data from open questions/sentence completion

Sample prompt:

> 'What I'm most looking for in a new car is _____.'

Sample individual response:

> 'What I'm most looking for in a new car is <u>low fuel consumption</u>.'

Sample data after data entry:

| Participant ID | Response |
| --- | --- |
| 1 | low price |
| 2 | low fuel consumption |
| 3 | best value for money |
| 4 | driving experience |
| 5 | vroom! |
| 6 | safety features |
| 7 | that it's cheap to maintain |
| 8 | that it gets good reviews |
| 9 | I can afford it |
| 10 | that it drives well |

**EXCEL**
- Enter the names of the variables in the first cell of the respective column, then enter the text as it is.
- If the text is too long for the width of the column, click Wrap Text so that the text is adjusted to the width of the column rather than running on and over the cell boundary.

**www ONLINE CONTENT**

You can find a sample Excel file with this data on the companion website.

**SPSS**
- Create a variable for the participant ID. Type is *Numeric*, and the Measure is *Nominal*.[2] Since the participant ID is counting up participants in increments of 1, you can set the Decimals to 0.
- Create a variable for the response. Type is *String*, and the Measure is *Nominal*.

**www ONLINE CONTENT**

You can find a sample SPSS file with this data on the companion website.

### 5.5.2 Data from single choice questions

Sample prompt:

> If you didn't vote in the last election please indicate below why (please select your main reason):

Sample response:

|     |                                            |
| --- | ------------------------------------------ |
| ☐   | I didn't think my vote would count         |
| [x] | None of the parties reflected my own values |
| ☐   | I didn't have time to vote                 |
| ☐   | I couldn't make up my mind                 |
| ☐   | I'm not interested in politics             |
| ☐   | I didn't know there was an election        |
| ☐   | Don't know                                 |
| ☐   | N/A                                        |

To record which option each participant chose, you have a few options. One option is to record it as a binary choice (yes/no) where for each answer option you record whether the participant

---

[2] This may seem counterintuitive, but the participant ID is purely a label and nothing which should be used in any calculations or analyses.

chose it or not; another option would be to record for each question only the answer the participant did select. Although they collect the same data the approaches differ slightly in the emphasis they put on the data: the former is equally interested in all options and you want to record whether they have been selected or not; the latter puts more emphasis on finding out which option is selected most frequently. Both options are demonstrated below.

### 5.5.2.1 Recording selection for each response

Sample data after data entry (Table 5.1):

*Table 5.1 Recording selection for each response*

| Participant ID | Vote Count | Reflect Values | No Time | Indecisive | Not Interested | No Election | Don't Know | N/A |
|---|---|---|---|---|---|---|---|---|
| 1 | 1 | 0 | 0 | 0 | 0 | 0 | 0 | 0 |
| 2 | 0 | 1 | 0 | 0 | 0 | 0 | 0 | 0 |
| 3 | 0 | 0 | 0 | 0 | 0 | 0 | 0 | 1 |
| 4 | 1 | 0 | 0 | 0 | 0 | 0 | 0 | 0 |
| 5 | 0 | 0 | 0 | 0 | 0 | 0 | 1 | 0 |
| 6 | 0 | 0 | 0 | 1 | 0 | 0 | 0 | 0 |
| 7 | 0 | 0 | 0 | 0 | 1 | 0 | 0 | 0 |
| 8 | 1 | 0 | 0 | 0 | 0 | 0 | 0 | 0 |
| 9 | 0 | 0 | 0 | 0 | 0 | 1 | 0 | 0 |
| 10 | 1 | 0 | 0 | 0 | 0 | 0 | 0 | 0 |

**EXCEL** To enter data into Excel, use a column for each possible response, including 'Don't know' and 'No response'. Record a 1 for the answer that was chosen, and 0 for the responses that were not selected.

**www ONLINE CONTENT**

You can find an Excel file with this sample data on the companion website.

**SPSS**
- Create a variable for the participant ID. Type is *Numeric*, and the Measure is *Nominal*. Since the participant ID is counting up participants in increments of 1, you can set the Decimals to 0.
- Create variables to record the selection for each possible response. The Type is *Numeric*, and the Measure is *Nominal*.

**www ONLINE CONTENT**

You can find an SPSS file with this sample data on the companion website.

### 5.5.2.2 Recording only selected response

Sample data after data entry:

*Table 5.2 Recording only selected response*

| Participant ID | Reason |
|---|---|
| 1 | 1 |
| 2 | 2 |
| 3 | 8 |
| 4 | 1 |
| 5 | 7 |
| 6 | 4 |
| 7 | 5 |
| 8 | 1 |
| 9 | 6 |
| 10 | 1 |

**EXCEL** To enter data into Excel, use one single column to track participant ID and one column to enter the data. You can either use a numerical code for each answer (as we have done in Table 5.2) or type out the answer option itself. If you chose the latter, keep in mind that any manual entry carries with it the risk of typos and mistakes, and the more you have to type, the higher the risk. Try to use autocomplete, where applicable, to cut down on the risk of typos, and make sure that you have recorded which code means which in an accessible place for you to look up.

**www ONLINE CONTENT**

You can find an Excel file with this sample data on the companion website.

**SPSS**
- Create a variable for the participant ID. Type is *Numeric*, and the Measure is *Nominal*.
- Create a variable to record the response. The Type is *String*, and the Measure is *Nominal*. Change Width to the number of characters you think you might need.
- Remember that you can use variable value labels to have the Data view display the actual responses instead of the numerical codes allocated to each answer (see Section 5.3.4).

**www ONLINE CONTENT**

You can find an SPSS file with this sample data on the companion website.

### 5.5.3 Data from multiple choice questions

Sample prompt:

If you applied for a job in the last six months, please indicate which criteria you used to select the positions you applied for (tick all that apply):

Sample response:

| [ ] | Geographical location |
| [x] | Salary |
| [ ] | Job description |
| [x] | Employer reputation |
| [ ] | Investor in People accreditation |

Sample data after data entry (Table 5.3):

*Table 5.3 Recording data from multiple choice questions*

| Participant ID | Geographical location | Salary | Job description | Employer reputation | IiP accreditation |
|---|---|---|---|---|---|
| 1 | 0 | 1 | 0 | 1 | 0 |
| 2 | 1 | 1 | 1 | 0 | 0 |
| 3 | 0 | 1 | 1 | 0 | 0 |
| 4 | 1 | 1 | 1 | 0 | 1 |
| 5 | 1 | 1 | 1 | 0 | 1 |
| 6 | 0 | 1 | 1 | 1 | 1 |
| 7 | 0 | 0 | 1 | 0 | 1 |
| 8 | 0 | 1 | 0 | 0 | 1 |
| 9 | 1 | 0 | 1 | 1 | 1 |
| 10 | 0 | 1 | 0 | 0 | 1 |

**EXCEL** To enter data into Excel, use a column for each possible response, including 'Don't know' and 'No response'. Record 1 for each response which was chosen, and choose 0 for each response which was not selected.

**www ONLINE CONTENT**

You can find an Excel file with this sample data on the companion website.

**SPSS**
- Create a variable for the participant ID. Type is Numeric, and Measure is Nominal..
- Create variables to record the selection for each possible response. The Type is Numeric, and the Measure is Nominal. Record 1 for each response which was chosen, and record 0 for each response which was not selected.

## ONLINE CONTENT

You can find an SPSS file with this sample data on the companion website.

### 5.5.4 Data from ordering/ranking tasks

Sample prompt:

Thinking about the five candidates whose CVs you have just read, please rank them from least qualified to most qualified for the job role:

Sample response:

| Rank (1 = Most qualified, 5 = Least qualified) | |
|---|---|
| 1 | Candidate ____4____ |
| 2 | Candidate ____3____ |
| 3 | Candidate ____5____ |
| 4 | Candidate ____1____ |
| 5 | Candidate ____2____ |

*Table 5.4 Recording data from ordering/ranking tasks*

| Participant ID | Candidate 1 | Candidate 2 | Candidate 3 | Candidate 4 | Candidate 5 |
|---|---|---|---|---|---|
| 1 | 4 | 5 | 2 | 1 | 3 |
| 2 | 1 | 2 | 3 | 4 | 5 |
| 3 | 5 | 3 | 2 | 1 | 4 |
| 4 | 2 | 1 | 3 | 4 | 5 |
| 5 | 5 | 2 | 1 | 3 | 4 |
| 6 | 2 | 3 | 1 | 5 | 4 |
| 7 | 1 | 4 | 5 | 3 | 2 |
| 8 | 3 | 4 | 2 | 5 | 1 |
| 9 | 5 | 4 | 3 | 2 | 1 |
| 10 | 2 | 3 | 4 | 1 | 5 |

Sample data after data entry (Table 5.4):

**EXCEL** To enter data into Excel, use a column for each ranked item and record the rank the participant allocated.

## ONLINE CONTENT

You can find an Excel file with this sample data on the companion website.

> **SPSS**
> - Create a variable for the participant ID. <u>Type</u> is *Numeric*, and <u>Measure</u> is *Nominal*.
> - Create variables to record the rank for each item. The <u>Type</u> is *Numeric*, and the <u>Measure</u> is *Ordinal*. For each item, record the rank it was allocated.

> **ONLINE CONTENT**
>
> You can find an SPSS file with this sample data on the companion website.

### 5.5.5 Data from rating scales and semantic differentials

Sample prompt:

> To what extent do you agree or disagree with the statement:
> "I'm willing to take risks and try new things"?

Sample response:

| ☐ | ☐ | [x] | ☐ |
|---|---|---|---|
| Disagree strongly | Disagree somewhat | Agree somewhat | Agree strongly |

Sample data after data entry:

| Participant ID | Willingness_risk |
|---|---|
| 1 | 2 |
| 2 | 4 |
| 3 | 2 |
| 4 | 3 |
| 5 | 3 |
| 6 | 1 |
| 7 | 3 |
| 8 | 2 |
| 9 | 2 |
| 10 | 4 |

*Data from a simple rating question*

> **EXCEL** To enter data into Excel, use a column for each ranked item and record the rank the participant allocated.

> **ONLINE CONTENT**
>
> You can find an Excel file with this sample data on the companion website.

> **SPSS**
> - Create a variable for the participant ID. <u>Type</u> is *Numeric*, and <u>Measure</u> is *Nominal*.
> - Create a variable to record the rating. The <u>Type</u> is *Numeric*, and the <u>Measure</u> is *Scale*. For each item, record the value given.
> - In this example, participants were presented with labels for the different values. Use variable labels (see Section 5.3.4) to see the labels displayed in your <u>Data</u> view.

> **ONLINE CONTENT**
>
> You can find an SPSS file with this sample data on the companion website.

> **REVIEW & REFLECT**
> - Why and how are data collection and data entry linked?
> - Which precautions should you take when handling data?

## 5.6 CHECK FOR DATA ENTRY ERRORS AND OUTLIERS

When you are checking your data before conducting your analysis, you are looking for three main sources of error:

1. Data that might have been entered incorrectly, ranging from typos to more severe data entry errors such as shifting of cells or columns.
2. Data which might indicate participants did not answer truthfully, carefully or in the spirit of the study.
3. Issues with the tool or the data collection process.

How do you know which is which? As with many things, there is no clear-cut answer; however, as a rule of thumb, irregularities across participants tend to suggest that there is a systemic issue, whether with data collection or data entry. Some of these irregularities you may be able to correct; others may mean that you decide to exclude the data from the analysis. But do exercise caution! None of the checks and questions listed below are failsafe. The decision to exclude data should never be taken lightly, because it can introduce or reinforce bias into your data and subsequent analysis. If you do decide to exclude data, whether individual participants or entire variables, it is important that you report this in your data analysis section (see Chapter 9). One possible way to reduce the number of potential issues and irregularities is to employ validation rules, where they are allowed, by electronic tools. Some allow you to define the range of valid answers for a question (e.g., age data only in a range from 18 to 120, answers between 1 and 6, and so on). This is helpful for rating scales or multiple choice questions, but it does not work for questions where you cannot confidently predict the range of possible answers in advance. Neither does it help you to avoid errors when transferring data from a paper questionnaire to an electronic version, although it will avoid very basic data entry problems by restricting entry to data of, for example, only numerical or text type.

These caveats in place, here are a few things that can indicate potential problems. You will see that we have also included suggestions to check basic descriptives when trying to discover possible data entry errors or outliers (to see how you can conduct those basic descriptive analyses, look at Chapter 6).

- Values are dramatically different from the rest
- Similar questions yield very different answers
- Answers to questions are too similar
- Range or mean are implausible
- Answers do not make sense or are not internally consistent
- Recorded times are too short or too long
- Participant answers indicate that they did not participate in a constructive or truthful way
- Last, but not least: simple typing errors.

**Values are dramatically different from the rest:** Before conducting any detailed data analysis, perform a quick check on the data to examine it for extreme values within the distribution. A frequencies analysis (see Section 6.1) can highlight values that occur only once. Are these values plausible? For example, extreme values in salary are more plausible than extreme values in age, particularly when the age indicates the participant should either not be literate yet (e.g., '3 years') or no longer capable of participating (e.g., '180'). Other variables are much more challenging to evaluate, such as reaction times or salary. One or two very extreme values may be treated as outliers and removed from the data; this should be recorded and explained in the data analysis section in the results. However, several outliers in otherwise unsuspicious data sets may mean that your initial assumptions concerning the data and its distribution were incorrect. The plausibility of an outlier also depends very much on the sample. A sample drawn randomly from a very diverse population will more likely show outliers than a sample drawn from a very homogenous population (i.e., a population with participants of the same class/age/ethnicity, etc.).

**Similar questions yield very different answers:** Rarely will you use two questions which ask the same exact thing because if you did, you would really only need one of the two. But broadly you expect answers to similar questions to be somewhat similar. For example, agreement with the statement 'I enjoy being busy' should go along with (some) disagreement with the statement 'I enjoy doing nothing'; similarly, you would not normally expect a participant to indicate that they are fairly happy with their life at the moment while simultaneously indicating that they would like to dramatically change their life or that they are, on the whole, very stressed. If you find that several participants have given opposing answers to the two questions, you need to check that you answered or coded the answers correctly. Maybe one of the questions was reverse-coded to check that participants read the questions and paid attention and you failed to take this into account when entering the data? That all said, this is no fool-proof strategy. We have stressed several times before that you need to be careful not to introduce your own bias into the data. What you consider mismatching answers could be an expression of your own bias and not a mistake on your participant's side. There may well be a context where what looks like a contradiction just reflects different interpretations or poorly worded questions: a participant may reasonably feel that they enjoy being busy when they are at work and doing nothing when they are at home.

**Answers to questions are too similar:** A series of identical answers to successive questions could indicate that the participant did not read the question but just chose the first, last or middle answer every time (see also **central-tendency bias** in the Glossary). If the data includes time taken to complete the questionnaire, this allows a cross-check: very short durations make it more likely the participant was not thinking about the answer. Consider including check items that reverse the scale or are phrased in a different direction; participants who do not read the items will tend to answer the same for all responses and should show a very different answer here than the other participants.

**Range or mean are implausible:** Look at the basic descriptives for your data (see Chapter 6). If your answer options for a question only range from 1 to 6, then the minimum value should not be below 1, the maximum value not above 6. If the descriptives show a maximum value of 7, this tells you that there is at least one inaccurate value in your data set. Similarly, a mean below the minimum or above the maximum value of your defined answers tells you something is wrong: if your options only ranged from 1 to 6, the mean should be greater than or equal to 1 and less than or equal to 6. An implausibly high mean could be caused, for example, when entering 16 into one field rather than 1 in one and 6 into the next. For example, consider the following description from a study by Lazar et al. (2007) which sought to establish what problems blind users encountered when using screen readers to access the Internet. As part of that study participants were asked how much time they lost when encountering technical problems. In their methodology section, Lazar et al. discuss in detail which data sets they excluded and why:

> The time data from only 90 users were included, as 10 users indicated that they wasted more than 100% of time. It is theoretically possible to lose more than 100% of the reported time spent during the session. For instance, in an extreme example, if you spent 2 hr on the computer and your hard drive crashed, you would have lost more than 100 hr of work. This is obviously an extreme example, and nothing like this occurred within the current study. However, it is possible that someone spent 3 hr on the computer but, due to a crash, lost work from a previous session and therefore lost 110% of their time. Although it is possible, we consider situations where users report losing more than 100% of their time to be outliers and would prefer to be conservative when reporting our data. We have therefore removed those outliers from the data reporting. (p. 259)

You may disagree with the decision to exclude these data sets, because it under-reports the amount of time lost to inaccessible websites. But because the authors report on their decision, you can form your own opinion on their approach and perhaps decide to do a similar study without such exclusion.

**Answers do not make sense or are not internally consistent:** This should be approached with caution and only applied as a means of checking overall data quality. Do birthdates and level of education match overall? In other words, do participants indicating they have a PhD also have a matching age? One or two cases of mismatch may indicate an unusual academic progression; more than a handful of cases could imply that data has been sorted incorrectly or copied into the wrong area. A common pattern to look out for are values offset by a cell, either across a row or a column. Look at the excerpt of a data file showing both participant age and work experience in years (Table 5.5).

*Table 5.5* Data file excerpt

| Participant ID | Age in years | Work experience in years |
|:---:|:---:|:---:|
| 7 | 27 | 1 |
| 8 | 21 | 38 |
| 9 | 66 | 15 |
| 10 | 45 | 17 |
| 11 | 38 | 22 |

Something does not seem to be adding up here. The 21-year-old participant shows up with 38 years of work experience, while the 66-year-old participant only accumulated 15. What happened? Have a look at a larger section of the table. We have highlighted the cells where the mistake happened (Table 5.6):

*Table 5.6* Data file showing data entry error

| Participant ID | Age in years | Work experience in years |
|---|---|---|
| 1 | 19 | 0 |
| 2 | 34 | 8 |
| 3 |  | 35 |
| 4 | 60 | 17 |
| 5 | 40 | 14 |
| 6 | 39 | 4 |
| 7 | 27 | 1 |
| 8 | 21 | 38 |
| 9 | 66 | 15 |
| 10 | 45 | 17 |
| 11 | 38 | 22 |
| 12 | 42 | 17 |
| 13 | 39 | 20 |
| 14 | 41 | 28 |
| 15 | 50 | 38 |
| 16 | 62 | 0 |
| 17 | 18 | 2 |
| 18 | 24 | 7 |
| 19 | 28 | 3 |
|  | 25 |  |

Because a cell was skipped in row 3, all the age data is offset by a cell. For the same reason you can see a single filled cell at the bottom of the middle column ('25'). And because of the offset, age and experience data do not match. In cases like these, you can correct the mistake by moving data back to where it belongs; here, each age value should be moved one cell up.

**Recorded times are too short or too long:** This concerns both recorded times within studies (reaction times, time to solve a problem) and overall completion times, as they would be recorded, for example, for people filling out an online questionnaire. A participant completing a 50-question questionnaire in a minute or less is unlikely to have read the questions and thought about the answers. On the other hand, a participant shown to have taken two hours from start to finish for what should have been a five-minute questionnaire may just have been distracted or called away from the computer, only to return later and finish it. While both times will skew any calculations of average, the latter is less critical in terms of quality than the former.

**Participant answers indicate that they did not participate in a constructive or truthful way:** Some of these are better to spot in free-text fields, for example answers such as 'asdflkjfa', '11111' or extremely short and unrealistic duration times.

**Simple typing errors:** Some errors are most likely down to simple typing errors on the keyboard, for example:

- Errors that are created by not holding down the shift key and thus producing the wrong symbols (e.g., 'blackcoffee'notamorningperson.com' suggests the shift key was not held down so instead of the desired '@' symbol the user typed').

- Holding the shift key down when it should not be held can create entries such as '23.)4.1976' where instead of the '0' holding down the shift key has produced ')'.
- Switched letters or numbers: Where dates read '60.01.1977' you can reasonably assume that it should have read '06.01.1977' instead. However, keep in mind that sometimes what looks like a typo or accidental reversal may be date in a different format (e.g., the American date format rather than the British one).

> **REVIEW & REFLECT**
>
> - Is there a way to reliably tell whether a particular value is an outlier?
> - How is data entry and handling related to the avoidance of bias?

## 5.7 CODE AND RECODE YOUR DATA

In some cases, it might be advisable to recode the data you have recorded. For example, you may have originally elicited agreement on a scale from 1 to 6, ranging from 1 = 'Strongly disagree' to 6 = 'Strongly agree', but now you would like to conduct an analysis that only distinguishes between agreement and disagreement.

Before we show you two options for how to recode, one word of caution. When you create new variables or recode data you need make sure to keep the old data by creating a new variable and clearly marking the new variables as recoded by affixing a code such as *rec_*, *RC_* or similar. This retains the original data and allows you to change data coding should your assumptions turn out to be incorrect. Another reason for this is that recoding usually subtracts information from data rather than adding it; therefore, recoding has consequences for the amount of information contained in the data. When writing up your study, detailing the rationale behind recoded data helps other researchers to understand the process from raw data to result more fully, and to question any assumptions that may have influenced the process.

### 5.7.1 Recoding data

For the next example, assume that you have collected agreement data offering a simple answering scale from 1 to 6 such as below:

| 1 | 2 | 3 | 4 | 5 | 6 |
|---|---|---|---|---|---|
| Strongly disagree | Mostly disagree | Somewhat disagree | Somewhat agree | Mostly agree | Strongly agree |

For some parts of your analysis you are only interested in whether participants agreed or disagreed. If participants answered '1', '2' or '3', you want to record that they disagreed; for '4', '5' or '6', you want to record that they agreed.

> **ONLINE CONTENT**
>
> You can find sample Excel and SPSS files with the original and recoded data on the companion website.

*Data Entry and Data Handling* 147

> **EXCEL** • To do so, first create a new variable by inserting a new column and entering the variable name into the first cell of the column. We have called it 'Rc_Agreement' to indicate that this is the recoded version of the 'Agreement' variable. Then place the cursor into the first data cell of the new column (that is, in the first cell below the cell containing the name of the variable) and go to Insert → Function (Figure 5.23).

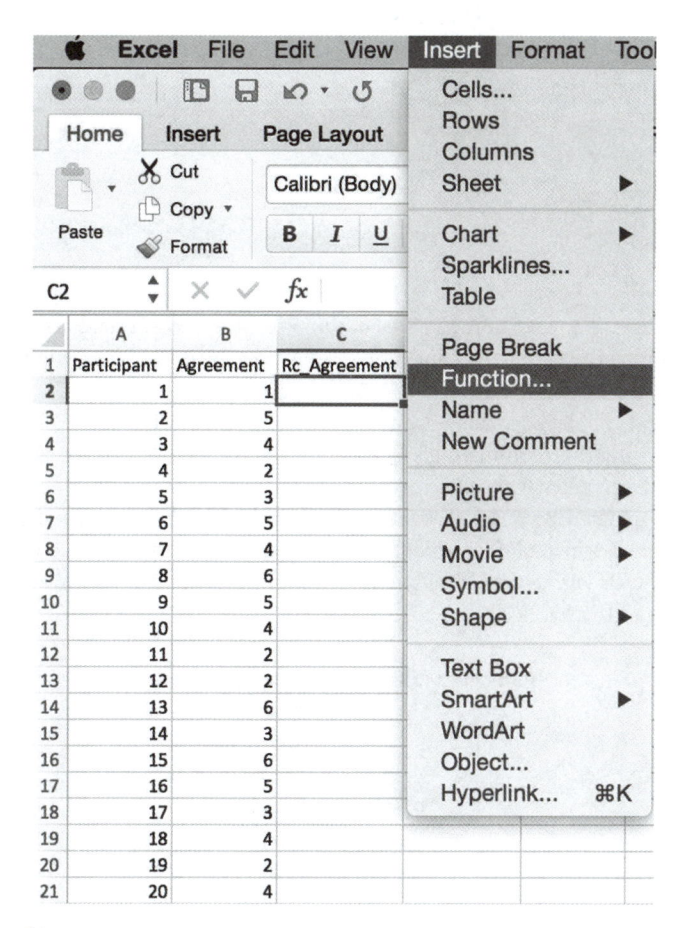

**Figure 5.23** *Excel insert menu*
Used with permission from Microsoft.

- In the window that appears, scroll down the list of functions to find and double-click on IF. This brings up the Formula Builder window. The IF function checks for a given range (here, a single cell) whether a specific condition is true and returns one value if the condition is met, another value if it is not. In this example, you want to know whether the value in the cell is either 1, 2 or 3 in which case you want to record this as disagreement; or 4, 5 or 6, in which case you want the recoded variable to indicate agreement. We have included a screenshot of a completed Formula Builder window below to explain its individual elements (Figure 5.24):

148    *Introducing Quantitative Methods*

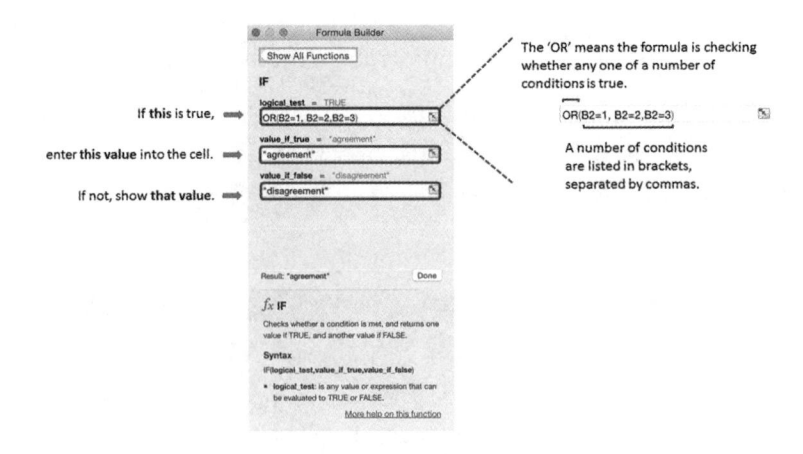

***Figure 5.24*** IF function
*Used with permission from Microsoft.*

- The first field lists the condition you are checking for; the second field notes what you want to be entered into the cell if the condition is met; the third field lists what you want to be displayed if the condition is not met.
- If you want text displayed make sure to enclose it in quotation marks "". Once you have completed entering this formula, click <u>Done</u> and then copy it down to all cells in the column.
- Make sure you drag it down with your cursor rather than simply copy and paste so that the cell reference is properly updated, because you want the third 'Rc_agreement' cell down the column to check the third cell in the original column, rather than all cells referring to the first cell on top of the column.
- This will fill all cells with either 'agreement' or 'disagreement', depending on the value of the original agreement variable (Figure 5.25):

| Participant | Agreement | Rc_agreement |
| --- | --- | --- |
| 1 | 1 | agreement |
| 2 | 5 | disagreement |
| 3 | 4 | disagreement |
| 4 | 2 | agreement |
| 5 | 3 | agreement |
| 6 | 5 | disagreement |
| 7 | 4 | disagreement |
| 8 | 6 | disagreement |
| 9 | 5 | disagreement |
| 10 | 4 | disagreement |
| 11 | 2 | agreement |
| 12 | 2 | agreement |
| 13 | 6 | disagreement |
| 14 | 3 | agreement |
| 15 | 6 | disagreement |
| 16 | 5 | disagreement |
| 17 | 3 | agreement |
| 19 | 4 | disagreement |
| 19 | 2 | agreement |
| 20 | 4 | disagreement |

***Figure 5.25*** Recoding in Excel

*Data Entry and Data Handling* 149

- **SPSS** • Go to Transform → Recode into Different Variables.³
- Move the variable you want to recode into the middle field (Input Variable → Output Variable) and enter the name of the new variable into the rightmost field; remember that you can assign both a name and a label (see Section 5.3.4). In this example, we choose 'Rc_disagreement' as the name and 'recoded agreement' as the label. Note that recoding changes values but not labels.
- Click on Old and New Values … to open the recoding window. In this window you have a range of options. On the left side you define which variables you want to change; on the right side you indicate what you want to change those variables to. You can recode values one by one or define a range of values that should be recoded into another one. The latter is what you are trying to do here, because you want to recode values 1 to 3 to agreement, and values 4 to 6 to disagreement (Figure 5.26).

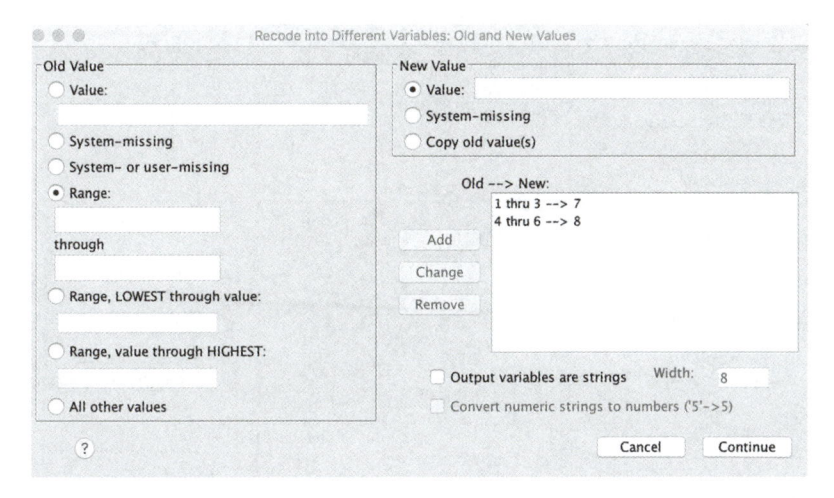

**Figure 5.26** *Recoding in SPSS*
Reprint Courtesy of International Business Machines Corporation, © International Business Machines Corporation.

- Click Continue and, in the next window, click OK.
- Having done that, you can now assign the label 'Agreement' to the value 7, and the label 'Disagreement' to the value 8.

## ❗ LOOK OUT!

When you recode old values into new values, try to make sure that the new values do not overlap with the old values. In the example above, we have recoded values 1 to 3 into 7, and values 4 to 6 into 8 so there is no mixing up old and new values.

### 5.7.2 Calculating new variables

Section 5.7.1 described the process of recoding a variable into either the same or another. Recoding relied on changing a variable's expression or changing its complexity by reducing the

---

³ When recoding variables, SPSS offers you two choices, recoding into the same or a different variable. We *strongly* recommend to always recode into a different variable.

150    *Introducing Quantitative Methods*

number of values. In contrast, this section will describe how to create a new variable based on information from existing variables.

> **EXCEL**  In Excel, the process of calculating a new variable from scratch is quite simple: The first step is choosing or developing the function that computes the new variable and entering the function into the top cell of the column (the first non-name cell, that is). The second step is copying in the function to the rest of the cells, which you can do by copying the function and then pasting it into all the cells it should apply to; all references to other cells will update automatically.

> **SPSS**  To compute a new variable, navigate to Transform → Compute Variable.

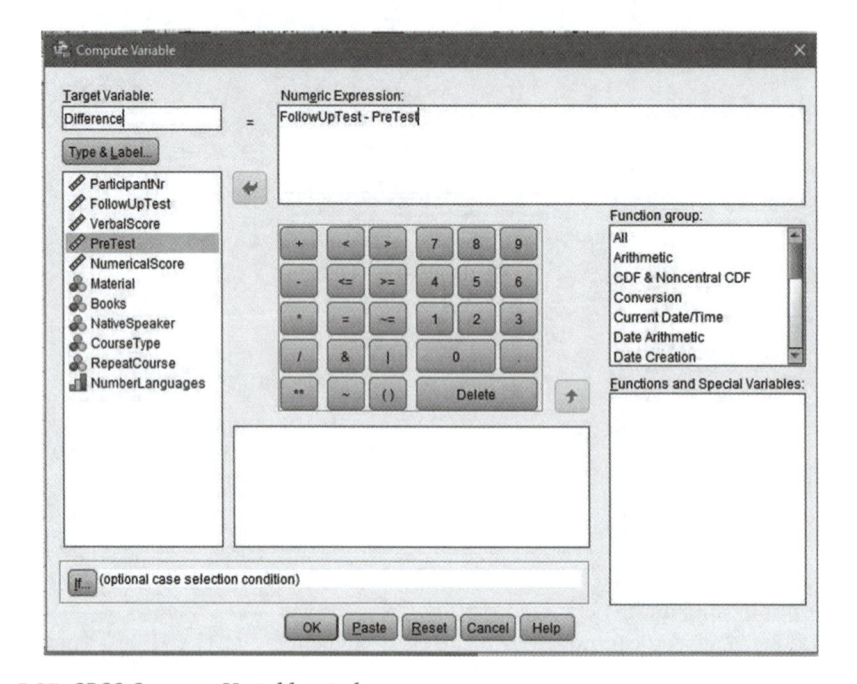

*Figure 5.27  SPSS Compute Variable window*
Reprint Courtesy of International Business Machines Corporation, © International Business Machines Corporation.

In the window that opens (see Figure 5.27), enter the name of the variable you want to compute into the top left field Target Variable. To the right of that field you see an equal sign, and to the right of that a field called Numeric Expression. This is the field in which you enter the formula to compute your new variable. In the example given above, the new variable is called 'Difference', and it is computed by deducting the value of one variable ('PreTest') off another ('FollowUpTest'). You can either type the variable names straight into the field or move them over from the left list of variables by clicking the arrow symbol when you have the variable you want to move selected.

### 5.7.3   Dummy variable

The term **dummy variable** refers to the step of creating a new binary variable from an existing variable which can be of any type (nominal, ordinal, interval or ratio). The resulting variable is categorical, which means it indicates whether a property exists or not (its scale type is nominal); it may also indicate to which of two groups a value belongs. For example, in Schmierbach and Oeldorf-Hirsch's (2012) study on the credibility of Twitter, information was presented in three conditions: as either a full New York Times (NYT) article; an opening NYT paragraph with a link to more information; or a link in a tweet. Schmierbach and Oeldorf-Hirsch then created a dummy variable indicating whether the information was presented via the New York Times or Twitter, thus using the dummy variable to transform the condition variable with three values to two.

### 5.7.4 Going further: Scale transformations

Section 2.2 introduced the different types of scale data – nominal, ordinal, interval and ratio – and pointed out the hierarchy within these scales: ratio scale data carries more information than interval scale data, which in turn carries more information than ordinal data, and so on. Having now looked at recoding data, you can see that this can sometimes change the scale type of the data. For example, in the example above, agreement data has been changed from interval data to nominal data (yes/no). This simplifies some calculations, but means there are fewer analyses available. Generally, recoding data only removes information and detail but never adds to it. When applied to scale types, this means that recoding only allows data to either stay at the same level in the hierarchy or move down one or more levels, but never move up. For example, interval data may be recoded into ordinal or nominal data, but nominal data cannot be recoded into ordinal, interval or ratio data.

### 5.7.5 Taking notes, taking names

We have mentioned before that you should note in your data analysis section if you exclude any values or entire variables. But that is not all – in fact, Chapters 6 and 12 will discuss in more detail what the data analysis section needs to cover. An essential part of your write-up is describing your treatment of the raw data. What changes did you make? What did you recode and why? To report on your data handling as truthfully as possible, remember to make notes as you go along. This is particularly important if you recode data in Excel, whereas SPSS makes it much easier for you to keep track if you use the Paste function to save the syntax for your changes or analysis in the Output document.

### RESEARCH METHODS AT WORK

Peggy is looking over the data collected from the latest consumer survey. This was quite a lengthy survey, so to boost response rates, upon completion participants could enter a raffle to win a £100 voucher for an online book store. This incentive meant the survey got a good number of responses, but Peggy now needs to make sure that the analysis is based on data from participants who took the survey seriously and did not just click through so they could participate in the raffle. She spots a data set where the respondent seems to have answered harshly throughout most of the survey: they selected '1 = Disagree very strongly' for most of the questions. On closer inspection Peggy see that the only times the participant answered '6 = Agree very strongly' was when the question's answer scale was reversed. This suggests to her that the participant always picked the first item of the scale, regardless of the answer. A further hint is that the participant's birthdate is given as January 1$^{st}$ 1900. If real, it would mean the participant was more than 118 years old – not impossible, just very, very unlikely. It is far more likely, however, that the participant just picked the first entry in the respective pick lists of the months, day and year questions. Lastly, Peggy checks the completion time for the survey: while other participants took around 16 minutes on average to complete the survey, this participant only needed 2 minutes to get to the end, and none of the optional free-text fields have been filled in. Taken together, this suggests to Peggy that the participant did not complete the survey in good faith and with real data. Therefore, although they still get to participate in the raffle, she marks the data set as one that should be excluded from the final analysis.

Joan had previously distributed a few dozen paper questionnaires at an exhibition and has just finished copying the questionnaire content into a file. She now wants to check that she did not make any mistakes in the process of copying over the data and so starts with calculating means and standard deviation. With 6.98 on a 7-point scale, the mean customer satisfaction score looks too good to be true, so Joan checks minimum and maximum values for this particular question and, alas, finds that the maximum is 71. This suggests that instead of a 7 in one cell and 1 in another, she must have entered 71 instead, thus artificially inflating the average. Upon double-checking the value in the original questionnaire she then corrects the data in the file, and on a second calculation the average drops to a less magnificent but much more plausible 5.25.

## A SHORT SUMMARY

- Data safety is paramount. Back up and save your data in at least two different locations and save your raw data before you make any changes whatsoever. Continue backing up frequently.
- Ensure data confidentiality and anonymity by splitting data into two files – one with identifying information and one with the information relevant for your analyses – and linking both files via the participant ID.
- Use encryption and safe passwords.
- Label your data by making sure that variable names are informative, short and consistent.
- Excel is a spreadsheet tool which can be used for some simple analyses.
- SPSS is a powerful analytical tool which can handle complex analyses; conducting an analysis involves handling a data and an output file as well as potentially a syntax file.
- Exercise caution when trying to identify outliers to make sure that your own assumptions do not bias your analyses and results.
- When checking data quality, look out for the following
  - Values that are dramatically different from the rest
  - Similar questions yielding very different results
  - Different questions yielding too similar answers
  - Implausible ranges or means
  - Internally inconsistent answers
  - Too long or too short completion times
  - Participant answers indicating lack of effort
- Recoding can be helpful to simplify analyses but decreases the level of detail and information in your data.

## CHECK YOUR UNDERSTANDING

1. We have outlined a simple study design below. Read through the description and then answer the following questions:
   a. How you would enter this data into Excel?
   b. Suggest a suitable name for each of these variables.
   c. Which data should be split off into a separate look-up file?

*This study uses a survey to examine to what extent agreement to ten statements regarding crime and sentencing is associated with a range of demographic criteria. Agreement is elicited on a six-point bipolar scale ranging from 'disagree absolutely' to 'agree absolutely'; the survey also asks about age, gender identity, household income, political affiliation. Participants are asked whether they would like to receive a summary of the study's results; those who are interested are asked to give their email address.*

2. For each of these statements, indicate whether they are true or false:
   1. In SPSS, variable names can contain any elements and symbols.
   2. In Excel, all data has to be entered through the data entry bar.
   3. In SPSS, variable names and variable labels are the same.
   4. In Excel, functions can only be entered through the Formula Builder.
   5. SPSS can be used for qualitative analysis.
   6. SPSS splits data analysis into three files: data, output and syntax.
   7. In Excel, a document always consists of one worksheet.

3. We have provided an excerpt of a raw data file for a study described below.

   www You will find this Excel file on the companion website.

   Imagine that you have entered the data by hand. Examine the data to identify potential issues. For each of the potentially problematic values, describe
   a. why is it problematic and
   b. what you suggest doing with it.

*This study examined which effect the mode and length of an ad have on the perceived value of the product. The study therefore has a 2 × 2 design with two independent variables: 'length of presentation' (short, long) and 'presentation format' (visual, aural). The dependent variable is 'perceived value'. Each participant only experiences one condition. You collect additional demographic information from your participants in the form of gender identity, age in years, email address, and you track for each of your participants whether they would want to be contacted with information on the outcome of the study.*

| Participant ID | Age | Gender | Contact | Length | Format | Estimated value |
|---|---|---|---|---|---|---|
| 37 |  | male | y | Long | Auditory | 474 |
| 38 | 23 | female | n | Short | Auditory | 484 |
| 39 | 43 | Non-binary |  | Long | Visual | 546 |
| 40 | 62 | male | y | Short | Auditory | 453 |
| 41 | 55 | female | n | Long | Visual | 410 |

| | | | | | | |
|---|---|---|---|---|---|---|
| 42 | 32 | female | y | Short | Auditory | 4935 |
| 43 | $$ | male | n | Long | Auditory | 23 |
| 44 | 2 | female | y | Short | Visual | 518 |
| 45 | 3 | male | y | Long | Visual | 390 |
| 46 | 45 | male | n | Short | Visual | 374 |
| 47 | 34 | male | n | Long | Auditory | 434 |
| 48 | 51 | female | n | Short | Visual | 462 |
| 49 | 18 | female | n | Long | Auditory | 508 |
| 50 | 39 | male | y | Short | Visual | 501 |
| 51 | 28 | female | y | Long | Visual | 425 |
| 52 | 37 | female | y | Short | Auditory | 380 |
| 53 | 51 | female | y | Long | Visual | 383 |
| 54 | 29 | female | y | Long | Auditory | 481 |
| 55 | 41 | male | y | Short | Visual | 494 |
| 56 | 28 | female | y | Short | Auditory | 422 |
| 57 | 46 | female | n | Length | V | 357 |
| 58 | 22 | female | y | Long | Auditory | 370 |
| 59 | 19 | female | y | Long | Visual | 401 |
| 60 | 31 | female | y | Short | Visual | 501 |
| 61 | 20 | female | y | L | Auditory | 385 |
| | 37 | | | | | |

# 6 Basic Concepts of Data Description and Analysis

## WHAT IS THIS CHAPTER ABOUT?

Chapter 6 discusses the core concepts of statistical analysis. It begins by introducing basic means of describing data. The chapter then moves to discuss measures of central tendency and to examine their advantages and disadvantages to help you choose appropriate descriptives for your research data. Following this, the chapter discusses variance and standard distribution and provides guidance on how to compute these measures. The chapter introduces and explain normal distribution, significance, power and effect size.

## WHY IS THIS IMPORTANT?

Choosing and interpreting descriptive data is yet another skill that helps you avoid bias; you will see this demonstrated, for example, in the discussion concerning which means of central tendency to use to describe your data. Understanding the basic concepts of data description and analysis such as variance, standard distribution and power prepares you for looking at more complex statistical analyses in Chapters 9, 10 and 11.

## WHAT ARE THE LEARNING OUTCOMES OF THIS CHAPTER?

At the end of this chapter you will be able to:
- Assess which measures are appropriate for which type of data and calculate them
- Understand and apply the concept of normal distribution
- Understand the differences between sample and population, and statistics and parameters and their implications
- Calculate variance and standard deviation
- Apply the concepts of effect size and power

## 6.1 FREQUENCIES

The most basic form of describing a set of data is simply counting how often every individual value occurs. For example, for a question asking 190 participants for their main reason for not voting during the last election, the resulting list could look like this (Table 6.1):

*Table 6.1 Frequencies of main reasons not to vote*

| Reason | Number of participants |
|---|---|
| I didn't think my vote would count | 23 |
| None of the parties reflected my own values | 34 |
| I couldn't make up my mind | 38 |
| I'm not interested in politics | 76 |
| Don't know | 19 |

Here, '23', '38', '76', etc. are the frequencies for how often participants gave individual reasons as their main reason. However, this is only suitable for variables with relatively few different values. For variables with many different values, this is not feasible. For example, if you are recording reaction times for 100 or more participants you could easily get a list of different values such as 456, 434, 235, 509, 457, 343, 454, which could be as long as the list of participants itself. To present data in frequency form, ideally data should consist of a limited number of possible values, for example number of smokers/non-smokers (two options); number of participants employed/unemployed/self-employed (three options); selections from a pick list; answers to a scale such as agree/agree somewhat/disagree somewhat/disagree (four options), standardised lists of countries/occupations/etc. Where you are presenting nominal data (see Section 2.2.1), frequencies are often the only way of presenting the results because you cannot calculate means or standard deviations for that data type.

### ONLINE CONTENT

You can find the SPSS file for this example on the companion website.

In SPSS, you can determine the frequencies of values via Analyze → Descriptive Statistics → Frequencies ... and moving the variables for which you want the frequencies to the Variable(s) field to the right.

### ONLINE CONTENT

You can find the Excel file for this example on the companion website.

To count values in Excel, you have at least two options:

- You can use the filter function via Data → Filter and then filter for each value in turn; the number of items returned is then visible in the status bar at the bottom right of the page.
- Alternatively, you can use the COUNTIF function which is explained in the Excel Functions Glossary.

- If your data consists of simple 1 or 0 entries to indicate whether a response was chosen or not, you can also use the AUTOSUM function to total up the number of 1s and therefore, the times that particular response was chosen.
- Having entered your data this way, you can then use the PIVOTTABLE function to count the occurrences of each variable value.
    - Select the range of the table and go to Data → Summarize with PivotTable (Figure 6.1):

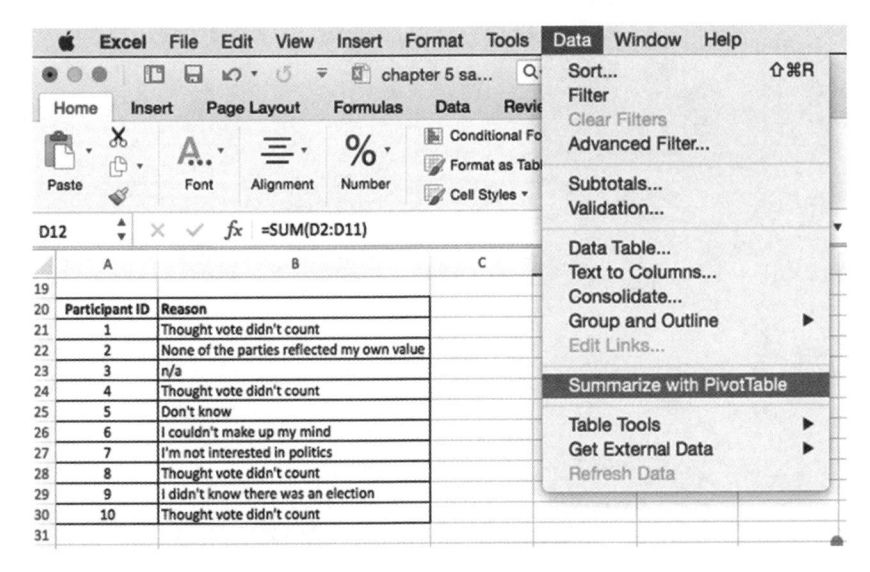

**Figure 6.1** *Excel PivotTable menu*
Used with permission from Microsoft.

- Confirm the range of cells you have selected or manually enter the range, then select whether you want the pivot table to appear on the same worksheet or on a new one. Click OK (Figure 6.2):

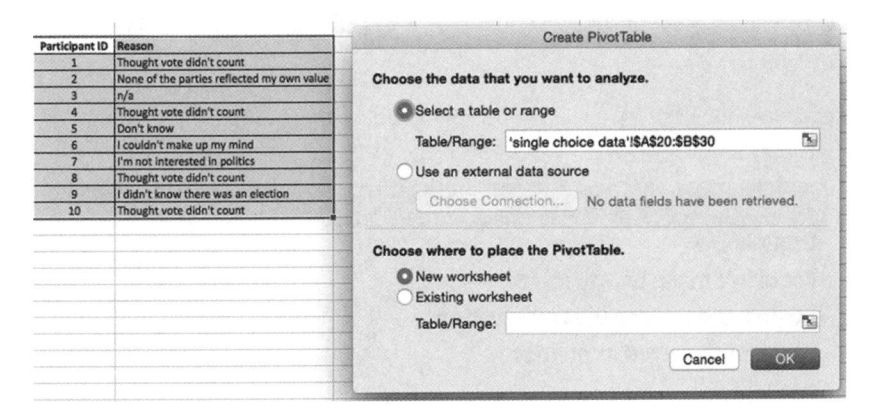

**Figure 6.2** *Excel PivotTable window*
Used with permission from Microsoft.

- In the PivotTable window that then pops up, drag the variable 'Reason' to the 'Rows' section, and drag the variable 'Participant ID' to the Σ Values section. Click on the (i) icon to change

158  *Introducing Quantitative Methods*

the function from SUM to COUNT. This will ensure that the pivot table counts the number of IDs for each value of the variable 'Reason' (rather than summing up the IDs!) (Figure 6.3):

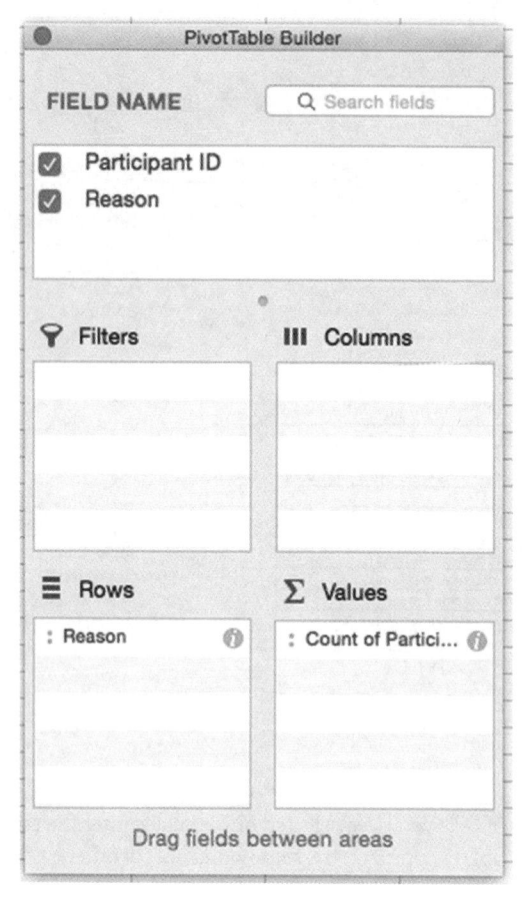

**Figure 6.3**  *Excel PivotTable Builder*
Used with permission from Microsoft.

Once you have done this, you will get this pivot table as the result (Figure 6.4):

| Row Labels | Count of Participant ID |
| --- | --- |
| Don't know | 1 |
| I couldn't make up my mind | 1 |
| I didn't know there was an election | 1 |
| I'm not interested in politics | 1 |
| n/a | 1 |
| None of the parties reflected my own value | 1 |
| Thought vote didn't count | 4 |
| Grand Total | 10 |

**Figure 6.4**  *Excel pivot table*
Used with permission from Microsoft.

## 6.2 PERCENTAGES

Other times, you might be interested in the distribution of values. Rather than displaying a mere count of values, you can present data as ratios or percentages such as in the following example (see also Section 4.2 on the calculation and interpretation of percentages):

*Table 6.2 Percentages of main reasons given*

| Main reason | Percentages |
| --- | --- |
| None of the parties reflected my own values | 10% |
| I'm not interested in politics | 10% |
| I thought my vote didn't count | 40% |
| I couldn't make up my mind | 10% |
| Don't know | 10% |
| I didn't know there was an election | 10% |
| Not applicable | 10% |

Table 6.2 is a simple example of data presented in percentage values. For a more complex example representing the same data, have a look at Table 6.3. In this table we have put the percentage values in the context of the overall sample (N = 1200) and split the individual values by age and political affiliation; note that for this example the percentages are markedly different because the sample size is much bigger than previously:

*Table 6.3 Complex table of percentages showing responses split by age and political affiliation*

| | In % | N | <20 | 21–40 | 41–60 | >60 | Subtotal | Strongly right-leaning | Somewhat right-leaning | Centrist | Somewhat left-leaning | Strongly left-leaning | Subtotal |
| --- | --- | --- | --- | --- | --- | --- | --- | --- | --- | --- | --- | --- | --- |
| None of the parties reflected my own values | 25 | **300** | 98 | 78 | 76 | 48 | 300 | 76 | 64 | 55 | 72 | 33 | 300 |
| I'm not interested in politics | 23 | **276** | 72 | 83 | 53 | 68 | 276 | 33 | 42 | 67 | 59 | 75 | 276 |
| I thought my vote didn't count | 18 | **216** | 24 | 47 | 95 | 50 | 216 | 54 | 23 | 61 | 22 | 56 | 216 |
| I couldn't make up my mind | 12 | **144** | 56 | 34 | 31 | 23 | 144 | 36 | 44 | 19 | 31 | 14 | 144 |
| Don't know | 9 | **108** | 35 | 26 | 26 | 21 | 108 | 25 | 27 | 19 | 23 | 14 | 108 |
| I didn't know there was an election | 8 | **96** | 24 | 32 | 25 | 15 | 96 | 22 | 37 | 21 | 7 | 9 | 96 |
| Not applicable | 5 | **60** | 7 | 5 | 24 | 24 | 60 | 14 | 6 | 5 | 22 | 13 | 60 |
| Total | 100% | 1200 | 316 | 305 | 330 | 249 | 1200 | 260 | 243 | 247 | 236 | 214 | 1200 |

160　*Introducing Quantitative Methods*

> **EXCEL** You can calculate the percentage by dividing the counts by overall N. For example, to calculate the percentage for the 'I thought my vote didn't count' answers, the Excel formula would look like = 216/1200; or you can make reference to the cells containing the data (i.e., = [cell range of share]/[cell range of count]).

> **SPSS** To derive percentages for the distribution of values, use the procedure described in Section 6.1 – the output of this analysis gives both absolute and relative numbers.

Talking about percentages introduces an important idea, namely that of describing a set of values in terms of how those values relate to each other. One way of looking at data is imagining the data values as a cloud of data points. You can describe this cloud by indicating where the centre of the cloud is and how dense the cloud is, that is, how tightly around the centre the individual points are spread out. The following graphic shows three different distributions of values along an axis – a simplified cloud, if you will. For each distribution individual values are shown as dots, and the centre is shown by a line drawn through the axis. Note how in the top distribution the values are clustered closely around the centre point. In the middle distribution the same centre point is surrounded by a much less dense distribution of values, and in the bottom distribution the values are spread out widely and loosely around a different centre than the other two. Note also that the centre of the distribution is not necessarily an existing data point – more on that later (Figure 6.5).

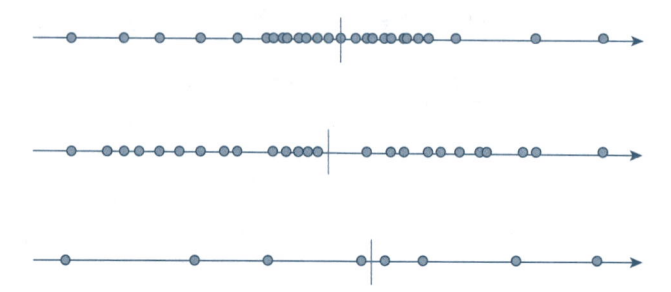

*Figure 6.5  Dispersal of data points around a central measure*

The centre can be described by measures of central tendency, and the density of the cloud by terms such as *standard deviation*. The next section will discuss measures of central tendency in more detail.

> **? REVIEW & REFLECT**
> 
> - When might percentages and frequencies not be suitable to describe data?
> - When might they be particularly suitable?

## 6.3　MEASURES OF CENTRAL TENDENCY

There are three **measures of central tendency**:

- Mean
- Mode
- Median

Each has a slightly different perspective on data and each comes with its own advantages and disadvantages. We will discuss their differences with an example set of eight values, for example, the age of eight participants:

$$17, 18, 18, 18, 17, 19, 19, 19$$

> **www ONLINE CONTENT**
>
> You can find the Excel and SPSS sample files for the following sections on the companion website.

### 6.3.1 Mean

The **mean** refers to the arithmetic average of all values and is calculated by adding up all individual values and dividing the total by the number of values. In the context of (statistical) formulas, X is often used to refer to an individual value and N to the total number of values in a distribution. The mean is also indicated by the letter $\overline{X}$, called 'x-bar', or by the Greek letter $\mu$ (*mu*). In this example, the mean is calculated by adding up all eight values and dividing the total by N (=8):

$$\mu = \frac{17+18+18+18+17+19+19+19}{8} = \frac{145}{8} = 18.125$$

Generally, $\mu$ is used when referring to *populations* and *population means*, and $\overline{X}$ when talking about *samples* and *sample means*. For now, we will be using $\mu$ since we are referring to the population mean. You will see further below why it makes sense to clearly distinguish between the two.

> **EXCEL** Use the AVERAGE function to calculate the mean (see Excel Functions Glossary).

> **SPSS** Go to <u>Analyze</u> → <u>Descriptive Statistics</u> → <u>Frequencies …</u> and move the variables for which you want to display the mean to the right. Click on <u>Statistics</u> and then tick the boxes for <u>Mean</u> in the <u>Central Tendency</u> window in the top right, then click <u>Continue</u>. Alternatively, go to <u>Analyze</u> → <u>Descriptive Statistics</u> → <u>Descriptives</u>, move the variables you are interested in to the right, then click <u>Options …</u> and tick <u>Mean</u> at the top.

### 6.3.2 Mode

The **mode** describes the most frequent value. If there is one single value which occurs most frequently, that value is the mode, but if there is a tie between several values all being equally frequent, those values are all considered modes. In this example, if you order the list of values, you will find that the two most frequent values are 18 and 19 because they both occur three times (Table 6.4).

*Table 6.4 Frequencies of individual values*

| X | Frequency of X |
| --- | --- |
| 17 | 2 |
| 18 | 3 |
| 19 | 3 |

Therefore, this distribution has two modes: 18 and 19. Because modes rely on establishing frequency of values but make no further requirements on the data, they are particularly suitable to describe sets of nominal data, which cannot readily be described by a mean or median.

> **EXCEL** There are two ways of identifying modes in Excel, depending on whether you are dealing with nominal data or numerical data (i.e., ordinal, interval, or ratio data). We will describe the slightly more straightforward way of calculating mode(s) from non-nominal data first, and then we will explain how to find the mode(s) from nominal data.

- To calculate the mode in Excel for numerical data, use the MODE.MULT function which allows identification of more than one mode.
- First, determine the range of cells for which you want to calculate the mode. Because we are using a small list of numbers arranged in one column, in this example the cell range is A1 to A8. Now select a number of cells within which the result will be displayed. Since you do not know ahead of time how many modes you will find, err on the side of caution and select more than you think you might need. To be on the safe side, we recommend selecting an entire column right next to the column of data values you are examining.
- *Whilst keeping the cells selected* (this is important!), write the following formula into the function bar: =MODE.MULT(A1:A8). Then hit Control + Shift + Enter (Windows) or Command + Shift + Enter (Mac) – this copies the function into all selected cells in one go – and you will see that Excel has correctly identified two modes, 18 and 19:

|   | A | B | C | D | E |
| --- | --- | --- | --- | --- | --- |
| 1 |   | 17 | 18 |   |   |
| 2 |   | 18 | 19 |   |   |
| 3 |   | 18 | #N/A |   |   |
| 4 |   | 18 | #N/A |   |   |
| 5 |   | 17 | #N/A |   |   |
| 6 |   | 19 | #N/A |   |   |
| 7 |   | 19 | #N/A |   |   |
| 8 |   | 19 | #N/A |   |   |
| 9 | Sum total | 145 |   |   |   |
| 10 |   |   |   |   |   |
| 11 |   |   |   |   |   |
| 12 | Average | 18.125 |   |   |   |

C8  fx  {=MODE.MULT(B1:B8)}

*Used with permission from Microsoft*

- You cannot use this function to count non-numerical values (e.g., a list of single-word answers), but you can use the pivot table as described in Section 6.1 to count occurrences of each item.

> **SPSS** Use the first of the two procedures described in Section 6.3.1 and instead (or additionally) tick the box for Mode in the Central Tendency window.

### 6.3.3 Median

Lastly, the **median** is used to split an ordered distribution of values in exactly half such that half of its values remain on one side of the median, half on the other. For example, in an ordered list of numbers from 1 to 5, 3 would be the median because there are two values to either side of it:

$$1 \quad 2 \quad \mathbf{3} \quad 4 \quad 5$$

Consider the following list of values:

$$17, 17, 18, 18 \mid 18, 19, 19, 19$$

In this example, the median is 18 because, in this ordered list, four values are greater than (or equal to) 18 and four are less than (or equal to) 18. However, the median does not have to be a number contained in the actual list of values. If instead the list would have looked like this:

$$17, 18, 19, 20 \mid 21, 22, 23, 24$$

the median would be calculated as the average of the two values to the immediate left and right of the centre:

$$\frac{20+21}{2} = \frac{41}{2} = 20.5; \text{ therefore, the median is 20.5.}$$

> **EXCEL** In Excel, you can calculate the median by using the function MEDIAN: =MEDIAN([range of cells for which you want to calculate the median]).

> **SPSS** Use the first of the two procedures described in Section 6.3.1, and instead (or additionally) tick the box for Median in the Central Tendency window.

Thus for the initial example of the set of 17, 17, 18, 18, 18, 19, 19, 19 the mean is 18.125, the two modes are 18 and 19, and the median 18. While these values seem fairly similar they focus on different aspects and can be skewed when the distribution of values is not as homogeneous as in the current example.

### 6.3.4 Going further: Median split

The median is often used to artificially split a set of values in two halves, for example to class participants as high or low in a particular trait, to distinguish between agreement and disagreement, and so on, in a context where these variables are used to allocate participants to a particular condition. This is called a **median split**. For example, you might want to study the relationship between a leader's confidence in their own leadership skills and their team members' assessment

164  *Introducing Quantitative Methods*

of those leadership skills. Leaders are asked to rate the confidence in their own leadership skills on a scale from 1 to 30, 1 being not at all confident, 30 being absolutely confident. Rather than picking an absolute value above which a leader classes themselves as high in confidence, you choose to perform a median split by ranking all test results in ascending order and then determining the median. In the example below, the left table shows the original data. In the right table, the values have been split into half by the median of 15.5; the scores below the median are considered 'low', the scores above it 'high' (Figure 6.6).

| Participant ID | Confidence in leadership skills |
|---|---|
| 1 | 11 |
| 2 | 2 |
| 3 | 22 |
| 4 | 23 |
| 5 | 10 |
| 6 | 16 |
| 7 | 25 |
| 8 | 25 |
| 9 | 25 |
| 10 | 8 |
| 11 | 16 |
| 12 | 5 |
| 13 | 10 |
| 14 | 18 |
| 15 | 13 |
| 16 | 15 |
| 17 | 23 |
| 18 | 7 |
| 19 | 22 |
| 20 | 25 |
| 21 | 19 |
| 22 | 7 |
| 23 | 7 |
| 24 | 7 |
| 25 | 12 |
| 26 | 9 |
| 27 | 21 |
| 28 | 8 |
| 29 | 23 |
| 30 | 27 |

| Participant ID | Confidence in leadership skills | |
|---|---|---|
| 2 | 2 | |
| 12 | 5 | |
| 18 | 7 | |
| 22 | 7 | |
| 23 | 7 | |
| 24 | 7 | |
| 10 | 8 | |
| 28 | 8 | 'Low' |
| 26 | 9 | |
| 5 | 10 | |
| 13 | 10 | |
| 1 | 11 | |
| 25 | 12 | |
| 15 | 13 | |
| 16 | 15 | |
| 6 | 16 | |
| 11 | 16 | |
| 14 | 18 | |
| 21 | 19 | |
| 27 | 21 | |
| 3 | 22 | |
| 19 | 22 | |
| 4 | 23 | 'High' |
| 17 | 23 | |
| 29 | 23 | |
| 7 | 25 | |
| 8 | 25 | |
| 9 | 25 | |
| 20 | 25 | |
| 30 | 27 | |

**Figure 6.6** *Example median split*

Yet the distinction is arbitrary because it depends on the specific values you find in your specific sample. As you can see in this example, the highest score of the 'low confidence in leadership skills' group is just one point away from the lowest score of the 'high confidence in leadership skills' group. Crawford (2005) used a similar approach when looking at project management competence and how managers were perceived by their superiors. As part of this study, Crawford performed a median split to categorise participants as either high or low performers, but noted that all participants would have to be considered effective performers anyway (p. 10). Therefore, when interpreting data keep in mind that this type of splitting data creates artificial groupings. Once upon a time there was a student who reported that they conducted a median split on the extraversion scores of their participants so they could class them as high or low in extraversion; the student then expressed concern that half of the sample turned out to be introverted! Do not be that student.

## 6.4 COMPARING MEASURES OF CENTRAL TENDENCY

We will now add another value to the distribution of values used in the example above. We said previously that the data represents the age in years of your small group of participants; now imagine adding a ninth participant who happens to be a mature student aged 88.

17, 17, 18, 18, 18, 19, 19, 19, 88

The average age is now 25.89, even though eight participants are younger than this, and one participant substantially older. The modes remain 18 and 19. The median is identified as the value that splits the set of values exactly in half – here, this value also remains 18.

17, 17, 18, 18   **18**   19, 19, 19, 88

If you compare the three measures of central tendencies now, you will find that you have a mean of 25.89, two modes of 18 and 19 and a median of 18. Of these three values, the mean is noticeably different from the other two values. This is no coincidence: the mean is particularly susceptible to extreme values. If you had replaced the value of 88 with 123,456 (even though this is not a valid age) both mode and median would remain unchanged: 18 and 19 remain the most frequent values, and there are still an equal number of values on either side of the value of 18. However, the mean would now be 13733.44.

Median and mode give a slightly more accurate picture of the actual description, whereas the mean will be skewed disproportionately by a single large value. This suggests that not every measure describes every distribution equally well; some measures are better suited to describe certain types of distributions than others.

Gravetter and Wallnau (2004, p. 90ff) describe three more scenarios where the median would be a better choice:

1. Distributions with undetermined values. (Note that 'undetermined' does not mean missing.) Gravetter and Wallnau give the example of a participant vastly exceeding the available time to complete a task such that the experimenter stops the participant after an hour. In this case the researcher wants to record this as an undetermined value rather than as a missing value, because the fact that the participant was unable to complete the task is still valuable information. However, the absence of a time value does not allow use of the mean. In contrast, when using the median, the values would simply be sorted in ascending order of size, and whether the hapless participant had to be stopped after an hour, two hours or five would not make a difference to the median itself.
2. Similarly, open-ended distributions (i.e., whenever data is elicited with one or more categories of the type 'X or more') do not carry enough information to allow calculation of

the mean. In Gravetter and Wallnau's example, a questionnaire enquires to the number of children per household, with the highest available options '5 or more'. Recording this means losing detail on whether a household described by this option has 5, 6 or 20 children. Again, the median is unaffected by this lack of detail.
3. Data elicited on an ordinal scale (see Section 2.2.2) would not allow calculation of a mean, whereas a median can be established.

When data is described by values which allow neither calculating a mean nor establishing a median, using the mode can be appropriate (after Gravetter and Wallnau, p. 92):

1. Data described on a nominal scale (see Section 2.2.1). For example, a question may have asked participants to list associations with the presented stimulus word. The results are best described by listing the associations in order of mentions or just naming the most frequently given one.
2. When variables exist in discrete categories (e.g., options such as 'smoker'/'non-smoker') status may be coded as '0' and '1' or '1' and '2' in whatever spreadsheet or data analysis software is used, but a mean or median (e.g., of 0.5 or 1.5) simply does not make any sense. The mode more usefully describes the distribution (e.g., by stating that most of the participants were non-smokers).

Two or more measures can also be combined to provide more detailed and useful information by supplementing the mean by the mode or median to give a more accurate picture of the set of values. For example, you might describe participant age by stating: 'Participants' mean age was 25.89, but this was disproportionately affected by a participant aged 88. Median age was 18.' This disproportionate effect of extreme values explains why the early (and appropriate!) identification of outliers is so important. While we can use the median to mitigate the outlier's effect in the descriptive data, much of the statistical analyses rely on the mean as a key element, and subsequently any such analyses can potentially be skewed by outliers.

## ❓ REVIEW & REFLECT

- Why is the mean a problematic measure of central tendency?
- When is the median a better choice?

## 6.5 MEASURES OF DISPERSION: VARIANCE AND STANDARD DEVIATION

Having introduced measures of central tendency as a description of the centre of the cloud, you now need a way to describe the density of the cloud, that is, how tightly data points are clustered around the centre – you need to describe the *spread* of the distribution. You have already seen one means of describing spread: the range, defined as the difference between the highest and the lowest value in the distribution. However, the range is imprecise because it tells you nothing about the shape of the distribution. Table 6.5 below has listed the values from a previous example and calculated the difference to the mean for every individual value. A quick reminder: X refers to the individual value; $\mu$ to the calculated population mean of 18.125; therefore, $X - \mu$ refers to the calculated difference between the average and the individual value. Unless otherwise specified, all values are rounded to three decimal places (see Section 4.3).

*Table 6.5* Mean and deviation from mean

| X | X − μ |
|---|---|
| 17 | 17 − 18.125 = −1.125 |
| 17 | 17 − 18.125 = −1.125 |
| 18 | 18 − 18.125 = −0.125 |
| 18 | 18 − 18.125 = −0.125 |
| 18 | 18 − 18.125 = −0.125 |
| 19 | 19 − 18.125 = 0.875 |
| 19 | 19 − 18.125 = 0.875 |
| 19 | 19 − 18.125 = 0.875 |

What happens if you add up all deviations (i.e., differences) from the mean? The process of 'adding up all values' is described by the symbol $\Sigma$ (sigma), therefore

$$\Sigma (X - \mu) = (-1.125) + (-1.125) + (-0.125) + (-0.125) + (-0.125) + 0.875 + 0.875 + 0.875 = 0$$

Calculating a total of 0 is a logical consequence of adding up values that are below and above the mean, resulting in both positive and negative numbers which will always be balanced such that the result of a simple addition of all deviations will always be 0. Because this holds true for all distributions, just adding up deviations does not help with the description of a set of data. To avoid this, a step is added to the calculation: after calculating the deviations, the values are squared. Since squaring a positive number always results in a positive number ($4^2 = 16$), and squaring a negative number also always results in a positive number (($-4)^2 = 16$, too), this ensures that all values are positive and can be added up to a number larger than 0. Compare the totals of the two right columns. In this example, $\mu = 18.125$ (Table 6.6):

*Table 6.6* Calculating the sum of squares

| X | X − μ | $(X - \mu)^2$ |
|---|---|---|
| 17 | 17 − 18.125 = −1.125 | $-1.125^2 = 1.265625$ |
| 17 | 17 − 18.125 = −1.125 | $-1.125^2 = 1.265625$ |
| 18 | 18 − 18.125 = −0.125 | $-0.125^2 = .015625$ |
| 18 | 18 − 18.125 = −0.125 | $-0.125^2 = .015625$ |
| 18 | 18 − 18.125 = −0.125 | $-0.125^2 = .015625$ |
| 19 | 19 − 18.125 = 0.875 | $0.875^2 = .765625$ |
| 19 | 19 − 18.125 = 0.875 | $0.875^2 = .765625$ |
| 19 | 19 − 18.125 = 0.875 | $0.875^2 = .765625$ |
| $\Sigma(X) = 145$ | $\Sigma(X - \mu) = 0$ | $\Sigma(X - \mu)^2 = 4.875$ |

The figure expressed by $\Sigma(X - \mu)^2$ is also referred to as the **sum of squares (SS)**. But while this formula is quite handy, it is not always easy to use for calculating by hand.

> **! LOOK OUT!**
>
> In the context of calculating statistics and parameters, SS refers to the formula as described above (i.e., the end result of a process of calculating deviations, squaring them and then adding them all up). However, in Excel the function SS conducts a different calculation: here, the sum of squares really just consists of the total of all squared values.

The following formula looks different, but calculates the exact same number. Note that it is shorter and you do not have to calculate the mean beforehand. The shorter formula is often referred to as the **definitional formula**, and the longer as the **computational formula**.

$$SS = \sum x^2 - \frac{(\sum x)^2}{N}$$

Have a look at the individual components of the computational formula:
$\sum x^2$ refers to the sum of the squared values, that is, the individual values are *first* squared, *then* totalled up:

$$\sum x^2 = 17^2 + 17^2 + 18^2 + 18^2 + 18^2 + 19^2 + 19^2 + 19^2$$
$$= 289 + 289 + 324 + 324 + 324 + 361 + 361 + 361$$
$$= 2633$$

For $(\sum x)^2$ the individual values are *first* summed up and *then* the total is squared:

$$\sum x^2 = (17 + 17 + 18 + 18 + 18 + 19 + 19 + 19)^2$$
$$= 145^2$$
$$= 21{,}025$$

**N** equals eight because the example used eight values.

Putting all of this together, you get: $2633 - \frac{21{,}025}{8} = 2633 - 2628.125 = 4.875$ which is equivalent to the value derived with the shorter formula. Once you have calculated the sum of squares, you can calculate the **variance**. The symbol for variance is $\sigma^2$ (for reasons that will become clear in a couple of paragraphs) and variance is calculated by dividing SS by the number of values:

$$\sigma^2 = \frac{SS}{N}$$

For the example above, this gives you

$$\sigma^2 = \frac{SS}{N} = \frac{4.875}{8} = 0.609.$$

Squaring the differences solves one problem – getting rid of negative values – but creates another one: the resulting sum is inflated. To resolve this issue, you need to take the square root of the variance to counteract this inflation.

$$\sqrt{\sigma^2} = \sqrt{\frac{SS}{N}} = \sqrt{0.609} = 0.781$$

This value is referred to as the **standard deviation**, and the symbol for standard deviation is $\sigma$. Now you can see why variance is described by the symbol $\sigma^2$. Variance is the squared standard deviation, and standard deviation is the square root of the variance:

| $\sqrt{variance}$ = Standard Deviation | $\sqrt{\sigma^2} = \sigma$ |
|---|---|
| (Standard Deviation)$^2$ = Variance | $(\sigma)^2 = \sigma^2$ |

The standard deviation allows you to describe the spread of the distribution around the mean. You will see in Section 6.7 that for a certain type of distribution, the so-called 'normal distribution', the standard deviation can provide information about the probability of specific values occurring in any one population or sample.

### ? REVIEW & REFLECT

- Why are the deviations from the mean squared rather than added up?
- Since standard deviation and variance are inexorably linked, why do we still use both?

## 6.6 PARAMETERS AND STATISTICS

At the beginning of the example we stated that these values were treated as a **population** rather than a sample. We introduced $\mu$ and $\bar{X}$ as population and sample means, respectively. Values relating to a population are called **parameters**; values relating to a sample are called **statistics**. It is easy to remember which is which: population and parameter both start with 'p', and sample and statistics both start with 's'. You have already seen that the standard symbol for a **population's standard deviation** is lowercase sigma ($\sigma$), and since the population variance is the squared population standard deviation, the symbol for **population variance** is $\sigma^2$. Using **N** to describe the number of observations similarly indicated that we referred to a population and hence a complete set of observations, that is, one where all data points are available. However, often you do not have access to the complete set of observations, and most of the time you are operating with a sample. The same basic principles apply, but with an added layer of complexity. The sample, by definition, is incomplete and gives an incomplete representation of the population. Thus you need to apply a correction to the formula to reflect this fact. How do you do this? To start off, small letter **n** is used to indicate that the number of observations is incomplete. Variance and standard deviation are still calculated in a similar way, but expressed by different symbols and a correction is applied by using n-1 rather than N. You will still often see N to apply to the size of a sample rather than a population; always make sure to check the context. To calculate the values previously calculated for a sample, the formulas are changed as below:

**Sample variance** is referred to as $s^2$ and calculated by $\frac{SS}{n-1}$.

**Sample standard deviation** is referred to as **s**, and calculated by $\sqrt{\frac{SS}{n-1}}$.

The following table gives a quick summary of the different notations. Parameters are, by convention, either described by Greek symbols or in capitals, whereas sample statistics are usually in lowercase (with the exception of x-bar) and do not use Greek letters (Table 6.7):

**Table 6.7** *Comparison of symbols for population parameters and sample statistics*

|  | Population parameters | Sample statistics |
| --- | --- | --- |
| Number of observations | N | n |
| Mean | $\mu$ | $\overline{X}$ |
| Variance | $\sigma^2$ | $s^2$ |
| Standard deviation | $\sigma$ | s |

It is important to distinguish between sample and population because it makes a huge difference whether you are working with a full data set or an incomplete data set. Whenever you work with samples you work with gaps (e.g., data you do not have), which may include values which may profoundly impact on the statistics you compute; your results and computations need to acknowledge that your data is incomplete.

How you draw your sample and how large your sample is determines how closely your results will resemble what the overall population looks like. We will show this with an example looking at a population of 120 values[1] (here, IQ test results) from which we have drawn four different samples of 30 values each. This example also shows how to calculate these parameters and statistics in Excel and SPSS.

### ONLINE CONTENT

You can find SPSS and Excel files with the data for the four samples on the companion website (Figure 6.7).

**Population**

|  Sample 1  | | | | Sample 2 | | |
| --- | --- | --- | --- | --- | --- |
| 80 | 94 | 112 | 95 | 94 | 78 |
| 113 | 91 | 134 | 113 | 75 | 83 |
| 94 | 91 | 108 | 93 | 98 | 84 |
| 99 | 114 | 87 | 126 | 81 | 88 |
| 114 | 116 | 92 | 113 | 110 | 130 |
| 120 | 110 | 122 | 116 | 63 | 105 |
| 91 | 82 | 78 | 94 | 101 | 88 |
| 102 | 102 | 117 | 108 | 80 | 121 |
| 91 | 131 | 116 | 113 | 128 | 92 |
| 127 | 104 | 120 | 81 | 112 | 80 |
| 115 | 104 | 90 | 108 | 101 | 117 |
| 88 | 89 | 105 | 109 | 106 | 89 |
| 89 | 119 | 114 | 97 | 94 | 86 |
| 85 | 95 | 100 | 112 | 117 | 80 |
| 74 | 84 | 109 | 139 | 111 | 77 |
| 101 | 128 | 115 | 92 | 104 | 112 |
| 110 | 100 | 97 | 115 | 81 | 96 |
| 85 | 107 | 115 | 107 | 122 | 115 |
| 74 | 119 | 96 | 77 | 88 | 116 |
| 112 | 93 | 108 | 120 | 80 | 115 |

Sample 3 — Sample 4

**Figure 6.7** *Four samples from the same population*

---

[1] The values used here are normally distributed (see section 6.7 for a definition of a normal distribution). They were generated in Excel by using the formula =NORMINV(RAND(), 100, 15) where 100 and 15 are parameters we chose: we wanted a distribution with a mean of 100 and a standard deviation of 15. Note that because the distribution is still quite small the calculated mean and standard deviation will approximate but not quite meet those parameters. If we had generated data for a population of 500, 800 or 1000, the values would get much closer to our chosen parameters.

We will first use data from Sample 1. We have reordered the data into one column in Excel to later allow better comparisons between samples, but the functions in Excel all work with the existing layout in the example. Go to Insert → Function … and open the Formula Builder to select the right function (Figure 6.8).

|  | A | B | C |
|---|---|---|---|
|  |  | Sample 1 |  |
|  |  | 80 |  |
|  |  | 113 |  |
|  |  | 94 |  |
|  |  | 99 |  |
|  |  | 114 |  |
|  |  | 120 |  |
|  |  | 91 |  |
|  |  | 102 |  |
|  |  | 91 |  |
|  |  | 127 |  |
|  |  | 94 |  |
|  |  | 91 |  |
|  |  | 91 |  |
|  |  | 114 |  |
|  |  | 116 |  |
|  |  | 110 |  |
|  |  | 82 |  |
|  |  | 102 |  |
|  |  | 131 |  |
|  |  | 104 |  |
|  |  | 112 |  |
|  |  | 134 |  |
|  |  | 108 |  |
|  |  | 87 |  |
|  |  | 92 |  |
|  |  | 122 |  |
|  |  | 78 |  |
|  |  | 117 |  |
|  |  | 116 |  |
|  |  | 120 |  |
| **Mean** |  | 105.07 |  |
| **Standard Deviation** |  | 15.416 |  |
| **Variance** |  | 237.651 |  |

Formula bar: $fx$ =VAR.S(B2:B31)

**Figure 6.8** Descriptives for Sample 1
Used with permission from Microsoft.

**EXCEL**
- First, calculate the mean as described in Section 6.3.1. To calculate the standard deviation for Sample 1, use the function STDEV.S (the 'S' denotes that this is the version for samples) either through the Formula Builder or by typing in directly =STDEV.S(B2:31). This will calculate the standard deviation for Sample 1 as 15.416.
- Then repeat these steps for Samples 2, 3 and 4. Across all samples, this gives you the following results (Figure 6.9):

172  Introducing Quantitative Methods

|  | Sample 1 | Sample 2 | Sample 3 | Sample 4 |
|---|---|---|---|---|
|  | 80 | 115 | 95 | 108 |
|  | 113 | 88 | 113 | 109 |
|  | 94 | 89 | 93 | 97 |
|  | 99 | 85 | 126 | 112 |
|  | 114 | 74 | 113 | 139 |
|  | 120 | 101 | 116 | 92 |
|  | 91 | 110 | 94 | 115 |
|  | 102 | 85 | 108 | 107 |
|  | 91 | 74 | 113 | 77 |
|  | 127 | 112 | 81 | 120 |
|  | 94 | 104 | 94 | 101 |
|  | 91 | 89 | 75 | 106 |
|  | 91 | 119 | 98 | 94 |
|  | 114 | 95 | 81 | 117 |
|  | 116 | 84 | 110 | 111 |
|  | 110 | 128 | 63 | 104 |
|  | 82 | 100 | 101 | 81 |
|  | 102 | 107 | 80 | 122 |
|  | 131 | 119 | 128 | 88 |
|  | 104 | 93 | 112 | 80 |
|  | 112 | 90 | 78 | 117 |
|  | 134 | 105 | 83 | 89 |
|  | 108 | 114 | 84 | 86 |
|  | 87 | 100 | 88 | 80 |
|  | 92 | 109 | 130 | 77 |
|  | 122 | 115 | 105 | 112 |
|  | 78 | 97 | 88 | 96 |
|  | 117 | 115 | 121 | 115 |
|  | 116 | 96 | 92 | 116 |
|  | 120 | 108 | 80 | 115 |
| Mean | 105.07 | 100.667 | 98.100 | 102.767 |
| Standard Deviation | 15.416 | 13.755 | 17.456 | 15.697 |

*Figure 6.9* Descriptives for all samples
Used with permission from Microsoft.

Note how different variance and standard deviations for each sample are, even though all samples have been drawn from the same population.

**SPSS** Use the first procedure described in Section 6.3.1 and instead (or additionally) tick the box for Std. Deviation and Variance in the Dispersion window in the bottom left. Alternatively, use the second procedure described in Section 6.1 and tick Std. Deviation and Variance in the Dispersion part of the Descriptives: Options window.

As a final step, we will calculate the population parameters by using the population variants of the same formulas we have used just now.

**EXCEL** Instead of STDEV.S, we are using STDEV.P and are going to select a wider range of cells to include all of them. In the table below we have listed the results for the population parameters next to the sample statistics (Table 6.8):

*Table 6.8 Mean and standard deviation for four samples from the same population, and for the overall population*

|  | Sample 1 | Sample 2 | Sample 3 | Sample 4 | Population |
|---|---|---|---|---|---|
| Mean | 105.07 | 100.667 | 98.100 | 102.767 | 101.650 |
| Standard deviation | 15.416 | 13.755 | 17.456 | 15.697 | 15.653 |

Compare sample statistics against population parameters and you will see how the values are very close, which makes sense – the five sets of values are related as four are a subset of the fifth, but they are not identical because the four subsets are incomplete parts of the whole.

> **SPSS** SPSS does not usually give the option to calculate population variance and standard deviation; the correcting factor is always applied, therefore there is no corresponding guidance for this calculation.

The concepts of variance and standard deviation are so important because the basic principle underlying almost all statistical tests is to compare the obtained difference between sample means, such as between the experimental and the control group's results, to the mean difference expected by chance. Another way to describe this would be to talk about the identification and classification of variance as variance *between* treatments and variance *within* treatments, and the contribution of each type to the overall variance.

Consider the concept of perceived stress. Peoples' perceived stress varies widely, and you will know from your own experience that some of your friends stress much more easily than others. If you were to collect data on peoples' perceived stress levels, you would not expect every participant to have the exact same result. In addition, within every individual, perceived stress varies too. You have good days and bad days, sometimes you feel more in control, sometimes you feel less in control and much more stressed. Now consider a study like the one described in Chapter 2 where you want to know whether offering meditation sessions to participants has an effect on participants' perceived stress. In this scenario, what you are really doing is trying to identify the sources of the variance of the test scores. Some of the variance will be due to the fact that people are different and have different base levels of stress; some of the variance will be due to the fact that individual participants have different stress levels at different times and in different contexts. Both types would be considered **error variance** and will be largely **unsystematic variance**. However, there may be sources of **systematic variance**, too: For example, if self-allocation to groups was allowed, participants' stress levels may influence their decision which group to join, thus introducing systematic differences. Any such variance introduced by confounds would be termed, unsurprisingly, **confound variance**. Lastly, you would hope that further systematic variance is introduced by the intervention, or treatment itself, aptly named **treatment variance**. You are therefore looking at total variance as the sum of both systematic and unsystematic variances. You aim to design your research methods in a way which focusses on identifying treatment variance and minimises or eliminates confound variance, while hoping to mitigate error variance through random allocation to conditions (Figure 6.10).

```
                    ┌─ ┌─ Treatment Variance
                    │  │  Variance introduced by treatment. For
                    │  │  example, reduced stress levels through
                    │  │  meditation sessions.
                    │  Systematic
                    │  Variance
                    │  │  Confound Variance
  Total             │  │  Variance not related to treatment. For
  Variance          │  │  example. self-allocation to treatment
                    │  │  group affected by participants'
                    │  └─ perceived stress levels.
                    │
                    │  ┌─ Error Variance
                    │  │  Random variance not related to the
                    │  Unsystematic treatment. For example, individual
                    │  Variance    difference between participants;
                    │  │  participants having good/bad days.
                    └─ └─
```

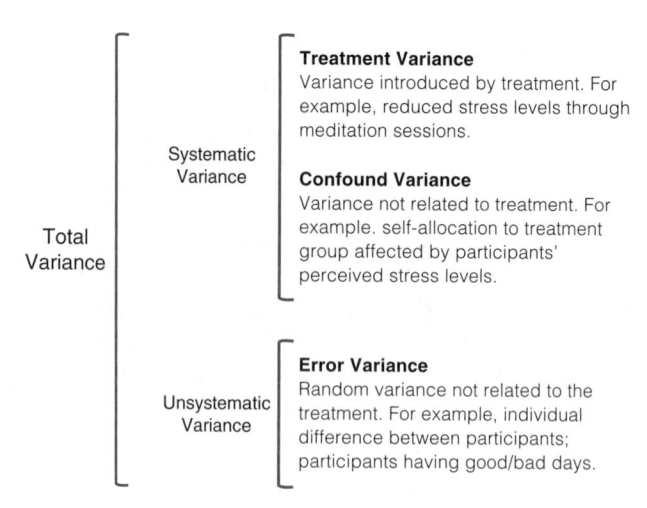

**Figure 6.10** *Example of sources of variance in perceived stress*

Granted, this is a somewhat simplified example, but identifying and examining variance is at the root of statistical analyses and you will encounter this concept frequently, including but not limited to the discussion of chi-square tests, ANOVAs, factor analysis or multiple regression. Knowing that overall variance is the sum of variances contributed from different sources also helps with understanding why statistical tests are categorised as independent, paired, repeated, etc. Calculations differ whether you compare the same group of participants before and after an intervention, or whether you compare two different groups of participants with and without the intervention. If you are comparing the same participant's score before and after an intervention, you expect most of the variance to be coming from the intervention. But if you are comparing two different groups, the composition of the overall variance is different. For example, Kirmani (1997) examined the effects of both print ad colour and exposure repetition in a 2 × 4 between-participants design, meaning that different groups of participants experienced the eight different conditions. When analysing the data, Kirmani's statistical analyses had to take into account that differences between the groups could not only have come from having seen different ads a different number of times, but also that the participants varied from group to group, thus adding additional variance.

### 6.6.1 Going further: Var-iations

You do not usually have to calculate the variance for your main descriptives and analyses, but if you wanted to, follow these instructions:

- Open the Formula Builder by navigating to Insert → Function ..., type 'var' (without quotation marks) and you will see that a number of possible functions are displayed: VAR, VAR.P, VAR.S, VARA, VARP and VARPA. Do not panic! You need only two of those. Those six versions are actually three sets of two, with each set consisting of a version for sample and population:
  - VAR (sample) and VARP (population) are only included for compatibility reasons with older Excel versions only and can safely be ignored.
  - VARA (sample) and VARPA (population) are used for value distributions which include logical values and text and can similarly be ignored for now.
  - This leaves VAR.S (sample) and VAR.P (population).

- You want to calculate the variance for a sample, so choose VAR.S. Click on Insert Function and tell Excel which cells to include by highlighting the relevant area in the worksheet. Alternatively, you can type the function in directly as =VAR.S(B1:B31).

## REVIEW & REFLECT

- Why is the concept of sources of variance particularly important for social science research?
- Would it make sense to focus on within-participants research to eliminate a source of variance? Why or why not?

## 6.7 NORMAL DISTRIBUTION

Earlier in this chapter we introduced measures of central tendency and the standard deviation as means of describing a distribution's centre and the spread of values around that centre. This section discusses the **normal distribution** as a special type of distribution which exhibits a number of specific properties:

1. Values cluster around the mean rather than spreading evenly and in a linear fashion around it.
2. The distribution is symmetric (i.e., the distribution of values above the mean value mirrors the distribution of values below the mean).

When plotted as a graph of values against frequencies, these properties mean that the resulting curve roughly resembles a bell-shaped curve where the exact shape is defined by the variance around the mean; the curve can be flat or very narrow or anything in between (Figure 6.11):

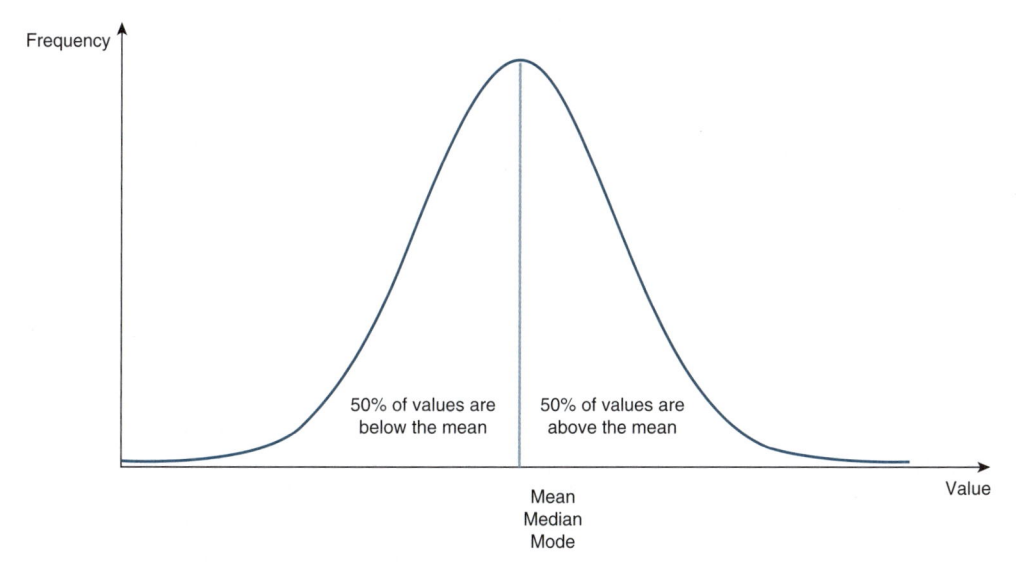

*Figure 6.11 A prototypical normal distribution*

A large number of phenomena and properties seem to be distributed in a normal distribution following the properties described above. Normal distribution allows you to identify

176  *Introducing Quantitative Methods*

and express probabilities for the values you can expect to observe. Note how the curve is highest around the mean, meaning that values close to the mean will occur most frequently; it then flattens towards the outside. This means that values further away from the mean are less likely to occur. For example, according to a 2014 Yougov poll (Yougov, 2014) the average body height for adult men is 178 cm (5'10"). If body height is a property which is normally distributed, it will mean that there are as many men taller than 178 cm as there are men smaller than 178 cm. A substantial number of men will be 178 cm or very close to it, with the frequencies diminishing the further you get away from the mean of 178 cm in either direction.

We have presented above an abstract, ideal form of the normal distribution, where mean, mode and median coincide: here, the mean is also the most frequent value (mode) and is the value dividing the distribution in half (median). In a normal distribution, 68% of the values are found within one standard deviation of the mean; 95% within two standard deviations; and 99.7% within three standard deviations. Turning this around it means that there is a 95.45% chance you will observe a value that falls within two standard deviations from the mean, but only a 4.55% chance of observing a value that falls outside two standard deviations (Figure 6.12).

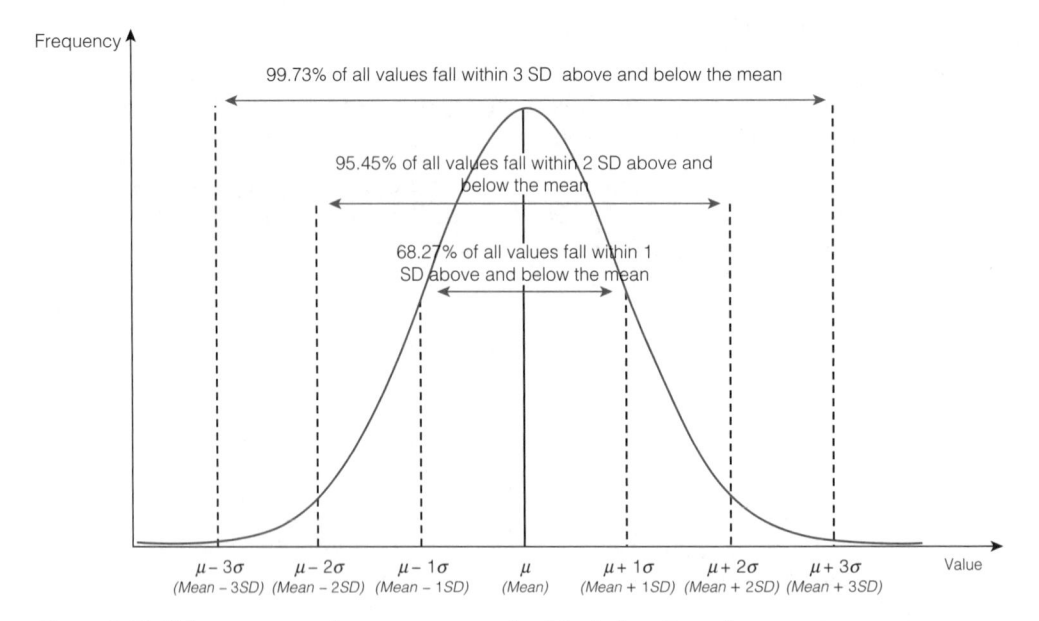

*Figure 6.12  Values one, two, three or more standard deviations from the mean*

Returning to the previous example of an adult population with a mean body height of 178 cm and a standard deviation of 15 (cm), this would mean that 68% of the population are of a body height 178 ±15 (i.e., between 163 and 193 cm). The normal distribution is an abstraction as it is difficult to observe a normal distribution in small samples. Only with large sample sizes will the distribution really be visible as you include more and more cases to fill out the shape of the curve. The following graph gives a very good illustration of how the increase in observations leads to the curve becoming more and more smoothly bell-shaped. Each column displays a series of samples from a normal distribution. Note how the initial curve is quite jaggy but grows smoother with growing sample size (Figure 6.13):

**Random samples from normal distributions—five samples of size 20, 50, 100, and 500.**

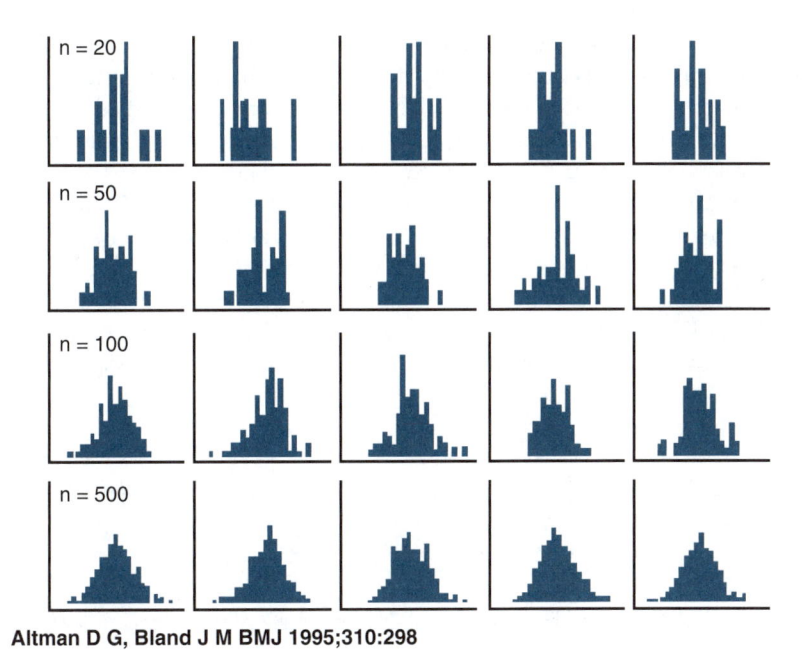

Altman D G, Bland J M BMJ 1995;310:298

*Figure 6.13* The shape of a normal distribution becoming more visible with growing sample size
Reproduced with permission from BMJ Publishing Group Ltd. (Altman and Bland, 1995).

Because of its bell-shape, the curve is also referred to as **bell curve**; alternatively you will see it referred to as a **Gaussian curve** named for Friedrich Gauss, the researcher who first described it.

Although the normal distribution is common it is by no means universal and the name thus probably slightly misleading. For example, ordinal data or nominal data is not normally distributed. In many countries, age is not normally distributed across a population but rather skewed towards older age; in war-torn countries where whole generations are lost to war, the reverse is true, with the age distribution skewed towards young age. Other times, the manner in which a sample was formed or data collected may in itself lead to a non-normal distribution. For example, depending on how the feedback is elicited, customer satisfaction surveys may be skewed towards both ends, with a distinct dip in the middle as very happy and very frustrated customers are more likely to respond than customers feeling indifferent or mildly pleased/peeved. Whether a distribution is normal or not has implications for the type of statistical analyses that can be conducted, and Chapter 8 will discuss this in more detail.

> **? REVIEW & REFLECT**
>
> - Are there any subject areas or types of variables that are more likely to be normally distributed than others?
> - What might be the implications of normal distributions for marking student work or assessing employee performance?

## 6.8  Z-SCORES

The 'standard' in the term 'standard deviation' alludes to its use as a tool to describe a value in terms of relative size and distance to the mean. In the previous example, a difference of 15 cm between values or sizes could also be expressed as a difference of exactly one standard deviation. This may sound not particularly useful at first glance, but it is extremely helpful to compare values coming from different distributions with vastly different means and standard deviations. For example, consider intelligence tests using different scales: Some will operate with a mean of 100 and a standard deviation of 15; others perhaps with a mean of 100 and a standard deviation of 24. Assume that you have a participant with a score of 130 in the first test; another participant scored 136 in the second test. Whose IQ is higher? Scores from tests with different standard deviations are not immediately comparable but first have to be converted from **raw scores** to **z-scores** which express values in relative terms (multiples of standard deviation) rather than absolute. The equation for a z-score is

$$z = \frac{X - \mu}{\sigma}$$

In simpler terms:

$$z = \frac{value - mean}{standard\ deviation}$$

We are applying this first to the raw score of 130 in a test using a mean of 100 and a standard deviation of 15:

$$z = \frac{130 - 100}{15} = \frac{30}{15} = 2$$

This participant's IQ is two standard deviations above the mean. Now have a look at the second participant's IQ score, 136 on a scale with a mean of 100 and a standard deviation of 24:

$$z = \frac{136 - 100}{24} = \frac{36}{24} = 1.5$$

This participant's score is 1.5 standard deviation above the mean. Using the z-score we can show that although the first participant's score is lower in absolute terms, their IQ is higher because the value is further away from the mean than the second participant's score. Positive z-scores indicate that the value is *above* the mean; negative z-scores indicate the value is *below* the mean, but both describe distance to the mean. Lastly, knowing the z-score and a distribution's mean and standard deviation means you can reconstruct the raw score by multiplying the z-score with the known standard deviation and adding it to the known mean. For example, assume you have a z-score of −0.7 and know that the mean is 10 and the standard deviation 3:

$$X = -0.7(3) + 10 = -2.1 + 10 = 7.9$$

You can easily check that the raw score was indeed 7.9 by calculating the z-score:

$$z = \frac{7.9 - 10}{3} = \frac{-2.1}{3} = -0.7$$

## 6.9  SKEW AND KURTOSIS

We have occasionally used 'skewed' synonymous with 'biased', but there is another meaning of skew which describes the shape of normal distributions. More specifically, **skewness** describes distributions that are not symmetrical and where one of the two tails is longer than the other. Look at the two distributions below (Figure 6.14):

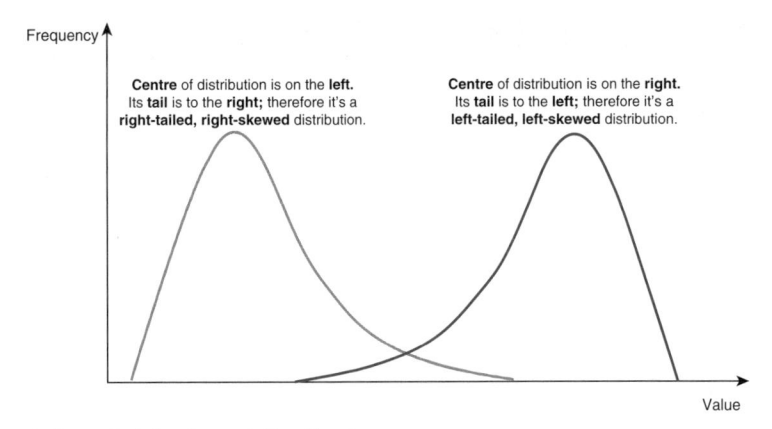

*Figure 6.14* Left- and right-skewed distributions

You can see that for the left distribution, the centre is more to the left, and the right tail is longer than the left tail. This distribution displays **positive skew**. The naming convention is based on which tail is longer; therefore, a distribution that skews to the right can also be described as **right-skewed** or **right-tailed**. In contrast, the centre of the right distribution is to the right, and the left tail is longer than the right. This distribution displays **negative skew**; it is **left-skewed** or **left-tailed**. For an example of skew consider Wu and Wang's study on the effect of word of mouth appeal and message source credibility on brand attitude. In their methods section, they acknowledge that their method of recruiting participants through an online survey resulted in more male than female participants and younger than average participants, resulting in a skew towards men and younger consumers (Wu and Wang, 2011); if you plotted the participants' age distribution, such a distribution would likely look left-skewed as the centre of the distribution would be towards the left (i.e., younger age values).

Another way of describing the shape of the distribution is **kurtosis**, which can be either positive or negative. **Positive kurtosis** means the distribution is steeper in the centre of the distribution and its tails are shorter; **negative kurtosis** means the distribution has a lower peak and longer tails. Distributions with positive kurtosis are also referred to as **leptokurtic**, distributions with negative kurtosis as **platykurtic**, and distributions with normal kurtosis as **mesokurtic** (see Figure 6.15):

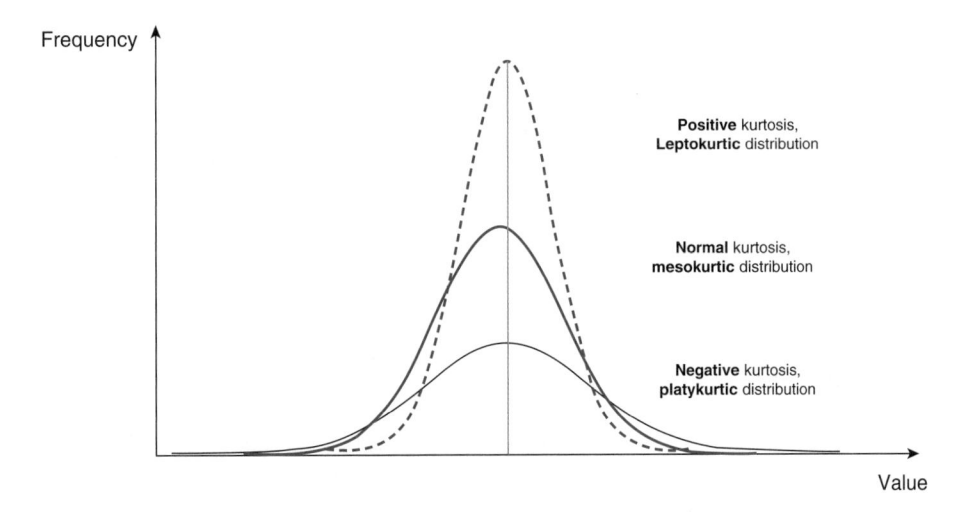

*Figure 6.15* Types of kurtosis

## 6.10 SIGNIFICANCE

Inferential analyses normally consist of two parts: a test parameter and a significance value. For example, conducting a correlation analysis will result in a correlation and a significance. This will become clearer in Chapter 8 when we discuss individual tests, but for now suffice it to say that the result of a test can only be properly interpreted in combination with the *p*-value.

Why *p*? The *p* stands for *probability*, and in this context the probability of the result being due to chance. When you observe a difference, a correlation, an association or an effect, you do not want this outcome to be due to chance. You want the difference between the test scores of two groups to accurately reflect a difference due to experimental manipulation or correctly reflect a genuine, existing difference; for example, you want the correlation between practice and performance to be an indication of a genuine relation between practising and performing. This means the lower the *p*-value, the better. The commonly accepted cut-off point is 5%, that means it is accepted – or tolerated – that there is an overall chance of 5% that the result does not reflect an actual difference in the two groups but that the difference in values is due to sheer chance. This cut-off point is referred to as the **alpha level** and describes the highest *p*-value one would still be willing to accept. If you look back to Figure 6.12 showing the distribution of values within one, two and three standard deviations from the mean, you will see that 95.45% of values fall within two standard deviations above and below the mean; a cut-off point of 5% is therefore roughly (but not exactly) equivalent to excluding values more than two standard deviations from the mean. Remember the concept of the null hypothesis, introduced in Section 2.10.4, describing the expectation that there is no effect, no difference, no correlation? A *p*-value of higher than 5% means that you have not enough reason to reject the null hypothesis; a value of 5% or lower means that the null hypothesis is rejected and the alternative hypothesis accepted.

How does this look in practice? Assume that a marketing agency trials two different ads. Each ad is shown to a different group. The agency expects ad 2 to be more memorable than ad 1:

- $H_1$: There is a difference between how memorable ad 1 and 2 are such that ad 2 is more memorable than ad 1.

Their corresponding null hypothesis is that both ads are equally memorable:

- $H_0$: There is no difference between how memorable ad 1 and 2 are.

Either of the two hypotheses has to be true. There are only two possibilities, or 'realities': the ads differ in how memorable they are or they do not. Equally, you could make one of two choices: accept or reject $H_1$. This means there are four different possible scenarios in total, illustrated in the table below (Table 6.9):

*Table 6.9* Type 1 and 2 errors

| Reality | The ads differ in how memorable they are. | | The ads are equally memorable. | |
|---|---|---|---|---|
| Decision | **Scenario 1a** You conclude that there is no difference and accept $H_0$. | **Scenario 1b** You conclude that there is a difference and reject $H_0$. | **Scenario 2a** You conclude that there is no difference and accept $H_0$. | **Scenario 2b** You conclude that there is a difference and reject $H_0$. |
| Outcome | You have committed a Type 2 error. | You are correct. | | You have committed a Type 1 error. |

- In scenario 1a, the ads differ in how memorable they are, but you conclude they are not. You therefore accept H$_0$ even though you should have rejected it: you have committed a **Type 2 error**.
- In scenario 1b, the ads differ in how memorable they are, and you correctly conclude that there is a difference. You correctly accept H$_1$ and reject H$_0$.
- In scenario 2a, the ads are equally memorable. You correctly conclude that they are equally memorable, and you correctly accept H$_0$ and reject H$_1$.
- In scenario 2b, the ads are equally memorable but you incorrectly conclude that there is a difference. You therefore accept H$_1$ even though you should have rejected it, and you reject H$_0$ even though it should have been accepted: you have committed a **Type 1 error**.

We have mentioned above that a 5% chance of the result being due not to a genuine difference or effect but rather due to chance is usually accepted. This amounts to a 5% chance of falsely rejecting the null hypothesis (i.e., committing a Type 1 error). Could we not use a more stringent *p*-value, for example, $p = 1\%$ or perhaps 1‰ (1 per mille = 1/1000)? Yes, we could and this would indeed reduce the likelihood of committing a Type 1 error. However, by introducing a stricter *p*-value, we are now more likely to falsely accept the null hypothesis when it is false, which would be committing a Type 2 error. The two types of error are inextricably linked and whatever precautions we take to reduce the likelihood of committing one increases the likelihood of committing the other. Ultimately it is your responsibility and your judgement which error would be the most detrimental to your research, and hence which error you prefer to avoid at the cost of being more likely to commit the other type of error.

Keep in mind that the 5% cut-off is usually interpreted as the cut-off for a two-tailed hypothesis: if your hypothesis is one-tailed, you are usually allowed to halve the calculated *p*-value and take the resulting value as 'your' *p*-value. For example, imagine that you conduct a t-test (see Section 9.4) to examine whether two groups differ from each other, and your hypothesis went beyond stating the existence of a difference but also stated a direction (e.g., predicted that the scores of group 2 would be higher than the scores of group 1). The descriptives indicate that the scores of group 2 are indeed higher than the scores of group 1, but the *p*-value for the t-test is .08 and therefore higher than the .05 you'd be looking for. In this case you are allowed to halve the *p*-value, resulting in .04, which would be considered significant. This serves as a good reminder that when interpreting data and test results you are always operating with probabilities. Studies rarely 'prove' or 'disprove' anything, but results may make certain assumptions more likely than others. Thus the absence of a significant difference between two groups' reading scores does not mean that there *is* no difference, but that a difference is *less likely*. Similarly, finding a statistically significant difference does not automatically mean that the two groups are indeed different. It just means that the chance of this being the case is less than 5%. Hopefully it has become clear by now that in the context of statistical analyses, the term **significance** has a very specific and limited meaning that has nothing to do with the more colloquial interpretation of 'significant' as 'important'. Non-significant results can be very important, for example, when a study fails to show a hypothesised difference between two groups (e.g., between people from different socioeconomic status, between genders, or between depressed and non-depressed participants). Conversely, a highly significant result showing a difference of a tenth of a point in a test score between two groups may be highly statistically significant but raise questions as to the practical relevance. For example, an intervention aimed at reducing alcohol consumption might show a highly significant effect which manifests as a difference of a quarter unit a week between the test group and the control group. Would this result justify spending large amounts of money on an intervention across a larger group of people? And what would it mean if a different intervention had a lower significance but the two groups' consumption differed by two units or more? In fact, questions like these have become increasingly more prominent and important in psychological research. Most of what we have described above reflects the traditional, classic understanding of the *p*-value and is likely to mirror how you have been taught to understand and interpret significance and *p*-value – but there is a lively academic debate about the meaning and value of alpha levels and significance; see, for example, McCloskey and Ziliak's (2008) book *The Cult of Statistical Significance*. One result of these discussions is the American Statistical Association's statement on statistical significance and *p*-values, which highlights the following six principles:

1. *p*-values can indicate how incompatible the data are with a specified statistical model.
2. *p*-values do not measure the probability that the studied hypothesis is true, or the probability that the data were produced by random chance alone.
3. Scientific conclusions and business or policy decisions should not be based only on whether a *p*-value passes a specific threshold.
4. Proper inference requires full reporting and transparency.
5. A *p*-value or statistical significance does not measure the size of an effect or the importance of a result.
6. By itself, a *p*-value does not provide a good measure of evidence regarding a model or hypothesis.
(*Source*: ASA, 2016)

In other words: Do not take *p*-values at face value. Interpret your data in context; do not mistake significance for truth or importance.

In Section 3.8.1 we described a simple way of calculating required sample sizes and introduced the concept of confidence level, which we described as a measure of confidence in your data. The *p*-value is linked to the confidence level because the confidence level is actually calculated by 1-*p*; for example, if you set alpha at 5%, your confidence level is 95% (1 − .05 = .95). Note that as your confidence level increases, *p* decreases: If you want a higher confidence level, you need a lower *p*.

> **! LOOK OUT!**
>
> When *p* is displayed as .000 it is reported not as .000 but as $p < .001$.

> **? REVIEW & REFLECT**
>
> - McCloskey and Ziliak (2008) talk about the 'cult of statistical significance'. Do you think that is an appropriate interpretation?
> - Do you think there is merit in still using *p*-values?

## 6.11 POWER

The term **power** is used to describe the probability that a statistical test will correctly reject a false null hypothesis and correctly identify a genuine effect (or difference or association). The larger the sample, the more likely it is therefore representative of the population it was drawn from and the more likely you are to make accurate judgements about the data. Consequently, power is influenced by N. In Section 3.8.2, we discussed the importance of choosing an appropriate sampling method to form a sample which is sufficiently representative of the population from which the sample has been drawn. We noted that in addition to the 'content' of the example, size was also important (You in the back row, stop snickering.) Having introduced the concepts of normal distribution and power, it should now become more apparent why a sufficiently large sample size is needed: the values you are going to observe in the sample will be distributed around the mean. The more data points you have, the closer you get to determining the spread and the centre of the distribution. With it you get closer to the real mean, and the more likely your results are to reflect the actual effect rather than being due to chance. This means that the quality of your analyses and the validity of your results depend on the number of data points. That all said, in smaller studies, particularly in the context of students conducting their final year research, it is known and accepted that sample sizes are rarely large enough to achieve high power. We have introduced the concept here so you are familiar with its implication but since power is affected by so many different factors – sample size, expected effect size, standard error/standard deviation – it is beyond the scope of this chapter to provide a satisfying guide for calculation.

## 6.12  EFFECT SIZE

While the concept of power relates to the accuracy of our result and our decision to reject or accept the null hypothesis, the **effect size** is used to express the magnitude of our finding. For example, we may want to know whether there is a difference in means between two populations. The effect size is then calculated as the ratio of the difference between the compared means and the standard deviation though different approaches vary as to which standard deviation value should be used – in effect telling you how big the difference in means is relative to the standard deviation. This way, the effect size provides a standardised way of looking at differences. If the spread of running ability is very large in the group you are competing in, running a tenth of a second faster will not make much of a difference; in the Olympics, it could win you a gold medal. A brewery will react differently to the content of their bottles deviating ±5 ml from the volume indicated than a company producing potent medical drugs. The former may consider this well within the normal range of variation; the latter an unacceptable error with potentially lethal consequences for the patient.

One of the standard measures of effect size is **Cohen's d** which is used to compute effect sizes for differences between two independent groups:

$$d = \frac{\bar{X}_1 - \bar{X}_2}{SD}$$

$\bar{X}_1$ and $\bar{X}_2$ are the means of the two groups, and $SD$ usually refers to the standard deviation of the control group (however, note the explanation in Section 6.13.1). If this concept looks familiar, it is because it is reminiscent of the z-score which also helps you standardise scores to compare them better.

When interpreting the result, anything above .80 is considered a large effect size. For a medium effect size, you need .50 or larger; to get at least a small effect size, you need .20 or more. Now compare the two calculations for the same absolute difference (3) but for populations with different standard deviations:

Example 1: A study looked at difference in reaction times with and without **priming**, that is, preceding one stimulus with another which prepares the participants for a subsequent stimulus (e.g., by activating certain concepts or increasing their attention). In your experimental group (with priming) you observed mean reaction times of 450 ms, with a standard deviation of 75 ms.

In your control group, you observed mean reaction times of 453 ms, with a standard deviation of 79 ms.

$$d = \frac{X_1 - X_2}{SD} = \frac{453 - 450}{79} = \frac{3}{79} = 0.038.$$

Example 2: A study compared the impact of ad repetition on attitude towards the brand. After the first repetition, mean attitude was found to be 9.5, with a standard deviation of 2.7; after the tenth repetition, mean attitude dropped to 6.5, with a standard deviation of 2.8.

$$d = \frac{X_1 - X_2}{SD} = \frac{9.5 - 6.5}{2.8} = \frac{3}{2.8} = 1.071$$

You can see how the same absolute difference translates into two very different ratios, reflecting the relative size of the difference between the two examples: While the first effect size does not even meet the threshold of a small effect size, the second one can be considered a very large effect. This is just one of the many ways of calculating effect sizes, and there is no consistent calculation or treatment of effect sizes in SPSS. It is beyond the scope of this book to present an exhaustive list. Thankfully there are a number of online calculators available to compute effect sizes for a variety of research designs, from paired groups to independent groups, and looking at differences, effects and correlations.

### ONLINE CONTENT

You can find a list of online calculators on the companion website.

Lastly, remember that the final interpretation of the importance and meaning of a result lies with you. All elements need to be considered in context. In Section 6.10 we already noted that significance does not equal importance. The significance tells you whether a difference exists; effect size tells you the size of the difference, but only you as the researcher can decide whether the difference is important in terms of real-world impact.

### REVIEW & REFLECT

- Can you think of examples where effect size might be more important than significance?
- What do you think is most important, and why: power, effect size or significance?

## 6.13 DEGREES OF FREEDOM

In Chapters 9, 10 and 11 you will see that conducting and particularly reporting statistical test results often requires stating **degrees of freedom**. What does that mean? Simply speaking, degrees of freedom is a measure of how many values in a calculation you are free to vary, and it is linked to N, the number of values in your sample or population. For example, assume that you know your sample has ten values and that the sample average is 25. Take a look at the table below. You can see that there are many different combinations of values which all come to the same average. In each case we have listed a set of nine numbers and then calculated the tenth number that was needed to bring the overall average to 25.

| 1 | 2 | 3 | 4 | 5 | 6 | 7 | 8 | 9 | 10 | Average |
|---|---|---|---|---|---|---|---|---|----|---------|
| 14 | 14 | 23 | 23 | 23 | 23 | 8 | 15 | 5 | 102 | 25 |
| 12 | 17 | 23 | 23 | 3 | 25 | 8 | 15 | 15 | 109 | 25 |
| 25 | 37 | 32 | 11 | 28 | 25 | 23 | 21 | 25 | 23 | 25 |
| 25 | 37 | 32 | 41 | 38 | 35 | 33 | 31 | 35 | −57 | 25 |

In this example, you can freely choose nine values, but to get the average you want, the tenth needs to be of a certain value. This means that you have nine degrees of freedom.

### 6.13.1 Going further: Yours or mine? Calculating effect sizes with pooled standard deviations

We have presented above a simpler version of calculating effect size. In the example given we divided the difference between the two means by the standard deviation of the control group. This formula should suffice for your statistical requirements. However, some argue that rather than the control group's standard deviation, a pooled standard variation should be used which takes into account both the control and the experimental group. If you would like to go for the added precision (and do not mind a challenge in Excel), you could use the formula below instead; it might look complex, but it actually consists mostly of elements you already know (Figure 6.16).

$$SD_{pooled} = \sqrt{\underbrace{\frac{(n_1 - 1)SD_1^2 + (n_2 - 1)SD_2^2}{n_1 + n_2 - 2}}_{\text{Variance}}}$$

**Figure 6.16** *Formula for pooled variance*

You already know that the standard deviation is the square root of the variance. This means that the part under the square root sign describes how to calculate the pooled variance for a number of groups (here, two). Each group is represented by an element in the equation above the fraction bar and an element beneath it (Figure 6.17):

$$\frac{\overbrace{(n_1 - 1)SD_1^2}^{\text{Group 1}} + \overbrace{(n_2 - 1)SD_2^2}^{\text{Group 2}}}{\underbrace{n_1}_{\text{Group 1}} + \underbrace{n_2}_{\text{Group 2}} - 2}$$

**Figure 6.17** *Two groups in the pooled variance*

Now look at the individual elements. For each group represented in the formula, you calculate that group's variance by multiplying the number of values in that group with that group's standard deviation; you then apply a correction by subtracting 1. In the denominator (the part under the fraction bar) of the fraction you add up the total number of values across all groups compared, correcting again (this time by the total number of groups). That is all. Once you have calculated the pooled variance, you compute its square root and thus calculate the pooled standard deviation. You can then plug the value of the pooled standard deviation into the formula for Cohen's d as given above, which would now look like this:

$$d = \frac{\bar{X}_1 - \bar{X}_2}{SD_{pooled}} = \frac{\bar{X}_1 - \bar{X}_2}{\sqrt{\frac{(n_1 - 1)SD_1^2 + (n_2 - 1)SD_2^2}{n_1 + n_2 - 2}}}$$

## ONLINE CONTENT

You can download a worksheet for calculating Cohen's d with a pooled standard deviation from the companion website.

## RESEARCH METHODS AT WORK

Björn is the regional manager of a large fast food chain selling mainly seafood meals. To improve customer service, Björn has asked his assistant Ragnar to lead a project with two regional branches to trial a different in-store ordering process and examine how changing it would affect customer satisfaction. Having run the trial for a couple of months, Ragnar excitedly reports the results: the difference in customer satisfaction is highly significant at $p < .0001$! Although pleased, Björn is cautious and asks Ragnar what the absolute difference in customer satisfaction is. It turns out that average customer satisfaction is 4.14 in the restaurant using the old ordering process, and 4.15 in the one using the new process. While this is statistically highly significant, Björn knows this is likely due to the large sample size (because the trial ran for two months, the data is based on more than 40,000 completed customer satisfaction surveys) and the difference in practice largely meaningless; it is certainly not worth a lengthy training and orientation process for employees across all branches in the region.

---

Helga is comparing the spread of house prices in two different parts of town. Initially, they look quite similar as in both areas the average house price is £240,000. However, looking at the standard deviation, Helga can tell that one area has a much larger variation in individual house prices. For the southern part of town, the standard deviation is £15,000, meaning that 68.27% of houses go for a price between £255,000 and £225,000 (one SD from the mean in both directions, that is, £240,000 ± £15,000), and 95.45% of houses go for a price between £270,000 and £210,000 (two SD from the mean in both directions, that is, £240,000 ± £30,000). Less than 5% of houses are sold at a price above £270,000 or below £210,000. For the eastern part of town, however, the standard deviation is £50,000 – meaning that for 68.27% of houses, the prices range between £290,000 and £190,000 (one SD from the mean in either direction, that is, £240,000 ± £50,000); 95.45% of houses go for a price between £340,000 and £140,000 (two SD in both directions, that is, £240,000 ± £100,000). Just looking at the average house prices is therefore misleading since price and quality of houses vary much more in the southern part of town.

## A SHORT SUMMARY

- A distribution of values is best described by a combination of a measure of central tendency (mean, mode or median) and the spread of values around that measure.
- The mode describes the most frequent value(s) in a distribution.
- In an ordered set of values, the median cuts the set exactly in half such that half of the values are above and half are below the median.
- The mean or average is calculated by adding up all values and dividing them by the number of values.

- Median and mode are less vulnerable to extreme values than the mean.
- Variance and standard deviation describe the spread of a distribution of values.
- The standard deviation is derived by calculating the square root of the variance.
- Values relating to a population are called parameters; values relating to samples are called statistics.
- The normal distribution is a special kind of distribution with three key properties: the values cluster around the mean and they do so in a roughly symmetrical and non-linear way.
- In a normal distribution, the standard deviation is linked to a given percentage of values falling within a certain distance from the mean.
- Z-scores help you to standardise and thus compare values from different distributions.
- The *p*-value describes the probability a result is due to chance.
- A chance of 5% is usually considered acceptable, leading to the cut-off point of $p = .05$.
- A *p*-value of equal or smaller than .05 means rejecting the null hypothesis.
- Falsely rejecting the null hypothesis (i.e., positing a difference or effect or correlation where there is none) is committing a Type 1 error. In contrast, falsely accepting the null hypothesis is committing a Type 2 error.
- Reducing the risk of committing a Type 1 error increases the risk of committing a Type 2 error, and vice versa.
- The probability of correctly rejecting a false null hypothesis is described by the power.
- The term effect size is used to describe the magnitude of the difference between two means.

## ONLINE CONTENT

On the companion website you can download the following worksheets:

1. A worksheet which will guide you through calculating variance and standard deviation by first calculating mean and sum of squares, as well as an already completed worksheet to show you an example.
2. A worksheet to help you calculate population parameters in Excel.

## CHECK YOUR UNDERSTANDING

1. A study collected data on job satisfaction, seniority and salary.

    The data is available in Excel and SPSS files on the companion website.

    Calculate mean, median and mode(s) each:

    | Job satisfaction | Seniority | Salary |
    |---|---|---|
    | 12 | 2 | 102,100 |
    | 99 | 3 | 45,000 |
    | 25 | 5 | 80,500 |
    | 84 | 4 | 26,400 |

|      |   |         |
|------|---|---------|
| 100  | 1 | 58,000  |
| 50   | 2 | 750,000 |
| 90   | 1 | 12,000  |
| 22   | 5 | 18,100  |
| 70   | 4 | 35,600  |
| 22   | 1 | 43,000  |
| 12   | 4 | 70,500  |
| 14   | 4 | 64,800  |
| 12   | 2 | 12,500  |
| 88   | 4 | 130,000 |
| 57   | 1 | 95,000  |
| 76   | 2 | 63,000  |
| 45   | 5 | 27,000  |
| 27   | 1 | 33,000  |
| 80   | 4 | 55,000  |
| 95   | 4 | 19,600  |

Mean

Median

Mode(s) _____

2. Which measure of central tendency is best to describe each of the sets of values in Exercise 1, and why?

   - Job satisfaction:
   - Seniority:
   - Salary:

3. Part of the product design process is determining the measurements and dimensions of the product that make the product usable by as large a part of the population as possible. Assume you want to determine the required dimensions for a chair and assume that you have the data (in terms of means and standard deviation) of what people have judged to be a comfortable sitting height, and that the data is normally distributed. How many standard deviations from the mean would you need to consider if you wanted 95% or more of the population to be able to comfortably use the chair?

4. www Download the sample data set for this exercise. In this study, participants were asked to provide a suggestion for the length of a sentence for assault; the cases described referred to either a defendant of the same gender as the participant or of a different gender. Defendants were also identified as either repeat offenders or first-time offenders. This is a 2 × 2 × 2 study with the factors gender of participant (identifies as male or female), gender of defendant (identified in the records as male or female), and whether defendant is a repeat offender (yes/no). Using either Excel or SPSS:
   a. Determine mean sentencing length across all records.
   b. Determine variance and overall standard deviation, keeping in mind that your data comes from a sample, not a population.

c. Find out how many modes the distribution has and what they are.
d. How many participants suggested sentences of more than 40 months?
e. Establish average sentence lengths for each of the eight conditions.

5. The following list of values represents the self-esteem scores taken from a participant sample of 20.

| 12 |
|---|
| 8 |
| 9 |
| 10 |
| 12 |
| 8 |
| 9 |
| 10 |
| 12 |
| 4 |
| 9 |
| 10 |
| 3 |
| 6 |
| 5 |
| 7 |
| 4 |
| 6 |
| 9 |
| 7 |

a. Calculate variance and standard deviation for this variable.
b. Now assume this is not a sample, but a population. Calculate variance and standard deviation with the appropriate formulas.

6. If you are looking at a normal distribution, what percentage of values fall in the area two standard deviations above and below the mean?

7. If a distribution skews to the right, does it display a positive or negative skew?

8. Calculate z-scores for the following values:
   a. 8.5 (for a distribution with a mean of 60 and a SD of 8)
   b. 8.5 (for a distribution with a mean of 50 and a SD of 10)
   c. 145 (for a distribution with a mean of 100 and a SD of 15)

9. Assume that you are given the following z-scores and know that they are coming from a distribution with a mean of 80, SD = 12. Calculate the original score.
   a. z-score = 1.5
   b. z-score = −0.8
   c. z-score = .03

10. What type of error are you committing if you falsely reject the null hypothesis?

11. What happens if you reduce the probability of falsely rejecting the null hypothesis?

12. You are comparing neuroticism scores between participants raised as single children (N=39) and participants raised with siblings (N = 42). The mean score for neuroticism for participants who were an only child is 14.5 (SD = 3.25), while for participants who had siblings the mean is 13.8 (SD = 3.5). Calculate the effect size (your choice whether with regular SD or pooled SD).

# 7 Presentation and Illustration of Data

## WHAT IS THIS CHAPTER ABOUT?

Chapter 7 first discusses different options to present quantitative data, such as in tables or in narrative form. A large portion of this chapter is then dedicated to examining options of data visualisation by presenting an overview of the advantages and disadvantages of the most frequently used chart types such as bar charts, histograms, pie charts, scatter plots, line charts, etc.

## WHY IS THIS IMPORTANT?

In almost all cases, you are conducting your research with the aim of presenting the data to a target audience, whether to your colleagues, your supervisor, your boss, your customer, an exam panel or other interested parties. Presenting your data clearly makes it easier for others to understand your research and makes it more likely that in turn your findings may inform other peoples' work and research. The right illustration can help clarify your argument or illustrate your findings, while an inappropriate illustration can weaken your argument or introduce bias into your presentation. This chapter will help you design your presentation in a way so as to make it accessible to a broad audience.

## WHAT ARE THE LEARNING OUTCOMES OF THIS CHAPTER?

At the end of this chapter you will be able to:
- Design a complex table to present your data
- Choose appropriate chart types to visualise your data
- Consider how to make your charts and figures accessible to your readers

First, a few clarifications. In the context of this book, 'data' usually means variables and relationships between variables – effects, differences, associations, etc. When we talk about presenting data, this refers both to the initial verbal description and any visualisation in the form of graphs and charts because both are needed to give the reader insight into your data. When writing up your data, these descriptives are usually followed by reporting the outcome of statistical tests. However, this chapter will focus on presenting and illustrating descriptive data; we will explain how to report test results whenever a test is explained in Chapters 9, 10 and 11.

> In this book, formatting is similar to but not fully compliant with the American Psychological Association's (APA 2010) guidelines. These may or may not apply to you so make sure you know if you are expected to follow particular discipline and/or institution guidelines.
>
> In most cases, it is best to start with a narrative description of your data's main properties, such as mean and standard deviation. This provides information about the basic shape of the variables used in your study. In a second step, you can then illustrate some of the key properties and relationships with other variables using visualisation. This chapter will follow this process by discussing first how to present basic descriptives and then looking at the advantages and disadvantages of the most frequently used chart types.

## 7.1 BASIC DESCRIPTIVES

In Chapter 6 we mentioned that the best way to describe a distribution or set of values is to describe the shape and density of values, and their centre point. The same information is used in the initial narrative description of your data, precisely because it is the most informative. A very basic description of data includes mention of appropriate measures of central tendency: usually mean and standard deviation but, for reasons discussed in Section 6.4, other measures such as the mode or the median may be more appropriate. For example, the results of a (fictitious) study might be summarised like this.

> At the second time of measurement across all participants, intent to purchase product A ranged from 4.5 to 19, $M = 12.5$ ($SD = 3.2$). For participants in the experimental condition, intent to purchase scores ranged from 5 to 19, $M = 14$ ($SD = 2.1$); for participants in the control condition, intent to purchase scores ranged from 4.5 to 19, $M = 12$ ($SD = 2.2$).

You can see in the example above that rather than using the full expressions 'standard deviation' and 'mean' we have used the abbreviation *SD* and *M*. Note that when describing data, abbreviations such as *SD* for Standard Deviation and *M* for Mean are written in italics.

Reporting in narrative form is most effective if you are describing only a few variables, or just a few conditions within a variable. With a higher number of conditions, this can quickly become unwieldy. Consider a study that looks at factors that might influence a participants' willingness to donate to a charity. The study uses the variables 'type of charity' (supporting a political party, supporting the elderly, supporting animal rescues); the amount of 'donation initially requested' (low, moderate, high); and the 'type of appeal' for donation (appeal to reason, appeal to emotion). Participants only experience one condition each; the dependent variable is the size of the donation. This is described as a $3 \times 3 \times 2$ between-participants design, and you already know how to calculate the number of individual conditions: 3 times 3 times 2 = 18. A verbal narrative is not the best way to present your data in this case because the amount of information would be overwhelming and difficult to digest. An alternative solution would be to use a table, and the next section will look into using tables effectively.

> **REVIEW & REFLECT**
>
> - Why is it important to clearly present your findings?
> - What are the consequences of biased presentations?

## 7.2 USING TABLES EFFECTIVELY

Tables are versatile and can present a large amount of information in a relatively small space. In Section 6.1 we used a table to describe frequencies of main reasons not to vote for 190 participants (Table 7.1):

*Table 7.1 Frequencies of main reasons not to vote*

| Reason | Number of participants |
|---|---|
| I didn't think my vote would count | 23 |
| None of the parties reflected my own values | 24 |
| I couldn't make up my mind | 38 |
| I'm not interested in politics | 76 |
| Don't know | 19 |

You could easily accommodate one or more additional variables to the table presented above. For example, in addition to the main reason not to vote you can include a rubric 'first-time voter?' by introducing one more level to the table. 'First-time voter' now serves as a heading to the sub-headings of 'yes' and 'no'. In the table below we have also introduced a 'Total' column and 'Total' row to allow a quick look at the total number of first-time eligible voters (=87) or participants who said that none of the parties reflected their own values across both types of voters (=24) (Table 7.2):

*Table 7.2 Reasons for non-voting by voting eligibility*

|  | First-time voter? |  | Total |
|---|---|---|---|
| Main reason not to vote | Yes | No |  |
| I didn't think my vote would count | 17 | 6 | 23 |
| None of the parties reflected my own values | 10 | 14 | 24 |
| I couldn't make up my mind | 14 | 24 | 38 |
| I'm not interested in politics | 35 | 41 | 76 |
| Don't know | 11 | 8 | 19 |
| Total | 87 | 93 | 180 |

Such a table is also referred to as a **contingency table**. The subtotals of the Yes and No column and of the individual rows are called **marginal totals**; the overall total in the bottom right corner the **grand total**.

Tables can be expanded quite substantially to allow the presentation of multiple variables and conditions. In the example below we have listed the results for a 3 × 3 × 2 study which looked at the impact of 'amount requested' (high, middle or low), the 'type of charity' (political party, supporting the elderly, animal rescue) and the 'type of appeal' (to emotion or to reason) on the size of the donation (Table 7.3).

*Table 7.3* Mean (SD) of average donation (in £) per condition

|  | Charity focus |  |  |  |  |  |
|---|---|---|---|---|---|---|
|  | Supporting political party |  | Supporting the elderly |  | Animal rescue |  |
|  | Type of appeal |  | Type of appeal |  | Type of appeal |  |
| **Amount requested** | Emotion | Reason | Emotion | Reason | Emotion | Reason |
| **High** | £12 (3.4) | £3 (1.3) | £12 (4.6) | £5 (2.1) | £12 (4.7) | £12 (6.4) |
| **Moderate** | £11 (2.4) | £7 (4.5) | £9 (3.5) | £5 (2.2) | £12 (5.2) | £16 (5.2) |
| **Low** | £9 (2.4) | £11 (3.4) | £7 (5.1) | £6 (2.3) | £15 (6.2) | £13 (4.1) |

Here we have given one row to each level of the variable donation requested; the three main columns display the headings for the type of charity and each column is further divided into the two types of appeal. For completeness' sake we are illustrating below how to use the same table format to further include subtotals (Table 7.4).

## 7.3 VISUALISING DATA

After providing the basic descriptives, it can be useful to visualise the data. Appropriate visualisation of your data can help you to illustrate your point and present your evidence in a manner easy to understand. But there are limits: You want to present your data in a neutral and unbiased way, and instead use the results of your statistical tests and your discussion of the theoretical framework to make your argument. Therefore, this chapter will not help you to show the data from its 'best' angle, but from the angle that is clearest and lets the data mostly speak for itself.

> **LOOK OUT!**
>
> **Visualisation is not proof.** A graph does not show an effect, a correlation or a difference. Displaying information in a graphical form does not add analytically relevant information. While graphical representation can help understanding relationships between variables, and identifying trends, it cannot, in and by itself, 'prove' anything. Often students mistake a visualised difference (e.g., by showing two non-overlapping lines in a chart) as 'evidence' for a difference, stating 'the means are different, and the graph shows that the means are indeed different'. This is not necessarily true. The graph is a different representation of the same underlying data as the mean and standard deviation. It may be a strong indication of a difference but only an analysis, for example a t-test, will provide evidence whether that difference is significant and reason enough to reject the null hypothesis that there is no difference.

The objective of visualising data is to aid understanding. Any graph or chart should be clear, uncluttered and concise. A good chart does not bias interpretation nor employ unnecessary extras – it only consists of elements aiding understanding and interpretation, which includes a clear and unambiguous title, clear labelling of axes, and a legend for explanation,

Table 7.4 Mean (SD) of average suggested donations in £*

| | Charity | | | | | | | | | Total per amount requested |
|---|---|---|---|---|---|---|---|---|---|---|
| | Supporting political party | | | Supporting the elderly | | | Animal rescue | | | |
| | Type of appeal | | Subtotal | Type of appeal | | Subtotal | Type of appeal | | Subtotal | |
| Amount requested | Emotion | Reason | | Emotion | Reason | | Emotion | Reason | | |
| High | £12 (3.4) | £3 (1.3) | £15 (2.3) | £12 (4.6) | £5 (2.1) | £17 (3.3) | £12 (4.7) | £12 (6.4) | £24 (5.1) | £56 (4.1) |
| Moderate | £11 (2.4) | £7 (4.5) | £18 (3.3) | £9 (3.5) | £5 (2.2) | £14 (3.1) | £12 (5.2) | £16 (5.2) | £28 (5.1) | £60 (4.8) |
| Low | £9 (2.4) | £11 (3.4) | £20 (2.9) | £7 (5.1) | £6 (2.3) | £13 (4.4) | £15 (6.2) | £13 (4.1) | £28 (5.4) | £61 (3.9) |
| Total | £32 (2.7) | £21 (3.7) | £53 (2.8) | £28 (4.1) | £16 (2.2) | £44 (3.4) | £39 (5.1) | £41 (5.1) | £80 (5.2) | £177 (4.3) |

*Do not try and interpret these mean and standard deviation values – they are all completely fictitious and will almost certainly not be consistent.

where necessary. At the same time, visualisation should be used sparingly and only to aid understanding and clarification. Do not use graphs where a well-phrased paragraph or a short table would suffice. If a single question had a yes/no answer, a sentence describing the distribution of yes/no answers will do and no additional pie chart is required. Be mindful of the potential of data misleading your readers' conclusions. For example, when presenting cross-sectional data (see also Section 3.1.1) it is important to keep in mind that it provides a snapshot only. Consider Caspersen et al. (2000) who conducted a cross-sectional study which looked at patterns of physical activity and inactivity. They found that regular, vigorous activity was highest in the group aged 14 and dropped to the lowest in the group aged 30–44. However, from this it would be wrong to conclude that across the population, physical activity is lowest between 30 and 44. Rather, the only conclusion that can be drawn is that physical activity is highest for people *currently* aged 14, and lowest for people *currently* aged between 30 and 44.

Last but not least, the use of visualising data extends beyond solely describing and displaying results. Bezerra et al. (1998) argue that graphical (re)presentations can also help develop hypotheses in innovative ways by clarifying complex relationships and influences.

### REVIEW & REFLECT

- What are the limits of presenting data in tables?
- When might it be most appropriate to present data in a table?

## 7.4 CREATING A CHART

**EXCEL** In Excel, go to Insert → Chart and then select the type of chart you'd like to create. In Word, the Chart menu item is in the same place – and it gets you to the same place, eventually: Go to Insert → Chart and the programme will open Excel so you can enter the relevant data. We recommend you use Excel if you have large data sets you would like to simply present in graphical form because the route via Word requires you to enter data anew. For completeness' sake, we should mention that there is of course a wider range of applications in which you could create charts, such as in PowerPoint or in Open Office's variants of Excel and Word. However, in this book we are focussing on Excel and SPSS as the two main examples. For the same reason, we are not covering data visualisation software such as Tableau, QlikView or Datawrapper.

**SPSS** In SPSS, go to Graphs → Chart Builder and pick the chart type you want to create, then move the variables into the axes or other relevant parts of the chart. Some analyses also contain graphical elements; always check under Options whether you can choose to have a chart created and displayed. To copy over content from SPSS output, click on the object you want to copy and go to File → Export. This opens the Export Output window. Note the file name and location provided in the middle (or change, if required) and make sure to tick Selected at the top of the window.

- If it is a table or text output you want to copy, click OK; this will copy the content into a Word document.
- If you want to copy a chart or graphic, make sure to change the Document Type to 'None (Graphics only)'; you can also change the graphics type to .jpg, .tif or whichever format you need in the Graphics Type field in the lower half of the window.

## 7.5 CHART TYPES

The following sections describe a range of different chart types in more detail, in particular:

- Column charts
- Bar charts
- Histograms
- Pie charts
- Scatter plots
- Line charts

### 7.5.1 Column chart

The **column chart** (sometimes also referred to as a **bar chart**, but see Section 7.5.2) is an extremely versatile visualisation tool and is particularly well suited to display or compare two or more variables. Column charts are often used in before/after comparisons across two or more groups, see Figure 7.1:

**Figure 7.1** *Sample bars chart showing customer satisfaction scores before and after staff training*

You can see that customer satisfaction scores were higher after the staff training, though whether that improvement over the control group is significant still needs to be examined.

## 7.5.2 Bar chart

In contrast to column charts, bar charts are useful to illustrate distributions of values between different groups. Figure 7.2 illustrates a stacked bar chart comparing a distribution of values across two different groups:

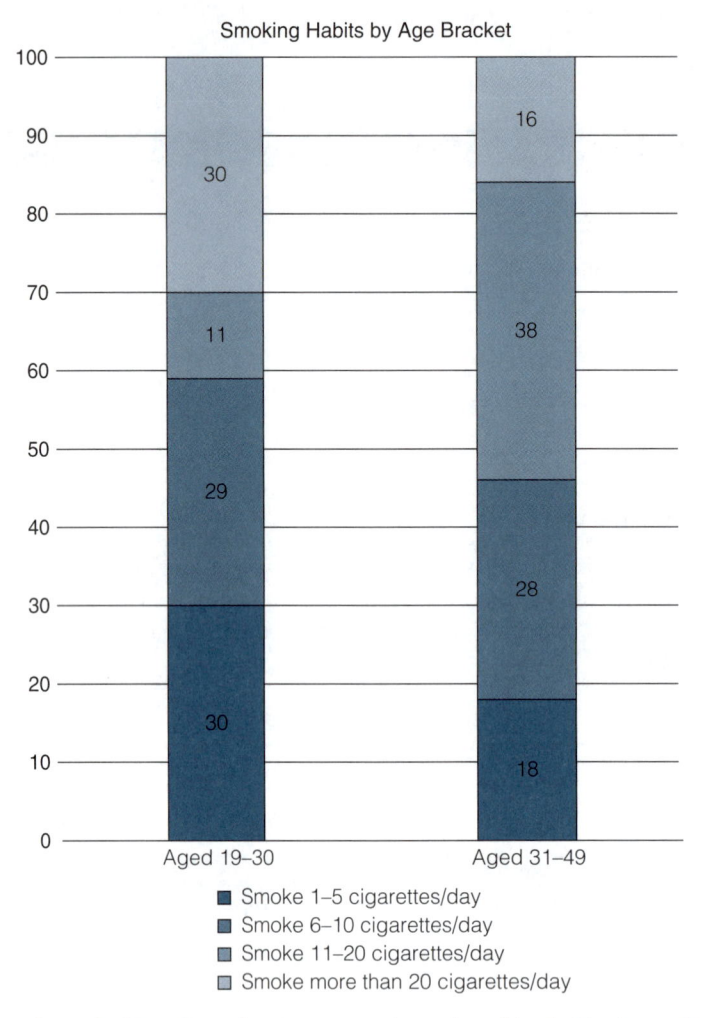

*Figure 7.2 Sample stacked bar chart showing comparison of smoking habits by age bracket*

In 'normal' bar charts, the different bars indicate different values of a variable and are compared on a horizontal basis. Stacked bar charts are more suitable for illustrating distributions of values within groups. The type of variable represented here on the x-axis is representative of the type of variables typically displayed by bar charts (i.e., categorical variables).

## 7.5.3 Histogram

To display continuous data, you can employ something similar to the bar chart, the **histogram**. The following histogram illustrates the distribution of answer scores to the question 'On a scale of 1 = Fully agree to 7 = Fully disagree, how much do you agree with the statement "I usually feel that I am in control of my own life"?' (Figure 7.3):

*Presentation and Illustration of Data* 199

Answers to Question 1: 'In control of my own life'

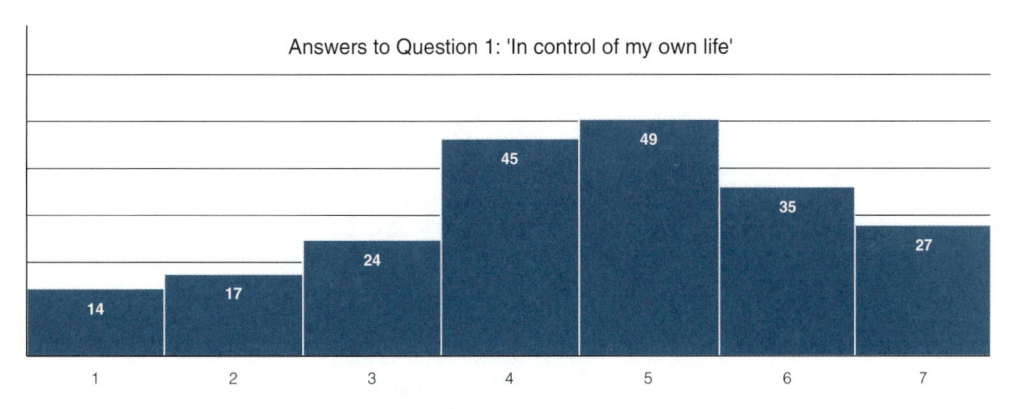

| 1 | 2 | 3 | 4 | 5 | 6 | 7 |
|---|---|---|---|---|---|---|
| 14 | 17 | 24 | 45 | 49 | 35 | 27 |

***Figure 7.3*** *Sample histogram showing frequencies of answers*

Rather than using categorical data, a histogram displays distinct values of a quantitative variable on the x-axis, and the y-axis defines the frequency of that variable. This makes it particularly useful for displaying distributions of values, with the individual variable's possible values marked on the x-axis and the frequency marked on the y-axis. A histogram is a type of bar chart but with no gaps between the individual bars.

### 7.5.4   Pie chart

**Pie charts** use the size of different segments ('slices') of a circle ('pie') to indicate variable values. Larger values are represented by larger slices. Although pie charts are used quite often, their actual usefulness is limited because it is difficult to meaningfully and accurately interpret the size of the individual pie section. They are best used to show distributions of a small number of values, particularly when the distribution is very obvious (see Figure 7.4), but it gets less informative even with a small number of values (see Figure 7.5) – and downright confusing with a larger number of values (see Figure 7.6).

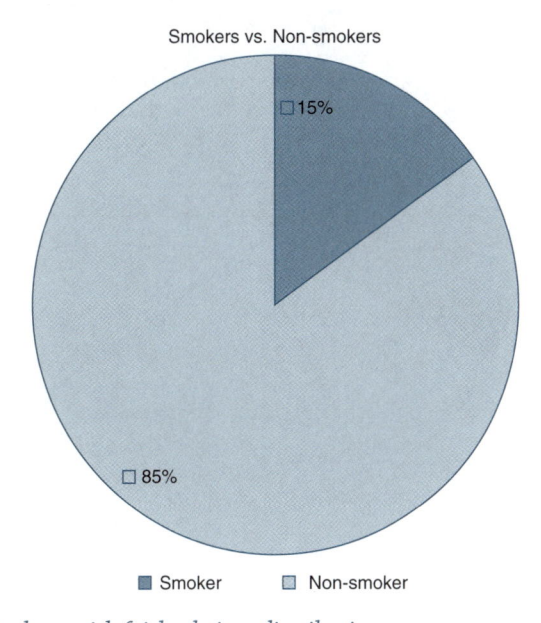

Smokers vs. Non-smokers

- 15% Smoker
- 85% Non-smoker

***Figure 7.4*** *Sample pie chart with fairly obvious distribution*

200　*Introducing Quantitative Methods*

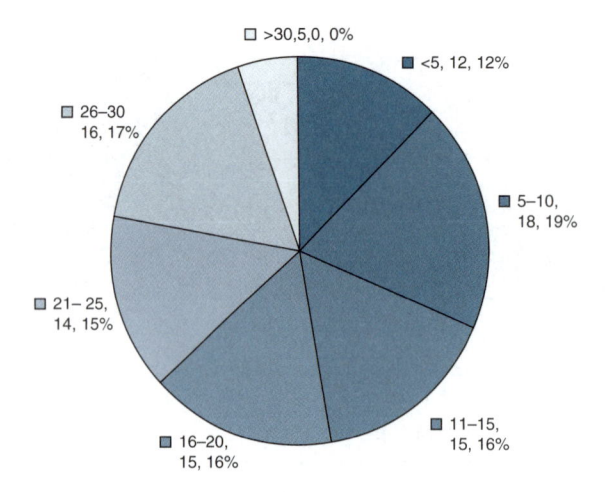

**Smoking Habits in Cigarettes Per Day**

- >30, 5, 0, 0%
- <5, 12, 12%
- 26–30, 16, 17%
- 5–10, 18, 19%
- 21–25, 14, 15%
- 11–15, 15, 16%
- 16–20, 15, 16%

*Figure 7.5* *Sample pie chart with small number of values*

However, you can already see that the pie chart itself is difficult to read. Readers will not always be able to really assess the size of individual 'slices'. It gets more confusing the more individual pie sections are used, as illustrated in Figure 7.6.

**Smokers' Brands Preferences**

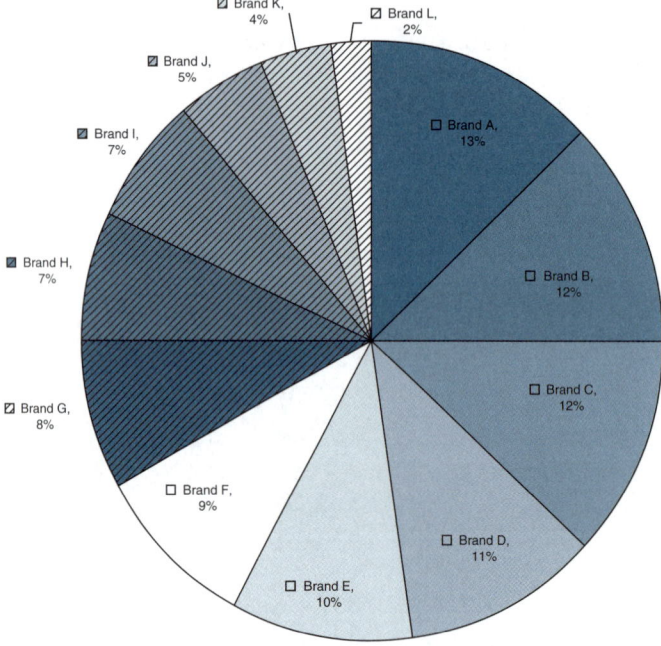

- Brand K, 4%
- Brand L, 2%
- Brand J, 5%
- Brand A, 13%
- Brand I, 7%
- Brand H, 7%
- Brand B, 12%
- Brand G, 8%
- Brand C, 12%
- Brand F, 9%
- Brand D, 11%
- Brand E, 10%

*Figure 7.6* *Sample pie chart with too many groups*

This suggests that pie charts are particularly useful when visualising data of a nominal type with a small number of variables.

## 7.5.5 Scatter plot

**Scatter plots** illustrate distributions of variable pairs. They show how often certain x-values are paired with certain y-values, and they also allow a first visual inspection of whether variables are correlated with each other. If they are, the scatter plot will show a tendency, a certain direction, allowing you to draw an imaginary line across the chart around which the value pairs are clustered (see Figure 7.7):

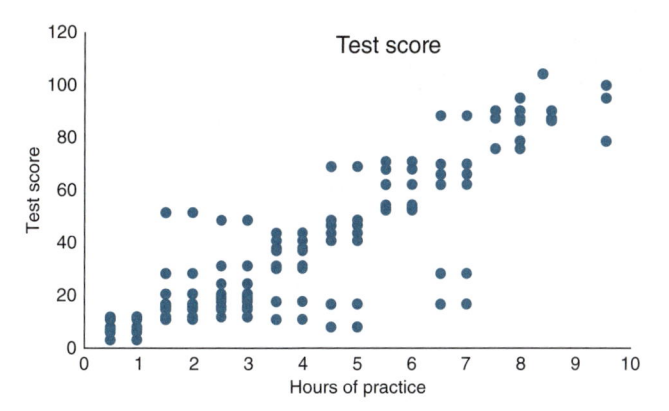

**Figure 7.7** *Sample scatter plot*

This scatter plot suggests that there is a positive correlation between practice and test performance (as expressed in a test score). However, as mentioned previously, a scatter plot or any other graphical representation would only be suitable to illustrate a relationship, but not to provide evidence for it.

## 7.5.6 Line chart

In Section 2.8 we used **line charts** to illustrate a variety of potential study outcomes, such as simple effects, interactions of variables, and a combination of an effect and an interaction, as illustrated below (Figure 7.8):

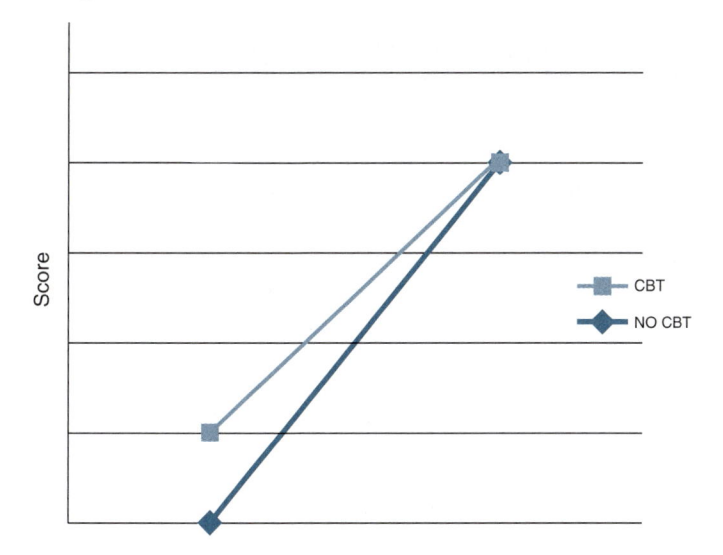

**Figure 7.8** *Sample line chart illustrating an interaction of Cognitive Behavioural Therapy (CBT) and exercise*

For simple studies with few variables, line charts can be extremely useful to illustrate results and describe individual variables. Line charts are well suited to show development of variables over time, for example at multiple points of testing, also allowing comparison across different groups (Figure 7.9):

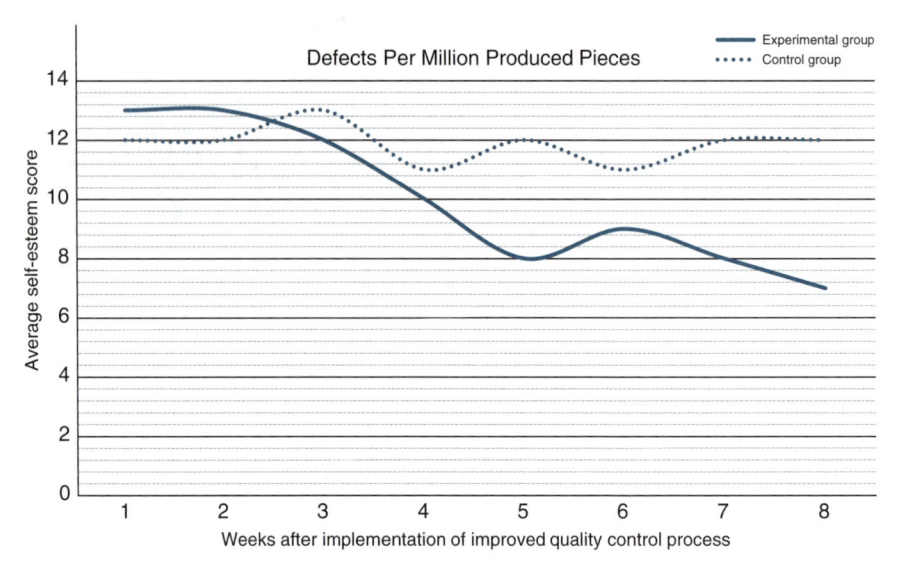

**Figure 7.9** *Comparison of quality control measures over time*

## REVIEW & REFLECT

- What are the limitations of pie charts?
- When might a scatter plot be particularly appropriate?

### 7.6 ACCESSIBILITY OF GRAPHS

Perhaps you have noticed that some of the charts we used above were displayed in shades of one colour or used different patterns to indicate the individual cases even though Word and Excel offer a multitude of colour schemes. Of course there are a variety of built-in colour schemes, and you can also design your own colour schemes. Colour itself is often used to make further statements about data values, such as using green and red to indicate values that are above or below certain thresholds. But using colour does not necessarily make charts easier to read for every reader. For example, green-red contrasts cannot be read and processed by colour-blind readers. If you try to communicate essential information through the red-green contrast, a colour-blind reader will miss out. But there are other types of colour blindness, so avoiding green-red contrasts will not always help. So what can you do? There are three broad options:

- Use appropriate colour schemes
- Use greyscale rather than colour
- Use textures rather than colours

**Use appropriate colour schemes:** There are online resources helping you to choose a good colour scheme which will be accessible to most if not all of your readers, for example http://dasplankton.de/ContrastA We have collected some links to those resources on the companion website.

**Use greyscale rather than colour:** Rather than using colour schemes, you could use greyscale. This will eliminate issues for readers with colour blindness but may still be difficult to read, particularly if you are using a wide range of shades which may be difficult to tell apart.

**Use textures rather than colours:** An alternative might be to use different textures rather than shades or colours (Figure 7.10):

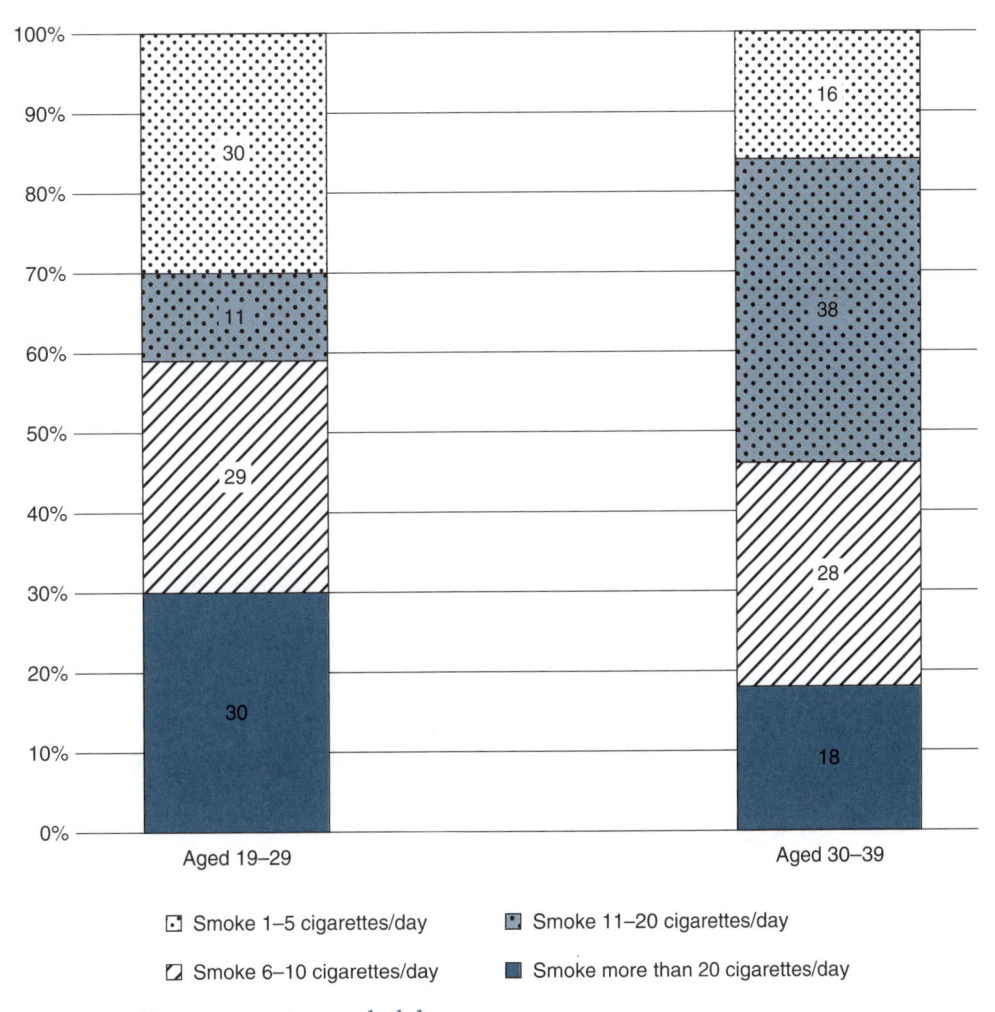

*Figure 7.10 Using textures in a stacked chart*

Textures also help with distinguishing different lines on a line graph (Figure 7.11):

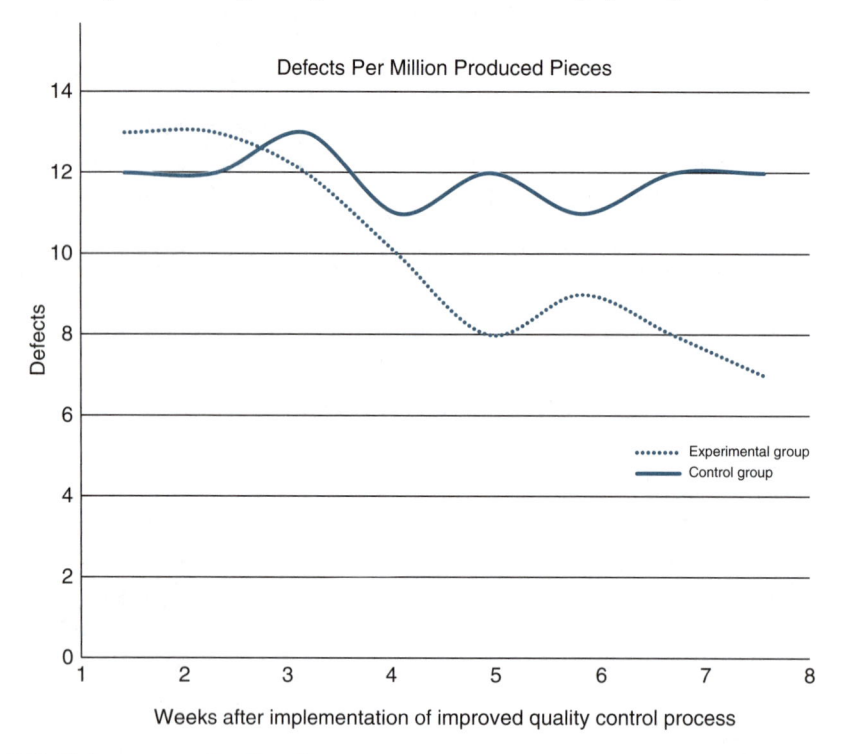

**Defects Per Million Produced Pieces**

*Figure 7.11 Using textures in a line chart*

But even the most wonderfully formatted and perfectly accessible chart is no substitute for your data and the results of your statistical analyses. This is what the next chapter will cover.

## ❓ REVIEW & REFLECT

- How might the requirement for accessible information link to the guidelines for ethical research mentioned in earlier chapters?
- Are there other ways in which you could make your research findings accessible for others?

## 7.7 GOING FURTHER: SIGNIFICANCE IN TABLES

So far this chapter has focussed on describing and illustrating data. In many cases it is sufficient to offer tables and graphs for description and then discuss results of any statistical analyses in the text. However, there are also ways to indicate significance (or the lack thereof) in tables[1] directly by using asterisks and subscripts.

---

[1] Excel and SPSS further offer options to display equivalent information in charts on whether values are significantly different, but to describe those would require more detail on the statistical background and go beyond the scope of this chapter for either Excel or SPSS. We will therefore limit ourselves to discuss the expression of significance and difference in tables (but not effects) and will describe here three possible ways of doing so, going from the simple to the more complex.

In the simple version, you include the significance data in the data presented in the table. In the table below we have included the t-test and the *p*-value (Table 7.5).

**Table 7.5** *Average reaction time in ms, depending on priming and task difficulty*

|            | Priming |     |               |         |
| ---------- | ------- | --- | ------------- | ------- |
| Difficulty | Yes     | No  | t-test        | *p*-value |
| Easy       | 160     | 220 | t(48) = 5.789 | .001    |
| Medium     | 190     | 204 | t(47) = 1.339 | .12     |
| Difficult  | 240     | 270 | t(48) = 3.536 | .04     |

If you have seen the output of correlation analyses in Excel or SPSS, you will have noticed that those tables have a unique shape. For example, the Excel output looks like this (Table 7.6):

**Table 7.6** *Correlation output in Excel*

|                | VerbalScore | FollowupTest | NumericalScore | PreTest |
| -------------- | ----------- | ------------ | -------------- | ------- |
| VerbalScore    | 1.000       |              |                |         |
| FollowupTest   | 0.986       | 1.000        |                |         |
| NumericalScore | 0.982       | 0.973        | 1.000          |         |
| PreTest        | 0.595       | 0.594        | 0.686          | 1.000   |

In SPSS, a table might look like this (Table 7.7):

**Table 7.7** *Correlation output in SPSS*

| Correlations |  |  |  |  |  |
|---|---|---|---|---|---|
|  |  | FollowUpTest | VerbalScore | PreTest | NumericalScore |
| FollowUpTest | Correlation Coefficient | 1.000 | .984** | .717** | .984** |
|  | Sig. (2-tailed) | . | .000 | .000 | .000 |
|  | N | 150 | 150 | 150 | 150 |
| VerbalScore | Correlation Coefficient | .984** | 1.000 | .736** | .998** |
|  | Sig. (2-tailed) | .000 | . | .000 | .000 |
|  | N | 150 | 150 | 150 | 150 |
| PreTest | Correlation Coefficient | .717** | .736** | 1.000 | .735** |
|  | Sig. (2-tailed) | .000 | .000 | . | .000 |
|  | N | 150 | 150 | 150 | 150 |
| NumericalScore | Correlation Coefficient | .984** | .998** | .735** | 1.000 |
|  | Sig. (2-tailed) | .000 | .000 | .000 | . |
|  | N | 150 | 150 | 150 | 150 |

What both tables have in common is that they follow a matrix pattern of correlating every variable with every other variable, including itself. If you look closely at the SPSS table, you can see that there is a diagonal of cells where the correlation coefficient is 1.000 – it is a perfect correlation because those are the cells where each variable is correlated with itself. The table below shows the idealised version of a correlation table (Table 7.8):

*Table 7.8* Prototypical correlation table

|  | Variable A | Variable B | Variable C | Variable D | Variable E |
|---|---|---|---|---|---|
| Variable A | A × A | A × B | A × C | A × D | A × E |
| Variable B | B × A | B × B | B × C | B × D | B × E |
| Variable C | C × A | C × B | C × C | C × D | C × E |
| Variable D | D × A | D × B | D × C | D × D | D × E |
| Variable E | E × A | E × B | E × C | E × D | E × E |

Tables are organised in this structure to help examine correlations for individual variables (i.e., to check for each individual variable whether or not it correlates with another variable); the table generated by SPSS is such an example. However, in logical and mathematical terms, there is no difference between correlating A with B or B with A, rendering half of the table redundant. Furthermore, since correlating a variable with itself will always yield a perfect correlation of 1, the diagonal of cells is redundant, too. In the following table we have shaded the redundant information to demonstrate the principle; this also includes cells that contain a perfect correlation by definition (i.e., A × A, B × B, etc.). This is the abridged form the table generated by Excel takes (Table 7.9):

*Table 7.9* Prototypical correlation table, with redundant cells shaded

|  | Variable A | Variable B | Variable C | Variable D | Variable E |
|---|---|---|---|---|---|
| Variable A | A × A | A × B | A × C | A × D | A × E |
| Variable B | B × A | B × B | B × C | B × D | B × E |
| Variable C | C × A | C × B | C × C | C × D | C × E |
| Variable D | D × A | D × B | D × C | D × D | D × E |
| Variable E | E × A | E × B | E × C | E × D | E × E |

The SPSS table also shows the level of significance for each individual correlation. When presenting your data, you can reduce the level of detail and present the outcome of your measurements while indicating the level of significance directly with one or two asterisks and an explanation of the levels in the footnotes (Table 7.10):

*Table 7.10* Indicating significance in tables

|  | Priming |  |  |
|---|---|---|---|
| Difficulty | Yes | No | Significant? |
| Easy | 160 | 220 | s** |
| Medium | 190 | 204 | ns |
| Difficult | 240 | 270 | s* |

\* significant at $p < .001$; ** significant at $p < .05$

Both versions work well if you have only a few comparisons and therefore the space to show significance values for each individual comparison. However, it gets more complicated if you are comparing many different groups with each other, for example in a post-hoc test after an initial ANOVA. In those cases, you can use subscripts to indicate values that *are not* significantly different from each other. For example, if you are looking at six groups of which none is different from any other, all groups would share only one subscript; conversely, you would at the most have six subscripts, one for each group, if all groups were significantly different from all other groups. Have a look at the following example taken straight out of my very own PhD thesis (Rudloff, 2011) (Table 7.11):

**Table 7.11** *Average arguments correctly and incorrectly recalled by time and type of recall*

|  | Recall period | | | | |
|---|---|---|---|---|---|
| Recall | 2 days | 12 days | 20 days | $F(2, 284)$ | $p$ |
| Correct | 4.11 (1.85)$_a$ | 3.78 (1.94)$_{a,b}$ | 3.72 (2.05)$_b$ | 4.349 | .014 |
| Incorrect | 0.35 (0.72)$_a$ | 0.22 (0.49)$_a$ | 0.37 (0.61)$_a$ | 1.726 | .180 |

*Note*: Means sharing a subscript are not significantly different

The figures show that number of correctly recalled arguments decreased over time (from 4.11 to 3.72), while the number of incorrectly recalled arguments did not change significantly over time. The *F*-value and *p*-value in the rightmost column show that there is an effect of recall period on the correctly recalled words but no effect on incorrectly recalled words. Therefore, all values in the bottom row share the same subscript; a different way of looking at this is that they all belong to the same group (i.e., they are *not* different). However, there was an effect of recall period on correctly recalled words as you can see from the significant result in the right column. Following that significant result, a number of post-hoc tests have been conducted which identified significant differences between the 2-day condition and the 20-day condition, therefore they have different subscripts; but no significant difference between the 2-day condition and the 12-day condition, therefore they share the same subscript $_a$; and no difference between 12 days and 20 days, therefore sharing the same subscript $_b$.

## RESEARCH METHODS AT WORK

Kira works for a medium-sized online bookstore and is responsible for the quality control process. She wants to present a comparison of the types of complaints the company has received in the two preceding quarters. Initially, she uses a 100% stacked bar chart (Figure 7.12):

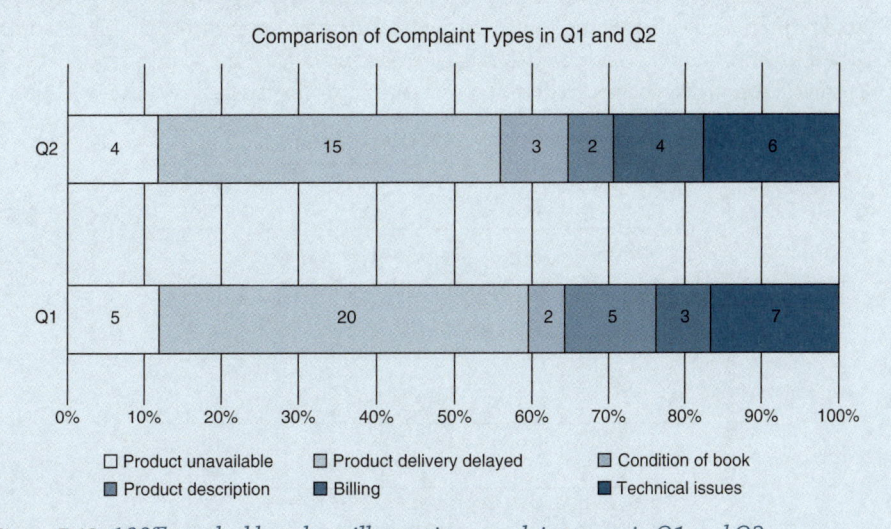

**Figure 7.12** *100% stacked bar chart illustrating complaint types in Q1 and Q2*

208 *Introducing Quantitative Methods*

However, she realises that the 100% charts only allow to compare the distribution of complaint types, giving no indication of how the absolute number of complaints has changed. She therefore changes the chart type to stacked bar chart, allowing her to compare both number and types of complaints (Figure 7.13):

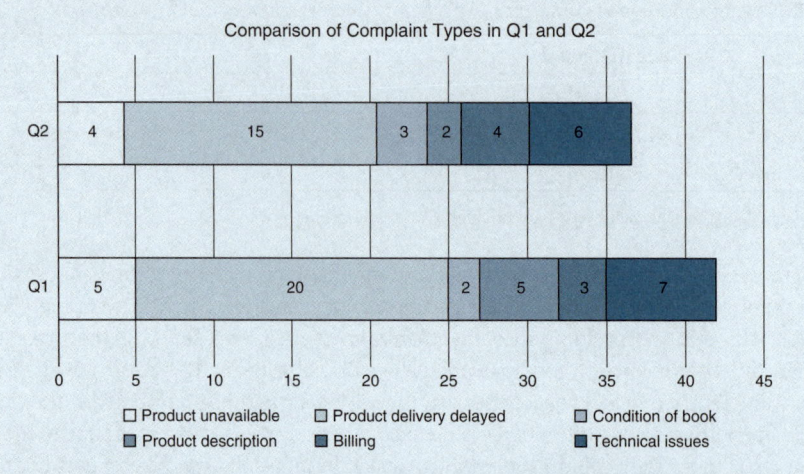

**Figure 7.13** *Stacked bar chart illustrating complaint types in Q1 and Q2*

Kira's boss Quincy is not impressed. He can see that the absolute number of complaints has gone up and worries that this indicates a decline in overall quality of service. Kira reassures him that in her opinion, this is not the case. Firstly, the increase in complaints is largely driven by the increase in complaints about delayed product delivery from 15 to 20. This is almost entirely due to one delivery of a newly published book several customers had already pre-ordered. This delay was on the publisher's side and not under the control of the bookstore. Other types of complaints varied by one or two from Q2 to Q1, but in Kira's experience the amount of variation shown is entirely normal. Quincy remains unconvinced for now, pointing out that he would expect the number of complaints go down and instead it seems to have grown over the years. Kira agrees; the absolute number of complaints has increased somewhat over the years. But, she argues, the absolute number is misleading since the number of customers has also grown over the years and so one would expect the absolute numbers to grow in line with it. A better expression of the quality of service would be the relative number of complaints. Kira has prepared such a graph and added a trend line which demonstrates clearly that over time, the share of customers complaining has decreased (Figure 7.14):

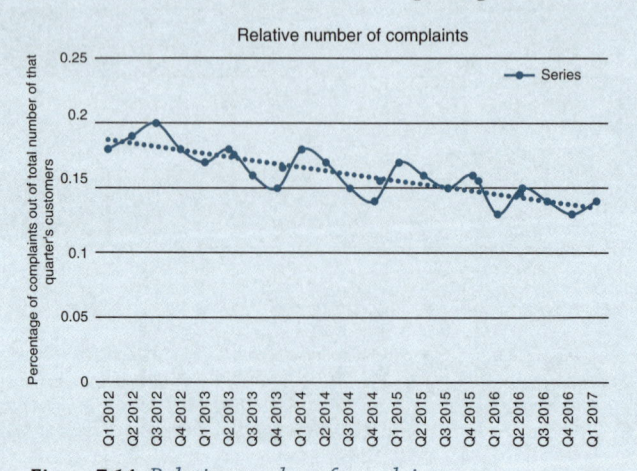

**Figure 7.14** *Relative number of complaints*

## A SHORT SUMMARY

- Choose graphs wisely. If you have only a few variables to describe, a narrative description is better.
- Tables can accommodate a large number of variables and conditions.
- Graphs and charts can only ever visualise and illustrate observations, never prove them.
- Pie charts are quite difficult to read and should only be used if few values are displayed.
- Column charts are great for comparisons of variables.
- Bar charts are good to compare distribution of values across groups.
- If you want to visualise frequency of different values, a histogram is a good choice.
- Scatter plots illustrate distribution of variable pairs and are great to visualise correlations.
- Line charts can be used to visualise effects and interactions between variables.
- All charts need to be backed up by statistical analyses and statements about the significance of differences or effects.
- Aim to make your charts accessible for all readers: avoid using red-green contrasts, use fewer colours or greyscale, and try textures rather than colours.

## CHECK YOUR UNDERSTANDING

1. You want to test the impact of scarcity and price on intent to purchase. Your study is a 2 × 2 between-participants study with two independent variables: 'price' (high or low) and 'scarcity' (abundant or rare). Participants are given information on a product and told it is either rare or easily available; half of them are given a high price for the product, and half of them are given a low price. The dependent variable is 'intent to purchase', measured on a scale from 1 to 20. The table presents average values of 'intent to purchase' (Table 7.12):

   **Table 7.12** *Intent to purchase*

   |  | Scarcity |  |
   |---|---|---|
   |  | Available | Rare |
   | Price: High | 15 | 13 |
   | Price: Low | 18 | 15 |

   a. Describe the results verbally.
   b. Visualise them with a chart.

2. Read the narrative description of this study's results:

   'Prior to the intervention, 19.5% of employees indicated that they never exercised; 50.3% said they exercised occasionally; and only 30.2% said they exercised regularly. Six months after introducing a points-based incentive system, 15.4% still indicated that they never exercised, while 44.6% reported that they exercised occasionally, and 40% now said they exercised regularly.'

   a. Present these results in a table.
   b. Visualise them with a chart.

3. The following chart visualises the responses to the question 'On a scale from 1 to 7, where 1 = Strongly agree and 7 = Strongly disagree, how much do you agree with the statement "On the whole, I'm in control of my own life."?' (Figure 7.15)

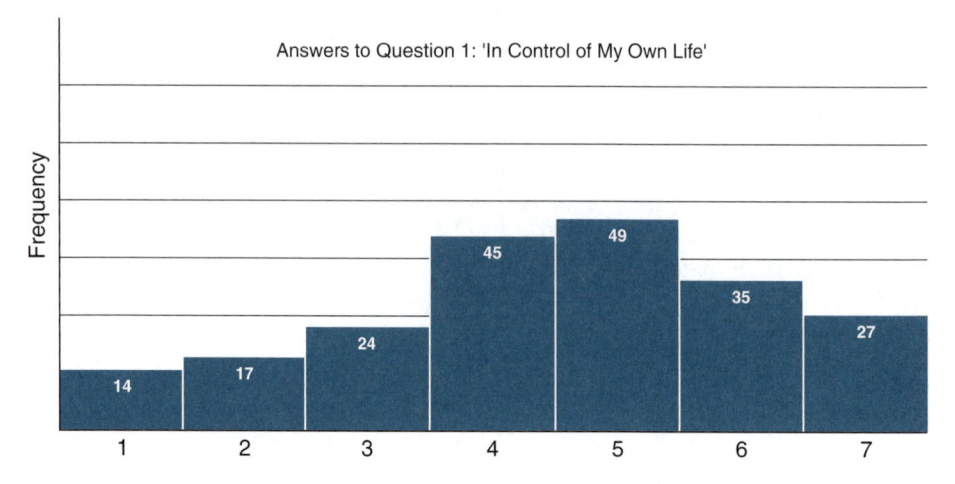

*Figure 7.15 Agreement data*

   a. Present these results in a table.
   b. Present these results in a narrative description.

4. What would be suitable chart types to display the type of information listed below, and why?
   a. Overview of survey respondents' highest level of education
   b. Reaction times in a 2 × 2 study with 'priming' and 'task difficulty' (easy/difficult) as the two independent variables
   c. Percentage of women in a group at three different points in time
   d. Projected fund development assuming risky and cautious investment strategy
   e. Reading age scores from two initial cohorts (parents of either high or low socioeconomic status) of primary school children tested at age 5, 6, 7, 8, 9 and 10
   f. Weekly work hours booked to a project for the last quarter, comparing actual versus projected hours
   g. Frequencies of answer responses on a scale from 1 to 7
   h. Percentage of respondents agreeing or disagreeing with a statement

5. You want to examine what compels participants to assist another person, or not. The factors you are interested in are whether participants know the person needing assistance or not, whether the need for assistance is salient or not, and how many other people are present (none, one, two or three). Your dependent variable is the amount of time it takes for the participant to offer assistance.

   Work out a possible layout of a table showing all of this information and sketch it in the space below:

# 8 Choosing Your Statistical Analysis

### WHAT IS THIS CHAPTER ABOUT?

This chapter begins by discussing the difference between parametric and non-parametric data and tests. It describes how to establish whether data is parametric or non-parametric by introducing the key criteria and explaining how to examine those criteria in Excel and SPSS. The chapter moves on to first giving an overview of the tests covered in this book and then explaining the basic principle of each of these tests in more detail.

### WHY IS THIS IMPORTANT?

The quality of your research relies not only on the quality of your data but also on the quality of your analyses. Using inappropriate analyses for the data you collected can compromise the integrity of your study; you might draw the wrong conclusion on whether a difference exists between groups; whether two factors are associated with each other; or whether a particular intervention had an effect (see also **conclusion validity** in the Glossary).

### WHAT ARE THE LEARNING OUTCOMES FOR THIS CHAPTER?

At the end of this chapter you will be able to:
- Determine whether data is parametric or non-parametric.
- Collect data on mean, median, skewness and kurtosis in both Excel and SPSS.
- Create a Q-Q plot in Excel and SPSS.
- Assess the data on mean, median, skewness, kurtosis and the Q-Q plot to establish whether you need to use parametric or non-parametric tests.
- Understand the use of a range of different statistical analyses and choose a test suitable for your requirements.

## 8.1 PARAMETRIC OR NON-PARAMETRIC?

So far we have focussed on descriptive tests and analyses. As the name indicates, those analyses only *describe* the general shape and form of your data. If you want to go beyond descriptives and look for relations between variables – and more importantly, draw conclusions from your data – then you need to employ different types of analyses: **inferential statistics**, so called because they help you make *inferences*, that is, draw conclusions. If you are looking at performance data for two groups, descriptive analyses allow you to describe the data in the form of means and standard deviations; inferential analyses allow you to determine whether the difference between the two groups is statistically significant and therefore potentially meaningful.

Section 6.7 introduced the normal, or Gaussian distribution as a special type of distribution, where values are symmetrically and in a non-linear fashion clustered around the mean. We mentioned that whether a set of values is **parametric** (i.e., normally distributed) or not has implications for the type of analyses that you can conduct. Nominal and ordinal data by definition cannot be considered to be normally distributed and is considered **non-parametric** data, allowing for non-parametric tests. The reverse is not automatically true: interval and ratio data are not always normally distributed. This means for interval and ratio data you still need to examine the data to establish whether or not it is normally distributed, as both types of data allow different types of statistical analyses.

> **ONLINE CONTENT**
>
> In the following section we describe how you can check whether values are normally distributed by performing calculations on sample data available on the companion website.

For this example, we are looking at a variable 'VerbalScore', which measures general language skills and was collected after participants attended a training course (the full scenario is explained in Section 8.9.1). We do so by considering a range of criteria:

- Mean and median
- Skewness
- Kurtosis
- Q-Q plot

Of those criteria, you have already been introduced to mean (see Section 6.3.1), median (see Section 6.3.3), skewness and kurtosis (both see Section 6.9). In addition, we are using a Q-Q plot. A **Q-Q plot** is called such because it plots quantiles of two data sets against each other – in other words, **q**uantiles versus **q**uantiles. We have previously introduced z-scores as a way of making values comparable by expressing them as ratio of score to standard deviation rather than absolute values. The basic principle of a Q-Q plot is comparing z-scores for your distribution's values against z-scores for an 'ideal', normal distribution. The more similar the two distributions are, the more closely their values will align on the Q-Q plot. A perfectly straight line would mean your distribution is identical to a normal distribution – the more curves and bends, the less similar.

## 8.2 DESCRIPTIVES IN EXCEL

### 8.2.1 Mean, median, skewness and kurtosis

Start by running a brief analysis in Excel:

1. Go to <u>Tools</u> → <u>Data Analysis</u> → <u>Descriptive Statistics</u>
2. Enter the range of the data you want to analyse (remember not to include the first row, i.e. the title row). Tick the box <u>Summary statistics</u>.

We have copied the result of this analysis below (note that we have formatted the results to be displayed with three decimal places) (Table 8.1):

**Table 8.1** *Descriptives of 'VerbalScore'*

| Mean | 133.947 |
|---|---|
| Standard Error | 1.482 |
| Median | 134.000 |
| Mode | 129.000 |
| Standard Deviation | 18.145 |
| Sample Variance | 329.259 |
| Kurtosis | -0.022 |
| Skewness | 0.069 |
| Range | 93.000 |
| Minimum | 90.000 |
| Maximum | 183.000 |
| Sum | 20092.000 |
| Count | 150.000 |

In addition, you have to work out the ratio between skewness and the *standard error of skewness*. The latter is calculated as follows:

$$\sqrt{\frac{6}{n}}$$

In Excel you can calculate this with the formula =SQRT(6/N), where n is the sample size of your sample.

$$\sqrt{\frac{6}{150}}$$
$$= \sqrt{.04}$$
$$= .20$$

Then, find the ratio between the skewness and the standard error of skewness you just calculated:

$$\frac{\text{sample skewness}}{\text{standard error of skewness}} \quad \frac{.069}{.20} = .345$$

You can calculate this in Excel by a simple division, using references to the table cells containing sample skewness and standard error skewness:

$$= \frac{\text{[CELL CONTAINING SAMPLE SKEWNESS]}}{\text{[CELL CONTAINING STANDARD ERROR OF SKEWNESS]}}$$

That said, some consider this a poor approximation for small samples. There is a more elaborate formula which works better but requires more steps. We have included this formula in Section 8.4.2.1; in case you would rather not work this out by hand you can also look up values for n between 1 and 20 in Appendix 1 "Standard Error of Skewness for Small Sample Sizes", p. 302.

### 8.2.2 Q-Q plot

Note: In the explanation that follows we will occasionally indicate that you should make sure a certain cell range is updated. This means that, rather than updating automatically when you copy the cell content to a different cell, the reference remains unchanged. You can do so by putting a $ sign before the part of the cell reference you do not want to update (i.e., $A2 if you do not want the column to update, A$2 if you do not want the row to update and $A$2 if you want neither column nor row to update).

> **ONLINE CONTENT**
>
> You can follow the calculations in the sample file available on the companion website.

#### 8.2.2.1 The basic principle

> **THE HEADLINES**
>
> - Sort values in ascending order.
> - Calculate z-scores for cumulative probabilities from 1 to N.
> - Calculate z-scores for each value in your sample.
> - Plot the two z-scores against each other.
> - Excel functions used: AVERAGE, COUNT, NORM.S.INV, STDEV.S.

You can do this either in the same or in a separate Excel sheet, but it is probably slightly easier to do this in a separate Excel sheet because you will need to add a few columns.

1. Sort values in ascending order.
   - Before you start to create a Q-Q plot for your variable, make sure that the values are sorted in ascending order, that is, from smallest to largest value.
2. Calculate z-scores for cumulative probabilities from 1 to N.
   - You will need three new columns for this.
   - First new column (here, column C, as data occupies columns A and B already):
     – In this column you are simply counting from 1 to N.
   - Second new column (column D):
     – Cells in this column will be filled by a function calculating cumulative probabilities.
       
       The formula for this function is $\frac{i - 0.5}{n}$, where i is your variable from the 'counting'

column and n is the number of values in your sample: ([cell reference]-0.5)/[number of values])
- You can either put in N directly as a number or have Excel count the number of values through the function COUNT(RANGE), where range is the range of cells with your data values. Make sure that you use the same range throughout – you do not want the range to update (see p. 214 for an explanation).
- Adjust the cell references to match your data and copy the formula to the entire column.
- Third new column (column E):
  - In this column you calculate the z-score for each probability in the second column (in this example, column D).
  - Use the function NORM.S.INV: =NORM.S.INV([Cell reference])
  - Adjust the cell references to match your data and copy the formula to the entire column.
3. Calculate z-scores for each value in your sample.
   - Insert a further column (E). The function takes the form [Value]-[Mean]/[Standard deviation], where Value refers to the original values in your sample, and mean and standard deviation are calculated by the AVERAGE and STDEV.S functions on the spot: =([cell reference]/AVERAGE([fixed range reference]))/STDEV.S([fixed range reference])
   - Adjust the cell references to match your data and copy the formula to the entire column. Make sure that you use $ to keep constant the range over which mean and standard deviation are to be computed.
4. Plot the two z-scores against each other.
   - Go to Insert → Chart → X Y (Scatter) and enter the data range for columns D and E. Click OK (Figure 8.1).

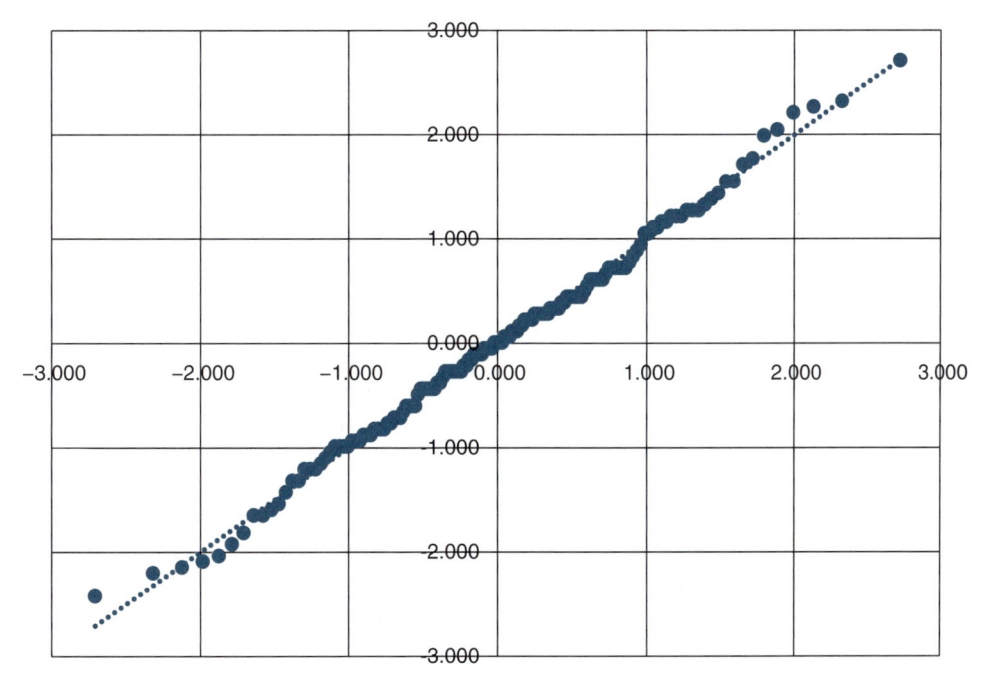

**Figure 8.1** *Excel Q-Q plot for 'VerbalScore'*

## 8.3 DESCRIPTIVES IN SPSS

### 8.3.1 Mean and median

Sections 6.3.1 and 6.3.3 describe how you can determine mean and median in SPSS, respectively.

### 8.3.2 Skewness and kurtosis

To find skewness and its standard error, go to <u>Analyze</u> → <u>Descriptive Statistics</u> → <u>Descriptives</u>… and move the variable 'VerbalScore' to the right. Click on <u>Options …</u> and tick the box next to <u>Skewness</u>. In the same window tick the box next to <u>Kurtosis</u>.

### 8.3.3 Q-Q plot

To create a Q-Q plot in SPSS, follow these steps:

- Open the menu <u>Analyze</u> → <u>Descriptive Statistics</u> → <u>Explore</u>.
- Click on <u>Plots</u> and tick the box <u>Normality plot with tests</u>, then click <u>OK</u>.
- Select the variable you want to explore and click on the topmost arrow to move it into the dependent list.
- Click <u>OK</u> to run.

## 8.4 INTERPRETING DESCRIPTIVES

Having computed the required descriptives, you can now have a closer look at them to assess whether the distribution is normally distributed.

### 8.4.1 Mean and median

In this example in Table 8.1, the mean 133.947 and the median 134 are very close together. This suggests that the distribution is symmetrical. If mean and median were substantially different, it would suggest asymmetry.

### 8.4.2 Skewness

For perfectly normal distributions, you would expect to see a skewness of 0. Negative skewness values indicate the distribution skews left whereas positive values indicate the distribution skews to the right. The skewness value here is very low (.07) and indicates a minor positive skew which does not cause any immediate concern. There is reason for concern if this value is either higher than 2, or lower than −2, as this would indicate a likely positive or negative skew, respectively. A value of .345 for the ratio of skewness to standard error of skewness lies perfectly within the two boundaries and is therefore less concerning. However, it still does not give a guarantee that the distribution is not skewed – the value just suggests that skew is not very likely.

***8.4.2.1 Going further: Standard error for skewness for smaller samples*** We mentioned above that there is a more complex formula to work out the standard error for skewness which is more accurate for smaller sample sizes. The formula is as follows (where $n$ = sample size):

$$SES = \sqrt{\frac{6n(n-1)}{(n-2)(n+1)(n+3)}}$$

You can either work this out by hand or paste the following formula into Excel, replacing N with your sample size:

$$= SQRT(6 \times N \times (N-1)/((N-2) \times (N+1) \times (N+3)))$$

If you look closely you can see how this formula replicates the formula given above: SQRT is the function to calculate the square root, and in this case the square root of the entire term within brackets. You can also see the '/' dash, which divides the formula into the **numerator** (see Glossary) and the **denominator** (see Glossary).

### 8.4.3 Kurtosis

To avoid any confusion, let us clarify straight away that both Excel and SPSS do not report actual kurtosis but **excess kurtosis**. For a normal distribution you would expect a kurtosis of 3 which is very different from the values you will find in SPSS or Excel. However, you can easily translate excess kurtosis to kurtosis and vice versa:

- Kurtosis = Excess kurtosis + 3
- Excess kurtosis = Kurtosis − 3

The lowest possible excess kurtosis value is −2, which is equivalent to kurtosis of 1, there is no upper limit. For a normal distribution, the reference value for excess kurtosis is 0. The closer to 0, the better. Excess kurtosis higher than 0 would indicate that the distribution has a stronger than usual peak and flatter tails, whereas excess kurtosis lower than 0 would indicate a flatter peak and stronger tails. In this example, Excel and SPSS report excess kurtosis of −0.022 which is close to 0, the reference value for excess kurtosis in a normal distribution.

### 8.4.4 Q-Q plot

We mentioned earlier that the Q-Q plot indicates normality by plotting two sets of data against each other – one of a hypothetical perfect normal distribution and one of your data. The closer those two data sets align, the closer the dots align to a line. In this example, you can see that the values cluster very closely along the trend line SPSS shows for comparison in Figure 8.1.

The SPSS analysis gives you additional information because the bottom table (below the Q-Q plot) displays the result of the tests of normality. Two tests have been conducted: Shapiro-Wilk is preferred for data sets of up to 50 cases; for data sets larger than that, the Kolmogorov-Smirnov (K-S) test is more appropriate. Since the sample data set consists of 50 cases, you can consider the Kolmogorov-Smirnov test result (in real research, this sample would most likely be considered too small). For the purpose of the normality test, the assumption of normality is your null hypothesis, and a statistically non-significant result means that you have no reason to reject the null hypothesis. In other words, if it is significant, the data is not normally distributed.

Based on mean, median, skewness, kurtosis and the Q-Q plot you can therefore conclude with reasonable confidence that the distribution is normally distributed. But what about 'NumericalScore'? We have repeated the analysis for 'NumericalScore' and have given the relevant values in Table 8.2 (again rounded to three decimal points).

> **ONLINE CONTENT**
>
> You can follow the calculations with the files available on the companion website.

**Table 8.2** Descriptives of 'NumericalScore'

| Mean | 110.780 |
| --- | --- |
| Standard Error | 0.405 |
| Median | 111.000 |
| Mode | 111.000 |
| Standard Deviation | 4.961 |
| Sample Variance | 24.616 |
| Kurtosis | −0.905 |
| Skewness | −0.142 |

**Mean and median:** Although mean and median are very close here, too, the standard deviation looks very small in comparison to the median. This gives you a first idea that maybe the distribution is not as wide as it should be.

**Skewness:** Skewness is given as −.142, which would indicate a minor left-skew. The standard error of skewness is $\sqrt{\frac{6}{n}} = .04$, because this sample has the same N as the previous one. The ratio between skewness and skewness standard error is $= \frac{skewness}{standard\ error\ of\ skewness}\ \frac{-.142}{.20} = -0.71$, a value larger than .345 from the previous example but still smaller than the cut-off value of 2 above which a distribution would be considered significantly skewed.

**Kurtosis:** Excess kurtosis is −0.905, which is quite different from an expected excess kurtosis of 0 for a normal distribution. Together, mean, median, skewness and kurtosis suggest that this distribution is not normally distributed.

**Q-Q plot:** The Q-Q plot shows the values substantially diverging from a diagonal line – the first half of the line has a 'C'-like shape, whereas the second half of the curve looks like an inverted 'C'. You can see how the curve moves towards and away from the trend line a couple of times (Figure 8.2).

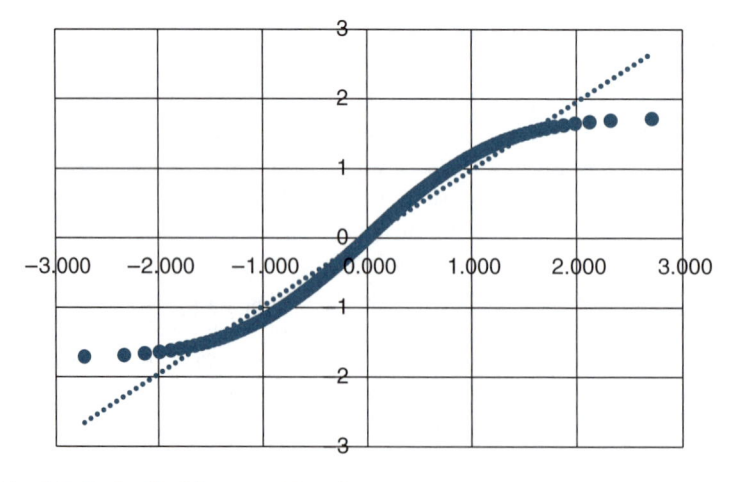

*Figure 8.2* Excel Q-Q plot for 'NumericalScore'

Although the standard error of skewness is within range, based on the combination of the other parameters – skew itself, kurtosis and Q-Q plot – it seems likely that this distribution is not normally distributed.

Lastly, a note of caution. These tests should not be the sole basis on which to make the decision whether to treat the data as parametric or non-parametric. A normality test is no substitute for a close look at the data, a consideration of the data source and, last but not least, common sense.

> **REVIEW & REFLECT**
>
> - Which criteria are used to assess whether a distribution is parametric or non-parametric, and why?
> - Why is nominal data considered non-parametric?

## 8.5 OVERVIEW OF ANALYSES

The next three chapters will describe individual analyses in more detail. This chapter served as an introduction to the test whether data is parametric or non-parametric because it influences which analyses are available to you; it is one of the main distinguishing factors. In addition, we are using a distinction between looking at relationships, differences or effects – a categorisation we also introduced in previous chapters. Table 8.3 below now gives you an overview of the analyses described in Chapters 9, 10 and 11 according to those two types of distinction we have just described. All tests are covered in SPSS; tests marked * are also explained for Excel.

***Table 8.3*** *Overview of statistical tests covered in Chapters 9, 10 and 11*

|  |  | **Parametric** | **Non-Parametric** |
|---|---|---|---|
| **Comparison/Difference** | To a given mean | One-sample t-test* | Wilcoxon signed rank test |
|  | In a paired sample | Paired-samples t-test* |  |
|  | Between two independent samples | Independent-samples t-test* | Mann-Whitney U* |
| **Effect** |  | Analysis of Variance (ANOVA)** Analysis of Covariance (ANCOVA) | Kruskal-Wallis |
| **Relationship** | Association | Chi-square test of independence* Chi-square test goodness of fit* |  |
|  | Correlation | Pearson's* | Spearman's* |

** *Of the types of ANOVA, only the one-way ANOVA is covered in Excel*

## 8.6 LOOKING AT COMPARISONS OR DIFFERENCES

### 8.6.1 One-sample t-test

***8.6.1.1 The basic principle*** The name of the test gives away one of its key features. It only applies to one sample, e.g. one group of participants. It is used to compare a group's values against one other fixed value; you will see in the description of the other tests that the **one-sample t-test** is unique in this as most of the other tests compare sets of values with each other. In Chapter 6 we emphasised the point that most statistical tests can be described in terms of identifying size and sources of variances. The t-test is one such test. It assesses the size of a difference in means (between sample and population mean) and examines how it compares to the variance within the sample itself. The larger the difference, the higher the t-test value. If the difference in means is very small in relation to the sample variance, then it is less likely that the measured difference is significant – it is more likely that it is the expression of the sample's natural variance. If the difference is very large in comparison to the sample variance, however, then it is more likely that this is due to a real difference in mean and not arising from the sample's variance.

***8.6.1.2 Example*** Wadlington and Wadlington (2005) looked at the beliefs different groups of educators (e.g., lecturers, undergraduate teaching students, etc.) held about dyslexia. As part of the study, participants completed a Dyslexia Belief Index (DBI) scale. Wadlington and Wadlington then used a one-sample t-test to establish which groups' scores were significantly lower than 108 on the scale. Groups which did score significantly lower than this were then classed as having a 'substantial number of misconceptions' (p. 22).

→ You can find guidance on how to perform a one-sample t-test in Section 9.1.

### 8.6.2 Paired-samples t-test

***8.6.2.1 The basic principle*** With a **paired-samples t-test**, all the data for the comparison still comes from one group but rather than against a fixed value, the group is compared against itself, like you would do in a within-participants design or in a before/after setup. In those same scenarios you could potentially also use a one-way ANOVA, but the paired t-test should be used if:

- The independent variable is nominal (e.g., smoker/non-smoker; low-involvement/high-involvement) or
- The sample is very small.

In addition, you will often find t-tests – either paired t-test or independent-samples t-test, see Sections 9.3 and 9.4, respectively – as post-hoc tests following two/three-/four-way ANOVAs comparing more than two groups, since ANOVAs only establish the existence of an effect but require additional tests to identify which of the groups differ from each other.

How does a t-test work? If you think about the paired-samples t-test (and by extension, the one-way ANOVA) in terms of variance, you have two potential sources of variance: the variance within the participants (e.g., participants' abilities and cognitions fluctuating naturally); and any potential variance introduced by the treatment or condition. A paired-samples t-test assesses the size of a difference in means between two groups and examines how it compares relative to overall variance. The larger the difference in means (as compared to overall variance), the higher the t-test value and the higher the chance that the two means are significantly different.

***8.6.2.2 Example*** Ineson et al. (2006) examined culture shock and culture surprise of UK students doing a placement in the United States. Ineson et al. wanted to find out whether there was a significant difference between 'Culture Shock' and 'Culture Surprise'. Because they compared two values (which were measured on similar scales) coming from the same group of participants, they could have used either a one-way ANOVA or a paired t-test. However, their sample was very small (N = 38) and so they used the more appropriate t-test.

→ Section 9.3 gives you guidance on how to conduct a paired-samples t-test.

### 8.6.3 Wilcoxon signed rank

***8.6.3.1 The basic principle*** The **Wilcoxon signed rank** test is the non-parametric alternative to both the one-sample t-test (see p. 220) and the paired-samples t-test (see p. 220), which means it can be used in the scenarios described for those tests if the data is not normally distributed (see Section 8.1 on how to establish whether data is normally distributed). The calculation that is behind the Wilcoxon signed rank rests on comparing how many values in your data set are above the value you are comparing against and how many below. A parameter is calculated which expresses the ratio of values above and below. This parameter is then compared to a reference value which is based on two distributions being equal (i.e., where the null hypothesis of no difference is true). The comparison of your value against the reference value tells you whether your two distributions are different.

***8.6.3.2 Example*** Fehr and Gächter (2002) looked at how freeriding behaviour was punished by a group. In their study, participants were given information on how much four other participants contributed. Of these, three contributed similar amounts; a fourth participant contributed either a bit less (scenario 1) or much less (scenario 2) than the other participants. Participants were asked to indicate feelings of anger towards the person contributing less than the others. Fehr and Gächter then used a Wilcoxon signed rank test to compare differences in anger expressed by participants in the two scenarios.

→ Section 9.2 describes how to conduct a Wilcoxon signed rank test.

### 8.6.4 Independent-samples t-test

***8.6.4.1 The basic principle*** Like the paired-samples t-test, the **independent-samples t-test** carries a partial clue to its purpose in its name. Unlike the paired t-test, where both halves of a comparison come from the same group, the independent-samples t-test compares two different groups. This means that in addition to variance within the participants (e.g., participants' abilities and cognitions fluctuating naturally) (source 1), and any potential variance introduced by the treatment or condition (source 2), we now also have variance coming from the differences between the two groups (i.e., between-participants variance) (source 3). An independent-samples t-test assesses the size of a difference in means between two groups and examines how this difference compares to the two groups' variances. Exact calculations differ based on whether the two groups' variances are equal or unequal, therefore the process of conducting an independent-samples t-test requires an extra step to establish whether variances are equal. The larger the difference in means (relative to the groups' variances), the higher the t-test value and the higher the chance that the two means are significantly different.

***8.6.4.2 Example*** In an earlier chapter we referred to a study by Chu and Kamal (2008) on blogger credibility. The study used a between-subjects design and included two conditions, high and low blogger trustworthiness, meaning that materials were manipulated in such a way to induce participants in one group to rate the blogger's trustworthiness as high, participants in the other group as low. Because participants were in two different groups, Chu and Kamal used an independent-samples t-test to check whether blogger trustworthiness differed significantly between the two groups.

→ Section 9.4 describes how to conduct an independent-samples t-test.

### 8.6.5 Mann-Whitney U-test

**8.6.5.1 The basic principle** The **Mann-Whitney U-test** is the non-parametric alternative to the independent-samples t-test (see Section 8.6.4), which means it is used in the same scenario but where the data is not normally distributed (see Section 8.1 on how to check for normal distribution). The Mann-Whitney U-test relies on ranking values across two groups and then computing a ratio (see Section 4.5) of ranks between groups. This ratio is compared to a reference value to establish whether the difference in ranks between the two groups is significant.

**8.6.5.2 Example** Gneezy and Rustichini (2000) examined whether participants who were paid more for correct answers would perform better in a test. In a between-participants design, participants were split across four groups with different levels of payment. Because the data was not normally distributed, Gneezy and Rustichini then used a Mann-Whitney U-test to find out whether the number of correct responses differed significantly between groups.

→ Section 9.5 describes how to conduct a Mann-Whitney U-test.

> **? REVIEW & REFLECT**
>
> - What do the t-tests have in common?
> - What is the main difference between t-tests and a Mann-Whitney U-test?

## 8.7 LOOKING AT EFFECTS

### 8.7.1 Analysis of variance (ANOVA)

**8.7.1.1 The basic principle** An **Analysis of Variance** (ANOVA) can generally be used to look at the same type of questions for which paired-samples t-tests (Section 8.6.2) or independent-samples t–tests (Section 8.6.4) are used, but it is more appropriate than t-tests if more than two groups are compared, that is, where the independent variable has more than two levels and/or if the sample size is large.

There are several different types of ANOVA which are distinguished by:

- Number of dependent variables: **Univariate ANOVAs** look at the effect on one dependent variable, **multivariate ANOVAs** look at the effect on two or more dependent variables
- Number of independent variables:
    - A **one-way ANOVA** looks at one independent variable.
    - A **two-way-ANOVA** looks at two independent variables.
    - A **three-way ANOVA** looks at three independent variables.
- Whether they are applied on between-participants or within-participants data, the default description of an ANOVA refers to a between-participants analysis. If you see the added description **repeat(ed) measures**, it refers to a within-participants analysis; if it is called mixed it contains both within- and between-participants analysis. In this book we are going to mostly focus on univariate analyses.

Because comparisons between groups have different sources of variance than comparisons within groups, different analyses are needed for each; you have seen this difference reflected in the distinction between an independent-samples t-test and a paired-samples t-test.

In order to conduct between-participants ANOVAs, the dependent variables generally need to meet four conditions. Where those tests are explained in the following chapters, we will also show how to test those assumptions.

1. Roughly similar variances: in Excel this is tested with the F-test for unequal variances described on page 239; SPSS includes the results for both variants (with and without unequal variance) in the output. You will also see this being referred to as **homogeneity of variance** or **homoscedasticity**.
2. Normality (or data normally distributed): see Section 8.1 for an explanation of the concept of normality.
3. Coming from independent groups (between-participants, not within).
4. Data on an interval scale or ratio scale: see Section 2.2 for an overview of the different scale types.

In order to conduct within-participants ANOVAs (that is, repeated measures ANOVAs), your data needs to meet the following conditions:

1. Normality (see Section 8.1 for an explanation of the concept of normality).
2. The dependent variable needs to be of interval or ratio type (see Section 2.2 for an overview of the different scale types).
3. Independent variable needs to come from two related groups or matched pairs (see Section 2.7 for an explanation of between- versus within-participants design).
4. No outliers.
5. **Sphericity** (this assumption is the repeated measure equivalent of homoscedasticity).

If any of these conditions are not met, it may be more appropriate to conduct a non-parametric test such as the Kruskal-Wallis test (Section 8.7.3).

Conducting an ANOVA boils down to comparing the variance between groups to the variance within groups. The formula does not use the simple idea of variance you have already encountered, but uses a measure called mean squares (degrees of freedom are also involved). However, at its very core the F-statistic is no more than an expression of the ratio between the variance that exists within groups and the variance that exists between groups. The greater the ratio, the more likely it is that there really is a difference.

**8.7.1.2 Examples** *Example one-way ANOVA:* Magnier and Schoormans' (2015) study looked on the impact of packaging design on perceived eco-friendliness as the dependent variable. The study used a 2 × 2 between-participants design with 'visual appearance' (conventional vs. eco-looking) and 'sustainability claim' (absent vs. present) as the two independent variables. For each of the two main variables the researchers used a separate *one-way ANOVA* to conduct a manipulation check. (Note that although there were two dependent variables, it was a univariate analysis as each analysis only looked at one dependent variable.)

*Example two-way ANOVA:* Miron-Shatz et al. (2009) wanted to know to what extent the format in which information on prenatal screening was presented affected participant comprehension and risk assessment. As part of their analysis they examined the effect of numeracy levels and presentation format on overall comprehension and a dummy variable (see Section 5.7.3) recording whether participants had correctly understood the information. A two-way multivariate ANOVA was then used to check whether there was an effect of numeracy and/or presentation format on overall comprehension and correct comprehension.

*Example repeated measures two-way ANOVA:* Furman and Buhrmester (1985) wanted to find out how children aged 11 to 13 perceived a range of personal relationships, for example with their parents, grandparents, siblings and teachers. The children were asked to complete a questionnaire rating each of those relationships along a number of relationship qualities such as importance of the relationship, satisfaction, conflict, etc. Because every participant answered all questions, this is considered a within-participants setup, and Furman and Buhrmester subsequently used a repeat measures two-way ANOVA to test for an effect of the child's gender and the relationship type on perceived relationship quality.

*Example three-way ANOVA:* Matz and Wood (2005) were interested in examining participants' coping with disagreement. Participants encountered a group that disagreed with them and were then instructed to pursue a strategy of either yielding to the group's opinion; changing the group's opinion; or joining a new group. During the study, participants' discomfort was measured twice, and at the end, participants were asked whether they assessed the group discussion as having resolved the conflict or not. In their analysis, Matz and Wood employed a three-way ANOVA with three independent variables ('Resolution Achieved', 'Strategy' and 'Time of Assessment') on 'Overall Discomfort' as a dependent variable.

### 8.7.2 Analysis of covariance (ANCOVA)

**8.7.2.1 The basic principle** A related form of the ANOVA is the **analysis of covariance**, also called **ANCOVA**, which controls for the influence of a confounding variable (a covariate) on the dependent variables. The underlying analysis is the same; the difference is that the part of the variance that is contributed by the confounding variable is removed before the basic analysis of variance is conducted.

In addition to the requirements for conducting an ANOVA (see Section 8.7.1), conducting an ANCOVA also requires the assumption of 'homogeneity of regression slopes' to be met. We will explain how to test for those assumptions in Section 10.5 when we explain how to conduct an ANCOVA.

**8.7.2.2 Example** In Schmierbach and Oeldorf-Hirsch's (2012) between-participants study on the question of credibility of Twitter and tweets, the same news story was presented in three different ways (a full news page, a first paragraph with a link for more details, or a tweet with a shortened link to the full story). The dependent variable in this study was credibility. To get a clearer picture of the impact of source on credibility, Schmierbach and Oeldorf-Hirsch also controlled for a number of variables they considered affecting overall perception of Twitter content: age, prior use of Twitter, gender and whether the participant was a student. By using an ANCOVA and controlling for those factors, it was more likely that any differences in perceived credibility were only due to the manipulation of the source of the news.

→ See Section 10.5 on how to conduct an ANCOVA.

### 8.7.3 Kruskal-Wallis

**8.7.3.1 The basic principle** Like the Wilcoxon signed rank or the Mann-Whitney U, the **Kruskal-Wallis test** relies on comparing ranks of values across and between groups. The Kruskal-Wallis uses those ranks to calculate a test statistic for which a significance value can then be established. This test is used if the conditions for an ANOVA (see Section 8.7.1) or ANCOVA (see Section 8.7.2) are not met, provided that there are more than five observations per group; that said, if you have fewer than five observations, it might not be appropriate to run any statistical test since the results will neither be informative or reliable.

***8.7.3.2 Example*** McCammon (2002) looked into the importance and effect of use of heuristics employed by people who were victims of an avalanche (when skiing). One of the factors examined was the size of groups in which people travelled. McCammon used Kruskal-Wallis to compare the level of exposure (to avalanches) between people travelling in groups of different sizes because one of the conditions for using an ANOVA was not met (see Section 8.7.1): in this case, the difference in variances between the groups was too big.

→ Section 10.6 describes how to conduct a Kruskal-Wallis test.

### ❓ REVIEW & REFLECT

- What is the role of variance in distinguishing an ANOVA from an ANCOVA?
- Why do we distinguish between within- and between-participants ANOVAs?

## 8.8 LOOKING AT RELATIONSHIPS

### 8.8.1 Chi-square test

***8.8.1.1 The basic principle*** Simply put, a **chi-square** test compares frequency distributions of categorical values against a distribution that would have occurred by chance; it compares the *observed* distribution of values against the *expected* distribution. An expected distribution can be the distribution you would expect if it was truly random, but it can also be an expectation based on previous research or additional information. For example, a study might have participants choose between three products which are identical except for colour – red, blue and green. If prior research has led you to believe that colour does not make any difference at all, your expected distribution would be roughly 33%/33%/33% (i.e., you expect each colour to be picked at fairly similar levels). However, if prior research indicates that red is strongly preferred, then depending on the information you have, your expected distribution might look more like this: 50%/25%/25%. The key point here is that for this test you need to consciously and in an informed way define and set the expected frequencies. A chi-square test comes in two flavours: *goodness-of-fit* and *test of independence*, but both work on the difference between expected and observed frequencies. Both will now be explained in more detail.

### 8.8.2 Chi-square test of independence

The **chi-square test of independence** calculates a ratio describing the difference between expected frequencies of values and observed frequencies of values. The size of the ratio describes the significance of the finding – higher ratios mean higher significance. In doing so, the test helps you establish whether there is any association between two (or more – but we will not cover this version here) variables. A significant results means the variables are not independent of each other and instead are *associated* with each other.

***8.8.2.1 Example*** Ball et al. (2015) researched nurses' work experiences and wanted to know whether workload was associated with attitude towards work. They used a chi-square test of independence to find out whether there was an association between attitudes towards work and average length of their shift, which was classified as either shorter than 12 hours or 12 hours or more.

→ See Section 11.4 on how to conduct a chi-square test of independence.

### 8.8.3 Chi-square test of goodness-of-fit

The **goodness-of-fit chi-square test** is used when you look at only one variable and its distributions and want to know whether the distribution of values is different from one expected by chance. (Note: You may also see this test referred to as **Pearson's Chi Square**). For example, if you have asked participants to choose between a number of options (yes/no; red or green urn; more/less/the same; pick the door to the left, the middle door, the door to the right), the goodness-of-fit chi-square helps you compare the observed distribution to the expected (50%/50% in the first example two examples, 33.3%/33.3%/33.3% in the second two examples) and tell you whether the difference between expected and observed frequencies is significant. The procedure is largely the same as the one described in Section 8.8.2 but focusses on a slightly different application. A goodness-of-fit test looks at the distribution of just one categorical (or nominal) variable's values rather than at the combination of two or more variables. In more advanced analyses, a chi-square goodness-of-fit is also used to test analytical models: Since models predict values of the involved variables, a chi-square test can then test the observed values against the values predicted by the model.

*8.8.3.1 Example* DeLong (2006) examined the motivation of college students to engage in physical activity. She looked at different stages of engaging in physical activity: contemplation, preparation, action and maintenance and compared students who had taken a physical activity class with students who had not. DeLong used the chi-square goodness-of-fit to establish whether students who had taken the class were distributed differently along the individual stages (e.g., had moved on to action and maintenance more frequently than others).

### 8.8.4 Pearson's correlation

*8.8.4.1 The basic principle* As with almost any other test, correlations are based on examining variances of two or more variables. To find out whether and how much variables correlate is to establish to what extent variables co-vary – in other words, what extent of variance is shared between two variables. In fact, you can calculate the explained variance by squaring the correlation: a correlation of .5 explains $.5^2 = .25 = 25\%$ of variance. A correlation can take a value between 0 and 1.0; the latter would be a perfect correlation. The larger the correlation coefficient, the more variance is shared: if two variables correlate at 1.0, they correlate perfectly and share the entirety of their variance.

*8.8.4.2 Example* Ali and Ahmed (2009) looked at associations between several types of rewards and work motivation and satisfaction. A Pearson's correlation analysis showed that of the examined factors, recognition and payment had the highest correlation with motivation and satisfaction, whereas the person of the leader/supervisor correlated only moderately with it.

→ See Section 11.1 on how to conduct a Pearson's correlation.

### 8.8.5 Spearman's correlation

*8.8.5.1 The basic principle* If the data is non-parametric, you use Spearman's correlation as an alternative to Pearson. Spearman's correlations work on the same principle as Pearson's correlations, with the only difference that the calculations are based on ranks.

*8.8.5.2 Example* Lu et al. (2007) surveyed 512 hospital nurses from the Chinese mainland to explore factors affecting overall job satisfaction. Because the data was not normally distributed (see Section 8.1), instead of Pearson's, a Spearman's correlation analysis was used to test the correlations between job satisfaction, organisational commitment, occupational stress, professional commitment, role conflict and role ambiguity.

→ See Section 11.2 on how to conduct a Spearman's correlation.

> **REVIEW & REFLECT**
>
> - Why does the chi-square goodness-of-fit test rely on your existing knowledge and assumptions?

## 8.9 HOW TO READ CHAPTERS 9, 10 AND 11

The following scenario and guidelines regarding how to read the instructions apply for all guidance in Chapters 9, 10 and 11.

### 8.9.1 Data set

Unless mentioned otherwise, examples in Chapters 9, 10 and 11 are based on one set of data describing the following experiment:

150 students with above average numerical aptitude (as established by a numeracy test and recorded in the variable 'NumericalScore') but low to average verbal skills have been recruited. All participants attend a general language course in one of three modes ('CourseType': either *online* as a course of ten sessions, as a *weekly* face-to-face one-hour course lasting ten weeks, or as a *weekend* face-to-face intensive course over two days) using either one of two types of material ('Material': existing or a newly developed set of materials). Language skills are assessed one week before the first session ('PreTest'), one week after completing the language course ('VerbalScore'), and again after four weeks ('FollowUpTest'). For each participant, the data set also includes the information whether they are a native English speaker (1 = yes, 2 = no) and the number of books they had read in the month prior to the first test ('Books'). Each participant was asked whether they would be interested in repeating the course at a later time ('RepeatCourse'), with 1 = yes and 2 = no (Figure 8.3).

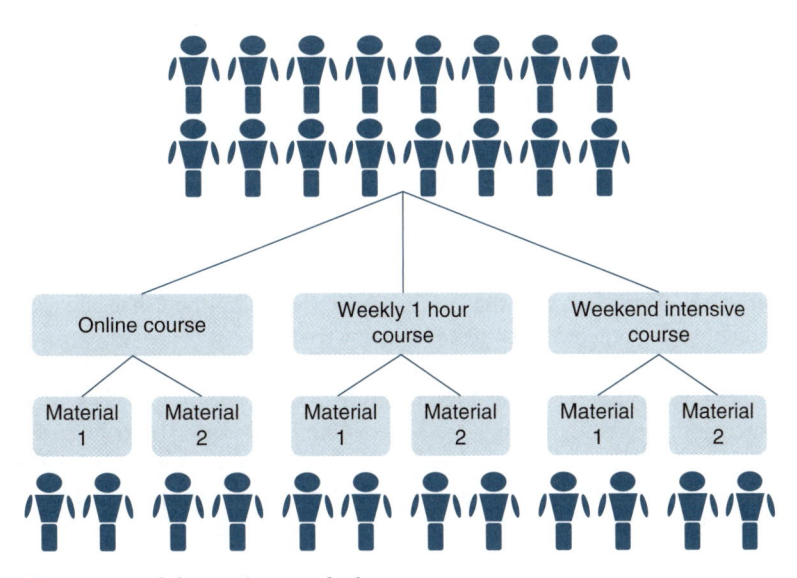

*Figure 8.3 Experimental design for sample data*

### 8.9.2 How to read instructions in the following chapters

Text that looks like this refers to Excel or SPSS formulas or menu items.

For all descriptions in curved brackets, '( )', are part of the formula and should be copied. Square brackets, '[Text]', will contain a description of a value or information which needs to be replaced by your specific data and should not be copied.

Example:

This requires you to fill in the cell range for your data, for example from cell A2 to cell A88. The final formula in Excel would look like this: =AVERAGE([cell range]), in this example =AVERAGE(A2:A88)

The text in square brackets has been replaced by specific cell references but the curved brackets are part of the Excel formula and have been kept.

Lastly, a disclaimer. It is beyond the scope of this handbook to provide a detailed, extensive description for every statistical analysis mentioned in this table – this would require an extensive SPSS manual and there are already several excellent books available, for example Brace, Kemp and Snelgar's (2016) *SPSS for Psychologists*. Instead the focus is on providing concise guidance for how these analyses can be conducted in SPSS and, for a range of those analyses, in Excel.

## A SHORT SUMMARY

- Most statistical tests are based on identifying sources of and comparing differences between types of variance.
- Most non-parametric tests adjust for the lack of normal distribution by basing calculations and comparisons on ranks of values rather than values themselves.

## CHECK YOUR UNDERSTANDING

1. Use the file available on the companion website to establish (either through Excel or SPSS) whether the variable 'Books' is normally distributed.
   a. Calculate or identify the following values for the variable 'Books':
      i. Mean
      ii. Median
      iii. Skewness
      iv. Kurtosis
   b. Create a Q-Q plot for 'Books'.
   c. Decide whether the variable is normally distributed.
2. For the following scenarios, which statistical analysis would be most appropriate?
   a. You ask participants to rate a candidate's CV in terms of suitability for a job. Half of the participants are told that the candidate is a man, the other half are told the candidate is a woman. Which test would you use:
      i. if the data is normally distributed
      ii. if the data is not normally distributed
   b. Participants are asked to complete a series of simple counting tasks twice. For half of the participants, the first task is completed while listening to white noise, the second task while listening to classical music; for the other half of the participants, the order is reversed. Assume that the data is normally distributed.

c. You want to know which of three TV ads appeals more to consumers. You play all three ads to a group of participants and ask them to pick their favourite. Assume that the data is normally distributed.
3. What is the non-parametric alternative to:
   a. A paired-samples t-test
   b. A one-sample t-test
   c. A one-way ANOVA
4. What is the parametric alternative to a Spearman's correlation?

# 9 Statistical Analyses: Looking at Differences

## WHAT IS THIS CHAPTER ABOUT?

This chapter describes in more detail the tests that we have previously introduced and categorised as tests looking at differences. You will find explanations of these analyses' concepts and use in Chapter 8; in this chapter we are looking at how to conduct them in practice. Each analysis will be explained using an example which you can follow in a file available from the companion website. For each analysis, we will also explain which information you need to report the results and how you use the information in writing up your findings.

## WHY IS THIS IMPORTANT?

Analysing data for differences between groups is a basic tool in the inventory of every researcher. In this chapter we want to make sure you are familiar with how to conduct these analyses, interpret the results, and report your findings, all in order to answer your research question.

## WHAT ARE THE LEARNING OUTCOMES FOR THIS CHAPTER?

At the end of this chapter you will be able to choose and run the appropriate test to analyse your data, including the following tests (tests marked with * are explained for both SPSS and Excel):

- One-sample t-test*
- Independent-samples t-test*
- Mann-Whitney U-test*
- Paired-samples t-test*
- Wilcoxon signed rank test

You can find a description of the data used for most of these scenarios as well as guidance on how to read the instructions in Section 8.9.

## 9.1 ONE-SAMPLE T-TEST

The concept and purpose of this analysis is described in more detail in Section 8.6.1.

Example question: Do the values for the variable 'VerbalScore' differ significantly from a given mean of 100?

### 9.1.1 One-sample t-test in Excel

> **ONLINE CONTENT**
>
> On the companion website you will find an Excel file you can use to follow the guidance in this section. You can also download and adjust it to fit your data.

> **THE HEADLINES**
>
> - Calculate the t-test statistic.
> - Identify t-value needed for significant result.
> - Excel functions used: AVG, STDEV.S, SQRT, T.INV.2T.

1. Calculate the t-test statistic.
   - This is the formula used to calculate the t-test statistic:

   $$\frac{\text{sample mean} - \text{population mean}}{\text{sample SD}/\sqrt{n}}$$

   - Establish the sample mean by using the AVG function (see Excel Functions Glossary).
   - Establish the standard deviation by using the STDEV.S function (see Excel Functions Glossary).
   - In this example:
     - The sample mean is 133.947.
     - The population mean is 100 – this is the value we want to compare against.
     - The standard deviation is 18.145.
     - N equals 150;

Plug all this back into the formula: $\frac{133.947 - 100}{18.145/12.247} = \frac{33.947}{1.482} = 22.913$

- Alternatively, you can calculate this all in one go. Use the following formula in Excel: =(AVERAGE([Cell range containing sample data])-[Mean you are comparing against])/((STDEV.S([cell range containing sample data]))/(SQRT(N))). Do not be intimidated by the long formula – you only need to plug in three different values. The figure below shows how the formula is constructed; we have highlighted the parts that require your input. Note: If you copy this formula into Excel, make sure you get the right number of brackets in the right place – this is important for the formula to work well – and remember to update the cell range to fit your data (Figure 9.1). In this example, the exact formula reads: =(AVERAGE(C2:C152)-100)/((STDEV.S(C2:C152))/(SQRT(150))).

This is your t-test statistic. But is it significant?

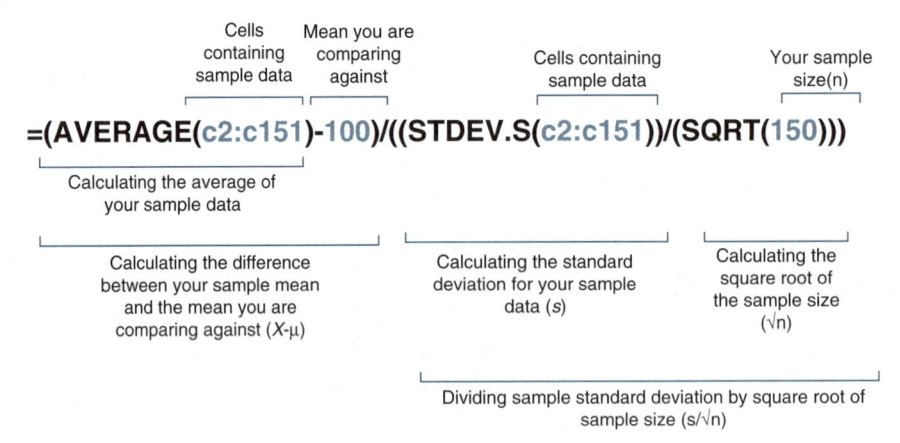

$$=(\text{AVERAGE}(c2:c151)-100)/((\text{STDEV.S}(c2:c151))/(\text{SQRT}(150)))$$

- AVERAGE(c2:c151): Cells containing sample data — Calculating the average of your sample data
- 100: Mean you are comparing against
- STDEV.S(c2:c151): Cells containing sample data — Calculating the standard deviation for your sample data (s)
- SQRT(150): Your sample size (n) — Calculating the square root of the sample size (√n)
- Calculating the difference between your sample mean and the mean you are comparing against (X-μ)
- Dividing sample standard deviation by square root of sample size (s/√n)

**Figure 9.1** *How the t-test statistic is calculated*

2. Identify t-value needed for significant result.
    - Find out what t-test value you would need for a significant result. The cut-off value for the t-test you need is also referred to as the 'critical value'.
    - You can identify the critical value by the Excel function =T.INV.2T. The '2t' part indicates that this is looking for a two-tailed significance. This function takes two arguments: alpha level and degree of freedom. For a sample of 150, the degree of freedom is n − 1 = 149, and you probably want to start testing for a significance at .05. If you calculate =T.INV.2T(.05, 149) in Excel, you get 1.976, which means that for a significance of .05, your critical value is 1.976. At t = 22.913, you have well and truly surpassed the critical value. Your sample's mean of 133.947 is significantly higher than the population mean of 100.
    - For $p = .01$: =T.INV.2T(.01, 149) = 2.609, thus your sample mean is different at $p < .01$, too.
    - For .001: =T.INV.2T(.001, 149) = 3.357 – again, your t-test value easily surpasses this critical value and your sample mean is significantly different from the population mean at $p < .001$.

### 9.1.2 One-sample t-test in SPSS

> **ONLINE CONTENT**
>
> On the companion website you will find SPSS data and syntax files you can use to follow the guidance in this section. You can also download and adjust them to fit your data.

1. Navigate to Analyze → Compare Means → One-Sample T Tests.
2. In the left side column, you see all variables available for this analysis; in the right column all selected variables will appear. Click on the name of the variable you want to compare against a fixed value. In this example, click on 'VerbalScore', then click on the arrow in the middle to move it to the right column (Figure 9.2)

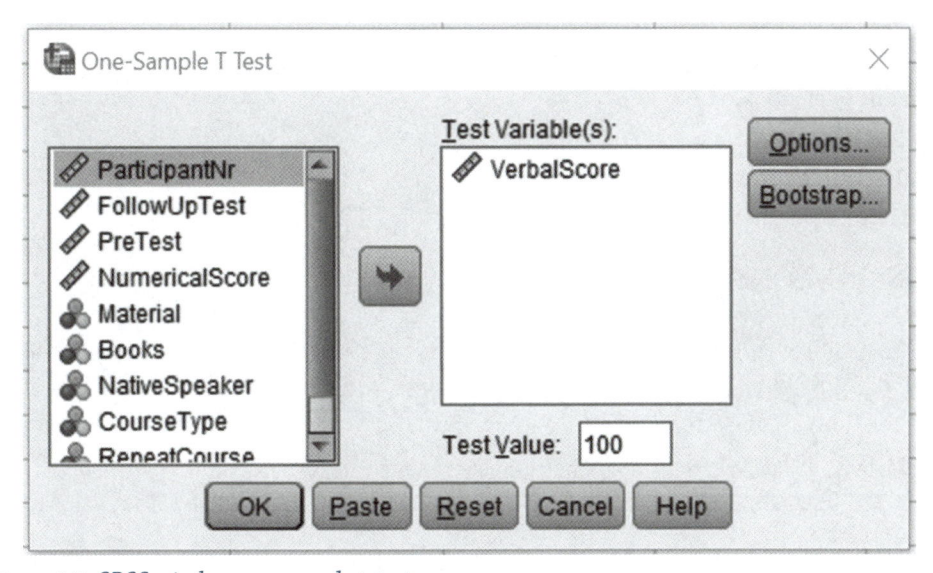

*Figure 9.2  SPSS window one-sample t-test*
Reprint courtesy of International Business Machines Corporation, © International Business Machines Corporation.

3. Enter the mean you are comparing the variable against into the field Test Value; in this example, 100.
4. Click OK.

### 9.1.3  Reporting the results of a one-sample t-test

#### 9.1.3.1  What you need to know

- Mean and standard deviation of the variable you are looking at (see Sections 6.3.1 and 6.5, respectively).
- Mean or value you are comparing it against: calculated or derived from literature research.
- Degrees of freedom (df): calculated in SPSS; manually calculated by you for Excel as N-1.
- t-test statistic, *p*-value: calculated in SPSS and Excel.

#### 9.1.3.2  What you need to do

- Describe your data and the value or sample mean you are comparing it against.
- Report the t-test statistic, including degrees of freedom and *p*-value.

For example:

> 'Participants' verbal scores showed a mean of 133.95 ($SD$ = 18.145). This was significantly higher than the comparison mean of 100, $t(149)$ = 22.913, $p$ <.001.'

## 9.2  WILCOXON SIGNED RANK

The concept and purpose of this analysis is described in more detail in Section 8.6.3.

Example question: Assume for the moment that the standard score in the numerical test you used (across all ages and backgrounds) is 100; you know that the variable 'NumericalScore' is

234  *Introducing Quantitative Methods*

not normally distributed. You have been given a reference score of 110 for numerically gifted pupils aged 15 and now want to know: Does your sample's 'NumericalScore' differ significantly from this reference score?

### 9.2.1 Wilcoxon signed rank in SPSS

> **ONLINE CONTENT**
>
> On the companion website you will find SPSS data and syntax files you can use to follow the guidance in this section. You can also download and adjust them to fit your data.

1. Navigate to <u>Analyze</u> → <u>Nonparametric Tests</u> → <u>One Sample</u>.
2. In the <u>Objectives</u> tab, click the first option: <u>Automatically compare observed data to hypothesized</u>.
3. In the <u>Fields</u> tab, select the second option: <u>Use custom field assignments</u> and make sure that the field you would like to compare (here, 'VerbalScore') is in the right column.
4. In the <u>Settings tab</u>, select <u>Customize tests</u>, and choose the second to last option, which is <u>Compare median to hypothesized (Wilcoxon signed/rank test)</u>. In the free field, you then enter the value to which you want to compare your sample mean to.
5. Click <u>Run</u> to start the test.
6. In the output window you will initially see a single, small table called 'Hypothesis Test Summary'. Double-click on this table to see more detailed results (Figure 9.3):

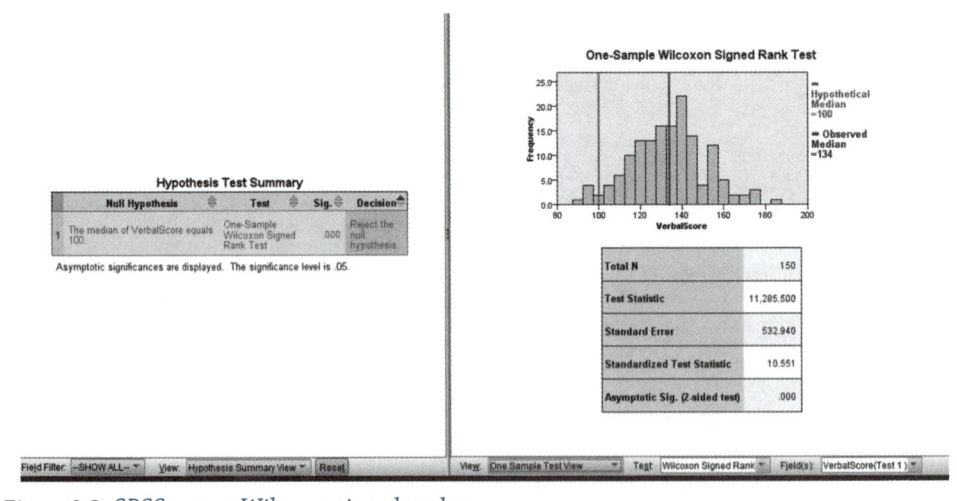

**Figure 9.3** *SPSS output Wilcoxon signed rank*
Reprint Courtesy of International Business Machines Corporation, © International Business Machines Corporation.

7. On the bottom right side, you see a pick list <u>View</u> which allows you to change to either <u>One Sample Test View</u> where you find the information for the test parameters, or <u>Continuous Field Information</u>, which gives you descriptives for 'VerbalScore'.

## 9.2.2 Reporting the results of a Wilcoxon signed rank test

### 9.2.2.1 What you need to know

- Median of the variable you are looking at: SPSS output.
- Median you are comparing it against: your data.
- Z-value: The value given as 'Standardised test statistic' in the SPSS output: here, 1.193.
- Significance value: here, given as <.001.

### 9.2.2.2 What you need to do

- Describe your data and the value or sample mean you are comparing it against.
- Report the Wilcoxon test statistic and *p*-value.

For example:

'A Wilcoxon signed rank test indicated that participants' numerical score (median = 111) did not differ significantly from the reference numerical score of 110, $z$ =1.930, $p < .001$.'

## 9.3 PAIRED-SAMPLES T-TEST

The concept and purpose of this analysis is described in more detail in Section 8.6.2.

Example question: Do participants' verbal scores differ before ('PreTest') and after the language training ('VerbalScore')?

### 9.3.1 Paired-samples t-test in Excel

### ONLINE CONTENT

You can use the Excel file provided on the companion website to follow the guidance in this section, or download and adjust it to fit your data.

Unlike SPSS, Excel does not apply any existing filters when running a statistical analysis. If, like in this example, you want to conduct analyses on only a subset of your data (first, on all participants using Material 1 then on all participants using Material 2), you therefore need to sort your data and then make sure to use the relevant range of cells. That said, running this test in Excel is surprisingly straightforward.

### THE HEADLINES

- Conduct a paired two-sample t-test using Data Analysis menu.
- Excel function used: t-Test: Paired Two Sample for Means.

1. Sort your data by 'Material'. 1
2. Navigate to Tools → Data Analysis and double-click on t-Test: Paired Two Sample for Means.

3. Enter the cell range for the data of your two variables. If you include the row heading in the cell range, make sure to tick the <u>Labels</u> box. Adjust the alpha level, if required. Click <u>OK</u>.
4. In the Excel output thus generated, 't Stat' refers to the t-test value. Note that the default formatting of the Excel output gives critical values and significance values in the exponential format as described in Section 4.9. If you want to view it in a more understandable format, just format the four cells through <u>Format</u> → <u>Cells</u> → <u>Number</u> to show as regular numbers with as many decimal places as you like (Table 9.1).

*Table 9.1* Results of a paired-samples t-test for Material 1

|  | PreTest | VerbalScore |
|---|---|---|
| Mean | 91.133 | 128.520 |
| Variance | 162.333 | 428.766 |
| Observations | 75.000 | 75.000 |
| Pearson's Correlation | 0.304 |  |
| Hypothesized Mean Difference | 0.000 |  |
| df | 74.000 |  |
| t Stat | −15.605 |  |
| P(T <= t) one-tail | 0.000 |  |
| t Critical one-tail | 1.666 |  |
| P(T <= t) two-tail | 0.000 |  |
| t Critical two-tail | 1.993 |  |

5. The results of the paired t-test (N = 75, which confirms that you have in fact only examined one group) show that the means of the pre-test and the post-test verbal score are 91.133 and 128.520, respectively. The t-test statistic is −15.605.
6. The table shows you the critical values for one and two-tailed tests at an alpha of .05. Both the one-tailed and two-tailed tests are well above the critical value required.
7. Note that this only covers half of the data set – this is the Pre/Post analysis for participants who were presented with Material 1. Now repeat the analysis for participants who were presented with Material 2 (Table 9.2):

*Table 9.2* Results of a paired-samples t-test for Material 2

|  | PreTest | VerbalScore |
|---|---|---|
| Mean | 105.387 | 139.373 |
| Variance | 120.321 | 174.507 |
| Observations | 75.000 | 75 |
| Pearson's Correlation | 0.981 |  |
| Hypothesized Mean Difference | 0.000 |  |
| df | 74.000 |  |
| t Stat | −91.305 |  |
| P(T<=t) one-tail | 0.000 |  |
| t Critical one-tail | 1.666 |  |
| P(T<=t) two-tail | 0.000 |  |
| t Critical two-tail | 1.993 |  |

8. The pre- and post-tests for group 2 show a mean of 105.387 and 139.373, respectively. The critical value for a two-tailed test is 1.993, and the given t-test statistic of −91.305 exceeds this by far.

### 9.3.2 Paired-samples t-test in SPSS

> **ONLINE CONTENT**
>
> On the companion website you will find SPSS data and syntax files you can use to follow the guidance in this section. You can also download and adjust them to fit your data.

1. If you were to simply run a paired t-test on the data as is, you would be comparing the pre-test scores of the entire sample with the post-test scores of the entire sample. However, you want to know whether either group A or B's scores differs significantly so you first need to select the cases you want to look at by going to Data → Select Cases (it is the second to last option in a very long list).
2. Choose the option If condition is satisfied. Click on If … which opens a new window. Here you can either move the selection variable (in this case, 'Material') to the right field via the arrow or type it in directly. 'Material = 1' means that only the cases where the value for 'Material' equals 1 are selected.
3. After clicking Continue and then clicking OK, SPSS applies the filter to the data.
4. If you look at the Data view again, a new column called filter_$ has appeared, and the row number of data sets where 'Material = 2' is crossed out. This affects data display and subsequent analyses until the filter is removed by entering the Data → Select Cases menu again and selecting the All Cases option.
5. For now, the filter excludes these cases and allows you to conduct a paired t-test of the pre- and post-test verbal scores of participants of group 1.
6. Navigate to Analyse → Compare Means → Paired Samples T Test. Here you will be asked to move the two variables you want to compare to the right; move the variables 'PreTest' and 'VerbalScore' to the right. Run the analysis (Figure 9.4).

**T-Test**

**Paired Samples Statistics**

|  |  | Mean | N | Std. Deviation | Std. Error Mean |
|---|---|---|---|---|---|
| Pair 1 | PreTest | 91.13 | 75 | 12.741 | 1.471 |
|  | VerbalScore | 128.52 | 75 | 20.707 | 2.391 |

**Paired Samples Correlations**

|  |  | N | Correlation | Sig. |
|---|---|---|---|---|
| Pair 1 | PreTest & VerbalScore | 75 | .304 | .008 |

**Paired Samples Test**

|  |  | Paired Differences ||||| t | df | Sig. (2-tailed) |
|---|---|---|---|---|---|---|---|---|---|
|  |  | Mean | Std. Deviation | Std. Error Mean | 95% Confidence Interval of the Difference ||  |  |  |
|  |  |  |  |  | Lower | Upper |  |  |  |
| Pair 1 | PreTest − VerbalScore | −37.387 | 20.749 | 2.396 | −42.161 | −32.613 | −15.605 | 74 | .000 |

**Figure 9.4** *SPSS output paired-samples t-test, group 1*
Reprint Courtesy of International Business Machines Corporation, © International Business Machines Corporation.

7. Now change the filter to only look at participants from group 2 (repeat steps 1 to 3).
8. When a new filter is entered, SPSS automatically assumes that the old one is no longer valid (see the USE ALL command in the first line) and starts from scratch.
9. To run the same paired t-test on group 2, repeat step 6 (Figure 9.5).

**Paired Samples Statistics**

|  |  | Mean | N | Std. Deviation | Std. Error Mean |
|---|---|---|---|---|---|
| Pair 1 | PreTest | 105.39 | 75 | 10.969 | 1.267 |
|  | VerbalScore | 139.37 | 75 | 13.210 | 1.525 |

**Paired Samples Correlations**

|  |  | N | Correlation | Sig. |
|---|---|---|---|---|
| Pair 1 | PreTest & VerbalScore | 75 | .981 | .000 |

**Paired Samples Test**

|  |  | Paired Differences |  |  |  |  | t | df | Sig. (2-tailed) |
|---|---|---|---|---|---|---|---|---|---|
|  |  | Mean | Std. Deviation | Std. Error Mean | 95% Confidence Interval of the Difference |  |  |  |  |
|  |  |  |  |  | Lower | Upper |  |  |  |
| Pair 1 | PreTest – VerbalScore | −33.987 | 3.224 | .372 | −34.728 | −33.245 | −91.305 | 74 | .000 |

*Figure 9.5* SPSS output paired-samples t-test, group 2
Reprint Courtesy of International Business Machines Corporation, © International Business Machines Corporation.

### 9.3.3 Reporting the results of a paired-samples t-test

#### 9.3.3.1 What you need to know

- Mean and standard deviation of the variable you are looking at for both groups: the SPSS input contains both; the Excel output contains mean and variance, and the standard deviation is the square root of the variance.
- T-test statistic, df, significance value: this is reported in both the SPSS and Excel output.

#### 9.3.3.2 What you need to do

- Describe the two groups you are comparing against in terms of mean and standard deviation.
- Report the t-test statistic, including degrees of freedom and *p*-value.

For example:

'For participants being taught with Material 1, verbal scores increased from a mean of 91.13.840 ($SD = 12.741$) at the initial test to a mean score of 128.520 ($SD = 20.707$) at the first test after the language classes. A paired-samples t-test confirmed that this increase was significant, $t(74) = -15.605$, $p < .001$.'

## 9.4 INDEPENDENT-SAMPLES T-TEST

The concept and purpose of this analysis is described in more detail in Section 8.6.4.
Example question:

Do the verbal scores after the training differ for participants who have been taught with Material 1 and those who have been taught with Material 2 (variable 'Material')?

### 9.4.1 Independent-samples t-test in Excel

> **THE HEADLINES**
>
> - Sort variables according to grouping variable.
> - Establish whether samples have equal or unequal variances.
> - Run appropriate test via Data Analysis extension. (see Section 5.2)
> - Excel functions used: n/a.

> **ONLINE CONTENT**
>
> You can use the Excel file provided on the companion website to follow the guidance in this section or download and adjust it to fit your data.

1. Sort variables according to grouping variable.
    - In this example you want to compare the 'VerbalScores' of group 1 with the 'VerbalScores' of group 2. To prepare for the analysis, sort the data in your Excel sheet by the variable 'Material'. The first 75 data sets belong to participants who received Material 1, and the next 75 data sets to participants who saw Material 2.

2. Establish whether samples have equal or unequal variances.
    - Navigate to Tools → Data Analysis and select F-Test Two-Sample for Variances. Enter the cell range of 'VerbalScore' for the first sample in the first field, and for the second sample in the second field. In this example, we have entered the range for the first 75 data sets in the first field, and the cell range for the next 75 data sets in the second field.
    - Adjust the alpha value if you prefer it to be more stringent.
    - Click OK. In this analysis, the variance of variable 1 needs to be higher than that of variable 2 in order to work. Check that this is the case (as in the table below); if not, run the analysis again but swap the cell ranges around.
    - Because the null hypothesis for the *F*-Test is that variances for the two variables are equal, a non-significant finding means variances are equal; a significant result means variances are unequal. In this example, the *F*-value is 2.457 with the critical value at 1.469. It is significantly above the critical value and we conclude that the variances are unequal (Table 9.3).

*Table 9.3 Excel result for f-test two-sample for variances*

| F-Test Two-Sample for Variances | | |
| --- | --- | --- |
|  | Variable 1 | Variable 2 |
| Mean | 128.520 | 139.373 |
| Variance | 428.766 | 174.507 |
| Observations | 75 | 75 |
| df | 74 | 74 |
| F | 2.457 |  |
| P(F<=f) one-tail | 0.000 |  |
| F Critical one-tail | 1.469 |  |

3. Run appropriate test via Data Analysis extension.
   - Navigate to Tools → Data Analysis. If the *F*-test confirms equal variances, select t-test: Two Samples Assuming Equal Variances. If the *F*-test showed unequal variances, select t-test: Two Samples Assuming Unequal Variances.
   - Enter the cell range for the first sample in the first field and for the second sample in the second field.
   - Adjust the alpha value if you prefer it to be more stringent. Click OK.
   - We have shown below the results for the first version. Note that we have reformatted the four bottom cells in the second column to show in non-exponential format (Table 9.4):

*Table 9.4* Excel result for t-test: Two-sample assuming equal variances

| t-Test: Two-Sample Assuming Equal Variances | | |
| --- | --- | --- |
|  | Variable 1 | Variable 2 |
| Mean | 128.520 | 139.373 |
| Variance | 428.766 | 174.507 |
| Observations | 75 | 75 |
| Pooled Variance | 301.637 | |
| Hypothesized Mean Difference | 0 | |
| df | 148 | |
| t Stat | −3.827 | |
| P(T<=t) one-tail | 0.000 | |
| t Critical one-tail | 1.655 | |
| P(T<=t) two-tail | 0.000 | |
| t Critical two-tail | 1.976 | |

## 9.4.2 Independent-samples t-test in SPSS

1. **www** On the companion website you will find SPSS data and syntax files you can use to follow the guidance in this section. You can also download and adjust them to fit your data.
2. Navigate to Analyze → Compare Means → Independent-Samples T Test.
3. In order to conduct an independent-samples t-test you need to tell SPSS which variable to examine (by moving 'VerbalScore' into the Test Variable box), and how to tell apart the two different groups. To do this, first move the variable 'Material' (which you used to record whether pupils had been allocated to group 1 or 2) into the Grouping Variable: Box.
4. Click on Define Groups and type the value of the grouping variable that defines group 1 in the Group 1 field, and the value that defines group 2 in the Group 2 field. In this example, type in '1' for group 1, and '2' for group 2.
5. Click Continue.
6. Note that the test output shows two possible results: One for 'Equal variances assumed' and one for 'Equal variances not assumed': (Figure 9.6)

### Group Statistics

| | Material | N | Mean | Std. Deviation | Std. Error Mean |
|---|---|---|---|---|---|
| VerbalScore | 1 | 75 | 128.52 | 20.707 | 2.391 |
| | 2 | 75 | 139.37 | 13.210 | 1.525 |

### Independent Samples Test

| | | Levene's Test for Equality of Variances | | t-test for Equality of Means | | | | | 95% Confidence Interval of the Difference | |
|---|---|---|---|---|---|---|---|---|---|---|
| | | F | Sig. | t | df | Sig. (2-tailed) | Mean Difference | Std. Error Difference | Lower | Upper |
| VerbalScore | Equal variances assumed | 8.917 | .003 | -3.827 | 148 | .000 | -10.853 | 2.836 | -16.458 | -5.249 |
| | Equal variances not assumed | | | -3.827 | 125.676 | .000 | -10.853 | 2.836 | -16.466 | -5.241 |

*Figure 9.6* SPSS output for independent-samples t-test
Reprint Courtesy of International Business Machines Corporation, © International Business Machines Corporation.

7. The second and third column from the left column contain the result for Levene's Test for Equality of Variance. Like the *F*-Test in Excel, the null hypothesis is that variances are equal and if Levene's test is not significant, it means that variances are equal and the first line of results relevant. If Levene's test is significant, then the second line of results is important. The test results confirm that the two groups differ significantly from each other such that the mean verbal score of group 2 is higher than the mean verbal score of group 1.

### 9.4.3 Reporting the results of an independent-samples t-test

#### 9.4.3.1 What you need to know

- Mean and standard deviation of the variable you are looking at for both groups: the SPSS input contains both; the Excel output contains mean and variance, and the standard deviation is the square root of the variance.
- Results of Levene's test or *F*-Test if unequal variances have been established: established through test in Excel; shown in SPSS output.
- T-test statistic, df, significance value: calculated and displayed by SPSS and Excel.

#### 9.4.3.2 What you need to do

- Describe the two groups you are comparing in terms of mean and standard deviation.
- Report the t-test statistic, including degrees of freedom and p-value; report Levene's test or *F*-Test if variances are unequal.

For example:

'An independent-samples t-test was used to compare verbal scores between participants taught with Material 1 and those taught with Material 2. An *F*-Test Two-Sample for Variances test established that variances were unequal ($F(74) = 2.457, p < .001$) therefore the results of a the t-test assuming unequal variances are reported. Verbal scores of participants being taught with Material 1 were at a mean of 128.52 ($SD = 20.707$) whereas participants taught with Material 2 had a mean verbal score of 139.3733 ($SD = 12.210$); this difference was significant at $t(126) = -3.827, p < .001$.'

## 9.5 MANN-WHITNEY U-TEST

The concept and purpose of this analysis is described in more detail in Section 8.6.5.

Example question: Do the numerical scores differ between participants who are or are not native English speakers?

## 9.5.1 Mann-Whitney U-test in Excel

> **THE HEADLINES**
>
> - Rank all values as part of one set of values. Award average ranks for tied values.
> - Sum up ranks for each sample individually.
> - Pick lower of the two rank sums.
> - Calculate Mann-Whitney U.
> - Calculate z-value for lower of two rank sums.
> - Calculate critical value of Mann-Whitney U.
> - Calculate significance value.
> - Excel functions used: IF, MIN, NORM.S.INV, NORM.S.DIST, RANK.AVG, SQRT.

> **www ONLINE CONTENT**
>
> You can use the Excel file provided on the companion website to follow the guidance in this section, or download and adjust it to fit your data.

We have provided below a screenshot from an Excel sheet showing the cells and their labels. Values in not-shaded cells are values you need to enter or calculate elsewhere in Excel (we will explain how); all shaded cells are computed through the formulas in the cells and we will explain those formulas below (Figure 9.7):

|   | A | B | C | D | E | F | G | H | I | J | K | L |
|---|---|---|---|---|---|---|---|---|---|---|---|---|
| 1 | Alpha | 0.050 |  | Sample 1 | n | 81 | Rank sum | 6907 | Mean rank | 72.93 | Mann-Whitney U | 3003 |
| 2 | Tails | 2.000 |  | Sample 2 | n | 69 | Rank sum | 5418 | Mean rank | 78.52 | Mann-Whitney U | 2586 |
| 3 | N | 150.000 |  |  |  |  |  |  |  |  |  |  |
| 4 | Mann-Whitney U | 2586.000 |  |  |  |  |  |  |  |  |  |  |
| 5 | Mean | 2794.500 |  |  |  |  |  |  |  |  |  |  |
| 6 | Variance | 70328.250 |  |  |  |  |  |  |  |  |  |  |
| 7 | Standard Deviation | 265.195 |  |  |  |  |  |  |  |  |  |  |
| 8 | Z-Score | 0.786 |  |  |  |  |  |  |  |  |  |  |
| 9 | Critical value for Mann-Whitney U test stati | 2274.678 |  |  |  |  |  |  |  |  |  |  |
| 10 | Significance (p-value) | 0.432 |  |  |  |  |  |  |  |  |  |  |

**Figure 9.7** *Excel sheet to calculate Wilcoxon signed rank*
Used with permission from Microsoft.

1. **Rank all values as part of one set of values. Award average ranks for tied values.**

   For this example, we are only concerned with two columns in this Excel sheet: 'NumericalScore', which contains the numerical score, and 'NativeSpeaker', which shows '1' for participants who are native speakers and '2' for participants who are not.
   - In a first step, the Mann-Whitney U-test ranks values of both groups you want to compare as if they formed one big group and for each value assigns a rank within this big, combined group. Where ties exist, average ranks are assigned.

     1. Create two new columns called 'MW_Rank_1' and 'MW_Rank_2' . The function for each column takes the following format:
        =IF([Criterion],[What to Do or Display if Criterion is True, What to Do or Display if Criterion is Not True]).
        In this example, the criterion is whether the value in the 'NumericalScore' column value belongs to group 1 or 2, which is shown in the 'NativeSpeaker' column. For example, O2=1 checks whether the value in cell O2 equals 1.

2. If the value belongs to group 1, the corresponding rank assigned to this value should be displayed: RANK.AVG([Location of cell],[Fixed range of cells],[type of ranking]). If the value does not belong to group 1, the cell should display '0'.
3. The first value here is the location of the cell you are examining – in this example, it is the first (non-heading) cell of column N (i.e., N2). The next part, the range for the ranking, needs to be entered in a certain format to make sure that the range does not update but remains fixed. The last part is this particular type of ranking, 1. We start by checking this for cell N2. If the cell content equals 1, we want to enter the rank out of the range between N2 to N151; if cell content does not equal 1, we want to display a zero. The full formula is therefore =IF(O2=1,RANK.AVG(N2,$N$2:$N$151,1),0).
4. Copy this formula to the entire column.
    - Repeat this for the second group in the second column, adjusting the formula accordingly. In this example, the adjusted formula reads =IF(O2=2,RANK.AVG(N2,$N$2:$N$151,1),0). Note that the only thing that changes here is the criterion at the start of the formula and that we have used '$' to make sure the references to the range do not change. Copy this formula to the entire column.
    - You should now have two columns showing a mixture of cells containing '0' and ranks.

2. **Sum up ranks for each sample individually.**
    - Use the AUTOSUM function at the bottom of each column to sum up ranks for each group. In this example, ranks for participants from group 2 sum up to 5418; ranks for participants from group 1 sum up to 5907.
    - Establish N for both groups by counting the number of participants in each. You can do so by filtering for either 1 or 2 in the 'NativeSpeaker' column. We count 81 participants in group 1, and 69 in group 2.
    - Now you have all the data you need to enter into the list of fields and functions in the file shown earlier on page 242. Note how the right part uses the data you have just collected – n and the rank totals (Figure 9.8):

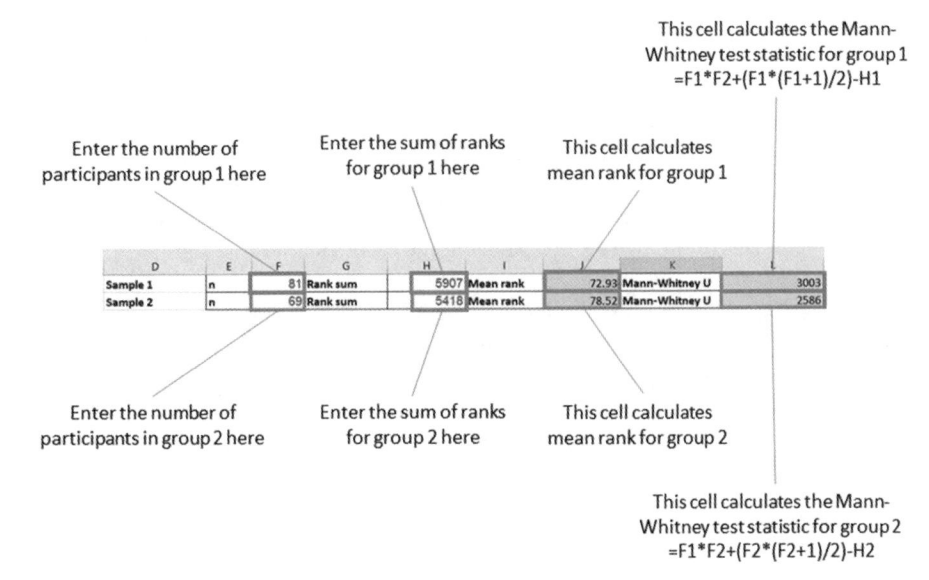

**Figure 9.8** Data for samples 1 and 2
Used with permission from Microsoft.

- Copy these cells into your Excel sheet, making sure that the cell references are updated. With these values calculated, you can now proceed to the left part of the overview shown above (Figure 9.9):

|   | A | B |
|---|---|---|
| 1 | Alpha | 0.050 |
| 2 | Tails | 2.000 |
| 3 | N | 150.000 |
| 4 | Mann-Whitney U | 2586.000 |
| 5 | Mean (rank) | 2794.500 |
| 6 | Variance (rank) | 70328.250 |
| 7 | Standard deviation (rank) | 265.195 |
| 8 | Z-Score | 0.786 |
| 9 | Critical value for Mann-Whitney U test statistic | 2274.678 |
| 10 | Significance (p-value) | 0.432 |

*Figure 9.9* Completing calculations for Mann-Whitney U-test in Excel
Used with permission from Microsoft.

- Alpha: Enter the alpha value (see Section 6.10) you want to test at. In this example, we used .05.
- Tails (see Section 2.10): Unless your hypothesis is directional, enter 2.
- N: Calculates N from the sample sizes you have entered for both groups with the following formula:
  =F1 + F2.

3. **Pick lower of the two rank sums.**
    - Mann-Whitney U: Chooses the smaller of the two Whitney U-values you have calculated previously with the following formula:
    = MIN(J1,J2).

Note that this refers to the columns from the rightmost part explained above.

4. **Calculate Mann-Whitney U.**
    - The next three values (mean, variance, and standard deviation) are values for Mann-Whitney U under the assumption that the null hypothesis is true.
    - **Mean:** calculates the mean (see also Section 6.3.1) for the reference value of U based on the sample sizes of the two groups by using the following formula:
    = (F1 + F2)/2.
    - **Variance:** Calculates the variance (see also Section 6.5) for the reference value of U based on the sample sizes of the two groups, using the following formula:
    = (F1 + F2 × (F1+F2+1))/12.
    - **Standard Deviation:** calculates the standard deviation (see also Section 6.5) for the reference value of U, based on the variance calculated earlier, and using the following formula:
    = SQRT(B6).

5. **Calculate z-value for lower of two rank sums.**
    - Z-Score: calculates the z-score (see also Section 6.8) based on U and the mean and standard deviation calculated earlier, using the following formula:
    = (B5-B4)/B7.

6. **Calculate critical value of Mann-Whitney U.**
   - Critical Value: calculates the critical value for U based on the mean, standard deviation and the arguments for tails and alpha-value you entered previously, using the following formula: = B5+B7*NORM.S.INV(B1/B2)-B1. You do not need this value to calculate the significance of your findings – it just tells you whether the U-value you found in your sample is lower or higher than the U-value calculated via the normal approximation.

7. **Calculate significance value.**
   - P-value: calculates *p* (see also Section 6.10) based on the z-score calculated above and the number of tails specified earlier, using the following formula:
   = B2*(1-NORM.S.DIST(B8,TRUE)).

### 9.5.2 Mann-Whitney U-test in SPSS

> **ONLINE CONTENT**
>
> On the companion website you will find SPSS data and syntax files you can use to follow the guidance in this section. You can also download and adjust them to fit your data.

- Navigate to <u>Analyze</u> → <u>Nonparametric Tests</u>. You are presented with three options: <u>One Sample</u>, <u>Independent Samples</u>, and <u>Related Samples</u>.
- Because the Mann-Whitney U-test tests two independent samples, click on the second option, <u>Independent Samples</u>.
- This window has three tabs – <u>Objective</u>, <u>Fields</u>, and <u>Settings</u>. The menu opens onto the <u>Objective</u> tab and you can select your objective in the middle – here, select <u>Compare medians across groups</u> since you want to know whether there is a significant difference in the performance of male and female participants.
- To tell SPSS which variables you want to examine, switch to the second tab, <u>Fields</u> and move the variable 'NumericalScore' into the top right <u>Test Fields</u> column (1). The bottom right <u>Group</u> field (2) receives the variable that defines your groups, in this case 'NativeSpeaker'.
- Switch to the <u>Settings</u> tab. If you are unsure which test to use you could select the first option <u>Automatically choose the tests based on the data</u> and have SPSS choose the appropriate tests. However, for your data the Mann-Whitney U-test is most appropriate. Tick the corresponding box <u>Mann-Whitney U (2 samples)</u>. Click <u>Run</u>.
- If you want to know more details about the test results, a double-click on this table calls up a more detailed view. Note: Make sure you click on the right row to get the right details! It shows the distribution of rankings and, in the second line of the table, the Mann-Whitney U-value.

### 9.5.3 Reporting the results of a Mann-Whitney U-test

#### 9.5.3.1 What you need to know

- Mean rank: computed in the Excel worksheet; in SPSS accessible through double-click on the graphical output.
- Mann-Whitney U-test statistic: calculated by both routes, SPSS and Excel.
- Z-score: calculated in Excel; given by SPSS.
- df: calculated as N1+N2-2.
- Significance value: determined by you; see Section 6.12 on the meaning and definition of the *p*-value.

### 9.5.3.2 What you need to do

- Describe the two groups you are comparing against in terms of mean and standard deviation.
- Report the Mann-Whitney U-test statistic, including z-score, degrees of freedom and *p*-value.
- Note that the values calculated for the Mann-Whitney U parameter by SPSS and Excel may differ. However, the calculated z-scores usually align and you may choose to report that value instead.

For example:

'Mean ranks for participants for whom English was their first language and for those where it was not were at 72.93 and 78.52, respectively. Mean ranks did not differ significantly, Mann-Whitney U = 2,586, $n_1 = 69$, $n_2 = 81$, $p > .05$.'

## A SHORT SUMMARY

- One-sample t-tests assess the size of a difference in means (between sample and population mean) and examine how it compares to the variance within the sample itself.
- A paired-samples t-test assesses the size of a difference in means between two groups and examines how it compares relative to overall variance.
- The Wilcoxon signed rank is the non-parametric alternative to both the paired t-test and the one-sample t-test. It relies on comparing how many values in your data set are above the value you are comparing against and how many below.
- An independent-samples t-test assesses the size of a difference in means between two groups and examines how this difference compares relative to the two groups' variances.
- The Mann-Whitney U-test is the non-parametric alternative to the independent-samples t-test. It relies on ranking values across two groups and then computing a ratio of ranks between the groups.

## RESEARCH METHODS AT WORK

Takeshi is a product development manager for a high-end chocolate confiserie. As part of their loyalty programme, they are running a tasting club for which they send out samples of their new developments with questionnaires for customers to rate the samples. Last month they sent out samples for two new products, Terrific Truffles and Awesome Almonds, and Takeshi now wants to know which of the two performed better. The rating data turns out to be normally distributed and Takeshi therefore uses a paired-samples t-test since each customer has rated both samples.

Ayodele is also interested in evaluating consumer feedback. In her case, a small independent tea shop, consumers ask for one of the two monthly tea samples to be sent out in return for their feedback. Because customers rate either one or the other tea sample, an independent-samples t-test would be more appropriate. However, Ayodele has also checked for normal distribution and found that the data is not normally distributed; she therefore uses a Mann-Whitney U-test for her analysis.

## CHECK YOUR UNDERSTANDING

1. What is the key difference between a paired-samples t-test and an independent-samples t-test? Why is this difference important?

2. In a study, participants rated an item on two different scales: one ranging from 'Good' to 'Bad' and one ranging from 'Like' to 'Dislike'. The output of a paired-samples t-test comparing 'Like' and 'Good' is given here (Figure 9.10):

**Paired Samples Statistics**

| | | Mean | N | Std. Deviation | Std. Error Mean |
|---|---|---|---|---|---|
| Pair 1 | Like | 3.7961 | 103 | 2.02126 | .19916 |
| | Good | 2.5922 | 103 | 1.25586 | .12374 |

**Paired Samples Correlations**

| | | N | Correlation | Sig. |
|---|---|---|---|---|
| Pair 1 | Like & Good | 103 | .581 | .000 |

**Paired Samples Test**

| | | Paired Differences | | | | | t | df | Sig. (2-tailed) |
|---|---|---|---|---|---|---|---|---|---|
| | | Mean | Std. Deviation | Std. Error Mean | 95% Confidence Interval of the Difference Lower | Upper | | | |
| Pair 1 | Like - Good | 1.20388 | 1.64710 | .16229 | .88198 | 1.52579 | 7.418 | 102 | .000 |

*Figure 9.10* A paired-samples t-test examining whether two variables are similar or different

   a. Looking at the output, do you think the two ratings are different enough to justify keeping them as separate variables?
   b. Write up the results of the test.

3. A study presented information to participants and asked them after 2, 12 or 20 days how many arguments presented to them initially they recalled. Two raters then scored participants' responses as to the number of correctly and incorrectly recalled arguments. Below you find the output for all three comparisons between the three groups of participants. Assume that the hypotheses were non-directional and that variances are equal (Figures 9.11, 9.12 and 9.13).

**Group Statistics**

| | Time_condition | N | Mean | Std. Deviation | Std. Error Mean |
|---|---|---|---|---|---|
| Agreed correct count, 2nd part | 2 days | 100 | 4.11 | 1.847 | .185 |
| | 12 days | 99 | 3.78 | 1.941 | .195 |

**Independent Samples Test**

| | | Levene's Test for Equality of Variances | | t-test for Equality of Means | | | | |
|---|---|---|---|---|---|---|---|---|
| | | F | Sig. | t | df | Sig. (2-tailed) | Mean Difference | Std. Error Difference |
| Agreed correct count, 2nd part | Equal variances assumed | .424 | .516 | 1.237 | 197 | .218 | .332 | .269 |
| | Equal variances not assumed | | | 1.237 | 196.306 | .218 | .332 | .269 |

*Figure 9.11* Independent-samples t-test examining recall data of 2 and 12 days

## 248  Introducing Quantitative Methods

**Group Statistics**

| | Time_condition | N | Mean | Std. Deviation | Std. Error Mean |
|---|---|---|---|---|---|
| Agreed correct count, 2nd part | 2 days | 100 | 4.11 | 1.847 | .185 |
| | 20 days | 94 | 3.26 | 2.290 | .236 |

**Independent Samples Test**

| | | Levene's Test for Equality of Variances | | t-test for Equality of Means | | | | |
|---|---|---|---|---|---|---|---|---|
| | | F | Sig. | t | df | Sig. (2-tailed) | Mean Difference | Std. Error Difference |
| Agreed correct count, 2nd part | Equal variances assumed | 2.353 | .127 | 2.869 | 192 | .005 | .855 | .298 |
| | Equal variances not assumed | | | 2.850 | 178.724 | .005 | .855 | .300 |

*Figure 9.12*  Independent-samples t-test examining recall data of 2 and 20 days

→ T-Test

**Group Statistics**

| | Time_condition | N | Mean | Std. Deviation | Std. Error Mean |
|---|---|---|---|---|---|
| Agreed correct count, 2nd part | 12 days | 99 | 3.78 | 1.941 | .195 |
| | 20 days | 94 | 3.26 | 2.290 | .236 |

**Independent Samples Test**

| | | Levene's Test for Equality of Variances | | t-test for Equality of Means | | | | |
|---|---|---|---|---|---|---|---|---|
| | | F | Sig. | t | df | Sig. (2-tailed) | Mean Difference | Std. Error Difference |
| Agreed correct count, 2nd part | Equal variances assumed | .930 | .336 | 1.713 | 191 | .088 | .522 | .305 |
| | Equal variances not assumed | | | 1.705 | 182.522 | .090 | .522 | .306 |

*Figure 9.13*  Independent-samples t-test examining recall data of 12 and 20 days

Write up the results of these tests.

# 10 Statistical Analyses: Looking at Effects

### WHAT IS THIS CHAPTER ABOUT?

This chapter provides guidance for the type of tests categorised in earlier chapters as looking at effects. This chapter will describe how to conduct several types of ANOVAs as well as the non-parametric alternative (for the one-way ANOVA, guidance will also be given for Excel). We will begin with one-way ANOVAs for between- and within-participants design, and we will then introduce the two- and three-way variants for both types of design. We will explain how to adjust these analyses for a mixed-method design. Additionally, this chapter describes the Kruskal-Wallis test in SPSS and provides guidance to conduct an ANCOVA.

### WHY IS THIS IMPORTANT?

The analyses described in this chapter are some of the most frequently used. Knowing how to conduct these analyses will equip you with the skills not only to run these yourself, but also to interpret the results presented by other researchers.

### WHAT ARE THE LEARNING OUTCOMES FOR THIS CHAPTER?

At the end of this chapter you should be able to conduct the following analyses in SPSS, as well as describe and interpret the results:
- One-way ANOVA between-participants
- One-way ANOVA within-participants
- Two- and three-way ANOVA between-participants
- Two- and three-way ANOVA within-participants
- Within-/Between-participants ANCOVA
- Kruskal-Wallis

## 10.1 ONE-WAY BETWEEN-PARTICIPANTS ANOVA

The concept and purpose of this analysis is described in more detail in Section 8.7.1.

Example: You want to examine whether the type of course had any effect on the verbal score immediately after the course.

First, you need to test the assumptions for the dependent variable:

1. Homogeneity of variance: In Excel this is tested with the *F*-test for unequal variances described on page 239; SPSS gives you the option to run this test alongside the ANOVA itself
2. Normality (that is, the data should be normally distributed): see Section 8.1
3. Coming from independent groups: this needs to be the case to conduct a between-participants analysis
4. Data on an interval scale or ratio scale: see Section 2.2

### 10.1.1 One-way between-participants ANOVA in Excel

**ONLINE CONTENT**

On the companion website you will find an Excel file you can use to follow the guidance in this section. You can also download and adjust it to fit your data.

**THE HEADLINES**

- Prepare your data such that the values for the groups you are comparing are aligned in columns next to each other.
- Conduct a one-way ANOVA using the Data Analysis menu.
- Conduct post-hoc tests if necessary, using independent-samples t-tests (or other appropriate tests).
- Excel functions used: Data Analysis extension (see page 120).

1. Prepare your data such that the values for the groups you are comparing are aligned in columns next to each other.
   - The easiest way to do this is to sort your data by your grouping variable (here, 'CourseType') and then copy each group into a separate column. In this example it means that you now have three columns headed 'VerbalScore CourseType1', 'VerbalScore CourseType2' and 'VerbalScore CourseType3', respectively.
2. Conduct a one-way ANOVA using the Data Analysis menu.
   - Navigate to Data Analysis → Anova: Single Factor. Enter the range for which you want to conduct your analysis – note that the range here spans *all columns* and includes values of all groups you compare. Tick whether the data is grouped by columns or rows and whether it includes headings (Figure 10.1).

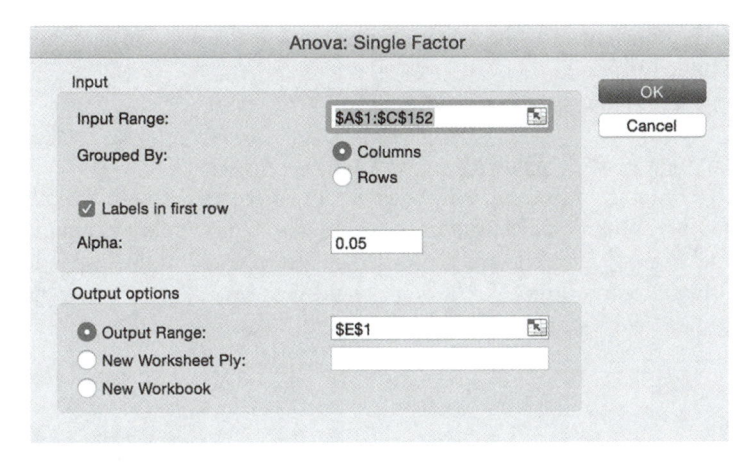

*Figure 10.1* Conducting a single factor ANOVA in Excel
Used with permission from Microsoft.

- Click OK. This gets you the following result (Figure 10.2):

*Figure 10.2* Output for a one-way ANOVA with the independent variable 'CourseType' and the dependent variable 'VerbalScore'
Used with permission from Microsoft.

- Look at the *F*-value: 0.240 at *p*=.786. This tells you that for the 'VerbalScore' variable, there is no effect of 'CourseType'.

### 10.1.2 One-way between-participants ANOVA in SPSS

> **ONLINE CONTENT**
>
> On the companion website you will find SPSS data and syntax files you can use to follow the guidance in this section. You can also download and adjust them to fit your data.
>
> *Multivariate one-way ANOVA:* You can adjust the guidance in this example. This requires you to pay particular attention to step 3.

Note: In SPSS, you have two choices to conduct a one-way ANOVA: one via Analyse → Compare Means (as described below) and one via Analyse → General Linear Model → Univariate. Of the

252  *Introducing Quantitative Methods*

two, the second is more powerful, the first is simpler to navigate. We have here chosen to explain the first for simplicity's sake.

Conducting the ANOVA:

1. Navigate to <u>Analyze</u> → <u>Compare Means</u> → <u>One-Way ANOVA</u>.
2. Since you are interested in comparing the verbal test scores between the different course type conditions, both immediately after the courses and four weeks after, move the variable 'CourseType' to the <u>Factor</u> field and the variables 'VerbalScore' to the <u>Dependent List</u>.
3. For a multivariate one-way ANOVA, you would move more than one variable into the <u>Dependent List</u> field (Figure 10.3).

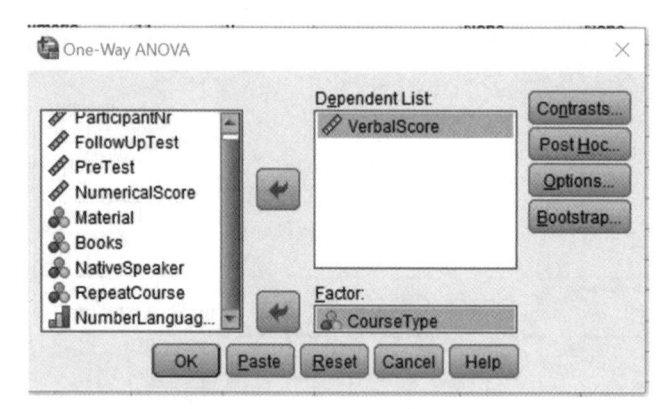

*Figure 10.3* Setting up a one-way ANOVA in SPSS

Reprint Courtesy of International Business Machines Corporation, © International Business Machines Corporation.

4. Click the <u>Options …</u> button and tick three options:
   a. <u>Descriptive Statistics</u> to get the descriptive data.
   b. <u>Homogeneity of variance test</u> to run the test for equality of variances.
   c. <u>Welch</u> as the alternative analysis in case variances are unequal and the assumptions violated (Figure 10.4).

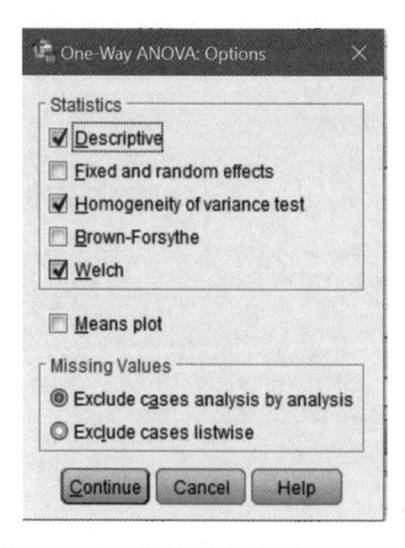

*Figure 10.4* Setting options for a one-way ANOVA in SPSS

Reprint Courtesy of International Business Machines Corporation, © International Business Machines Corporation.

5. Click Continue, then click Post Hoc ... : The choice of post-hoc tests can be quite overwhelming, but the most frequently used tests are Bonferroni, LSD or Tukey. In your case, select 'Bonferroni' and 'Games-Howell': the former is used if variances are equal, the latter if they are not (Figure 10.5).

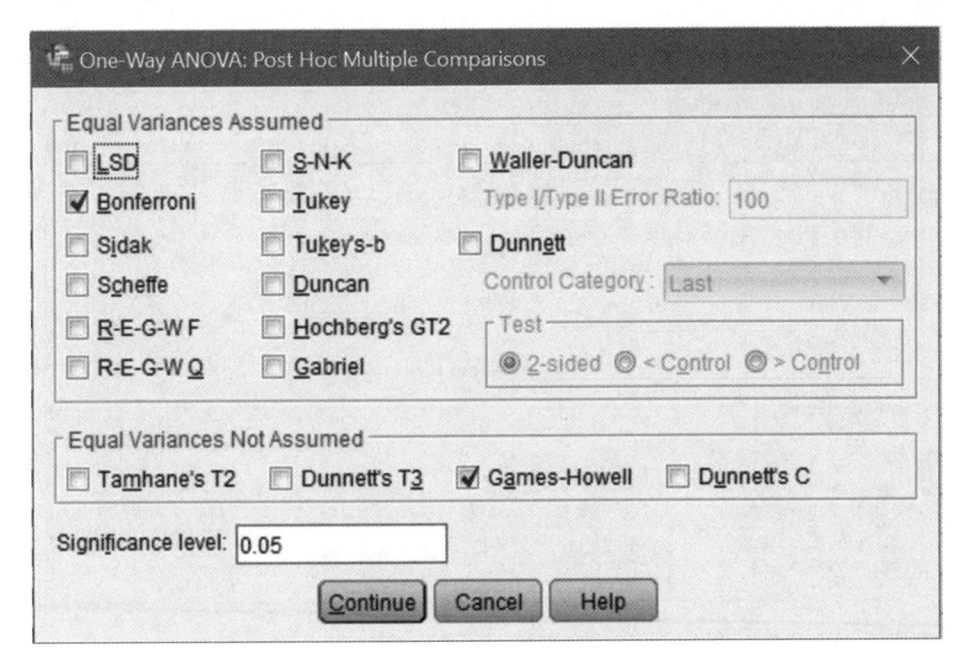

*Figure 10.5* Setting post-hoc multiple comparisons for a one-way ANOVA in SPSS
Reprint Courtesy of International Business Machines Corporation, © International Business Machines Corporation.

6. Click OK to run the analysis.
7. The output starts with the descriptives for the dependent variable for each of the independent variables' levels (Figure 10.6):

**Descriptives**

VerbalScore

|  | N | Mean | Std. Deviation | Std. Error | 95% Confidence Interval for Mean Lower Bound | 95% Confidence Interval for Mean Upper Bound | Minimum | Maximum |
|---|---|---|---|---|---|---|---|---|
| 1 | 50 | 135.14 | 22.570 | 3.192 | 128.73 | 141.55 | 96 | 183 |
| 2 | 50 | 132.62 | 17.040 | 2.410 | 127.78 | 137.46 | 90 | 165 |
| 3 | 50 | 134.08 | 14.078 | 1.991 | 130.08 | 138.08 | 94 | 159 |
| Total | 150 | 133.95 | 18.145 | 1.482 | 131.02 | 136.87 | 90 | 183 |

*Figure 10.6* Descriptives for variable 'VerbalScore' across three conditions of 'CourseType' and overall
Reprint Courtesy of International Business Machines Corporation, © International Business Machines Corporation.

8. The next table (Figure 10.7) shows the results of the test for homogeneity of variance. The Levene's test has equality of variances as the null hypothesis which means that a significant result indicates that variances are *not* homogenous. In our example, the Levene's test has a significant result, which means that the assumption of homogeneity of variance is not met.

## Test of Homogeneity of Variances

VerbalScore

| | Levene Statistic | df1 | df2 | Sig. |
|---|---|---|---|---|
| Based on Mean | 7.158 | 2 | 147 | .001 |
| Based on Median | 6.747 | 2 | 147 | .002 |
| Based on Median and with adjusted df | 6.747 | 2 | 135.047 | .002 |
| Based on trimmed mean | 7.078 | 2 | 147 | .001 |

*Figure 10.7* Test of homogeneity of variances for variable 'VerbalScore'
Reprint Courtesy of International Business Machines Corporation, © International Business Machines Corporation.

9. The next table (Figure 10.8) gives the ANOVA results assuming variances are equal:

## ANOVA

VerbalScore

| | Sum of Squares | df | Mean Square | F | Sig. |
|---|---|---|---|---|---|
| Between Groups | 160.093 | 2 | 80.047 | .241 | .786 |
| Within Groups | 48899.480 | 147 | 332.650 | | |
| Total | 49059.573 | 149 | | | |

*Figure 10.8* Result of ANOVA testing for effect of 'CourseType' on 'VerbalScore'
Reprint Courtesy of International Business Machines Corporation, © International Business Machines Corporation.

10. The table after that (Figure 10.9) gives the results of the Welch test which we clicked in the <u>Options</u> window above. This is the alternative to the ANOVA for when the assumption of homogeneity is violated. Because the Levene's test was significant, this is the result we need to use:

## Robust Tests of Equality of Means

VerbalScore

| | Statistic[a] | df1 | df2 | Sig. |
|---|---|---|---|---|
| Welch | .216 | 2 | 94.904 | .806 |

a. Asymptotically F distributed.

*Figure 10.9* Test for equality of means for variable 'VerbalScore'
Reprint Courtesy of International Business Machines Corporation, © International Business Machines Corporation.

11. You can see that the statistical parameters such as the significance values are slightly different but not substantially so. However, in some cases a difference of .02 can make the difference between a significant and a non-significant result.
12. The last table *Multiple Comparisons* (Figure 10.10) is the list of post-hoc tests which tell you for which pairings (if any) the difference is significant. Since we have ticked two post-hoc tests, you see two different versions in this output:

**Multiple Comparisons**

Dependent Variable: VerbalScore

| | (I) CourseType | (J) CourseType | Mean Difference (I-J) | Std. Error | Sig. | 95% Confidence Interval Lower Bound | Upper Bound |
|---|---|---|---|---|---|---|---|
| Bonferroni | 1 | 2 | 2.520 | 3.648 | 1.000 | -6.31 | 11.35 |
| | | 3 | 1.060 | 3.648 | 1.000 | -7.77 | 9.89 |
| | 2 | 1 | -2.520 | 3.648 | 1.000 | -11.35 | 6.31 |
| | | 3 | -1.460 | 3.648 | 1.000 | -10.29 | 7.37 |
| | 3 | 1 | -1.060 | 3.648 | 1.000 | -9.89 | 7.77 |
| | | 2 | 1.460 | 3.648 | 1.000 | -7.37 | 10.29 |
| Games-Howell | 1 | 2 | 2.520 | 3.999 | .804 | -7.01 | 12.05 |
| | | 3 | 1.060 | 3.762 | .957 | -7.92 | 10.04 |
| | 2 | 1 | -2.520 | 3.999 | .804 | -12.05 | 7.01 |
| | | 3 | -1.460 | 3.126 | .887 | -8.90 | 5.98 |
| | 3 | 1 | -1.060 | 3.762 | .957 | -10.04 | 7.92 |
| | | 2 | 1.460 | 3.126 | .887 | -5.98 | 8.90 |

*Figure 10.10* Multiple comparisons table listing post-hoc tests comparing all three groups
Reprint Courtesy of International Business Machines Corporation, © International Business Machines Corporation.

## 10.1.3 Reporting results

### 10.1.3.1 What you need to know

- Mean and standard deviation of the variable you are looking at for both groups: the SPSS input contains both (see Sections 6.3.1 and 6.5, respectively, how to establish mean and SD in Excel).
- $F$-statistic, df (given in both Excel and SPSS as df for Between Groups and Within Groups), significance value: calculated by SPSS and Excel.
- Whether variances are equal or not.
- Results of post-hoc t-tests, where applicable. Report as full statistical analysis, including degrees of freedom, test statistics and $p$-value.

### 10.1.3.2 What you need to do

- Describe the means and standard deviations of the relevant variables.
- Is the result for the Levene's test significant?
  - Yes: report on the outcome of the Welch test. Use 'Welch's $F$' instead of $F$, and use the df1 and df2 given in the Welch's result.
    Is there a significant effect?
    ◦ Yes: report on the outcome of the Games-Howell post-hoc test.
    ◦ No: nothing else needed.
  - No: report on the outcome of the ANOVA.
    Is there a significant effect?
    ◦ Yes: report on the outcome of the Bonferroni post-hoc test.
    ◦ No: nothing else needed.
- Report the $F$-value with the two degrees of freedom (between groups, within groups) and the significance level. If the result is found to be significant, report results of post-hoc tests and indicate which comparisons yielded significant results.

### 10.1.3.3 Example 
'On average, participants in the online group achieved a verbal score of 135.14 ($SD = 22.570$) at the first test after the training, for participants in the weekly 1 hr class a mean of 132.62 ($SD = 17.040$) was observed; and for participants in the weekend intensive course it was a mean of 134.08 ($SD = 147.078$). A test of homogeneity of variance showed that

256  Introducing Quantitative Methods

variances were unequal ($F$ (2,147) = 7.158, $p$ = .001). There was no effect of course type on verbal scores immediately after the training, Welch's $F$(2, 94.904) = 0.216, $p$ > .05.'

## 10.2  ONE-WAY WITHIN-PARTICIPANTS ANOVA/REPEATED MEASURES ANOVA

The concept and purpose of this analysis is described in more detail in Section 8.7.1.

### ONLINE CONTENT

On the companion website you will find SPSS data and syntax files you can use to follow the guidance in this section. You can also download and adjust them to fit your data.

*Multivariate one-way ANOVA:* You can adjust the guidance in this example. This requires you to pay particular attention to step 3 in the guidance.

*Mixed one-way within-participants ANOVA:* You can adjust the guidance in this example. This requires you to pay particular attention to steps 6 and 15 in the guidance.

Example question: In this study, we asked participants to estimate how much people would be able to recall if they had been presented with information in one of three formats: text alone, text with numbers, or text with graphs; every participant was asked to make these three estimates. We want to know whether the presentation format influenced the size of the estimate participants made.

### 10.2.1  SPSS guidance

1. The first step is to tell SPSS which variables to compare with each other. In our example, the participants' estimates are recorded in three different variables, and we need to tell SPSS to treat each of these variables as one level, or condition, of a factor. Navigate to <u>Analyze</u> → <u>General Linear Model</u> → <u>Repeated Measures</u>. This opens the <u>Repeated Measures</u> window (Figure 10.11):

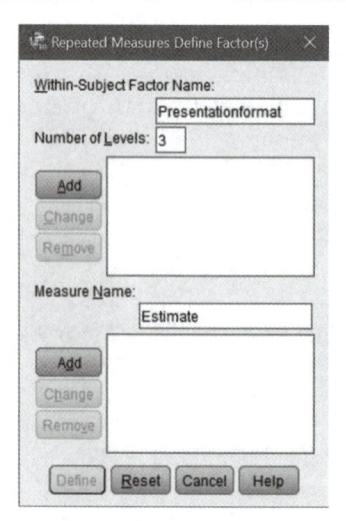

*Figure 10.11* Repeated measures: defining factors

Reprint Courtesy of International Business Machines Corporation, © International Business Machines Corporation.

2. In this window we have named the Within-Subject Factor 'Presentationformat' and indicated that it has three levels. Once you have named your variables, click Add. Similarly, name the Measure (the dependent variable); in this example we have named it *Estimate*. Click Add to add it to the definition.
3. *Multivariate one-way ANOVA*: You can conduct a multivariate variant of this analysis by defining more than one Measure in this window (Figure 10.12).

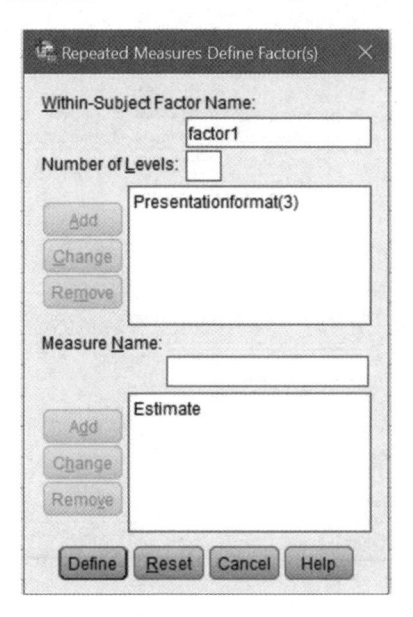

***Figure 10.12*** *Repeated measures: defining measures*

Reprint Courtesy of International Business Machines Corporation, © International Business Machines Corporation.

4. Then click Define. This brings you to the next window (Figure 10.13):

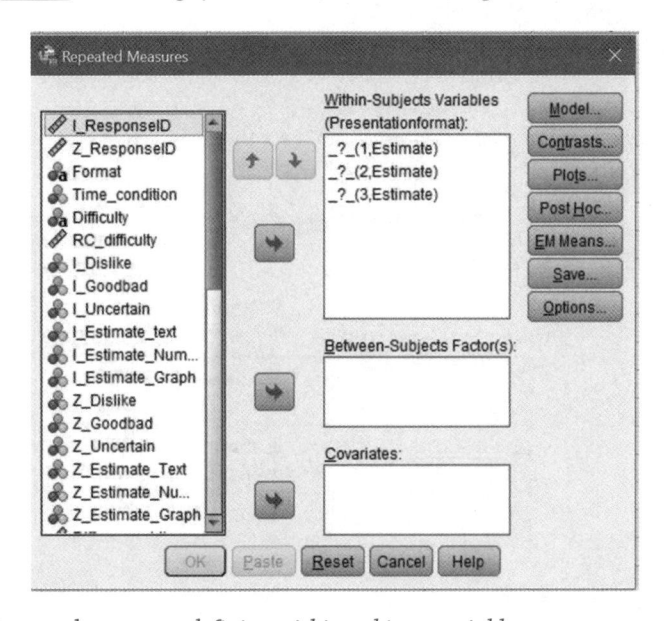

***Figure 10.13*** *Repeated measures: defining within-subjects variables*

Reprint Courtesy of International Business Machines Corporation, © International Business Machines Corporation.

258  Introducing Quantitative Methods

5. Now we need to explain to SPSS which three variables are recording the estimates for the three different formats. In this example, we are looking at 'I_Estimate_text', 'I_Estimate_Numerical' and 'I_Estimate_Graph'. Click on the first of the three, then click the arrow to move it to the right into the Within-Subjects Variables box. Repeat for the other two variables (Figure 10.14):

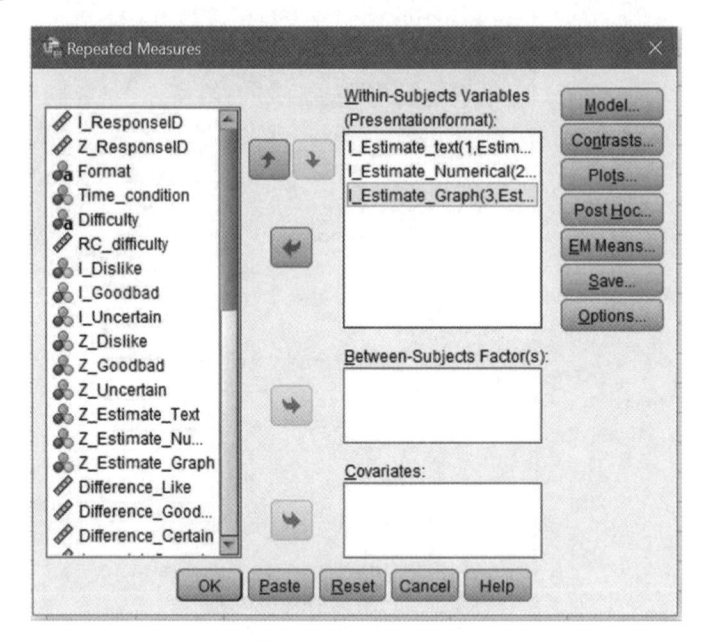

*Figure 10.14* Repeated measures: completed within-subjects variables field
Reprint Courtesy of International Business Machines Corporation, © International Business Machines Corporation.

6. *Mixed one-way ANOVA*: If you want to conduct a Mixed One-Way ANOVA, you can add one or more Between-Subjects Factors here.
7. Then click on Options… and tick Descriptive Statistics. You can also tick Estimates of effect size and Observed power if you are required to report on those.
8. Click OK.
9. The *Within-Subjects Factors* table (Figure 10.15) lists the variables whose values are compared against each other:

**Within-Subjects Factors**

Measure: Estimate

| Presentationformat | Dependent Variable |
|---|---|
| 1 | I_Estimate_text |
| 2 | I_Estimate_Numerical |
| 3 | I_Estimate_Graph |

*Figure 10.15* Within-subjects factors
Reprint Courtesy of International Business Machines Corporation, © International Business Machines Corporation.

10. The *Descriptive Statistics* table (Figure 10.16) gives you mean, standard deviation and N for each of the variables:

**Descriptive Statistics**

|  | Mean | Std. Deviation | N |
|---|---|---|---|
| 1st Estimate Text | 4.27 | 1.581 | 293 |
| 1st Estimate Numerical | 5.21 | 1.526 | 293 |
| 1st Estimate Graph | 6.61 | 1.457 | 293 |

***Figure 10.16*** *Descriptive statistics*

Reprint Courtesy of International Business Machines Corporation, © International Business Machines Corporation.

11. You will find the values for effect size (partial eta squared) and observed power under the heading *Multivariate Tests* (Figure 10.17):

**Multivariate Tests[a]**

| Effect | | Value | F | Hypothesis df | Error df | Sig. | Partial Eta Squared | Noncent. Parameter | Observed Power[c] |
|---|---|---|---|---|---|---|---|---|---|
| Presentationformat | Pillai's Trace | .625 | 242.616[b] | 2.000 | 291.000 | .000 | .625 | 485.233 | 1.000 |
| | Wilks' Lambda | .375 | 242.616[b] | 2.000 | 291.000 | .000 | .625 | 485.233 | 1.000 |
| | Hotelling's Trace | 1.667 | 242.616[b] | 2.000 | 291.000 | .000 | .625 | 485.233 | 1.000 |
| | Roy's Largest Root | 1.667 | 242.616[b] | 2.000 | 291.000 | .000 | .625 | 485.233 | 1.000 |

a. Design: Intercept
   Within Subjects Design: Presentationformat
b. Exact statistic
c. Computed using alpha = .05

***Figure 10.17*** *Repeated measures: multivariate tests for variable 'Presentationformat'*

Reprint Courtesy of International Business Machines Corporation, © International Business Machines Corporation.

12. Figure 10.18 shows the outcome of *Mauchly's Test of Sphericity*, which is one of the assumptions for a repeated measure ANOVA.

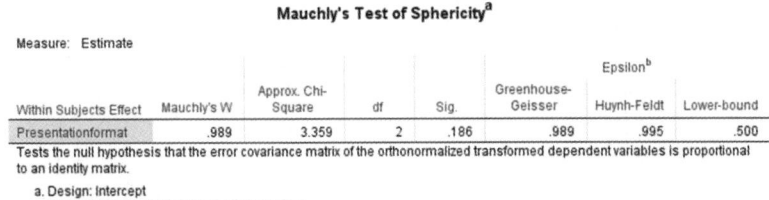

**Mauchly's Test of Sphericity[a]**

Measure: Estimate

| Within Subjects Effect | Mauchly's W | Approx. Chi-Square | df | Sig. | Greenhouse-Geisser | Huynh-Feldt | Lower-bound |
|---|---|---|---|---|---|---|---|
| Presentationformat | .989 | 3.359 | 2 | .186 | .989 | .995 | .500 |

Epsilon[b]

Tests the null hypothesis that the error covariance matrix of the orthonormalized transformed dependent variables is proportional to an identity matrix.

a. Design: Intercept
   Within Subjects Design: Presentationformat
b. May be used to adjust the degrees of freedom for the averaged tests of significance. Corrected tests are displayed in the Tests of Within-Subjects Effects table.

***Figure 10.18*** *Repeated measures: Mauchly's test of sphericity for variable 'Presentationformat'*

Reprint Courtesy of International Business Machines Corporation, © International Business Machines Corporation.

13. *Tests of Within-Subjects Effects* (Figure 10.19) lists the result of the ANOVA. We are interested in the results for the source 'Presentationformat':

**Tests of Within-Subjects Effects**

Measure: Estimate

| Source | | Type III Sum of Squares | df | Mean Square | F | Sig. | Partial Eta Squared | Noncent. Parameter | Observed Power[a] |
|---|---|---|---|---|---|---|---|---|---|
| Presentationformat | Sphericity Assumed | 813.586 | 2 | 406.793 | 266.009 | .000 | .477 | 532.017 | 1.000 |
| | Greenhouse-Geisser | 813.586 | 1.977 | 411.462 | 266.009 | .000 | .477 | 525.980 | 1.000 |
| | Huynh-Feldt | 813.586 | 1.991 | 408.692 | 266.009 | .000 | .477 | 529.545 | 1.000 |
| | Lower-bound | 813.586 | 1.000 | 813.586 | 266.009 | .000 | .477 | 266.009 | 1.000 |
| Error(Presentationformat) | Sphericity Assumed | 893.081 | 584 | 1.529 | | | | | |
| | Greenhouse-Geisser | 893.081 | 577.373 | 1.547 | | | | | |
| | Huynh-Feldt | 893.081 | 581.287 | 1.536 | | | | | |
| | Lower-bound | 893.081 | 292.000 | 3.058 | | | | | |

a. Computed using alpha = .05

***Figure 10.19*** *Repeated measures: test of within-subjects effects for variable 'Presentationformat'*

Reprint Courtesy of International Business Machines Corporation, © International Business Machines Corporation.

14. The SPSS output also contains a Table "Tests of Within-Subjects Contrasts" which is relevant if your independent variable has three or more levels. However, the decision whether to use the values from "Tests of Within-Subjects Contrasts" or "Tests of Within-Subjects Effects" is very complex and beyond the scope of this guidance. In most cases, it is perfectly appropriate to report the results of the "Effects" table and we will therefore not discuss the "Contrasts" table.
15. *Mixed One-Way ANOVA*: The output also lists a *Tests of Between-Subjects Effects* table which is only relevant if you added any between-subjects effect. For a regular repeated measure ANOVA the table would not be relevant.

### 10.2.2 Reporting results

#### 10.2.2.1 What you need to know

- Mean and standard deviation of the dependent variable you are analysing: in the *Descriptives* table.
- Outcome of the sphericity test: in the *Mauchly's Test of Sphericity* table.
- *F*-value, degrees of freedom and significance for effect of independent variable, plus power and effect size, if required: in the *Test of Within-Subjects Effects* table.

#### 10.2.2.2 What you need to do

- Give mean and standard deviation for the individual levels of the dependent variable; describe what this means.
- Report result of the repeated measure analysis of variance.
    - Was Mauchly's Test of Sphericity significant?
        - Yes: the assumption of sphericity has been violated. Report the result with the values from 'Greenhouse-Geisser' line.
        - No: the assumption of sphericity has been met. Report the result with values from the 'Sphericity assumed' line.
    - Was the result of the ANOVA significant?
        - Yes: if your dependent variable has more than two levels, conduct post-hoc t-tests. Report on the results of the post-hoc tests.
        - No: nothing else needed.

#### 10.2.2.3 Example
'When participants were asked to estimate other participants' recall, their estimates put average recall at 4.27 (*SD* = 1.58) arguments in the Text Only condition, 5.21 (*SD* = 1.53) for the Text Numerical condition and 6.61 (*SD* = 1.46) for the Text Graphical condition. Participants expected participants in the Text Graphical condition to remember most and participants in the Text Only condition to remember least. A repeated measures analysis of variance observed an effect of presentation format on estimate, $F(2, 584) = 266.009$, $p < .001$, $\eta 2 = .477$, power = 1.0. A series of paired-samples t-tests showed all differences to be significant at $p < .001$.'

## 10.3 TWO- OR THREE-WAY BETWEEN-PARTICIPANTS ANOVA

The concept and purpose of this analysis is described in more detail in Section 8.7.1.

### ONLINE CONTENT

On the companion website you will find SPSS data and syntax files you can use to follow the guidance in this section. You can also download and adjust them to fit your data.

Example question: In this study, a group of participants completed a confidence questionnaire. Participants identified as either male or female and went to either a private or public school. We want to find out whether gender and type of school affect the confidence as measured through this score.

*Three-way ANOVA*: Follow the guidance in this section but add a third independent variable wherever the instructions mention two independent variables.

### 10.3.1 SPSS guidance

1. First, you need to test the assumptions for the dependent variable:
   a. Homogeneity of variance: SPSS gives you the option to run this test alongside the ANOVA itself.
   b. Normality (that is, the data should be normally distributed): see Section 8.1.
   c. Coming from independent groups: this needs to be the case to conduct a between-participants analysis.
   d. Data on an interval scale or ratio scale: see Section 2.2.
2. Navigate to Analyse → General Linear Model → Univariate.
3. Move the dependent variable (here, 'C_Testscore') into the Dependent Variable field, and move the two independent variables (here, 'P_Gender' and 'P_EduType') into the Fixed Factor(s) field (Figure 10.20):

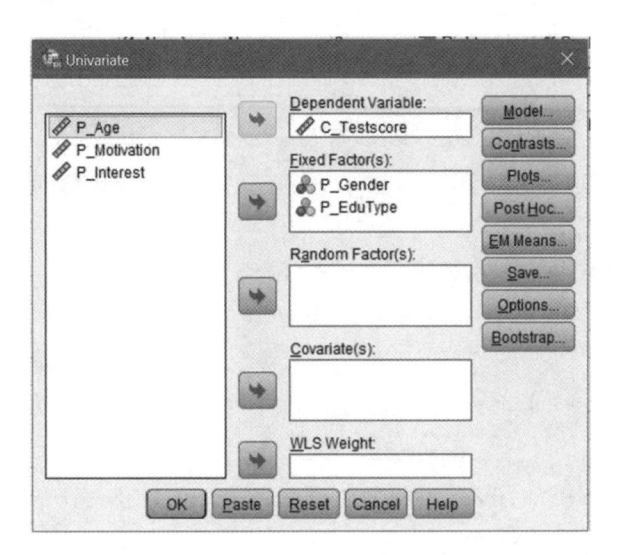

*Figure 10.20* Setting up two-way univariate analysis in SPSS
Reprint Courtesy of International Business Machines Corporation, © International Business Machines Corporation.

4. Click Options… and tick Descriptive statistics, Estimates of effect size, Observed power and Homogeneity tests. Click Continue.
5. If your independent variables have more than two levels, click Post Hoc… and move them to the right field, then tick Bonferroni. In our example, we do not need post-hoc tests for either of the two variables because both have only two levels.
6. Click Continue, then click OK.
7. The output is very similar to the output of a one-way ANOVA and you can look up the descriptions for the individual tables in steps 7 to 12 in Section 10.1.1. It starts with a list of the between-subjects factors and is followed by a table *Descriptive Statistics* (Figure 10.21):

**Descriptive Statistics**

Dependent Variable: C_Testscore

| P_Gender | P_EduType | Mean | Std. Deviation | N |
|---|---|---|---|---|
| Male | Public | 101.9167 | 18.26595 | 24 |
|  | Private | 105.8182 | 16.19147 | 11 |
|  | Total | 103.1429 | 17.49814 | 35 |
| Female | Public | 106.1429 | 16.51506 | 14 |
|  | Private | 99.4000 | 18.00741 | 10 |
|  | Total | 103.3333 | 17.10496 | 24 |
| Total | Public | 103.4737 | 17.53566 | 38 |
|  | Private | 102.7619 | 16.96439 | 21 |
|  | Total | 103.2203 | 17.19068 | 59 |

*Figure 10.21* Descriptive statistics for test scores across gender and education type
Reprint Courtesy of International Business Machines Corporation, © International Business Machines Corporation.

This is followed by the *Levene's Test of Equality of Error Variances* (Figure 10.22):

**Levene's Test of Equality of Error Variances[a,b]**

|  |  | Levene Statistic | df1 | df2 | Sig. |
|---|---|---|---|---|---|
| C_Testscore | Based on Mean | .120 | 3 | 55 | .948 |
|  | Based on Median | .145 | 3 | 55 | .932 |
|  | Based on Median and with adjusted df | .145 | 3 | 54.558 | .932 |
|  | Based on trimmed mean | .140 | 3 | 55 | .935 |

Tests the null hypothesis that the error variance of the dependent variable is equal across groups.

a. Dependent variable: C_Testscore
b. Design: Intercept + P_Gender + P_EduType + P_Gender * P_EduType

*Figure 10.22* Levene's test of equality of error variances for variable 'C_Testscore'
Reprint Courtesy of International Business Machines Corporation, © International Business Machines Corporation.

8. In this example the Levene's test is not significant and the assumption of equality of variance is met.
9. The next table (Figure 10.23) lists the between-subjects effects, which is what we are interested in. In our example, there are no main effects of either of the two independent variables nor an interaction of the two.

**Tests of Between-Subjects Effects**

Dependent Variable: C_Testscore

| Source | Type III Sum of Squares | df | Mean Square | F | Sig. | Partial Eta Squared | Noncent. Parameter | Observed Power[b] |
|---|---|---|---|---|---|---|---|---|
| Corrected Model | 380.552[a] | 3 | 126.851 | .416 | .742 | .022 | 1.249 | .128 |
| Intercept | 561829.045 | 1 | 561829.045 | 1843.757 | .000 | .971 | 1843.757 | 1.000 |
| P_Gender | 15.805 | 1 | 15.805 | .052 | .821 | .001 | .052 | .056 |
| P_EduType | 26.556 | 1 | 26.556 | .087 | .769 | .002 | .087 | .060 |
| P_Gender * P_EduType | 372.701 | 1 | 372.701 | 1.223 | .274 | .022 | 1.223 | .192 |
| Error | 16759.584 | 55 | 304.720 |  |  |  |  |  |
| Total | 645752.000 | 59 |  |  |  |  |  |  |
| Corrected Total | 17140.136 | 58 |  |  |  |  |  |  |

a. R Squared = .022 (Adjusted R Squared = -.031)
b. Computed using alpha = .05

*Figure 10.23* Tests of between-subjects effects for dependent variable 'C_Testscore'
Reprint Courtesy of International Business Machines Corporation, © International Business Machines Corporation.

## 10.3.2 Reporting results

### 10.3.2.1 What you need to know

- Mean and standard deviation of the dependent variable you are analysing for each of the different conditions: in the *Descriptives* table.
- F-value, degrees of freedom and significance – plus power and effect size, if required – for (potential) main effects and interactions of the two independent variables: in the *Test of Within-Subjects Effects* table.
- Where more than one independent variable is involved, calculating degrees of freedom becomes a bit more complicated. For the following calculations, assume that j equals number of levels for independent variable 1 (two levels for variable 'Gender'), k equals number of levels of the independent variable 2 (two levels for variable 'EduType'), and N equals number of observations.
  - *For the main effects*, for the independent variable 1 the first value (df1) is calculated as: j – 1, that is, in our example df1 = 2 – 1 = 1. For the independent variable 2 the first value (df1) is calculated as: k – 1, that is, in our example df1 = 2 – 1=1. Df2 is calculated as N – j and N – k, respectively.
  - *For the interaction*, df1 is calculated as (j – 1) × (k – 1), which for our example means (2 – 1) × (2 – 1) = 1×1 = 1. Df2 is calculated as N-(j × k), which for our example means df2 = 59 – (2 × 2) = 59 – 4 = 55.

### 10.3.2.2 What you need to do

- Give mean and standard deviation for the individual levels of the dependent variable; describe what this means.
- Report main effects and interactions. For each effect and interaction:
  - Was the result significant?
  - Yes: if your dependent variable has more than two levels, conduct post-hoc t-tests, for example with an independent-samples t-test. Report on the results of the post-hoc tests.
  - No: nothing else needed.

**10.3.2.3 Example** 'Participants who identified as male scored an average of 101.917 (*SD* = 18.266) if they went to a public school and an average of 105.818 (*SD* = 16.191) if they went to a private school. Participants who identified as female scored an average of 106.143 (*SD* = 16.515) if they went to a public school and 99.400 (*SD* = 18.007) if they went to a private school. A two-way ANOVA observed no effect of gender on confidence, $F(1,57) = .052$, $p > .05$, $\eta2 = .001$, power = .56, nor of schooling on confidence, $F(1,57) = .087$, $p > .05$, $\eta2 = .002$, power = .60. There was no interaction, $F(4,55) = 1.223$, $p > .05$, $\eta2 = .022$, power =.192.'

## 10.4 TWO- OR THREE-WAY WITHIN-PARTICIPANTS ANOVA

### ONLINE CONTENT

On the companion website you will find SPSS data and syntax files you can use to follow the guidance in this section. You can also download and adjust them to fit your data.

264  *Introducing Quantitative Methods*

Example question: In this study we want to find out how much participants liked ads that followed the same structure and advertised the same product but differed in 'Difficulty' of the presented information (difficult or easy) and 'Length' (short, medium, long). Each participant was presented with all six versions. The dependent variable was liking on a scale of 1 to 20. The question for the within-participants ANOVA is whether there is an effect of either 'Difficulty' or 'Length', and whether there is an interaction of both on the dependent variable.

*Three-way within-participants ANOVA*: Follow the guidance in this section but add a third independent variable wherever the instructions mention two independent variables.

*Mixed two- or three-way within-participants ANOVA*: You can adjust the guidance in this example. Pay particular attention to step 7 in the guidance and step 7 in the output description.

### 10.4.1  SPSS guidance

A two- or three-way repeated measures ANOVA is conducted very similarly to a one-way repeated measures ANOVA, described in Section 10.2, with only few modifications required.

1. Navigate to Analyse → General Linear Model → Repeated Measures. This opens the Repeated Measures window (see also Figure 10.24)
2. Instead of only one, add two or three Within-Subject Factors, depending on whether it is a two- or three-way ANOVA. In this example, we define two factors, one with three levels ('Difficulty') and one with two levels ('Length'):

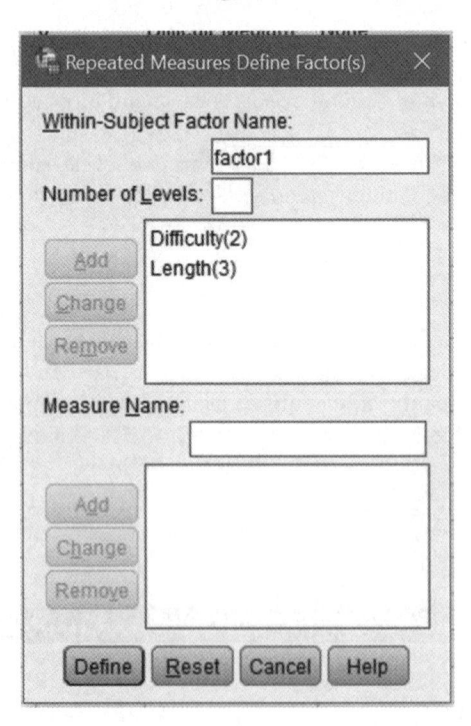

**Figure 10.24**  *Repeated measures: defining two factors in SPSS*
Reprint Courtesy of International Business Machines Corporation, © International Business Machines Corporation.

3. Click Define.
4. In the next window, assign your variables to the correct combinations (Figure 10.25):

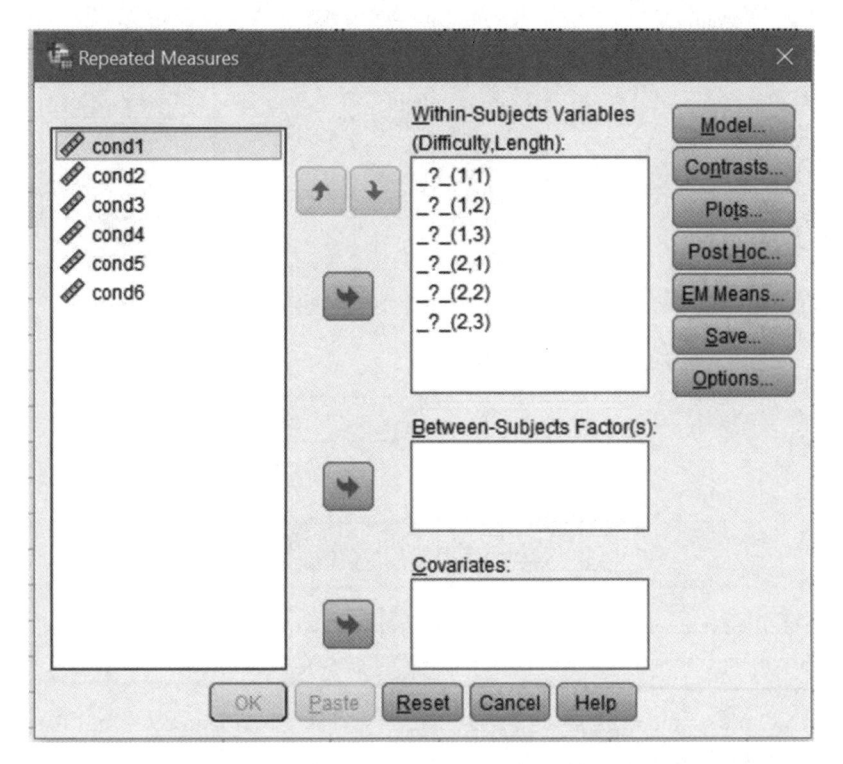

*Figure 10.25* Repeated measures: defining individual within-subjects variables in SPSS
Reprint Courtesy of International Business Machines Corporation, © International Business Machines Corporation.

5. In this example, we have 2 × 3 conditions (i.e., six in total). Because this is completely within-participants, each participant experienced each condition which we therefore recorded in six separate variables. For simplicity's sake we have called those variables 'cond1', 'cond2', and so on, and have put an explanation in the variable label (see Section 5.3.4) to explain what each variable measures. The sequence in which you move those variables over matters: You need to make sure that the data really matches the variable combination listed in the window. Note that the Within-Subjects Variables window has listed them in the order (1,1), (1,2), (1,3), then (2,1), (2,2) and (2,3); that is, the first value of the two-level variable is first paired with all levels of the three-level variable and then the second value of the two-level variable is paired with all levels of the three-level variable. We have mirrored this by moving the variables in this sequence (Figure 10.26):

- Cond1 = Difficult, Short
- Cond2 = Difficult, Medium
- Cond3 = Difficult, Long; then
- Cond4 = Easy, Short
- Cond5 = Easy, Medium
- Cond6 = Easy, Long.

266  Introducing Quantitative Methods

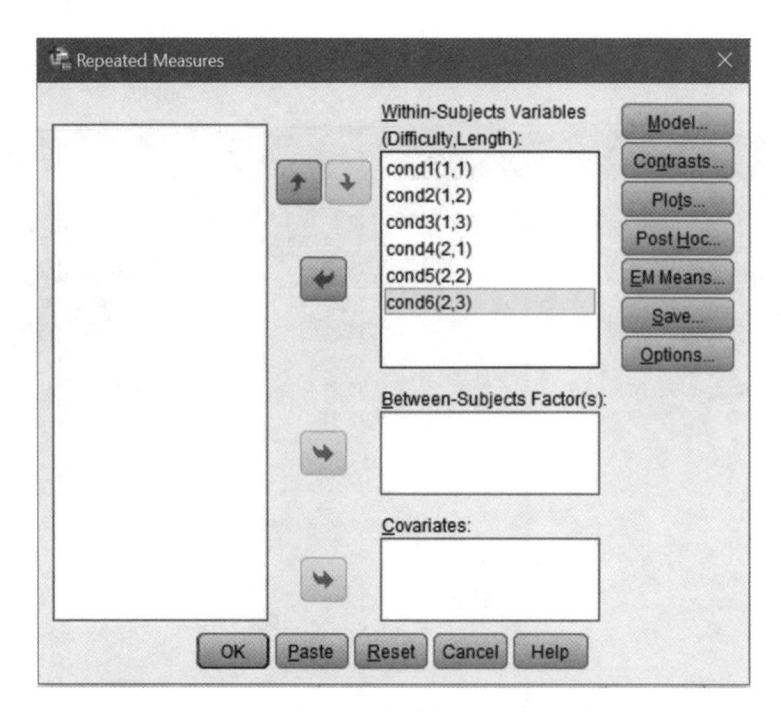

**Figure 10.26** *Repeated measures: completed definitions of within-subjects variables*
Reprint Courtesy of International Business Machines Corporation, © International Business Machines Corporation.

6. Go into Options and click Descriptive Statistics; click Observed power and Estimates of effect size if required.
7. Note that if you wanted to conduct a mixed ANOVA you could add a between-subjects factor here.
8. Click OK.

Similar to the output described in steps 7 to 13 in Section 10.2.1, the output for a two-or three-way within-participants ANOVA consists of the following:

9. The *Within-Subjects Factors* table (Figure 10.27) lists the variables whose values are compared against each other.

**Within-Subjects Factors**
Measure: MEASURE_1

| Difficulty | Length | Dependent Variable |
|---|---|---|
| 1 | 1 | cond_1 |
|   | 2 | cond_2 |
|   | 3 | cond_3 |
| 2 | 1 | cond_4 |
|   | 2 | cond_5 |
|   | 3 | cond_6 |

**Figure 10.27** *Repeated measures: list of within-subjects factors 'Difficulty' and 'Length'*
Reprint Courtesy of International Business Machines Corporation, © International Business Machines Corporation.

10. The *Descriptive Statistics* table (Figure 10.28) gives you mean, standard deviation and N for each of the variables:

**Descriptive Statistics**

|  | Mean | Std. Deviation | N |
|---|---|---|---|
| Easy,Short | 3.97 | 2.048 | 293 |
| Easy,Medium | 4.09 | 2.130 | 293 |
| Easy,Long | 3.75 | 2.073 | 293 |
| Difficult,Short | 3.30 | .657 | 293 |
| Difficult,Medium | 3.22 | .495 | 293 |
| Difficult,Long | 3.79 | 2.081 | 293 |

***Figure 10.28*** *Repeated measures: descriptive statistics for six conditions*
Reprint Courtesy of International Business Machines Corporation, © International Business Machines Corporation.

11. The next table (Figure 10.29) shows the outcome of Mauchly's Test for Sphericity, which is one of the assumptions for a repeated measure ANOVA. Note that there is no result for 'Difficulty' as it has only two levels; the sphericity test makes only sense for variables with more than two levels.

**Mauchly's Test of Sphericity[a]**

Measure: MEASURE_1

| Within Subjects Effect | Mauchly's W | Approx. Chi-Square | df | Sig. | Greenhouse-Geisser | Huynh-Feldt | Lower-bound |
|---|---|---|---|---|---|---|---|
| Difficulty | 1.000 | .000 | 0 | . | 1.000 | 1.000 | 1.000 |
| Length | .314 | 336.739 | 2 | .000 | .593 | .594 | .500 |
| Difficulty * Length | .408 | 260.537 | 2 | .000 | .628 | .630 | .500 |

Tests the null hypothesis that the error covariance matrix of the orthonormalized transformed dependent variables is proportional to an identity matrix.

a. Design: Intercept
Within Subjects Design: Difficulty + Length + Difficulty * Length

b. May be used to adjust the degrees of freedom for the averaged tests of significance. Corrected tests are displayed in the Tests of Within-Subjects Effects table.

***Figure 10.29*** *Repeated measures: Mauchly's test of sphericity for variables 'Difficulty' and 'Length'*
Reprint Courtesy of International Business Machines Corporation, © International Business Machines Corporation.

12. You will find the values for effect size (partial eta squared) and observed power under the heading *Multivariate Tests*. Note that unlike in Section 10.2.1, we now see tests for two variables and the interaction of the two. If you had run a three-way ANOVA, you would see here the results of all possible two- and three-way interactions (Figure 10.30).

**Multivariate Tests[a]**

| Effect |  | Value | F | Hypothesis df | Error df | Sig. | Partial Eta Squared | Noncent. Parameter | Observed Power[c] |
|---|---|---|---|---|---|---|---|---|---|
| Difficulty | Pillai's Trace | .117 | 38.806[b] | 1.000 | 292.000 | .000 | .117 | 38.806 | 1.000 |
|  | Wilks' Lambda | .883 | 38.806[b] | 1.000 | 292.000 | .000 | .117 | 38.806 | 1.000 |
|  | Hotelling's Trace | .133 | 38.806[b] | 1.000 | 292.000 | .000 | .117 | 38.806 | 1.000 |
|  | Roy's Largest Root | .133 | 38.806[b] | 1.000 | 292.000 | .000 | .117 | 38.806 | 1.000 |
| Length | Pillai's Trace | .013 | 1.942[b] | 2.000 | 291.000 | .145 | .013 | 3.883 | .401 |
|  | Wilks' Lambda | .987 | 1.942[b] | 2.000 | 291.000 | .145 | .013 | 3.883 | .401 |
|  | Hotelling's Trace | .013 | 1.942[b] | 2.000 | 291.000 | .145 | .013 | 3.883 | .401 |
|  | Roy's Largest Root | .013 | 1.942[b] | 2.000 | 291.000 | .145 | .013 | 3.883 | .401 |
| Difficulty * Length | Pillai's Trace | .152 | 26.109[b] | 2.000 | 291.000 | .000 | .152 | 52.219 | 1.000 |
|  | Wilks' Lambda | .848 | 26.109[b] | 2.000 | 291.000 | .000 | .152 | 52.219 | 1.000 |
|  | Hotelling's Trace | .179 | 26.109[b] | 2.000 | 291.000 | .000 | .152 | 52.219 | 1.000 |
|  | Roy's Largest Root | .179 | 26.109[b] | 2.000 | 291.000 | .000 | .152 | 52.219 | 1.000 |

a. Design: Intercept
Within Subjects Design: Difficulty + Length + Difficulty * Length
b. Exact statistic
c. Computed using alpha = .05

***Figure 10.30*** *Repeated measures: multivariate tests for variables 'Difficulty' and 'Length'*
Reprint Courtesy of International Business Machines Corporation, © International Business Machines Corporation.

13. The *Tests of Within-Subjects Effects* table (Figure 10.31) lists the result of the ANOVA. We are interested in the results for main effects and interactions. :

| | | Type III Sum of Squares | df | Mean Square | F | Sig. | Partial Eta Squared | Noncent. Parameter | Observed Power[a] |
|---|---|---|---|---|---|---|---|---|---|
| Difficulty | Sphericity Assumed | 111.129 | 1 | 111.129 | 38.806 | .000 | .117 | 38.806 | 1.000 |
| | Greenhouse-Geisser | 111.129 | 1.000 | 111.129 | 38.806 | .000 | .117 | 38.806 | 1.000 |
| | Huynh-Feldt | 111.129 | 1.000 | 111.129 | 38.806 | .000 | .117 | 38.806 | 1.000 |
| | Lower-bound | 111.129 | 1.000 | 111.129 | 38.806 | .000 | .117 | 38.806 | 1.000 |
| Error(Difficulty) | Sphericity Assumed | 836.205 | 292 | 2.864 | | | | | |
| | Greenhouse-Geisser | 836.205 | 292.000 | 2.864 | | | | | |
| | Huynh-Feldt | 836.205 | 292.000 | 2.864 | | | | | |
| | Lower-bound | 836.205 | 292.000 | 2.864 | | | | | |
| Length | Sphericity Assumed | 6.315 | 2 | 3.158 | 3.349 | .036 | .011 | 6.697 | .632 |
| | Greenhouse-Geisser | 6.315 | 1.187 | 5.322 | 3.349 | .061 | .011 | 3.973 | .486 |
| | Huynh-Feldt | 6.315 | 1.189 | 5.313 | 3.349 | .061 | .011 | 3.980 | .486 |
| | Lower-bound | 6.315 | 1.000 | 6.315 | 3.349 | .068 | .011 | 3.349 | .446 |
| Error(Length) | Sphericity Assumed | 550.685 | 584 | .943 | | | | | |
| | Greenhouse-Geisser | 550.685 | 346.458 | 1.589 | | | | | |
| | Huynh-Feldt | 550.685 | 347.055 | 1.587 | | | | | |
| | Lower-bound | 550.685 | 292.000 | 1.886 | | | | | |
| Difficulty * Length | Sphericity Assumed | 66.643 | 2 | 33.321 | 36.508 | .000 | .111 | 73.016 | 1.000 |
| | Greenhouse-Geisser | 66.643 | 1.257 | 53.032 | 36.508 | .000 | .111 | 45.878 | 1.000 |
| | Huynh-Feldt | 66.643 | 1.260 | 52.911 | 36.508 | .000 | .111 | 45.983 | 1.000 |
| | Lower-bound | 66.643 | 1.000 | 66.643 | 36.508 | .000 | .111 | 36.508 | 1.000 |
| Error(Difficulty*Length) | Sphericity Assumed | 533.024 | 584 | .913 | | | | | |
| | Greenhouse-Geisser | 533.024 | 366.944 | 1.453 | | | | | |
| | Huynh-Feldt | 533.024 | 367.784 | 1.449 | | | | | |
| | Lower-bound | 533.024 | 292.000 | 1.825 | | | | | |

a. Computed using alpha = .05

**Figure 10.31** *Repeated measures: tests of within-subjects effects for variables 'Difficulty' and 'Length'*
Reprint Courtesy of International Business Machines Corporation, © International Business Machines Corporation.

14. The SPSS output also contains a Table "Tests of Within-Subjects Contrasts" which is relevant if your independent variable has three or more levels. However, the decision whether to use the values from "Tests of Within-Subjects Contrasts" or "Tests of Within-Subjects Effects" is very complex and beyond the scope of this guidance. In most cases, it is perfectly appropriate to report the results of the "Effects" table and we will therefore not discuss the "Contrasts" table.
15. The output also lists a table entitled *Tests of Between-Subjects Effects*. Since this was a repeated measure ANOVA and not a mixed repeated measures ANOVA, this table is not relevant for this analysis. However, if you had added a between-subjects factor in step 7 in Section 10.4.1, you would see the results here.

### 10.4.2  Reporting results

#### 10.4.2.1  *What you need to know*

- Mean and standard deviation of the dependent variable you are analysing for each of the different conditions: in the *Descriptives* table.
- Outcome of the sphericity test: in the *Mauchly's Test of Sphericity* table.
- F-value, degrees of freedom and significance – plus power and effect size, if required – for (potential) main effects and interactions of the two independent variables in the *Test of Within-Subjects Effects* table. Look up how to calculate degrees of freedom in Section 10.3.2.1.

### 10.4.2.2 What you need to do

- Give mean and standard deviation for the individual levels of the dependent variable; describe what this means.
- Report result of the repeated measure analysis of variance.
  - If the independent variable had more than two levels: was Mauchly's Test of Sphericity significant?
    - Yes: the assumption of sphericity has been violated. Report the result with the values from 'Greenhouse-Geisser' line.
    - No: the assumption of sphericity has been met. Report the result with values from the 'Sphericity assumed' line.
  - Report main effects and interactions. For each effect and interaction:
    - Was the result significant?
    - Yes: if your dependent variable has more than two levels, conduct post-hoc t-tests. Report on the results of the post-hoc tests.
    - No: nothing else needed.

### 10.4.2.3 Example
The average liking scores are listed in the table below.

|  | Difficulty | |
| --- | --- | --- |
| **Length** | Easy M (SD) | Difficult M (SD) |
| Short | 3.97 (2.048) | 3.30 (.657) |
| Medium | 4.09 (2.130) | 3.22 (.495) |
| Long | 3.75 (2.073) | 3.79 (2.081) |

'A repeated measures analysis of variance observed an effect of 'Difficulty' on liking such that more difficult items had lower liking scores, $F(2, 292) = 38.806$, $p < .001$, $\eta 2 = .117$, power = 1.0. For the variable 'Length' and the interaction of 'Length' and 'Difficulty', the assumption of sphericity was violated and results are reported with Greenhouse-Geisser correction. No effect of 'Length' was found on *liking*, $F(1.187, 346.458) = 3.349$, $p > .05$, $\eta 2 = .011$, power = .486. There was an interaction of 'Length' and 'Difficulty' on liking, $F(1.257, 366.944) = 36.508$, $p < .001$, $\eta 2 = .111$, power = 1.0.'

## 10.5 ANCOVA

The concept and purpose of this analysis is described in more detail in Section 8.7.2.

### ONLINE CONTENT

On the companion website you will find SPSS data and syntax files you can use to follow the guidance in this section. You can also download and adjust them to fit your data.

Example: In this study, information was presented to participants in a number of different *formats* (text only, text with numbers, text with graphs, extended text). Participants had to indicate to what extent they thought about the information (dependent variable 'Thought').

'Numeracy' was collected as a potential covariate. The study wanted to find out whether presentation format had an effect on the extent to which participants thought about the information, while controlling for numeracy.

*Multivariate ANCOVA*: Follow the guidance in this section; skip steps 2, 5, 6 and 9; add additional dependent variables wherever the instructions mention a dependent variable.

### 10.5.1 SPSS guidance

Describing the ANCOVA in a separate section is actually a bit misleading since it is not really a separate analysis but a potential addition to another analysis of variance. The main analysis can be within or between, and can be a one-, two- or three-way ANOVA. The C in ANCOVA means that the main analysis controls for, that is, disregards, the variance introduced by one or more variables – the covariates. That said, not all variables can be considered covariates; rather, a set of assumptions has to be met. One of those assumptions can be tested in advance:

If we are examining more than one covariate, we first need to check that they are not too highly correlated with each other. To do so, conduct a **bivariate correlation** analysis on the potential covariates: see Sections 11.1 or 11.2 on how to do that.

The remaining two assumptions are tested while conducting the analysis itself:

1. Homogeneity of variance: This assumption is checked through the Levene's Test of Equality of Error Variances while conducting the analysis
2. Normal distribution of residuals (a part of the variance that is examined): To check this assumption, you need to perform an extra step during the ANCOVA itself to create new variables and then conduct your standard tests of normality on those variables. We will explain this further below.
3. For an ANCOVA, first follow the steps of the underlying analysis you are conducting until you are at either the Repeated Measures window, the Univariate window or the Multivariate window.
4. In our example, we are conducting a between-participants analysis.
5. You will see a field Covariates. Move the variable(s) you want to control for into that field; here, 'Numeracy'.
6. Click the Save button. Under Residuals, tick Standardized, then click Continue; this allows you to test one of the assumptions.
7. Go into Options and click Descriptive Statistics and Homogeneity tests; click Observed power and Estimates of effect size if required. Click Continue.
8. Click OK to run the test.
9. There is one additional step you need to perform before analysing the output. If you go back to your data file, you will see that it now contains an additional variable starting with something like ZRE_ and with the description 'Standardised Residual for [Variable]' in the variable label (see Section 5.3.4). You now need to check whether this variable is normally distributed. You can find guidance about how to do this in Section 8.2. In our example, 'Numeracy' is fairly normally distributed and the assumption met.

The output then follows the same structure we have described before:

- For a between-participants analysis, you can find a description of the output in steps 7 to 9 in Section 10.3.1.
- For a within-participants analysis, you can find a description of the output in steps 9 to 15 in Section 10.4.1.

### 10.5.2 Reporting results

#### 10.5.2.1 What you need to know

- If you are conducting a between-participants analysis, follow the guidance in Section 10.3.2.
- If you are conducting a within-participants analysis, follow the guidance in Section 10.4.2.

#### 10.5.2.2 What you need to do

- If you are conducting a between-participants analysis, follow the guidance in Section 10.3.2. You only need to adjust the reporting by including 'with [Variable] as a covariate'.
- If you are conducting a within-participants analysis, follow the guidance in Section 10.4.2. You only need to adjust the reporting by including 'with [Variable] as a covariate'.

**10.5.2.3 Example** 'A one-way univariate analysis of variance with numeracy as a covariate was conducted, showing that presentation format had no significant effect on the extent to which participants thought about the information, $F(3, 98) = 0.436, p > .05$.'

## 10.6 KRUSKAL-WALLIS

The concept and purpose of this analysis is described in more detail in Section 8.7.3.

Example question: Do participants who are native speakers have a higher numerical score than participants who are not?

> **ONLINE CONTENT**
>
> On the companion website you will find SPSS data and syntax files you can use to follow the guidance in this section. You can also download and adjust them to fit your data.

### 10.6.1 SPSS guidance

1. Navigate to Analyze → Nonparametric Tests → Independent Samples which brings up a window consisting of Objective, Fields, and Settings tabs. In the Objective tab select Customize Analysis.
2. In the Fields tab, move the variables you want to examine (here, 'NumericalScore' to the Test field and 'NativeSpeaker' to the Groups field).
3. In the Settings tab select Customize Test, then select Kruskal-Wallis 1-way ANOVA (k samples), which is the top option in the right-hand column. (Note: There is a left-hand column of options, make sure you are on the first option Choose Tests.) Make sure that the pick list for Multiple comparisons is set to All pairwise. Click Run.
4. The test result is displayed in a manner similar to the Mann-Whitney U-test: a very basic table displaying whether to reject or retain the null hypothesis which can be expanded to a more detailed overview.

### 10.6.2 Reporting results

#### 10.6.2.1 What you need to know

- Median for both groups: navigate to Analyze → Descriptive Statistics → Explore, move 'NativeSpeaker' into the Factor List, 'NumericalScore' into the Dependent List.

272  *Introducing Quantitative Methods*

- Mean ranks for both groups: expand the table of the Kruskal-Wallis test, set view to Independent Samples Test View, and mouse over the boxplots for each variable (Figure 10.32):

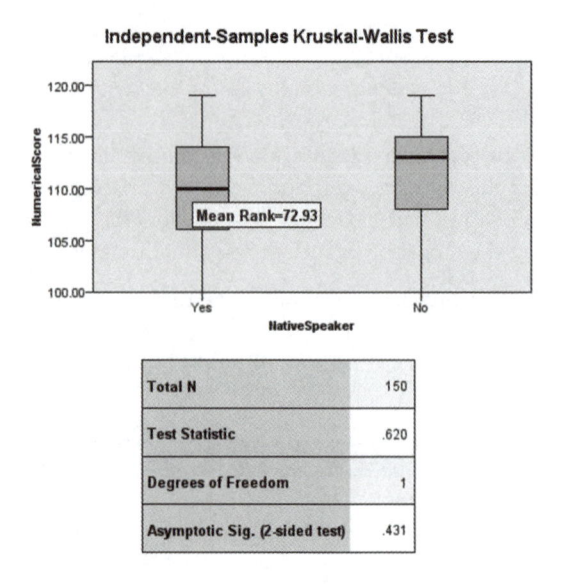

*Figure 10.32 Results of an independent-samples Kruskal-Wallis test in SPSS*
Reprint Courtesy of International Business Machines Corporation, © International Business Machines Corporation.

- The *H*-value, here listed under Test Statistic; degrees of freedom
- Significance value: see Section 6.10.
- Results of post-hoc t-tests, where applicable.

### 10.6.2.2  What you need to do

- Report the *H*-value with the reported degrees of freedom and the significance level.
- If the result is found to be significant, report results of post-hoc tests and indicate which comparisons yielded significant results.

### 10.6.2.3  Example '

The median numerical score for participants who were native speakers of English was 110 (mean rank = 72.93); for participants who were not native speakers of English it was 113 (mean rank = 78.52). A Kruskal-Wallis found no effect of 'NativeSpeaker', H(1) = .620, *p* = .431.'

### RESEARCH METHODS AT WORK

Calvin is a training and development manager in the HR department of a big organisation which is spending over three million pounds a year on sending employees to external training providers. One of the training sessions offered to employees is the industry-relevant certification IPSO700. This is offered by five training providers and so far Calvin's employer has been sending employees to whichever provider had the next training session scheduled. However, the organisation now wants to know whether the choice of provider makes any difference on either employees' satisfaction with the course or how their productivity is rated by their superior after course completion. There is only one independent variable (or factor) – the type of provider – which makes this a one-way ANOVA; because Calvin is looking at two dependent variables, he needs to conduct a multivariate one-way ANOVA.

Susie helps Calvin to conduct this analysis. While looking at the descriptives, she wonders whether productivity rating after course completion will be affected by how the course participants were rated before they went on the course. She expects productive employees to continue being productive after the course, so she wonders whether pre-course productivity might be a confound and suggests to run an ANCOVA instead, controlling for pre-course productivity.

## A SHORT SUMMARY

- Repeated measures ANOVAs analyse data coming from the same source or sample; taking into account that the variance composition is different than if two different groups were compared.
- For most ANOVAs, the process includes the tests required to test for assumptions.
- The steps to conduct a one-way ANOVA can be adjusted to conduct a multivariate one-way ANOVA.
- Most ANOVAs can be adjusted to account for a mixed-methods design.
- The process to conduct a two-way ANOVA can be easily adjusted to conduct a three-way ANOVA.

## CHECK YOUR UNDERSTANDING

1. Download the sample data set for this exercise, either for SPSS or for Excel. In this study, participants who identified as female had to complete a numerical test, after having been presented with one of three types of instruction: one activated a stereotype referring to the participants' gender (activated_same) by referring to the myth of women's inferior numerical skills; one activated a stereotype by referring to the myth of men's superior numerical skills (activated_different); the third instruction did not make any mention of either men or women's numerical skills.
   a. What are mean and standard deviation of the test score for the three individual conditions?
   b. Find out whether there is an effect of stereotype threat on test score. If required, conduct post-hoc analyses. Write up the results as you would report them in a paper or thesis.

2. A study was conducted to see whether the way in which information was presented to participants (IV 'Condition') had an effect on the extent to which they thought about the topic (DV 'Thought') or paid attention to the information (DV 'Attend'). Participants' numeracy was measured as a potential confounding variable and controlled for in the analysis. Look at the output below. What is missing for you to fully report on the results of this test?

### Between-Subjects Factors

|  | | Value Label | N |
|---|---|---|---|
| Condition | 1 | TextOnly | 25 |
|  | 2 | TextNumbers | 25 |
|  | 3 | TextGraphs | 26 |
|  | 4 | ExtendedTxt | 27 |

### Multivariate Tests

| Effect | | Value | F | Hypothesis df | Error df | Sig. |
|---|---|---|---|---|---|---|
| Intercept | Pillai's Trace | .361 | 27.386[a] | 2.000 | 97.000 | .000 |
|  | Wilks' Lambda | .639 | 27.386[a] | 2.000 | 97.000 | .000 |
|  | Hotelling's Trace | .565 | 27.386[a] | 2.000 | 97.000 | .000 |
|  | Roy's Largest Root | .565 | 27.386[a] | 2.000 | 97.000 | .000 |
| Numeracy | Pillai's Trace | .047 | 2.378[a] | 2.000 | 97.000 | .098 |
|  | Wilks' Lambda | .953 | 2.378[a] | 2.000 | 97.000 | .098 |
|  | Hotelling's Trace | .049 | 2.378[a] | 2.000 | 97.000 | .098 |
|  | Roy's Largest Root | .049 | 2.378[a] | 2.000 | 97.000 | .098 |
| Condition | Pillai's Trace | .057 | .953 | 6.000 | 196.000 | .459 |
|  | Wilks' Lambda | .944 | .948[a] | 6.000 | 194.000 | .462 |
|  | Hotelling's Trace | .059 | .944 | 6.000 | 192.000 | .465 |
|  | Roy's Largest Root | .048 | 1.566[b] | 3.000 | 98.000 | .202 |

a. Exact statistic
b. The statistic is an upper bound on F that yields a lower bound on the significance level.
c. Design: Intercept + Numeracy + Condition

### Tests of Between-Subjects Effects

| Source | Dependent Variable | Type III Sum of Squares | df | Mean Square | F | Sig. |
|---|---|---|---|---|---|---|
| Corrected Model | Thought | 8.338[a] | 4 | 2.085 | .971 | .427 |
|  | Attend | 15.679[b] | 4 | 3.920 | 2.260 | .068 |
| Intercept | Thought | 82.744 | 1 | 82.744 | 38.533 | .000 |
|  | Attend | 77.846 | 1 | 77.846 | 44.879 | .000 |
| Numeracy | Thought | 5.546 | 1 | 5.546 | 2.583 | .111 |
|  | Attend | 7.673 | 1 | 7.673 | 4.423 | .038 |
| Condition | Thought | 2.810 | 3 | .937 | .436 | .728 |
|  | Attend | 7.658 | 3 | 2.553 | 1.472 | .227 |
| Error | Thought | 210.439 | 98 | 2.147 | | |
|  | Attend | 169.991 | 98 | 1.735 | | |
| Total | Thought | 1606.000 | 103 | | | |
|  | Attend | 1308.000 | 103 | | | |
| Corrected Total | Thought | 218.777 | 102 | | | |
|  | Attend | 185.670 | 102 | | | |

[a] R Squared = .038 (Adjusted R Squared = −.001)
[b] R Squared = .084 (Adjusted R Squared = .047)

# 11 Statistical Analyses: Looking at Associations and Relationships

### WHAT IS THIS CHAPTER ABOUT?

Chapter 11 provides guidance for the type of tests categorised in earlier chapters as looking at associations and relationships. It describes how to conduct correlation analyses both for parametric and non-parametric data as well as explains the different types of chi-square tests.

### WHY IS THIS IMPORTANT?

Both correlation analyses and chi-square tests are a staple of quantitative research methods. Knowing how to conduct these analyses will equip you with the skills not only to run these yourself, but also how to interpret the results presented by other researchers. Lastly, this chapter completes the overview on basic methods of statistical analysis. In combination with the other two chapters on statistical analyses you should have a good foundation from which to approach quantitative research.

### WHAT ARE THE LEARNING OUTCOMES OF THIS CHAPTER?

At the end of this chapter you will be able to choose and run the appropriate test to analyse your data, including the following tests:
- Pearson's correlation
- Spearman's correlation
- Chi square

## 11.1 PARAMETRIC DATA CORRELATION (PEARSON'S)

The concept and purpose of this analysis is described in more detail in Section 8.8.4.
Example question:

In this study, data was collected on participants' verbal and numerical skills. Although these two scores measure separate abilities, it could be argued that both are an indication of participants' overall intellectual capabilities. You would therefore be justified in expecting the two scores to be highly positively correlated. The following example is going to test this hypothesis. (For the sake of this example we will assume that both variables are normally distributed.)

### 11.1.1  Pearson's in Excel

#### ONLINE CONTENT

On the companion website you will find an Excel file you can use to follow the guidance in this section. You can also download and adjust it to fit your data.

#### THE HEADLINES

- Calculate correlation coefficient.
- Calculate *p*-value.
- Excel functions used: CORREL, F.DIST. Optional: Data Analysis tool.

1. Calculate correlation coefficient.
   - There are two ways of calculating correlation coefficients, either via Tools → Data Analysis → Correlation, or via the Excel function CORREL.
   - For two variables:
     – If you want to correlate only two variables, CORREL is faster and easier to use. You cannot do correlations on more than two variables at a time, however.
     – CORREL takes two arguments, which are the cell ranges for both variables: =CORREL(Cell range variable 1, Cell range variable 2).
   - For three or more variables:
     – If you want to correlate more than two variables at a time, you need to use the Excel Data Analysis tool. However, this requires you to enter the data you want to correlate to be entered in a continuous cell reference (i.e., the data needs to be stored in adjacent columns or rows).
     – We want to calculate a correlation between three variables. For this we need to use the Data Analysis function, and we need to move columns so that the columns for all three variables are next to each other.
     – Prepare your Excel sheet such that all variable data is next to each other. In this example, the three verbal scores (pre-test, post-test and follow-up in the form of the variables 'PreTest', 'VerbalScore' and 'FollowUpTest', respectively) are in columns A, B and C, respectively.
     – Navigate to Tools → Data Analysis → Correlation.
     – Enter the range for all variables together, from the top cell of the leftmost column to the bottom cell in the rightmost column. Note that you can tick Labels in First Row so Excel knows not to count the first row for the analysis (Figure 11.1).

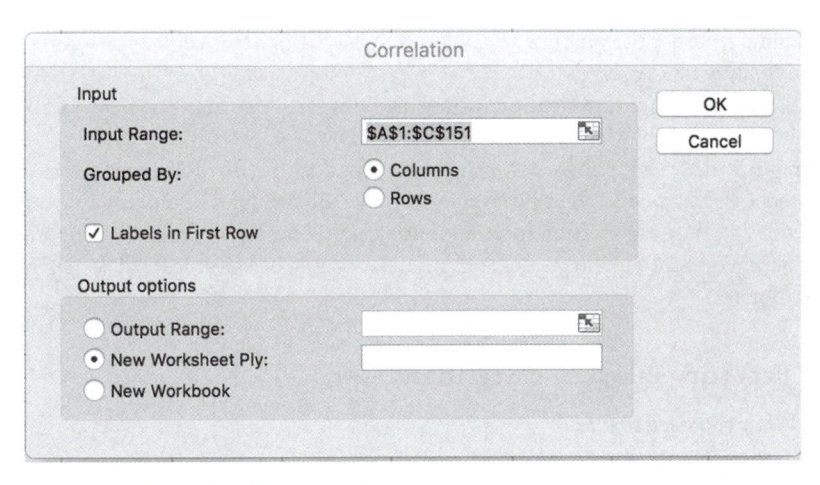

*Figure 11.1* Data analysis: Correlation window
Used with permission from Microsoft.

And this is an example result (Table 11.1):

*Table 11.1* Correlation scores

|  | PreTest | VerbalScore | FollowupTest |  |
|---|---|---|---|---|
| PreTest | 1.000 |  |  | PreTest |
| VerbalScore | 0.595 | 1.000 |  | VerbalScore |
| FollowupTest | 0.594 | 0.986 | 1.000 | FollowupTest |

- Both methods give a correlation size. But now we need to find out whether those correlations are significant.

2. Calculate *p*-value.
    - There is a formula to calculate the *p*-value based on the correlation size and the degrees of freedom. You can calculate this in one go, using the following formula: = 1−F.DIST(((X*Y^2)/(1−Y^2)),1,X−2,TRUE). X stands for N, the number of cases (X-2 calculates the degrees of freedom) and Y for r, the size of the correlation. You can either insert the values directly or enter correlation size and N into two cells in Excel and then replace X and Y with the respective cell references. In this example, N = 150, the correlation size of the correlation between 'VerbalScore' and 'PreTest' is in cell B3, and the full formula would look like this:

    $$= 1 - \text{F.DIST}(((150 \times B3^{\wedge}2)/(1 - B3^{\wedge}2)),1,150 - 2,\text{TRUE})$$

    - The result of this formula is 0.000, which means p <.001.

## 11.1.2 Pearson's in SPSS

**ONLINE CONTENT**

On the companion website you will find SPSS data and syntax files you can use to follow the guidance in this section. You can also download and adjust them to fit your data.

1. To examine whether the amount of books read and the pre-test verbal score correlate, navigate to <u>Analyze</u> ➔ <u>Correlate</u>.
2. Choose <u>Bivariate…</u> to examine the relationship between amounts of books read and pre-test score.
3. The menu for bivariate correlation includes the options for both parametric and non-parametric correlation. Select <u>Pearson</u> and move all variables you want to examine into the right <u>Variables</u> field. To help you identify significant correlations (which is particularly useful when you examine more than just a couple of variables), click <u>Flag significant correlations</u>.

### 11.1.3 Reporting Pearson's correlations

#### 11.1.3.1 What you need to know

- Correlation size $r$: calculated in Excel and SPSS.
- Degrees of freedom: here, N-2.
- Significance value: calculated in Excel and SPSS.

#### 11.1.3.2 What you need to do

- List $r$ and the degrees of freedom, followed by the significance level.
- Then briefly describe how the correlation is manifested.

**11.1.3.3 Example** 'Participants' pre-test verbal scores showed a high positive correlation with their post-test 'VerbalScore', $r(148) = .595, p < .001$, such that higher pre-test verbal scores were associated with higher verbal scores after the training course.'

When interpreting correlation values, a correlation consists of a direction (positive or negative) and a size which is assessed independent of the direction of the correlation. A correlation is considered strong at $r = .80$ (i.e., $-.80$ or $+.80$), moderate at $r = (\pm).50$, and weak at $r = (\pm).30$. The squared value of $r$, $r^2$ describes the portion of shared variance between the two variables. In the example above, $(r = .595)$ the amount of shared variance is calculated by squaring .595:

$$.595^2 = .354.$$

This means that the two variables share 35.4% of the variance (i.e., that the two variables account for 35.4% of the variance in the data).

## 11.2 SPEARMAN'S CORRELATION

The concept and purpose of this analysis is described in more detail in Section 8.8.5.

Example question:

In this study, data was collected on participants' verbal and numerical skills. Although these two scores measure separate abilities, it could be argued that both are an indication of participants' overall intellectual capabilities. You would therefore be justified in expecting the two scores to be highly positively correlated. The following example is going to test this hypothesis.

### 11.2.1 Spearman's in Excel

> **ONLINE CONTENT**
>
> On the companion website you will find an Excel file you can use to follow the guidance in this section. You can also download and adjust it to fit your data.

> **THE HEADLINES**
>
> - Calculate correlation coefficient.
> - Calculate *p*-value.
> - Excel functions used: CORREL, F.DIST, RANK.AVG.

1. Calculate correlation coefficient.
   - The overall process of calculating a correlation on non-parametric data is very similar to calculating this on parametric data. The only difference is that Spearman's correlation does not calculate a correlation on the individual values but on their rankings.
   - To calculate a correlation, you can use the same CORREL function described on page 276 and just adapt the arguments slightly since you do not correlate values, but ranks of values. In brief, the structure of the function is: =CORREL([Range 1], [Range 2]). This means it correlates the values in range 1 with the values in range 2. But since you are correlating ranks of values rather than values themselves, the function needs to be adjusted slightly: =CORREL(RANK.AVG([Range 1], [Range 1],1),RANK.AVG([Range 2], [Range 2],1)). In our example, the ranges for the variables are A2:A151 and B2:B151, respectively and the full formula is therefore as follows:
   =CORREL(RANK.AVG([A2:A151], [A2:A151],1),RANK.AVG([B2:B151], [B2:B151],1)).
   - Note that this function now correlates the outcome of two other functions with each other:
   =RANK.AVG[A2:A151], [A2:A151],1) with the result of =RANK.AVG([B2:B151], [B2:B151], 1).[1]

2. Calculate *p*-value.
   - Having calculated the correlation size itself, you now need the *p*-value. For this you use the F.DIST function in Excel which takes the following format: 1−F.DIST(((X*Y^2)/(1−Y^2)),1,X−2,TRUE).
   - X stands for N, the number of cases, and Y for r, the size of the correlation. You can either insert the values directly or enter correlation size and N into two cells in Excel and then replace X and Y with the respective cell references. For example, if N=150 and the correlation size is stored in cell B3, then the full formula would look as follows:
   =1−F.DIST(((150*B3^2)/(1−B3^2)),1,150−2,TRUE). In our example, the result of this formula is 0.000, which means that $p < .001$.

---

[1] Look up the explanation to the RANK.AVG function in the Excel Functions Glossary to understand why it contains the same range: in brief, it means looking at each value *of* range X to sum them *in relation* to the same range X.

## 11.2.2 Spearman's in SPSS

A correlation analysis for non-parametric data is conducted in a way very similar to the parametric type which we have described in Section 8.8.4.

To conduct a Spearman's analysis in SPSS you can therefore follow the steps 1 to 3 in Section 11.2.2. The only difference is that rather than ticking the Pearson box as you would for a correlation analysis with parametric data, you tick the third box Spearman. This will calculate **Spearman's rho** as a correlation coefficient in a table identical to the table that was produced for the Pearson's correlation coefficient. Despite their similarities, however, the two analyses are not interchangeable. Calculations for Spearman's rho apply certain corrections to the data to compensate for the non-parametric nature.

## 11.2.3 Reporting Spearman's correlations

Correlations are reported in the same way, regardless of whether they are calculated as Spearman's or Pearson's (see p. 278 on how to report Pearson's correlation).

For example:

'A Spearman's correlational analysis found a correlation of .735 between participants' numerical score and their pre-test verbal score, $p < .001$.'

## 11.3 COMPARING EXPECTED VERSUS OBSERVED FREQUENCIES: CHI-SQUARE GOODNESS-OF-FIT

The concept and purpose of this analysis is described in more detail in Section 8.8.3.

Example question: Do the observed frequencies of native versus non-native speakers differ significantly from the expected frequencies?

### 11.3.1 Goodness-of-fit chi-square in Excel

**ONLINE CONTENT**

On the companion website you will find an Excel file you can use to follow the guidance in this section. You can also download and adjust it to fit your data.

**THE HEADLINES**

- Establish actual frequencies.
- Calculate expected frequencies.
- Calculate $\chi^2$ (= chi square) value based on comparing the two.
- Calculate *p*-value.
- Excel functions used: SUM, CHISQ.TEST.

1. Establish actual frequencies.
   - In this example, we find that there are 81 native speakers out of a sample of 150, and 69 non-native speakers. These are our observed frequencies (Figure 11.2):

|   | A | B | C |
|---|---|---|---|
| 1 |   | Yes | No |
| 2 | Native speaker | 81 | 69 |

*Figure 11.2 Observed frequencies*

2. Calculate expected frequencies.
   - The expected frequencies can depend on your knowledge of the data. Barring any specific expectations, calculate what the chance distribution would be by dividing N by the number of possible outcomes. In this example, we assume that our expected frequencies are based on statistics that put the distribution at 75% and 25%, respectively.

|   | A | B | C |
|---|---|---|---|
| 1 |   | Yes | No |
| 2 | Native Speaker | 112.5 | 37.5 |

3. Calculate $X^2$ value based on comparing the two.
   - $X^2$ is calculated by the following formula.

$$X^2 = \sum \frac{(Observed\ frequency - Expected\ frequency)^2}{Expected\ frequency}$$

   - That means summing up the results for each value's equation; in this example, replace the observed and expected frequency in the equation once with the frequencies for native speakers then for the non-native speakers.
   - For native speakers, the equation looks like this:

$$\frac{(81 - 112.5)^2}{112.5} = \frac{(-31.5)^2}{112.5} = \frac{992.25}{112.5} = 8.82$$

   - Repeating this for non-native speakers, the result is 26.460. Add the two together: 8.82 + 26.460 = 35.28. This is your $X^2$ value.

4. Calculate *p*-value.
   - Use the Excel function CHISQ.TEST, which takes two pieces of information: the range of cells containing the observed value and the range of cells containing the expected value: =CHISQ.TEST[Range 1, Range 2]. In our example, the observed values are in cells B3:C3, the expected values are in cells E6:F6, and the resulting formula is therefore =CHITEST( B6:C6, E6:F6 ). The result is 0.000, which means p < .001.

### 11.3.2 Goodness-of-fit chi-square in SPSS

> **ONLINE CONTENT**
>
> On the companion website you will find SPSS data and syntax files you can use to follow the guidance in this section. You can also download and adjust them to fit your data.

1. Navigate to Analyze → Nonparametric Tests → One Sample … .
2. In the Objective tab, choose Customize analysis.

3. In the Fields tab, SPSS has by default moved all variables into the Test Fields column; make sure to move all variables back except the one whose distribution you want to test.
4. In the Settings tab, tick Customize tests, then Compare observed probabilities to hypothesized (Chi-Square test).
5. Click on Options to specify the probabilities against which you would like to conduct the test. In this example, we want to find out whether the distribution of native to non-native speakers differs significantly from the 75% : 25% distribution we expect to see. Select Customize expected probability. For the variable 'NativeSpeaker', 1 = yes and 2 = 0, therefore we enter 1 for the category in the first row, and 75 in the corresponding column; we then enter 2 in the second row and 25 for the respective column.
6. Click OK, then click Run.

### 11.3.3   Reporting the outcome of a goodness-of-fit chi-square test

#### 11.3.3.1 What you need to know

- The expected frequencies
- The observed frequencies
- Chi-square value
- *p*-value
- Degrees of freedom: For the goodness-of-fit chi-square, df is calculated as k −1, where k is the number of categories; for example, if we are looking at the two categories 'native speaker' and 'non-native speaker', we only have one degree of freedom.

#### 11.3.3.2 What you need to do

- Report the distribution you expected.
- Report chi-square statistics with N and degrees of freedom.
- Report the *p*-value.

**11.3.3.3 Example** 'In this sample, 81 participants were native speakers, 69 people were not. Demographic statistics suggest that for this sample we would expect a distribution of 113 and 37, respectively. A goodness-of-fit chi-square test compared the observed frequencies of native and non-native speakers against the hypothesised frequencies and found a significant difference, $X^2 (1, N = 150) = 35.28, p < .001$.'

## 11.4   COMPARING EXPECTED VERSUS OBSERVED FREQUENCIES: TEST OF INDEPENDENCE CHI-SQUARE

The concept and purpose of this analysis is described in more detail in Section 8.8.2.
    Example question:

In the sample study, participants of all three groups (online, weekly sessions, weekend training) were asked whether they would be interested in participating in a similar training session again. Their responses were as follows (Table 11.2):

*Table 11.2* Observed frequencies

|  | Yes | No |
| --- | --- | --- |
| Online course | 19 | 31 |
| Weekly 1 hr course | 38 | 12 |
| Weekend intensive course | 27 | 23 |

We will be conducting a chi-square test of independence to establish whether participants' stated preference is independent of the type of course they attended.

### 11.4.1 Test of independence chi-square in Excel

#### ONLINE CONTENT

On the companion website you will find an Excel file you can use to follow the guidance in this section. You can also download and adjust it to fit your data.

#### THE HEADLINES

- Establish actual frequencies.
- Calculate expected frequencies.
- Calculate $X^2$ value.
- Calculate $p$-value.
- Excel functions used: SUM, CHISQ.TEST.

1. Establish actual frequencies.

We have already established actual frequencies – they are the frequencies listed in the table above. So you can follow the example below, we have copied the table including the row and column labels in Excel (e.g., cell B2 contains the number of people who participated in the online course and responded 'Yes' when asked whether they would like to participate in another course of the same type) (Figure 11.3).

|   | A | B | C |
|---|---|---|---|
| 1 |   | Yes | No |
| 2 | Online course | 19 | 31 |
| 3 | Weekly 1 hr course | 38 | 12 |
| 4 | Weekend intensive course | 27 | 23 |

*Figure 11.3* Actual frequencies

- Before you can move to calculate expected frequencies, you need to expand the table of observed frequencies by adding column, row and overall totals (calculated with the SUM function) (Figure 11.4):

|   | A | B | C | D |
|---|---|---|---|---|
| 1 |   | Yes | No |   |
| 2 | Online | 19 | 31 | **50** |
| 3 | Weekly 1 hr course | 38 | 12 | **50** |
| 4 | Weekend intensive course | 27 | 23 | **50** |
| 5 |   | 84 | 66 | **150** |

*Figure 11.4* Actual frequencies with row totals

284  *Introducing Quantitative Methods*

- Cells B5 and C5 contain the column totals; cells D2, D3 and D4 contain the row totals; and cell D5 contains N, that is, the overall total of 150.

2. Calculate expected frequencies.
   - In this step you are working towards filling a table with the results of the following formula (Figure 11.5):

|   | A | B | C |
|---|---|---|---|
| 1 |   | Yes | No |
| 2 | Online | $\frac{Column\,Total}{N} \times Row\,Total$ | $\frac{Column\,Total}{N} \times Row\,Total$ |
| 3 | Weekly 1 hr course | $\frac{Column\,Total}{N} \times Row\,Total$ | $\frac{Column\,Total}{N} \times Row\,Total$ |
| 4 | Weekend intensive course | $\frac{Column\,Total}{N} \times Row\,Total$ | $\frac{Column\,Total}{N} \times Row\,Total$ |

*Figure 11.5*  *Formulas to calculate expected frequencies*

- To illustrate better what the formula means, we have replaced the formula with the actual values for each cell (Figure 11.6):

|   | A | B | C |
|---|---|---|---|
| 1 |   | Yes | No |
| 2 | Online | $\frac{84}{150} \times 50 = .56 \times 50 = 28$ | $\frac{66}{150} \times 50 = .44 \times 50 = 22$ |
| 3 | Weekly 1 hr course | $\frac{84}{150} \times 50 = .56 \times 50 = 28$ | $\frac{66}{150} \times 50 = .44 \times 50 = 22$ |
| 4 | Weekend intensive course | $\frac{84}{150} \times 50 = .56 \times 50 = 28$ | $\frac{66}{150} \times 50 = .44 \times 50 = 22$ |

*Figure 11.6*  *Calculated expected frequencies*

- You could of course calculate each cell individually, but you can also use Excel functions with references to the column and row totals. We have copied in the formulas we have used in the table below. This is a new table which makes reference to the original table's cells (Figure 11.7):

|   | E | F |
|---|---|---|
| 2 | =($B$5/$D$5)*$D2 | =($C$5/$D$5)*$D2 |
| 3 | =($B$5/$D$5)*$D3 | =($C$5/$D$5)*$D3 |
| 4 | =($B$5/$D$5)*$D4 | =($C$5/$D$5)*$D4 |

*Figure 11.7*  *Sample Excel formulas to calculate expected frequencies*

- Note the use of the '$' in the formulas to ensure that the reference to the column total doesn't change but remains static. For example, the formula in cell B2 consists of a static reference ($B$5) to the column total (84) and a static reference ($D$5) to N (150), whereas the reference to the row total only keeps the column constant but allows for the increase in the row.

3. Calculate $X^2$ value.
   - The overall $X^2$ is calculated as follows:

$$X^2 = \Sigma \frac{(Observed\ frequency - Expected\ frequency)^2}{Expected\ frequency}$$

   - The sigma sign tells you that you need to do this for all values (i.e., for all cells of the table). We have here created a new table which only contains the results of the formulas for all cells of the original table (Figure 11.8):

|   | H | I |
|---|---|---|
| 2 | =(B2–E2)^2/E2 | =(C2–F2)^2/F2 |
| 3 | =(B3–E3)^2/E3 | =(C3–F3)^2/F3 |
| 4 | =(B4–E4)^2/E4 | =(C4–F4)^2/F4 |

**Figure 11.8** *Sample Excel formulas to calculate expected frequencies*

   - Use the =SUM function (or navigate there via the $\Sigma$ symbol) to sum up the values of all cells. This is your chi-square value.

4. Calculate *p*-value.
   - The last element to calculate is the level of significance. Thankfully, this only requires a simple Excel function aptly named CHISQ.TEST, which takes two pieces of information: the range of cells containing the observed value and the range of cells containing the expected value, that is, = CHISQ.TEST[Range1, Range2].

The significant chi-square test tells you that the two variables are not independent, that is, there is an association between which group participants attended and their willingness to attend a similar training.

### 11.4.2 Test of independence chi-square in SPSS

**ONLINE CONTENT**

On the companion website you will find SPSS data and syntax files you can use to follow the guidance in this section. You can also download and adjust them to fit your data. There are two ways to conduct this analysis in SPSS, and we will briefly explain both of them. Use the first analysis if your data is in the form we have seen so far, that is, one data set per item or participant. Use the second form if your data is already consolidated and you have a list of frequencies but no individual cases.

Version 1

1. Navigate to Analyze → Descriptive Statistics → Crosstabs.
2. Move 'CourseType' to the Row(s) field, and move 'RepeatCourse' to the Column(s) field.

3. Click Statistics and tick Chi Square. Click Continue, then Run.
4. The SPSS output tells you that there is a significant difference in the frequencies with which participants indicated their willingness to attend a similar course. Note the comment on the bottom of the table advising that 0 cells have an expected count of less than 5 – SPSS would not be able to compute a chi-square test if that were the case. However, an *observed* count of 5 or less is fine.

Version 2

1. Make sure that your data is prepared the right way. For this analysis, you need to define your variables such that you have one frequency value for each individual condition. For this example, you have two variables: one with three levels and one with two. Therefore, you have six total conditions and six individual frequencies (Figure 11.9):

| CourseType | RepeatCourse | Frequency |
|---|---|---|
| Online | yes | 19.00 |
| Weekly | yes | 38.00 |
| Weekend | yes | 27.00 |
| Online | no | 31.00 |
| Weekly | no | 12.00 |
| Weekend | no | 23.00 |

*Figure 11.9* SPSS data for chi-square test
Reprint Courtesy of International Business Machines Corporation, © International Business Machines Corporation.

5. Before conducting the chi-square test, navigate to Data → Weight Cases. Select Weight Cases By and move the data which contains your frequency data (here helpfully named Frequency) into the Frequency Variable field. Click OK.
   Note: Make sure to switch back to Do not weigh cases before conducting another analysis!
6. Navigate to Analyze → Descriptive Statistics → Crosstabs.
7. Move 'CourseType' to the Row(s) field, and move 'RepeatCourse' to the Column(s) field.
8. Click Statistics and tick Chi Square. Click Continue, then Run.

### 11.4.3 Reporting a chi-square test of independence

#### 11.4.3.1 What you need to know

- Chi-square value: calculated in SPSS and Excel.
- Degrees of freedom: The degrees of freedom are calculated through the following formula: (number of rows – 1) × (number of columns – 1). They are given in the SPSS output.
- N: established in Excel, calculated in SPSS.
- Significance value: calculated in SPSS and Excel.

#### 11.4.3.2 What you need to do

- List the chi-square value with N and the degrees of freedom in brackets.
- Report level of significance.

***11.4.3.3 Example*** 'A chi-square test of independence established that the type of course participants attended was associated with their willingness to attend a second time, $X^2$ (2, $N = 150$) = 14.773, $p = .001$.'

We want to conclude on (yet another) cautionary note: Although this book has discussed different types of research questions, and although these types of questions are often associated with specific tests, there is no absolute, fixed mapping between research question and test. Rather, the choice of test is based on the type of data available. Whether the result of a t-test is indicative of a difference between groups (or whether you can talk of a causal link between independent and dependent variables which is manifested in a difference between two groups) depends on your research question, the theoretical assumptions your research was based on, your experimental setup and how variables were controlled. A t-test result might tell you whether there is a difference and whether it is statistically significant, but it is your responsibility to put meaning and context to the result.

> ### RESEARCH METHODS AT WORK
>
> In the previous chapter Calvin, the training and development manager, looked at his colleagues' satisfaction with a training course and their productivity ratings later to get an idea regarding the effectiveness of the training courses. After a conversation with his manager Teddy, he starts to doubt whether satisfaction with the course was really a good variable to choose. He vaguely remembers having read that satisfaction as rated immediately after training is more likely to relate to having felt comfortable and not bored rather than to having learned a lot. However, Calvin knows that training participants also fill out a feedback form four weeks after the training, which gives them the opportunity to reflect on how they have used the training content in their workplace. He therefore decides to look into the training feedback forms again and conduct a correlational analysis to see how well satisfaction immediately after the training relates to satisfaction as measured four weeks later.
>
> Lilly is the Business Development Manager of one of the training providers that Calvin and Susie's employer regularly employs. She is thinking of ways to expand the course portfolio and wants to know which training appeals to which participant groups. Lilly suspects that the day-time courses are more likely to be booked by participants who are already in a well-established job and that the evening courses are more likely to be taken up by people who are trying to get better qualifications to apply for a job. She wants to know whether level of work experience (entry level/experienced) is associated with the kind of training booked (evening/day) and therefore conducts a chi-square test of independence.

### A SHORT SUMMARY

- Chi-square tests exist in two variants, goodness-of-fit and test for independence; both versions are based on comparing expected frequencies with observed frequencies.
- Both Pearson's correlation and Spearman's correlation establish the amount of shared variance between two or more variables. Pearson's is used for parametric data, while Spearman's is used for non-parametric data.

## CHECK YOUR UNDERSTANDING

1. A group of 113 smokers and 110 non-smokers were asked whether they support a smoking ban in pubs and restaurants. The results appear below:

|  | Smoker | Non-Smoker | Total |
|---|---|---|---|
| *Supports the ban* | 61 | 72 | 123 |
| *Does not support the ban* | 52 | 38 | 90 |
| *Total* | 113 | 110 | 223 |

   a. The table above presents the observed values. Assume that you have no reason to expect that either group will have a preference for or against the ban. What are the expected values?

|  | Smoker | Non-Smoker |
|---|---|---|
| *Supports the ban* |  |  |
| *Does not support the ban* |  |  |

   b. Conduct a chi-square test of independence in Excel to establish whether being a (non-)smoker is independent of the support of a smoking ban. Report chi-square value, degrees of freedom and *p*-value.

2. As part of a study, three variables collected aspects of attitude certainty by asking participants to what extent they were certain, sure and confident of their attitude. They then ran a correlation analysis to see how closely related the answers were.
   a. Examine the table below and report on the results.
   b. Would you recommend the researcher to combine the three measurements into one composite measure? Why or why not?

**Correlations**

|  |  | AT_Certain | AT_Sure | AT_Confident |
|---|---|---|---|---|
| AT_Certain | Pearson Correlation | 1 | .820** | .808** |
|  | Sig. (2-tailed) |  | .000 | .000 |
|  | N | 103 | 103 | 103 |
| AT_Sure | Pearson Correlation | .820** | 1 | .807** |
|  | Sig. (2-tailed) | .000 |  | .000 |
|  | N | 103 | 103 | 103 |
| AT_Confident | Pearson Correlation | .808** | .807** | 1 |
|  | Sig. (2-tailed) | .000 | .000 |  |
|  | N | 103 | 103 | 103 |

**. Correlation is significant at the 0.01 level (2-tailed).

Reprint Courtesy of International Business Machines Corporation, © International Business Machines Corporation.

# 12 Writing Up Research

## WHAT IS THIS CHAPTER ABOUT?

This chapter concludes the book by guiding you through the process of writing up a research project. It examines the main elements of writing up quantitative research, ranging from the individual elements required in a write-up such as introduction and literature review to methods, data analysis and discussion. The chapter starts by describing a basic template of a write-up and listing possible variations and additional requirements. It then moves to a more detailed description of individual elements, noting what is needed and what you should consider while writing.

## WHY IS THIS IMPORTANT?

If you are conducting research in an academic setting, sharing your findings is what makes a research culture possible in the first place. You build upon other researchers' findings and allow others in turn to build upon yours. For this to happen, your research and your findings need to be written in a clear and largely standardised structure so that others can easily access the information.

If you are conducting research in an industry or organisational setting, it is equally important that the findings be communicated to the interested parties in order to draw the right conclusions and/or implement your recommendations.

## WHAT ARE THE LEARNING OUTCOMES FOR THIS CHAPTER?

At the end of this chapter you will be able to:
- Inform other researchers (as well as other potential readers) about your research in a way that is comprehensive and accessible
- Make an informed choice regarding which elements to include to create a complete documentation of your research
- Understand the purpose of individual sections and know what you need to consider
- Structure a report writing up your research and your results

We have previously talked about the process of research as comprising trial and error – testing hypotheses and revising models based on observations. We have also mentioned the importance of formulating falsifiable hypotheses and protecting yourself from bias. All of this (and more) is important, but the real contribution lies in disseminating research findings. Scientific progress happens when researchers communicate, either directly through collaboration or indirectly through reading other people's research and learning from it. Therefore, most academic writing serves at least two purposes:

1. To potentially enable other researchers to conduct a similar study: Just as you have read and critically evaluated existing research, other people will cast a critical eye on your findings. Some may disagree with your findings. Some may want to conduct a similar study to see whether they can replicate your findings. Others may want to adjust your research design to address what they conceive to be a flaw or room for improvement. Your write-up has to be detailed enough to allow other researchers to potentially conduct the same study – and hopefully come to the same conclusions.
2. To document your research process and present your findings: Not only will other researchers be interested in *what* you found, but also *how* – how you designed your method, why you made the choices you made, and how you fared. Perhaps you tried a particular approach which turned out to not be very fruitful, or you built on previous research but found that adjusting the methodology yielded much more useful results. Reading about your research process helps other researchers learn from your experiences, the good *and* the bad.

The second point is particularly important if you are writing a thesis, dissertation, project report or similar as a student and are worried that your project is too small or too broad or the methodology did not work or you did not find the results you were expecting. In most cases, the process of writing up is not about the perfect study or the perfect result: It is about how you as researcher made your decisions and how you dealt with the limitations and constraints you encountered. Of course, individual requirements may vary from institution to institution and from degree programme to degree programme, but it is perfectly possible to write an excellent dissertation or report about a study that has gone awry. What matters is that you show awareness of the shortcomings, for example by outlining how the shortcomings may have affected the results and by discussing how you would adjust the methods in future research.

There is no one perfect structure for a write-up. Requirements can vary from institution to institution, and sometimes even from teacher to teacher or supervisor or manager. A sample structure is shown below but there are many variations (Figure 12.1):

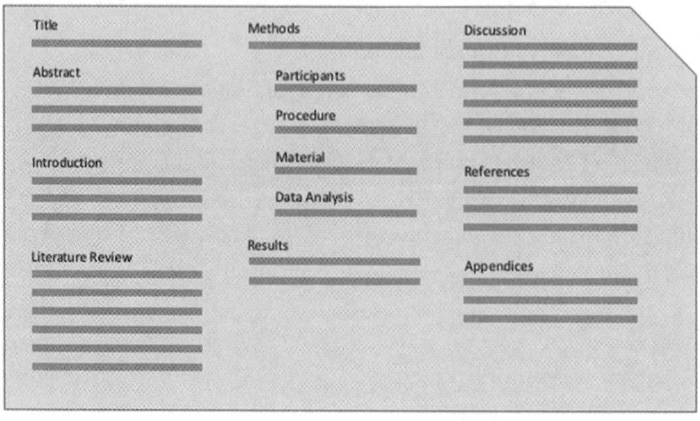

*Figure 12.1* A sample outline

- You may be required to write an abstract.
- You may be asked to provide a separate list of tables, figures and abbreviations used in the text.
- You may be asked to write a separate literature review or to combine it with the introduction.
- You may be asked to provide a separate section on your research rationale or to include it in the literature review.
- In a more applied context, a separate background chapter on the relevant sector, industry or organisation may be required.
- You may be asked to include a separate data analysis section or to split the information instead between the methods and results sections.
- You may be asked to state your hypotheses towards the end of your literature review or in your data analysis section.
- The order of sections can vary, for example appendix and references – you may be asked to provide your references before or after the appendix.

We strongly recommend you get in touch with whoever is in a position to define the requirements. Although the outline presented should be suitable for most cases, your specific institution's rules will always trump a textbook's suggestions.

The advice in this chapter is not specific to a report, a paper, a thesis or a dissertation: all have a roughly similar structure, though the length of individual sections will vary. This chapter will describe each individual section's purpose and the information it should contain so that you will be able to adjust the sequence of sections to suit your requirements.

This book has adopted a chronological approach of describing the process in the order in which individual stages occur. This chapter maintains this approach, which means you will see the individual sections presented in a counterintuitive sequence. Rather than starting with abstract and introduction, we will start with the literature review and end with abstract, introduction and title. Although a reader will first encounter the title, abstract and introduction, the process of writing up flows more smoothly if you approach them last. It is easier to start by writing up the methods section – you can do that while still collecting data. Once you have described your methods, explained your results and discussed your findings, you are in a much better position to summarise your research in an abstract and a title, and you will find it easier to outline the report in the introduction.

Regardless of the individual components and their exact sequence, the key ingredient for a well-written dissertation is *continuity* – the sense that your dissertation forms one coherent whole, with a clear beginning and end and with the component parts connecting with each other (Figure 12.2):

What is your research question? > Why does it matter? > How does your question fit with existing research? > How did you go about answering the research question? > What did you find? > How does your answer fit with existing research?

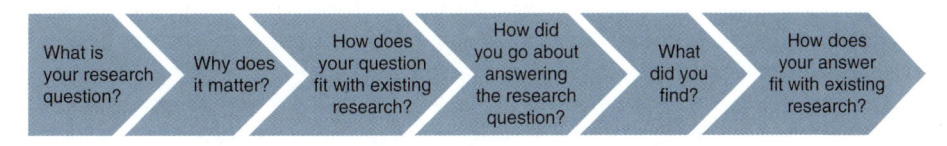

*Figure 12.2  Continuity in writing up*

- Your title and abstract let the reader know what your dissertation/report/paper is about.
- Your introduction sets the scene. It tells the reader why the area of research is important and what they can expect when reading your report.
- Your literature review tells the reader what your research question is and how it fits into the existing research.
- Your methods section builds on the literature research and explains how you went about answering the question.

- Your results section builds on the methods section and describes what you found.
- Your discussion builds on the results section and the literature review and puts the results into context.

Keep this sequence of interlinking elements in mind as we turn to discussing the individual components.

> **REVIEW & REFLECT**
>
> - How do concepts introduced in earlier chapters, such as reliability and validity, relate to the need for continuity in the structure?
> - What are the advantages and disadvantages of one fixed structure for all types of studies?

## 12.1 LITERATURE REVIEW

Chapter 1 noted that one requirement for a research question is that it contributes usefully to the academic discussion. However, as always, there are exceptions. You may have had no influence on the research question – for example, you may be a student writing up the results of a study that was conducted in the course of a particular module. You may have been allocated a certain research question or data set. Or you may have opted to conduct a replication study which, for the reasons outlined in Chapter 1, is an entirely worthwhile endeavour. Whatever your reasons, in your literature review you need to set out how the question fits into existing research. How does your research contribute to the existing body of knowledge? What is known already, and what is still missing? The challenge in writing a literature review is to present the state of existing research as an ongoing debate. You are reporting on this debate as an impartial observer, weighing the pros and cons of individual arguments. Rather than merely rephrasing or repeating what other researchers have said, take a broader perspective by summarising. Instead of 'Jones (2000) asserts A and B, while Smith (2010) states A and C', try 'Jones (2000) and Smith (2010) agree on A. However, Jones argues in favour of B while Smith maintains C is more appropriate.' Then you can focus on the different arguments for B and C and critically evaluate their individual merits or outline how your research attempts to settle the question between B and C.

Students often struggle with the concept of 'critical evaluation', worrying that it means they have to judge and 'criticise' every paper. You do not have to do that. Instead, keep in mind the criteria of reliability and validity (these concepts are discussed in Chapter 2) as you read other researchers' papers and studies, and think about to what extent you consider them useful, plausible, well-executed and appropriately interpreted:

- Is their methodology suitable to answer their chosen research question?
- Have they chosen appropriate measurements?
- Are their test instruments reliable?
- Is the sample size big enough, and is the sampling population adequate?
- Have they considered potential confounding variables?
- Do you agree with their interpretation of the results?

You do not have to subject each paper you read to a checklist of this type, though. Instead, make it a habit of recording your responses and thoughts as you read each paper. Where you have concerns or questions, where you can see links or contradictions with existing research, make a note for further discussion during the literature review.

We have said above that the individual parts of your write-up connect with each other, and the research methodology builds on the literature review. Put another way, the literature review can set up the methodology. You can provide a rationale not (only) for your research question but also for your method, by using a review of the existing research to identify which methodology is appropriate. For example, you might find that for your particular question there already exist tried and tested experimental protocols which would give you the best chance to collect useful data. Or perhaps in the process of critically evaluating existing papers you have come to the conclusion that previous methodologies have particular flaws which your method aims to redress.

## 12.2 RATIONALE

In many cases, the rationale for a particular research is expressed implicitly in the literature review by outlining which gap in the existing research the study sets out to fill. In some cases, a more explicit rationale is required, spelling out the reasons for the research and the original contribution it makes under a separate heading. The rationale for your research is the gap in existing research that your literature review identified; more precisely, it is the gap that your research study attempts to fill. Because this gap is your rationale, it is important to keep up to date with the relevant literature and start working on your literature review before you conduct your empirical research: *as the gap disappears, so does your rationale*. You do not want to be halfway through your research project only to discover that someone already conducted this very study, thus making your research obsolete. That said, this is more of an issue if you are working on your PhD thesis or towards a publication in a scholarly journal – it is unlikely that your Bachelor's or even your Master's thesis or your research report's success will be affected by the publication of a similar study.

### REVIEW & REFLECT

- How are the literature search and the rationale linked?
- In planning your research, which should come first, and why?

## 12.3 HYPOTHESES

Chapter 2 introduced hypotheses as the hallmarks of good science and scientific research. Hypotheses state your expectations; they make you paint the bullseye *before* you fire the first shot. Hypotheses require you to explicitly state what kind of evidence you are looking for, and they thus help you reduce experimenter bias. In addition, the exact phrasing of your hypotheses restricts the type of statistical analyses you can later conduct. Often hypotheses are stated at the end of the literature review. This reflects how closely linked they are with existing research as your knowledge of the existing variables and your expectations towards the results will be based on that. Each hypothesis should make reference to one or more specific variables and indicate the type of expected behaviour in relation to other specific variables. For example:

- Children with more affluent parents will perform better academically than children with less affluent parents.

- Under conditions of uncertainty, participants will tend to favour a more conservative investment strategy.
- Patients who have been given the revised information brochure will show more compliance with the treatment regimen.

In some cases, you may be required to state a null hypothesis in addition to or instead of the alternative hypothesis. Make sure to clearly mark your hypotheses: While 'regular' hypotheses are numbered from $H_1$, $H_2$, etc., a null hypothesis is always $H_0$. Even if you conduct exploratory research, you still have to provide hypotheses. However, they can be phrased quite broadly and are often non-directional.

> **! LOOK OUT!**
>
> Make sure that your hypotheses match your statistical tests! If your hypothesis is directional, you need to conduct one-tailed tests; if it is non-directional, you can use two-tailed tests.

## 12.4 METHODS

In this section you describe in detail how you conducted your empirical research. If not specified otherwise, the methods section is usually divided into smaller subsections:

- Participants
- Procedures
- Design
- Data analysis

### 12.4.1 Participants

This section describes who participated in your study and why. How many participants took part? How old were they? What gender did they identify with? It also describes their main demographic characteristics: Are they students of a particular university, children at a particular school, or people recruited through an online questionnaire? Use demographic information such as region/country, first language, level of occupation, etc. to give a better impression of the spread and diversity of your sample. You can also use the range here, a concept we introduced in Section 4.7. If you used specific criteria to approach and recruit your participants (e.g., handedness, scoring above or below a certain cut-off point on a particular test, or any other physical or psychological traits), you need to mention it in this section. Indicate why your participants took part. Were they students who participated for credit? Were they recruited through specific channels? Were they offered any incentives for participation?

### 12.4.2 Design

Describe the form your study took – was it conducted as a correlational study, a quasi-experiment, or a (true) experiment? Note whether you employed a within- or between-participants design, or a mixture of both. List the number of factors, dependent and independent variables and their individual levels. Describe how your sample was determined and how many participants were allocated to each condition.

### 12.4.3 Procedures

Describe your procedure in sufficient detail that other researchers have enough information to potentially conduct the same study. Start with how participants were introduced to the study, what material and which instruments you used and why, and how the testing or study took place, up to and including debriefing and thanking participants. Mention any time constraints participants might have been given. If you conducted computer-based testing, describe the sequence of tasks and how responses were recorded. If you used any imaging technology, describe the exact setup and resolution in which data was presented and how responses were recorded.

We mentioned earlier that writing up your research is as much about documenting the process as it is about presenting your findings. Documenting the process means showing that your choices were informed choices and explaining what guided your decisions. For example, you might outline that although online questionnaires have distinct disadvantages, the fact that you could more easily reach a more diverse group of participants from a wider range of cultures outweighed the disadvantages for you. A reader (or fellow researcher) might agree or disagree with you, but what matters is that you showed that you did not randomly decide to use the online version; instead, you made an informed choice.

### 12.4.4 Data analysis

The data analysis section bridges the gap between data collection and results. It explains what you did with the data after you collected it and before you started conducting your statistical analyses. Describe how many data sets you ended up with and, if applicable, how many of those are complete. If you discarded any data sets because you identified them as outliers, explain your reasoning for this. How did you treat missing data or data entry errors? Mention any recoding you might have done and where you transformed data from one scale to another.

> **REVIEW & REFLECT**
>
> - Why do you need to document your hypotheses in writing up your study?
> - How would relaxing this requirement impact on your research's validity?

## 12.5 RESULTS

Considering its overall importance, the results section is generally surprisingly short. In fact, it is the discussion section which usually takes up more space and focus because it is there where the findings are, well, discussed and put into context. In contrast, the results section is fairly short. Report the results of any manipulation check (see Section 2.6.1) as this will establish whether you were able to conduct the study as planned and will also inform the validity of your conclusions. Then describe your variables before you report the results of statistical analyses. Include any testing of assumptions to establish whether a particular statistical analysis was appropriate or feasible, also include post-hoc tests, where applicable. Chapter 6 provided guidance on how to determine and present the main descriptives while Chapter 7 discussed different options on how to present data, either in text, through tables or figures.

## 12.6 DISCUSSION

This is where you interpret your findings and put them into context. First, relate the results to your hypotheses. How do they fit? Does the data confirm your hypotheses or not? Then take a step back. How do the findings relate to your research question? To discuss this, you need to link your results to research and findings mentioned in the introduction and the literature review. Do your findings agree with previous research? Are there contradictions? Can you think of possible reasons, ideally also rooted in existing literature, why your results are not in line with existing research? What might be a plausible next step to resolve those contradictions? What data might it be useful to collect now?

### 12.6.1 Limitations

Sometimes the discussion of limitation forms part of the general discussion; sometimes it is treated as a separate section. In either case, it means acknowledging the limits within which your study's results can be generalised, based on the restricted method and sample available to you; it also means discussing assumptions you have made in designing and conducting your research and which will have impacted your findings. For example, in using an online questionnaire you have made the assumption that most if not all of your potential participants in your target population are willing and able to use the Internet and that you will get a representative sample using this method. Lastly, it means reflecting on the quality of your methodology, from sampling and the material used to the data quality and the quality of the analyses. For example, you might have concluded that there was a confounding variable you did not control for, or your analyses may show that the experimental manipulation was not successful. Other things to look out for are (note that the list is by no means exhaustive!):

- The sample was too homogenous and only comprised participants of a very narrow (sub) population. Example: You only recruited students aged 21 to 23.
- You identified either a **floor effect** or **ceiling effect** in your response data, indicating that you did not see the full possible range of data. Example: You used a seven-point scale to collect agreement, but participants only used the two highest response options, giving you little variation in the scope of agreement.
- Participant feedback suggests that participants may have misinterpreted instructions. Example: Instructions were phrased ambiguously, and instead of aiming for speed, participants aimed for accuracy.
- The sample is heavily biased towards a certain participant characteristic *relevant to the research question*. Example: You conducted a study on helping behaviour but relied exclusively on volunteer participants.[1]
- Participants from a particular condition were more likely to not complete the task or study. Example: You conducted the same survey in two forms, as a structured interview and a purely online survey. You found that participants starting on the online survey disproportionately failed to complete the survey, which leads you to conclude that the electronic form leads to testing fatigue and frustration.

---

[1] Admittedly, this is a tricky one. By its very nature (and as per ethics guidelines) research usually takes place only with willing and voluntary participants. But for some variables and research question this is more a problem than for others.

- You realise that there would have been a better way to operationalise one of your variables. Example: You asked participants to indicate their level of self-esteem on a five-point scale, but you later learned of the Rosenberg self-esteem scale.
- The data is not detailed enough or is collected in a less suitable format. Example: You collected age data in age brackets rather than in years.

Be critical, but not overly so – if you find that you criticise every aspect of your methodology, it will be hard to argue why you conducted your study in the first place!

> **LOOK OUT!**
>
> Students often point out that ecological validity is threatened with the use of very limited samples (i.e., university students). This is true, but only to a point. Ecological validity is at risk only where the behaviour, skill or response examined is one where you have good reason to assume that university students are different from the population you want the results to apply to. For example, a student-only sample in a study looking at the relationship between frustration and aggression would likely not compromise ecological validity because you have little reason to believe that students react to frustration any differently from the general population. However, a study dependent on or measuring educational background, political affinities or career aspirations would most likely yield results that cannot be generalised because you can reasonably expect students to differ from the population in those respects (i.e., be politically less conservative than average and have higher education and higher career ambitions than the average, too).

> **REVIEW & REFLECT**
>
> - Why do you need to discuss the limitations of your research? How might the reasons differ for a paper for publication and a student thesis?
> - Discussions often include a passage on the need for specific future research. To what part of the overall writing up of your research might this relate, and why?

## 12.7 REFERENCES

There are two main rules for the references: know the rules, apply the rules consistently and – okay, there are three main rules for references: (1) know the rules, (2) apply the rules consistently and (3) make sure that in-text citations and references match.

**Know the rules:** Most likely you will know which set of formatting rules you are expected to follow, whether they are discipline- or subject-specific, your institution's house rules or a mixture of both. If you do not know yet, ask; if you are not given any guidance, pick one set and apply it consistently. This brings us to the second rule.

**Apply the rules consistently:** Formatting rules vary from subject to subject, and often from journal to journal. Even if you are not fully sure whether you are using the right set of guidelines, pick one and stick with it: a reference list formatted consistently throughout with the wrong set of rules still looks better than a reference list where individual items have been copied and pasted from a range of different sources and no two list entries look alike.

**Make sure that in-text citations and references match:** If you mention a source in the text, you need to have a matching reference in the reference list. And vice versa: For every item in the reference list, there should be at list one citation in your main text.

## 12.8 APPENDIX

The appendix contains all the information that is useful and relevant for your study but is too long or too detailed to be included in the main text, including but not limited to:

- Copies of the material you used such as participant information sheets, instructions, debriefing sheets and any material you developed yourself. You can include copies of existing questionnaires if they are short and easily included; otherwise a reference to the full version is sufficient.
- Any output from software packages showing the results of your statistical analyses. When working results out by hand, you need to include a sheet which – either typed or in tidy handwriting – shows your work so other people can follow and check your calculations.
- A copy of the letter giving you ethics approval.

While chapters are usually numbered (Chapters 1, 2, 3 and so on) appendices are usually titled by letters: Appendix A is followed by Appendix B is followed by Appendix C. They are titled in order of appearance in the text so that whatever is first mentioned in the text is found in Appendix A, the next one is Appendix B, and so on.

The APA *Publication Manual* (2010, p. 39) covers the online storage of supplementary material and suggests that it may be suitable for:

- Lengthy computer code
- Details of mathematical or computational models
- Audio or video clips
- Oversized tables
- Detailed intervention protocols
- Primary or supplementary data sets
- Expanded methodology sections
- Colour figures

None of these are likely to be an option for module assignments, Bachelor's or even Master's dissertations, although you may be asked to provide a USB-stick or CD with relevant documents. So if you do plan on using any of the above, do make sure to check first in which form you may be asked (and allowed) to provide documentation.

## 12.9 INTRODUCTION

Now that you have written most of your report or thesis, you should be in a much better position to write your introduction. Requirements for introductions vary. In some cases, an introduction is a lengthy part of the whole work and includes the literature review; in other cases, it is a separate section between the abstract and the literature review. Regardless of its location, the introduction serves to briefly outline why your research is important and how your writing work will be structured. It is for those latter cases where the counterintuitive approach of writing the introduction last really helps because at this point you have already written most of your work and you can let your introduction be guided by the existing structure of the work rather than the other way around.

## 12.10 TITLE

Why should the title come this late? Should that not be the first thing you should have decided on, even before you started your data collection? Well, no. You should have decided on your *research question*, which of course will be your provisional title – but research question and title are two different things, not only because a title can hint at or disclose your main finding. Investigating the effect of employee appraisals on employee satisfaction is a research question; 'Performance appraisal and employee outcomes: Mediating and moderating roles of work motivation' (Kuvaas, 2006) is one of the possible titles describing the outcome of a study which found work motivation to be a mediating and moderating variable. 'Examining memory beliefs' may be a research question, but 'Womb with a view: Memory beliefs and memory-work experiences', the title given by Garry et al. to their 1997 paper, is interesting, smart and funny (the title is a play on the researchers' observation that some participants seemed to remember experiences from before they were born). That said, you can be playful with your title, but you do not have to. Often the title is the very first thing other researchers will see of your research; therefore, the title has to be informative enough for them to decide whether it is worth reading the abstract for more information.

## 12.11 ABSTRACT

At last, the abstract. Two-hundred to 250 words to summarise the entirety of your research, often a daunting task! This is not made easier by knowing that both abstract and title are particularly outward-focussed – they are the primary source for other researchers or interested readers to decide whether your work is relevant to their interests and worthwhile reading. Perhaps you have already been through the experience of trying to buy a paper from a journal or having to procure it through an inter-library loan, or perhaps you had to register with a site first before being allowed to access a paper … only to find that the paper was not relevant after all because it looked at different variables or the sample size was too small or it was a review paper on existing research rather than an empirical paper. Even if you can access most of the papers for free through your university library, spending time and effort on the 'wrong' papers can be a very frustrating experience. Try to save your fellow researchers from this by being as accurate and informative as possible. Focus on study design, sample and findings.

- **Study design:** What variables did you examine? Did you conduct an experiment/quasi-experiment/correlational study? What was the design (e.g., 2 × 4 × 2, etc.)? Describe the main conditions and summarise any manipulations.
- **Sample:** What was the (rough) composition of your sample? Describe sample size and main demographic characteristics so the reader knows whether participants were mostly students or recruited to specific parameters.
- **Findings:** What were your hypotheses and what effects (if any) did you find? If you still have word count left, what are the implications of your research? If your research contradicts existing research, this is particularly noteworthy.

## REVIEW & REFLECT

- Why does it make sense to write the abstract last?
- How do you decide what is important enough to be in the abstract?

## RESEARCH METHODS AT WORK

Edith works in the HR department of a large education provider which offers online learning courses across the public sector. Recently the organisation has asked its students to fill out a student satisfaction survey, and Edith has been tasked with analysing and writing up the results. Since this is a business research report, for the introduction Edith describes the demographics of the current students and the current national regulatory and political context of education but does not discuss any academic literature or findings. In the results and discussion she focusses on recommendations for specific, practical measures the organisation can take now to improve the experience for students. Lastly, Edith makes sure to emphasise that these recommendations are based on the assumption that the regulatory context will remain largely the same and that recommendations will have to be reviewed should the situation change.

---

Charlie is writing up his Bachelor's thesis for which he conducted a large online survey on attitudes towards hybrid and electric cars among his student peers. Because the survey had so many questions, Charlie decides to summarise only the main variables' descriptives and supply the detailed descriptives on a number of other variables in the appendix. Charlie also provides a link to a copy of the questionnaire so readers can have a close look at the whole instrument. Although with 250 participants the final sample was quite large for a Bachelor's thesis, Charlie notes in the limitations sections that the sample consisted only of student peers. University students tend to be more educated and more affluent than average, and both factors may have skewed this sample's views.

## A SHORT SUMMARY

- Your write-up needs to tell one coherent story; the individual sections need to be linked. Make sure that your results and discussion answer the research question outlined in the introduction and literature review.
- The title gives a concise summary of your research findings.
- The abstract summarises methods, findings and discussion.
- The introduction explains why your research is important.
- The literature review outlines what is already known, how your research contributes to existing research (rationale) and what you expect to find (hypotheses).
- The methods section describes the nuts and bolts of your empirical research – what did you do and why – including your sample (participant section), your method (procedure and design section), and whatever you did with the data before you ran your descriptive and inferential statistics (data analysis).
- The results section *describes* your findings, including any assumption testing and post-hoc tests.
- The discussion section *interprets* your findings and relates them to your hypotheses. It puts your findings into the context of existing research and discusses any potential shortcomings (limitations). Be critical, but not overly so.

## ONLINE CONTENT

You can find a write-up checklist on the companion website.

### CHECK YOUR UNDERSTANDING

1. Number the elements so that they appear in the correct order.
   [ _____ ] Brief summary of main variables, methodology, findings and implications (max 250 words)
   [ _____ ] Detailed explanation of procedure
   [ _____ ] Copy of any testing material used
   [ _____ ] Description of recoded variables and data sets identified as outliers
   [ _____ ] Descriptives for main variables
   [ _____ ] Detailed description of sample
   [ _____ ] Discussion of potential improvements in the methodology
   [ _____ ] Outline of gap in research
   [ _____ ] Discussion to what extent results can be generalised outside the sample
   [ _____ ] Discussion to what extent results confirm hypotheses or not
   [ _____ ] Expectations towards result
   [ _____ ] Detailed description of materials used
   [ _____ ] Explanation why topic is important
   [ _____ ] Outline of existing research
   [ _____ ] References
   [ _____ ] SPSS output or manual working out of detailed statistical analyses
   [ _____ ] Statistical tests and analyses to confirm or reject hypotheses
   [ _____ ] Suggestion of potential future research
   [ _____ ] Discussion how current results fit with existing research
   [ _____ ] Very brief summary of main finding (max 20 words)

2. Note for each statement whether it is true or false, and why.
   a. In the literature review you need to provide a short summary of each paper you cite. (T/F)
   b. Appendices are numbered, beginning with 1. (T/F)
   c. A rationale can either be included as a separate section or integrated into the overall literature review. (T/F)
   d. You do not need hypotheses if you conduct exploratory research. (T/F)
   e. You always need to provide hypothesis **and** null hypothesis. (T/F)
   f. In your data analysis section, you mention whether you identified any data sets as outliers. (T/F)
   g. It is easier to write your abstract and introduction before you write your methodology. (T/F)
   h. You do not have to critically evaluate every individual reference you use. (T/F)
   i. Your statistical tests need to match your hypotheses. (T/F)
   j. You can be brief in describing your methods – if other researchers have any questions, they can always email you. (T/F)

# Appendix 1 - Standard Error of Skewness for Small Sample Sizes

This table contains values for the Standard Error of Skewness for sample sizes up to N = 20. Values have been calculated after the following formula and then rounded to three decimal places:

$$SES = \sqrt{\frac{6n(n-1)}{(n-2)(n+1)(n+3)}}$$

| N | Standard Error of Skewness |
| --- | --- |
| 1 | – |
| 2 | – |
| 3 | 1.225 |
| 4 | 1.014 |
| 5 | 0.913 |
| 6 | 0.845 |
| 7 | 0.794 |
| 8 | 0.752 |
| 9 | 0.717 |
| 10 | 0.687 |
| 11 | 0.661 |
| 12 | 0.637 |
| 13 | 0.616 |
| 14 | 0.597 |
| 15 | 0.580 |
| 16 | 0.564 |
| 17 | 0.550 |
| 18 | 0.536 |
| 19 | 0.524 |
| 20 | 0.512 |

For larger samples, you can use the standard equation: $SES = \sqrt{\frac{6}{n}}$

# Appendix 2 - Critical Values for Wilcoxon Signed Rank test

|     | 2-tailed test |              | 1-tailed test |              |
| --- | --- | --- | --- | --- |
| N   | For $\alpha = .05$ | For $\alpha = .01$ | For $\alpha = .05$ | For $\alpha = .01$ |
| 6   | –   | –   | 2   | –   |
| 7   | 2   | –   | 3   | –   |
| 8   | 3   | –   | 5   | 1   |
| 9   | 5   | 1   | 8   | 3   |
| 10  | 8   | 3   | 10  | 5   |
| 11  | 10  | 5   | 13  | 7   |
| 12  | 13  | 7   | 17  | 9   |
| 13  | 17  | 9   | 21  | 12  |
| 14  | 21  | 12  | 25  | 15  |
| 15  | 25  | 15  | 30  | 19  |
| 15  | 29  | 19  | 35  | 23  |
| 17  | 34  | 23  | 41  | 27  |
| 18  | 40  | 27  | 47  | 32  |
| 19  | 46  | 32  | 53  | 37  |
| 20  | 52  | 37  | 60  | 43  |
| 21  | 58  | 42  | 67  | 49  |
| 22  | 65  | 48  | 75  | 55  |
| 23  | 73  | 54  | 83  | 62  |
| 24  | 81  | 61  | 91  | 69  |
| 25  | 89  | 68  | 100 | 76  |

N here refers to the number of ranks not overall values. Values for which the difference to the compared value is 0 (and therefore no rank assigned), do not count for the purpose of identifying the critical value.

# Exercise Solutions

*Note:* Unless otherwise specified, all numerical values are rounded to three decimal points.

## CHAPTER 1

1. When might it make sense to repeat a study that has already been conducted? For example, when political or social circumstances change, either over time or suddenly through the course of an event; the researcher believes a variable has been neglected or the wrong measurement used; a researcher believes a confound has not been taken into account.
2. Are some areas of research more likely to benefit from replicating studies than others? Why or why not? Areas of research where circumstances change quickly (e.g., medical research, political attitudes); areas that are likely to have been subject to bias.
3. Assume that you want to find out why people still use their mobile phones while driving and how their usage of phones might affect their driving. List at least eight different research questions that could help shed light on this issue:
   There are many possible questions, here are just a few:
   a. What reasons for using their mobile phones do drivers self-report?
   b. Is there a difference in personality traits between people who use their phones while driving and those who don't?
   c. Is extraversion linked to mobile phone use while driving?
   d. How accurately do drivers perceive their own driving skills while using their phone?
   e. Do drivers who use their mobile phone make more mistakes than drivers who don't?
   f. Are all types of mobile phone usage equally dangerous for driving?
   g. How is talking on the phone while driving different from talking to a passenger in the car?
   h. Which personality traits predict phone usage?
4. Now work through as many questions in Exercise 3 as you think are necessary:
   a. What would an answer to this question look like?
   b. Does it indicate which type of data analysis is likely needed?
   c. Does it indicate which variables need to be examined?
   d. Does it contribute usefully to existing research? For this exercise, the fourth criterion can be relaxed not to require extensive literature research. Which theoretical concepts you can usefully discuss in the context of your question(s)?
5. Of your eight questions in Exercise 3, which (if any) are suitable for quantitative research and why?

# CHAPTER 2

1. For each of the following information, list an option to perform measurements in continuous or discrete form (one example is given):

   |                      | Discrete                                                                                  | Continuous                                                           |
   |----------------------|-------------------------------------------------------------------------------------------|----------------------------------------------------------------------|
   | Reaction time        | <200<br>201–300<br>301–400<br>>400ms                                                      | In ms as measured                                                    |
   | Temperature          | Below –10°<br>Between –10° and 0°<br>Between 1° and 10°<br>Between 11° and 20°<br>Higher than 20° | In degrees Celsius                                                   |
   | Literacy             | Very high<br>Moderately high<br>Average<br>Below average<br>Very low                      | Reading time                                                         |
   | Socioeconomic status | Upper class<br>Working class<br>Middle class<br>Lower class                               | Monthly/Annual income                                                |
   | Risk aversion        | Willingness to take risk as answer to a Yes/No question                                   | Amount of money participant is willing to risk in a gamble/bet       |
   | Willingness to donate| Yes<br>No<br>Maybe                                                                        | In currency units (e.g., dollars, Great British pounds, euros)       |

2. Looking at the following topics, describe how you might phrase and examine research questions in terms of associations, differences or effects:
   a. Type of information provided and compliance with medication regimen
      **Association**: To what extent do amount of information and duration of compliance correlate?
      **Difference**: Do participants provided with more detailed information show more compliance than participants who were not?
      **Effect**: Is there an effect of information on extent of compliance?
   b. Educational background and reading skill
      **Association**: Are reading skill and educational background independent of each other?
      **Difference**: Is there a difference in reading skills between people with higher and lower educational background?
      **Effect**: What is the effect of educational background on reading skill?
   c. Product scarcity and perceived product value
      **Association**: To what extent does perceived product value vary with product scarcity?
      **Difference**: Do consumers perceive scarce products to be more valuable than non-scarce products?
      **Effect**: What is the effect of scarcity on perceived product value?

d. Socioeconomic status and political affiliation
**Association**: Are classes of socioeconomic status associated with political affiliation?
**Difference**: Are people of lower socioeconomic status more conservative than people of higher socioeconomic status?
**Effect**: Is there an effect of socioeconomic status on political affiliation?

3. How would you describe the following study in the shorthand of the 'A by B' type: an examination of the relationship between 'product price', 'product scarcity' and 'intent to purchase', with the independent variables 'product price' (high/medium/low), 'product scarcity' (rare/common) and the dependent variable 'intent to purchase'? 3 × 2. How many unique conditions does this study have? 3 × 2 = 6 unique conditions.

4. If you want to compare willingness to donate between participants identifying as either liberal or conservative, would this be within-participants or between-participants? Would you refer to this as an experiment? Why or why not? Between-participants, because you can't have participants undergo both the 'liberal' and 'conservative' condition.

   Would you refer to this as an experiment? Why or why not? No. At the most it could be a quasi-experiment because participants are allocated to groups on the basis of political affiliation which cannot be manipulated by the experimenter.

5. For each of the following variables, determine whether this can be used as an independent variable:
   a. Age No
   b. Time allowed to complete a task Yes
   c. Importance of individual answer Yes
   d. Time pressure to complete a task Yes
   e. Life satisfaction No
   f. Familiarity with a task Yes
   g. Numeracy No

6. Note for each statement whether it is true or false, and why.
   a. Participants do not have to be told the purpose of a study before they participate. True if the study design requires it; they then will have to be informed during debriefing.
   b. Once participants have completed a questionnaire, they cannot withdraw from the study anymore. False. Participants can withdraw from the study at any time, without having to give any reason; this also means withdrawing their data (and thus their participation) afterwards.
   c. Participants have to sign a consent form before you can collect data. True.
   d. Participants have to explain their reasons if they want to withdraw participation in the middle of the study. False. Participants can unequivocally withdraw from the study at any time, without having to give any reason.
   e. It is always okay to coerce participants to do things as long as that is part of the research question. False. It depends on the kind of coercion and, even where coercion is appropriate, it can only be minimal.
   f. Debriefing is also a way of checking whether participants feel okay after participation and offering potential further sources of support. True.

7. Are the following hypotheses directional or non-directional?
   a. Depressed participants will report less exercise per week than non-depressed participants. Directional
   b. Contacting customers by email and text leads to different retention rates than contacting customers by email alone. Non-directional

c. There will be no significant difference in self-esteem between participants high or low in extraversion. Non-directional
d. There will be an association between age and musical preference. Non-directional
e. Participants who kept a diary are more likely to report a change in exercise habits than participants who did not. Directional

8. For each of the hypotheses listed in Exercise 7, state the null hypothesis.
   a. There is no difference in self-reported exercise between depressed and non-depressed participants.
   b. There is no difference in retention rates for customers who are contacted by email and customers who are contacted by email and text.
   c. There will be a difference in self-esteem between participants high or low in extraversion.
   d. There is no association between age and musical preference.
   e. There will be no difference in reported exercise habits between participants who kept a diary and participants who did not.

9. The following are all potential operationalisations of the abstract concept of hunger. To what extent do you think they adequately reflect the underlying concept, and why? There are no clear-cut answers to this. The following answers are possible considerations.
   a. Volume of rumbling stomach noise. A purely physiological measurement, but volume may also be affected by individual characteristics (e.g., size of participant, muscle density, fat density, etc.).
   b. Answer to the question 'On a scale from 1 to 10, how hungry are you right now?' Assumes that participants can accurately assess own level of hunger.
   c. Speed with which participant reaches for food offered. May be affected by individual differences in initiative, extraversion, willingness to appear greedy, worry to be rude, etc.
   d. Amount of money participant is willing to pay for food. May differ based on participants' financial background. May be more suitable in measuring participants' willingness to eat rather than be hungry.
   e. Combination of skin conductivity and heart rate measurements. Purely physiological measurement, but may primarily measure arousal rather than hunger.

10. Assume that you want to examine whether there is an association between numeracy and risk-taking in financial decisions. How could you operationalise numeracy:
    a. In a questionnaire setting: a questionnaire setting a range of numerical questions and calculating an overall numeracy score.
    b. In a lab-based study: a timed paper or computer questionnaire using both accuracy of answers as well as time used to complete questionnaire to calculate overall numeracy score.
    c. Relying only on secondary data: looking for data indicating numeracy, such as school grades in relevant subjects (mathematics, physics, etc.).
    Can you think of other possible operationalisations? What are their advantages and disadvantages?

# CHAPTER 3

1. You want to know whether the depiction of violence on TV can raise aggression levels in the short term. You could design your own experiment, for example, presenting either violent or non-violent TV clips to participants and then measuring aggression by examining behaviour in a co-operation task or a negotiation exercise. Alternatively you could use data collected by Tel-Stats, an organisation run and funded by ten major private broadcasters. Tel-Stats has recently published a report looking into the prevalence of crime on TV in relation to the crime rates developing over the past ten years, using data from over one million hours of television material. What are the advantages and disadvantages of using Tel-Stats data or developing your own study?
   **Advantages** (the list of advantages and disadvantages is by no means exhaustive): You would have access to a far larger data set than you could ever collect on your own. The data set would also allow you to look at the development of crime rates over time.
   **Disadvantages**: Using Tel-Stats data would mean you are conducting a correlational study, but not an experiment since you would not be actively manipulating any variables. Because Tel-Stats is funded and run by broadcasters, it could be argued that they have a vested interested in showing that violence on TV *does not* affect aggression. You would have only limited opportunities to detect and mitigate possible bias in data collection and analysis.

2. Using the Excel tool on the companion website, calculate the required sample size for a study with the following parameters:
   a. Population size 800, alpha level 5%, margin of error 5%. 260
   b. Population size 430,000, alpha level 1%, margin of error 2%. 4120
   c. Population size 60,000, alpha level .5%, margin of error 5%. 382

3. A local school has recently trialled a new anti-bullying scheme. This consisted of mandatory training sessions for all pupils across all years and classes. The school now wants to find out whether and to what extent pupils' attitudes towards bullying have changed. You want to survey a sample of 100 out of the 1500 pupils. Identify the sampling techniques listed below:
   a. You position yourself at the entrance of the cafeteria at 12:30 and approach every tenth pupil. Systematic sampling
   b. You have a numbered list with the names of all 1500 pupils. You use a random number generator to generate random numbers between 1 and 1500 and pick the student listed at that position on the list. Simple random sampling
   c. You have a numbered list with the names of all 1500 pupils. You generate a random number between 1 and 15. Starting with the pupil listed at that position on the list, you then pick every 15th pupil. Systematic sampling
   d. You send around an email to all pupils asking them to fill out an online questionnaire at a link given in the email. Opportunity sampling/accidental sampling
   e. You are given a list with class cohorts. From that list you establish that there are 30 class cohorts in the school. You randomly pick 20 classes from the list and subsequently randomly pick five students per class. Cluster sampling
   f. You think that bullying might be perceived differently by pupils of different ages. You consider age a relevant variable to the study and thus want to re-create the distribution of age across the school in your sample. You establish that 40% of the pupils are aged 14 or under, 40% between 15 and 16, and 20% are aged 17 and above. When approaching pupils, you recruit as many pupils as you need until your sample consists of 40 pupils aged 14 or under, 40 pupils aged between 15 and 16, and 20 pupils aged 17 or older. Stratified sampling

g. You are particularly interested in comparing male versus female pupils' views on the anti-bullying campaign. You are approaching students identifying as one of either gender until your sample consists of exactly 50% male- and 50% female-identifying students. Quota sampling

4. (Content Note: Weight loss.) You are interested in people's weight loss successes and failures. You want to know which diets people may have attempted in the past and how effective they were. How could you phrase related questions in each of the formats listed below, and what would the data look like?
    a. Open-ended. Please list which diets have you attempted in the past:
    b. Multiple choice. Which of the following diets have you attempted in the past? Tick each that apply.
    c. Rank order. Please rank the following diets in order of most effective to least effective.
    d. Semantic differential. For each diet, please indicate how you felt about it:
       Dieting was easy. ←-----------------→ Dieting was difficult.
       I felt encouraged. ←-----------------→ I felt discouraged.
       The diet was effective. ←-----------------→ The diet was ineffective.
    e. Sentence completion. The most effective diet I tried was _____. The least effective diet I tried was _____.

5. How many pairwise comparisons would you need for 7 items?
$$\frac{7 \times 6}{2} = \frac{42}{2} = 21$$

6. Design both a unipolar and a bipolar scale to ask participants how happy they are with their life at the moment.
    a. **Unipolar**: How happy are you with your life at the moment? 1 = Not at all happy, 2 = Only a bit happy, 3 = Moderately happy, 4 = A lot, 5 = Very happy
    b. **Bipolar**: How happy are you with your life at the moment? 1 = Very unhappy, 2 = Unhappy, 3 = Rather unhappy, 4 = Rather happy, 5 = Happy, 6 = Very happy

7. Look at your scales from Exercise 6. Are they symmetric or asymmetric?
   The unipolar scale is an example of an asymmetric scale; the bipolar scale is an example of a symmetric scale.

8. Consider the following set of response options to the question: 'What is your employment situation right now?' Unemployed/Employed (part-time)/Employed (full-time)/In full-time education.
    a. Why would this not be considered 'MECE'? The question conflates education and employment. A participant might be unemployed *and* in full-time education.
    b. What could you do to make the set of options mutually exclusive and comprehensively exhaustive? Split the question into two (or three) questions:
       '1. What is your employment situation right now? Unemployed/Employed (part-time)/Employed (full-time)
       2. Are you in education right now? Yes/No
       3. If yes, are you in part-time or full-time education? Part-time/Full-time'

9. For each of the following variables, note whether it is data on a ratio, interval, ordinal or nominal scale:
    a. Level of education: Nominal, possibly ordinal
    b. Products ranked by perceived quality: Ordinal
    c. Outside temperature: Ratio
    d. Satisfaction with service: Interval

e. Distance between home and workplace: Ratio
f. Agreement with a statement: Interval
g. Time per day spent at the computer: Ratio
h. Traits to describe self, ranked from most applicable to least applicable: Ordinal

10. How are the following questions biased and how could you change them to reduce bias?
    a. 'Do you agree that it is important to give to charity?' Potential social desirability bias; few people will disagree (publicly, at least). Bias could be (somewhat) reduced by rephrasing as asking 'How important do you think it is to give to charity?' or ask when and how much participant has recently donated.
    b. 'Many people oppose the recent cuts in benefits, saying that they hit the poorest most. Are you for or against benefit cuts?' This is a loaded question; the context provides potential endorsement of one option over the other. To reduce bias either only ask second question and/or present the first part as a separate statement to which participant can express degree of (dis-)agreement.
    c. 'How often do you ask your boss for his opinion?' This question expresses a gender bias because it assumes the boss identifies as male. Reduce bias by asking 'How often do you ask your boss for their opinion?'
    d. 'At what age did you start cheating in school exams?' This question implies that it's taken for granted the participant cheated in school exams. You could reduce bias by splitting into two questions: 'Did you cheat in school exams?' 'If so, when did you start?'
    e. To male participants, 'How would you describe your relationship with your partner? To what extent do you feel supported by her?' This question expresses bias towards heterosexual (and monogamous) relationships by assuming that there is only one partner of a male participant and that the partner is female. You can reduce bias by rephrasing this as 'To what extent do you feel supported by your (main) partner(s)?'
    f. 'With which character from Hollyoaks do you identify most?' This question expresses cultural bias by assuming that participants are familiar with the TV series Hollyoaks. You could reduce bias by splitting this up into two questions: 'Are you familiar with the TV series Hollyoaks?' 'If so, with which character do you identify most?'

11. You are conducting a 2 × 2 within-participants study. Your two independent variables are 'background noise' (absent/present) and 'task difficulty' (high/low). This gives you four different conditions:

    AH: Background noise absent, high difficulty

    AL: Background noise absent, low difficulty

    PH: Background noise present, high difficulty

    PL: Background noise present, low difficulty

    Create a Latin Square which gives you four different sequences in which participants can experience all four conditions. There are many different solutions to this. We are presenting one possible solution here. Remember, Latin Squares work like sudoku puzzles. If your solution would pass as the sudoku test with no repeats within columns or rows, it is probably a correct solution.

    | AH | AL | PH | PL |
    | --- | --- | --- | --- |
    | PL | AH | AL | PH |
    | PH | PL | AH | AL |
    | AL | PH | PL | AH |

# CHAPTER 4

1. Decide for every statement whether it is true or false:
   a. $X < X+1$     T
   b. $X > X+1$     F: X cannot be greater than X+1.
   c. $7 \leq 5$     F: 7 is greater than 5, not equal to or smaller.
   d. $.05 \leq .05$     T
   e. $.01 \leq .05$     T
   f. $.03 \geq .001$     T
   g. $.2 \leq .05$     F: 0.2 is greater than, not equal to or smaller than .05.
   h. $5 \geq 4$     T
   i. $5 \leq 7$     T

2. Express the following statements using the correct greater than/less than sign:
   a. 3 is smaller than 5               $3 < 5$
   b. .001 is smaller than or equal to .01     $.001 \leq .01$
   c. X is larger than X-1            $X > X-1$
   d. .04 is smaller than .4          $.04 < .4$

3. Calculate the following percentages:
   a. 15 of 58           = 25.86%
   b. 34 of 200         = 17%
   c. 3000 of 23,481    = 12.78%
   d. 17 of 100         = 17%
   e. 5% of 17          = 0.85
   f. 50% of 170       = 85
   g. 150% of 20       = 30

4. Give the results for taking off ten percent points from the results of 3a-d:
   a. = 15.86%
   b. = 7%
   c. = 2.78%
   d. = 7%

5. Move the decimal point in 9.34281 four places to the right. 93,428.1
6. Move the decimal point in 0.0342 six places to the left. 0.0000000342 (that's seven zeroes after the decimal point)
7. Multiply .009 by 1000. $.009 \times 1,000 = 9$
8. Divide 1,202,094 by 10,000. $\frac{1,202,094}{10,000} = 120.2094$
9. Round the following numbers to the second decimal place:
   a. 2.874          2.87
   b. 35.988        35.99
   c. 9.809348     9.81
   d. 234.54        234.54
   e. 98.870        98.87
10. Round the following numbers to the third decimal place:
    a. .0094         .009
    b. .8721         .872
    c. 1.8379       1.838
    d. .0121         .012
    e. 1.2098       1.210

11. In the fraction $\frac{17}{18}$, which is the numerator and which is the denominator? 17 is the numerator, 18 is the denominator.
12. In a group of 20 consumers, there are 15 non-smokers and 5 smokers. Express this as a ratio of
    a. Smokers to non-smokers 5 to 15
    b. Non-smokers to smokers 15 to 5
13. Express the statements below in the form of 'Of ____ treatments, ____ succeed and ____ fail.'
    a. 'This treatment has a 1 in 5 success rate.' Of five treatments, one succeeds and four fail.
    b. 'This treatment has a 1 to 5 success ratio.' Of six treatments, one succeeds and five fail.
14. Perform the calculations expressed in the formulas below based on the following set of values: 10, 12, 20, 15, 22, 25
    a. $\sum X = 10 + 12 + 20 + 15 + 22 + 25 = 104$
    b. $\sum (X - 5)$
       $=(10-5)+(12-5)+(20-5)+(15-5)+(22-5)+(25-5)=5+7+15+10+17+20=74$.
    c. $\sum X^2 = 10^2 + 12^2 + 20^2 + 15^2 + 22^2 + 25^2 = 100 + 144 + 400 + 225 + 484 + 625 = 1978$
    d. $(\sum X)^2 = (10 + 12 + 20 + 15 + 22 + 25)^2 = 104^2 = 10816$
15. What is the range for the following sets of values (note that the sets are not ordered)?
    a. 5, 10, 12, 16, 20, 22, 20, 20. Highest value = 22, lowest value = 5. Range = 22 − 5 = 17.
    b. 123, 155, 167, 188, 120, 125. Highest value = 188, lowest value = 120. Range = 188 − 120 = 68.
    c. 4, 6, 2, 5, 8, 4, 12, 16. Highest value = 16, lowest value = 2. Range = 16 − 2 = 14.
    d. 1.23, 1.45, 1.17, 1.18, 1.22, 2.01. Highest value = 2.01, lowest value = 1.17. Range = 2.01 − 1.17 = 0.84.
16. For the following set of values, first calculate the average, then the total of the absolute differences to the average: 12, 16, 24, 26, 28, 30, 32, 35, 40. Average =
    $\frac{12 + 16 + 242 + 256 + 28 + 30 + 32 + 35 + 40}{9} = \frac{243}{9} = 27$
    $|(12-27)|+|(16-27)|+|(24-27)|+|15|+|(26-27)|+|(28-27)|+|(30-27)|+$
    $|(32-27)|+(35-27)|+|(40-27)|=|15|+|11|+|3|+|1|+|1|+|3|+|5|+|8|+|13|=60$
17. Work out the results for the following equations:
    a. −3 −4 = −7
    b. (−3) × (−4) = 12
    c. 3 × (−4) = −12
    d. |7| + |−5| + |−12| = −10
18. Calculate the following exponential expressions. First express them as a fraction, then work out the result. The solution for the first item is provided:
    a. $3^{-7}$    $3^{-7} = \frac{1}{3 \times 3 \times 3 \times 3 \times 3 \times 3 \times 3} = \frac{1}{2187} = 0.000457247$
    b. $2^6$    $2^6 = 2 \times 2 \times 2 \times 2 \times 2 \times 2 = 64$
    c. $4^{-3}$    $4^{-3} = \frac{1}{4 \times 4 \times 4} = \frac{1}{64} = 0.015625$

d. $13^{-2}$     $13^{-2} = \dfrac{1}{13 \times 13} = \dfrac{1}{169} = 0.005917159$

e. $980^2$     $980^2 = 980 \times 980 = 960400$

f. $(1.5)^{-2}$     $1.5^{-2} = \dfrac{1}{1.5 \times 1.5} = \dfrac{1}{2.25} = 0.444$

g. $(0.6)^2$     $0.6^2 = 0.6 \times 0.6 = 0.36$

h. $(0.06)^2 =$     $0.06^2 = 0.06 \times 0.06 = 0.0036$

19. Work out the results for the following exponential expressions:
    a. $1.2398E\text{-}04$     $0.00012398$
    b. $9.82E07$     $98200000$
    c. $1.09385E\text{-}08$     $0.0000000109385$
    d. $5.342342E06$     $5342342$

20. Express the following numbers in scientific notation:
    a. 2,983,000     $2.983E06$
    b. 4398     $4.398E03$
    c. .0000456     $4.56E{-}05$
    d. .0000000384     $3.84E{-}08$
    e. 983,349,923,982     $9.83349923982E11$
    f. 1500     $1.5E03$
    g. .0034928736     $3.4928736E{-}03$

21. Express the square of the following numbers as a product, then calculate the result. The first solution has been provided for you:
    a. $25^2$     $= 25 \times 25 = 625$
    b. $17^2$     $= 17 \times 17 = 289$
    c. $(-45)^3$     $= (-45) \times (-45) \times (-45) = -91{,}125$
    d. $9^3$     $= 9 \times 9 \times 9 = 729$
    e. $.5^4$     $= (.5) \times (.5) \times (.5) \times (.5) = 0.0625$
    f. $(-14)^2$     $= (-14) \times (-14) = 196$
    g. $(-2.3)^2$     $= (-2.3) \times (-2.3) = 5.29$

22. Calculate the result of the following expression: $\sqrt{70} \times \sqrt{70} = 70$

23. Assume that you are taking a multiple choice test on a topic you do not know anything about. There are four questions, each with three answer options. What are your overall chances to get a perfect score if you guessed the answer for every single question?

    $\dfrac{1}{3} \times \dfrac{1}{3} \times \dfrac{1}{3} \times \dfrac{1}{3} = \dfrac{1}{81} = .012 = 1.2\%$

24. You and your colleagues are drawing straws to determine who is to work on the boring task you all dislike. You are in a group of 7 people in total, and there are six long straws and one short one. What is your chance to draw a short straw if it is your turn after two people already drew a long straw? At that point there are four long straws left and one short one. Your chance is one out of five, or one-fifth.

## CHAPTER 5

1. We have outlined a simple study design below. Read through the description and then answer the following questions:
   a. How you would enter this data into Excel?
   b. Suggest a suitable name for each of these variables.
   c. Which data should be split off into a separate look-up file?
   
   This study uses a survey to examine to what extent agreement to ten statements regarding crime and sentencing is associated with a range of demographic criteria. Agreement is elicited on a six-point bipolar scale ranging from 'disagree absolutely' to 'agree absolutely'; the survey also asks about age, gender identity, household income, political affiliation. Participants are asked whether they would like to receive a summary of the study's results; those who are interested are asked to give their email address.
   
   a. 'Agreement' in *number* format, with values from 1 to 6; 'age' and 'household income' similarly in *number* format. 'Gender identity' and 'political affiliation' depending on how they've been collected in the survey. If in free-text form, then store in Excel in *general* format as a free-text field; possibly recode into values denoting specific terms once a list of all terms used in the responses has been compiled. If already collected through a pick list, then store a single value in the Excel cell. 'Interested in summary report' as a yes/no response; 'email address' in a *general* format field.
   b. *Agreement*, *age*, *h_income*/*household_income*, *gender_identity*/gender_id, *affiliation*, *interest*, *email*.
   c. The most important thing is to store the email address separately. If you want to make sure, you can store household income and gender identity in a third file, again only linked through the participant ID.

2. For each of these statements, indicate whether they are true or false:
   1. In SPSS, variable names can contain any elements and symbols. False: Spaces and some symbols are not permitted.
   2. In Excel, all data has to be entered through the data entry bar. False: You can also enter straight into the cell although it will appear in the data entry bar at the same time.
   3. In SPSS, variable names and variable labels are the same. False.
   4. In Excel, functions can only be entered through the Formula Builder. False: You can enter functions straight into the cell.
   5. SPSS can be used for qualitative analysis. True, but with limitations.
   6. SPSS splits data analysis into three files: data, output and syntax. True.
   7. In Excel, a document always consists of one worksheet. False: A document can consist of several worksheets.

3. We have provided an excerpt of a raw data file for a study described below.
   
   www You will find this Excel file on the companion website.
   
   Imagine that you have entered the data by hand. Examine the data to identify potential issues. For each of the potentially problematic values, describe
   a. why is it problematic and
   b. what you suggest doing with it.

*This study examined which effect the mode and length of an ad have on the perceived value of the product. The study therefore has a 2 x 2 design with two independent variables: 'length of presentation' (short, long) and 'presentation format' (visual, aural). The dependent variable is 'perceived value'. Each participant only experiences one condition. You collect additional demographic information from your participants in the form of gender identity, age in years, email address, and you track for each of your participants whether they would want to be contacted with information on the outcome of the study.*

| | |
|---|---|
| Age for participant ID 37 is blank | Several possible solutions. The age 37 below participant ID 61 suggests that age data may have been shifted one cell below by mistake. But it's unclear whether this is due to the missing age for participant 37, or whether that age is genuinely missing and the offset is due to a mistake with the age for participant 44 which should have been 23. This can't be rectified without going back to the original data and checking. |
| There is an otherwise empty row below the data for participant 61 | |
| Age for participant 44 has been entered as 2, age for participant 45 has been entered as 3 | |
| Age for participant 43 is entered as '$$' | Likely data entry error where shift key has been pressed by mistake. Could be corrected to 44. |
| Missing contact info for participant 39 | If in doubt, assume participant does not want to be contacted. |
| Entry 'Length' for the length of presentation condition for participant 57 | Most likely a data entry mistake with choosing the wrong autocomplete for the entry. Change to 'Long'. |
| Entry 'L' for the prime condition for participant 61 | Most likely a data entry mistake with the autocomplete for the entry. Change to 'Long'. |
| Entry 'V' for the prime condition for participant 57 | Most likely a data entry mistake with the autocomplete for the entry. Change to 'Visual'. |
| Very high value for participant 42 | Suggests data entry mistake, most likely 493 and 523 instead of 4935 and 23. However, needs to be checked against original data. If it cannot be confirmed, value needs to be deleted and cannot be use for these participants. |
| Very low value for participant 43 | |

# CHAPTER 6

1. A study collected data on job satisfaction, seniority and salary.

   The data is available in Excel and SPSS files on the companion website.

   Calculate mean, median and mode(s) each:

   |  | Job satisfaction | Seniority | Salary |
   |---|---|---|---|
   |  | 12 | 2 | 102,100 |
   |  | 99 | 3 | 45,000 |
   |  | 25 | 5 | 80,500 |
   |  | 84 | 4 | 26,400 |
   |  | 100 | 1 | 58,000 |
   |  | 50 | 2 | 750,000 |
   |  | 90 | 1 | 12,000 |
   |  | 22 | 5 | 18,100 |
   |  | 70 | 4 | 35,600 |
   |  | 22 | 1 | 43,000 |
   |  | 12 | 4 | 70,500 |
   |  | 14 | 4 | 64,800 |
   |  | 12 | 2 | 12,500 |
   |  | 88 | 4 | 130,000 |
   |  | 57 | 1 | 95,000 |
   |  | 76 | 2 | 63,000 |
   |  | 45 | 5 | 27,000 |
   |  | 27 | 1 | 33,000 |
   |  | 80 | 4 | 55,000 |
   |  | 95 | 4 | 19,600 |
   | Mean | 54 | 2.95 | 87,055 |
   | Median | 53.5 | 3.5 | 50,000 |
   | Mode(s) | 12 | 4 | n/a |

2. Which measure of central tendency is best to describe each of the sets of values in Exercise 1, and why?
   a. Job satisfaction: Both median or mean could be argued here. Mode is not representative of the distribution. Mean and median are different, but there is no immediately obvious outlier.
   b. Seniority: (1, 2, 4, 5 but not 3) therefore it could be argued that mean and median represent a value that was not selected frequently (or indeed, at all). The mode might be a good choice here.
   c. Salary: There is no one most frequent value in this distribution so the mode is not suitable. The mean is skewed by one very high outlier, thus the median is the best choice.

3. Part of the product design process is determining the measurements and dimensions of the product that make the product usable by as large a part of the population as possible. Assume you want to determine the required dimensions for a chair and assume that you have the data (in terms of means and standard deviation) of what people have judged to be a comfortable sitting

height, and that the data is normally distributed. How many standard deviations from the mean would you need to consider if you wanted 95% or more of the population to be able to comfortably use the chair? For a normally distributed trait, values two standard deviations in either direction (i.e., above and below the mean) will cover 95.45% of the population (see Figure 6.12, page 176).

4. Download the sample data set for this exercise. In this study, participants were asked to provide a suggestion for the length of a sentence for assault; the cases described referred to either a defendant of the same gender as the participant or of a different gender. Defendants were also identified as either repeat offenders or first-time offenders. This is a 2 × 2 × 2 study with the factors gender of participant (identifies as male or female), gender of defendant (identified in the records as male or female), and whether defendant is a repeat offender (yes/no). Using either Excel or SPSS:
   a. Determine mean sentencing length across all records. 40.85
   b. Determine variance and overall standard deviation, keeping in mind that your data comes from a sample, not a population. Sample variance =48.117, sample standard deviation 6.397
   c. Find out how many modes the distribution has and what they are. The distribution has only one mode, 47.
   d. How many participants suggested sentences of more than 40 months? 93
   e. Establish average sentence lengths for all eight conditions.

|          |                      |               | Participant          |                    |
|----------|----------------------|---------------|----------------------|--------------------|
|          |                      | First offense? | Identifies as female | Identifies as male |
| Offender | Identifies as female | Yes           | 48.12                | 44.26              |
|          |                      | No            | 37.50                | 33.39              |
|          | Identifies as male   | Yes           | 45.84                | 48.58              |
|          |                      | No            | 34.86                | 35.83              |

5. The following list of values represents the self-esteem scores taken from a participant sample of 20.

| 12 |
|----|
| 8  |
| 9  |
| 10 |
| 12 |
| 8  |
| 9  |
| 10 |
| 12 |
| 4  |
| 9  |
| 10 |
| 3  |
| 6  |
| 5  |
| 7  |
| 4  |
| 6  |
| 9  |
| 7  |

318    *Exercise Solutions*

   a. Calculate variance and standard deviation for this variable.
      Variance = 7.368, SD = 2.714
   b. Now assume this is not a sample, but a population. Calculate variance and standard deviation with the appropriate formulas.
      Variance = 7.000, SD = 2.646

6. If you are looking at a normal distribution, what percentage of values fall in the area two standard deviations above and below the mean? 95.45%

7. If a distribution skews to the right, does it display a positive or negative skew? Right-skewing distribution displays positive skew.

8. Calculate z-scores for the following values:
   a. 8.5 (for a distribution with a mean of 60 and a SD of 8) −6.4375
   b. 8.5 (for a distribution with a mean of 50 and a SD of 10) −4.15
   c. 145 (for a distribution with a mean of 100 and a SD of 15) 3

9. Assume that you are given the following z-scores and know that they're coming from a distribution with a mean of 80, SD = 12. Calculate the original score.
   a. z-score = 1.5     98
   b. z-score = .8      89.6
   c. z-score = .03     80.36

10. What type of error are you committing if you falsely reject the null hypothesis? Type 1 error.

11. What happens if you reduce the probability of falsely rejecting the null hypothesis? You increase the probability of committing a Type 2 error.

12. You are comparing neuroticism scores between participants raised as single children (N=39) and participants raised with siblings (N=42). The mean score for neuroticism for participants who were an only child is 14.5 (SD = 3.25), while for participants who had siblings the mean is 13.8 (SD = 3.5). Calculate the effect size (your choice whether with regular SD or pooled SD).

With regular SD = $\frac{14.5 - 13.8}{3.25} = .215$

With pooled SD: Pooled standard deviation =

$\sqrt{\frac{(39-1)3.25^2 + (42-1)3.5^2}{39+42-2}} = 3.382$. Effect size = $\frac{14.5 - 13.8}{3.382} = .207$

# CHAPTER 7

1. You want to test the impact of scarcity and price on intent to purchase. Your study is a 2 × 2 between-participants study with two independent variables: 'price' (high or low) and 'scarcity' (abundant or rare). Participants are given information on a product and told it is either rare or easily available; half of them are given a high price for the product, and half of them are given a low price. The dependent variable is 'intent to purchase', measured on a scale from 1 to 20. The table presents average values of 'intent to purchase' (Table 7.12):

    Table 7.12 *Intent to purchase*

    |  | Scarcity |  |
    |---|---|---|
    |  | Available | Rare |
    | Price: High | 15 | 13 |
    | Price: Low | 18 | 15 |

    a. Describe the results verbally.
    Participants who were told that the product was available tended to rate intent to purchase higher than participants who were told that the product was rare. When participants were told that the product was easily available, intent to purchase was rated at an average 15 for the high price condition and 18 for the low price condition; when participants were told the product was scarce, average intent to purchase was rated as 13 in the high price condition and 15 in the low price condition.
    b. Visualise them with a chart.

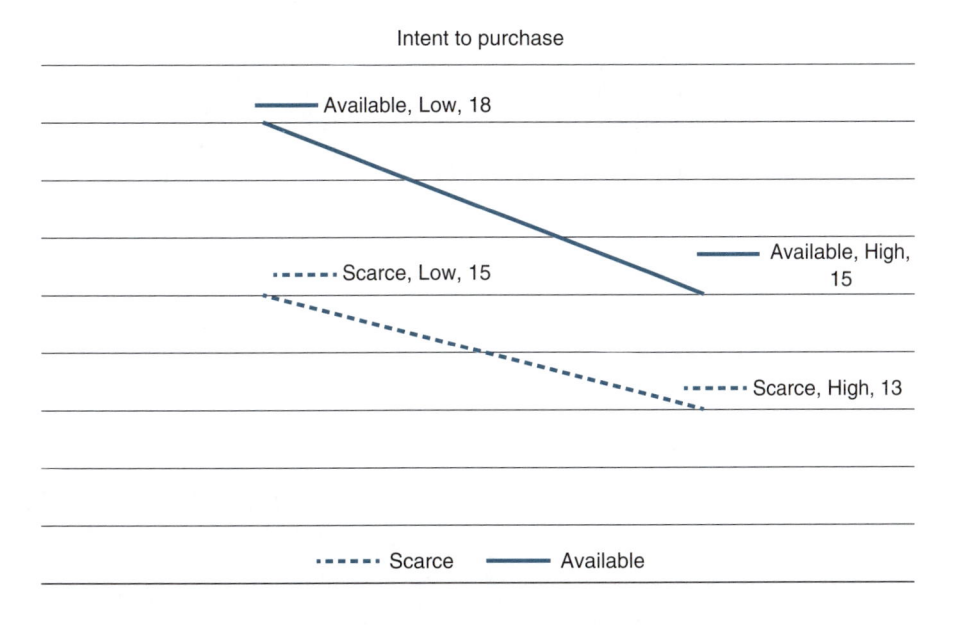

    Intent to purchase

    - Available, Low, 18
    - Scarce, Low, 15
    - Available, High, 15
    - Scarce, High, 13

    ····· Scarce ——— Available

2. Read the narrative description of this study's results:
   'Prior to the intervention, 19.5% of employees indicated that they never exercised; 50.3% said they exercised occasionally; and only 30.2% said they exercised regularly. Six months

after introducing a points-based incentive system, 15.4% still indicated that they never exercised, while 44.6% reported that they exercised occasionally, and 40% now said they exercised regularly.

a. Present these results in a table.

|  | Exercise frequency (in %) | | |
|---|---|---|---|
|  | 'Never' | 'Occasionally' | 'Frequently' |
| Before the intervention | 19.5 | 50.3 | 30.2 |
| After the intervention | 15.4 | 44.6 | 40 |

b. Visualise them with a chart.

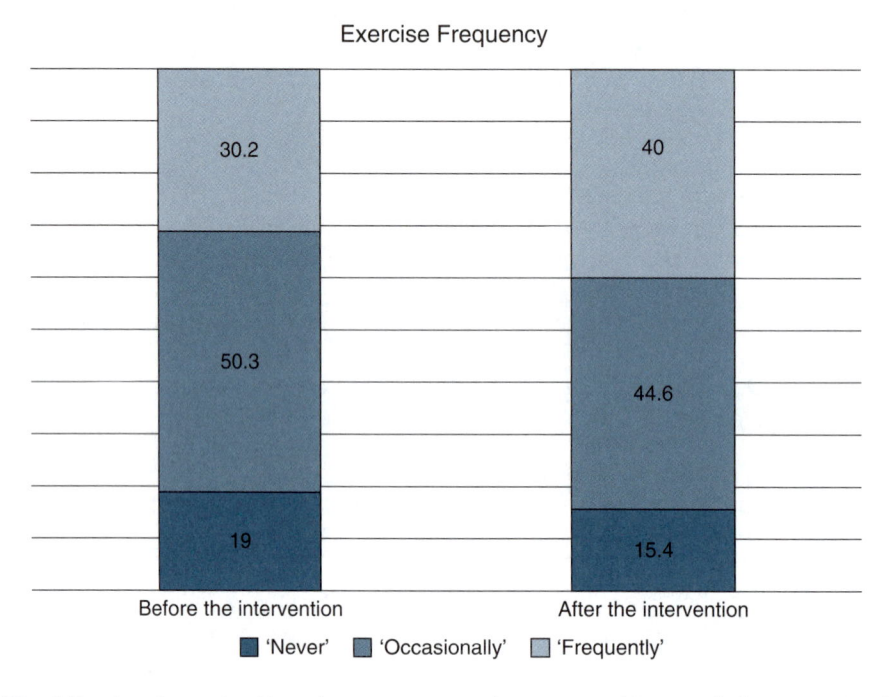

**Exercise Frequency**

| Before the intervention | After the intervention |
|---|---|
| Frequently: 30.2 | Frequently: 40 |
| Occasionally: 50.3 | Occasionally: 44.6 |
| Never: 19 | Never: 15.4 |

■ 'Never'  ■ 'Occasionally'  ☐ 'Frequently'

3. The following chart visualises the responses to the question 'On a scale from 1 to 7, where 1 = Strongly agree and 7 = Strongly disagree, how much do you agree with the statement "On the whole, I'm in control of my own life."?'

**Answers to Question 1: 'In control of my own life'**

| 1 | 2 | 3 | 4 | 5 | 6 | 7 |
|---|---|---|---|---|---|---|
| 14 | 17 | 24 | 45 | 49 | 35 | 27 |

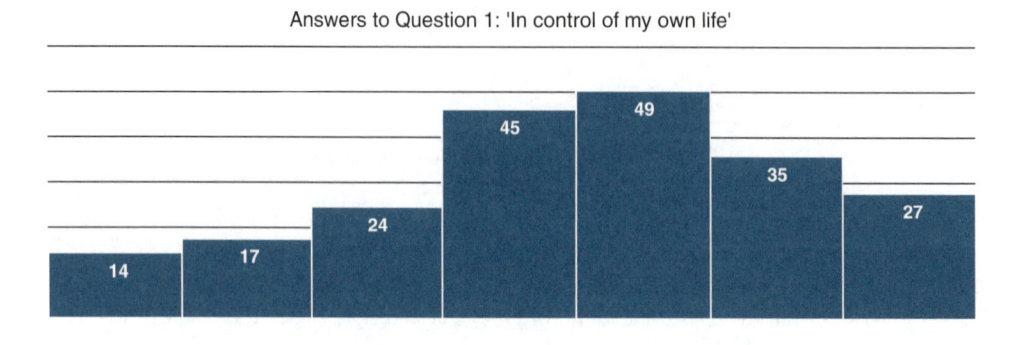

a. Present these results in a table.

|  | Value | Frequency of response |
|---|---|---|
|  | 1 | 14 |
|  | 2 | 17 |
|  | 3 | 24 |
|  | 4 | 45 |
|  | 5 | 49 |
|  | 6 | 35 |
|  | 7 | 27 |
| **Total** |  | **211** |

b. Present these results in a narrative description.
Fourteen participants responded that they strongly agreed with the statement "On the whole, I'm in control of my own life". Seventeen participants indicated they mostly agreed, and 24 participants agreed somewhat. Forty-five participants neither agreed nor disagreed. Forty-nine participants somewhat disagreed, while 35 participants mostly disagreed. Twenty-seven participants said they strongly disagreed with the statement.

4. What would be suitable chart types to display the type of information listed below, and why?
   a. Overview of survey respondents' highest level of education. Only one variable with a handful of different values: table or narrative.
   b. Reaction times in a 2 × 2 study with 'priming' and 'task difficulty' (easy/difficult) as the two independent variables. Line chart can illustrate possible main effects and interactions.
   c. Percentage of women in a group at three different points in time. Narrative, line chart or table all work for this since only one variable is involved with three different values.
   d. Projected fund development assuming risky and cautious investment strategy. A line chart would nicely demonstrate the different paths the two strategies are taking (or not).
   e. Reading age scores from two initial cohorts (parents of either high or low socioeconomic status) of primary school children tested at age 5, 6, 7, 8, 9 and 10. Line chart: two lines can show the two cohorts' development over time.
   f. Weekly work hours booked to a project for the last quarter, comparing actual versus projected hours. A line chart would be well suited to demonstrate the gap between projected vs. actual.
   g. Frequencies of answer responses on a scale from 1 to 7. A histogram would be well suited to illustrating distribution of frequencies of values.
   h. Percentage of respondents agreeing or disagreeing with a statement. Narrative; alternatively, one of the few cases where a pie chart may be suitable.

5. You want to examine what compels participants to assist another person, or not. The factors you are interested in are whether participants know the person needing assistance or not, whether the need for assistance is salient or not, and how many other people are present (none, one, two or three). Your dependent variable is the amount of time it takes for the participant to offer assistance.

Work out a possible layout of a table showing all of this information and sketch it in the space below:

|  | \multicolumn{4}{c}{Knows whether assistance is needed} |  |  |  |
|---|---|---|---|---|
|  | Yes |  | No |  |
| Number of people present | Salient | Not salient | Salient | Not salient |
| 1 | *Time* | *Time* | *Time* | *Time* |
| 2 | *Time* | *Time* | *Time* | *Time* |
| 3 | *Time* | *Time* | *Time* | *Time* |

## CHAPTER 8

1.  Use the file available on the companion website to establish (either through Excel or SPSS) whether the variable 'Books' is normally distributed.
    a. Calculate or identify the following values for the variable 'Books':
        i. Mean: 5.44
        ii. Median: 4
        iii. Skewness: .938
        iv. Kurtosis: .311
    b. Create a Q-Q plot for 'Books'.

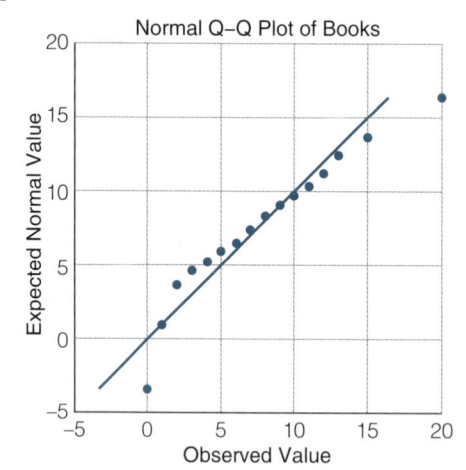

    Normal Q-Q Plot of Books

    c. Decide whether the variable is normally distributed. Mean and median are dissimilar. Skewness is quite high, but still within the two boundaries of 2 and −2. Kurtosis is within normal parameters. However, the Q-Q plot shows that the values do not cluster closely around the line; on balance, it would be better to treat this variable as not normally distributed.
2. For the following scenarios, which statistical analysis would be most appropriate?
    a. You ask participants to rate a candidate's CV in terms of suitability for a job. Half of the participants are told that the candidate is a man, the other half are told the candidate is a woman. Which test would you use:
        i. if the data is normally distributed: Independent-samples t-test.
        ii. if the data is not normally distributed: Mann-Whitney U-test
    b. Participants are asked to complete a series of simple counting tasks twice. For half of the participants, the first task is completed while listening to white noise, the second task while listening to classical music; for the other half of the participants, the order is reversed. Assume that the data is normally distributed. Paired-samples t-test; all participants experience all conditions even if they are in reversed order.
    c. You want to know which of three TV ads appeals more to consumers. You play all three ads to a group of participants and ask them to pick their favourite. Assume that the data is normally distributed. Chi-square goodness-of-fit.
3. What is the non-parametric alternative to:
    a. A paired-samples t-test: Wilcoxon signed rank.
    b. A one-sample t-test: Wilcoxon signed rank.
    c. A one-way ANOVA: Kruskal-Wallis.
4. What is the parametric alternative to a Spearman's correlation? Pearson's.

Exercise Solutions 323

## CHAPTER 9

1. What is the key difference between a paired-samples t-test and an independent-samples t-test? A paired-samples t-test is used in within-participants design; an independent-samples t-test is used in a between-participants design. This matters because a between-participants design has an additional source of variance.
2. In a study, participants rated an item on two different scales: one ranging from 'Good' to 'Bad' and one ranging from 'Like' to 'Dislike'. The output of a paired-samples t-test comparing 'Like' and 'Good' is given here (Figure 9.10):

**Paired Samples Statistics**

|  |  | Mean | N | Std. Deviation | Std. Error Mean |
|---|---|---|---|---|---|
| Pair 1 | Like | 3.7961 | 103 | 2.02126 | .19916 |
|  | Good | 2.5922 | 103 | 1.25586 | .12374 |

**Paired Samples Correlations**

|  |  | N | Correlation | Sig. |
|---|---|---|---|---|
| Pair 1 | Like & Good | 103 | .581 | .000 |

**Paired Samples Test**

|  |  | Paired Differences |  |  |  |  | t | df | Sig. (2-tailed) |
|---|---|---|---|---|---|---|---|---|---|
|  |  | Mean | Std. Deviation | Std. Error Mean | 95% Confidence Interval of the Difference Lower | Upper |  |  |  |
| Pair 1 | Like - Good | 1.20388 | 1.64710 | .16229 | .88198 | 1.52579 | 7.418 | 102 | .000 |

*Figure 9.10* A paired-samples t-test examining whether two variables are similar or different
Reprint Courtesy of International Business Machines Corporation, © International Business Machines Corporation.

   a. Looking at the output, do you think the two ratings are different enough to justify keeping them as separate variables? The difference between the two variables is highly significant, although the correlation is medium-sized. The two variables can be kept distinct.
   b. Write up the results of the test. Participants' mean 'Like' scores were 3.796 (SD=2.021), and their mean 'Good' scores were 2.592 (SD=1.256). A paired-samples t-test showed that this difference was significant, $t(102) = 7.418$, $p < .001$. The two scores showed a medium-sized positive correlation with their 'Good' score, $r(103) = .581$, $p < .001$, such that higher 'Like' scores were associated with higher 'Good' scores.
3. A study presented information to participants and asked them after 2, 12 or 20 days how many arguments presented to them initially they recalled. Two raters then scored participants' responses as to the number of correctly and incorrectly recalled arguments. Below you find the output for all three comparisons between the three groups of participants. Assume that the hypotheses were non-directional and that variances are equal (Figures 9.11, 9.12 and 9.13).

**Group Statistics**

|  | Time_condition | N | Mean | Std. Deviation | Std. Error Mean |
|---|---|---|---|---|---|
| Agreed correct count, 2nd part | 2 days | 100 | 4.11 | 1.847 | .185 |
|  | 12 days | 99 | 3.78 | 1.941 | .195 |

**Independent Samples Test**

|  |  | Levene's Test for Equality of Variances |  | t-test for Equality of Means |  |  |  |  |
|---|---|---|---|---|---|---|---|---|
|  |  | F | Sig. | t | df | Sig. (2-tailed) | Mean Difference | Std. Error Difference |
| Agreed correct count, 2nd part | Equal variances assumed | .424 | .516 | 1.237 | 197 | .218 | .332 | .269 |
|  | Equal variances not assumed |  |  | 1.237 | 196.306 | .218 | .332 | .269 |

*Figure 9.11* Independent-samples t-test examining recall data of 2 and 12 days
Reprint Courtesy of International Business Machines Corporation, © International Business Machines Corporation.

**Group Statistics**

| | Time_condition | N | Mean | Std. Deviation | Std. Error Mean |
|---|---|---|---|---|---|
| Agreed correct count, 2nd part | 2 days | 100 | 4.11 | 1.847 | .185 |
| | 20 days | 94 | 3.26 | 2.290 | .236 |

**Independent Samples Test**

| | | Levene's Test for Equality of Variances | | t-test for Equality of Means | | | | |
|---|---|---|---|---|---|---|---|---|
| | | F | Sig. | t | df | Sig. (2-tailed) | Mean Difference | Std. Error Difference |
| Agreed correct count, 2nd part | Equal variances assumed | 2.353 | .127 | 2.869 | 192 | .005 | .855 | .298 |
| | Equal variances not assumed | | | 2.850 | 178.724 | .005 | .855 | .300 |

*Figure 9.12* Independent-samples t-test examining recall data of 2 and 20 days
Reprint Courtesy of International Business Machines Corporation, © International Business Machines Corporation.

→ **T-Test**

**Group Statistics**

| | Time_condition | N | Mean | Std. Deviation | Std. Error Mean |
|---|---|---|---|---|---|
| Agreed correct count, 2nd part | 12 days | 99 | 3.78 | 1.941 | .195 |
| | 20 days | 94 | 3.26 | 2.290 | .236 |

**Independent Samples Test**

| | | Levene's Test for Equality of Variances | | t-test for Equality of Means | | | | |
|---|---|---|---|---|---|---|---|---|
| | | F | Sig. | t | df | Sig. (2-tailed) | Mean Difference | Std. Error Difference |
| Agreed correct count, 2nd part | Equal variances assumed | .930 | .336 | 1.713 | 191 | .088 | .522 | .305 |
| | Equal variances not assumed | | | 1.705 | 182.522 | .090 | .522 | .306 |

*Figure 9.13* Independent-samples t-test examining recall data of 12 and 20 days
Reprint Courtesy of International Business Machines Corporation, © International Business Machines Corporation.

Write up the results of these tests.

Mean agreed count was 4.11 ($SD$=1.847) for participants in the 2-days condition, 3.78 ($SD$=1.941) in the 12-days condition and 3.26 ($SD$=2.290) in the 20-days condition. The only significant difference was between the 2-days and 20-days condition, with $t(192) = 2.869$, $p = .005$. There was no significant difference between the 12-days and 20-days condition ($t(191) = 1.713$, $p > .05$), or between the 2-days and 12-days condition ($t(197) = 1.237$, $p > .05$).

# CHAPTER 10

1. 🌐 Download the sample data set for this exercise, either for SPSS or for Excel. In this study, participants who identified as female had to complete a numerical test, after having been presented with one of three types of instruction: One activated a stereotype referring to the participants' gender (activated_same) by referring to the myth of women's inferior numerical skills; one activated a stereotype by referring to the myth of men's superior numerical skills (activated_different); the third instruction did not make any mention of either men or women's numerical skills.

   a. What are mean and standard deviation of the test score for the three individual conditions?
   Mean test scores when no stereotype threat: 40.22, SD = 5.285
   Mean test scores when stereotype for different gender activated: 34.57, SD = 6.703
   Mean test scores when stereotype for same gender activated: 33.30, SD = 6.588.

   b. Find out whether there is an effect of stereotype threat on test score. If required, conduct post-hoc analyses. Write up the results as you would report them in a paper or thesis. When no stereotype threat was present, female participants scored an average 40.22 ($SD = 5.285$). When a stereotype of men's superior skills was activated, participants averaged test scores of 34.57 ($SD = 6.703$), and when a stereotype on women's numerical skills was activated, test scores dropped to 33.30 ($SD=6.588$). A one-way ANOVA showed an effect of stereotype activation, $F(2,149) = 17.755, p < .001$. Post-hoc tests showed that the significant differences were between the activated and non-activated conditions (both differences significant at $p < .001$) but that there was no difference between the scores of the two activated conditions ($p > .05$).

2. A study was conducted to see whether the way in which information was presented to participants (IV 'Condition') had an effect on the extent to which they thought about the topic (DV 'Thought') or paid attention to the information (DV 'Attend'). Participants' numeracy was measured as a potential confounding variable and controlled for in the analysis. Look at the output below. What is missing for you to fully report on the results of this test? Information on whether 'Thought' or 'Attend' are normally distributed. Descriptive information on mean and standard deviation of the dependent variables across the four conditions. Descriptive information on numeracy. Post-hoc analyses.

### Between-Subjects Factors

|  |  | Value Label | N |
|---|---|---|---|
| Condition | 1 | TextOnly | 25 |
|  | 2 | TextNumbers | 25 |
|  | 3 | TextGraphs | 26 |
|  | 4 | ExtendedTxt | 27 |

### Multivariate Tests[c]

| | Effect | Value | F | Hypothesis df | Error df | Sig. |
|---|---|---|---|---|---|---|
| Intercept | Pillai's Trace | .361 | 27.386[a] | 2.000 | 97.000 | .000 |
|  | Wilks' Lambda | .639 | 27.386[a] | 2.000 | 97.000 | .000 |
|  | Hotelling's Trace | .565 | 27.386[a] | 2.000 | 97.000 | .000 |
|  | Roy's Largest Root | .565 | 27.386[a] | 2.000 | 97.000 | .000 |

|  |  |  |  |  |  |  |
|---|---|---|---|---|---|---|
| Numeracy | Pillai's Trace | .047 | 2.378[a] | 2.000 | 97.000 | .098 |
|  | Wilks' Lambda | .953 | 2.378[a] | 2.000 | 97.000 | .098 |
|  | Hotelling's Trace | .049 | 2.378[a] | 2.000 | 97.000 | .098 |
|  | Roy's Largest Root | .049 | 2.378[a] | 2.000 | 97.000 | .098 |
| Condition | Pillai's Trace | .057 | .953 | 6.000 | 196.000 | .459 |
|  | Wilks' Lambda | .944 | .948[a] | 6.000 | 194.000 | .462 |
|  | Hotelling's Trace | .059 | .944 | 6.000 | 192.000 | .465 |
|  | Roy's Largest Root | .048 | 1.566[b] | 3.000 | 98.000 | .202 |

a. Exact statistic
b. The statistic is an upper bound on F that yields a lower bound on the significance level.
c. Design: Intercept + Numeracy + Condition

### Tests of Between-Subjects Effects

| Source | Dependent Variable | Type III Sum of Squares | df | Mean Square | F | Sig. |
|---|---|---|---|---|---|---|
| Corrected Model | Thought | 8.338[a] | 4 | 2.085 | .971 | .427 |
|  | Attend | 15.679[b] | 4 | 3.920 | 2.260 | .068 |
| Intercept | Thought | 82.744 | 1 | 82.744 | 38.533 | .000 |
|  | Attend | 77.846 | 1 | 77.846 | 44.879 | .000 |
| Numeracy | Thought | 5.546 | 1 | 5.546 | 2.583 | .111 |
|  | Attend | 7.673 | 1 | 7.673 | 4.423 | .038 |
| Condition | Thought | 2.810 | 3 | .937 | .436 | .728 |
|  | Attend | 7.658 | 3 | 2.553 | 1.472 | .227 |
| Error | Thought | 210.439 | 98 | 2.147 |  |  |
|  | Attend | 169.991 | 98 | 1.735 |  |  |
| Total | Thought | 1606.000 | 103 |  |  |  |
|  | Attend | 1308.000 | 103 |  |  |  |
| Corrected Total | Thought | 218.777 | 102 |  |  |  |
|  | Attend | 185.670 | 102 |  |  |  |

a. R Squared = .038 (Adjusted R Squared = -.001)
b. R Squared = .084 (Adjusted R Squared = .047)

# CHAPTER 11

1. A group of 113 smokers and 110 non-smokers were asked whether they support a smoking ban in pubs and restaurants. The results appear below:

   |  | Smoker | Non-Smoker | Total |
   |---|---|---|---|
   | Supports the ban | 61 | 72 | 133 |
   | Does not support the ban | 52 | 38 | 90 |
   | Total | 113 | 110 | 223 |

   a. The table below presents the observed values. Assume that you have no reason to expect that either group will have a preference for or against the ban. What are the expected values?

   |  | Smoker | Smoker |
   |---|---|---|
   | Supports the ban | $\frac{113}{223} \times 133 = 67.39$ | $\frac{110}{223} \times 133 = 65.61$ |
   | Does not support the ban | $\frac{113}{223} \times 90 = 45.61$ | $\frac{110}{223} \times 90 = 44.39$ |

   b. Conduct a chi-square test of independence to establish whether being a (non-)smoker is independent of the support of a smoking ban. Report chi-square value, degrees of freedom and $p$-value. A chi-square test of independence showed no association between being smoker status and support of the ban, $X^2$ (1, $N$=223) = 3.048 $p > .05$.

2. As part of a study, three variables collected aspects of attitude certainty by asking participants to what extent they were certain, sure and confident of their attitude. They then ran a correlation analysis to see how closely related the answers were.
   a. Examine the table below and report on the results. The three measures all show high, positive correlations. 'AT_Certain' and 'AT_Sure' show a positive correlation of .82, 'AT_Certain' and 'AT_Confident' correlate at .808, and 'AT_Confident' and 'AT_Sure' correlate at .807; all correlations are significant at $p < .001$.
   b. Would you recommend the researcher to combine the three measurements into one composite measure? Why or why not? Yes, because the three measures correlate highly and at a highly significant level.

**Correlations**

|  |  | AT_Certain | AT_Sure | AT_Confident |
|---|---|---|---|---|
| AT_Certain | Pearson Correlation | 1 | .820[**] | .808[**] |
|  | Sig. (2-tailed) |  | .000 | .000 |
|  | N | 103 | 103 | 103 |
| AT_Sure | Pearson Correlation | .820[**] | 1 | .807[**] |
|  | Sig. (2-tailed) | .000 |  | .000 |
|  | N | 103 | 103 | 103 |
| AT_Confident | Pearson Correlation | .808[**] | .807[**] | 1 |
|  | Sig. (2-tailed) | .000 | .000 |  |
|  | N | 103 | 103 | 103 |

[**]. Correlation is significant at the 0.01 level (2-tailed).

*Reprint Courtesy of International Business Machines Corporation, © International Business Machines Corporation.*

# CHAPTER 12

Number the elements so that they appear in the right order.
- [2] Brief summary of main variables, methodology, findings and implications (max 250 words)
- [9] Detailed explanation of procedure
- [19] Copy of any testing material used
- [10] Description of recoded variables and data sets identified as outliers
- [11] Descriptives for main variables
- [7] Detailed description of sample
- [15] Discussion of potential improvements in the methodology
- [5] Outline of gap in research
- [16] Discussion to what extent results can be generalised outside the sample
- [13] Discussion to what extent results confirm hypotheses or not
- [6] Expectations towards result
- [8] Detailed description of materials used
- [3] Explanation why topic is important
- [4] Outline of existing research
- [18] References
- [20] SPSS output or manual working out of detailed statistical analyses
- [12] Statistical tests and analyses to confirm or reject hypotheses
- [17] Suggestion of potential future research
- [14] Discussion how current results fit with existing research
- [1] Very brief summary of main finding (max 20 words)

Order of 15,16 may be reversed; order of 19,20 may be reversed

2. Note for each statement whether it's true or false, and why.
    a. In the literature review you need to provide a short summary of each paper you cite. F: You do not have to provide a short summary of every paper; you need to consolidate and summarise across papers, too.
    b. Appendices are numbered, beginning with 1. F: Appendices are given letters, starting with A.
    c. A rationale can either be included as a separate section or integrated into the overall literature review.    T
    d. You don't need hypotheses if you conduct exploratory research. T
    e. You always need to provide hypothesis *and* null hypothesis. F: Requirements vary. You may be asked to only provide your hypothesis, or a hypothesis and null hypothesis.
    f. In your data analysis section, you mention whether you identified any data sets as outliers.    T
    g. It is easier to write your abstract and introduction before you write your methodology. F: It's easier to write most of your report before you write the abstract and introduction because those two are the most high-level summaries of your research.
    h. You do not have to critically evaluate every individual reference you use. T
    i. Your statistical tests need to match your hypotheses. T
    j. You can be brief in describing your methods – if other researchers have any questions, they can always email you. F: You need to be thorough enough that researchers can re-create your study in its main parameters relying on your write-up alone.

# General Glossary

**Accidental Sampling**: See *convenience sampling*.

**Alpha Level**: Level of *significance* that is still considered acceptable. Commonly chosen levels are $p = .05$, $p = .01$ or $p = .001$.

**Alternative Hypothesis**: See *hypothesis*.

**ANCOVA, Analysis of Covariance**: Statistical analysis examining the *effect* of one *independent variable* on one or more *dependent variables*, while *controlling* for the *effect* of a *covariate*.

**ANOVA, Analysis of Variance**: Statistical analysis examining the *effect* of one *independent variable* on one or more *dependent variables*. A *one-way ANOVA* looks at one independent variable, a *two-way ANOVA* at two independent variables, and so on.

**Archival Data**: *Secondary data* (i.e., data which is not collected by the researchers themselves but is analysed and examined throughout their research).

**Association**: A relation between two or more *variables*, either through a *correlation* or a cause-and-effect relationship.

**Asymmetric Rating Scales**: Scales providing an unbalanced set of response options, unlike *symmetric rating scales*.

**Bar Chart** (also referred to as *column chart*): A chart type where the size of two or more bars helps compare values of different *variables*.

**Base**: In a formula of the form $X^y$ ('x to the power of y'), x is the base and y is the *exponent*.

**Beck's Depression Inventory**: A questionnaire consisting of 21 questions relating to day-to-day behaviour and feelings. The total score is used to classify the extent and severity of depression, ranging from not depressed to extreme depression.

**Bell Curve**: *Normal distribution* curve.

**Between-Participants** (also referred to as **between-subjects**): *Variables* of which a participant experiences only one *level*, as opposed to *within-participants variables*, where participants experience all *levels*.

**Bivariate Correlations**: *Correlations* between two *variables*.

**Blind, Blinded, Blind Study, Blind Trial**: Refers to a research design where participants are not told which *condition* they are in to avoid the *placebo effect*. If neither researcher nor participants (but a neutral third observer) know who has been allocated to which *condition*, this is referred to as a **double-blind study**.

**Block Randomisation**: Splitting a large item pool up into chunks or blocks of several items each and applying *randomisation* techniques to the resulting blocks.

**Categorical Data**: See *nominal scale* type data.

**Ceiling Effect**: When a *variable* cannot progress/increase beyond a certain point, called the ceiling, either because of an inherent quality (e.g., human beings do not grow taller than 2.30 m) or because the instrument does not allow measurement of higher values (e.g., the *scale* is capped).

**Central-Tendency Bias**: Tendency to choose the middle or neutral option. Particularly prevalent when presenting participants with an uneven number of response items (e.g., 3 on a scale from 1 to 5; 4 on a scale from 1 to 7).

**Chi Square**: A statistical analysis which compares distributions of observed *frequencies* with expected *frequencies*. There are two versions of the chi-square test: **chi-square test of independence** (checking whether two variables are independent of each other) and **goodness-of-fit chi-square** (comparing observed frequencies of one nominal or categorical variable to specific hypothesized frequencies).

**Cluster Sampling**: Sampling technique to deal with very large and often geographically widespread *populations* where *sampling* is done on one or more levels of clusters rather than on individual respondents only (e.g., first region, then organisation, then department, then employee).
**Cohen's d**: A measure of effect size calculated by dividing the difference of two group means by one of the groups' standard deviation.
**Column Chart** (also referred to as *bar chart*): A chart type where the size of two or more bars helps compare values of different *variables*.
**Composite Measure**: A measure such as a *scale* or an index combining several individual measures into one.
**Computational Formula**: A shorter and slightly easier to compute variant of the formula to calculate the *sum of squares*; alternative to the *definitional formula*. Both formulas yield the same results.
**Conclusion Validity**: Extent to which a study is adequately designed to justify your conclusion.
**Condition**: Value of an *independent variable* or *factor*.
**Conditional Probability**: Probability of an event which is dependent on the outcome of another event.
**Confidence Interval**: The confidence interval *ranges* from (Given Result − *Margin of Error*) to (Given Result + *Margin of Error*).
**Confidence Level**: Level of certainty with which results would be replicated if the study were repeated. Calculated as (1-*alpha level*).
**Confound/Confounding**: *Variables* interfering in the relationship between *independent variable*(s) (or *factors*) and *dependent variable*(s). Confounds need to be *controlled* for, or eliminated.
**Confound Variance**: A type of *systematic variance* introduced by one or more *confounds*.
**Consent Form**: A form informing research participants of their rights in regards to their participation, such as the right to withdraw at any point without having to give a reason.
**Construct**: An abstract concept (e.g., motivation, need for cognition, verbal ability, attitude) which is not tangible and cannot be directly measured.
**Construct-Irrelevant Variance**: *Variance* contributed by a *variable* not immediately related to the main *construct* of interest.
**Construct Underrepresentation**: A methodology which fails to identify and assess all relevant facets of a *construct*. Identified by Messick (1995) as one of the threats to *validity*.
**Construct Validity**: Extent to which a study and its instruments are measuring the *construct* you intend to measure.
**Content Note**: A note indicating that content may be upsetting or disturbing to readers. Most frequently relates to descriptions of abuse, discussions of weight loss or body image, or mentions of subjects that may be upsetting to people with phobias.
**Contingency Table**: A table containing frequency information on two or more *variables*, providing *marginal totals* and a *grand total*.
**Continuous Variable**: *Variable* which can assume any value on a continuum (e.g., salary, reaction time, etc.).
**Control**: Degree to which researcher/experimenter can influence change in *variables* and environment. Control can be achieved by eliminating *confounds* or accounting for their effect in the choice of statistical tests.
**Control Condition**: Condition or *level* of a *variable* where the *independent variable* is not manipulated. Allows comparison to the condition where the *independent variable* is manipulated.
**Control Group**: Group of participants who do not receive any *treatment* or experience no *condition* where the *independent variable* is manipulated.
**Convenience Sampling**: Approaching members of the *population* in a manner that does not give everyone equal chances to be included in the *sample* (i.e., at limited times, in limited locations, etc.).
**Convergent Validity**: Different *measures* of the same *construct* yielding the same or similar results.

**Correlation**: Systematic non-causal relationship between *variables* such that the *variables* share an amount of *variance* ($r$ = correlation coefficient, $r^2$ = *percentage* of *variance* shared).

**Correlation, Negative**: As values for one *variable* increase, values for the other *variable* decrease.

**Correlation, Positive**: As the values for one *variable* increase so do the values for the other *variable*.

**Counterbalancing**: A method of reducing the likelihood of *order* and *sequence effect* by reversing the order of test items (e.g., items are presented in order ABCDEF in one *condition* and in order FEDCBA in another).

**Covariate**: A *variable* interfering with/mediating the *effect* of the *independent variable* on the *dependent variable* (e.g., motivation could be a covariate to the *effect* of practice on test performance).

**Cronbach's Alpha**: A measure of *scale reliability*, expressing the degree of internal consistency and overall inter-*correlation* between items.

**Data Transformation**: Changing the data type of a *variable*, for example from *interval* (motivation measured on a scale from 1 to 10) to *nominal* by classifying motivation as either 'high' or 'low'.

**Debriefing**: Generally, talking to (or interacting with) participants after their participation to enquire after their experience with and perception of the study; to find out whether they are feeling okay or require support if the study was potentially upsetting; to explain the purpose of the study, particularly if deception was involved.

**Definitional Formula**: The longer, more extensive version of the formula to calculate the *sum of squares*. Alternative to the *computational formula*. Both formulas yield the same results.

**Degrees of Freedom**: A *parameter* establishing contingency and flexibility of values within a distribution, indicating how many values are not fixed and therefore free.

**Demographic Questions**: Questions establishing the demographic properties of a *population* or *sample*, such as age, gender, occupation, etc.

**Denominator**: In the expression $\frac{6}{3}$, 6 is the *numerator* and 3 is the denominator.

**Dependent Variable**: *Variable* which is influenced by changes to the *independent variable* or *factor*.

**Directional Hypothesis**: See *one-tailed hypothesis*.

**Discrete Variable**: *Variable* where possible values can be expressed only in distinct categories (e.g., gender, occupation).

**Dummy Variable**: A dichotomous variable (i.e., one that has only two values, 'yes' or 'no') which transforms and simplifies another variable's values into two mutually exclusive terms. For example, if you have a variable 'pet owned' with the values 'cat', 'dog', 'fennec fox', 'rat', 'piranha', 'alligator', a dummy variable might be 'has exotic pet' with the value 1 for the owners of the fennec fox, the piranha and the alligator, and the value 0 for everyone else.

**Ecological Validity**: Subtype of *external validity*. Describes the extent to which findings from limited set of tasks and materials in study can be generalised or extrapolated to the 'real world'.

**Effect**: Causal relationship between two or more *variables* where a change in the *independent variable* leads to a change in the *dependent variable*.

**Effect Size**: Relative size of the difference between two groups, possibly (but not necessarily) indicating a causal relationship.

**Epistemology**: The science and philosophy of knowing, describing different ways of knowing and limits of knowledge.

**Error Variance**: Random *unsystematic variance* which is not related to the *treatment/conditions* (e.g., individual differences within/between participants).

**Experiment**: Methodology employing one or more *independent variables* and *random allocation* of participants to different *conditions*. In a true experiment the researcher is able to *control* for potential *confounds*.
**Explanatory Variable**: See *independent variable*.
**Exponent**: In a formula of the form $X^y$ ('x to the power of y'), y is the exponent and x is the *base*.
**External Validity**: Extent to which findings can be generalised outside the testing environment (e.g., other people, other times, other locations).
**Factor**: A *variable* which affects one or more other *variables* but is not an *independent variable* – a *variable* that cannot be actively manipulated (e.g., gender, age, etc.).
**Falsifiable**: A property of *hypotheses*. For falsifiable hypotheses, there exist *conditions* which could theoretically disprove them. 'I'm not me, but my identical clone' cannot be disproven.
**Floor Effect**: Where a *variable* cannot progress/decrease below a certain point, called the floor, either because of a quality or property inherent to the *variable* or because the instrument does not allow measurement of lower values (e.g., the *scale* is capped).
**Forced-Choice Method**: A design that excludes 'no response' options (i.e., 'Don't know'). Response *scales* may include an even number of responses so participants have no recourse to choose the middle (neutral) option. Can be used to minimise the impact of the *central-tendency bias*.
**Frequency**: Number describing how often a specific value occurs.
**Gaussian Curve**: The shape described by a graph plotting a *normal distribution*.
**Grand Total**: Overall total in a *contingency table*; also either the sum of all column *marginal totals* or the sum of all row *marginal totals*.
**$H_0$**: See *null hypothesis*.
**$H_1$**: See *hypothesis*.
**Histogram**: A chart displaying distinct values of a quantitative *variable* on the x-axis, with the size of the *variable* displayed on the y-axis; in contrast to a *bar graph*, the individual bars in a histogram are not separated by gaps.
**Homogeneity of Variance**: Simply speaking, that all values of the predictor *variable* have roughly the same variance.
**Homoscedasticity**: See *homogeneity of variance*.
**Hypothesis**: An statement explicitly describing the type of relationship a researcher expects to observe between two or more *variables* (also referred to as H1).
**Independent-Samples t-test**: Analytical tool used to compare the *means* of two independent *samples*.
**Independent Variable**: *Variable* which exerts an *effect* on one or more *dependent variables*.
**Indicator**: An indirect *measure* of a *construct* or concept, based on assumption through which *variables* a concept might be expressed or measured.
**Inferential Statistics**: Statistical analyses that go beyond a description of data and aim at drawing conclusions about relationships between *variables*.
**Interaction**: When the *effect* of one *independent variable* is linked to another *independent variable* assuming a particular value (as opposed to a *main effect*).
**Internal Validity**: Extent to which you can adequately conclude a causal relationship between *independent variables* (or *factors*) and *dependent variables*.
**Interpretivist**: A type of *epistemology* stating that knowledge and definitions are subjective and that reality cannot be measured objectively.
**Interval Scale**: Data which can be categorised and ordered in a meaningful way, with the intervals between individual values considered equivalent.
**Intervening Variable, Confounding Variable, Confound**: A *variable* other than the *independent variable* (or *factor*) influencing the *dependent variable*.
**Kruskal-Wallis Test**: *Non-parametric* alternative to the *ANOVA*.

**Kurtosis, negative/positive**: Describes the shape of a curve's arch as applied to the shape of a *normal distribution*. Higher kurtosis means a higher density in the centre of the distribution, leading to a steeper curve. Steeper curves represent *positive kurtosis*, flatter curves *negative kurtosis*. Distributions can be *mesokurtic*, *platykurtic* or *leptokurtic*.
Closely related: **Excess Kurtosis**: A different way of measuring the same property by only indicating the deviation of a curve's kurtosis from a standardised shape.
**Latin Square**: A method of *randomising* items or tasks within an *experimental* design.
**Left-Skewed**: See *left-tailed*.
**Left-Tailed**: A *skewed* distribution whose centre is on the right.
**Leptokurtic**: A distribution with *positive kurtosis*. The distribution has a narrower peak and flatter tails.
**Level(s)**: The discrete values an *independent variable* can assume within an *experimental* design.
**Likert Scale**: *Bipolar rating scale* expressing extent of agreement/disagreement.
**Line Chart**: Graphical representation of data. *Variable* categories are shown on the x-axis, the size of the category is shown on the y-axis, and the individual data points are connected by one continuous line.
**Longitudinal**: Research taking place over a longer period of time with multiple points of measurement. Often used to measure progress of year cohorts in terms of health outcomes or career trajectories.
**Lost-Letter Setup**: A technique whereby people's attitude towards organisations or members of certain groups is measured by researchers dropping pre-stamped and addressed letters and counting the number of letters picked up and posted by people.
**Main Effect**: An effect of an *independent variable* on a *dependent variable* which is not contingent on a specific value of one or more additional *independent variables*.
**Manipulation**: Actively changing values of the *independent variable(s)* to potentially observe changes in the dependent *variable(s)*.
**Manipulation Check**: Including items or tasks to assess to what extent the manipulation of the *independent variable* has been successful. For example, when examining the *effect* of motivation on test performance by offering different incentives, a manipulation check could include questions assessing participants' motivation.
**Mann-Whitney U-test**: *Non-parametric* alternative to the *independent-samples t-test*.
**Margin of Error**: Usually given as a *percentage*. States the difference (+/−) by which the real result may differ from the given result.
**Marginal Total**: Subtotal for a row or a column in a *contingency table*.
**Matching**: Alternative to *randomised* allocation of participants to allocation which ensures that participants in different *conditions* are similar in terms of age, gender, and any other *variables* potentially relevant (or intervening) with any of the *dependent* or *independent variables*.
**Mean (M)**: A *measure of central tendency*, calculated by adding up all individual values and dividing the total by the number of values.
- Symbol for sample mean: $\bar{x}$ ('x-bar')
- Symbol for population mean: $\mu$ ('mu')

**Measure**: A *variable* which is very closely related to or a direct expression of what is being measured.
**Measures of Central Tendency**: Used to provide a basic description of a distribution, often in combination with values indicating spread or *range*. *Mean*, *mode* and *median* are all measures of central tendency.
**MECE** (Mutually Exclusive, Comprehensively Exhaustive): A rule of thumb to apply to the development of a set of response options stating that the options should not overlap (mutually exclusive) and should cover all possibilities (comprehensively exhaustive).

**Median**: A *measure of central tendency*. Describes the point at which exactly half of the distribution's values fall below and half above.
**Median Split**: Splitting a distribution of values into exactly two halves based on the median.
**Mesokurtic**: A *normal distribution* with neither negative nor *positive kurtosis*.
**Mixed Between-Within**: Methodology using both *between-participants* and *within-participants variables* or *factors*.
**Mixed Factorial**: Methodology using both true *independent variables* and *factors*.
**Mixed-Method Approach**: Study design using both quantitative and qualitative methods.
**Mode**: A *measure of central tendency* describing the value occurring at the highest *frequency*.
**Multifactorial**: A study employing more than one *factor*.
**Multivariate ANOVA**: An analysis of variance employing more than one *independent variable*.
**N (uppercase N)**: Number of observations within a *population*.
**n (lowercase n)**: Number of observations within a *sample*.
**Negative Skew**: See *left-tailed*.
**Neurotypical**: As opposed to non-neurotypical. People on the autism spectrum are also referred to as non-neurotypical whereas people not on the spectrum would be considered neurotypical.
**Nominal Scale**: Data which can be categorised and named (e.g., gender, colours, occupation). Allows description in terms of *frequencies* only.
**Non-directional Hypothesis**: See *two-tailed hypothesis*.
**Non-parametric**: Not fulfilling the requirements for a *normal distribution*.
**Non-probability Sampling**: Any sampling technique where the requirements for *probability sampling* are not met (e.g., *snowball sampling, convenience sampling, opportunity sampling, accidental sampling, quota sampling* and *panel sampling*).
**Normal Distribution**: A type of symmetric distribution (of values) characterised by values clustering around the *mean* in the shape of a *bell curve*.
**Null Hypothesis**: A statement explicitly describing the *alternative hypothesis* to the *hypothesis*. Phrased in terms of absence of an *effect*, difference or *association*.
**Numerator**: In the expression 6/3, 6 is the numerator and 3 is the *denominator*.
**One-Sample t-test**: T-test comparing a given *sample's mean* against a known value.
**One-Tailed Hypothesis**: A *hypothesis* which not only specifies the existence of a difference, association or effect but also its direction.
**One-Way ANOVA**: Statistical test examining the *effect* of one *independent variable* on one or more *dependent variables*.
**Operationalisation**: The process of turning an abstract concept of interest (motivation, intelligence, attention, age) into a concrete, measurable *variable*.
**Opportunity Sampling**: See *convenience sampling*.
**Order Effects**: Where an item in a test or *scale* may affect a participant's response to a later item.
**Ordinal Scale**: Data which can be categorised and ordered in a meaningful way.
**Outlier**: Value substantially and markedly different from the rest of the distribution. Identifying an outlier is a subjective process and dependent on the researcher's knowledge and assumptions.
**Paired Samples t-test**: Comparing two *means* (of the same *variable*, measured twice) from the same *sample*.
**Pairwise Comparison**: Type of task where participants are asked to compare a pair of items; often used to split up the task of ordering and comparing a number of items to make it more manageable.
**Panel Sampling**: Randomly selected panel of participants. The panel is asked the same set of questions repeatedly over a longer period of time.
**Parameter**: A *measure* relating to a *population* rather than a *sample*.
**Parametric**: Data which is considered to be *normally distributed*, allowing for more complex analytical tests.

**Parametric Data Correlation (Pearson's Chi Square)**: *Correlation* analysis using *parametric* data.
**Participant Information Sheet**: Information given to participants in advance of their participation, explaining as much as possible about the purpose of the study and what participants can expect in terms of time and effort required.
**Percentage**: Describes a ratio of one group of items or entities to another group on the basis of 100.
**Percent Points**: Units in which *percentages* are expressed.
**Pie Chart**: Type of graphical representation where the distribution of values is illustrated by the respective sizes of the segments of a circle.
**Pilot Studies**: Small-scale studies conducted before the main study to test suitability and feasibility of materials and instructions.
**Placebo**: Mostly used in medical studies; a control substance (usually but not always inert) that is administered instead of the *treatment* substance since not administering any *treatment* would make it obvious to a participant which *condition* they are in and potentially affect *treatment* outcome. Usually employed within a *blind* or *double-blind* research design.
Closely related: **Placebo effect**, wherein participants gain benefits and positive outcome from a placebo because of their positive expectations towards the *treatment's* effectiveness.
**Platykurtic**: A distribution with *negative kurtosis*. Distribution has a flatter peak and shorter tails.
**Population**: Set of entities (most frequently, people) to which you want to generalise your research's findings. A representative selection, a *sample*, is drawn from the population.
**Positive Skew**: See *right-tailed*.
**Positivist**: A type of *epistemology* stating that knowledge and definitions are objective and that reality can be measured objectively.
**Power**: Power of a test describes the probability that the test will correctly reject a false *null hypothesis*.
**Primary Data**: Data collected by the researcher.
**Priming**: In the broadest sense, preparing participants for a subsequent stimulus.
**Practice Effect**: Effect of completing a task or a test for the second time and being more experienced and/or less nervous.
**Probability Sampling**: Any sampling technique where every item in the *population* has at least a theoretical chance to be included in the *sample* and that probability can be determined (e.g., *simple random sampling*, *stratified sampling*, *systematic sampling* and *cluster sampling*).
**Procedural Questions**: Questions eliciting data not immediately relating to the *(in)dependent variables* and *factors*. Allow a *manipulation check* as well as checking for understanding of testing instructions and materials.
**Q-Q Plot**: A plot comparing the quantiles of two distributions (i.e., your data's distribution against a *normal distribution*). The plot is used to assess whether data is normally distributed.
**Quasi-experiment**: Study design fulfilling all requirements for an *experiment except* the requirement of *random allocation* to groups.
**Quota Sampling**: Sampling technique to provide a fixed *ratio* of respondent categories (e.g., male/female, etc.) without the requirement that the *ratio*, the number and the selection of categories or the resultant *sample* are representative of the *population*.
**Random Allocation**: Assigning participants randomly to *conditions* to avoid *self-selection bias*.
**Randomisation**: 1) Process of ensuring a random presentation of all or a subset of items. 2) Process of ensuring *random allocation* of participants to *conditions*.
**Randomised Presentation**: Ensuring a random presentation of all or a subset of items or stimuli to participants.
**Range**: The difference between the highest and lowest value of a distribution.
**Rank**: An item's position in an ordered list (e.g., the second item in the list has the rank 2.)

**Rank Ordering**: Creating an ordered list to allocate *ranks* to individual items.
**Rating Scales**: Set of related response options relating to one single question.
**Ratio**: A ratio of X:Y means values are distributed in such a way that for every X of one thing there are Y of the other thing.
**Ratio Scale**: Data assuming the properties of *nominal*, *ordinal* and *interval scales* with the addition of a non-arbitrary point of zero.
**Raw Score**: Non-standardised value; value before it has been converted to a *z-score*.
**Reliability**: Extent to which an *experiment* or instrument measures consistently.
**Repeated Measures**: A *within-participants* design with one or more *independent variables* measured two or more times.
**Replication, Replication Studies**: Conducting a study which has already taken place to see whether it yields the same results with minor or no amendments to the original research design.
**Response Variable**: See *dependent variable*.
**Reverse Coding**: Usually done for individual items in a list of several items (e.g., reversing the direction of answer options). For example, switching from 'Not at all' to 'Very much' for most items to 'Very much' to 'Not at all' for a single item.
**Right-Skewed**: See *right-tailed*.
**Right-Tailed**: A distribution with its tail to the right.
**Sample**: The group of participants you are using in your study. A sample is a subset of the *population*.
**Sampling**: Process of selecting the group of participants or respondents for a study.
**Scale**: 1) A means of presenting more than two answer options to a single question or item, see for example Likert Scale. 2) A series of questions designed to measure a specific construct, for example the Perceived Stress Scale referred to on p. 26.
**Scale Reliability Testing**: Statistical analysis examining the consistency of a *scale* containing several items. *Reliability* can expressed in a *parameter* called *Cronbach's alpha*.
**Scale Types**: Classification of types of data which allow for different analyses. Data is either of *nominal*, *ordinal*, *interval* or *ratio* scale type.
**Scale Transformation**: see *Data Transformation*.
**Scatter Plot**: Graphical representation of data. Shows data as data points representing pairs of *variable* values. Allows first indication of spread of data and possible *correlation*.
**Secondary Data**: Data which has been collected by someone other than the researcher.
**Self Selection**: Participants self-allocating to *conditions* rather than being allocated by the researcher.
**Self Selection Bias**: Bias introduced to a study by participants self-selecting to *conditions* based on personal interest/motivation/traits/attitudes, etc. Self-selection means any difference in groups cannot be exclusively explained by the *factor* or *independent variable*.
**Semantic Differential**: A list of opposing pairs of descriptive labels (e.g., good – bad, high - low), requiring the participant to locate their answer on a point between the two poles.
**Sentence Completion**: Type of task asking the participant to complete a given sentence with a response (e.g., 'I'd describe the relationship between me and my colleagues as _____').
**Sequence Effects**: Where a participant's response to an item is affected by the item immediately preceding this item.
**Significance**: Probability to which the result is due to chance; expressed in the *p*-value. More precisely, a finding is considered statistically significant if the *p*-value is lower than a previously determined cut-off point (*alpha level*).
**Simple Random Sampling**: Most basic form of *probability sampling* where each entity in the *population* has an equal chance of being included in the *sample*.

**Skew, Skewness**: A measure of how (a)symmetric a distribution is. If the centre of the distribution is left, the longer tail is right; this is a *right-tailed* or *right-skewed* distribution. If the centre of the distribution is right, the longer tail is left; this would be a *left-tailed* or *left-skewed* distribution.

**Snowball Sampling**: Sampling technique whereby participants are asked to recruit/recommend further participants. Called snowball sampling because the number of potentially contacted participants increases exponentially.

**Social Desirability Bias**: Human participants' urge to be seen as a person who complies with society's norms and standards, therefore potentially giving answers which reflect what participants *think* is socially desirable but not necessarily reflecting their own behaviour or values.

**Spearman's Rho**: *Non-parametric* alternative to *Pearson's correlation* coefficient.

**Sphericity**: Simply speaking, the non-*parametric* version of *homogeneity of variance*.

**Standard Deviation (SD)**: Square root of the *variance*.
- Symbol for **Population Standard Deviation**: $\sigma$
- Symbol for **Sample Standard Deviation**: s

**Statistic**: A *measure* relating to a *sample* rather than a *population*.

**Stratified Sampling**: Sampling technique whereby a *population* is examined in terms of existing strata relevant to the research question (i.e., income, role in organisation, education level). The *sample* is then built to either contain all strata in equal measures or to accurately reflect the distribution of strata in the *population*.

**Sum of Squares (SS)**: For a *population* (or *sample*), the sum of all values' squared differences to the *mean*.

**Survey**: In the context of social science research, usually a means of collecting data by presenting a (large) number of participants with a questionnaire.

**Symmetric Rating Scales**: Scales providing a balanced set of options (e.g., an equal number of response options to either side of a neutral response or an equal number of options relating to either poles of the scale).

**Systematic Sampling**: Determining the *ratio* of *sample* to *population* as 1:N and a random starting point between 1 and N, then proceeding to select every $N^{th}$ item out of a list of the entire *population*.

**Systematic Variance**: Part of the total *variance*; comprises *treatment* and *confound variance*.

**Testing Fatigue**: Fatigue or demotivation due to very long or very challenging tasks, leading to results that do not necessarily represent the participant's true ability.

**Three-Way ANOVA**: Statistical test examining the *effect* of three *independent variables* on one or more *dependent variables*.

**Treatment**: A different term for *condition*.

**Treatment Variance**: The type of *variance* you are most interested in as it is the *variance* introduced by the *treatment*.

**Triangulation**: Using multiple methods of enquiry and testing to corroborate the findings.

**Trigger Warning**: A type of *content note*. Originally referring to content which may trigger (i.e., cause) an episode of Post Traumatic Stress Disorder; now more commonly used for content that might be upsetting or disturbing.

**Two-Tailed Hypothesis**: A *hypothesis* concerning an *association* or difference between *variables* or a difference which only posits the existence of a difference or *association* but does not specify the manner.

**Two-Way ANOVA**: Statistical test examining the *effect* of two *independent variables* on one or more *dependent variables*.

**Type 1 Error**: To falsely reject the *null hypothesis*.

**Type 2 Error**: To falsely accept the *null hypothesis*.
**Unconditional Probability**: Probability of an event which is not dependent on the outcome of a previous event.
**Unifactorial**: A study design employing only one *factor*.
**Unipolar Rating Scales**: Response options are phrased as referring to the extent of a single *variable* or criterion (e.g., from 'agree not at all' to 'agree very much').
**Univariate ANOVA**: An analysis of variance employing only one *independent variable*.
**Unsystematic Variance**: Part of the overall *variance*; *error variance*. Random *variance* not introduced by the *treatment*.
**Validity**: Extent to which conclusions from the study are sound and a true reflection of the real relationships between *variables*.
**Variable**: Any entity within the context of a study the existence of which is acknowledged and which is labelled and measured, be it as an *independent* or *dependent variable*, a *factor*, or a potential *confound*.
**Variance**: *Sum of squares* divided by N (or N-1, see page 169). Also defined as the squared *standard deviation*.
Symbol for **Sample Variance**: $s^2$
Symbol for **Population Variance**: $\sigma^2$
**Wilcoxon Signed Rank Test**: *Non-parametric* alternative to the *paired-samples t-test*.
**Within-participants** (also referred to as **within-subjects**): *Variables* of which a participant experiences all *levels* – as opposed to *between-subject variables*, where participants experience one *level*.
**Z-score**: Helps comparing values from different distributions by standardising values by expressing them as multiples of the *standard deviation* from the *mean*.

# Excel Functions Glossary

- This glossary contains explanations for all Excel functions used in this book, plus some of their useful variants, where appropriate.
- Where cell ranges are given, and unless otherwise mentioned, they refer to the sample data set below.
- An expression in square brackets (for example, [value], [date], [range]) stands for the value itself and should be entered without the square brackets.
- Most formulas allow *nesting* – the use of formulas within formulas, for example =AVERAGE (SQRT(20),SQRT(40),SQRT(60)) calculates the average of the results of a series of square root equations.
- We have used uppercase letters for the formulas for clarity; Excel is not case-sensitive.

|    | A   | B   |
|----|-----|-----|
| 1  | 116 | 50  |
| 2  | 84  | 148 |
| 3  | 148 | 88  |
| 4  | 122 | 14  |
| 5  | 37  | 195 |
| 6  | 49  | 175 |
| 7  | 61  | 148 |
| 8  | 85  | 167 |
| 9  | 202 | 165 |
| 10 | 215 | 199 |

### ABS

Creates absolute values. Positive values remain positive; negative values become positive.

**Structure**
ABS([Number])
- [Number] – the number for which you want the absolute value

**Examples**
- =ABS(−25)=25
- =ABS(25)=25

## AVERAGE

Computes the average of a number of values.

**Structure**
AVERAGE([Range]) or
AVERAGE([Number1],[Number2] ... [Number 255])
- [Range] – range of cells with values for which the average will be computed
- [Number] – 1 to 255 numbers for which the average should be computed

**Examples**
- =AVERAGE(A1:B10)=123.4
- =AVERAGE(116,84,148,122,37,49,61,85,202,215)=111.9

## CHISQ.DIST

Calculates the probability density function for the chi-square distribution.

**Structure**
CHISQ.DIST([VALUE],[Degrees of freedom],[Parameter])
- [Value] – value for which you want to establish the *p*-value
- [Degrees of freedom] – degrees of freedom for the distribution
- [Parameter] – if set to 1, gives cumulative probability; if set to 0, gives individual probability (density)

**Examples**
CHISQ.DIST(0.236,2,1) = 0.111303947

Note: If you wanted to calculate the *p*-value associated with a Kruskal-Wallis test, you would need to deduct the result of this formula from 1 (i.e., 1- CHISQ.DIST(0.236,2,1) = 0.888696053 → your relevant *p*-value is .889).

## CHISQ.TEST

Calculates the level of significance for a chi-square test over a set of expected and observed values.

Note: Somewhat counterintuitively, this formula does not calculate the p $X^2$ -value itself, only the level of significance.

**Structure**
CHISQ.TEST([Range of actual values],[Range of expected values])
- [Range of actual values] – describes the range of cells which contain the actual (i.e., observed) values
- [Range of expected values] – describes the range of cells which contain the calculated expected values[1]

**Example**
For this example, we are using the data from Chapter 11's explanation on how to conduct a chi-square test.
- =CHISQ.TEST(B2:C4,E2:F4)=.001. Cells B2 to C4 contain the observed frequencies, cells E2 to F4 the expected frequencies. The $X^2$ -value needs to be calculated separately and is significant at the .001 level.

---

[1] See Section 11.4.1 on how to calculate expected values.

## CORREL

Computes correlations between two distributions.

A few important notes:

1. This is the *Pearson's* correlation coefficient since it is calculated directly on the values, not on their ranks.

2. The distributions (that is, the cell ranges) need to be of equal size, otherwise Excel will give out 'n/a'. If the two distributions are not of equal size, it is better to use Tools → Data Analysis → Correlations instead.

3. This function will only give you the correlation coefficient; you will still need to calculate the *p*-value for the correlation.[2]

**Structure**
CORREL([Range 1,Range 2])
- [Range1] – cell range of distribution A which is being correlated with distribution B
- [Range2] – cell range of distribution B which is being correlated with distribution A

**Examples**
- =CORREL(A1:A10,B1:B10)=−0.082406888. The two distributions show a very small, negative correlation of −.082.
- =CORREL(A1:A10,B1:B9)=#N/A. Because the two ranges aren't of equal sizes, Excel cannot calculate a correlation.

## COUNT

Counts number of values.

**Structure**
COUNT([Range]) or
COUNT([Number1],[Number2] ... [Number 255])
- [Range] – range of cells with values which will be counted
- [Number] – 1 to 255 numbers which will be counted

**Examples**
- =COUNT(A1:B10)=20
- =COUNT(1,5,7)=3

## COUNT A

Counts number of values that are not empty.

**Structure**
COUNTA([Range]) or
COUNTA([Number1],Number2] ... [Number 255])
- [Range] – range of cells with values which will be counted
- [Number] – 1 to 255 numbers which will be counted

---

[2] The formula for this is =1-F.DIST((($X \times Y^2$)/($1 - Y^2$)),1,X − 2,TRUE) where X is the number of cases and Y is the size of the correlation.

**Examples**
- =COUNT(A1:B20)=20
- =COUNT(A1,A2,A12)=2

## COUNTIF

Counts number of values which meet a criterion.

**Structure**
COUNTIF([Range],[Criterion])
- [Range] – range of cells with values which will be counted
- [Criterion] – criterion which values need to meet in order to be included in the count

**Examples**
- =COUNTIF(A1:B10,">200")=2. Counts all cells in the range between A1 and B10 which are larger than 200.
- =COUNTIF(A1:B10,148)=3. Counts all cells in the range given where the value is 148.
- =COUNTIF(A1:B10,">"&B5) = 3. Counts all cells which contain a value that is larger than the value in cell B5. Note the format for the criterion: the operator '>' is in quotation marks, and there is an ampersand ('&') before the cell reference.

## IF

Checks whether a condition is met and displays one value if the condition is met, another value if the condition is not met.

**Structure**
IF([Condition], [Value if true],[Value if not true])
- [Condition] – condition which is checked (e.g., whether a value in a cell or cell range is larger, smaller or equal to another value; whether a cell or cell range contains a certain string of characters, etc.).
- [Value if true] – value which is displayed if the condition above is met
- [Value if not true] – value which is displayed if the condition is not met

**Examples**
- =IF(B5>A5, "is larger than","is smaller than")='is larger than'. Checks whether value in cell B5 is larger than value in cell A5. If it is true, the cell displays value 'is larger than'; if it is not true, cell displays 'is smaller than'.
- =IF(SQRT(A6)=7,"yes","no")='yes'. Checks whether the square root of cell A6 is equal to 7. If it is true, the cell displays 'yes'; if it is not, 'no'.

## F.DIST

The $F$-value describes the ratio between the variances of two distributions. You have seen $F$ used in Section 9.4.1, where we used the $F$-Test Two-Sample for Variances, which tests whether two samples have equal or unequal variances. The $F$-distribution describes the spread and distribution of this $F$-value; depending on the parameter you set, the F.DIST function tells you the percentage of $F$-values smaller or equal to this $F$-value *or* the probability of this $F$-value occurring.

**Structure**
F.DIST([F-value], [Degrees of freedom 1],[Degrees of freedom2],[Parameter])

- [*F*-value] – ratio between the two distributions you are comparing; for example,

$$F = \frac{\text{Variance A}}{\text{Variance B}}$$

- [Degrees of freedom 1] – degrees of freedom of distribution A
- [Degrees of freedom 2] – degrees of freedom of distribution B
- [Parameter] – can be 0 or 1. If set to 0, tells you the individual probability for this *F*-value to occur; if set to 1, tells you the cumulative probability for the *F*-value to be at or below the value given.

**Examples**
- The first example is based on the tests for unequal variances described in Chapter 9 on page 239 mentioned above. =F.DIST(2.457,74,74,1)= 0.999925154. Here 2.457 is the *F*-value calculated previously;[4] degrees of freedom are 74 for both distributions because both have 75 values; the parameter is set to 1 because we want to see the cumulative probability.
But the F.DIST function gives you the left-tailed probability, and what you are interested in is the right-tailed probability. Easily solved: Calculate the inverse probability by deducting the result from 1. 1 − 0.999925154 = 0.000075. And this, in turn, tells you that the probability is less than .001: This *F*-value is highly significant at $p < .001$.
- The second example is based on the example conducting a one-way ANOVA in Excel: =F.DIST(0.271,2,147,1)= 0.237. Again, the formula yields the left-tailed probability and you want to know the right-tailed probability. =1−0.237 = 0.763.

## MEDIAN

Calculates the median of either a group of numbers or a range of cells.

**Structure**
MEDIAN([Cell range]) or
MEDIAN([Number1], [Number2], ... up to [Number255])
- [Cell range] – cell range containing values for which median is determined
- [Number1], etc. – up to 255 numbers forming the distribution of values for which the median is determined

**Examples**
- =MEDIAN(B1:B10)=156.5
- =MEDIAN(116,84,148, 122,37,49,61,85,202,215)=100.5

## MIN

Identifies the smallest number in a given set of numbers.

**Structure**
MIN([Cell range]) or
MIN([Number1], [Number2], ... up to [Number255])

---

[4] You can calculate the F-value yourself to check: simply divide the variance of one distribution by the other distribution's variance. In this example they are given as 428.766 and 174.507, respectively; $F = \frac{428.766}{174.507} = 2.4570$ – which is the same (rounded) F-value calculated by Excel in this example.

- [Cell range] – cell range containing values from which minimum is determined
- [Number1], etc. – up to 255 numbers forming the distribution of values from which the minimum is determined

**Examples**
=MIN(B1:B10)=14
=MIN(116,84,148, 122,37,49,61,85,202,215)=37

## MODE.SNGL

Identifies a single most frequently occurring value in a given set of numbers.

Note: Returns '#n/a' if there is no single most frequent value (i.e., all values are equally frequent). May produce inaccurate results if there is more than one mode – in those cases, **MODE.MULT** would be more appropriate.

**Structure**
MODE.SNGL([Cell range]) or
MODE.SNGL([Number1], [Number2], … up to [Number255])
- [Cell range] – cell range containing values from which the mode is determined
- [Number 1], etc. – up to 255 numbers forming the distribution of values from which the mode is determined

**Examples**
- =MODE.SNGL(B1:B10)=148
- =MODE.SNGL(116,84,148, 122,37,49,61,85,202,215)=#n/a

## MODE.MULT

Identifies the most frequently occurring values in a given set of numbers.

Note: This formula needs to be entered as an array formula[5] because the result may appear in more than one cell and you cannot be sure how many results you will be getting. We suggest using an array as large as the original data set to be on the safe side.

**Structure**
MODE.MULT([Cell range]) or
MODE.MULT([Number1], [Number2], … up to [Number255])
- [Cell range] – cell range containing values from which the mode(s) is/are determined
- [Number1], etc. – up to 255 numbers forming the distribution of values from which the mode(s) is/are determined

**Examples**
- =MODE.MULT(1,4,1,4,2,5,6,7,8) produces values in two cells of the array into which it was copied, '1' and '4'
- =MODE.MULT(B1:B10)=148 produces only one value because there is only one mode

---

[5] Highlight all cells in which you want the formula to apply – here the cells in which you want to see the results, not the cells containing the data. Keeping the cells selected, write the formula into the function bar and hit Control + Shift + Enter (Windows) or Command + Shift + Enter (Mac) to complete the entry.

## NORM.DIST

Tells you the probability of a specific value A in relation to a specific distribution; either in terms of being above/below another specified value B, or the exact likelihood of that value B occurring.

Note: This is the inverse version of the NORM.INV function: NORM.INV calculates a *value* based on a probability, a mean and a standard deviation; NORM.DIST calculates a *probability* based on a value, a mean and a standard deviation.

**Structure**
NORM.DIST([Value], [Reference mean], [Reference standard deviation],[True or False])
- [Value] – the number or value for which you want to know more
- [Reference mean] – the mean for the distribution you want to compare [value] against
- [Reference standard deviation] – the standard deviation for the distribution against which you want to compare [value]
- [True or False] – specifies what you want the formula to do
  - If set to 'False' or '0', this function tells you – for the distribution you have specified – how likely it would be that any single value from the distribution would be exactly [value]
  - If set to 'True' or '1', the function tells you the probability that a value would be equal to or smaller than [value]

**Examples**
For the first two examples we are using a distribution with a mean of 100 and a standard deviation of 15; the comparison value is 115.
- =NORM.DIST(115,100,15,0) = 0.016131382. For such a distribution, there is a probability of 0.016 (i.e., 1.6%) of the specific value 115 to occur.
- =NORM.DIST(115,100,15,1) = 0.841344746. In this case 0.8413 (i.e., 84.13%) of the distribution would have a value equal to or lower than 115.

This example relates to the sample data given above.
- =NORM.DIST(115,AVERAGE(A1:A10),STDEV.P(A1:A10),1) = 0.521253098. This is an example of a nested function: We are calculating mean and standard deviation of the distribution *within* the function. For the example distribution, 52.13% of its values are equal to or smaller than 115.

## NORM.INV

Calculates the value that corresponds to a given probability for a given distribution.

Note: This is the inverse version of the NORM.DIST function. The NORM.DIST function calculates a *probability* based on a value, a mean and a standard deviation, whereas NORM.INV calculates a *value* based on a probability, a mean and a standard deviation.

**Structure**
NORM.INV([Probability],[Mean],[Standard deviation])
- [Probability] – is the probability for which you want to calculate a score from the distribution
- [Mean] – mean of the distribution you are observing
- [Standard deviation] – standard deviation of the distribution you are observing

**Examples**
- =NORM.INV(0. 841344746,100,15)=115. For a distribution with a mean of 100 and a standard deviation of 15, 115 is the value for which 84.13% of the distribution's values are equal to or below.

- =NORM.INV(0.521253098,AVERAGE(A1:A10),STDEV.P(A1:A10))=115. This is an example of a nested function. We want to find out for which number it is true that 52.13% of the distribution's value fall at or below, and we are calculating the distribution's parameter within the formula.

## NORM.S.DIST

Tells you the probability of a specific value A in relation to a standardised distribution – a mean of 0 and a standard deviation of 1 – either in terms of being above/below another specified value B, or the exact likelihood of that value B occurring. It works like the NORM.DIST function but with standardised instead of absolute values.

### Structure
NORM.S.DIST([Z-value],[True or False])
- [Z-Value] – the number or value for which you want to know more (see Chapter 6 for an explanation of z-value, also referred to as *z-score*)
- [True or False] – specifies what you want the formula to do
  - If set to 'False' or '0', this function tells you – for the distribution you have specified – how likely it would be that any single value from the distribution would be exactly [z-value]
  - If set to 'True or '1', the function tells you the probability that a value would be equal to or smaller than [z-value]

### Examples
- =NORM.S.DIST(0.7,1) = 0.758036348. For a standard normal distribution, 0.758 (75.80%) of its values would be at or below a z-value of 0.7.
- =NORM.S.DIST(0.7,0)=0.312253933. For a standard normal distribution, the change for any single value to equal a z-value of 0.7 is 0.3122 (31.22%) =NORM.S.DIST(((115−100)/15),1)= 0.841344746. This is an example of a nested function. We are calculating the z-score[6] for which we want a probability attached *within* the function.

## NORM.S.INV

Calculates the z-score that corresponds to a given probability for a standardised distribution with a mean of 0 and a standard deviation of 1.
Note: This is the standardised inverse version of the NORM.S.DIST function. The NORM.S.DIST function calculates a *probability* based on a z-score and a standardised mean and standard deviation, whereas NORM.S.INV calculates a *value* based on a probability value.

### Structure
NORM.S.INV([Probability])
- [Probability] – is the probability for which you want to calculate a z-score from the distribution

### Example
- =NORM.S.INV(0.758036348)=0.7. For a standardised distribution, 75.80% of all values are equal to or below a z-score of 0.7

## RANK.AVG

Returns the rank for a value in relation to a specified range of values.

---

[6] The z-score is calculated by calculating the difference between individual value and the mean and then dividing the outcome by the standard deviation for the distribution.

**Structure**
=RANK.AVG([Value],[Reference range],[Order parameter])
- [Value] – value or cell reference for value for which you want to know the rank
- [Reference range] – range of values within which you want [value] to be ranked
- [Order parameter] – specified order of ranking. If 0 or not given, values are ranked in descending order; any value except 0 or not given, values are ranked in ascending order

Note: [Value] needs to be a part of [Reference range] (i.e., you cannot rank a value that is not included in the reference range). Excel will return an error message if you try.

**Examples**
- =RANK.AVG(148,A1:A10,1)=8. 148 is ranked eighth if values are ranked in ascending order.
- =RANK.AVG(148,A1:A10,0)=3. 148 is ranked third if values are ranked in descending order.
- =RANK.AVG(A3,A1:A10,0)=3. The function works with cell ranges or values.
- =RANK.AVG(B4,A1:A10)=#N/A. Function returns an error message because the value in B4 is not included in the range from A1:A10.

## SQRT

Calculates the square root of a cell or a number.

**Structure**
SQRT([Cell]), or
SQRT([Number])
- [Cell] – Individual cell reference containing the value for which the square root should be calculated
- [Number] – Individual number of which the square root should be calculated

**Examples**
- =SQRT(B3)= 9.38083152
- =SQRT(195)=13.96424004

## STDEV.P

Calculates the standard deviation for a range of values coming from a population.

**Structure**
STDEV.P([Cell range])
STDEV.P([Number1], [Number2], ... up to [Number255])
- [Cell range] – cell range containing values for which the population standard deviation is determined
- [Number1], etc. – up to 255 numbers forming the distribution of values for which the population standard deviation is determined

**Examples**
- =STDEV.P(B1:B10)= 59.69329946
- =STDEV.P(116,84,148,122,37,49,61,85,202,215)= 58.16261686

## STDEV.S

Calculates the standard deviation for a range of values coming from a sample.

**Structure**

STDEV.S([Cell range])

STDEV.S([Number1], [Number2], ... up to [Number255])

- [Cell range] – cell range containing values for which the sample standard deviation is determined
- [Number1], etc. – up to 255 numbers forming the distribution of values for which the sample standard deviation is determined

**Examples**

- =STDEV.S(B1:B10)= 62.92226244
- =STDEV.S(116,84,148,122,37,49,61,85,202,215)= 61.30878132

## SUM

Calculates the sum of either a range of cells or a series of numbers.

**Structure**

SUM(Cell range]) or

SUM([Number1], [Number2], ... up to [Number255])

- [Cell range] – cell range containing values for which the sum is determined
- [Number1], etc. – up to 255 numbers forming the distribution of values for which the sum is determined

**Examples**

- =SUM(A1:A10)=1119
- =SUM(50,148,88,14,195,175,148,167,165,199)=1349

## SUMIF

Looks at two ranges of cells and only sums up cells of range A if a criterion is met in the corresponding cell of range B.

**Structure**

SUMIF([Range A],[Condition],[Range B])

- [Range A] – range of which cells will be checked for the condition specified in the formula
- [Condition] – specifies the condition for which cells of range A are checked
- [Range B] – for each cell of range A which meets the condition, the *corresponding* cell in range B is included in the sum. Two important notes:

    1. If the specified ranges are not of equivalent length, Excel will automatically size range B to be of equivalent length. For example, if both ranges are 10 cells long and in range A the second, fourth and sixth cell meet the criterion, the sum includes the second, fourth and sixth cell of range B. If you only specified the first four cells of range B, Excel will nevertheless include the second, fourth and sixth cell of range B.

    2. Range B is optional – if you do not include a second range in the formula, Excel will automatically sum up the cells of range A which meet the criterion.

**Examples**

- =SUMIF(A1:A10,">200",B1:B10)=364. In this example, only the last two cells of range A meet the criterion, therefore only the last two cells of range B are summed up

- =SUMIF(A1:A10,">200",B1:B4)=364. Even though the second range has been entered as only having four cells, Excel automatically extends it to have the same length as range A; it therefore gives the same result as the previous formula
- =SUMIF(B1:B8,"<100")=152. In this example, we have omitted the second range; Excel thus sums up all the cells of the range given for which the criterion is met.

## T.INV

Returns the *one-tailed* critical value of the t-test statistic for a given alpha-value and degrees of freedom; in other words, tells you the minimum t-value at which it would be significant for a distribution with the amount of degrees of freedom given.

**Structure**
T.INV([Probability],[Degrees of freedom])
- [Probability] – the *p*-value at which you want it to be significant (e.g., .05, .01, .001 or any other level)
- [Degree of freedom] – degrees of freedom of the distribution for which you want to calculate the critical value. Usually df = n−1, but check individual test requirements.

**Examples**
Note that although Excel gives negative values, t-values are read as absolute values (i.e., for the first example, a t-value of either −1.7 or 1.7 would be considered significant at an alpha level of .05). You can see how increasing the alpha level requires higher t-values.
- =T.INV(.05,149)=−1.655144534
- =T.INV(.01,149)=−2.351634895
- =T.INV(.001, 149)=−3.145829198

## T.INV.2T

Returns the *two-tailed* critical value of the t-test statistic for a given alpha-value and degrees of freedom; in other words, tells you the minimum t-value at which it would be significant for a distribution with the amount of degrees of freedom given.

**Structure**
T.INV.2T([Probability],[Degrees of freedom])
- [Probability] – the *p*-value at which you want it to be significant (e.g., .05, .01, .001 or any other level)
- [Degree of freedom] – degrees of freedom of the distribution for which you want to calculate the critical value. Usually df = n−1, but check individual test requirements.

**Examples**
Note that although Excel gives negative values, t-values are read as absolute values (i.e., for the first example, a t-value of either −1.7 or 1.7 would be considered significant for a two-tailed test at an alpha level of .05). You can see how increasing the alpha level requires higher t-values.
- =T.INV.2T(.05,149)=−1.976013178
- =T.INV.2T(.01,149)=−2.609227907
- =T.INV.2T(.001, 149)=3.357020283

# References

Aaker, J. L. (1997). Dimensions of brand personality. *Journal of Marketing Research*, *34*(3), 347–356.

Achtnicht, M. (2012). German car buyers' willingness to pay to reduce CO2 emissions. *Climatic Change*, *113*(3–4), 679–697.

Agnew, M. D., & Thornes, J. E. (1995). The weather sensitivity of the UK food retail and distribution industry. *Meteorological Applications*, *2*(2), 137–147.

Aitken, P. P., & Jahoda, G. (1983). An observational study of young adults' drinking groups—i. drink preferences, demographic and structural variables as predictors of alcohol consumption. *Alcohol and Alcoholism*, *18*(2), 135–150.

Ali, R., & Ahmed, M. S. (2009). The impact of reward and recognition programs on employee's motivation and satisfaction: An empirical study. *International Review of Business Research Papers*, *5*(4), 270–279.

Altman, D. G., & Bland, M. (1995). Statistics notes: The normal distribution. *British Medical Journal*, *310*, 298.

Altarriba, J., & Canary, T. M. (2004). The influence of emotional arousal on affective priming in monolingual and bilingual speakers. *Journal of Multilingual and Multicultural* Development, *25*(2–3), 248–265.

Ambady, N., Shih, M., Kim, A., & Pittinsky, T. L. (2001). Stereotype susceptibility in children: Effects of identity activation on quantitative performance. *Psychological Science*, *12*(5), 385–390.

American Psychological Association. (2010). *Publication manual of the American Psychological Association* (6th ed.). Washington, DC: American Psychological Association.

American Statistics Association. (2016). The ASA's statement on p-values: Context, process, and purpose. http://amstat.tandfonline.com/doi/abs/10.1080/00031305.2016.1154108. (Accessed 30 April 2016).

Asch, S. E. (1951). Effects of group pressure upon the modification and distortion of judgment. In H. Guetzkow (Ed.), *Groups, leadership and men*. Pittsburgh, PA: Carnegie Press.

Ball, J., Maben, J., Murrells, T., Day, T., & Griffiths, P. (2015). *12-hour shifts: Prevalence, views and impact*. National Nursing Research Unit.

Bamberg, S., & Möser, G. (2007). Twenty years after Hines, Hungerford, and Tomera: A new meta-analysis of psycho-social determinants of pro-environmental behaviour. *Journal of Environmental Psychology*, *27*(1), 14–25.

Banbury, S. P., & Berry, D. C. (2005). Office noise and employee concentration: Identifying causes of disruption and potential improvements. *Ergonomics*, *48*(1), 25–37.

Barr, R., Muentener, P., Garcia, A., Fujimoto, M., & Chávez, V. (2007). The effect of repetition on imitation from television during infancy. *Developmental Psychobiology*, *49*(2), 196–207.

Bates, T. C. (2015). The glass is half full and half empty: A population-representative twin study testing if optimism and pessimism are distinct systems. *The Journal of Positive Psychology*, *10*(6), 533–542.

Beck, A. T., Steer, R. A., & Brown, G. K. (1996). *Manual for the Beck Depression Inventory-II*. San Antonio, TX: Psychological Corporation.

Benedict, R. H., & Zgaljardic, D. J. (1998). Practice effects during repeated administrations of memory tests with and without alternate forms. *Journal of Clinical and Experimental Neuropsychology*, *20*(3), 339–352.

Bennett, R. (2003). Factors underlying the inclination to donate to particular types of charity. *International Journal of Nonprofit and Voluntary Sector Marketing*, *8*(1), 12–29.

Bezerra, R. F., Jalloh, S., & Stevenson, J. (1998). Formulating hypotheses graphically in social research. *Quality & Quantity*, *32*, 327.

Biklen, D., & Schubert, A. (1991). New words: The communication of students with autism. *Remedial and Special Education*, *12*(6), 46–57.

Binet, A., & Simon, T. (1916). The development of intelligence in children: The Binet-Simon Scale (No. 11). Williams & Wilkins Company.

Boake, C. (2002). From the Binet–Simon to the Wechsler–Bellevue: Tracing the history of intelligence testing. *Journal of Clinical and Experimental Neuropsychology*, *24*(3), 383–405.

Boncori, I. (2017). *Personal communication*.

Booth, A. L., Leigh, A., & Varganova, E. (2012). Does ethnic discrimination vary across minority groups? Evidence from a field experiment. *Oxford Bulletin of Economics and Statistics*, *74*(4), 547–573.

Brace, N., Kemp, R., & Snelgar, R. (2016). *SPSS for Psychologists* (6th ed.). Basingstoke: Palgrave Macmillan.

British Academy of Management. (2013). The British Academy of Management's code of Ethics and Best Practice for Members. Available at https://www.bam.ac.uk/sites/bam.ac.uk/files/The%20British%20Academy%20of%20Management's%20Code%20of%20Ethics%20and%20Best%20Practice%20for%20Members.pdf. (Accessed 12 January 2018).

British Psychological Society. (2014). Code of Human Research Ethics. Available at http://www.bps.org.uk/system/files/Public%20files/code_of_human_research_ethics_dec_2014_inf180_web.pdf. (Accessed 17 June 2016).

Campbell, N. C., Graham, J. L., Jolibert, A., & Meissner, H. G. (1988). Marketing negotiations in France, Germany, the United Kingdom, and the United States. *The Journal of Marketing*, *52*(2), 49–62.

Carlsson, M., & Rooth, D.-O. (2008). Is it your foreign name or foreign qualifications? An experimental study of ethnic discrimination in hiring, *IZA Discussion Papers*, No. 3810, http://nbn-resolving.de/urn:nbn:de:101:1-20081126850. (Accessed 02 July 2018)

Casey, M. B., Pezaris, E., & Nuttall, R. L. (1992). Spatial ability as a predictor of math achievement: The importance of sex and handedness patterns. *Neuropsychologia*, *30*(1), 35–45.

Caspersen, C. J., Pereira, M. A., & Curran, K. M. (2000). Changes in physical activity patterns in the United States, by sex and cross-sectional age. *Medicine & Science in Sports & Exercise*, *32*(9), 1601–1609.

Cassidy, G., & MacDonald, R. A. (2007). The effect of background music and background noise on the task performance of introverts and extraverts. *Psychology of Music*, *35*(3), 517–537.

Cattell, R. B. (1963). Theory of fluid and crystallized intelligence: A critical experiment. *Journal of Educational Psychology*, *54*(1), 1.

Chu, S. C., & Kamal, S. (2008). The effect of perceived blogger credibility and argument quality on message elaboration and brand attitudes: An exploratory study. *Journal of Interactive Advertising*, *8*(2), 26–37.

Cohen, S., Kamarck, T., & Mermelstein, R. (1983). A global measure of perceived stress. *Journal of Health and Social Behavior*, *24*(4), 385–396.

Collie, A., Maruff, P., Darby, D. G., & McStephen, M. (2003). The effects of practice on the cognitive test performance of neurologically normal individuals assessed at brief test–retest intervals. *Journal of the International Neuropsychological Society*, *9*(3), 419–428.

Coyle-Shapiro, J., & Kessler, I. (2000). Consequences of the psychological contract for the employment relationship: A large scale survey. *Journal of Management Studies*, *37*(7), 903–930.

Crawford, L. (2005). Senior management perceptions of project management competence. *International Journal of Project Management*, *23*(1), 7–16.

Crossley, R. (1992). Getting the words out: Case studies in facilitated communication training. *Topics in Language Disorders*, *12*(4), 46–59.

DeLong, L. L. (2006). College students' motivation for physical activity. Doctoral Thesis. Available at http://web.ftvs.cuni.cz/hendl/metodologie/dis2006motivacesport.pdf. (Accessed 31 January 2018).

Desimone, L. (1999). Linking parent involvement with student achievement: Do race and income matter? *The Journal of Educational Research*, *93*(1), 11–30.

Dixon, H., Scully, M., Wakefield, M., Kelly, B., Chapman, K., & Donovan, R. (2011). Parent's responses to nutrient claims and sports celebrity endorsements on energy-dense and nutrient-poor foods: An experimental study. *Public Health Nutrition*, *14*(6), 1071–1079.

Eberlin, M., McConnachie, G., Ibel, S., & Volpe, L. (1993). Facilitated communication: A failure to replicate the phenomenon. *Journal of Autism and Developmental Disorders*, *23*(3), 507–530.

Economic and Social Research Council. (2015). ESRC Framework for Research Ethics. Available at http://www.esrc.ac.uk/files/funding/guidance-for-applicants/esrc-framework-for-research-ethics-2015/. (Accessed 12 January 2018).

Evans, G. W., & Johnson, D. (2000). Stress and open-office noise. *Journal of Applied Psychology*, *85*(5), 779.

Fehr, E., & Gächter, S. (2002). Altruistic punishment in humans. *Nature*, *415*(6868), 137.

Fiedler, K., Messner, C., & Bluemke, M. (2006). Unresolved problems with the "I", the "A", and the "T": A logical and psychometric critique of the Implicit Association Test (IAT). *European Review of Social Psychology*, *17*(1), 74–147.

Flanagin, A. J., & Metzger, M. J. (2000). Perceptions of Internet information credibility. *Journalism & Mass Communication Quarterly*, *77*(3), 515–540.

Frei, H., & Thurneysen, A. (2001). Treatment for hyperactive children: Homeopathy and methylphenidate compared in a family setting. *British Homoeopathic Journal*, *90*(4), 183–188.

Furman, W., & Buhrmester, D. (1985). Children's perceptions of the qualities of sibling relationships. *Child Development*, 448–461.

Furnham, A., Trew, S., & Sneade, I. (1999). The distracting effects of vocal and instrumental music on the cognitive test performance of introverts and extraverts. *Personality and Individual Differences*, *27*(2), 381–392.

Garry, M., Loftus, E., Brown, S. W., and DuBreuil, S. C. (1997). Womb with a view: Memory beliefs and memory-work experiences. In D. G. Payne and F.G. Conrad (Eds), *Intersections in basic and applied memory research* (pp. 233–255). Mahwah, NJ: Lawrence Erlbaum Associates, Inc.

Gneezy, U., & Rustichini, A. (2000). Pay enough or don't pay at all. *The Quarterly Journal of Economics*, *115*(3), 791–810.

Gravetter, F. J., and Wallnau, L. B. (2004). *Statistics for the behavioural sciences* (6th ed.). London: Thomson Wadsworth.

Grimes, D. R. (2012). Proposed mechanisms for homeopathy are physically impossible. *Focus on Alternative and Complementary Therapies*, *17*(3), 149–155.

Hambleton, R. and Rodgers, J. H. (1995). Item bias review. *Practical Assessment, Research & Evaluation*, *4*(6), 1–3.

Haney, C., Banks, C., & Zimbardo, P. (1972). Interpersonal dynamics in a simulated prison (No. ONR-TR-Z-09). Stanford University, CA: Department of Psychology.

Haney, C., Banks, W. C., & Zimbardo, P. (1973a). A study of prisoners and guards in a simulated prison. *Naval Research Reviews*, *9*, 1–17.

Haney, C., Banks, C., & Zimbardo, P. (1973b). Interpersonal dynamics in a simulated prison. *International Journal of Criminology and Penology*, *1*, 69–97.

Harris, R. and Jarvis, C. (2013). *Statistics in geography and environmental science*. London: Routledge.

Harrison, K. (1992). Whether the weather be good. *Super Marketing*, *13*, 15–17.

Haskel, J., & Slaughter, M. J. (2001). Trade, technology and UK wage inequality. *The Economic Journal*, *111*(468), 163–187.

Henrich, J., Heine, S. J., and Norenzayan, A. (2010). The weirdest people in the world? *Behavioral and Brain Sciences*, *33*(2–3), 61–83.

Hentschel, J., Lanjouw, J. O., Lanjouw, P., & Poggi, J. (2000). Combining census and survey data to trace the spatial dimensions of poverty: A case study of Ecuador. *The World Bank Economic Review*, *14*(1), 147–165.

Hinkin, T. R., & Schriesheim, C. A. (2008). A theoretical and empirical examination of the transactional and non-leadership dimensions of the Multifactor Leadership Questionnaire (MLQ). *The Leadership Quarterly*, *19*(5), 501–513.

Hyland, M. E. (2005). A tale of two therapies: Psychotherapy and complementary and alternative medicine (CAM) and the human effect. *Clinical Medicine*, *5*(4), 361–367.

Ineson, E.M., Lyons, A., & Branston, C. (2006). Cross cultural change, adjustment and culture shock: UK to USA. *Turizam: Međunarodni Znanstveno-stručni časopis*, *54*(4), 355–365.

Keating, J., Van Boven, L., & Judd, C. M. (2016). Partisan underestimation of the polarizing influence of group discussion. *Journal of Experimental Social Psychology*, *65*, 52–58.

Kirmani, A. (1997). Advertising repetition as a signal of quality: If it's advertised so much, something must be wrong. *Journal of Advertising*, *3*, 77–86.

Kolek, E. A., & Saunders, D. (2008). Online disclosure: An empirical examination of undergraduate Facebook profiles. *NASPA Journal*, *45*(1), 1–25.

Kressmann, F., Sirgy, M. J., Herrmann, A., Huber, F., Huber, S., & Lee, D. J. (2006). Direct and indirect effects of self-image congruence on brand loyalty. *Journal of Business Research*, *59*(9), 955–964.

Kuvaas, B. (2006). Performance appraisal satisfaction and employee outcomes: Mediating and moderating roles of work motivation. *The International Journal of Human Resource Management*, *17*(3), 504–522.

LaPiere, R. T. (1934). Attitudes vs. actions. *Social Forces*, *13*(2), 230–237.

Lazar, J., Allen, A., Kleinman, J., & Malarkey, C. (2007). What frustrates screen reader users on the web: A study of 100 blind users. *International Journal of Human-Computer Interaction*, *22*(3), 247–269.

Lee, K., Agrawal, A., & Choudhary, A. (2013, August). Real-time disease surveillance using twitter data: Demonstration on flu and cancer. In *Proceedings of the 19th ACM SIGKDD International Conference on Knowledge Discovery and Data Mining* (pp. 1474–1477). Chicago, IL: ACM.

Lercher, P., Evans, G. W., & Meis, M. (2003). Ambient noise and cognitive processes among primary schoolchildren. *Environment and Behaviour*, *35*(6), 725–735.

Linke, L., Saribay, S. A., & Kleisner, K. (2016). Perceived trustworthiness is associated with position in a corporate hierarchy. *Personality and Individual Differences*, *99*, 22–27.

Løken, T. (2002). Alternative therapy of animals–homeopathy and other alternative methods of therapy. *Acta Veterinaria Scandinavica*, *43*(1), S47.

Lu, H., While, A. E., & Louise Barriball, K. (2007). A model of job satisfaction of nurses: A reflection of nurses' working lives in Mainland China. *Journal of Advanced Nursing*, *58*(5), 468–479.

Madlock, P. E. (2008). The link between leadership style, communicator competence, and employee satisfaction. *The Journal of Business Communication*, 45(1), 61–78.

Magnier, L., & Schoormans, J. (2015). Consumer reactions to sustainable packaging: The interplay of visual appearance, verbal claim and environmental concern. *Journal of Environmental Psychology*, 44, 53–62.

Matz, D. C., & Wood, W. (2005). Cognitive dissonance in groups: The consequences of disagreement. *Journal of Personality and Social Psychology*, 88(1), 22.

McCammon, I. (2002, September). Evidence of heuristic traps in recreational avalanche accidents. In *Proceedings ISSW* (pp. 244–251).

McCloskey, D. N., & Ziliak, S. (2008). *The cult of statistical significance*. Ann Arbor, MI: University of Michigan Press.

Messick, S. (1995). Validity of psychological assessment: Validation of inferences from persons' responses and performances as scientific inquiry into score meaning. *American Psychologist*, 50(9), 741–749.

Milgram, S. (1963). Behavioural study of obedience. *The Journal of Abnormal and Social Psychology*, 67(4), 371.

Mir, P., Trender-Gerhard, I., Edwards, M. J., Schneider, S. A., Bhatia, K. P., & Jahanshahi, M. (2011). Motivation and movement: The effect of monetary incentive on performance speed. *Experimental Brain Research*, 209(4), 551–559.

Miron-Shatz, T., Hanoch, Y., Graef, D., & Sagi, M. (2009). Presentation format affects comprehension and risk assessment: The case of prenatal screening. *Journal of Health Communication*, 14(5), 439–450.

Mischel, W., Ebbesen, E. B., & Raskoff Zeiss, A. (1972). Cognitive and attentional mechanisms in delay of gratification. *Journal of Personality and Social Psychology*, 21(2), 204.

Nichols, A. L., & Maner, J. K. (2008). The good-subject effect: Investigating participant demand characteristics. *The Journal of General Psychology*, 135(2), 151–166.

North, A. C., & Hargreaves, D. J. (2007). Lifestyle correlates of musical preference: 1. Relationships, living arrangements, beliefs, and crime. *Psychology of Music*, 35(1), 58–87.

Nyhan, B., & Reifler, J. (2015). Does correcting myths about the flu vaccine work? An experimental evaluation of the effects of corrective information. *Vaccine*, 33(3), 459–464.

Olsen, S. O. (2003). Understanding the relationship between age and seafood consumption: The mediating role of attitude, health involvement and convenience. *Food Quality and Preference*, 14(3), 199–209.

Pope-Davis, D. B., & Twing, J. S. (1991). The effects of age, gender, and experience on measures of attitude regarding computers. *Computers in Human Behaviour*, 7(4), 333–339.

Prieto, M., & Caemmerer, B. (2013). An exploration of factors influencing car purchasing decisions. *International Journal of Retail & Distribution Management*, 41(10), 738–764.

Raymond, M., & Pontier, D. (2004). Is there geographical variation in human handedness? *Laterality: Asymmetries of Body, Brain and Cognition*, 9(1), 35–51.

Reichheld, F. F. (2003). The one number you need to grow. *Harvard Business Review*, 81(12), 46–55.

Research Council UK. (2013). Policy ad guidelines on governance of food research practice. Available at http://www.rcuk.ac.uk/RCUK-prod/assets/documents/reviews/grc/RCUKPolicyandGuidelinesonGovernanceofGoodResearchPracticeFebruary2013.pdf. (Accessed 12 January 2018).

Rosenthal, R. (1963). On the social psychology of the psychological experiment: The experimenter's hypothesis as unintended determinant of experimental results. *American Scientist*, 51(2), 268–283.

Rotter, J. B. (1990). Internal versus external control of reinforcement: A case history of a variable. *American Psychologist*, 45(4), 489.

Rudloff, D. (2011). Exploring perceptions of presentation formats: Antecedents and consequences, PhD thesis, awarded 22 December 2011.

Saulnier, A., & Sivasubramaniam, D. (2015). Effects of victim presence and coercion in restorative justice: An experimental paradigm. *Law and Human Behavior*, 39(4), 378.

Schlam, T. R., Wilson, N. L., Shoda, Y., Mischel, W., & Ayduk, O. (2013). Preschoolers' delay of gratification predicts their body mass 30 years later. *The Journal of Pediatrics*, 162(1), 90–93.

Schmierbach, M., & Oeldorf-Hirsch, A. (2012). A little bird told me, so I didn't believe it: Twitter, credibility, and issue perceptions. *Communication Quarterly*, 60(3), 317–337.

Schubert, R., Brown, M., Gysler, M., & Brachinger, H. W. (1999). Financial decision-making: Are women really more risk-averse? *The American Economic Review*, 89(2), 381–385.

Shang, A., Huwiler-Müntener, K., Nartey, L., Jüni, P., Dörig, S., Sterne, J. A., Pewsner, D., & Egger, M. (2005). Are the clinical effects of homoeopathy placebo effects? Comparative study of placebo-controlled trials of homoeopathy and allopathy. *The Lancet*, 366(9487), 726–732.

Spearman, C. (1946). Theory of general factor. *British Journal of Psychology*, 36(3), 117–131.

Steele, C. M. and Aronson, J. (1995). Stereotype threat and the intellectual test performance of African Americans. *Journal of Personality and Social Psychology*, 69(5), 797–811.

Stonewall. (2016). Do ask, do tell: Capturing data on sexual orientation and gender identity globally. Available at https://www.stonewall.org.uk/sites/default/files/do_ask_do_tell_guide_2016.pdf. (Accessed 15 February 2017).

Stroop, J. R. (1935). Studies of interference in serial verbal reactions. *Journal of Experimental Psychology*, 18(6), 643–662.

Struthers, C. W., Perry, R. P., & Menec, V. H. (2000). An examination of the relationship among academic stress, coping, motivation, and performance in college. *Research in Higher Education*, 41(5), 581–592.

Tang, F. C. (2009). Electricity consumption, income, foreign direct investment, and population in Malaysia: New evidence from multivariate framework analysis. *Journal of Economic Studies*, 36(4), 371–382.

Thurstone, L. L. (1934). The vectors of mind. *Psychological Review*, 41(1), 1.

Underwood, R. L., & Klein, N. M. (2002). Packaging as brand communication: Effects of product pictures on consumer responses to the package and brand. *Journal of Marketing Theory and Practice*, 10(4), 58–68.

Velasco, C., Salgado-Montejo, A., Marmolejo-Ramos, F., & Spence, C. (2014). Predictive packaging design: Tasting shapes, typefaces, names, and sounds. *Food Quality and Preference*, 34, 88–95.

Wadlington, E. M., & Wadlington, P. L. (2005). What educators really believe about dyslexia. *Reading Improvement*, 42(1), 16–33.

Wagner, K. D., Robb, A. S., Findling, R. L., Jin, J., Gutierrez, M. M., & Heydorn, W. E. (2004). A randomized, placebo-controlled trial of citalopram for the treatment of major depression in children and adolescents. *American Journal of Psychiatry*, 161(6), 1079–1083.

Wahab, E. A. A., & Rahman, R. A. (2009). Institutional investors and director remuneration: Do political connections matter? In *Corporate Governance and Firm Performance* (pp. 139–169). Emerald Group Publishing Limited.

Weibel, D., Wissmath, B., & Groner, R. (2008). How gender and age affect newscasters' credibility—an investigation in Switzerland. *Journal of Broadcasting & Electronic Media*, 52(3), 466–484.

Wellcome Trust. (2005). Guidelines on Good Research Practice. Available at http://www.wellcome.ac.uk/About-us/Policy/Policy-and-position-statements/WTD002753.htm. (Accessed 12 January 2018).

Wood, S., Nolte, S., Burridge, M., Rudloff, D., & Green, W. (2015). Dimensions and location of high-involvement management: Fresh evidence from the UK Commission's 2011 Employer Skills Survey. *Human Resource Management Journal*, *25*(2), 166–183.

Woodzicka, J. A., & LaFrance, M. (2005). The effects of subtle sexual harassment on women's performance in a job interview. *Sex Roles*, *53*(1), 67–77.

World Health Organisation. (2001). Putting women's safety first: Ethical and safety recommendations for research on domestic violence against women. Geneva: Global Programme on Evidence for Health Policy. Available at http://www.who.int/gender/violence/womenfirtseng.pdf. (Accessed 15 January 2018).

Wu, P. C., & Wang, Y. C. (2011). The influences of electronic word-of-mouth message appeal and message source credibility on brand attitude. *Asia Pacific Journal of Marketing and Logistics*, 23(4), 448–472.

Yougov. (2014). The ideal height: 5'6" for a woman, 5'11" for a man. Available at https://yougov.co.uk/news/2014/07/11/ideal-height-56-woman-511-man/. (Accessed 17 February 2017).

# Index

absolute numbers
　general, 106–7
　in Excel, 107
　in SPSS, 107
abstract, 299–300
academic debate, 4–5
accessibility
　of methods, 85
　of charts, 202–4
alpha level, 180
　see also p-value
alternative hypothesis, 42
　contrast with null hypothesis
analyses overview, 219–226
ANCOVA (Analysis of Covariance)
　example, 224
　general principle, 224
　in SPSS, 269–270
　reporting, 271
anonymity, 38
ANOVA (Analysis of Variance)
　between participants,
　　assumptions, 223
　multivariate, 222
　within participants, assumptions,
　　223
　see also one-way ANOVA,
　　repeated measures ANOVA,
　　two- or three-way ANOVA,
　　three-way ANOVA
appendix, 298
archival data, 56
associations, 5, 24
　causal, 22
　non-causal, 23
　see also analyses looking at
　　associations: chi square
　　goodness-of-fit, chi square
　　test of independence,
　　Pearson's correlation,
　　Spearman's correlation
asymmetric (rating scale), 70

backing up, 119
bar chart, 198
base, 107–8
Beck's depression inventory, 49
bell curve, 177
between-participants, 31
　contrast with within-participants
between-subjects, see between-
　participants, 31
bias, 28, 31, 77, 84, 142
　avoidance of, 83
　by making assumptions, 78
　by using loaded language, 78
　regarding gender, 77
bipolar (rating scale), 69

blind/blind studies/blind trials, 28
block randomisation, 86–7
branching, in online surveys, 63

categorical data, 17–8
causality, 5
central-tendency bias, 70, 143
charts
　elements of, 194–5
　in Excel, 196
　in SPSS, 196–7
chi square goodness-of-fit
　example, 226
　general principle, 226
　in Excel, 280–281
　in SPSS, 281–2
　reporting, 282
chi square test of independence
　example, 225
　general principle, 225
　in Excel, 283–5
　in SPSS, 285–6
　reporting, 286
choice question, 65
coercion, 37
comments (in SPSS), 130
confidence interval, 80
Cohen's d, 183–4
colours, use of, 64
column chart, 197
comparisons, 5
　see also tests looking at
　　comparisons/differences:
　　one-sample t-test, Wilcoxon
　　signed rank, paired-sample
　　t-test, independent-samples
　　t-test, Mann-Whitney U
composite measure, 49
computational formula (of SS), 168
conclusion validity, 47, 74
condition, 27
conditional logic, in online
　surveys, 63
confidence level, 80
confidentiality, 38
confound variance, 173–4
confound, see confounding variable
confounding variable, 25, 27
consent form, 39
construct underrepresentation,
　48–9
construct, 59
　see also construct validity
construct-validity, 47
construct-irrelevant variance, 48
constructivist, 6
content note, 63
contingency table, 193

continuous variables, 15–7
　contrast with discrete variables
control, 29–30, 47
control condition, 25–9, 46
control group, 25–9, 46
convergent validity, 47, 59
correlation, 23–4
　analysis output, in Excel, 205
　analysis output, in SPSS, 205–6
　negative, 23
　positive, 23
　tables, 206
counterbalancing, 87
"counting" questions, 4
covariates, 25
　see also Analysis of Covariance
　　(ANCOVA)
Cronbach's alpha, 90–91

data analysis, writing up of, 295
data entry
　errors in, 142–6
　multiple choice questions, 139
　open questions/sample questions,
　　135–6
　ordering/ranking tasks, 140–141
　rating scales/semantic
　　differentials, 141–2
　single choice questions, 136–8
data management, 118–120
data transformation, 60, 151
data, backing up of, 119
debriefing, 39
deception, 37, 39
decimal points, 100–101, 109
definitional formula (of SS), 168
degrees of freedom, 184–5
demographic question, 72
denominator, 103
dependent variable, 24–5, 30
　contrast with independent
　　variable,
descriptives, 192
design, shorthand for, 31–2
differences, 23–5
directional hypotheses, see one-
　tailed hypotheses
discrete variables, 15–7
　contrast with continuous variables
discussion, 296–7
double-blind study, 28
dummy-variable, 150

effect, 22, 24
effect size, 183
e-notation, see scientific
　notation, 108
epistemology, 6

error variance, 173–4
ethics approval, 39
ethic guidelines, 36
excel, 120–7
    applying a filter in, 126–7
    copying a function to other cells, 125
    entering a function, 123–5
    entering data in, 121–2
expected frequency, 281, 284–5
experiment, 29–31
explanatory variable, *see* independent variable
exponent, 107–8

facilitated communication, 7
factor, 27, 30
forced-choice method, 70
fractions, 103
frequencies, 98–9
    describing of, 156
    calculating in Excel, 156–7
    calculating in SPSS, 156
    expected, 281, 284–285
    observed, 280–281, 283

Gauss curve, *see* bell curve
gender
    identity, 15, 73–4
    asking about, 73–4
    fluid, 15
    non-binary, 15
    gender vs. sex, 21
grand totals, 193
graphs
    in test material, 63
    colour scheme of, 203
    greyscale, 203
    texture of, 203–4
greater than or equal sign, 97
greater than sign, 97

hazard perception test (HPT), 63
histogram chart, 198–9
homogeneity of variance, 223
homoscedasticity, *see* homogeneity of variance
hypotheses, 40
    and associations, 42
    and differences, 41
    and effects, 40, 43
    falsifiable, 40
    writing up of, 293–4

IAT, *see* implicit association test
implicit association test (IAT), 50
independent variable, 24–5, 30
    *contrast with* dependent variable
independent-sample t-test
    example, 221–2
    general principle, 221
    in Excel, 239–240
    in SPSS, 240–241
    reporting, 241
indicator, 21–2, 75
inferential statistics, 212
intelligence, 47

interaction, 32–5
interpretivist, 6
interval scale data, 19–20
intervening variable, *see* confounding variable
introduction, 298–9

Kruskal-Wallis
    example, 225
    general principle, 224
    in SPSS, 271
    reporting, 271–2
kurtosis, 179
    in Excel, 213–14
    in SPSS, 216
    interpretation of, 217
    negative kurtosis, 179
    positive kurtosis, 179
    normal kurtosis, 179
La Piere, 50
Latin square, 87
left-skewed, 179
left-tailed, *see* left-skewed
leptokurtic, *see* positive kurtosis
less than or equal sign, 97
less than sign, 96–97
level, *see* condition
Likert scale, 70
limitations, writing up of, 296–7
line chart, 201–2
literature review, writing up of, 292–3
logs, in online surveys, 63
longitudinal, 56

main effect, 32–5
manipulation check, 27, 75
Mann-Whitney U
    example, 222
    general principle, 222
    in Excel, 242–6
    in SPSS, 245
    reporting, 245
margin of error, 80
marginal totals, 193
matching, 29
Mauchly's test of sphericity, 259–260
mean, 143, 161, 166
    and effect size, 183–4
    and power, 183
    calculating in Excel, 161
    calculating in SPSS, 161
measure, 21–22
measures of central tendency, 160, 165
    *see also* mean, mode, median
measures of dispersion, 166–9
MECE, 75–7
median, 163–6
    in Excel, 163
    in SPSS, 163
median-split, 163–5
mesokurtic, *see* normal kurtosis
method section 294–5
mixed between-within, *see* mixed design

mixed design, 31
mixed factorial, 31
mixed-method approach, 15
mode, 161–2, 165–6
    in Excel, 162
    in SPSS, 163
model, 57
Monte-Carlo effect, 111–12
Multifactorial, 31
multiple choice question, 66
multivariate, 31

negative numbers, 105–8
net promoter score, 113
neurotypical, non-neurotypical, 63
neutral option (on rating scale), 70
nominal data, 17–8, 177
non-directional hypotheses, *see* two-tailed hypotheses
non-normally distributed, *see* non-parametric
non-parametric, 212–9
    *contrast with* parametric
normal distribution, 175–9
normally distributed, *see* parametric
null hypothesis, 42–3, 180
    *contrast with* alternative hypothesis
numerator, 103

observations, 61
observed frequency, 280–281, 283
observer reliability, 61
one-sample t-test
    example, 220
    general principle, 220
    in Excel, 231–2
    in SPSS, 232–3
    reporting, 233
one-tailed hypotheses, 40
one-way ANOVA, 222
    *between participants*
    assumptions, 250
    in Excel, 250–1
    in SPSS, 251–6
    reporting, 255–6
    *within participants*
    example, 223
    repeated measures ANOVA, in SPSS, 256–260
    repeated measures ANOVA, reporting, 260
open question, 64–5
operationalisation, 49–50
order effect, 88
ordinal data, 18–9, 177
outliers, 57, 142–3

paired-sample t-test
    example, 221
    general principle, 220
    in Excel, 235–8
    in SPSS, 237
    reporting, 238
pairwise comparison, 67–8
parameters, 169–170
    *contrast with* statistics

# Index

parametric, 212–19
   *contrast with* non-parametric
participant information sheet, 39
participants
   communicating with, 118
   writing up of recruitment, 294
Pearson's correlation
   example, 226
   general principle, 226
   in Excel, 276–7
   in SPSS, 277
   reporting, 278
percent points, 99–100
percentages
   calculating, 98–9
   presenting in tables, 159
pie chart, 199–200
pilot study, 58, 62, 74, 88–9
pivot table, 157–8
placebo, 28
platykurtic, *see* negative kurtosis
population, 79–80, 84, 169–173
   *contrast with* sample
positivist, 6
post-hoc tests, 253, 255
power, 182
practice effect, 46
prejudice, 49
primary data, 58
   *contrast with* secondary data
priming, 183
probabilities, 111–12
procedural question, 74–5
procedures, writing up of, 295
project
   resources for, 10
   stages of, 11
p-value, 180, 182
   *see also* alpha level

q-q plot, 212–15
   in Excel, 214–15
   in SPSS, 216
   interpretation of, 212
quantitative research, 45, 60
quasi-experiment, 30
questionnaire, 62

random allocation, 29–30, 47
random number generator, 86
randomisation, 29
randomised presentation, 85
range, 104–5, 143
rank, 18
rank ordering, 66–7
ranking question, 66–7
rating scales, 68
ratio scale data, 20–21
rationale, writing up of, 293
ratios, 103
raw score, 178
recoding, 146
   in SPSS, 149–150
   in Excel, 147–9
references, 297–8
relationships between variables, 22
reliability, 43–5, 61, 90

repeated measures ANOVA, 222, 224
replication studies, 7
response variable, *see* dependent variable
research project, 11–2
research question
   development of, 8–12
   requirements for, 2–5, 9
results, writing up of, 295
reverse coding, 72
right-skewed, 179
right-tailed, *see* right-skewed
rounding, 101–2

sample, 79–80, 169–173
   composition of, 72, 81
   variance, 169
   standard deviation, 169
   *contrast with* population
sampling
   accidental sampling, *see* opportunity sampling
   and power, 183
   cluster sampling, 82
   convenience sampling, *see* opportunity sampling
   non-probability sampling, 84
      *contrast with* probability sampling
   opportunity sampling, 84
   panel sampling, 84
   probability sampling, 82
      *contrast with* non-probability sampling
   procedure, 57, 79
   quota sampling, 84
   simple random sampling, 82
   snowball sampling, 84
   stratified sampling, 83
   systematic sampling, 82
scale
   type of data, 17
   set of items, 59
scale reliability testing, 89–91
scale transformation, *see* data transformation
scale type, 17, 21, 60, 68
scale, measuring responses with, 64
scatter plot, 201
scientific notation, 108–9
scientific process, 7–8
screen readers, 64
secondary data, 56–8
   *contrast with* primary data
self-selection, self-selection bias, 29
semantic differential, 71–2
sentence completion, 65
sequence effect, 88
sigma, 104–5
significance, 180–2, 204–7
single choice question, 66
skew, 179
skewness, 178
   in Excel, 213–14
   in SPSS, 216
   interpretation of, 216

social desirability bias, 78
Spearman's correlation
   example, 226
   general principle, 226
   in Excel, 279
   in SPSS, 280
   reporting, 280
Spearman's Rho, 280
sphericity, 223
   *see also* Mauchly's test of sphericity
SPSS
   data file, 128–130
   data view, 128–9
   naming and labelling a variable, 131–2
   naming and labelling variable values, 132–4
   output file, 130–131
   syntax file, 130
   variable view, 129
square root, 110
squares, squaring, 110
SS, *see* sum of squares
standard deviation, 169–173, 176
   and effect size, 183
   calculating in Excel, 171
   calculating in SPSS, 172
   pooled, 185
standard error of skewness, 213–14
statistical analyses, overview of 219–226
statistics, 169–170
   *contrast with* parameters
sum of squares, 167–8
survey, 56, 62
symmetric (rating scale), 70
systematic variance, 173–4
   *see also* treatment variance and confound variance
   *contrast with* unsystematic variance

tables, presenting data in, 193–4
test variants, 46
testing fatigue, 46
tests, 63
three-way ANOVA, 222, 224
title, writing of, 299
treatment variance, 173–4
treatment, *see* condition
triangulation, 50
trigger warning *see* content note
t-test, 181
   independent sample, 238–241
   one-sample, 231–3
   paired-sample, 235–8
t-test statistic, 231
two- or three-way ANOVA
   *between participants*
      in SPSS, 261–2
      reporting, 263
   *within participants*
      in SPSS, 264–9
      reporting, 268–9
two-tailed hypotheses, 40

two-way anova, 222–3
type 1 error, 180–181
    *contrast with* type 2 error
type 2 error, 180–181
    *contrast with* type 1 error

unifactorial, 31
unipolar (rating scale), 69
univariate, 31
univariate ANOVA, 222
unsystematic variance, 173–4
    *contrast with* systematic variance

validity, 46–9
    conclusion validity, 47
    construct validity, 47
    convergent validity, 47
    ecological validity, 48
    external validity, 47
    internal validity, 47
variable, 15
    *see also* independent variable, dependent variable, confound variable
variance, 168–170, 174–5
    in Excel, 171, 173
    in SPSS, 172
visualisation of data, 194–204

Welch test, 252, 254–5
Wilcoxon signed rank
    example, 221
    general principle, 221
    in SPSS, 234
    reporting, 235

within-participants, 31
    *contrast with* between-participants
within-subjects, *see* within-participants
writing up, 290–291
    of abstract, 299
    of data analysis
    of discussion, 296
    of hypotheses, 293–4
    of introduction, 298–9
    of literature review, 292–3
    of methods, 294–5
    of rationale, 293
    of results, 295
    of title, 299

z-score, 178, 212
    *contrast with* raw score